History of
Modern Design

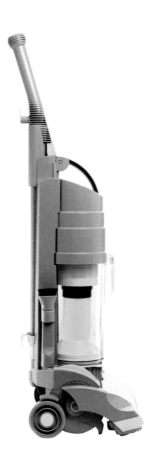

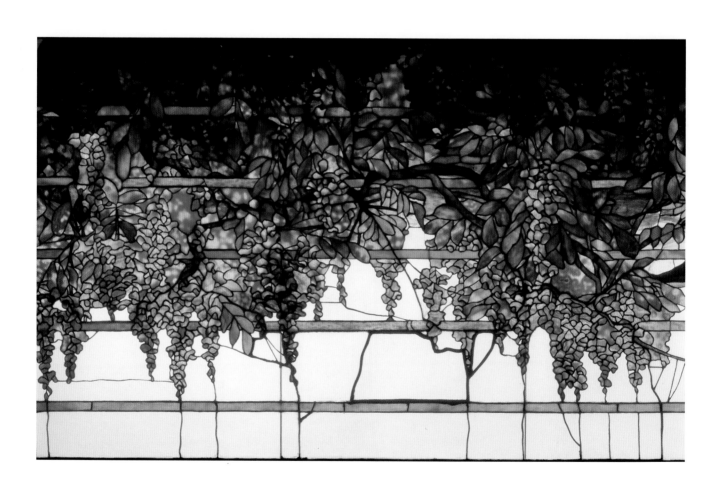

History of Modern Design

Second Edition

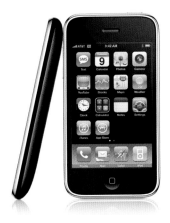

David Raizman

Pearson Prentice Hall
Upper Saddle River, N.J. 07458

For Pearson Education, Inc.:
Editor-in-Chief: Sarah Touborg
Editorial Assistant: Carla Worner
Assistant Managing Editor: Melissa Feimer
Project Liaison: Marlene Gassler
Senior Operations Supervisor: Brian K. Mackey
Director of Marketing: Brandy Dawson
Senior Marketing Manager: Kate Mitchell
Marketing Assistant: Craig Deming

This book was set in 10/13.5 Scala.

Credits and acknowledgments borrowed from other sources
and reproduced, with permission, in this textbook appear on
pages 422–423.

This book was designed and produced by
Laurence King Publishing Ltd, London
www.laurenceking.co.uk

For Laurence King Publishing:
Development Editor: Kara Hattersley-Smith
Senior Editor: Susie May
Copy Editor: Nicola Hodgson
Designer: Robin Farrow
Picture Researcher: Peter Kent
Production Manager: Simon Walsh

Printed in China

Author's dedication
To my brother, Dr. Richard E. Raizman (1945–2009), who defined courage.

Frontispiece: Louis Comfort Tiffany, Wisteria panel, leaded Favrile glass, manufactured by Tiffany Studios, New York, 1910–1920.
    © The Charles Hosmer Morse Foundation, Inc.
Part One: Robert Adam, Library, Kenwood House, Hampstead, London, 1767–1769.
    Alamy/© Bildarchive Monheim GmbH/Florian Monheim/Ronan von Götz.
Part Two: J. Parry, London Street Scene, Courtesy Alfred Dunhill Museum and Archive, London.
Part Three: Charles Rennie Mackintosh and Margaret MacDonald Mackintosh, interior, Buchanan Street Tearooms, Glasgow, 1896–1897.
    Culture and Sport Glasgow (Museums).
Part Four: Henriette Reiss, Rhythm Series, Goldstein Gallery, University of Minnesota.
Part Five: Marianne Straub, Surrey, Courtesy Warner Archive.
Part Six: Ron Arad, Big Volume 2, Courtesy Ron Arad Associates Limited.

Library of Congress Cataloging-in-Publication Data

Raizman, David Seth.
   History of modern design / David Raizman. -- 2nd ed.
      p. cm.
   Includes bibliographical references and index.
   ISBN-13: 978-0-205-72850-3 (hardcover : alk. paper)
   ISBN-10: 0-205-72850-2 (hardcover : alk. paper)
   1. Design--History. I. Title.
   NK1175.R35 2010
   745.409--dc22

                                        2010010528

10 9 8 7 6 5 4 3 2 1

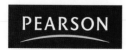

Prentice Hall
is an imprint of

www.pearsonhighered.com

ISBN 10: 0-20-572850-2
ISBN 13: 978-0-20-572850-3

Contents

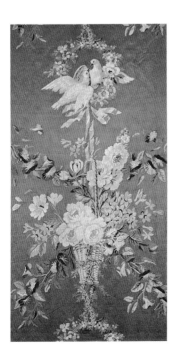

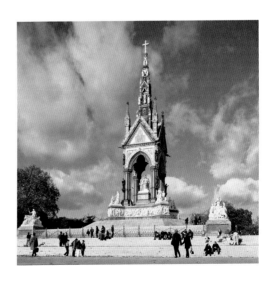

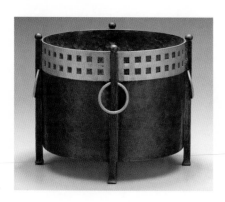

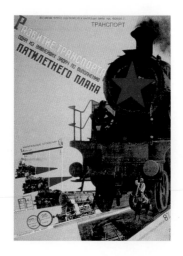

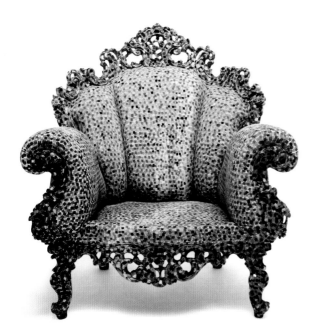

Preface

I have developed and revised the material and methodology for this book during 15 years of teaching the History of Design at the Westphal College of Media Arts & Design at Drexel University in Philadelphia, Pennsylvania. When Laurence King Publishing asked whether I would be interested in producing a second edition of *History of Modern Design*, I accepted the offer, based upon the success of the first book and the opportunity to make improvements using the knowledge and experience I have gained since completing the original manuscript. It has proven to be a challenging task. Any introductory book on a rich and expanding subject such as design requires a degree of simplification and reduction to help make material accessible to a general undergraduate audience. At the same time, adding new material and attempting to acknowledge and present more than a single viewpoint in the analysis and interpretation of that material is also important in order to make that material stimulating and interesting. Balancing these demands creates a tension whose resolution has been more difficult than I imagined.

There are many viable resources available to introduce the subject of design history to students. Dictionaries and encyclopedias of design are useful reference works that provide information on designers and movements. Standard works include Honour and Fleming's reliable and comprehensive *Penguin Dictionary of Decorative Arts* (new edition, 1989) and more recently Jonathan Woodham's *A Dictionary of Modern Design* (2005) as well as Gordon Campbell's two-volume *Grove Encyclopedia of Decorative Arts* (2006). Museum websites also provide information pertaining to the objects in their collections and current exhibitions. Another resource is case studies focusing upon themes such as the home, office, or corporate identity, as presented so provocatively in Adrian Forty's seminal study *Objects of Desire* (1986). Also useful are an increasing number of edited anthologies of readings from primary sources, including Carma Gorman's *The Industrial Design Reader* (2003) and Isabelle Frank's *The Theory of Decorative Art: An Anthology of European and American Writings 1750–1940* (2000). Several readers focusing upon critical literature in design history have been published more recently, such as Ben Highmore's *The Design Culture Reader* (2008), Hazel Clark and David Brody's *Design Studies: A Reader* (2009) and Grace Lees-Maffei and Rebecca Houze's *The Design History Reader* (2009). These complement Dennis Doordan's *Design History: An Anthology* (1995). In addition, several readers are available for the study of graphic design history and fashion, many of which are included in the bibliography of this book. The appearance of dictionaries and readers demonstrates rising interest in the academic and wider public to provide basic information and texts that help acquaint students with the history of design and establish its parameters and methods.

The method of this book, however, is narrative and chronological; it is a survey of objects chosen to familiarize students with the products of design, the processes by which they were created and the functions they serve for their designers, patrons, or manufacturers, and users. I have tried to approach the history of design in a framework that acknowledges a variety of perspectives through which it might be understood and appreciated, and that represent the dynamic interplay of multiple voices and forces within a given society and historical moment. It is my hope that the narrative is consistent and communicates the visual and intellectual rewards of studying the history of design. The selection of material, its organization, and the critical perspectives presented build upon the small number of previous surveys of the subject, numerous exhibitions as well as manufacturer and retail catalogues, and advertisements that remind us that museums and the statements of designers are not the only repository or source for learning about design. I have also included textual excerpts from a variety of primary sources, references to published studies of periods, movements, and designers by other historians and critics, as well as the author's synthesis of these sources and direct study of examples over a period of more than 25 years. In addition, classroom experience has helped considerably to shape the selection and presentation of material in the text.

The book is divided into 16 chapters and six major parts. Each part presents and compares different and sometimes conflicting approaches and attitudes to design during a particular period and in relationship to particular historical circumstances and events. Each of the parts listed below, supported with introductory and concluding sections within the text, presents material as paired (or triadic) responses to modern developments in politics, economics, and technology, and attempts to show the contingency between design and culture. This conceptual and organizational framework might be summarized as follows:

I. Demand, Supply, and Design (1700–1800):
    Chapters 1 and 2
    a. Design and Monarchy: France
    b. Design and Fashion: England
    c. Design and Popular Taste: The United States

II. Expansion and Taste (1800–1865): Chapters 3 and 4
    a. Industrial and Commercial Expansion
    b. The Meanings and Control of Taste; Reform

III. Arts, Crafts, and Machines – Industrialization: Hopes and Fears (1865–1914): Chapters 5, 6, and 7
    a. The Equality of the Arts and the Arts and Crafts Movement
    b. The Elevation of Craft and the Aesthetic Movement
    c. Efficiency and Early Modernity

IV. After World War I: Art, Industry, and Utopias (1918–1944): Chapters 8, 9, and 10
    a. Designing the Future: Modernism

b.   Luxury and Industry: the Moderne (Art Deco) ideal

c.   The Beginnings of Industrial Design in the US

V.   Humanism and Luxury: International Modernism and
      Mass Culture After World War II (1945–1960):
      Chapters 11, 12, and 13
      a.   International Modernism and the Cold War
      b.   Mass taste and the Cold War

VI.   Progress, Protest, and Pluralism (1960–2010):
      Chapters 14, 15, and 16
      a.   Alternative Voices: Protest and Design
      b.   Pluralism and Postmodernism
      c.   Design and Information in Contemporary Life

The second edition of the *History of Modern Design* includes several new illustrations, an expanded bibliography and timeline, and a larger section on contemporary design. In addition, the text has been organized into six rather than five parts in order to separate the early nineteenth from the eighteenth century and to present concepts relating to that material more clearly. A number of illustrations replaced existing ones to better communicate particular qualities of design in terms of techniques, or to relate with material presented elsewhere. New sections, such as Barcelona in the later nineteenth century, have also been added. Other new features include the placement of the American System of Manufacture in Chapter 3, the inclusion of additional examples of fashion and textiles into each part of the text, and placing the discussion of the Arts and Crafts Movement first in Part II rather than after the Aesthetic Movement and Art Nouveau. I have made an effort both to illustrate as well as to discuss objects in interiors rather than in isolation, so that their relation to lifestyles and lived experience becomes a more relevant and important part of their context. Also, a significant amount of new material has been added to reflect recent trends and perspectives in design, including digital technology, information, and interactivity.

In preparing this survey I have benefited from the work of many authors who have published chronological surveys beginning with most students' (of my generation anyway) introduction to modern design history, Sir Nikolaus Pevsner's *Pioneers of Modern Design*, and including Penny Sparke's *An Introduction to Design and Culture in the Twentieth Century* (1986), and Jonathan Woodham's *Twentieth-Century Design* (1997). There is also the excellent series of books by a range of specialists published by Oxford University Press. These include a number of volumes devoted to period styles (Arts and Crafts, Art Nouveau, Art Deco, Bauhaus, for example), as well as John Heskett's *Industrial Design* (1980) and more recently Jeffrey Meikle's illuminating *Design in the USA* (2004).

Phillip Meggs's *History of Graphic Design*, now in its fourth edition as *Meggs' History of Graphic Design* by Allston Purvis (2005), remains an informative and well-established survey of that material with an emphasis on the nineteenth and twentieth centuries. This survey is joined by newer voices in this field,

including the Richard Hollis's brief but highly engaging *Graphic Design: A Concise History* (2nd edition, 2001), Roxane Jubert and Serge Lemoine's *Typography and Graphic Design: From Antiquity to the Present* (2006), Stephen Eskilson's *Graphic Design: A New History* (2007), and Johanna Drucker and Emily McVarish's *Graphic Design History: A Critical Guide* (2008).

Surveys of interior design include John Pile's *History of Interior Design* (3rd edition, 2009), and for fashion, standard histories include Christopher Breward's *Fashion* (2003) and James Laver et al's *Costume and Fashion: A Concise History* (2002). For the area of craft, in addition to surveys such as Edward Lucie-Smith's 1981 *The Story of Craft: the Craftsman's Role in Society*, Glenn Adamson's *Thinking Through Craft* (2007) is a thoughtful and stimulating approach to craft and its place within the history and theory of modern art.

As with the first edition of *History of Modern Design*, I have also benefited from the opportunity of seeing numerous exhibitions that have contributed to this second edition. These include the Victoria and Albert Museum's exhibitions on Art Deco, Modernism, and Cold War Modern, MoMA's Safe Design and Design and the Elastic Mind, the Cooper Hewitt National Design Museum's triennial exhibition Design Life Now, the Venice Biennale (2008), and smaller exhibitions held at the Philadelphia Museum of Art, London's Design Museum, the Museum of Decorative Arts in Paris, the Courtauld Institute, the Metropolitan Museum of Art in New York, and elsewhere. Recent bibliography is simply too rich to mention even a few specific titles of articles and books, but the Bibliography and Suggested Reading sections have been expanded and provide those titles that have assisted in the preparation of this volume and might be consulted for students' further investigation. Once again, the *Journal of Design History*, *Design Issues*, and more recently the *Journal of Modern Craft* and *Design and Culture* provide regular reading material for keeping up with scholarship through articles and reviews of books and exhibitions. These and other journals are available to subscribers and libraries online, but there are also several free web-based journals, newsletters, edited blogs, and other resources that introduce and comment on design and design history. *Nineteenth-Century Art Worldwide* is a scholarly journal that frequently includes articles and review on design (http://www.19thc-artworldwide.org/), while *Design Observer* (http://designobserver.com/), developed and launched by designers Michael Bierut, William Drenttel, Jessica Helfand, and Julie Lasky, has recently expanded to include a wide range of related sites and links.

As a teacher I have always enjoyed the challenge of comparing works of art from different or even successive time periods that share formal or ideological similarities. I am happy for the students in the Westphal College of Media Arts & Design who have made the study of design history part of their education and hope that what they have learned, both in Philadelphia and in our Study Abroad Program in London, will in some way be incorporated into the contributions they are certain to make to their chosen design professions.

London, August 2009

Acknowledgments

I would like to thank my editors at Laurence King Publishing, Lee Ripley and Kara Hattersley-Smith, for their support of this project, including permission to add so many new illustrations and additional time to make extensive revisions. Thanks are also due to my dean, Allen Sabinson, and department head Joseph Gregory, for acknowledging and encouraging my research efforts in numerous ways, and Provost Mark Greenberg and Associate Provost John DiNardo for granting my sabbatical for 2009–2010. I would also like to recognize the Foundation for International Education, Drexel's Study Abroad partner in London, whose staff assisted with my summer teaching in 2006, 2007, and 2009 and who in many other ways have made summers in London so rewarding.

As with the first edition of *The History of Modern Design*, the most substantial debt I owe for this book is to my students at Drexel University, who have continued to listen and contribute to the trial-and-error presentation of its ideas since their initial publication in 2004. The choice of material, its organization, and the framework for presenting that material have all have taken shape in the context of the classroom term-by-term over several years. Testing new approaches, introducing new examples, and revising content and assignments remain a constant challenge, and I learned much from students' thoughtful responses, essays, and evaluations while revising and expanding the text and illustrations. Observing the creative work of our students as a guest at critiques remains a great source of satisfaction, for it permits me to see that the future of design is in able hands and imaginative, engaging minds.

Since the publication of the first edition of *History of Modern Design* I've been fortunate to meet and correspond with several scholars, curators, and teachers currently engaged in design history research through organizations such as the College Art Association (CAA), Design Studies Forum (DSF), the Association of Art Historians (AAH), and the Design History Society (DHS). Attending and participating in conferences and symposia, and corresponding with new colleagues in the field have contributed considerably to the revisions contained in this edition. I would like to thank Carma Gorman, Dennis Doordan, Elizabeth Guffey, Gabe Weisberg, Linda Shanahan, Gerry Beegan, Dennis Wardlesworth, Glenn Adamson, David Comberg, Joe Cunningham, Ezra Shales, Jennifer Zwilling, Christopher Storb, Martina Droth, Vladimir Kulic, and Klaus Krippendorf for their friendship and the insights they've provided through conversation, correspondence, and their own work in the field. Also, there were nine readers of the proposal I prepared for the second edition of *History of Modern Design*, and many of their thoughtful ideas have been incorporated into the finished text and illustration program. Especially helpful were the comments and suggestions of Professor James Slauson of the Milwaukee Institute of Art and Design, who later provided detailed suggestions for content and organization to the revisions of Parts V and VI, and George Marcus, whose careful reading of the first edition brought to my attention a number of errata and matters for further clarification and investigation. Graduate interior design student Lisa Priborsky worked with me on several aspects of the revisions as research assistant, and was responsible for checking information of the final version of the expanded timeline.

As ever, the Hagerty Library at Drexel University, and our College librarian Ann Keith Kennedy, have been responsive to requests for new materials in the form of books, periodicals, and online resources that aided considerably in the preparation of this volume.

Obtaining photographs and permissions for the 550+ illustrations contained in a book of such wide-ranging material represents an enormous behind-the-scenes effort, and the layout and design also presented challenges that required a great deal of dialogue and compromise. Much of this work was expertly done by picture editor Peter Kent, designer Robin Farrow, and senior editor Susie May at Laurence King Publishing. Mike Froio of the Photography Program in our College provided high-quality scans for a number of images in periodicals at Drexel's Hagerty Library, and Joe Cunningham and Bruce Barnes of the American Decorative Arts Foundation 1900 kindly provided images and rights for a number of Arts and Crafts objects in their collection that are illustrated in this revision. I'm also grateful to Sarah Touborg at Pearson Prentice-Hall for her assistance as the project moved toward completion.

I want to thank my wife, Lucy S. Raizman, for her patience during the year-long period of concentrated effort on the revisions for this book. What promised to be an intermittent task turned into an obsessive one that included long periods away from home, and so I'm especially grateful for her understanding and support. Including an illustration of Tom Wesselman's *Still-Life Number 30* (page 360), stemming from an afternoon's visit together at the Museum of Modern Art, is but one of several examples of the moments we shared in the preparation of this edition.

I only wish that my parents, Albert and Adele Raizman, and my dear brother, Dr. Richard Raizman, were alive to see the second edition of this book in print. Its first edition was a source of pride for each of them; their encouragement of my professional efforts was unwavering, and has meant more to me than I was ever able to express. Richard's interest in the book and the material it presents were subjects of conversations and travels over many years that I will always treasure.

Miami Beach, Fall 2009

Most scholars agree that an important characteristic of modern design was a growing separation of designing from making, incipient in the eighteenth century and more widespread in the nineteenth. The separation between designing and making provides the rationale for beginning this survey in the eighteenth century. During that century we can observe the effects of this separation, and recognize the differences between designers who provided models or sketches to manufacturers and artists who most often were responsible for executing their own, often unique, works; it also distinguishes the designer and the craftsperson or group of craftspeople who also work directly with materials. The separation focuses well-deserved attention upon manufacturers and consumers as important "stakeholders" in the history of design. Thus, despite similarities between art, craft, and design, most observers remind us that designers are concerned with meeting clients' needs rather than their own, as well as with producing instructions for serial rather than unique artifacts. Such distinctions are central to any history of design, as they bring into play the role and motivations of manufacturers and provide alternatives to writing the history of design (or explaining design) as though it were an "artistic" and individual activity. They also reveal the constraints under which designers often work and that lie at the heart of their activity. Creating products that provide efficient, economical "solutions" to consumer problems or needs held appeal for designers for several reasons, not only because it suggested the relevance of design to the lives of working-class people, but also because it lent credibility to design as a problem-solving activity that produced measurable results, making the profession seem substantive and serious, rather than simply a matter of taste.

Even when considering works that seem to fall squarely in the category of design, it is not always easy to distinguish clearly between commercial and artistic motivations. Advertising posters in the later nineteenth century were often promoted and produced for collectors by critics and printers, as well as to identify and make products appealing; similarly, the small, mass-produced chromolithographic trade cards printed during the same period were collected and pasted into albums or scrapbooks. Another point of connection between artist and designer concerns the status of each profession: as a 'liberal art,' the arts of painting, sculpture, and architecture were seen to have an intellectual and creative rather than a technical and material basis. The separation of

designing from making
design with a respected
with a less prestigious n

DISCOURSE

One of the more enjoy
history is the sense of
those who contribute to
brings together differen
enterprise, based upon
that provide the basis
viewpoints, and further
Yet certainly there can b
history of design; even i
tions as this one, almost
elicit charges of exclusiv
work such as *History of M*
as an attempt to provi
artifacts and perspectiv
framework for study an
ongoing discourse. The
vessels and other obje
plastic, or metal; tablew
curtains, carpets, uphols
patterns printed or wove
housings for electric ap
books, posters, magazir
digital devices, and so
exhaustive, is sufficient
that design is a pheno
familiar, embedded in ou

It is my hope that the
material will encourage
objects and phenomena
circumstances and pers
While it may be useful a
objects such as chairs, or
to one another chronolog
seek to explain those dii
social change or the inno
is also important to see
lived experience of cons
conditions that produced
that design reveals a part
a form of knowledge th
shaping, and choosing a

PRODUCTS, TECHNOLOGY, AND PROGRESS

During the week of March 20, 2000, the feature story for the weekly magazine *Time* was "the Rebirth of Design." The cover image illustrated photographs of a rubber-coated portable radio (designed in 1997 by Marc Berthier and called the Tykho) inside a crystal bowl. At the bottom left, the copy announced: "Function is out. Form is in. From radios to cars to toothbrushes, America is bowled over by style." The *Time* cover (below right) offers one of the most common and basic definitions of design, not only in the United States, but internationally: first, it identifies design with mass-produced domestic and personal products, and second, it suggests that design refers to "style," those characteristics – for instance, the crisp rectangular housing and bright green color of Berthier's radio, or the pleasingly spherical contour of the crystal-clear bowl in which it rests – that endow functional products with an aesthetic bonus that increases their appeal to consumers.

The *Time* cover is somewhat misleading because "design," of course, never died; all human products and processes, whether "stylish" or not, are, in some sense, designed. The *Time* definition, referring to products of everyday use with an added aesthetic value and appeal, provides a starting point for thinking about and studying the history of modern design. But appealing forms are only one reason for design's social and cultural significance, and probably not the most important one. Design has long been understood to have economic, social, and political functions at which the *Time* cover does not even hint. In the eighteenth century, for example, some observers noted with optimism that design (here used in the sense of stylish objects that went in and out of fashion) was an important element in a competitive economy, since it stimulated commerce and thus produced increased levels of employment. In the early nineteenth century, many writers added that design (used here in the sense of a shared notion of "good" taste) held the promise of disseminating "culture" and a higher standard of living to the masses. The association of design with innovation in materials and production technologies is clearly seen in the immensely popular mid- and late-nineteenth-century

World's Fairs, beginning with the Crystal Palace exhibition in London (The Great Exhibition of the Works of Industry of All Nations) in 1851 (see pages 63–70). At the same time, however, such visions of progress did not apply equally to all social groups, and it is possible to critique the relationship between design and technology in terms of liabilities as well as benefits, as a "choice" of possible alternatives rather than as an inevitable development. In addition, the cultural significance of design also involves the attitudes and active role of consumers, the meanings they attach to artifacts as encountered in shop windows, as photographs in a printed advertisement, as images in a television commercial, and the wide range of associations consumers bring to designed products.

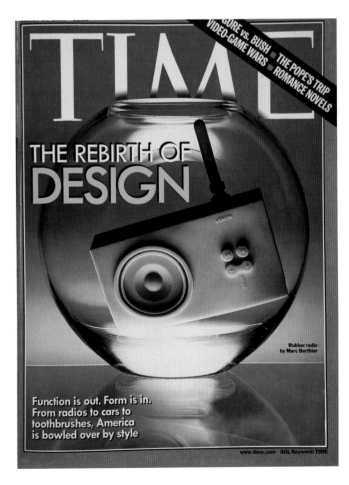

Designers and the Expansion of Design

The *Time* magazine cover also touches on several associations of the term "designer." The most common association is that of "giving form," as in the soft, waterproof synthetic rubber housing of Berthier's radio, or even the unusual choice of green for a product generally associated with more neutral hues. That the designer's contribution is often visual can hardly be denied, and that his or her formal invention constitutes added value is also apparent. Yet we might consider not only the Tykho radio's novel visual form, but also the ways it promotes interaction between product and user, for instance, its simple and very basic push-button controls and ease of operation, its tactile surface, or perhaps more importantly, its ability to contribute to a more pleasurable shower or bath, whether that means gauging the morning traffic, hearing the news stories of the day, or practicing karaoke.

In recent years, "design" has taken on new meanings and functions. Certainly the idea of interactivity, of "user-centered" design, has become a significant extension of design practice in the later twentieth century, contemporary with the shift from a mechanical to an information age

populated by increasi[...]
similar electronic an[...]
design often requires [...]
approaches, and m[...]
paradigm. It is wort[...]
offered by economis[...]
Simon in 1969; he w[...]
of action aimed at [...]
preferred ones" (see [...]
traditionally "designed[...]
in other fields who en[...]
that they do. This mo[...]
in a brochure from [...]
Week, sponsored by t[...]
Museum in New Yor[...]
featured a photograp[...]
include furniture, a[...]
electronic products su[...]
thinking certainly pre[...]
often associated with a[...]
such as Charles Ear[...]
sense of the word, usi[...]
process of arranging g[...]
party in order to avoi[...]
and to contribute to [...]
"software design" als[...]
expansion or applicati[...]
the software designer [...]
they certainly entail a[...]
choices or decisions [...]
navigate through a se[...]
history of design shoul[...]
practices and contexts [...]
encompasses activities[...]
patterns and typefaces[...]
production processes, [...]

Just as it is not a[...]
design and engineerin[...]
between design, art, [...]
changed in meaning ([...]
few centuries. Today, [...]
design in most univer[...]
whether they choose t[...]
sculpture, or ceramics,[...]
ities among these fie[...]
Indeed, many of the [...]
were inspired by a bel[...]
such beliefs repres[...]
understood only by a[...]
number of manufactu[...]
the establishment of o[...]
shaping more widespr[...]

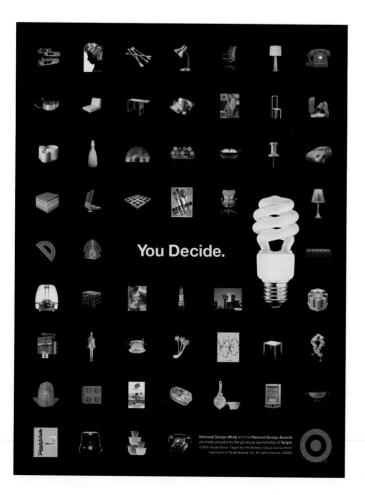

You Decide.

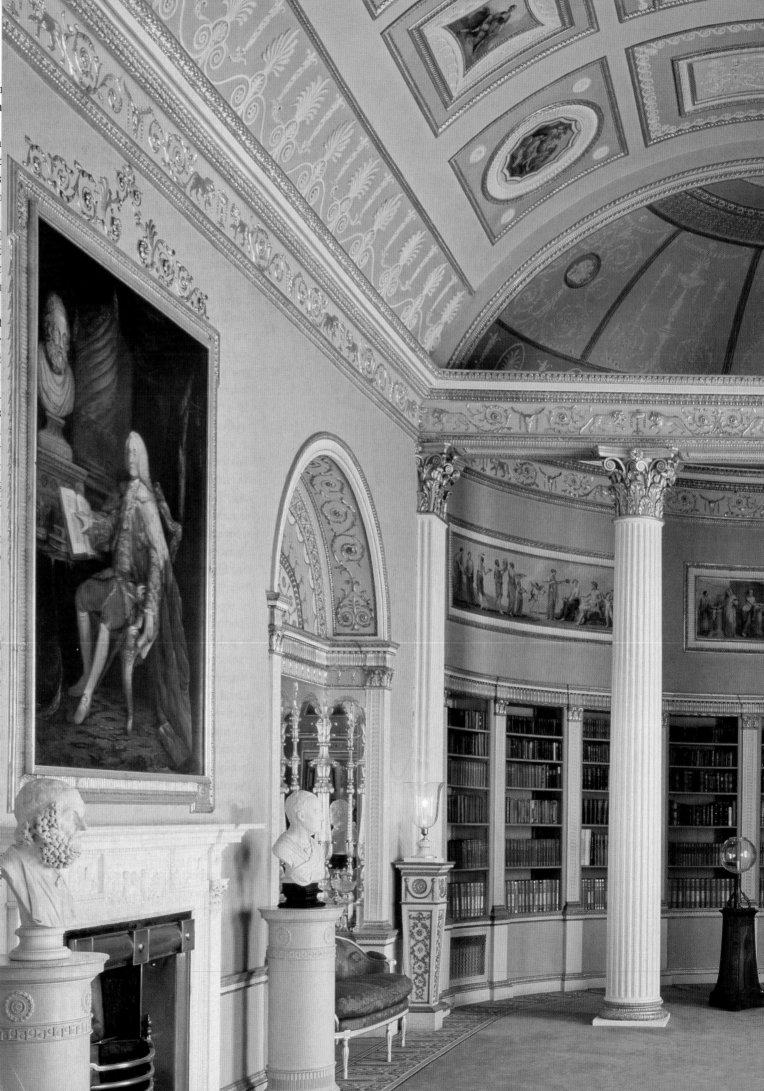

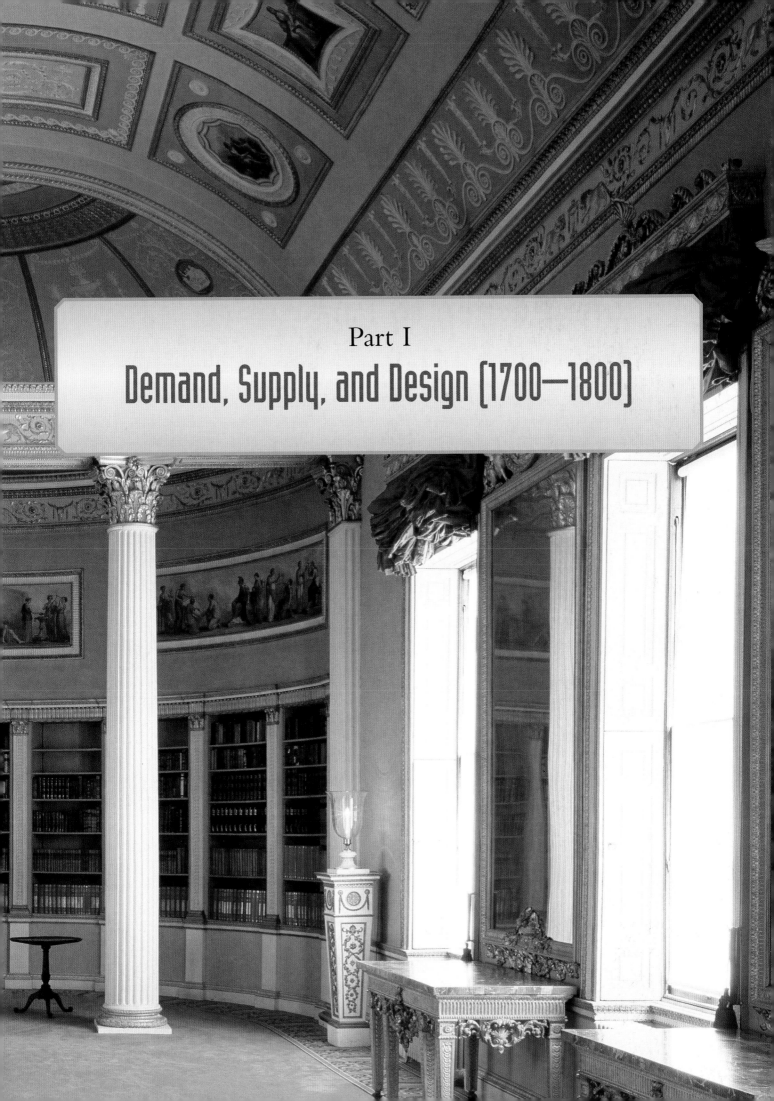

Part I
Demand, Supply, and Design (1700—1800)

Introduction to Part I

In the course of the eighteenth century, parallel revolutions in methods of production and patterns of consumption profoundly affected the history of manufactured products in Europe and in North America. Amid the consolidation of the monarchy in France, Louis XIV gave visual expression to his political authority and majesty through artistic patronage on a grand scale, overseeing the administration of modern facilities for the production of the decorative arts. In Great Britain, as an elastic growth in consumer demand stretched across geographic and social boundaries in the second half of the century, a generation of entrepreneurial manufacturers and merchants introduced changes in the organization of labor and the technology of production that recognized the roles of design and marketing in an expanding economy. New materials and processes took shape, greater productivity was achieved, and a confidence in the attainment of middle-class material comfort emerged, linked to the desire for social mobility and individual fulfillment. This dynamic, interdependent relation between production and consumption, involving new technologies, marketing, communications, and competitive commercial practices, provides the foundation for the study of modern design.

Chapter 1

Royal Demand and the Control of Production

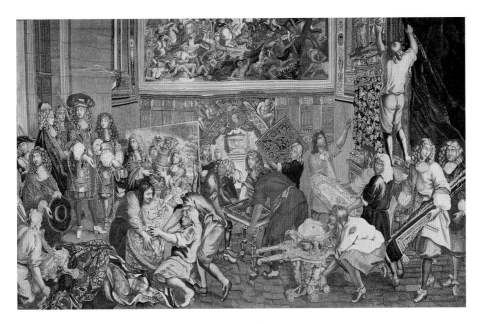

1.1 Charles Le Brun, *Louis XIV Inspecting the Gobelins Manufactory*, tapestry, manufactured at the Gobelins Tapestry Manufactory, 12 ft 2 in x 19 ft (3.7 x 5.8 m), *c.* 1662–78. Palace of Versailles, France.

STATE-OWNED MANUFACTORIES

During the age of absolutism in the later seventeenth century, monarchs often invested directly in the large-scale production of luxury goods as a visible expression of royal hegemony. In addition to commissioning furnishings from independent craft workshops (see page 23), royal patrons also sponsored the construction and oversaw the management of large facilities for the manufacture of goods under centralized control. Design was an integral element in creating distinctive, "branded" products that communicated the aura of majesty and prestige associated with monarchical power. Manufactories also associated monarchs with higher levels of productivity that characterized a civilized nation. In France, for instance, the growing demand for luxury goods and furnishings at the court of Louis XIV (1638–1715) stimulated the establishment of the state-owned manufactory just south of Paris at Gobelins in 1662, eventually employing 250 workers in the production of tapestries and other furnishings. In one of a series of 14 tapestries (1662–1678) designed by the court painter Charles Le Brun (1619–1690), who served as "director" of

the Gobelins, a distinctively attired Louis XIV is depicted at the upper left visiting the Royal Manufactory at Gobelins in the company of ministers including (to the king's left) his minister of finance Jean-Baptiste Colbert (1619–1683) as well as Le Brun to his right (fig. 1.1). The king enters a large room from the rear, filled with a lavish array of textiles and furnishings such as gold and silver urns and trays and an elaborately inlaid table, all products of the Gobelins workshops. In the right half of the tapestry, a standing figure points to a tall cabinet with twisted columns of carved foliage against a deep blue ground, while to his right a figure carries on his shoulder a large wooden floor tile with inlaid decoration. Scholars have identified these figures respectively as Pierre Gole (c. 1630–1705) and Domenico Cucci (c. 1620–1684), the former a cabinet-maker of Dutch descent working in Paris and the latter an artist trained in Italy and brought to the Gobelins at the king's request. Seventeenth-century traditions of virtuoso craftsmanship in furniture-making, involving intricate marquetry in stone or in precious materials such as ivory and tortoiseshell, were especially strong both in Holland and in Italy, and the importance of these kinds of skills in projecting

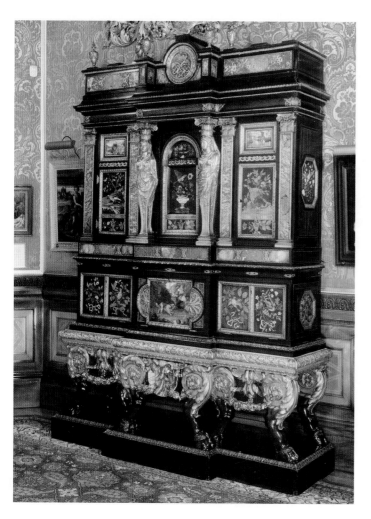

1.2 Domenico Cucci, cabinet, pine and oak with ebony veneer, set with pietra dure plaques with gilt bronze mounts, 117 9/16 x 77 3/16 x 25 1/2 in (299 x 196 x 65 cm), 1683–4, from the Palace of Versailles. Alnwick Castle, Northumberland.

cultural exclusivity are demonstrated by the king's efforts to install both masters at the newly established manufactory. While few royal commissions from Louis XIV's court of Versailles have survived, figure 1.2 illustrates one of two grand cabinets designed by Cucci, featuring carved and gilded figures as well as deeply carved naturalistic decoration along with marble and wood marquetry panels in a variety of colors. This cabinet is over 9 feet tall, resembles an elaborate façade for a building, and utilizes the most precious of raw materials as well as the most consummate skills associated with painting and sculpture to transform and ennoble those materials.

A consciously overwhelming display, the abundance of goods depicted in the Gobelins tapestry reinforces visually the social prestige and political power associated with the arts. The richness of the setting and feeling for display (rather than for the *use* of the furnishings themselves) emphasizes a direct relationship between absolute monarchy and the flourishing of culture. The series of which this

tapestry is a part illustrated 14 events in the life of the king, and it is worthwhile noting that in addition to battles, treaties, births, and marriages, the patronage of the arts, including the decorative arts, is also included and therefore significant. While the products of Gobelins and other manufactories may have served the needs and political interests of a small and wealthy elite, economists such as Jean-Baptiste Say (1767–1832) articulated the principle that royal and aristocratic investment and consumption meant material progress for all of society, stimulating the economy on a more general level by employing more people at all levels of production, and promoting exports of such goods abroad; the result was a favorable trade balance as well as an international reputation for luxury living. As historian Caroline Weber relates, when Queen Marie Antoinette was asked by her husband Louis XVI to curb her personal expenditure on clothing and jewelry as public criticism of royal indulgence swelled in the 1780s, the queen replied that to do so would put 200 shops out of business. In the mid-nineteenth century, the Empress Eugénie of France, who supposedly never wore the same gown more than once, remarked that in maintaining her wardrobe she was helping to provide the silk workers of Lyon with their livelihood.

Grandeur and projection of majesty were certainly the goals of Louis XIV's palace at Versailles, designed by architect Jules Hardouin-Mansart (1646–1708) and built primarily between 1678 and 1684. In order to create the palace's Hall of Mirrors (begun 1678), which connected the king's private apartments with the palace's chapel and was used to receive visitors (fig. 1.3), Colbert created a manufactory to produce the large mirrors and windows of the hall. Later known as St. Gobain (and still in business today), the manufactory rivaled glass production in the Republic of Venice, known at the time for its high quality and technical expertise in glass production. It is hardly a surprise that such investment and patronage confirmed the role of the decorative or mechanical arts in stimulating the economy, demonstrating technical achievement, as well as adding beauty and prestige to objects of use.

In much of Europe, only royalty possessed sufficient wealth to realize such high levels of productivity and style. Large-scale facilities such as Gobelins required significant investment in raw materials, equipment, space, and labor, as well as the costs of oversight and administration. As the scale of operations increased, the need to achieve greater volume, efficiency, and control led to specialization. Among the best-informed guides to the practices of labor and industry at the time were the French writers Denis Diderot (1713–1784) and Jean le Rond d'Alembert (1717–1783), whose *Encyclopédie*, first published between 1751 and 1772, contains hundreds of engraved illustrations

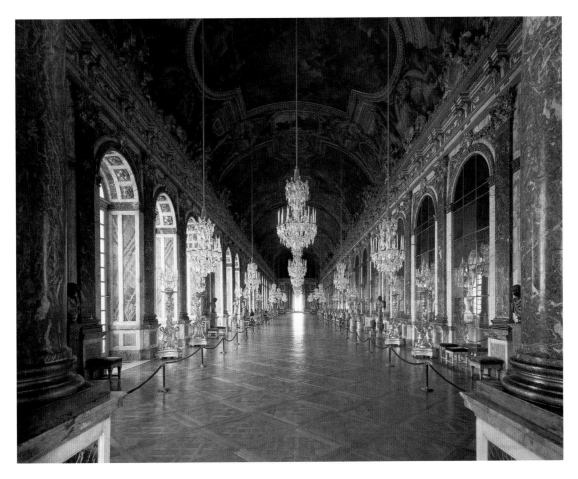

1.3 Jules Hardouin-Mansart, Palace of Versailles, Hall of Mirrors, 1678–1684. Mirrors manufactured at St. Gobain, Paris.

documenting the accumulated practical knowledge and industry of their time. The degree of specialization in both labor and tools is remarkable in its complexity and rationalization. An engraved plate from the *Encyclopédie* (fig. 1.4) gives some indication of the size of the tapestry manufactory at Gobelins in the mid-eighteenth century and the orderly arrangement of a large number of high-warp looms in a spacious, well-lit interior (one of three tapestry-

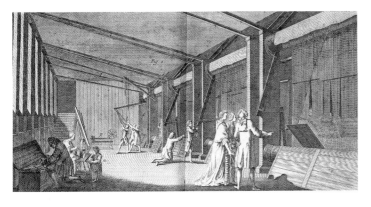

1.4 Interior, Gobelins Factory, High Warp Looms, engraved plate from Denis Diderot and Jean le Rond d'Alembert, *Encyclopédie*, Paris, 1751–1772.

weaving facilities at the Gobelins). Later in the nineteenth century, illustrated books, often printed in series, depicted the rational organization of labor as a series of specialized tasks in large, well-organized facilities to produce a wide variety of "useful manufactures." Such volumes were often published by manufacturers themselves as a form of advertising, or in small formats for children as a means of education and entertainment (storybooks for children were also among the earliest genres for printed color illustrations). The connection between specialization, efficiency, and progress became commonplace in the nineteenth century, though its emergence earlier at the Gobelins and in other industries subsidized or stimulated by royal demand or investment was highly developed during the eighteenth century.

Under the conditions of royal patronage, the division of labor improved efficiency but did not lead to a decline in quality or to the dry and repetitive work associated with mass production in the more competitive economic conditions of the nineteenth century; in fact, specialization inspired innovation and experiment. Translating the sketches or cartoons of court painters into tapestries was a challenge demanding collaboration and skill. It required the development of a wide array of dyes to match the range of the painter's palette, increased attention to delicate details, and the preservation of the overall unity and integrity of monumental compositions. During the eighteenth century, the Gobelins tapestry manufactory developed a palette of more than 10,000 vegetable dyes for their products to approximate the varied tonalities and hues of the sketches (cartoons) they transformed into wall-hangings on the loom. In the mid-nineteenth century the chief of this department, Michel-Eugène Chevreul (1786–1889), was among the most respected color theorists of his day, and his books on the subject were frequently read by late-nineteenth-century artists such as Georges Seurat (1859–1891). Using models provided by "designers," as in the royal manufactories, was not a servile act of copying; rather it involved a creative transformation from one medium to another demanding great knowledge of materials, cooperation with other phases of production, and a keen interest in process.

ARTISTS AND CRAFTSMEN

The state-owned system of manufacture encouraged the participation of painters and sculptors in the applied arts. Court painters such as Le Brun and later François Boucher (1703–1770) were responsible for supplying designs to the manufactories at Gobelins and the porcelain manufactory at Sèvres (see page 22), and both artists held the position of "director" for the activities of these large workshops. Such a practice ensured unity of style and expression in all aspects of interior decoration, and corresponded to an ideal image projected by the monarchs and courts that were their primary, if not exclusive, patrons. The decorative arts of the period bear the name of the French kings, from the Baroque grandeur of Louis XIV, to the more intimate and sensual Rococo of Louis XV (r. 1723–1774), and finally to the restrained classicism of Louis XVI (r. 1774–1791). The products and furniture from all three styles demonstrate the most refined levels of skill and craftsmanship, from the carving and joinery of the chassis and mechanical parts such as drawers or doors, to the more sculptural carved decoration, intricate marquetry, and inset plaques, to the casting and gilding of metal fittings.

Painters or sculptors who provided models to manufactories enjoyed a higher professional status than the craftsmen who produced those models. The elite audience for painting and sculpture acknowledged the fine arts as "liberal" rather than manual or mechanical, and judged their value along moral and intellectual lines as well as technical ones. The artist's choice and development of a subject was expected to educate as well as to please the patron, and the training of fine artists in academies rather than in workshops, as well as the exhibition of their works at the biennial Parisian Salons further confirmed this difference. Despite the general acknowledgment of such distinctions, there appears to have been a healthy collaboration between artists and craftsmen in France throughout much of the eighteenth century, which contributed to the quality and reputation of luxury goods and furnishings produced for a discriminating clientele. Under the French monarchy, *all* the arts possessed political as well as social meanings that reinforced the role of the state in overseeing and regulating the means of production.

In working closely with weavers or other craftsmen, the artist–designer balanced concerns for a convincing image or narrative with respect for the integrity of surface reinforced by borders and other areas of patterned, planar decoration. Perhaps unlike some of their revolutionary counterparts at the end of the eighteenth century, who dismissed craftsmen as servile employees dependent upon the favor of wealthy and aristocratic clients, court painters such as Boucher would hardly have been offended to see their sketches embroidered on a fire screen or on the back of an upholstered chair. These artists moved freely and seemingly without conflict between the Salon and the drawing room, the official and the private, the serious and the sensual. Indeed, the quality, refinement, and well-being associated with the decorative arts of the pre-revolutionary period would become an inspiration for a number of later French Art Nouveau and Art Moderne designers seeking to revitalize the French national heritage in the competitive international economy of the late nineteenth and early twentieth centuries.

Aspects of the eighteenth-century design process may be seen in the tapestry *The Chinese Fair* (fig. 1.5), designed by Boucher and woven at the Beauvais manufactory (also subsidized by the French monarchy) in 1742. The tapestry, more than 18 feet long, depicts a series of well-dressed and well-attended figures examining a variety of wares aligned along a road that proceeds diagonally from the lower left toward the upper right corner. In addition to the figures and their exotic costumes are palm trees and pagodalike architecture. China was a popular source of mostly genre and pastoral subjects (often known as chinoiserie) in the early to mid-eighteenth century. Not only does the scene convey the hazy atmosphere of a summer afternoon, but details, such as the deep red parasol held by a young curly-haired servant at the lower left, with its spontaneous flecks of lavender highlights, seem to test the limitations of the medium and expand its range of expression in response to Boucher's feeling for the beauty of afternoon light.

In addition to tapestry, the silk-weaving trade also flourished in the eighteenth century. The silk industry served the demand for both dress as well as material for

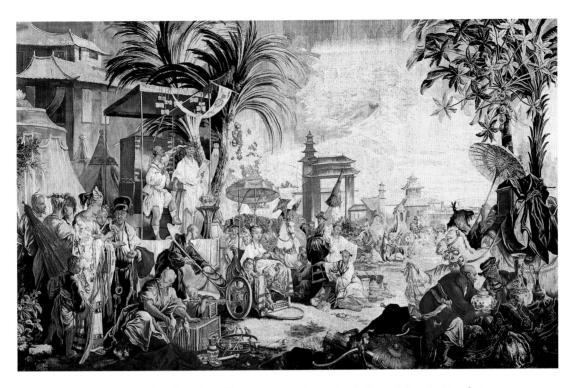

1.5 François Boucher, *The Chinese Fair*, tapestry, manufactured at the Beauvais Tapestry Manufactory, 11 ft 11 in x 18 ft 2 in (363.2 x 553.7 cm), 1742. Minneapolis Institute of Arts.

interior wall-coverings, draperies, and upholstery, and expanded with increased royal patronage in response to the impulse for distinction and luxury living. One of the leading centers for silk weaving in eighteenth-century Europe was the French city of Lyon. The growth of this industry demonstrated both an inventiveness of techniques for exploring textures and effects and collaboration with designers who drew patterns that were transformed into woven silk. An example of a delicate floral pattern for a dress fabric, dating to around 1770, is illustrated in figure 1.6. The designer was Philippe de LaSalle (1723–1805), a merchant–manufacturer who trained as a painter and whose teachers included François Boucher. De LaSalle designed fabrics for royal residences at Versailles and Fontainebleau and worked for other royal patrons in Spain as well as in Russia. His designs frequently employ floral and bird motifs in a pictorial style suggesting deft brushwork set against rich, highly saturated backgrounds. Their production involved a technique known as *point rentré*, which interlocked threads of different colors in order to produce more subtle shading. The technique was developed earlier in the century by Jean Revel (1684–1751), also from Lyon; Revel's father was a painter who worked under Le Brun at Versailles.

De LaSalle also developed a device that accelerated the production process on hand-drawn looms in order to facilitate the weaving of new patterns. His combination of design innovation and technical knowledge is characteristic of the

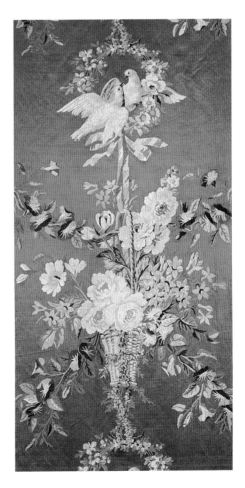

1.6 Philippe de LaSalle, pattern for a dress fabric, silk, 149 ½ x 22 in (380 x 55.6 cm), c. 1770. Musée des Arts Decoratifs, Paris.

interrelationship between the arts and business acumen that produced the flowering of luxury decorative arts in pre-revolutionary France. Jean le Rond d'Alembert, Diderot's coeditor of the *Encyclopédie* (see pages 18–19), expressed wonder at the level of expertise achieved by weavers: "Has anything ever been imagined, in any domain, more ingenious than the process of weaving striped velvet?" The remark is yet another testimony to the awareness of and admiration for the technical expertise and creativity associated with the applied arts during the *ancien régime*.

In the later eighteenth century, a synergy existed between the luxury textile industry and the aristocratic focus upon dress. At the court of Versailles, dress clearly conveyed royal splendor and provided a recognizable visual code of formal social distinctions. In the urban and increasingly fashionable quarters of Paris, dress communicated social aspirations and pretensions as well as personal identity, giving rise to boutiques and to *marchands de mode* or fashion merchants, such as Rose Bertin (1747–1813), who designed outfits and accessories, including elaborate coiffures, for Marie Antoinette and other royal and wealthy customers. In the 1770s, fashion illustrations (or plates) in journals replaced fashion dolls as a means for circulating the latest Parisian fashions to courts and tailors throughout Europe. Formal dress for women consisted of hips accentuated by layers of skirts, underskirts, and petticoats supported by hoops or panniers, a tightly corseted bodice, and a low neckline. The flowing silhouette that resulted from such an ensemble emphasized an idealized sensuality associated with the female body, but required elaborate undergarments that restricted physical activity. As prints and paintings of the period suggest, women trained to walk in such dresses appeared to glide or hover over the floor, heightening the desired effect of idealization and distinction. The connection between royal patronage of design, productivity, and economic stability, implied in the tapestry representing Louis XIV inspecting the workshops at the Gobelins (see fig. 1.1), continued to provide a rationale for monarchical authority and prerogative even as more democratic attitudes emerged that challenged this established order in a variety of ways.

PORCELAIN

As seen in Boucher's *The Chinese Fair* above (see fig. 1.5), Asia generated much intrigue and excitement in Europe during the later seventeenth and eighteenth centuries, both as a source of adventure and of economic expansion. In the arts, interest accrued to imported lacquer furnishings and to porcelain – a smooth, refined combination of ceramic materials fired at high temperatures (and producing a distinctive ring when tapped), possessing translucent surfaces. The ingredients and techniques of porcelain production were unknown in Europe until the early eighteenth century in Germany. In 1710, a royal manufactory for the production of highly prized hard-paste porcelain was established under Augustus II, elector of Saxony and king of Poland (1670–1733) at Meissen. In France, a manufactory founded in 1738 to produce soft-paste porcelain was relocated in 1756 from Vincennes to Sèvres near Paris. Its range of wares satisfied both royal demand and the tastes of a sophisticated urban elite in the later eighteenth century.

Porcelain from the royal manufactory at Sèvres ranged from extensive dinner services consisting of plates, saucers, and cups for multi-course meals, to display pieces such as candelabra and pot-pourri containers featuring carved and painted decoration and more fanciful shapes as well as brilliant glazes. Sèvres porcelain also included carved figurines based upon classical themes or upon subjects derived from contemporary popular theater and entertainment. Upon close observation, dinner plates reveal smooth surfaces, precisely patterned scalloped edges, and delicately painted borders with floral patterns that appear to float against a polished, milk-white translucent ground. It is generally agreed that such elaborate services, numbering to hundreds of individual pieces, were of distinctly higher quality than the Chinese export pottery specifically manufactured for European (and American) markets at the request of trading companies that began to face competition from the more recently established domestic manufactories. Services of export porcelain often were individualized through the inclusion of coats of arms for the families who commissioned them, and were generally based upon designs supplied to the Chinese manufactories by merchants. At manufactories such as Sèvres or Meissen, a closer collaboration between designers and craftsmen generally produced more symbiotic results.

Better known for their display in eighteenth-century period rooms in major museum collections throughout Europe and the United States are the pink and turquoise, green, or even violet and yellow vases with delicately painted scenes and patterns, elaborately carved handles, relief decoration, and gilded accents. Such display pieces reveal greater specialization of labor and a resulting brilliance of effect. Among the most complex and fanciful of this type is the monumental pot-pourri container (fig. 1.7) in the shape of a tall boat, the sweeping pyramidal "sail" of which is perforated to allow fragrances to escape. On either side, a carved personification of a "wind" blows in either direction, alluding to the freshness of sea breezes. The container dates to around 1761 and was modeled by the Italian-born goldsmith Jean-Claude Duplessis (c. 1695–1774), who worked at Sèvres and was responsible for some of the more inventive production at the manufactory.

THE GUILDS

Alongside the large state-owned industries that flourished in France and elsewhere during the eighteenth century there coexisted a longstanding tradition of independent craft organizations known as guilds (*corps* in French), many of which were organized as early as the thirteenth century. Guilds generally consisted of smaller workshops employing apprentices and journeymen working under the direction of a master who was trained in all aspects of a particular skill such as furniture-making, glass manufacture, or metalwork. Masters owned or rented space for manufacturing their goods on commission directly from a patron. During the course of the eighteenth century, masters also operated through merchants acting as intermediaries with clients; their role increased in importance and included aspects of design (see page 24). Guilds maintained high standards of craftsmanship and, aside from the state-owned manufactories whose products they

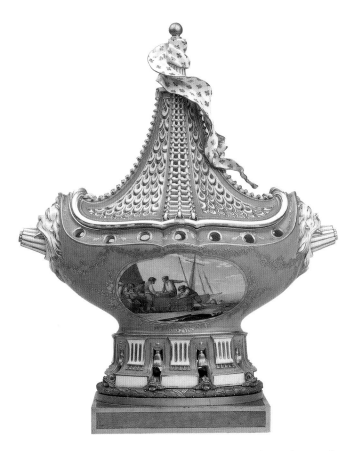

1.7 Jean-Claude Duplessis, pot-pourri container in the shape of a masted ship, soft-paste porcelain, 14 ¾ x 13 ³⁄₁₆ x 6 ½ in (37.4 x 33.5 x 14.5 cm), c. 1761, manufactured at the Royal Porcelain Manufactory at Sèvres. Waddesdon Manor, Aylesbury.

reserved the right to inspect, enjoyed a relative monopoly of craft production. In the later nineteenth century, the founders of the Arts and Crafts movement romantically recalled, in an age of increased mechanization and mass production, the technical knowledge, high levels of skill, and independence associated with the guilds. Even in the early twentieth century, faculty at the Bauhaus in Weimar were given the title of "master" rather than "professor" to reflect associations with the guild tradition (see page 197), and direct experience with materials and craft production still remain part of both art and design education in many colleges and universities. For admission to a guild as a master, journeymen were required to produce a "*master-piece*," judged by guild members and providing evidence of skill as well as invention. The trades of metalwork, particularly in precious materials, and wood carving and marquetry in the furniture trade, were among the most highly respected crafts during the eighteenth century, with closer ties to the fine art of sculpture. And as noted above, the design of patterns for silk weaving was often undertaken by artists trained as painters, at least at the higher end of the market.

Guild organizations paid taxes to a monarch or prince in exchange for exclusive rights to manufacture and distribute their products in a particular region, enabling the guild to set prices and protecting them from open competition. Low prices were equated with reduced quality, and thus were judged by the guilds as not being in the best interests of the consumer. Like state-owned or subsidized manufactories, the guilds depended for the most part upon the patronage of a privileged clientele who commissioned unique and individual works either directly from a master or through the intermediary of a merchant. These two systems of production coexisted in eighteenth-century France. Scholars have explained that the craftsmen working directly for the crown, such as Pierre Gole or Domenico Cucci, were exempt from guild restrictions; this enabled them to combine skills with a greater degree of novelty and originality.

Although luxury works such as Domenico Cucci's cabinet (see fig. 1.2) were made to order, expanding demand in the eighteenth century often led to the establishment of basic types of furniture rather than entirely unique pieces, and during this time a typology of standard pieces such as commodes, consoles, sofas, bergères, and secretaries emerged. In response to the development of typologies, and the accompanying specialization of production, entirely new guilds also emerged. The industry of furniture-making is one such example; the growing complexities of production were illustrated in the plates of Diderot and d'Alembert's *Encyclopédie*. In the mid-eighteenth century, the making of a luxury item such as a dressing table or bureau might involve the efforts of a number of distinct crafts. A basic carved chassis might be the responsibility of the carpenter or *menusier*, while the veneers and marquetry designs were the work of an *ébéniste*. A goldsmith or porcelain manufactory supplied gilt fittings or ceramic plaques, while a separate group of craftsmen was responsible for upholstery, utilizing woven fabrics ordered from yet another manufactory, usually located in the French city of Lyon (see page 21).

Specialization also resulted in the development of other varied areas of expertise that continue to form part of our understanding of the history of design. In addition to determining the size, overall form, and different types of materials, construction, and decoration of a particular table or chest of drawers, artisans also gave careful consideration to the mechanical functions of individual parts – that is, the way these pieces "interacted" with their users. The efficiently designed sliding table with pop-up mirrors combined the function of a desk with that of a vanity, as seen in figure 1.8, an example from the workshop of German-born master Jean-Henri Riesener (1734–1806) made for Marie Antoinette (1755–1793). As noted above, specialization increasingly necessitated the services of the *marchand mercier*, a merchant (mercer) or furniture dealer who often liaised between customer and craftsmen. These individuals often subcontracted a commission to several shops, coordinating the efforts of a number of master craftsmen to create furniture for sale in the merchant's shop. In Paris, many of the merchants' retail premises were located on the Right Bank in the fashionable rue Saint-Honoré, still a center for upscale retail and designer shops today. Mercers were often trained as craftsmen and may have worked as designers; but their role is perhaps best understood as being in direct contact with customers, catering to as well as shaping their desires.

In the eighteenth century, commercially minded mercers attracted customers with shop signs hanging outside the door (an example is Antoine Watteau's sign for the merchant Edmé-François Gersaint's store Au Grand Monarque, though located at the Pont Notre-Dame rather than on the rue Saint-Honoré and dating to 1720) and framed portraits of royal clients hanging on the walls. The mercer's role is a telling feature of eighteenth-century commerce. It demonstrates that the production of luxury goods involved a broad range of interdependent activities that included designing and various kinds of "making" as well as an ability to translate or stimulate the desire of a wealthy and cultured client for a combination of beauty, comfort, display, practicality, and convenience into a manufactured object that remains part of our understanding of the term "design" as the value added to articles of use, often in a domestic setting.

Many products of this manufacturing system remain among the most celebrated examples of eighteenth-century comfort. A good example is a secretary (fig. 1.9) dating to around 1787 that combines marquetry designs from the workshop of Adam Weisweiler (1744–1820; like Riesener, a German master craftsman working in Paris) and a series of Sèvres plaques used as surface decoration. This piece is remarkable less for its grandeur or elaborate decoration than for the precision of its manufacture and the ingenuity of its pull-down writing surface, which takes up less space than a large desk. Such furniture was designed with spatial efficiency in mind for clients furnishing apartments in the city rather than more expansive country estates. The plaques illustrate scenes of comfortably dressed shepherds dancing or resting in a landscape, and closely resemble similar subjects painted by François Boucher, such as a 1749 canvas entitled *An Autumn Pastoral* in the Wallace Collection in London.

Since the furnishings of a single room of luxury furniture might cost more than the annual salary of a skilled worker, only an exclusive clientele could enjoy the beauty and comfort of such furniture. The literary pastimes of this elite clientele are the subject of Jean-François de Troy's *La Lecture de Molière* (c. 1725; fig. 1.10), a painting whose

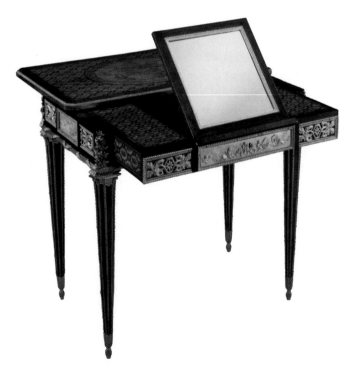

1.8 Jean-Henri Riesener, writing table with pop-up mirrors, oak veneered with *bois satiné* (bloodwood), holly, black-stained holly, amaranth, berberis, stained sycamore, and green lacquered wood, gilt-bronze mounts, 31 x 44 ½ x 27 in (78.7 x 113 x 68.6 cm), 1778. Metropolitan Museum of Art, New York.

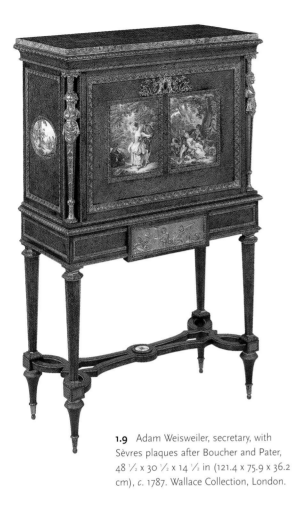

1.9 Adam Weisweiler, secretary, with Sèvres plaques after Boucher and Pater, 48 ½ x 30 ½ x 14 ½ in (121.4 x 75.9 x 36.2 cm), c. 1787. Wallace Collection, London.

interior setting is less frequently depicted by De Troy's contemporaries such as Boucher, Jean-Baptiste-Joseph Pater, Nicolas Lancret, or Jean-Honoré Fragonard, artists who preferred scenes of music parties or picnics in park-like surroundings. The furniture depicted in De Troy's interior contributes more than a measure of comfort and informality to the gathering and the participants' relaxed enjoyment of the pleasures of reading and listening.

Along with intimate reading and listening, interiors were also the setting for cultivated conversation in the homes of the wealthy known as salons, named for the drawing rooms in which such gatherings occurred (not to be confused with the official "Salons" where sculpture and painting were exhibited in public; see page 20). Eighteenth-century salons were often organized by women and offered an alternative to court formality and protocol. Salons also cultivated intellectual curiosity and freedom in the Age of Enlightenment. As art historian Leora Auslander has explained, features of eighteenth-century furniture relate both to the salon and to women, particularly the drawer mechanisms on secretaries or dressing tables that facilitated their ease of use (see page 24). The intellectual climate of the period is suggested in the interior design of the Grand Salon of the Hôtel Gaillard de la Bouëxière in Paris (now in the Minneapolis Institute of Arts) dating to the reign of Louis XV (c. 1735; fig. 1.11).

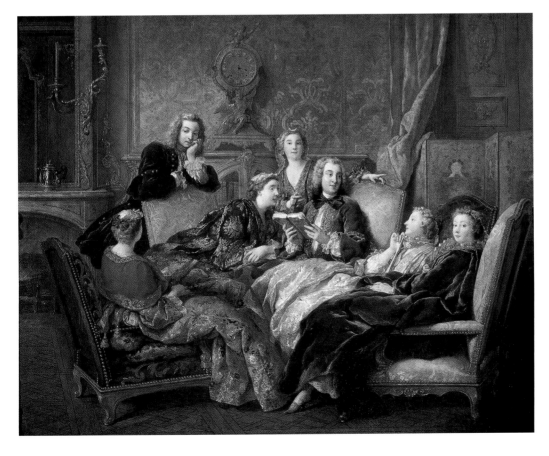

1.10 Jean-François de Troy, *La Lecture de Molière* (*The Reading from Molière*), oil on canvas, 29 ⅛ x 36 ⅝ in (73.7 x 93.4 cm), c. 1725. Private collection.

The salon is an oval room decorated with carved and gilded trophies and friezes relating to the arts, to nature's abundance, and to amusement – here in the form of monkeys inhabiting vine scrolls and playing musical instruments. Only an educated audience familiar with allusions to classical mythology would have appreciated the invention, skill, and literary associations inherent in the ensemble, in which a sophisticated and coordinated approach to design is evident.

As well as furniture and interior design, other decorative objects designed for the domestic interior demonstrate the cultivated sensibilities of the period, and in particular the close relationship between fine and applied art that existed in the luxury trade. In De Troy's *La Lecture de Molière*, a large clock rests on a table at the back of the room. Charles Cressent (1685–1768) was a master *ébéniste* working in Paris; he was also trained as a sculptor and manufactured his own gilded metal mounts or fittings. Among his most intricate creations are clock cases, such as the cartel or wall clock made of gilded bronze illustrated

in figure 1.12 and dating to 1740–1745 during the reign of Louis XV. Atop the clock is an allegorical figure representing Time wielding a scythe above the circular clock. Below, contained within a C-shaped scroll, is Cupid, reaching out as if to interrupt the motion of Time. Asymmetrically surrounding the figures is a rich array of thick foliage that suggests an overgrowth in need of pruning. The ensemble suggests that love conquers time, appropriate for an object that keeps and measures time's passage and also reveals how we may defeat its ravages. Clocks combined the most complicated mechanical ingenuity of the period with reflection upon the meaning of time on a symbolic level.

In 1791, the revolutionary government in France abolished the monopolies enjoyed by the guilds for craft production as vestiges of monarchy and privilege. The guild system, which had been responsible both for the education of craftsmen and the protection of exclusive production values, had to adjust to a succession of new official patrons, from the revolutionary government to the

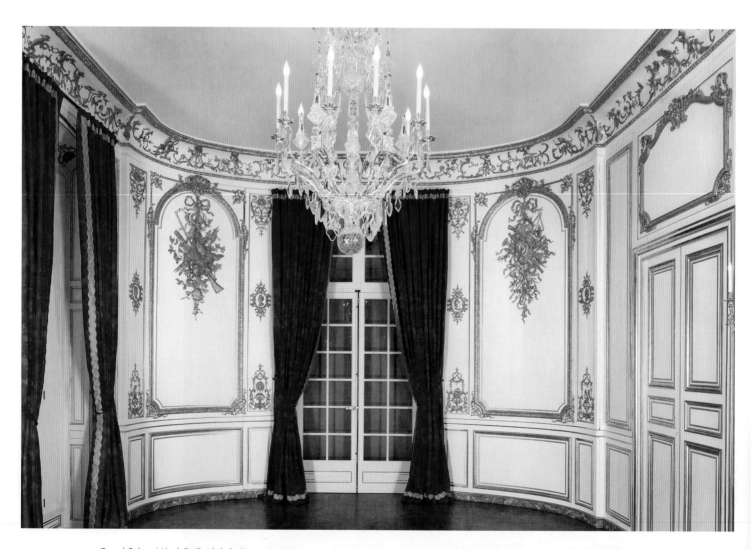

1.11 Grand Salon, Hôtel Gaillard de la Bouëxière, Paris, 190 ⅝ x 349 ½ x 230 ³⁄₁₆ in (484 x 888 x 585 cm), c. 1735. Minneapolis Institute of Arts.

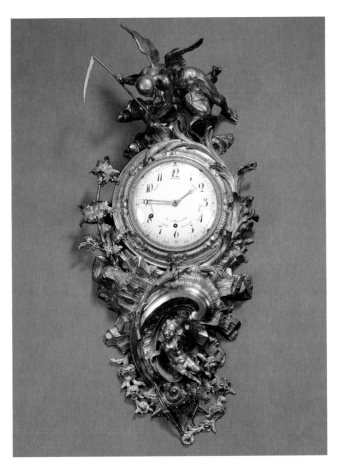

Directory (1792–1795), Consulate (1799–1804), Empire (1804–1814), and finally the restored monarchy after 1815. Those governments continued to assume responsibility for patronage and education, sponsoring "official styles" and establishing schools for the training of designers to replace or supplement earlier workshop practice. At the same time, merchants and manufacturers were generally forced to adjust to more entrepreneurial conditions, including international trade and resulting competition. The return of centralized authority in France under Napoleon Bonaparte (1769–1821) in 1804 led to renewed royal patronage and an official "Empire" style in the decorative arts, created in part by the architects Charles Percier (1764–1838) and Pierre Fontaine (1762–1853), who produced severe Neoclassical designs for furniture and furnishings, meant to embody the enduring spirit of reason and repudiate the decorative excess associated with the *ancien régime*. Percier and Fontaine published their designs in *Receuil des décorations intérieures* in 1801. The engraved plates from this work (fig. 1.13) show forms inspired by the study of Greek as well as Roman imperial art, and decoration utilizing Classical figures alluding to time-honored themes such as military victory, fame, and love. By invoking the sober forms of an ancient past, the designers and craftsmen of the decorative arts under the Empire believed that transforming taste would restore and promote values of reason embodied in the forms of Classical art.

1.12 Charles Cressent, cartel clock, copper alloy and mercury gilding with wood, enamel face, 45 ½ x 19 ½ in (115.5 x 49.5 cm), 1740–1745. The Nelson-Atkins Museum of Art, Kansas City, Missouri.

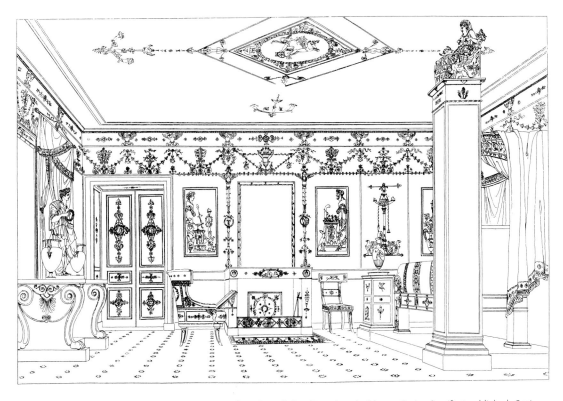

1.13 Charles Percier and Pierre Fontaine, interior, from *Receuil des décorations intérieures*, Paris, 1812 (first published 1801).

Although the royal laws that protected the guilds from competition had been abolished after the Revolution, furnishings designed and manufactured during the Empire show remarkable continuity with the traditions of luxury craft: the techniques of woodworking and metals continued to be practiced at the highest and most demanding levels of skill and with patronage provided by a restored central authority. Design remained a tool of statecraft under Napoleon and designers such as Percier and Fontaine were responsible for creating his public image, transforming Neoclassicism into a style of authority *and* of a new rational order extending to the organization of French society. Indeed, the fine *and* decorative arts were an important part of Napoleon's ambitions to reshape French society after the Revolution.

Despite the restoration of centralized political authority, the new circumstances created in the aftermath of the French Revolution were not always conducive to maintaining an effective and progressive collaboration and interchange between craftsmen, artists, mercers, and clients that had contributed to the quality and reputation for luxury goods both in France and abroad during most of the eighteenth century. Tracing the history of the decorative arts in the aftermath of the revolutionary period involves a consideration of many factors, such as introducing steam power in production technologies for some industries (for instance in weaving), promoting efforts on the part of government to identify and maintain standards for design, supporting the French reputation for luxury goods, as well as developing new commercial strategies in retailing and merchandising for expanding consumption in a more competitive international economic climate. The effects of such developments are more fully explored in the next chapter.

Despite the exclusivity that dominated the production and consumption of the decorative arts during the later seventeenth and eighteenth centuries, the efforts of the guilds to limit competition, and the tensions between government and guild, between court and salon, and between fine and mechanical arts, the *ancien régime* provided the political, social, and aesthetic context for the development of a highly successful approach to luxury design that was the envy of other nations during the eighteenth century. Whether through the *marchand mercier* who catered to the tastes of a cultivated elite, or through Le Brun or Percier and Fontaine, who established through their efforts the prestige and aura of royal and aristocratic authority, design emerged as a task or skill related to and yet distinct from making, connecting finished products to the ideals and aspirations of their audience. Those values linked manufactured goods to art, to industry, to nationalism, and to the quality of life in a society with a hierarchical social and political order; in time that order came under pressure from the democratic forces of political revolution and its economic as well as social consequences.

THE PRINTER'S ART

Diderot and d'Alembert's *Encyclopédie* is noteworthy not only for what its engraved plates reveal about the complex organization and practice of many industries, including the decorative arts, but also for its ambitious scope as a publishing venture. In its first edition, the *Encyclopédie* comprised 17 volumes of text and thousands of engraved illustrations released over 21 years, and earned a considerable profit for its publisher through subscription sales. The search for and dissemination of knowledge, the formation of private libraries by aristocratic and other wealthy patrons, the pastime of reading aloud or privately (as illustrated in fig. 1.10), as well as the emergence of newspapers (broadsides) and other popular and ephemeral printed materials, stimulated significant changes in the craft of printing that also form a part of the history of modern design. While the *Encyclopédie* generated interest for the currency of information it contained on the widest range of subjects, its publisher was also concerned with the quality of its production in terms of printing, binding, and the overall presentation of the text and images for a wealthy and discriminating clientele. Each aspect of printing production, from papermaking (from boiling rags into pulp rather than from wood) to punch-cutting, matrix-casting, page design, and scrupulous editing, had become a specialized task by the eighteenth century, achieving high levels of expertise and skill for a market that valued the book as an object of beauty and a sign of cultivation as well as a product of use.

The types for the *Encyclopédie* were purchased from Pierre Simon Fournier le jeune ("the younger," 1712–1768), among the best-known type founders of the period. Fournier developed an early version of the point system for measuring type, and had published his own specimens of type and printers' decorations for borders and frames (known as fleurons) in his *Modèles des Caractères* in 1742. He also published a manual presenting and celebrating the achievements of the printing profession. Fournier's types display refined characteristics derived from the "King's Roman" (*romain du roi*) designed at the direction of Louis XIV for the exclusive use of the crown. Historians of type often use the adjective "mechanical" in describing these letterforms, signaling a shift from the freer forms of calligraphically inspired letters (derived from traditions of writing with a quill pen) toward more precise and rational ("typographic") letters featuring hairline (rather than bracketed) serifs, stronger contrasts between thick and thin strokes, vertical rather than slanted shading or stress of letters, and greater uniformity in the width of all thick strokes. Following Fournier, the Didot family of printers in Paris, beginning with François-Ambroise (1730–1804) and spanning several generations from the later eighteenth to the early nineteenth centuries, also mastered the new concerns with typography, page design, and the overall quality of production. The portability of books and the printers' practice of publishing specimen books of their typefaces and fleurons for publishers and workshop use (or for posterity in the more luxurious examples) created a good deal of communication and cross-fertilization both in Europe and across the Atlantic. The reputation of the Didot family, for instance, was recognized by the American printer and statesman Benjamin Franklin, himself a printer, who apprenticed his grandson to a branch of the Parisian firm in 1785.

Generally, historians of typography, such as Philip Meggs, view the late eighteenth century as "an epoch of typographic genius." Examining a leather-bound volume published by the firm of Didot more than justifies this claim. The reduction of crowding between letters as well as lines, the ample margins, and the precise contours of letterforms result from careful planning and execution, and from attention to the role of each element both separately and in relation to one another. Letters of the Didot typeface, illustrated in a volume of the poetry of Virgil (fig. 1.14) published in 1798 by Pierre Didot (François-Ambroise's son, 1760–1853), are crisply cut and employ hairline serifs and a distinct contrast between thick and thin strokes of uniform width. Uniformity was also applied to the height of each line of text (sometimes known as the x-height, the heights of capital letters being the same as lower-case ascenders) and to the repetition of shapes among the bodies of individual letterforms. Careful examination and comparison with earlier eighteenth-century books also shows that faces such as Didot increase the length of lower-case letters like "g" or "d" that reach above or below the x-height, creating the impression of wider space between lines and less crowding of the text. Pierre Didot and other typographers also devoted attention to the serifs or letter endings of their fonts. While retaining curved brackets on capital letterforms such as the horizontal arms of the "L" or "E," such transitional elements were eliminated at the bases and tops of other letters. These changes are usually attributed to the printers' desire to reduce the calligraphic character of fonts and their association with the inconsistency of handwritten letters. Considered together, the characteristics of the Didot font are usually described as "Modern" (or "Didonic" in another system of classification), whereas less contrast between thick and thin strokes, shorter ascenders and descenders,

AENEIDOS

LIBER OCTAVUS.

Ut belli signum Laurenti Turnus ab arce
Extulit, et rauco strepuerunt cornua cantu,
Utque acres concussit equos, utque impulit arma;
Extemplo turbati animi; simul omne tumultu
Conjurat trepido Latium, sævitque juventus
Effera. Ductores primi, Messapus, et Ufens,
Contemptorque deûm Mezentius, undique cogunt
Auxilia, et latos vastant cultoribus agros.
Mittitur et magni Venulus Diomedis ad urbem,
Qui petat auxilium, et Latio consistere Teucros,
Advectum Aenean classi, victosque Penates
Inferre, et fatis regem se dicere posci,
Edoceat, multasque viro se adjungere gentes
Dardanio, et latè Latio increbrescere nomen:
Quid struat his cœptis, quem, si fortuna sequatur,
Eventum pugnæ cupiat, manifestiùs ipsi,
Quàm Turno regi aut regi apparere Latino.
   Talia per Latium: quæ Laomedontius heros
Cuncta videns, magno curarum fluctuat æstu,
Atque animum nunc huc celerem, nunc dividit illuc,
In partesque rapit varias, perque omnia versat.
Sicut aquæ tremulum labris ubi lumen ahenis,

23

1.14 Page from Virgil's *Bucolica, Georgica, et Aeneis*, Paris (Pierre Didot), 6 ⅛6 x 3 ½ in (15.3 x 8.9 cm), 1798. Hagerty Library, Drexel University, Philadelphia.

angled shading or stress, and bracketed serifs are features associated with "Old Face" (Humanistic and Garaldic). Both families of fonts belong to the broad category of typefaces known as "Roman," based in the upper case upon the carved inscriptions (epigraphy) known from Roman Imperial monuments such as the Pantheon and Trajan's Column and in the lower case upon early medieval scripts revived by writing masters and early printers in Italy at the end of the fifteenth century.

Historians of typography have also noted that printers were interested in achieving a balance between the elegance of the letterforms, the organization of the page, and the legibility of the text. This in turn may be seen as a parallel to transformations in other crafts where specialized expertise and experiment led to new levels of practical as well as aesthetic achievement. Increasing the amount of white space on a page of printed type tends to make it more inviting to the reader – something that appears to have been taken into account by the printer in the design of the page layout. On the other hand, thin strokes may lack the strength to stand out on the page and consequently may tire the reader's eye. Creating the desired effect – the balance between delicate effect and legibility – constitutes an important part of the printer's art and has remained a subject of debate among typographers and typographic historians.

As mentioned above, a number of eighteenth-century printers published extensive specimen books exhibiting the range of their achievement and providing models for others to follow. Among the most comprehensive is Giambattista Bodoni's (1740–1813) *Manuale Tipografico*, published in two volumes in 1818 (fig. 1.15) by his wife after the printer's death. Recruited as court printer to the duke of Parma (who was at the same time acquiring an important collection of books for his private library), Bodoni enjoyed the creative freedom to produce the *Manuale* as a luxury work, with examples of dozens of typefaces in standard and italic fonts, as well as alphabets in Greek and Hebrew. The text of each page is framed by a bold double band with very wide margins on all sides. Other contemporary printers often employed borders around their texts, but also developed a vocabulary of patterned geometric or floral patterns (fleurons) that complemented the visual weight of the typeface, and recalled the intricate decorative flourishes of medieval scribes who copied their texts by hand in manuscripts. Bodoni limited this practice in his *Manuale*, concentrating more upon the letterforms themselves and the overall design or architecture of the page.

Other typographic innovations were meant to ensure consistency in measurement and standards among the fonts developed by different printers. Drawing upon earlier initiatives to create families of type (fonts) in standardized sizes of uniform quality, François-Ambroise Didot further developed a standard system of measurement in which the sizes of letters were referred to by points, 72 to an inch. The point system gained currency in France, was later adopted in Britain and in Germany, and is still in use today (the type sizes that we effortlessly manipulate on our computer screens are based on the same system). Innovations in eighteenth-century printing occurred in an exclusive milieu dominated by wealthy patrons with discriminating and exclusive taste. It is hardly surprising that the model for so-called "Modern" or "Didonic" typefaces emerged from the court of Louis XIV and was yet another aspect of the monarchy's effort to brand the products of the court, control their production and use, and monitor printed materials and their dissemination through official channels of production. Even in his admiration for the King's Roman, Fournier had to be careful not to raise the eyebrows of government officials by imitating too closely the types of the National Printing House (Imprimérie Royale). Modern typefaces, like the contemporary crafts of the *ébéniste* or worker in precious metals (*ciseleur*), exemplified the progress of the mechanical arts through specialization, skill, and rationally developed methods of professional design and practice.

Quousque tan-
dem abutêre,Ca-
tilina, patientiâ

Quousque tan-
dẽ abutêre, Ca-
tilina, patientiâ

Quousque tan-
dem abutêre,
Catilina, pati-

1.15 Specimen of Ducale in three weights, detail from *Manuale Tipografico del cavaliere Giambattista Bodoni*, Parma, 1818.

Fine printing, as practiced and perfected by Fournier, Didot, or Bodoni, was not the only achievement of eighteenth-century publishing. While it is difficult to trace and study the history of decorative arts for a non-elite audience during this period, the existence of a popular art for a broader public can be appreciated in the practice of printing. While perhaps less aesthetically refined and not always exhibiting the highest levels of craftsmanship, more topical forms of print, such as newspapers or broadsides, almanacs, or the expression of controversial religious and political opinions in the form of pamphlets or inexpensively bound volumes, reached a broad and increasingly literate public during the eighteenth century and constitute an equally important and inspiring legacy of printing as a popular, accessible medium for expression and communication. Such material reminds us that the mechanical arts, however rudimentary, reached beyond the authority of official policy and served needs beyond those of a cultural elite. Works such as Joseph Moxon's *Mechanick's Exercises on the Whole Art of Printing*, published in England in 1683–1684 to provide an illustrated guide to the practice of printing, informed readers that knowledge was something to be shared rather than too closely guarded. These democratizing views will be treated in relation to the American colonies, where the press was less regulated and printed opinion circulated more freely and publicly (see page 39 and fig. 2.10).

Chapter 2

Entrepreneurial Efforts in Britain and Elsewhere

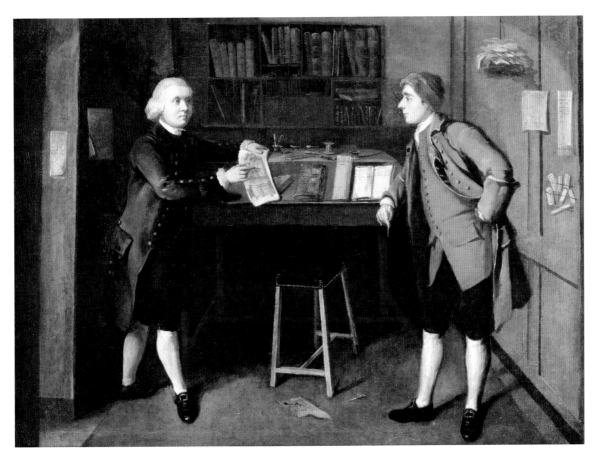

2.1 Anonymous, *A Cabinet-Maker in His Office*, oil on canvas, 20 ⅝ x 27 ½ in (52.7 x 70.2 cm), 1770. Victoria and Albert Museum, London.

In eighteenth-century Britain, the initiatives of a new breed of craftsman–merchant led to a number of successful enterprises in the decorative arts that both competed with continental luxury production and expanded the trade in such goods to include an upwardly mobile middle class. The inherent flexibility of technology and the specialization of labor, together with the ingenuity of entrepreneurs and their recognition of the roles of design and marketing in stimulating desire, combined to make such successes possible. Once again, such efforts required not only capital investment and oversight of a number of interdependent activities involving both manufacture and marketing, but also the existence of more competitive economic conditions and opportunities that made both efforts and results more varied and dynamic.

DESIGN IN AN EXPANDING MARKET

We may begin with the career of London cabinet-maker Thomas Chippendale (1718–1779). Chippendale published the illustrated furniture catalogue known as *The Gentleman and Cabinet-Maker's Director* in 1754, whose designs demonstrate an awareness of an expanding audience for luxury furnishings to decorate apartments and houses. Unlike earlier pattern or model books intended for workshop use (although it was certainly used as such by other cabinet-makers), Chippendale's *Director* targeted prospective *customers*; its publication was timed to coincide with the opening of parliament after a general election, when new members would be relocating to London and looking to furnish their apartments or town houses. Although

Chippendale trained as a cabinet-maker, his London shop provided complete services for custom interior design including upholstery and wall-coverings, and he was the overseer of a large workshop employing more than 150 craftsmen. The publication of the illustrated *Director*, the scale of operations, and the range of services all indicate Chippendale's attention to design and a growing interest in the decorative arts as an accompaniment to refined living and a mark of social distinction. The anonymous portrait dating to 1770 and reproduced in figure 2.1 represents the shop of an unidentified cabinet-maker who is preparing a drawing of a cabinet and bookcase to show to a prospective client. The younger man to the right has been identified as an employee, possibly the owner's bookkeeper. It is instructive to note that the cabinet-maker is not depicted as a craftsman in working attire but rather as a gentleman wearing breeches, a wig, and stockings – it is the retail end of the trade that is depicted, emphasizing the higher social standing connected with the roles of designer/merchant–manufacturer in fulfilling the aspirations of a client, and illustrating as well the distinctions and relationships among designing, making, and selling.

Chippendale's designs show a preference for contemporary French taste in the style of Louis XV, but the illustrated plates in the *Director* also include variations of this style such as Chinese motifs (chinoiserie) as well as furniture with decorative features based upon the Gothic style in architecture (figs. 2.2 and 2.3), which appealed to English taste at the time. Indeed, this heterogeneity and consciousness of style was characteristic of later eighteenth-century dress and other applied arts.

To what factors are we to attribute the eclecticism that emerged in the mid-eighteenth century in Britain? After all, the very coexistence of different styles in art challenges the general view of a successive and linear view of artistic change – the phenomenon of different tastes or styles existing at the same time suggests that ideals of beauty were contested among different individuals and groups rather than reflecting the shared outlook of a single, hegemonic taste. Indeed, we might suggest two explanations, the first acknowledging a broader and more heterogeneous market that reveals diverse rather than the shared or uniform tastes of a narrow elite; and the second recognizing that the acquisition of commodities is a powerful and self-conscious expression of personal and social identity. Styles drew from history (more properly historicism, the tendency to attribute values and attitudes to the past) and travel, and acknowledged an emerging sense of individualism, far less monolithic and authoritarian than under centralized monarchical control. There was an accompanying tendency toward competition and change that increased more rapidly after political revolutions in the United States (1775) and France (1789), and the Peace of Vienna in 1815 following the defeat of Napoleon (see page 43). Some styles adopted the curved surfaces and delicate carving associated with French luxury furniture, while others indulged a penchant for heightened emotionalism associated with nature, the Middle Ages, or exotic places in the Near and Far East.

In this new era, royalty were not the only authorities in the creation of ideal images for imitation. Questioning tradition was an expression of freedom and independence, parallel to the growing and prized emancipation of the artist that emerged with the Romantic movement in the late eighteenth and early nineteenth centuries (and that was later commercially exploited by manufacturers). An expanding, elastic market, by nature, reflected more diverse tastes than those of a homogeneous, aristocratic patronage. Thus, in general terms, such variety was a result of an incipient democratization of culture based upon commerce and the enjoyment and consumption of commodities.

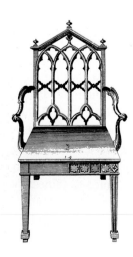

2.2 Thomas Chippendale, Gothic chair, detail of plate from *The Gentleman's and Cabinet-Maker's Director*, London, 17 ¾ x 12 ¼ in (45.1 x 31.1 cm), 1754.

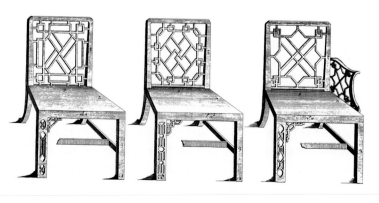

2.3 Thomas Chippendale, Chinese chairs, detail of plate from *The Gentleman's and Cabinet-Maker's Director*, London, 17 ¾ x 12 ¼ in (45.1 x 31.1 cm), 1754.

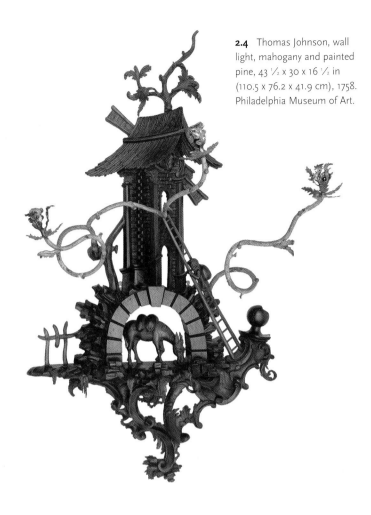

Johnson's girandoles, like the clocks of Charles Cressent in France (see fig. 1.12), demonstrate that the desire for luxury living stimulated a healthy dialogue between fine and applied arts, by which the latter could rise above the merely mechanical or useful, acquiring both beauty, intellectual value, and conferring distinction upon their owners.

WEDGWOOD AND ANTIQUITY

Younger than Chippendale, another ingenious entrepreneur of this period in England was Josiah Wedgwood (1730–1795), who came from a family of potters in Staffordshire, an area known throughout Britain at the time for the production of earthenware. As a trained craftsman, Wedgwood's early contribution was primarily technical. He successfully developed a process for making a cream-colored glazed earthenware (called creamware) that was considerably more refined than other local products, and that adopted the then-current preference in the luxury market for simple, regular shapes and a restrained approach to painted decoration. A friendship (and eventual partnership) with Thomas Bentley of Liverpool that began in 1762 was instrumental in connecting Wedgwood with the market for luxury ceramics, for Bentley traveled frequently to London and was aware of shoppers' preferences, information that contributed to the choice of pottery shapes and painted patterns for their embellishment. The decoration, eventually using stenciled transfer-printing rather than hand-painting, was supplied by a firm in the city of Liverpool, and may be seen in examples of creamware plates and serving dishes dating from 1790 (fig. 2.5). Wedgwood's experiments, both technical and in

This phenomenon provided the political and social framework not only for the variety of styles in Chippendale's *Director* but also for even more curious invention and ingenuity. Thomas Johnson (1714–c. 1778) was a British designer and craftsman who specialized in the design of decorative frames and particularly of wall-mounted candelabra known as girandoles. Although the asymmetrical composition and spiral pendants seen in his published designs may have been inspired by the contemporary French taste for chinoiserie, many of Johnson's works demonstrate startling originality. A carved wooden wall light attributed to him (fig. 2.4) represents a rustic narrative scene complete with figures, architecture, and landscape. The freedom of invention is hardly conceivable without the existence of a public with disposable income eager for novelty, even fantasy. Thus we may conclude that the accelerated pace of change and variety in commodities, linked with the expression of Romantic ideals of individuality and a willingness to break with tradition, were potent social as well as economic catalysts to inventiveness in the decorative arts. Fashionable design and an eclectic range of products satisfied both the psychological and social aspirations of consumers and stimulated the entrepreneurial efforts of merchants, manufacturers, and artists.

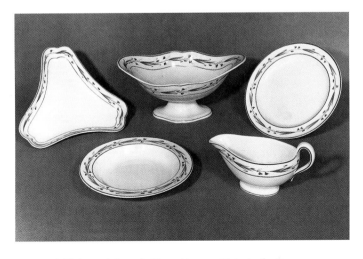

2.5 Josiah Wedgwood, Queen's Ware with green *Water Leaf* pattern, earthenware, *c.* 1790. Wedgwood Museum, Stoke-on-Trent.

terms of design and marketing, resulted from a worldly outlook not uncommon among manufacturers and merchants of the time, and his creamware competed with more costly imported porcelain wares being produced in France and Germany for an exclusive market in the urban centers of Europe. With Bentley's privileged social connections, Wedgwood produced a large service of his creamware for Queen Charlotte of England (1744–1817), and this royal commission helped significantly to establish his firm's reputation for quality and fashion; indeed, after 1765 the design was known as Queen's Ware. Following this success he built a larger factory that he named Etruria in 1769. In the editions of his published catalogues, Wedgwood praised the influential patrons whose approval meant so much to the success of his wares:

> The demand for this said Creamcolour, alias Queen's Ware, Alias Ivory, still increases. It is really amazing how rapidly the use of it has spread almost over the whole Globe, and how universally it is liked. How much of this general use, and estimation, is owing to the mode of its introduction – and how much to its real utility and beauty? are questions in which we may be a good deal interested for the government of our future Conduct ... For instance, if a Royal, or Noble introduction be as necessary to the sale of an Article of Luxury, as real Elegance and beauty, then the Manufacturer, if he consults his own interest will bestow as much pains, and expence too, if necessary, in gaining the former of these advantages, as he would in bestowing the latter.

Wedgwood capitalized on the enlarged Etruria facility to increase production. His efforts included the division of labor, the use of a small number of standardized shapes that were customized through being matched with a variety of decorative patterns, and the use of molds rather than potters' wheels. Sometimes referred to as "batch production," Wedgwood's initiatives and innovations saved time and ensured uniformity and high quality, maximizing consumer choice within a limited range of shapes and decorative patterns. Since sets of creamware and other Wedgwood products were selected either from catalogues or ordered in showrooms, it was essential to maintain consistency and quality, and in the course of his career Wedgwood developed thermometers to measure more accurately the temperature of his kilns. For this and other inventions he was elected a Fellow of the Royal Society (Britain's national academy of science) in 1783.

Wedgwood also was attuned to considerations of distribution and retailing: he helped to finance the construction of canals near the Etruria manufactory to control transport, supply, and delivery, and always looked for ways to expand the market for his wares, for instance by opening a showroom in London and publishing an illustrated catalogue from which retail merchants could select and purchase samples. Wedgwood's career is a far cry from the image of the village craftsman. His skills and interest in quality may have initially been nourished in that milieu, but they matured and prospered amid increasingly entrepreneurial and competitive economic conditions, less strictly regulated than in France and directed toward an expanding market.

While the catalogues of Wedgwood ceramic wares display a variety of styles that catered to diverse tastes at mid-century, the patronage of wealthier clients and the appeal to their tastes was paramount to the company's success and reputation, as suggested by references in Wedgwood's correspondence (as noted above). Subsequent technical experiments by Wedgwood led to new stoneware products known as basalt and jasper wares, whose opaque surfaces in black and blue respectively were cast in molds with figural relief decoration in white, imitating friezelike compositions.

In recalling the stability and enduring humanistic values of the classical past, such stoneware catered to contemporary aristocratic taste for Greco-Roman antiquities, the rediscovery of the ancient Roman cities of Pompeii and Herculaneum, and the popularity of visiting these and other ancient sites on the Grand Tour (often in the company of knowledgeable guides). One of the most

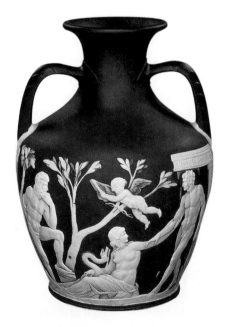

2.6 Josiah Wedgwood, the Portland (Barberini) vase, black jasper ware, 10 x 7 ⅜ in (25.4 x 18.7 cm), *c.* 1790. Wedgwood Museum, Stoke-on-Trent.

celebrated Roman objects of this period was the so-called Portland or Barberini vase, a cameo glass original of the first century BCE brought to Britain from Italy by an antiquities dealer and manufactured by Wedgwood in a series of stoneware copies beginning in 1790 (fig. 2.6). Wedgwood's stoneware designs such as the Barberini vase, or plaques with friezes, were based upon antique originals or upon models that Wedgwood commissioned from artists, including sculptor John Flaxman (1755–1826). These models (or designs) then become the basis for relief molds to create a variety of vases and plaques for firing and serial production.

Wedgwood marketed his classically inspired stoneware by successfully combining technical innovation and the most modern manufacturing methods with designs appealing to a sophisticated taste that recalled an idealized image of a past age. His success was also due in no small part to working closely with fine artists such as Flaxman, who championed the Neoclassical style and the enduring values it represented. In addition to his expertise as an innovative craftsman in the broadest sense of the word, Wedgwood's vision extended to design, marketing and merchandising, involving collaboration with artists.

Wedgwood's letters and project records provide a lively account of his business and the complex interrelationships among design, production, and marketing.

The emergence of the designer in craft production in Britain is also seen in the career of Robert Adam (1728–1792), an architect who supplied drawings of furniture and other interior furnishings to manufacturers (including Chippendale) for wealthy clients. Furniture designed by Adam incorporates elements of classically inspired architecture and decoration, often formal but enlivened by gilding and brightly colored silk fabrics or painted wall decorations. Kenwood, the estate of William Murray, the first Earl of Mansfield (1705–1793) in Hampstead Heath, London, was remodeled by Adam between 1764 and 1773, and its vaulted library was the public receiving room for the earl's guests (fig. 2.7). As an important judge serving under King George III, William Murray's library gives visual form to the education of its owner, with busts of Homer and Zeus located on either side of the earl's own painted portrait. Neoclassicism satisfied nostalgia for a golden age and gave reassurance of continuity with an imagined past. Classical motifs appear in the columns, garlands, and gilding that decorate the

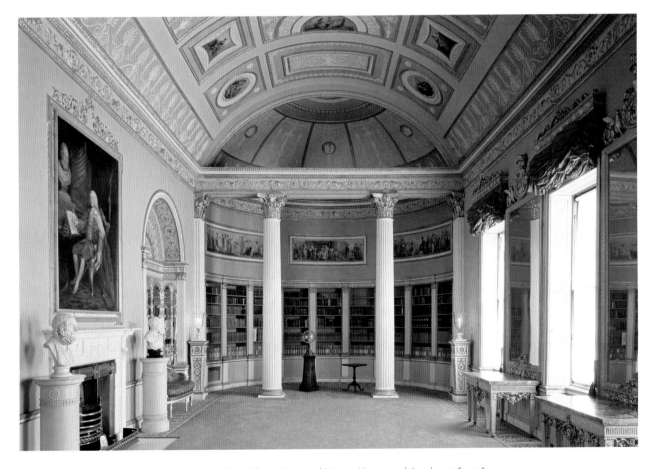

2.7 Robert Adam, Library, Kenwood House, Hampstead, London, 1767–1769.

mirrors, which in turn reflect light throughout the interior from large windows across the room. Frescoes by the Italian painter Antonio Zucchi (1728–1795) depict allegories of the arts as related to learning and civilization. Here the theme alludes to humanity's use of nature for peaceful enjoyment of her bounty, which in turn is amplified by learning. The sensual themes are also interesting – a marriage and a Bacchanal (albeit in a relatively chaste version) are depicted among the benefits of nature's gifts.

The interiors of Kenwood reveal a learned and sophisticated taste distinct from the solid carved mahogany furniture and coarser fabrics of earlier Georgian interiors; they indicate as well a new appreciation for the decorative arts in communicating the enlightened attitudes and distinction of their owners. One wonders what motivated so many traditionally wealthy and more recently successful and powerful families to build or more often to remodel their estates in the later eighteenth century and hire Adam to give expression to their ideals and values. One might see the popularity of Adam's Neoclassical design as an assertion of cultivated taste and privilege in a period when official views were challenged by public opinion, when traditional class distinctions were undermined by a more socially mobile society, and when change and the threat it posed to the established order produced a longing for the stability of a golden age as a source not only of nostalgia for the past but of hope for the present and future. Murray himself was not born into great privilege or wealth. He rose to become a high court chief justice respected for fair but often liberal views, including his support for legislation to outlaw slavery in Great Britain.

COMMODITIES AND FASHION

In an age of material progress and commercial expansion, Chippendale and Wedgwood's success underscores the significant role commodities played in communicating social status and individual identity, particularly in an economic and political climate in which opportunities for upward social mobility existed. According to a number of historians, the market for commodities in England became "elastic" when traditional class distinctions were blurred by new wealth amassed through trade, industry, and manufacturing, by fewer restrictions on entrepreneurship, and by the mingling of social classes that constitutes an aspect of an emerging urban life. Within this context of social aspiration and ambiguity, the desire for manufactured products acquired new and complex levels of meaning.

New wealth held the promise of personal improvement and social acceptance; consumption was one of the visible signs of social status, through the emulation of fashion in dress and the display of furnishings in the home. Fashions and manners might as easily reveal as provide the pretense of wealth, but it is the real prospect of social progress in Britain that provides the backdrop for the expanding market in the decorative arts and for experiments in design, production, and merchandising undertaken by Wedgwood and others.

Eighteenth-century attitudes toward the decorative arts appear in the novels of Jane Austen (1775–1817), for instance, in *Northanger Abbey* (begun 1798 but published posthumously) when the protagonist, Catherine Morland, comments favorably upon the elegance of her host's breakfast set. The host, General Tilney, responds that the English set compares favorably with continental porcelain production, but is already two years old; the sight of much improved specimens in town had almost tempted him to purchase an entirely new service. Such remarks reveal both a consciousness of design and the role played by novelty in home furnishings and suggest that designed goods are associated with improvement. Did the new tea set mentioned by the general pour more easily or preserve the flavor of the tea? It seems more likely that the new design possessed some perceived advantage that contributed to quality of life beyond its use value. It is the effort, or perhaps the game, of discerning wealth and position for the purposes of arranging marriages or favorable relationships, that lies at the heart of the novel and in which fashion, and manners, play a considerable part. In these circumstances, upwardly mobile middle-class buyers were beginning to experience and enjoy the comforts and convenience that commodities provided as well as the status they conferred, all formerly associated with a small and generally privileged landed aristocracy. Portraits from this period often register the pride and self-assurance of self-made individuals and their families through the possessions that surround them in their homes (including taking afternoon tea), the visible signs of self-improvement and upward social mobility.

However, even as the social motivations and pressures of modern fashion emerged in the eighteenth century, conflicting attitudes toward the phenomenon were also voiced. Novelty and change in design may indeed attest to democratization and signify a relaxation of social boundaries and opportunities for social advancement. Yet at the same time fashion was also criticized for the emphasis it placed upon ostentation and its conformity to values rooted in materialism – increasingly fashion was blamed for a decline in traditional values and the emphasis it placed upon the opinions of others. In contrast to the neutral observation on consumer attitudes in *Northanger Abbey*, Jane Austen's later novel *Mansfield Park* (1814) treats fashion with decided disdain. Here the acquisition of commodities alone never substitutes for the pleasures and sensibilities of the "good" life. For instance, Edmund, a cousin of the novel's central character, Fanny Price, laments that his friend and romantic interest, Mary Crawford, has fallen victim to the lure of fashion and materialism: "It is the influence of the fashionable world altogether that I am jealous of. It is the habits of wealth that I fear." Fashion allows people to pretend to be that which they are not, and attitudes of the period reveal an interesting mix of attraction as well as suspicion toward consumption that persists throughout the history of modern design.

Not surprisingly, the "habits of wealth" were often associated with dress. In the course of the early eighteenth century, fashionable clothing was made of silk fabric, and in England silk weaving was centered in the east end of London at Spitalfields. The English monarchy took an interest in promoting silk weaving domestically, attracting French weavers and guaranteeing their rights in the industry. Trading companies brought raw silk for production, and from the 1730s designers operated within the industry, creating and selling patterns based upon the adaptation of designs from Lyon (see page 21). One of the best-known English designers from the 1730s through the mid-1750s was Anna Marie Garthwaite (1690–1763), who worked as a freelance designer, selling patterns to a number of weavers, primarily for silk fabrics to be used for dresses. The pattern illustrated in figure 2.8 is an example of her work from the 1740s, a brocade woven with a rich palette of bright lavender, yellow, blue, and green against a pale pink ground and a loose pattern of flowers, leaves, and a curved, twisting stem. A guide to English industries published in 1751 noted that Garthwaite had introduced the principles of painting to the art of weaving. Spitalfields silk was a successful export product to the British colonies, including North America, where it can be seen in portraits from the later eighteenth century. While the dominant approach to dress in the later eighteenth century in England reflected the French courtly example, costume historians often note a greater informality in English dress that is parallel to the more democratic tendencies of the period. Rather than overtly expressing distinctions, some examples of English eighteenth-century dress are simple and "natural," as if conveying a certain egalitarianism, a recognition that, beneath the clothes we wear to communicate difference and individual identity, we are all basically the same. Writing on the subject of fashion and clothing in the early nineteenth century, the Scottish-born writer Thomas Carlyle (see page 58) stated that "within the most starched cravat there passes a windpipe and wesand, and under the thickest embroidered waistcoat beat a heart." This more natural attire is seen in Angelica Kauffmann's (1741–1807) portrait of Lady Elizabeth Foster

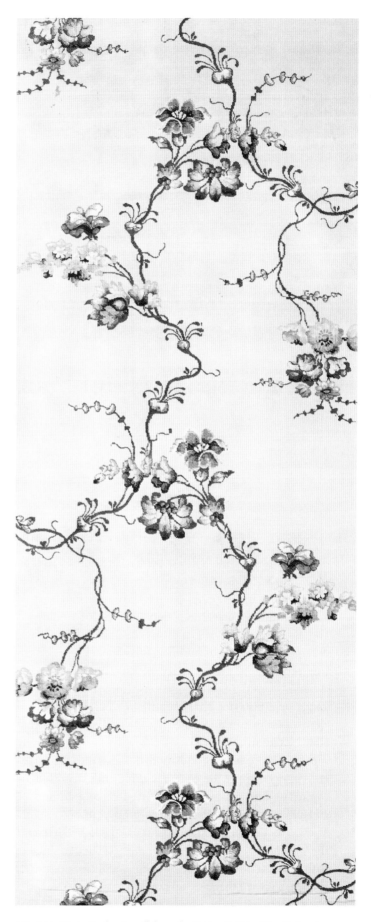

2.8 Anna Marie Garthwaite, silk brocade, 45 ¹/₁₆ x 23 ¹/₂ in (115 x 59.8 cm), c. 1740–50. Victoria and Albert Museum, London.

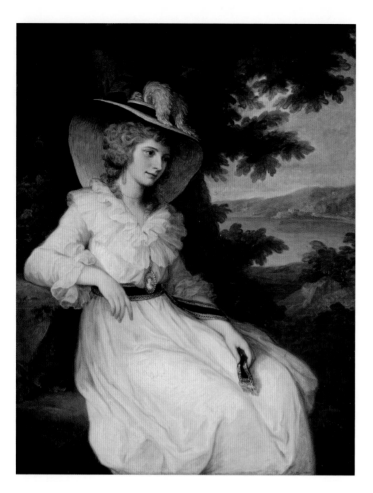

2.9 Angelica Kauffmann, *Portrait of Lady Elizabeth Foster*, oil on canvas, 50 x 40 in (127 x 101.6 cm), 1784. Ickworth House, Suffolk.

THE UNITED STATES

In the United States, the production and consumption of the decorative arts during the eighteenth century was much influenced by European trends and tastes. Spitalfields silks were imported to the colonies, and colonial craftsmen and workshops, inspired by the pages of Chippendale's *Director* and other contemporary model books, produced technically accomplished and distinctive carved furniture for well-to-do families in cities such as Boston and Philadelphia in the second half of the eighteenth century.

Thomas Jefferson (1743–1826) purchased a creamware dinner service manufactured by Wedgwood for his estate at Monticello in Virginia, and in the dining room the fireplace is decorated with inset Wedgwood jasper-ware plaques (fig. 2.11). He also acquired a Sèvres dinner service following an extended visit to France from 1784 to 1789. In addition, Jefferson designed his own practical, often ingenious furniture, constructed by craftsmen on the premises of the estate. These were intended to increase his own productivity and efficiency, and included such items as a revolving bookstand and a table with a revolving top for his study.

dated 1784, featuring a straw bonnet and soft as well as plain muslin fabric (fig. 2.9).

To sum up, whether in the furniture business of Thomas Chippendale, the pottery business of Wedgwood and Bentley, or the silk industry in Spitalfields, design emerged in England as an integral component in expanding production of a variety of consumer products. Whether based upon adaptations from French luxury goods or a taste for classical antiquity beginning in the 1760s, design communicated a cultivated sensibility that added value to a variety of useful products. Increasingly separated from making and attuned to marketing, designers emerged from the manufacturing industry itself or worked as fine artists or architects publishing designs or consulting with manufacturers to produce their designs. The role of designer and merchant in England, like that of the *marchand mercier* in France, was to connect buyers with manufacturers. Primarily designs reflected aristocratic taste, but even that taste allowed for variety and a degree of democratization in a social and economic climate that offered opportunities for self-improvement, individual expression, and social advancement.

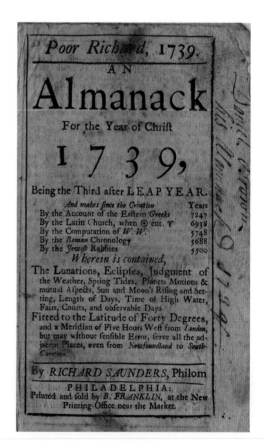

2.10 Benjamin Franklin, *Poor Richard's Almanack*, front cover, height 7 ⅛ in (18.1 cm), 1739. Van Pelt-Dietrich Library, University of Pennsylvania.

Popular Literature and the Freedom of the Press

Readers familiar with the career of Benjamin Franklin (1706–1790) are aware that this colonial founding father, inventor, and diplomat emerged from a craft background as printer and newspaper editor. Franklin was aware of continental developments in fine printing (see pages 28–30) and published some volumes of translations of classical literature in handsomely bound editions with spaciously designed text pages. He also selected the fine types of English type founder William Caslon (1692–1766) for the printing of the *Declaration of Independence* in 1776. Yet Franklin is perhaps best known as the publisher of printed ephemera, most notably *Poor Richard's Almanack*, published annually between 1732 and 1757 (fig. 2.10). *Poor Richard's Almanack* contained varied commentaries and aphorisms as well as calendars and weather predictions, and were aimed at farmers and tradespeople of diverse backgrounds, providing a combination of practical information and wisdom, humor, and popular fiction in a serialized format. Distinguished neither by the excellence of their typography nor their single-column layout or crude illustrations and tables, the *Almanack* is significant in revealing Franklin's desire and ability to direct topical printed materials toward a broad and inclusive readership with common interests. The design of such printed material involved the use of inexpensive materials for paper and covers, maximizing space with narrow margins and reduced leading between lines of type, and title pages featuring large sizes of bold type and italic letters to attract attention.

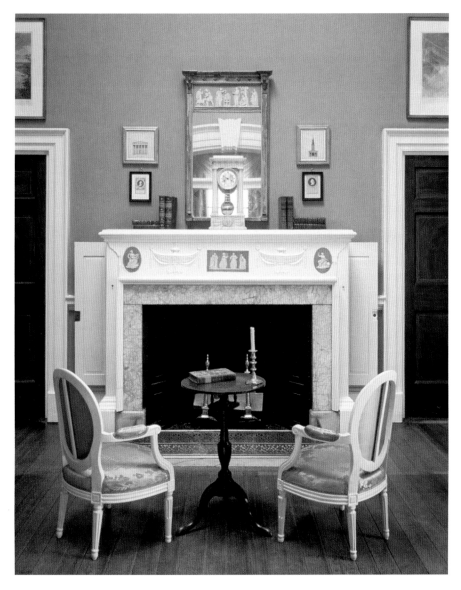

2.11 Thomas Jefferson, dining room with fireplace and Wedgwood jasperware plaques, Monticello, Virginia, 1808–9.

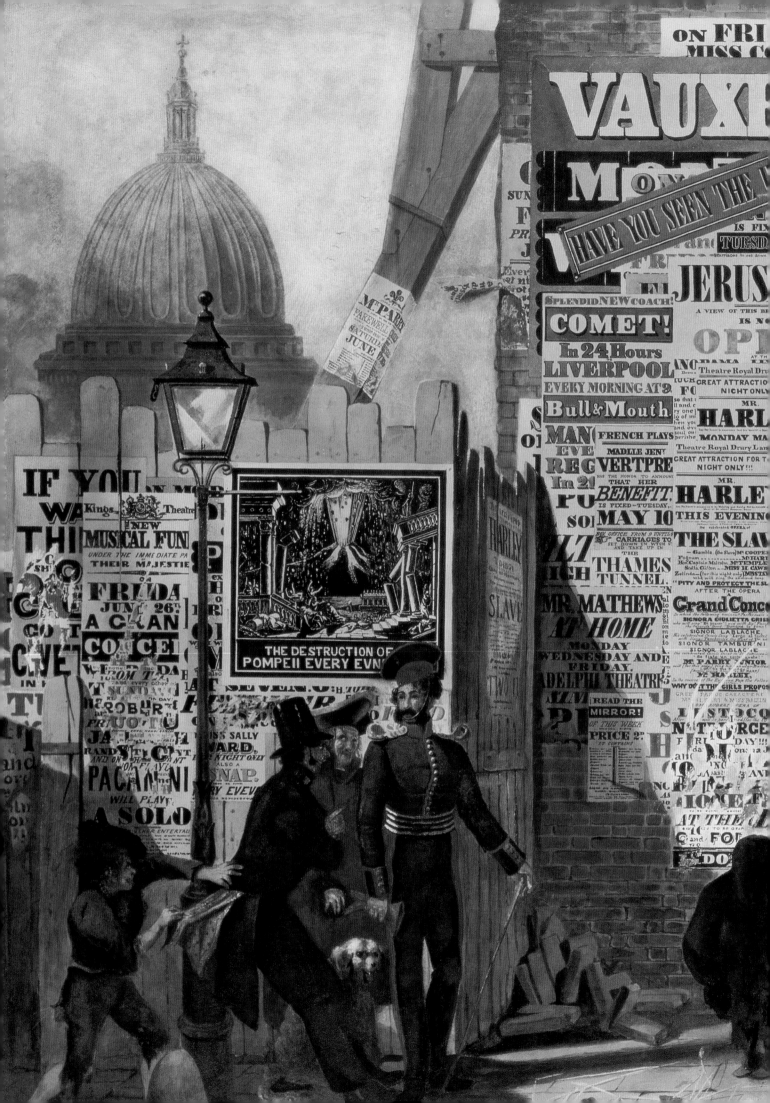

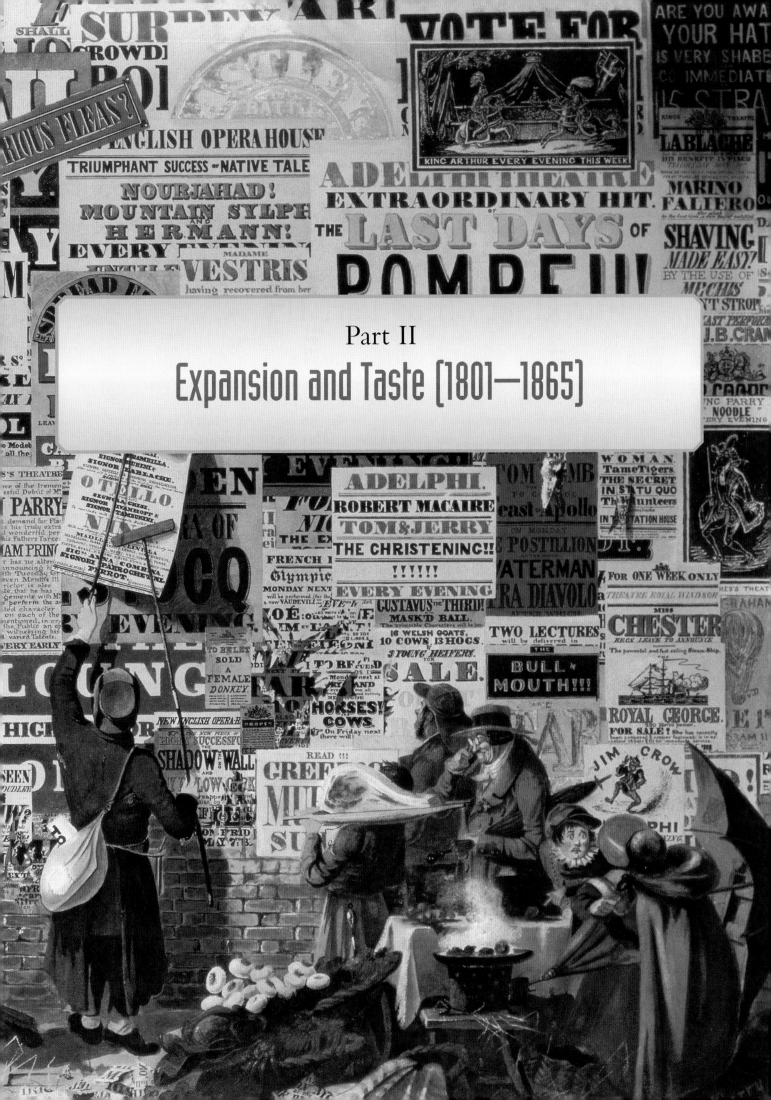

Part II
Expansion and Taste (1801—1865)

Introduction to Part II

The early nineteenth century witnessed the further expansion and acceleration of manufacturing amid continued technical advances in a political and economic climate generally favorable to trade and international competition. Yet with expansion came a host of new concerns. While merchants and manufacturers competed in the expanding market for goods and furnishings by offering an array of styles to appeal to varied tastes, others expressed fears for the erosion of quality as craft production became increasingly separated from "art." Government-sponsored organizations called for reform, and numerous efforts aimed at educating designers and regulating (if not controlling) the practice of design emerged. Government-sponsored schools, and prescriptions for the proper role of decoration in the applied arts were part of an attempt to promote common principles for an increasingly diverse consuming public. The culmination of these competing interests was the Great Exhibition (the Crystal Palace) in London held in 1851 and other international exhibitions that took place in the major urban and industrial capitals of Europe and the United States throughout the later nineteenth century. These hugely successful World's Fairs sought to promote trade, stimulate production, and entertain as well as educate the public.

Chapter 3

Growing Pains — Expanding Industry in the Early Nineteenth Century

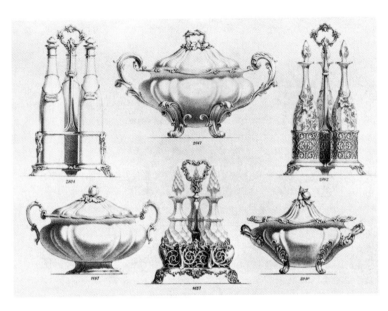

3.1 George Elkington, designs for electroplated silver tureens from *Elkington's Catalogue*, Birmingham, UK, 1847.

A CULTURE OF INDUSTRY AND PROGRESS

Following the war of 1812, Britain enjoyed peaceful relations with the United States, while the Peace of Vienna, forged in the wake of Napoleon's defeat at Waterloo in 1815, inaugurated a period of reduced political hostility in Europe that encouraged trade and the growth of markets for manufactured goods. Among the numerous technical advances of the time was the invention of the cotton gin (1793) by the American Eli Whitney (1765–1825). The cotton gin mechanically removed seeds from balls of raw cotton, a task that had previously been done painstakingly by hand, and this greatly increased the cultivation of raw cotton in the southern states. Whitney's invention, coupled with the introduction of steam power to the process of spinning in British factories, reduced prices for woven textiles and made cotton fabric (until this time usually imported from manufactories in India) available to middle-class buyers. Lower prices were also maintained through the use of slave labor on southern plantations, newer

mechanical methods of pattern printing on cloth, and finally the use of the sewing machine for stitching garments and trim by mid-century. In turn, these technologies contributed to the expansion of women's fashion and the manufacture of ready-to-wear clothing, stimulated further by printed fashion plates that provided ideals of feminine beauty and propriety in dress in popular illustrated magazines such as *Godey's Lady's Book*. This dynamic and interdependent development in the cotton industry, involving changes in technology, labor, and an elastic market, presents an image of progress and optimism, but also was accompanied by fears regarding the human consequences of unfettered economic expansion that characterizes the history of manufacturing and design in Europe and the United States beginning in the early nineteenth century. This culture is also global in scope, since expansion included colonial territories, their raw materials, markets, and labor.

Advances in printing technology, including the introduction of steam-powered cylinder presses, lithography and chromolithography, papermaking machines, and continuous-feed paper, helped to create a better informed and literate public. This was especially evident in the widespread proliferation of popular illustrated weekly broadsides and journals. Continuous printing processes were also introduced for patterned or scenic wallpapers, using longer lengths of paper and making paper wall-coverings and the cultivation of design in the home an attainable luxury for the middle class. The construction of railroads, first in Britain and then throughout Europe and the United States, stimulated the expansion of commerce, as the speed and ease of transportation of raw materials and commodities increased. The railroad also contributed to the ease of personal travel and its accompanying commercial activity in the form of tourism. Finally, it is worthwhile to connect the development of design and manufacturing in the first two-thirds of the nineteenth century with the beginnings of the advertising industry and to retail shopping experiences familiar to today's consumers (the first advertising agency, Volney Palmer, in Philadelphia, dates to the early 1840s, and the first modern department store, the Bon Marché, opened in Paris in the 1860s). Advertising in posters, in magazines, and in newspapers, along with lighting, fixed prices, and displays behind expanses of plate glass all defined the character of urban life and the experience of shopping. Writers and illustrators of the period document displays of goods in store windows, attractive salesgirls behind counters, and the use of signs, handbills, and sandwich boards to attract shoppers.

New Materials and Processes

The range of products and processes that emerged during the first half of the nineteenth century is overwhelming, but even a sampling may suffice to represent the expanding scope of manufacturing activity. During this period, for instance, the process known as silver electroplating was developed by George Elkington of Birmingham, England (1801–1865). The process was patented by 1840 and improved through further experiment by 1847. Electroplating involved a chemical reaction created by electricity that attached a thin coating of silver to base metals such as nickel to produce a wide variety of metal wares for use and display in the home (today the same process is used to protect metal automobile parts with a coating of chromium). Electroplating quickly competed with pewter, eclipsed a mid-eighteenth century method of plating using copper between layers of silver, and made "silverware" and silver tea services popular as symbols of comfort and leisure in many middle-class homes. The process also was employed for tableware manufactured for purchase in large quantities by hotels, clubs, passenger ships and rails, and restaurants, all

suggesting the expansion of middle-class leisure and entertainment. The illustration from Elkington's 1847 catalogue of designs (fig. 3.1) features highly wrought footed tureens that combine a new technology with the forms and decoration associated with the Renaissance. Elkington hired highly trained artists and silversmiths from France to design his electroplated wares in traditional styles associated with the highest levels of artistic invention and skill from the past; to market his process, unique specimens were exhibited as presentation pieces at World's Fairs beginning with the Crystal Palace in London in 1851 and again in 1862 (see pages 63–68), where they were praised by many observers as examples of the beneficial relationship between art and manufacturing. The designers hired by Elkington were the highest-paid of the many employees at the company, which by the 1880s employed more than 1,000 workers. A slightly later innovation in metallurgy was the discovery and first applications of aluminum, dating to around 1855. Early experimental uses of the new material were for jewelry, which is not surprising since its price was comparable to that of silver or gold. Only when electrolytic processes for extracting aluminum more cheaply were introduced industrially toward the end of the nineteenth century did applications expand to include casting for architecture, furniture, and other products (see page 131 and fig. 6.44).

Examples of this manufacturing expansion also include new materials for furniture such as cast iron and bentwood for chairs and benches. In 1830, German-born cabinet-maker Michael Thonet (1796–1871) used steam to bend beechwood rods into curved shapes that were then assembled to make chairs, hatstands, and supports for tables (fig. 3.2). His bentwood process eliminated the need for carving and other costly handwork, and came to the attention of Prince Klemens Metternich (1773–1859), advisor to the Austrian emperor, who commissioned a large order of furniture from Thonet for the emperor's palace at Liechtenstein. The example illustrated in figure 3.2 is lightweight, employing a woven cane seat and a restrained curvilinear form with decorative back and stretchers in a contemporary Neoclassical style.

German architect Karl Friedrich Schinkel (1781–1841) designed chairs made of both cast and wrought iron, primarily for use in gardens and public parks. The chairs (fig. 3.3) are constructed from identical sidepieces with X-shaped supports connected by cylindrical rods at the seat and the upper back, where a filling of foliate and other decorative motifs was attached and molded to fit the concave shapes of the connecting rods. As with the bentwood example of similar date, despite the modern method of production, the design of the chair, particularly the lyre and vine scrolls of the upper back portion, recall

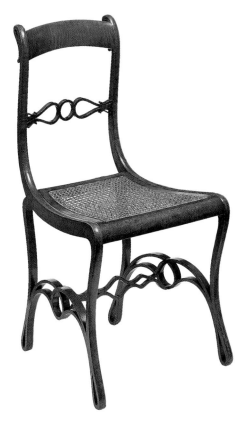

3.2 Michael Thonet, side chair, beechwood with wicker seat, approx. 35 in (88.5 cm) high, 1836–40. Victoria and Albert Museum, London.

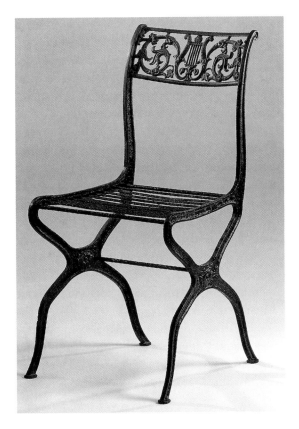

3.3 Karl Friedrich Schinkel, outdoor side chair, cast iron, 33 ¼ x 18 x 21 in (86 x 46 x 54 cm), *c*. 1821. Vitra Design Museum, Germany.

the Neoclassical style found in Schinkel's architectural designs and furniture in more traditional materials. The design and construction of these early-nineteenth-century examples of cast-iron furniture are remarkably similar to benches used today in parks or commuter rail stations, where simple cast-iron supports connect to riveted planks of painted or varnished wood. It also marks the beginning of a long tradition of using cast or bent metals for furniture.

Yet another material that was used for furniture during the first half of the nineteenth century was papier-mâché, made from wood pulp, then molded, baked, and finished often at great expense with elaborate finishes resembling lacquer surfaces with colorful inlay patterns in precious stones and mother-of-pearl. Manufacturers experimented with more durable forms of the material that achieved popularity, particularly in Britain (fig. 3.4). Papier-mâché was also used in the newspaper printing industry during the nineteenth century where the material was pressed into flat formes of type; it was then bent into a curved surface that served as a mold to make metal cylinders for newly invented and faster rotary presses (see page 52).

Materials technology was not the only dimension of change in the design and production of the decorative arts.

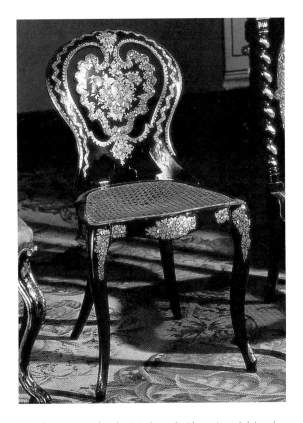

3.4 Side chair, japanned and painted wood with papier-mâché and mother-of-pearl, height 34 in (86.4 cm), probably manufactured by Jennens and Bettridge, Birmingham, *c*. 1850. Victoria and Albert Museum, London.

Invention is also demonstrated in the style of German and Austrian interior design known as Biedermeier that evolved in the second quarter of the nineteenth century (though the term "Biedermeier" did not emerge until after 1850). This new style embraced an almost abstract simplicity, emphasizing the beauty of natural woods and plain polished surfaces as seen in the writing desk illustrated in figure 3.5. Such restraint certainly shares common aesthetic principles with Neoclassicism, as seen, for instance, in the cast-iron chairs of Schinkel (see fig. 3.3), or in the bentwood chairs of Thonet in the 1830s (see fig. 3.2). While the style seems to have originated in aristocratic households as a kind of refuge from the formality and pomp of more extravagant spaces and furnishings, Biedermeier also appealed to values of comfort, convenience, and leisure for a prosperous middle class of merchants and professionals with considerable disposable income. Beyond issues of style, practical considerations were also important. For example, manufacturers of Biedermeier furniture made extensive use of coil-spring upholstery, patented by an upholsterer named Georg Junigl in Vienna in 1822.

Although Biedermeier furniture is known and admired today chiefly for the quality of its craftsmanship and an emphasis on practicality, simplicity, and comfort, toward mid-century much nineteenth-century furniture assumed a sense of grandeur both in scale and decoration that suggests an interest in public display rather than convenience or private enjoyment. In the wake of the French Revolution, Napoleon and his ministers cultivated an imperial or Empire style that was clearly designed to use hard-edged Neoclassical forms that embodied ideals of permanence and reason. The style was exemplified in designs by architects Charles Percier and Pierre Fontaine and manufactured by craftsmen who had been trained prior to the French Revolution of 1789 (see page 27 and fig. 1.13). The function of such furniture was to project an aura of imperial dignity and refinement, with forms based upon those found in examples of Roman wall painting, ancient Greek vase painting, or in subjects from Roman history painted by Neoclassical artists such as Jacques-Louis David (1748–1825). Decorative features, such as sphinxes (associated with the emperor's attempt to

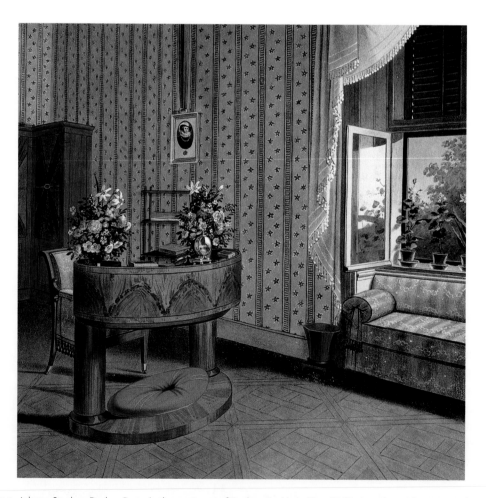

3.5 Johann Stephan Decker, *Room in the apartment of Duchess Sophie in Bluer Hof in Laxenburg, Vienna*, gouache, 9 ⅞ x 10 in (25 x 25.5 cm), 1826. Foundation for Prussian Palaces and Gardens, Berlin-Brandenburg, Germany.

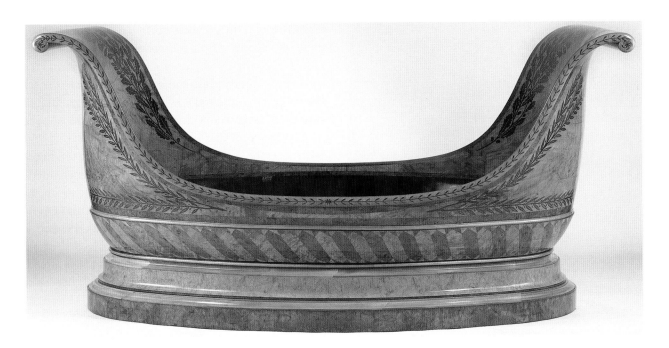

3.6 François Baudry, bed, mahogany with burr wood, elm, amaranth and lemonwood veneers, 53 ¹⁵⁄₁₆ x 84 ⁵⁄₈ x 66 ⁷⁄₈ (137 x 213 x 170 cm), 1827. Musée des Arts Decoratifs, Paris.

conquer Egypt) or the letter "N" referred directly to the emperor himself.

Following Napoleon's exile and the Peace of Vienna (1815), the French government began to organize exhibitions of national industry to re-establish (after the disruption of the revolution and its aftermath) its reputation for luxury products and to stimulate the export trade. The first two of these national industrial showcases were held in 1819 and 1834 in Paris, and were a means for manufacturers to demonstrate the quality of their products and have a venue to market them to visitors from other nations. Exquisite display pieces, such as the gondola-shaped bed designed by François Baudry and dating to 1827 (fig. 3.6), maintained the highest levels of skill and continuity with the reputation for luxury and high-end manufacture that France enjoyed prior to the Revolution and the breakdown of the monopolistic guild system for both craft training and production.

National industrial fairs also paved the way for the even more ambitious international exhibitions, beginning with the Crystal Palace in London in 1851 (see pages 63–68). The furniture presented at the fairs was often large and imposing in both size and scale and was usually not in any sense typical, since its purpose was to attract attention within a vast space with visitors' attention divided among a bewildering number of displays by manufacturers from all over the world – to truly be showpieces. The competitive atmosphere of the exhibitions, along with their sheer marketing potential, encouraged manufacturers to distinguish their products through skill, size, and complexity, and even to rival the allegorical subjects of sculptors (see fig. 4.9).

While specialization and other technical advances in woodworking made the manufacture of such pieces feasible, often the nature of display seemed to preclude either practicality or subtlety of effect. That such grandeur or grandiosity was a tendency in the furnishings of this period may be inferred from a passage from Stendhal's (Marie-Henri Beyle, 1783–1842) novel *Le Rouge et Le Noir* (*The Red and the Black*), published in 1830. Toward the end of the novel, Mathilde, a member of a privileged and well-bred aristocratic family, is pleasantly surprised by the furnishings in a parlor where she is waiting for the Bishop of Bescançon, and contrasts their "refinement and delicate luxury" (presumably a reference to pre-revolutionary elegance) with the "vulgar magnificence" one finds today in Paris in the "best houses." Perhaps the extreme of such magnificence is the apartments designed for Napoleon III (r. 1852–1870) in Paris, now installed in the Louvre and designed under the direction of architect Hector Martin Lefuel (1810–1880) between 1856 and 1861. Carved, gilded, and utilizing the newer technique of "tufted" upholstery in red silk and damask throughout, the furniture and setting embody a mid-nineteenth century ideal of luxury conveyed through richness and abundance of material as well as elaborate carving and construction. While frequently borrowing from the past for inspiration, the furnishings in the apartments display a remarkable

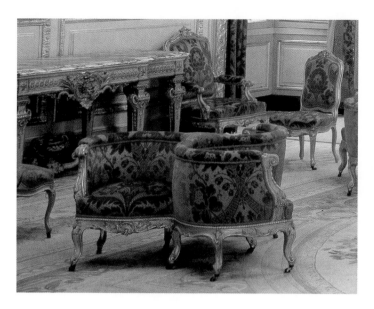

3.7 Interior with linked armchairs, gilded mahogany, apartments of Napoleon III, 1856–1861. The Louvre, Paris.

originality of form, for instance, in the odd combination of three connecting armchairs, apparently to facilitate conversation (fig. 3.7). Such novelty reveals an inventiveness associated with progress and competition, yet at the same time suggests continuity with established traditions of decoration associated with monarchy and national pride.

In England, the collector and amateur architect Thomas Hope (1769–1831) published *House Furniture and Decoration* in 1807, featuring drawings of formal interiors in a somewhat severe Neoclassical style. Drawing upon his own travels to Greece and the type of antique and Egyptian sources mined by the French architects Percier and Fontaine, Hope created designs with carved decoration and frequent inclusion of animal forms, such as table feet ending in claws and chair arms carved and gilded in the form of sphinxes or winged lions (fig. 3.8). The text of Hope's book explains his intention to influence behavior through design, elevating the taste of the poor and middle classes, and reigning in the excess and extravagance of the wealthy.

Hand-colored engravings of Hope's designs were printed in monthly magazines beginning around 1809. *Repository of the Arts*, published by the German emigré Rudolph Ackermann (1764–1834), is a good source for the furniture designs (as well as fashion) from this period. But along with the designs of Thomas Hope, Ackermann also included a wider variety of styles, reflecting an expanding trade as well as more pluralistic tastes: one example from the magazine is a reclining chair (fig. 3.9) with front legs and an attached footrest carved in the form of winged beasts, and a reading lectern, which appears to swivel, in the form of an attacking snake! While such an object was certain to make a visitor take notice and be a source of pride

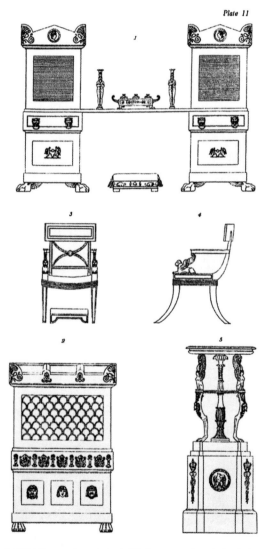

3.8 Thomas Hope, designs for writing table, armchair, and pedestal, drawing, 1807.

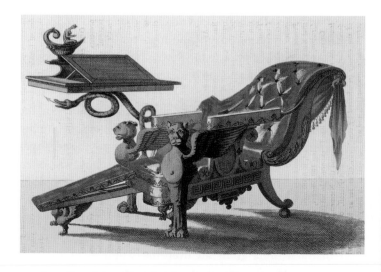

3.9 Pocock's reclining patent chair, hand-colored illustration from *Repository of the Arts*, Rudolph Ackermann, March, 1813.

for its owner, its sheer mass and complexity seem to interfere with any practical advantages the chair might offer.

In terms of extravagance, little compares with the fantasy created for the Prince of Wales (later King George IV, 1762–1830) at the Royal Pavilion at Brighton, built between 1815 and 1817 as a summer residence and designed by John Nash (1752–1835). Combining traditional classicizing forms with exotic elements such as twisting dragons and palm fronds inspired by the decorative arts of China, and onion-shaped domes based upon traditions of architecture of India, Nash created a decorative ensemble of great originality and extravagance (fig. 3.10). George IV was no doubt England's greatest patron of the arts at the time. At Brighton he commissioned grand and original design to express his individuality and rival earlier monarchical projects and pretensions, although the economic and social climate of the period demonstrate that wealth was no guarantee of emulation and influence upon popular taste. The Royal Pavilion at Brighton was seen by many critics as decadent and hedonistic, and George IV was the target of bitter criticism in print and in published cartoons of the period; rather than projecting an image of grandeur appropriate to kingship and serving the purpose of stimulating industry at all levels as at Versailles (see page 18 and fig. 1.3), the Royal Pavilion was popularly viewed as lavish and self-indulgent. The challenges that the Romantic spirit of individualism and invention posed to tradition worked in both directions in the early nineteenth century: markets and taste expanded dynamically but were difficult to guarantee or control.

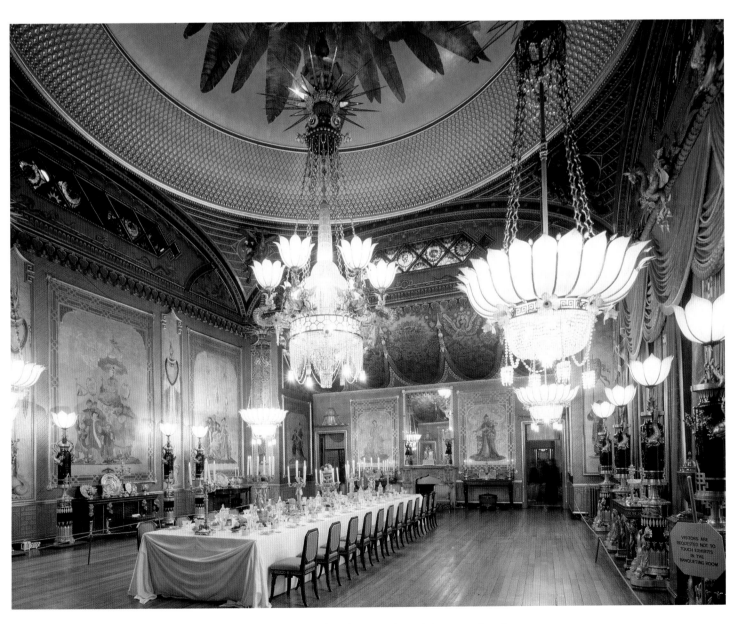

3.10   John Nash, Royal Pavilion at Brighton, dining room, 1815–1823.

In the eighteenth century, the printing industry was geared primarily to the production of books for a limited readership. Newspapers, broadsides, and other ephemeral material, such as Benjamin Franklin's *Poor Richard's Almanac* (see fig. 2.10), are examples of more popular kinds of printed information, and existed at the fringes of the traditional printing industry. During the early nineteenth century, printers and typographers greatly expanded the range of their production to meet the needs of an increasingly literate public that read daily and weekly broadsides, and to compete for public attention in advertising. Larger type sizes, new fonts, wood rather than metal type, and the introduction of the process of lithography to create or transfer images for illustrations exemplify the inventiveness in materials and production techniques that transpired during this time. Such changes affected both the printed word and the printed image, laying the groundwork for new professions in the printing industry such as illustrators, cartoonists, and eventually designers who could effectively combine type and image to fulfill new purposes and reach new audiences in the expanding industries of advertising, journalism, and other forms of printed communication.

Printers in urban centers, and particularly in the commercially active city of London, designed a wide variety of new display typefaces and a wide range of sizes for signs, handbills, and newspaper advertisements in an effort to grab the attention and interest of consumers or to influence public opinion. Casting large letters in metal proved expensive and unwieldy, so typographers cut type in wood. By the second half of the nineteenth century, wood type was cut with the help of templates and routing machines that cut grooves more quickly and precisely than handheld knives and chisels. Wood type was a response to the expansion of trade, free enterprise, and competition. Printers seized the opportunity of meeting the needs of businesses to print ephemeral materials to attract a buying public, inventing an array of new letterforms designed to communicate with immediacy and expression.

If the terminology used today by historians of the printing industry seems arcane, there is good reason. Much of this specialized vocabulary has not changed since the early expansion of the industry. For example, new faces developed in the early nineteenth century were generally called "fat," and are characterized by very large letters with proportionally thicker heavy strokes, often contrasted with thin strokes. The extreme contrast between thick and thin strokes recalls the new and rational later-eighteenth-century "Modern" faces (see pages 28–29), but on a scale much larger than that of the printed book. Fat faces appeared

3.11 Vincent Figgins, six-line pica no. 1 (fat face), cast type and matrices, from a specimen book, London, 1821.

3.12 William Thorowgood, six-line pica Egyptian (slab serif), from a specimen book, London, 1821.

early in the nineteenth century, often accompanied by simplified bracketed serifs that looked triangular and tended to make letters appear dense and closely spaced (fig. 3.11). The term "Egyptian" is also often used to refer to fat faces. One type of "Egyptian" face uses "slab serifs," heavy letter endings that anchor the letters to an insistent horizontal line as well as reduce the space between them, strengthening the immediate impact of each word (fig. 3.12). Designers in the twentieth century returned to such slab serif lettering for visual impact in developing corporate logos (see figs. 11.82 and 11.83). Perhaps for this reason it is common to refer to such letterforms as "display faces," as distinguished from "text faces" for use in books.

Also appearing during the same period are three-dimensional letters featuring shadows to one side, or faces that appear in the white of the paper against a border of pure black (fig. 3.13). Finally, the most varied faces are those where the fat letterforms are filled with scrolls and other patterned decoration. A number of British printers contributed to these developments. Specimen books from this period feature several of the new typefaces, though even these are quite conservative when compared with a watercolor painting by John Parry from 1835 of a wall

R. THORNE. BRIGHTON

WITHOUT RESERVE; HOUSEHOLD FURNITURE, PLATE, GLASS,

3.13 William Thorowgood, five-line pica shaded no. 2, from a specimen book, London, 1821.

3.15 Vincent Figgins, two-line great primer sans serif, from a specimen book, London, 1830.

covered with advertising posters and announcements (fig. 3.14), which reveals the busy commercial and public context that fueled these typographic developments, the ancestors of twentieth-century highway billboards and neon signs. Such inventiveness was not entirely new – engraved title pages produced during the seventeenth century in France and Belgium, especially elaborate frames designed by painters such as Rubens, also might violate the integrity of the two-dimensional page by creating illusionistic space, but even in these instances, later criticized by proponents of the Private Press Movement (see page

86), three-dimensional forms did not impinge upon the traditional look of printed pages of text for books.

Curiously, another new face linked to the growing demand for advertising eliminated serifs altogether and often used strokes of uniform thickness, also permitting the very close spacing of letters and giving a strong sense of overall density. Known at the time as a form of "Egyptian" type or sometimes as "Grotesque" or "Grotesk," these letters (fig. 3.15) were also appropriately called "sans serif." Sans serif typography was adopted as an article of faith among Modernist designers beginning in the

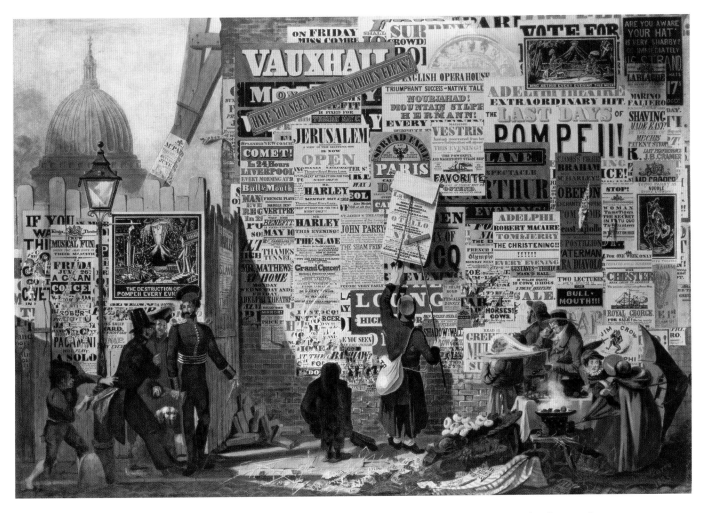

3.14 John Parry, *London Street Scene*, watercolor, 30 x 43 in (76 x 106.5 cm), 1835. Alfred Dunhill Museum and Archive, London.

mid-1920s as an approach that was sympathetic to the modern age of mechanized rather than handicraft production. Ironically, such Modernist typographers felt that serifs belonged to an outdated calligraphic tradition and that their elimination hastened the triumph of cleaner-looking pages, the interrelationship of type and graphic or photographic image, and more easily understood messages in a fast-paced modern world (see pages 206–211). In the post-World War II period, many multi-national corporations also favored sans serif faces as the basis for their logos and identity programs, building upon the close similarity among letterforms to create a strong sense of visual unity (the Mobil logo is one example; see fig. 13.20).

The technology of the printing press also developed rapidly in the early nineteenth century, primarily as a result of the increased circulation of newspapers. Efforts concentrated upon speeding up the production process, first with larger and easier to operate presses, often made of cast iron rather than wooden parts, then with the use of steam to provide mechanical power. Steam-powered presses, first introduced by a German engineer working in London named Friedrich Koenig (1774–1833), operated on a principle derived from copper-plate printing, where the type forme moved horizontally on a bed, first under an inking roller and then under a cylindrical press. These steam-powered presses were installed in 1814 at the London newspaper offices of *The Times*. Later versions printed simultaneously on both sides of a sheet of paper. Print historian Michael Twyman, who has traced these developments and their impact, relates that circulation of *The Times* from the late eighteenth century to 1830 grew from 1,500 copies per day to 11,000. The next major development, occurring simultaneously in Britain and in the United States, was the use of continuous rolls rather than individually cut sheets of paper to further increase the speed of production. Continuous-feed presses required transferring the flat type formes to a curved surface, accomplished by using the malleable material of papier-mâché to make curved impressions that were then used for creating cylindrical metal formes (the process is known as stereotyping; see page 45). By 1850, circulation for *The Times* had reached 38,000 copies daily.

Lithography, meaning literally "stone writing," was the name given to a planographic printing process developed in Germany by Alois Senefelder (1771–1834) in the early nineteenth century. Based on the chemical repellence of oil and water, a design was drawn with greasy ink or crayons on a flat limestone surface (the best limestone was known to come from Bavaria). The stone surface was then coated with water, which was absorbed by the stone only in those areas not covered with the crayon. An oily printing ink was next applied to the surface of the stone, which

adhered only to the drawing, being repelled by the wet part of the surface. The stone was then covered with a sheet of paper and placed beneath a press to make a printed impression.

Lithography has been called the most significant development in printing in the nineteenth century, although its progress in the early nineteenth century was hampered first by the slow progress of the technology during the Napoleonic Wars and second by the lack of machine presses to speed up printing until after 1850. Known for its versatility and the relative ease of the process in comparison with intaglio and relief methods of printing, lithography could be used for reproducing both illustrations and text, and thus became a popular medium for the design of early advertising posters as well as magazine covers and illustrations. Its commercial success was ensured as well by the use of color inks and the development of a complicated but effective process called chromolithography, patented in 1839 and used increasingly after mid-century for a wide range of printed materials such as book illustration, journal covers, and advertising posters.

WALLPAPER AND FABRIC PRINTING

The technology of continuous printing transformed other industries in the nineteenth century, particularly the manufacture of printed wallpapers. Though printing by hand from engraved wooden blocks continued as a production method for a number of wallpaper manufacturers, the introduction of patterns engraved on metal cylinders fed continuously by rolls of paper dramatically increased production and created a much broader market by the early 1840s. Even before the advent of rotary printing and steam-powered pressing machines, wallpaper manufacturers had produced a wide range of styles. A typical selection available to clientele ranged from scenic papers involving several blocks carefully registered and separately inked to produce the effect of painted frescoes, to papers that reproduced repeated vignettes of village life or chinoiserie, to imitated textures such as marble to "flocked" papers produced from pulverized silk or wool attached to glue-coated patterns. Also popular were geometric patterns or those derived from nature or historicizing decorative motifs. The adoption of industrial technology increased the output of all types of printed wall coverings, stimulating widespread invention and borrowing from a variety of sources such as wall painting, tapestry, and the imitation of other woven fabrics, creating an even wider array of patterns, simulated textures, and scenes. These range from elaborate imitation ironwork to patterned architectural decoration in the Gothic style (fig. 3.16), or to a trompe l'oeil garden scene (fig. 3.17).

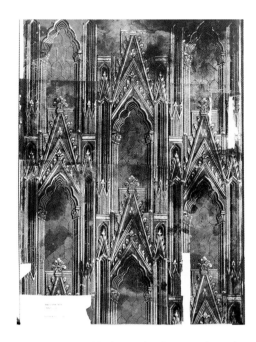

3.16 Anonymous, block-printed wallpaper in the Gothic style, *c.* 1820. Victoria and Albert Museum, London.

Methods for mechanically printing relief patterns in color on wallpaper were similar to methods for printing on textiles, chiefly on calico cloth. This fabric, formerly imported from India, became a middle-class commodity with the invention of the cotton gin in the United States and the industrialization of the textile industry in Britain, including the introduction of steam-powered spinning to roller rather than hand-applied printing. In Stendhal's novel *Le Rouge et Le Noir* (*The Red and the Black*, from 1830), the author refers to the social pretensions of the "wealthy calico printers" in the French town of Verrières, an indication of the prosperity enjoyed by these new industrial manufacturers.

In the early nineteenth century, the manufacture of machine-printed cotton was simultaneous with the introduction of more automated methods for the weaving of silk. The center of this latter development remained the French city of Lyon, which had supplied the fashionable capital of Paris and other European cities with woven silk since the early eighteenth century, when the industry employed more than 20,000 silk workers (see pages 20–22). The industry was disrupted during the French Revolution, but revived after the Peace of Vienna (1815), when a new type of hand-operated loom was introduced that manipulated the weaving of silk threads through a series of cards that were punched to create patterns. Although usually named the "Jacquard" loom for one of its innovators, Joseph Marie Jacquard (1752–1834), several individuals were responsible for equally significant contributions to this ingenious process.

The developments in the silk and cotton industries during the first half of the nineteenth century also helped to expand the market for women's clothing. Two valuable indications of this expansion are the interest of portrait painters in depicting with painstaking detail the wardrobes of their wealthy subjects, and the more numerous and stereotypical hand-colored woodblock and engraved illustrations of contemporary dress known as fashion plates. Fashion plates appeared as a feature in monthly subscription magazines (sometimes as few as two or four at the beginning of each issue) with included commentaries on the fashion trends and advice on matters relating to public appearance and behavior. Although there are examples of fashion plates in both France and England from the 1770s, publishers substantially expanded the practice of issuing colored illustrations by subscription or including them in more general publications during the early nineteenth century.

With the revival of its center for silk manufacturing in Lyon, and the restoration of the monarchy after 1815, France set the tone for fashion and for fashion plates. As the popularity of the genre increased, artists and amateurs specialized in the production of drawings that were then engraved, printed, and colored. Fashion plates both reflected as well as stimulated a feeling for the importance of a more "public" social life in the early nineteenth century: there was an increasing consciousness not only of one's dress but also its relation to proper social behavior

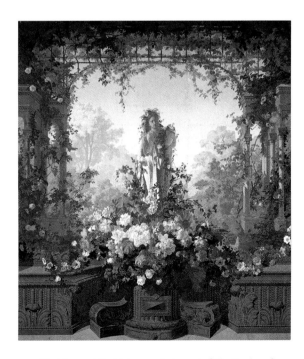

3.17 *The Vices and the Virtues*, central panel of *The Garden of Armida*, block-printed wallpaper, 12 ft 8 in x 11 ft (386.1 x 335.3 cm), designed by Edouard Muller and produced by Jules Desfosse, Paris, *c.* 1855. Musée des Arts Decoratifs, Paris.

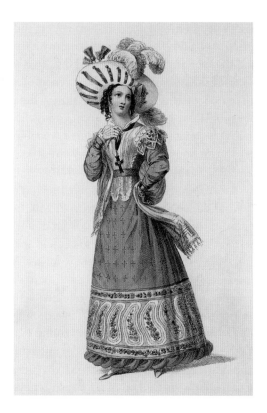

3.18 Fashion plate, hand-colored engraving, 9 ³/₈ x 5 ¹¹/₁₆ in (24 x 14.6 cm), from *Repository of the Arts*, Rudolph Ackermann, 1827. Hagerty Library Archive, Drexel University, Philadelphia.

for women. In the fashion plate (fig. 3.18) from Rudolph Ackermann's *Repository of the Arts* (1827), accessories and props such as chairs or benches provide an added context or even implied a narrative or "story" for such images. They reveal foremost a feeling for activities associated with family and leisure (rather than work or more active physical pursuits). These often include reading, playing an instrument (after the 1840s the most popular instrument was the piano), walking in the park, attending dances, or spending time with friends and children, all presented with idealized young women in relaxed, informal poses. Until the 1820s, the preference in women's fashion was for high-waisted long dresses (a legacy of the classically inspired Empire style), enlivened by satin ribbons or velvet borders and elaborate coiffures. During the second third of the century, fuller skirts and patterned cloth, both printed and woven, become more common, and pastimes illustrated in the fashion plates grew to include attendance at leisure activities such as horse races and concerts. The popularity of these plates demonstrates that dress was a way in which the habits of the wealthy were communicated to an increasing number of those with sufficient means to aspire to such practices, and who might use the plates to plan their own wardrobes. Through marketing, merchandising, and less costly methods for the color reproduction of illustrations,

the second half of the nineteenth century brought such habits into an even broader and competitive commercial realm. Design was an indispensable aspect of all of these activities, increasingly distinct from production, invaluable to manufacturers in helping to make their products more desirable in a climate of increasing social change and mobility. Designers, as well as publishers such as Ackermann, navigated a new and contested territory between the interests of consumers and manufacturers, and between tradition and novelty. The role they assumed was sometimes that of "tastemaker," improving or educating the public through design. We can appreciate this role in the text of *An Encyclopedia of Cottage, Farm, and Villa Architecture and Furniture* (1833) by the English designer and author J. C. Loudon (1783–1843), who remarked that beauty as well as comfort were concerns of the cottager (not just the concerns of the wealthy); that is, design was a means to improve the human condition. Such views formed the basis of the movement of design reform that was taking root at the same time – the arts were a form of knowledge once limited to the wealthy, now capable of being shared with the many. Loudon acknowledged the coexistence of a variety of styles, from the Grecian style as seen in the work of Thomas Hope (see page 48), to the Gothic, the Tudor, and the Italian; all styles signaled a belief in progress, a standard of living and quality of life beyond subsistence, an achievement now made possible for a broader public by the spread of knowledge, by technology, and by the efficiency and skill of increasingly rationalized labor.

A less "top-down" approach to design was taken by manufacturers and retailers who served the emerging mass market in inexpensive ceramic and glassware. In these industries, merchants relied upon observing the habits of shoppers who seemed to prefer a variety of fancy goods in which decoration was identified with both aesthetic and social progress.

THE AMERICAN SYSTEM

In North America, the demand for commodities accompanying westward expansion in the early nineteenth century and the scarcity of skilled labor hastened the adoption of rationalized production methods and the beginnings of mechanization. One of the key elements, according to the design historian John Heskett, was the mass production of interchangeable parts in the manufacture of firearms in the early nineteenth century, a process that required precision and careful oversight in order to ensure exact uniformity. At the outset the high capital costs of experiments with machine-made parts and rationalized methods of production were underwritten through government contracts to manufacturers for substantial quantities of uniform goods.

The main advantages to this method were the ease of repair and replacement of parts, and the vast savings in the cost of labor, especially in the time-consuming tasks of filing and fitting parts to each product. The principle upon which this productivity was based, once again, was the division of labor; the virtues of a rational approach to production were praised by British economist Adam Smith (1723–1790), whose description of a pin factory extols the virtues of dividing tasks and links such developments to productivity and general material progress:

> One man draws out the wire, another straightens it, a third cuts it, a fourth points it, a fifth grinds it at the top for receiving the head ... and the important business of making a pin is, in this manner, divided into about eighteen distinct operations, which in some manufactories are performed by distinct hands ... This separation too is carried furthest in those countries which enjoy the highest degree of industry and improvement; what is the work of one in a rude state of society being generally that of several in an improved one.

The American tendency to extend Smith's principles to specialized sequences of machine operations designed to fabricate increasingly complicated products with precise interchangeable parts may be seen in a number of goods, from rifles manufactured by Simeon North and later by Samuel Colt in Hartford, Connecticut, in the 1840s (under contract from the American government), to the clock mechanisms made by Eli Terry at around the same time, and also to the early development of the sewing machine around 1850 by Isaac M. Singer and other companies for factory rather than domestic use. The success of this approach to production, which became known as the "American System of Manufacture," should also be viewed in light of the absence of guilds or strong craft traditions, whose working methods and continued emphasis upon skill could not easily be adapted to the strict uniformity imposed by Jerome and others. Historians such as David Hounshell remind us, however, that the transition to this "American System" was slow, and that even successful companies such as Singer continued to employ workers to finish individual parts until demand forced greater attention to ensuring quality through increased reliance upon the sequence of special-function machines.

For many Europeans, the "utilitarian" approach of these early American manufacturers was on the one hand praised for its efficiency and "practicality," often described as uniquely American values. But it was also criticized as being "artless" for its lack of those outward signs of beauty, workmanship, and culture that linked products with luxury living and the decorative arts with progress. In an expanding consumer economy, "design" began to play an increasing role. As historian Jeffrey L. Meikle has observed, the self-sufficiency and practicality praised by many observers of Colonial America was somewhat of a myth – decoration and democratic variety came to characterize the expanding American market for ceramic and glassware and demonstrate middle-class aspirations of social progress in a fluid, heterogeneous society. While the production side of American design emphasized rationalized unskilled labor, standardization, and the introduction of machines, the consumption side turned to fashion and a parade of eclectic, quickly changing patterns and methods of decoration. As an example we might cite the shelf clocks manufactured by Eli Terry in Connecticut beginning in 1816 that used wooden rather than brass gears and required winding every 30 hours as opposed to every eight days. Many of Terry's wooden clock cases were designed by Chauncey Jerome (1793–1868) in a restrained Neoclassical style featuring columns to each side, a scrolled pediment above (fig. 3.19) and a painted scene inside of the glass panel that protected the painted dial.

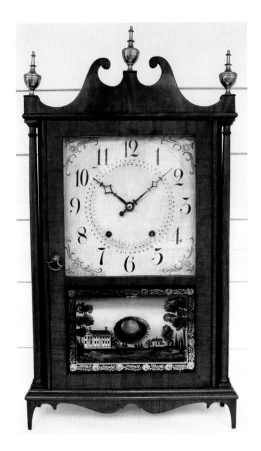

3.19 Eli Terry, "Pillar and scroll" shelf clock, mahogany veneer, hand-painted poplar dial and verse painting on glass, 29 x 16 x 4 ⅛ in (73.7 x 30.6 x 10.5 cm), manufactured by Eli Terry, c. 1822. American Clock and Watch Museum, Bristol, CT.

But such a standard approach soon expanded to include a variety of styles with painted and carved decoration. Ornament was not a requirement of the manufacturing process, but seemed to be an essential component of the consumption side of the American system. Decoration gave consumers a sense of individual choice and thus identity; these circumstances allowed design to assume an important place in the American System.

The glass industry also reveals the result of cost-effective production technologies such as the manufacture of pressed glass for inexpensive imitations of what had formerly been labor-intensive and expensive techniques of cutting glass. Here technology had a democratizing effect upon design for tableware that expressed individual and social aspirations connected to entertaining guests or celebrating special occasions, as in the two examples of celery vases (celery was considered a delicacy at the time) dated between 1820 and 1840 from the eastern United States (figs. 3.20 and 3.21). In this case, as described by historian Regina Blaszczyk, mold-makers often served as craftsmen–designers to expand the range of imagery and decoration on glass objects to appeal to the wide-ranging tastes and desires of a diverse market. In these two examples, a more or less standardized shape and surface is divided into fields covered with diamond or striped patterns that can be varied to create different effects and expand consumer choice. Such circumstances encouraged creativity and ingenuity in assessing, and in a sense respecting (rather than dictating) consumer preferences. In addition, advertising helped to influence the tastes of consumers and to mitigate the uncertainties of the competitive marketplace.

Craftsmen and labor organizations, especially in Britain, often viewed mechanization as a threat to jobs and to their status and independence as artisans. They lobbied for restricted use of machines by manufacturers, and such restrictions eventually allowed American goods to compete for British markets. By the second half of the nineteenth century, design, eclectic historicism, and printed advertising had become prominent features of manufacturing in the United States, as techniques of mass production were adapted to supply variety and choice in stimulating consumer demand for goods and furnishings. Changing styles were often viewed as a barometer of progress and ingenuity – just as new frontier settlements, reaping machines, and railways were transforming nature by making it more productive and "civilized," manufacturers were transforming raw materials into finished products with ingenuity as well as with design.

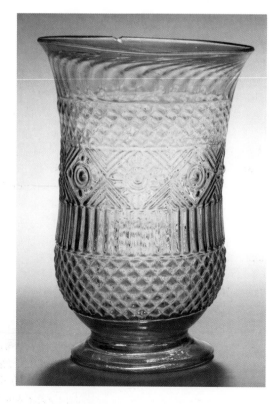

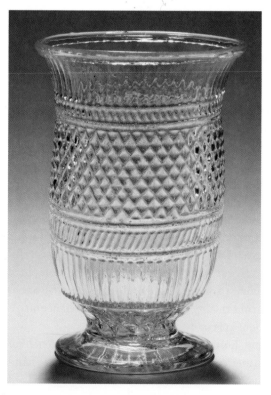

3.20 Celery vase, blown and molded glass, 7 ¼ x 4 ⅝ in (18.4 x 11.7 cm), 1825–1840, Philadelphia Museum of Art.

3.21 Celery vase, blown and molded glass, 7 ½ x 4 ⅞ in (19.1 x 12.3 cm), 1820–1840, Philadelphia Museum of Art.

Chapter 4

Design, Society, and Standards

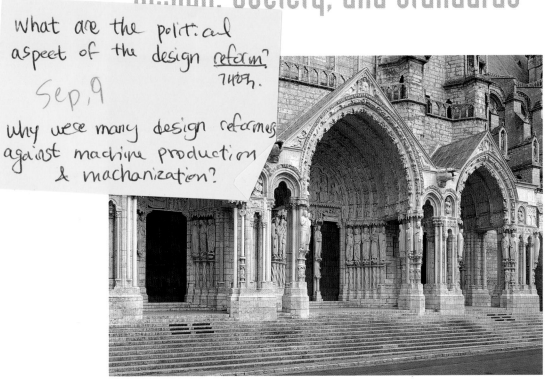

[Handwritten note: What are the political aspect of the design reform? 제도자. Sep,9 why were many design reformers against machine production & machanization?]

4.1 North transept portal, Chartres Cathedral, France, *c.* 1210–1220.

EARLY DESIGN REFORM

Cities were the focus of industrial and commercial activity throughout the nineteenth century, and the growth of urban populations throughout Europe presented challenges to governments in terms of housing, sanitation, unemployment, safety, as well as conflicts among classes and their developing identities. The year 1830 saw outbreaks of social unrest in Europe and working-class rebellion leading to armed conflict and its suppression through stronger central authority.

A portion of the emerging class of industrialists, merchants, and professionals during the first half of the nineteenth century took an interest in the living and labor conditions of factory workers and other artisans whose numbers swelled in the cities of Europe. Along with industrial wealth came a desire, even a sense of obligation, to address social and economic inequity, even if the motivation toward reform was often tied to reinforcing and shaping the values of a hierarchical social order within a more commercial, complex, and diverse society.

Reform efforts touched upon the role of the arts in promoting progressive social values (for instance, the establishment of government-sponsored collections of art such as the National Gallery in London in 1824), as well as the role of design in manufacturing as a means of increasing the appeal and value of useful goods. While some reformers presented moral arguments supporting the Gothic style as the model both of beauty and of a unified faith and a harmonious social order, other reformers took more practical initiatives to establish schools of design and cultivate a shared and discriminating taste in the public at large. Design "reform" aimed to set standards for taste in the public interest and was part of a broad response to industrial and commercial expansion toward the middle of the nineteenth century. Self-interest merged with group-interest, as reformers argued that manufactures were a source of wealth, prestige, and social progress in a competitive, international market economy. While reformers often employed zealous and polemic rhetoric for effect, their efforts seldom achieved the reception they intended, took account of the increasingly heterogeneous market for manufactured products, or fully understood the commercial forces that operated across the broad spectrum of interest in such goods. For this reason, until the 1860s design reform was mostly limited to the luxury market and to those manufacturers that catered to that market. From the 1860s until the end of the nineteenth century, elements of design reform appear in the form of consumer guides, published as books or as installments in periodicals, often directed toward women, who bore the responsibility for creating a proper home and family environment. Throughout both periods, however, reform attitudes and projects had the effect of further investing the decorative arts with cultural meanings, and are a significant part of the dialogue that informs the history of modern design.

Industry and Its Discontents

Not all observers welcomed the expansion of production and the demand for goods and furnishings with the same enthusiasm as economist Adam Smith. In the early nineteenth century, Britain experienced a staggering growth of industrial manufacturing, particularly in the production of textiles in steam-powered mills, cast iron, and in the construction of railroad engines, rolling stock, and track, which was accompanied by an increasing pressure to mine coal as a source of fuel. Industrialized production of commodities and related resources strained the dynamic relationship between production and consumption created by rationalized labor and increasing demand from an elastic market for manufactured commodities. Free trade, competition, and overproduction in an expanding market combined to make large-scale manufacturing a volatile and uncertain business, often with decidedly negative consequences for a new class of industrial workers. Optimism fueled by technological invention and harnessing the power of natural resources was tempered by the social consequences of an unequal distribution of wealth and the emergence of a chiefly urban laboring class tied to the long hours and increasingly monotonous routine of a factory system of production, often living in squalid and undesirable housing barely at the level of subsistence.

Even as emerging urban industrial areas in Britain such as Manchester, Birmingham, and Liverpool gained a voice in parliament, and as the industrialists who were chosen to represent their interests lobbied for free trade and the further expansion of markets for their products, there was ample cause for concern about the negative human consequences of these early stages of industrialization. The demand for labor in industrial centers resulted in problems of crowding, sanitation, disease, and increasing alcoholism. Workers remained socially and politically marginalized, without electoral power and with little

choice but to suffer low wages, poverty, dangerous working conditions, and long hours, the last made possible through the new technology of gas lighting that extended evening working hours. Working-class discontent led to uprisings and revolts between 1810 and 1830, followed by the beginnings of workers' organizations (trade unions) and the practice of organizing strikes to protest against low wages. The circumstances of factory life also led to legislative reforms such as child labor laws and the first experiments in Socialism in Great Britain and the United States by Robert Owen (1771–1858). In Owens' New Harmony community in Indiana, workers' lives were organized along collective rather than individual and familial lines with communal responsibility for education and child-rearing.

The exploitation of the working class was a theme among a number of writers, including Scottish-born Thomas Carlyle (1795–1881), who, lamenting the extreme contrast between the prosperity of the upper and middle classes and the poverty of the working class, pleaded for some sort of reform:

> The condition of England ... is justly regarded as one of the most ominous, and withal one of the strangest, ever seen in this world. England is full of wealth, of multifarious produce, supply for human want in every kind; yet England is dying of inanition. With unabated bounty the land of England blooms and grows; waving with yellow harvests; thick-studded with workshops, industrial implements, with fifteen millions of workers, understood to be the strongest, the cunningest and the willingest our earth ever had; these men are here; the work they have done, the fruit they have realised is here, abundant, exuberant on every hand of us: and behold, some baleful fiat as of Enchantment has gone forth saying, "touch it not, ye workers, ye master-workers, ye master-idlers; none of you can touch it, no man of you shall be the better for it; this is enchanted fruit!" On the poor workers such fiat fall first, in its rudest shape; but on the rich master-idlers nor any richest or highest man escape, but all are like to be brought low with it, and made "poor" enough, in the money sense or in a far fataler one.

In response to the needs and demands of an expanding working class in Britain, and fearing that unrest might lead to revolution, parliament undertook efforts to implement standardized codes for the due process of law, pursue broad-based educational opportunities, establish public museums and parks, restrict employers' use of child labor, and reform the prison system. Just as attempts were made to regulate working conditions, so too were efforts undertaken to regulate and standardize aspects of industrial production, as seen, for instance, in the adoption of standardized widths for the laying of railroad track in England. With many privately owned and competing companies, such shared standards ensured the ease of connecting one railroad line to another. In such circumstances design also took on a political dimension.

Increasing use of steam-powered engines to run machines, along with the further division of labor, contributed to making design a distinct part of the manufacturing process. For these reasons reformers focused their attention on the training of individuals to create patterns for textiles, wallpapers, ceramics, as well as wrought and cast metals. Rather than acquiring the technical knowledge of processes or a familiarity with materials gained from years of apprenticeship, designers mined the past and looked to nature as sources for decorative patterns that provided goods and furnishings with added value for an expanding commercial market.

Whether stirred by the fiery rhetoric of Carlyle or by progressive calls to action and responsibility, many reformers, whether artists, architects, industrialists, or politicians, were motivated by a sense of social responsibility and a desire to improve the lives of working people. As noted above, such attitudes may be viewed as a genuine concern for improving the quality of life and serving the public interest, or as efforts to exert social control, promoting values "imposed" from above in order to ensure compliance and prevent disruptive protest or revolution. Understanding the nature of early design reform involves reconciling these conflicting views and motivations, and recognizing that reform embodied complex attitudes aimed at balancing common values with a recognition and appreciation for the democratic, spontaneous impulses of an emerging popular culture.

Early design reformers in Britain directed their efforts toward creating standards and models for designers and manufacturers to follow. Many, including Matthew Digby Wyatt (1820–1877), welcomed technology in the form of new materials and processes to which guidelines might be applied, especially in relation to metals and casting; others, such as A. W. N. Pugin (1812–1852), called attention to the moral and ethical implications of design, ignoring the varied tastes and motivations of consumers. Still others, such as Sir Henry Cole (1808–1882), lobbied for schools of design, a museum devoted primarily to the decorative arts, and exhibitions to display national and international contemporary design to inform manufacturers and educate the public. In all cases, however, reformers believed in the existence of a fixed set of standards for design that applied to all, and the need to establish and implement them in the common culture – standards that they felt ultimately would be in the best economic, social, and moral interests of an ever-expanding consuming public. Thus design reform was in this basic sense political, and many reformers understood that in order to be effective, it was necessary to be persuasive. They used the latest technology in the printing industry to publish illustrations of their designs in books and journals as part of an effort to familiarize an expanding middle-class readership with the practice of good design, and to stage exhibitions that promoted their point of view.

REFORM AND THE GOTHIC REVIVAL

One of the strongest advocates for standards or principles of design was A. W. N. (Augustus Welby Northmore) Pugin. Pugin, an architect, designer, and author who collaborated with Sir Charles Barry on the design and interior decoration for London's Houses of Parliament (1837 ff.), contrasted the eclectic tastes in contemporary English architecture and design with the stylistic unity of its medieval and specifically Gothic past. For Pugin the consistency of the latter expressed morality as well as aesthetic harmony. Pugin's conversion to Roman Catholicism in 1835 and his enthusiasm for the beauty and "truth" of the Gothic style led him to a passionate investigation of and appreciation for the style. As a result he criticized the indiscriminate and superficial application of any type of carved, printed, and painted decoration to a wide variety of furnishings and utilitarian goods, which he felt was motivated by commercial greed and self-interest. The moralizing equation of decoration with excess was not entirely new (see page 27 and page 48), but the focus upon the Gothic style as the purest expression of such attitudes and the urgent pleas for change in Pugin's writings are characteristic of a polemic tone and ethical undercurrent in the nineteenth-century design reform movement.

Pugin's "principles" of design derived from his understanding of Gothic architecture. He believed that painting and sculpture (whether decorative or figural) were essentially embellishments of architecture and as such should be subordinated to, rather than independent from, the structure they decorate. This rational, subordinating principle of organization is certainly not absent from other architectural styles, including examples of classically inspired furniture discussed in Chapter 1 (see figs. 1.2 and 1.9), but for Pugin the principle is best exemplified in the Gothic style. Looking at the early-thirteenth-century north transept portal of Chartres Cathedral, for example (fig. 4.1), one can observe that the jamb statues maintain their character as columns supporting a porch, other carved figures do not project beyond their containing niches, and virtually all individual elements are part of a larger unit that is in turn related to the tripartite division of the doorway. As suggested by art historian Margaret Belcher, within such a framework a unity is imposed upon all of the arts that might also serve as a metaphor for an ideal society in which all individuals are unified by a single faith and live in harmony – individual difference yields to an ideal unity. In addition, Pugin advised respect for the characteristics of materials and argued, for instance, that carved materials, such as wood, should not look as if they are molded (like bentwood), and that while it is natural for artists and artisans to transform the materials they work with, stone should always retain in some measure its essential "stony" character, and should not pretend to be something else. The arbitrary use of pointed arches and quatrefoils for the base of a lamp or the back of a chaise was for Pugin a superficial appropriation of details, which revealed a lack of understanding of both the stylistic and symbolic unity of the Gothic style. Other grievances against contemporary design included the use of scenic or illusionistic patterns for wallpapers or carpets since the modeling of forms might be inconsistent with the effects of natural light, and such views interfered with the structural function of walls and floors. He registered some of his objections in a satirical drawing of "monstrosities" where the Gothic style is used to construct a collection of elaborately decorated doorstops, lamps, and other objects that make use of Gothic characteristics in varying degrees. His disdain for the modeled forms and detail in examples such as the Gothic wallpaper design illustrated in figure 3.16 was registered in the following comments: "What are commonly termed Gothic pattern papers for hanging on walls, where a wretched caricature of a pointed building is repeated from skirting to cornice, door over pinnacle and pinnacle over door." He is condescending in both social as well as aesthetic criticism, commenting that a particular misguided style of decoration was "a great favourite with hotel and tavern keepers". Pugin's own approach to decoration for walls is seen in the more two-dimensional pattern of the block-printed curtain illustrated in figure 4.2.

In 1841, Pugin enumerated his principles derived from the Gothic style in *True Principles of Pointed or Christian Architecture*, illustrated with engravings based on the author's drawings. In this book he wrote that "there should be no features about a building which are not necessary for convenience, construction, or propriety," and "all ornament should consist of enrichment of the essential construction of the building." He also published books of illustrations intended as models for the design of furniture, metalwork, ceramic plates and tiles, and ecclesiastical garments. A number of firms manufactured his designs, the moral as well as aesthetic dimension of which can be seen in a plate manufactured by Minton in 1849

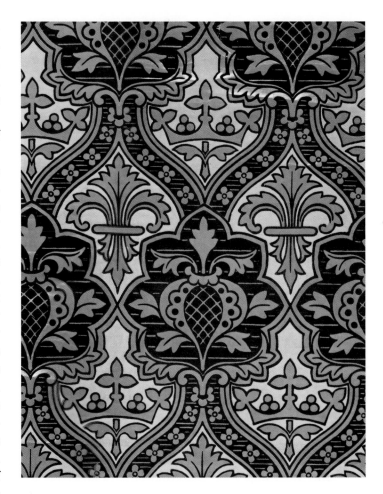

4.2 A. W. N. Pugin, *Fleur-de-Lys and Pomegranate* pattern, block-printed and glazed curtain, 88 ²⁄₃ x 59 in (225.2 x 150 cm), 1851. Private collection.

whose border is inscribed with the admonishment "Waste Not Want Not" in bold Gothic letters. Elaborated in many forms by other contemporary designers and authors, Pugin's "true principles" became the basis for many nineteenth-century approaches to design standards that refer to the "harmony between utility and beauty."

Art criticism for Pugin was inseparable from social criticism, and a disregard for design principles as he defined them was also a deviation from both beauty and moral truth. Eclecticism and lack of discrimination were signs of decay, and disregarding the "proper" use of materials was deceitful as well as ignorant of enduring standards. On the positive side, the understanding of and adherence to fixed principles were socially as well as aesthetically desirable, and in this way the decorative arts could contribute to the well-being of society, instilling common values during a time of uncertainty and change brought about by industrialization and rising demand. Wedded to a discriminating historicism and looking to the past to influence the future, the moral dimension of Pugin's views lent a polemic urgency to his writings. His views were based on a firm belief in the ability of the arts to influence culture, and were shared by a number of important artists, manufacturers, and politicians during the Victorian Age.

Many of Pugin's designs for patterns and interior furnishings were inspired by fourteenth- and fifteenth-century examples he studied and recorded in England and on visits to France. Motifs such as the quatrefoil or *fleur-de-lys* are common, as are other plant or lobed forms that share the same characteristics – repetition or symmetry, crisp contours, and flat shapes. This approach can be seen in the bright *Fleur-de-Lys and Pomegranate* wallpaper pattern used for a number of conference and committee rooms at the Palace of Westminster in London.

Many of Pugin's designs for furniture and interiors were commissioned by or intended for august religious or other ceremonial settings and circumstances, especially parish churches and in particular the chambers of the Houses of Parliament. The House of Lords adhered to Pugin's *True Principles*, but its deeply coffered ceilings, carved wall paneling, gilt screens, and carved stone figures were more appropriate to the public display of authority than to private comfort or daily living. While he holds a well-deserved place in the history of modern design, Pugin's direct legacy is perhaps best seen in the widespread construction of Gothic Revival churches in Britain and North America in the late nineteenth and early twentieth centuries. A more modest example of his design is a cast-iron umbrella stand manufactured by the firm of John Hardman in London from around 1850 (fig. 4.3). Here Pugin applied his principles to a contemporary household object made using a modern manufacturing process; a twisted vertical stem serves as an axis for eight circles above and a related octagonal tray below to hold dripping water. The base is supported by four feet attached to sweeping curved straps that also are repeated inversely above. There is little if any molded decoration to interfere with holding the umbrellas, and the visual organization is both practical and sophisticated.

Henry Cole and the "Cole Group"

Beginning in the 1830s the British government, fearing foreign competition for its manufactured goods, took an interest in design, primarily through the establishment of schools devoted to the education of artists to produce designs specifically for manufactured goods. A lengthy government report of 1835–6, prepared by Parliament's Select Committee on Arts and Manufactures under the auspices of the Board of Trade, noted that the arts in Britain had received very little encouragement and that the result was both a decline in demand abroad for British

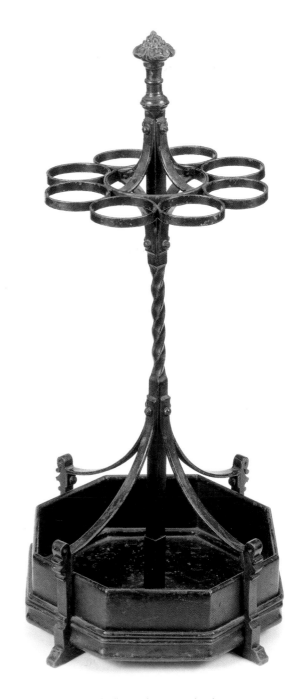

4.3 A. W. N. Pugin, umbrella stand, cast iron, height 30 in (76.2 cm), manufactured by John Hardman, c. 1850. Victoria and Albert Museum, London. Courtesy of the Palace of Westminster Collection.

goods and an increase in foreign imports at home (a negative trade balance, in contemporary economic terms). There was a belief among a number of committee members that the arts of painting and sculpture should form the basis for the education of designers in "manufactures." Drawing was an essential component of this education, based upon the belief that the noble and didactic aims of the fine arts would also elevate the general standards of public taste in useful goods. The Select

Committee also advocated specific recommendations for such standards, based, not surprisingly, upon a balance between utility and beauty and the use of decorative patterns derived from the study of botanical forms and select examples from the past.

Among the most prominent advocates for design education was Sir Henry Cole (1808–1882), a civil servant who believed that "an alliance between fine art and manufactures would promote public taste" as well as restore Britain's competitive edge in the expanding world market for manufactured goods. Cole's attitudes were strongly influenced by the House Report of 1835–6. Under the pseudonym Felix Summerly, Cole edited a series of illustrated travel books and storybooks intended for children (known as the *Home Treasury*) that were intended to "improve" upon the quality of children's literature currently available in the market. Throughout his long career in public service he argued that public museums should serve the interests of the working class and be "the antidote to brutality and vice," providing models for responsible behavior and social harmony. Turning to design, the harmony of utility and beauty in the decorative arts also served as a metaphor for the socially acceptable virtues of moderation and restraint, and government-sponsored design education provided practical training for artisans as a necessary element in those expanding industries producing a wide range of domestic products. As a model business venture, Cole furnished designs (both his own and those of his artist friends) for tea sets and other manufactured goods, founding Summerly Art Manufactures in 1847 as a model for manufacturers.

Richard Redgrave (1804–1888) was a painter of frequently moralizing subjects who participated in a number of Cole's initiatives, providing illustrations for the *Home Treasury* and designs for Summerly Art Manufactures. As a designer, Redgrave's glass *Well-Spring* carafe of 1847 (fig. 4.4) is an example of early design reform movement efforts. The painted decoration of reeds, appropriate as a subject to the vase's function as a water container, is based upon direct studies from nature, but the drawing results in a simplified, linear style that grows from a more abstract crisscross pattern of roots at the base. Glass allows for the tentative exploration of three-dimensional space, since it is naturally transparent and thus permits such effects. Summerly's products did not always adhere to such concern for the "truth to materials" dictum: Redgrave's *Well-Spring* design was later produced by the Minton Company in porcelain, where at least some of the subtlety of its effect is lost.

Neither Pugin nor Cole condemned the use of unskilled and increasingly divided labor or the use of new technologies to increase the efficiency of production.

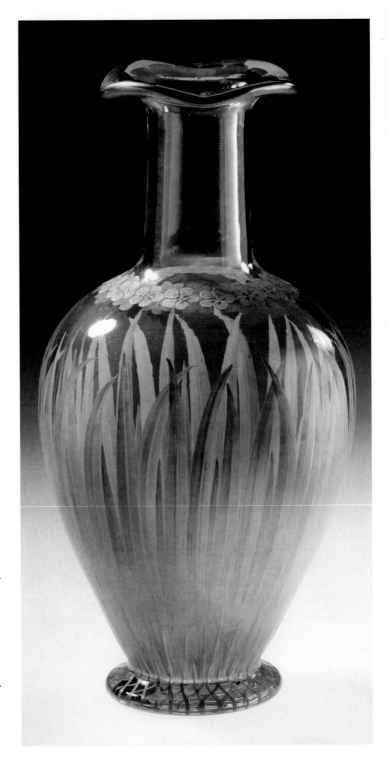

4.4 Richard Redgrave, *Well-Spring* carafe, glass, painted in enamel, 10 ³/₁₆ x 5 ¹/₁₆ in (26 x 13 cm), manufactured by A. J. F. Christy, Stangate Glass Workshop, Lambeth, London, 1847. Victoria and Albert Museum, London.

Rather, they were interested in articulating, practicing, and disseminating common standards of taste in *design* that might inform the production of useful goods by manufacturers in a competitive economy at home and abroad. If machines or specialization (sometimes taking the form of piecework, that is, the hiring out or subcontracting of particular parts of a product that are later assembled and sold) could increase efficiency and lower cost, it was only natural that manufacturers employ such means. While concerned with the welfare of working people, the reform efforts of Cole and his group applied more to finished products and the specific function of design for those products than to the process of labor by which they were manufactured. Unlike Pugin's insistence upon the morality and unity of the Gothic style, however, Cole and his group accepted a broader range of styles within their approach to reform, and direct studies from nature formed an integral part of their program to educate designers for industry. Designers might work from nature or in a variety of historic styles yet still adhere to a balanced relationship between utility and beauty, as well as be concerned with appropriate representational imagery that contradicted neither function nor the nature of the materials employed.

Cole recognized that his ideas would never gain acceptance without lobbying for education and attempting to shape public opinion. He helped to sponsor a periodical entitled *The Art Journal* (1849–51) that published illustrations for designers and manufacturers to follow, and also played a role with the reform of Britain's government-run schools of design, whose curricula focused upon drawing as a mainstay of training. Following the Crystal Palace exhibition of 1851 (see directly below), Cole realized his longstanding ambition to establish the South Kensington (later Victoria and Albert) Museum as a collection devoted to the decorative arts and the improvement of public taste (his portrait, in mosaic, is still found in a stairwell in the older part of the building). From the 1860s onward the South Kensington Museum installed gas lighting to permit working people to view the collections until ten o'clock three nights each week.

In addition to Redgrave, the sculptor Matthew Digby Wyatt was an advocate of design reform. He devoted much of his attention to the proper use of decoration in the manufacture of cast-metal objects such as coal-burning stoves and fireplaces used increasingly for household heating, and published books with detailed illustrations of product designs based on reform principles. Such principles were incorporated by the well-known sculptor Alfred Stevens (1817–1875) in his design for a stove in the Renaissance style dating from 1851 (fig. 4.5). The stove uses cast sculptural ornament in high relief as well as ceramic tile to help conduct heat; in the language of design reform, the stove illustrates the alliance of art with industry, and even decoration with functional efficiency. Such an approach was intended to promote the reputation of British manufactured goods for a discriminating and affluent market.

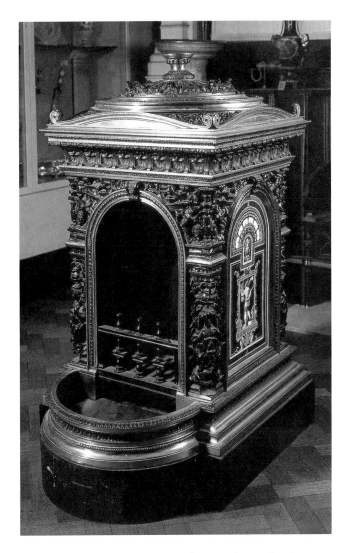

4.5 Alfred Stevens, warm-air stove, cast bronze with printed earthenware panels by Minton, 50 x 28 in (127 x 71.1 cm), manufactured by Hoole, Sheffield, England, 1851. Victoria and Albert Museum, London.

THE GREAT EXHIBITION OF 1851

The Exhibition of Art and Industry held in London at Hyde Park in 1851 served as a watershed for design at mid-century and emphatically confirmed the reality of a heterogeneous middle-class consumer culture in Europe that associated commodities with ideas of progress, abundance, individual identity, and social transformation. Never before had the decorative and industrial arts been the focus of such widespread attention and interest, crossing class boundaries and stirring the popular imagination. Supported by royal consort Prince Albert (1819–1861) and organized by Cole and his group of reformers, the Great Exhibition of 1851 expanded upon earlier national exhibitions of industry in France and created the framework for numerous international exhibitions in the late nineteenth and twentieth centuries both in Europe and in the United

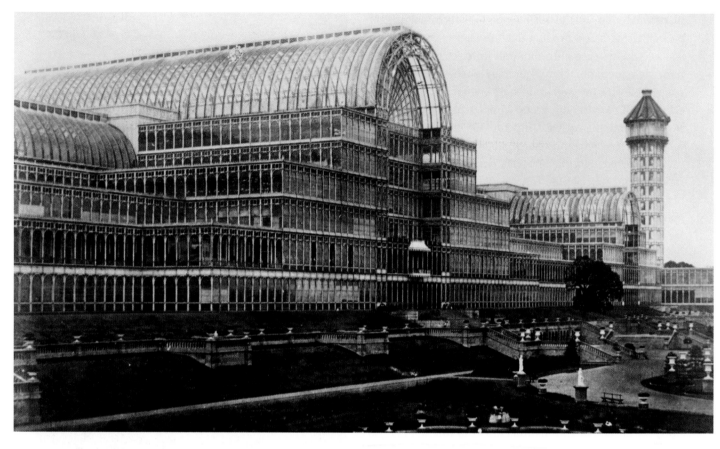

4.6 Joseph Paxton, Crystal Palace, north water tower and transept, London, built 1851, photographed by Francis Frith.

States. Entitled The Exhibition of the Art and Industry of All Nations, the fair originally was conceived as a national fair, but in the process of planning became international, attracting 14,000 producers, half of whom were from outside Britain. It was housed in a temporary structure (fig. 4.6) designed by architect Joseph Paxton (1801–1865), attracting great interest by its frank use of cast and wrought iron, its breathtaking expanses of glass, and the complete absence of traditional building materials such as stone and load-bearing walls. Relying upon uniform pre-fabricated parts, the Exhibition Hall was built in the short span of eight months, a necessity resulting from a lack of agreement among organizers in earlier planning and construction efforts. Although Paxton's choice of materials and method of construction had previously been used in utilitarian structures such as railroad stations and green-houses, the Crystal Palace, as it was dubbed at the time, with its colorful painted railings, high vaults, rhythmic arcades, and cast structural elements, aspired to rival if not to surpass the great architectural landmarks of the past, sounding a note of modernity, progress, and confidence in the aesthetic possibilities of industrialized technology.

Although the goods on display were not for sale, the sense of abundance and the display of products in close proximity to the spectator linked the exhibited objects to the promise of unlimited availability to the middle class and the fulfillment of dreams and desires. Historian Thomas Richards has placed the exhibition in the context of nineteenth-century theatrical spectacle, suggesting the transformation of goods as they entered a "vast space of association." Such magical, quasi-religious reactions to the Crystal Palace and its exhibition were not uncommon. Queen Victoria herself remarked that when standing inside the structure she was "filled with devotion." By the early 1860s, enterprising investors and merchants had translated the magical associations of such vast spaces into a new kind of shopping experience with the first depart-ment store, the Bon Marché in Paris in 1869, followed shortly after in the United States with Wanamaker's in Philadelphia, Macy's in New York, and then in Britain with Selfridges in London. These large, multi-storied business-es competed with boutiques and other smaller, specialized retail establishments. They also introduced uniform pricing (rather than bargaining with merchants), seasonal sales, and a large and diverse inventory of ready-made goods and fabrics.

The combination of optimism, belief in progress, and materialism seen in the broad public reaction to the

Crystal Palace is mirrored in the confident social aspirations of characters in contemporary fiction on both sides of the Channel. In Honoré de Balzac's (1799–1850) novel *César Birotteau* (1837), the protagonist comes to Paris as a poor provincial with no formal education or connections and rises, through hard work and prudent investment, to become a respected and successful Parisian perfume merchant. Upon being awarded the prestigious medal of the Legion of Honor for his support of the monarchy, César undertakes the expansion and decoration of his apartment with the help of an aspiring architect in order to give a ball celebrating his financial and social achievement. While subsequent investments and speculations bring disaster to César, and demonstrate the unpredictability of both fortune and the friendship based upon it, self-improvement and social advancement are portrayed as realistic middle-class aspirations in this nineteenth-century novel.

The spirit of progress and expansion associated with manufactured goods also forms part of the iconography of the Albert Memorial in Hyde Park (fig. 4.7), built between 1864 and 1876 and dedicated to the Prince Consort, who died in 1861 and who had strongly supported the Crystal Palace exhibition. Albert peers out over the four corners of the earth, each represented by a beast and symbolized by an allegorical figural group referring to the continents of Asia, Africa, Europe, and America. Matching the four continents are four categories of productive human endeavor, including the representation of manufactures,

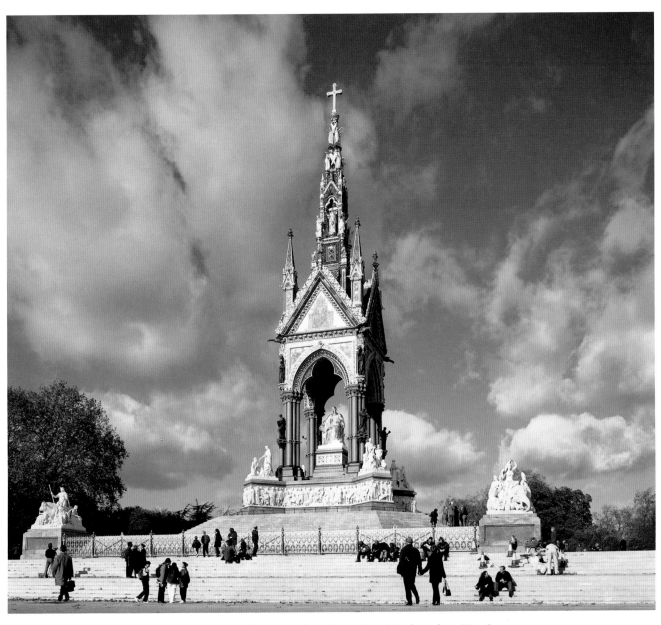

4.7   Sir George Gilbert Scott, Albert Memorial, Hyde Park, London, 1864–76.

along with agriculture, engineering, and commerce. The Manufactures group includes a Hercules-like figure representing labor and a seated figure holding a plate and urn. The symbolism of this orderly vision of the world is clear: Britain stands at the intersection of heaven (note the cross at the top of the baldachin) and earth: the riches of nature under God's watch are multiplied and extended by the creativity and ingenuity of the human race, creating an ideal vision of prosperity and peace. It is not surprising that the Albert Memorial was built during a time of aggressive colonial expansion, which brought the raw materials of an expanding industrial empire into the service of Britain.

Popular interest in the Great Exhibition may also be gauged from the proliferation of printed materials in the form of illustrated catalogues, books of illustrations featuring "masterpieces" from the exhibition or views of its varied displays, and smaller-scale ephemera in the form of sheet music, note cards, and Christmas cards celebrating the event and printed using the recently developed process of chromolithography.

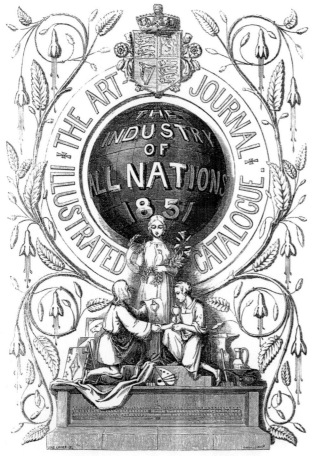

LONDON : PUBLISHED FOR THE PROPRIETORS, BY GEORGE VIRTUE.

4.8 Catalogue of the Great Exhibition of the Works of Industry of All Nations, front cover, published in *The Art Journal*, London, 1851.

While the Great Exhibition celebrated productivity and progress in manufacturing, the organizers themselves expressed disappointment in the results, for there was little evidence that public taste had been improved or that standards of design in British goods had been widely adopted by manufacturers. The cover page illustration that appeared on the issue of Cole's *Art Journal* devoted to the exhibition aptly expresses the didactic aspirations of the organizers (fig. 4.8). An allegorical figure of Peace holding a dove stands in front of a globe and is flanked by two kneeling figures – a designer and a craftsman. To her right, a well-groomed gentleman, clearly designated as the designer, holds a drawing of a chalice and is surrounded by books. These attributes – in combination with his long stylish hair and long-sleeved tunic, both of which are impediments to physical labor – associate the designer with the fine arts and their inclusion in the liberal arts. In contrast, the craftsman kneeling opposite him, and whose hand he clasps, wears cropped hair and a worker's smock with rolled-up sleeves, and is surrounded by the tools of his trade, including an anvil, and some finished products. The scene demonstrates the role of designer and the increasing separation of design from production, along with suggesting that the healthy (if subservient) collaboration between craftsman and artist contributes to global prosperity and peace.

Ralph Wornum, the Keeper of the Queen's Collection of Pictures, won a prize for his essay devoted to the goods on display at the exhibition, published in the *Crystal Palace Illustrated Catalogue*. Wornum expressed belief in the harmony of utility and beauty, and criticized the use of naturalistic flowers and plants for the decoration of carpets and other floor coverings as a violation of fitness to purpose. He was critical as well of the whims of fashion and argued that principles of good taste provided a reliable and permanent foundation for excellence in design. Readers today may be mystified by much of Wornum's analysis. For instance, two examples of wood-carving illustrated in his essay (figs. 4.9 and 4.10) are similar in their overall rectangular form, multi-tiered composition, relation to the theme of food and the hunt, and their abundance of deeply carved relief decoration. However, Wornum lauded the former, a sideboard exhibited by the large and well-known Parisian workshop of Fourdinois, for its appropriate use of imagery (the subjects include allegories of the continents of Europe, Africa, Asia, and America, foods associated with them, and four hunting hounds, all relating to the setting of a dining room); at the same time he condemned the latter carving for being overwrought. Such analysis might well have appeared too "elevated" for the general public to grasp or even care about. Moreover, it ignored the motivations of many middle-class consumers, who

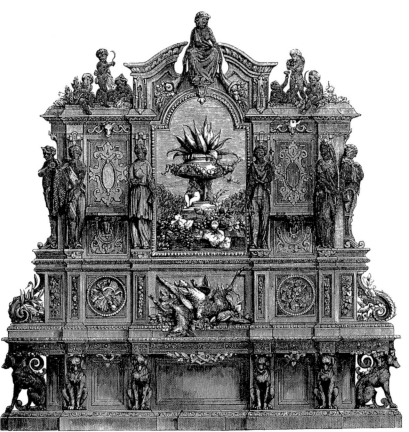

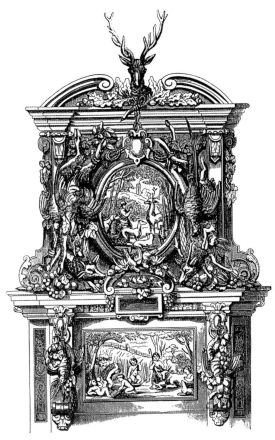

4.9 Henri-Auguste Fourdinois, sideboard, manufactured in Paris. Wood engraving from *The Art Journal* catalogue of the Great Exhibition, London, 1851.

4.10 Michel-Victor Crutchet, carved wall panel, manufactured in Paris. Wood engraving from *The Art Journal* catalogue of the Great Exhibition, London, 1851.

looked to commodities not for instruction or narrative meaning, but rather as symbols of luxury and social aspiration. Wornum further lamented an overabundance of luxury furniture and other products at the expense of less costly and more practical examples of good taste directed toward shaping the needs of average middle-class consumers. This theme would find an echo in subsequent World's Fairs as well, an indication of competing, conflicting attitudes among manufacturers, designers, reformers, craftsmen, and consumers.

Indeed, public reaction to aspects of early design reform was sometimes critical, and reveals the variety of responses to design in a diverse society, and in particular the difficulty of reconciling competing and contradictory points of view. For his efforts to establish standards for taste through exhibitions, publications, and education, Sir Henry Cole was much in the public eye, and was frequently a target of ridicule. In the novel *Hard Times*, which appeared in serial form in 1854, Charles Dickens (1812–1870) poked fun at government efforts to impose standards of taste. A commissioner (a thinly veiled portrait of Cole) visits a government-run school and asks the students whether they would use a carpet bearing

representations of flowers. A young girl, sent to the school by a well-meaning benefactor, replies that indeed she would, because she is very fond of flowers. But the commissioner sternly asks whether in that case "she would put tables and chairs upon them and have people walking over them with heavy boots." "It wouldn't hurt them, sir – they wouldn't crush and wither if you please, sir. They would be the pictures of what was very pretty and pleasant, I would fancy." But the commissioner replies, "Ay, ay, ay. But you *mustn't* fancy" [italics added]. While the motives behind reform were perhaps well-intentioned in a paternalistic sense, Dickens is here defending the democratic freedom of choice as inherently more fundamental than issues of good taste, whether or not it results in excess, sentimentality, and all that we tend to refer to as "kitsch." Dickens effectively used the example of a child to connect the absence of "good taste" with innocence rather than vulgarity or dishonesty.

While critics found examples to support principles of good design and the harmony of utility and beauty, there is generally little acknowledgment of the innovative, exuberant, and even playful qualities found in many objects on display at the Crystal Palace. These include a

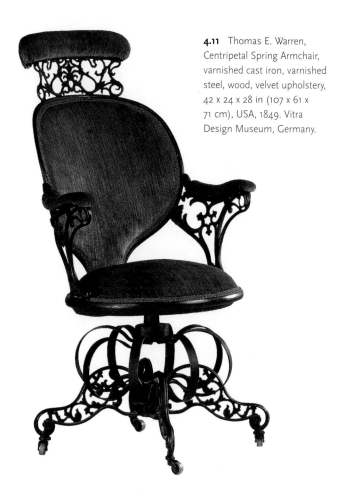

4.11 Thomas E. Warren, Centripetal Spring Armchair, varnished cast iron, varnished steel, wood, velvet upholstery, 42 x 24 x 28 in (107 x 61 x 71 cm), USA, 1849. Vitra Design Museum, Germany.

"Centripetal Spring Armchair" (fig. 4.11) designed in the United States by Thomas E. Warren in 1849 and manufactured by the American Chair Company of Troy, New York. The chair, complete with a rotating seat, is upholstered in velvet and is made from cast iron and wood. It also features eight bent steel strips connected under the seat to a cone-shaped piece in the center to provide a springing mechanism for the seat. The principle was adapted for use in railroad carriages and on other forms of transport to absorb the shock of motion, though one can only presume that such innovations would have been less important to reformers who would have thought the appearance of the cast-iron armrests far too delicate for the purpose of support.

Many of the critics of the Great Exhibition were architects and fine artists. For instance, the German architect and theorist Gottfried Semper (1803–1879), who lived for a time in London and taught at the government-sponsored School of Design there, was dismayed by the uneven quality at the Great Exhibition and compared it to the Tower of Babel. Richard Redgrave arrived at much the same conclusion, writing that "the absence of any fixed principle in ornamental design is most apparent in the Exhibition." Semper, however, was optimistic that the

study of the exhibition's "best" objects should form the basis of standards that took into consideration the rational use of new materials and techniques, function, and considerations of decoration.

Following the opening of the Great Exhibition, Owen Jones (1809–1874), an architect and designer who also was an organizer for the exhibition and advocate of design reform, wrote that the majority of goods on display demonstrated "novelty without beauty, beauty without intelligence, and all work without faith." One can understand his disappointment, for Jones had spent nearly two decades designing illustrations and decorations for books printed using the most recent developments in chromolithography and color wood-engraving, and had also published examples of decorative patterns based upon drawings from the fourteenth-century Nasrid Alhambra palace in Granada, Spain. The plates of Jones's Alhambra volume were intended not only as illustrations of a famed site for a travel book, but rather as didactic models for designers. In spite of his reaction to the Great Exhibition, Jones continued his reform efforts, both as a designer and as the author of *The Grammar of Ornament* (1856), the most extensive "dictionary" of design standards at that time. *The Grammar of Ornament* contained 100 color illustrations (using the chromolithographic process, see page 72) of patterns based upon Western and non-Western examples, in media ranging from carpets to ceramic tiles, from relief sculptures to illuminated manuscripts. Jones advocated a broad historicism based upon principles (32 in all) that appear at the end of the volume. The principles are related to those established by Pugin from the study of Gothic architecture, but extend to a wider variety of examples both geographically and chronologically. Jones's principles include: "Construction should be decorated. Decoration should never be purposely constructed"; "Flowers or other natural objects should not be used as ornaments, but conventional representations founded upon them sufficiently suggestive to convey the intended image to the mind, without destroying the unity of the object they are employed to decorate. Universally obeyed in the best periods of Art, equally violated when Art declines."

The Grammar of Ornament went through numerous printings throughout the late nineteenth century, and its approach to ornament and color was adopted for the decoration of numerous buildings and interiors during this period. By using a variety of historical examples from different cultures, the *Grammar* suggests the universality of standards that can form a basis for all designers (fig. 4.12). In addition to advocating the use of models from other periods and cultures, Jones included the possibility of constructing original patterns based upon the study of

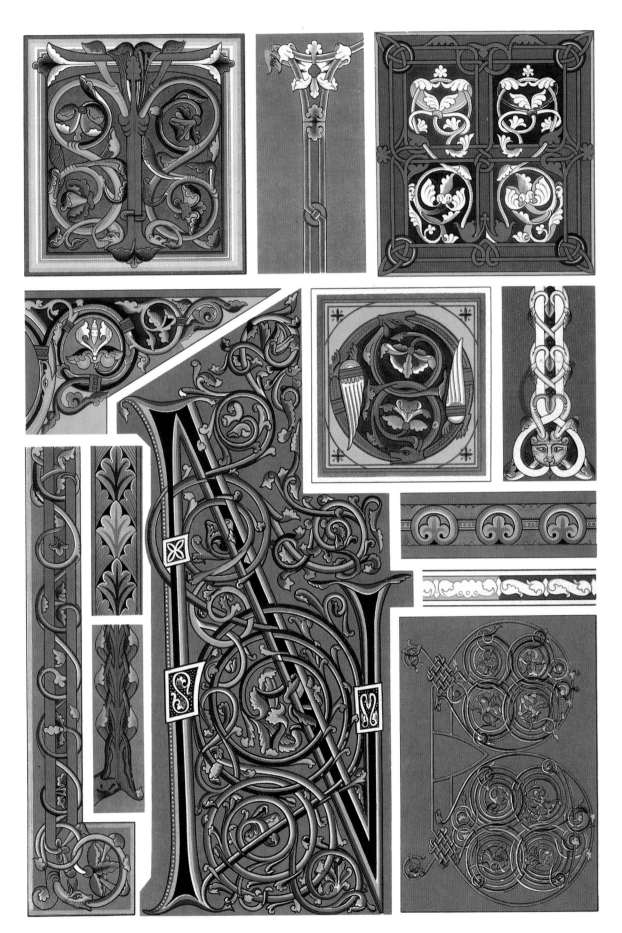

4.12   Owen Jones, Illuminated manuscrips no. 1, plate LXXI, color lithograph, 13 ¼ x 8 ⅞ in (33.7 x 22.5 cm), from the *Grammar of Ornament*, London, 1856. Private collection.

nature tempered by the rules he enumerated and as taught in the British Schools of Design. The British designer Christopher Dresser (1834–1904) contributed original plates to the *Grammar* featuring ornamental shapes based upon leaf and floral motifs in a style that simplified organic forms into flattened linear contours (see fig. 6.1 and chapter 6). Dresser was a student at the London School of Design and collaborated with manufacturers in creating a number of novel designs for industrial production. During his career, along with other contemporary artist- and architect-designers, Dresser attempted to expand the reformers' standards by advocating greater originality in pattern design and greater invention in the treatment of historical styles, including Japanese design, which he became interested in during the 1860s.

Although elevating the taste of the public remained part of the political mission of design reformers, the polemic tone and moralizing arguments of Pugin were less pronounced in the work of Jones. Later, reform efforts generally took the form of advice books by "tastemakers" such as Charles Eastlake (1836–1906). Eastlake's *Hints on Household Taste in Furniture, Upholstery, and Other Details* was published in 1868 and was popular in both the United Kingdom and the United States. Directed toward a mostly female readership who were expected to be concerned with creating a restful home environment, Eastlake wrote:

> We require no small amount of art and instruction and experience to see why direct imitation of natural objects is wrong in ornamental design. The quasi-fidelity with which the forms of a rose, or a bunch of ribbons, or a ruined castle, can be produced on carpets, crockery and wallpapers will always possess a certain kind of charm for the uneducated eye, just as the mimicry of natural sounds in music, from the rolling of thunder to the crackling of poultry, will always delight the vulgar ear. Both are ingenious and amusing but neither lie within the legitimate province of art.

A comparison between one of Eastlake's wallpaper designs (fig. 4.13), manufactured by Jeffery & Company and appearing in *Hints*, and the printed or woven designs at the Great Exhibition (fig. 4.14) reinforces the principles underlying design reform. Eastlake criticized the lack of discrimination in matters of design, but his prose focuses less upon the moral dimensions of design than upon the cultivation of taste as a vehicle for self-improvement as well as reinforcing middle-class cultural attitudes that identified the home as the sphere for women's activities. Such attitudes also pertain to women's activities as designers and are discussed in Chapter 6 (pages 116–118).

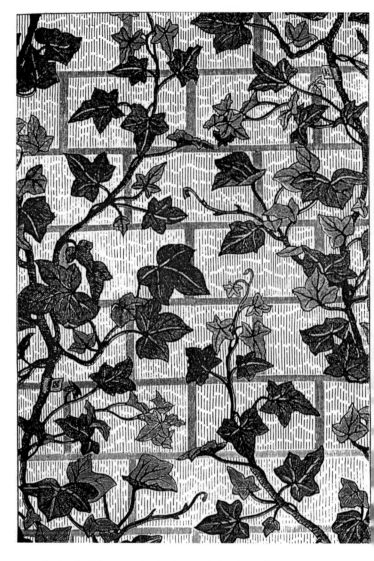

4.13 Charles Eastlake, example of wallpaper design from *Hints on Household Taste*, London, 1868.

IMAGES FOR ALL

The expansion of design in manufactured goods and the creation of a consumer economy was accompanied and stimulated by the expansion of print technology, particularly in the reproduction of images for illustrations and advertising. Competitive free-market conditions, coupled with production technology and the gradual elimination of taxes on paper and printed materials, helped to create the circumstances for the success of illustrated weekly journals aimed at an emerging mass-market, including working people, that reached a circulation in Britain of over 200,000 copies by the middle of the nineteenth century. One of the earliest examples of this type of affordable illustrated journals is *The Penny Magazine* (beginning in 1832), published by Charles Knight (1791–1873), who began his career as a craftsman and printer. Knight is known for his development of an economical method for

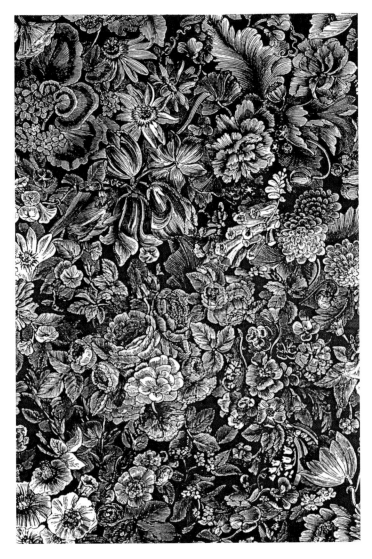

4.14 Carpet, from *The Art Journal* catalogue of the Great Exhibition, 1851, manufactured by Messrs. Turberville Smith, London.

producing color images from multiple engraved woodblocks. *The Penny Magazine* contained wood-engraved reproductions of works of art (part of an emerging "canon" of masterpieces) whose subject matter was intended to provide examples of personal and social virtue. Knight's venture was endorsed by the Society for the Distribution of Useful Knowledge, which supported the role of the arts as a civilizing force in Victorian society, again linking design to progress. Knight's magazine was joined by other weekly journals, often called *Miscellanies*, that included illustrations of examples of decorative art. While a painting's narrative might provide edifying models of behavior, the decorative arts also could convey through form and decoration an appropriate balance between utility and beauty that elevated ordinary goods into artistic ones. In addition to Knight's didactic messages, *Miscellanies* also featured illustrations accompanying

popular serialized and sensationalized fiction dealing with crime, intrigue, sex, and the occult. Thus illustrations and articles that encouraged self-improvement, restraint, temperance, and social harmony coexisted with the broader commercial appeal of aberrant behavior, escapism, and political radicalism – a rich and diverse combination best characterized by the term "popular culture."

Aside from lithography, other methods of satisfying a growing demand for black-and-white as well as color illustrations for reproduction in books, magazines, advertisements, and newspapers were developed during the first half of the nineteenth century. One of these techniques was wood engraving. Owing to the efforts of printer Thomas Bewick of Newcastle-upon-Tyne in northern England (1753–1828), the technique of producing woodblocks by cutting with engraving tools against rather than with the wood grain produced greater precision and a broader tonal range in the rendering of subtle textures and three-dimensional form. Prior to the invention of the half-tone photomechanical process, wood engravers worked directly from blocks printed with photographs.

Fine detail was also achieved beginning in the 1820s using a process that created steel-engraved plates, replacing previously used copper plates. The surface of steel plates was more durable than copper – greater numbers of prints could be run on a steel plate with minimal loss of quality. Steel plates also offered more precision when printing large quantities of thin lines to suggest subtle gradations of tone in relief. The method, developed in the United States by Jacob Perkins (1766–1849), was particularly effective in the creation of plates for secure forms of printing such as postage stamps and paper currency, where their complexity made counterfeiting more difficult.

English printers such as Charles Whittingham, Joseph Cundall, and Henry Shaw were knowledgeable in all phases of book production, and combined a respect for craft with the benefits of new techniques of mechanical reproduction. Whittingham worked in collaboration with the publisher Thomas Pickering at the Chiswick Press in a London suburb for the publication of a number of titles, and was respected for maintaining the highest standards of typography, illustration, layout, and binding (though generally on cardboard rather than more expensive leather). Whittingham and other book printers rejected modern typefaces with their stronger contrast of thick and thin strokes (more common in the nineteenth century for larger display types; see fig. 3.11) and returned to more traditional faces derived from William Caslon. Many printers took an avid interest in illustrated books for children, printed from wood engravings in both black-and-white as well as color. The firm of Robson, Levey & Franklyn

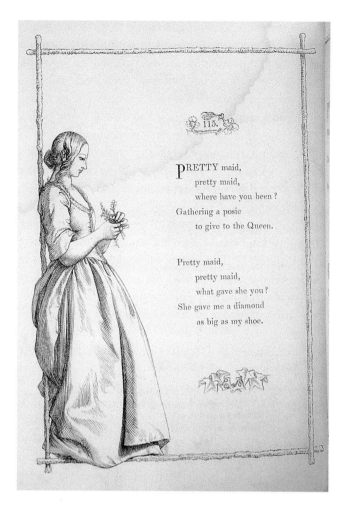

4.15 James Burns, drawings printed from woodblocks, 6 x 8 in (15.2 x 20.8 cm), *Nursery Rhymes, Tales and Jingles*, 1844.

through less expensive illustrated broadsides and weekly journals such as *The Penny Magazine*.

Images in popular weekly journals and broadsheets were printed in black-and-white. But concurrently with these strictly tonal processes, a significant development in color printing, known as chromolithography, was also emerging. Patented in the 1830s by Godefroy Engelmann (1788–1839) in France, the new technology quickly spread to England, Germany, and the United States. Chromolithography produced images in color using a series of stones with flat, polished surfaces, each inked with a different color and printed in succession using exact registration of the paper. The process, as perfected in England by William Savage (1770–1843), was used initially for the accurate color reproduction of paintings for expensive, high-quality prints and illustrated books beginning in the 1840s.

A number of early books with illustrations produced by chromolithography were facsimile editions of manuscripts such as the ninth-century Hiberno-Saxon Gospel book known as the *Book of Kells*. Others were private devotional books meant to rival their older medieval counterparts, such as H. Noel Humphrey's chromolithographed plates for *The Miracles of Our Lord*, published in 1848 (fig. 4.16).

In the late nineteenth century, the chromolithographic process was adopted for the color printing of popular greeting cards and souvenirs. The application of chromolithography to trade, business cards, and advertising (often a giveaway inside a product box) would soon follow, and attain immense popularity in the United States (see page 76).

Popular nineteenth-century color woodcut and chromolithographic images in France were known as *images d'Épinal*, named for the city in northeastern France where they were printed. Subjects ranged from portraits of heroes and political leaders to saints, representations of virtues and vices, to illustrations of contemporary events and disasters along with advertisements, board games, aids to learning the alphabet for children, and playing cards. They demonstrate the increasing role images were playing in the dissemination of information for political, religious, and commercial purposes. Popular prints varied in technique and quality, though a tendency toward simplified and easily recognized flat areas of color, undifferentiated by modeling, is frequently the case. An example is a colored lithograph illustrating a flood of the Loire River dating to 1866 (fig. 4.17). Here the colors are limited to primaries and the secondary color green, against a pale tan and gray ground. The scene shows the rescue of a farm family from the roof of their cottage by three figures on a boat. The gestures are theatrical and the pyramidal

published James Burns' *Nursery Rhymes, Tales and Jingles* in 1844, using Caslon types, rustic frames sometimes hung with vines, and wood-engraved illustrations (fig. 4.15). The asymmetrical yet balanced relationship between framed text and illustration provided both consistency and variety from poem to poem, and suggested a desire to create designs that were visually appealing to young readers. Other contemporary publishers were more lavish in the use and variety of decoration and typefaces. This is most evident in the title pages of contemporary fiction that often appeared in serialized form. George Routledge (1812–1888) of London published a series of novels known as the "Railway Library," presumably meant for reading while traveling and a forerunner of paperback fiction that, along with the daily news, occupies commuters on today's suburban trains and airlines. The cost of most illustrated books was generally beyond the means of working people. But the appeal of stories told with pictures, before the widespread popularity of photography and the advent of film (and later of television) was strong, and was satisfied

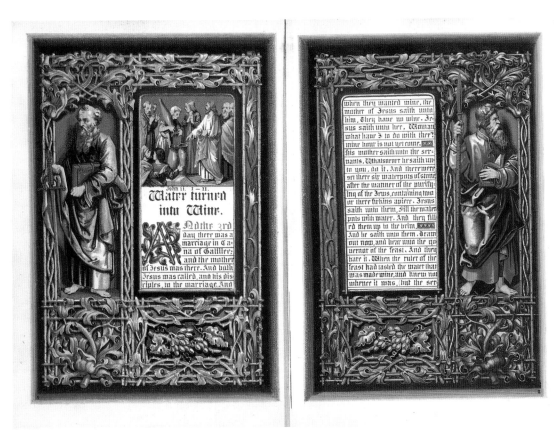

4.16 H. Noel Humphreys, chromolithograph in about 12 colors,
6 ½ x 4 ½ in (16.5 x 11.4 cm), from *The Miracles of Our Lord*, London, 1848.

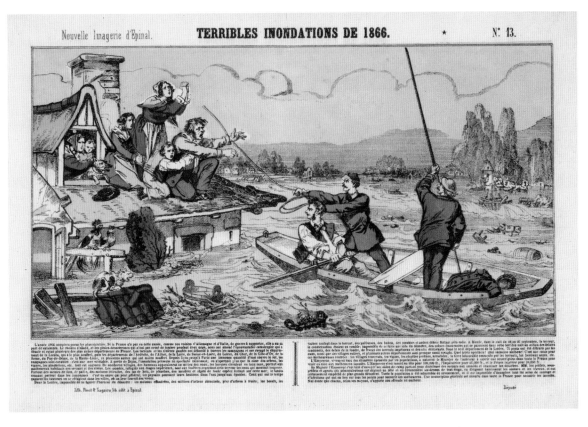

4.17 *Image d'Épinal*, 11 ¹/₁₆ x 16 ³/₁₆ in (28 x 41.1 cm), depicting the rescue of a farm family
from a flood of the Loire River, 1866. Philadelphia Museum of Art.

composition dramatic rather than journalistic. Such conventions rely heavily upon academic convention combined with modern techniques of production to record current events. For printed advertisements, many *images d'Épinal* featured a narrow range of colors and increasingly simplified drawing and modeling.

POPULAR GRAPHICS IN THE UNITED STATES

Illustrated weekly magazines were also popular in the United States, beginning in the 1850s with the publication of *Leslie's Weekly* and *Harper's Weekly* in New York. *Harper's Weekly* covered contemporary events and used the process of wood engraving to reproduce drawings by a number of artists who served as visual reporters, recording events based upon first-hand observations. The artist Winslow Homer (1836–1910), for instance, supported himself early in his career by documenting battles of the American Civil War for *Harper's Weekly*. Later his paintings and those of other fine artists were reproduced as wood-engravings in the weekly magazine. Another illustrator for *Harper's* was Thomas Nast (1840–1902), a gifted draftsman whose family moved to New York from Germany in 1846. As a young man, Nast traveled at the magazine's expense to Europe to cover a prizefight in Britain, as well as reporting on Giuseppe Garibaldi (1807–1882), who led military

campaigns to create the nation of modern Italy in 1860–61; Nast was also sent to report first-hand on some of the events of the American Civil War. Both during and after the Civil War, Nast was interested in shaping public opinion through illustrations aimed at a broad readership. In addition to documenting actual events, he illustrated themes relating to the Civil War and to war in general that had tremendous popular appeal. One of numerous examples, *Christmas Furlough* (fig. 4.18) appeared in late 1863 during the second full year of the Civil War. The design consists of several separately titled and framed scenes set against a background suggestive of a winter landscape. The focus is upon a returning officer visiting his wife and family, with all of the common, safe, and reassuring associations of a homecoming. The theme is reinforced by Nast's composition and use of light. Our attention is drawn immediately to the pyramidal unit formed by the embracing couple in the center vignette. In a smaller vignette to the left, a warm glow of light envelops sleeping children, enhancing the homespun ambiance. One might note that to the left of the main scene the sleeping children are visited by one of Nast's most popular inventions, the image of Saint Nicholas or Santa Claus, made popular by Clement Moore's 1823 poem "A Visit from St. Nick"; Nast's enduring version of Santa Claus combines Moore's description of a jolly, bearded, diminutive, and

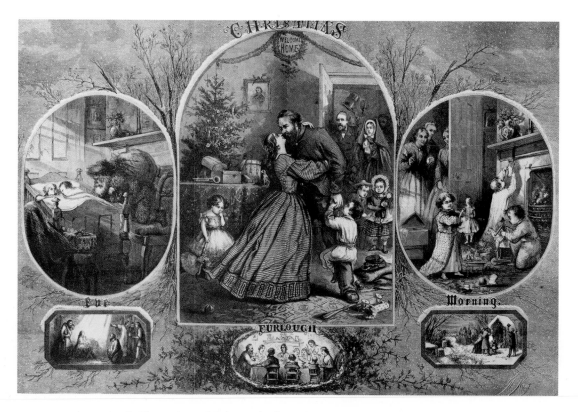

4.18 Thomas Nast, *Christmas Furlough*, wood-engraved illustration from *Harper's Weekly*, double-page spread, 16 x 22 ½ in (40.6 x 57.2 cm), December 26, 1863.

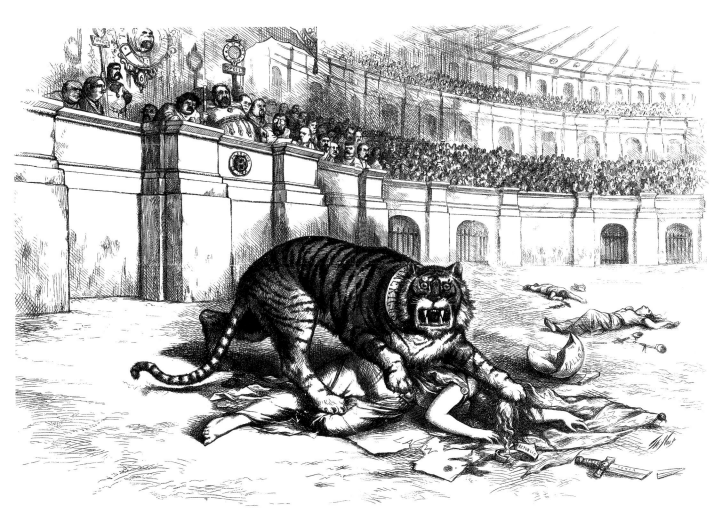

4.19 Thomas Nast, *The Tammany Tiger Loose – What are you Going to Do About it?*, wood-engraved illustration from *Harper's Weekly*, double-page spread, 16 x 22 ½ in (40.6 x 57.2 cm), November 11, 1871.

mischievous St. Nick with the artist's own memories of folk traditions in his native Germany that included a figure known as Pelznickel or "furry Nicholas."

Frequently carefully staged and employing figural arrangements dependent upon the Western academic tradition of religious and historical painting, Nast's approach to drawing often emphasized bold tonal contrast and a reduced interest in detailed description. His original drawings were translated into the medium of the engraved woodblock by other artisans. Nast popularized the use of human and animal figures such as Uncle Sam, Columbia, the Republican Party's Elephant, and the Democratic Party's Donkey as metaphors for collective entities or concepts.

Yet another aspect of Nast's output was political cartoons that made use of exaggeration or caricature. While Nast certainly had precursors who used caricature as a tool of political change (George IV, patron of the Royal Pavilion at Brighton, was a frequent target of satire; see page 49), and may have borrowed from them, the combination of clearly recognizable images of contemporary political figures and an inexpensive vehicle for circulation gave new power to the role of illustration in shaping and mobilizing public opinion. Public officials feared Nast's pen and were well aware of his ability to influence opinion against the untrammeled greed and corruption of public officials. The most celebrated of his campaigns was directed toward a New York State senator named William "Boss" Tweed, from 1869 to 1871. With both *Harper's Weekly* and the *New York Times* supporting the reform of city government, Tweed and his so-called "Ring" were indicted on charges of fraud, bribery, and corruption; in time the reign of the "Ring" came to an end, in no small measure due to the role played by the popular press and Nast's cartoons. Weekly journals such as *Harper's*, and editors such as Fletcher Harper, who supported freedom of expression through the popular press, helped to demonstrate the impact of the emerging profession of illustration. Nast's image of Tweed is seen in an 1871 illustration entitled *The Tammany Tiger Loose – What are you Going to Do About it?*

(fig. 4.19). Nast portrays the heavy, bearded Boss ("B") seated in a Roman amphitheater behind the familiar image of a tiger, symbolizing the Democratic Party machine in New York (Tammany Hall) maiming a victim. In this display of ruthless and brazen power, the artist draws upon audience familiarity not only with Tweed's own image, but also with Roman history and its various associations with emperors, gladiatorial contests, and the persecution of Christians. These themes were frequently depicted in paintings of the period and thus were part of a common cultural literacy that was able to stretch across boundaries of education and class. The development of any "mass" media depends not only upon technology that is able to reach a large audience but also upon the ability to communicate to a socially diverse cultural formation. The emerging art of illustration in wood engraving and chromolithography accomplished this during the later nineteenth century, reflecting and shaping common experiences and attitudes through a range of representational images that readily communicated with an expanding reading and viewing public. Many of these images were exploited by being "appropriated" by graphic designers during the 1960s and invested with oppositional meanings (see page 342 and fig. 13.27).

The efforts of chromolithographic printers in the United States in the field of color reproduction were even more enterprising and widespread than their European counterparts. Louis Prang (1824–1909) was a German-born printer who emigrated to Boston before 1850 and, using the painstaking methods of other experimenters in the field such as William Savage in Britain, produced a wide range of chromolithographic reproductions of paintings that were distributed in albums or individually. Marketed as "chromos," such prints satisfied a demand for works of art among the middle class, tied to the desire for social progress through education and an appreciation for art. Prang extended his market by printing small popular color images for a variety of new purposes, including trade cards, advertising cards, and "decalcomania" that people cut out and pasted on pieces of paper to exchange notes and greetings, or collected in scrap books as a personal gallery of familiar images. Beginning in the 1850s, color images on decals and cards were reproduced on large sheets that were cut and sold separately in packaged sets. Produced by Prang as well as other commercial printers, their initial success soon led to their application on product labels, eventually leading to the proliferation of brands and images that would characterize the broad public experience of the urban scene in the late nineteenth century. Examples range from bizarre anthropomorphic carrots, corncobs, and peapods recalling the type of playful invention sometimes seen in medieval decorated initials,

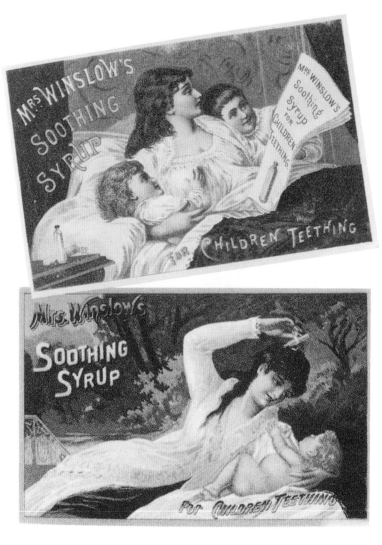

4.20 Trade cards for Mrs. Winslow's Soothing Syrup, chromolithographs, 2 ½ x 3 in (6.4 x 7.6 cm), c. 1885.

to innocent images of children or cats linked to a variety of domestic products (fig. 4.20). Such persuasive techniques, which became more common in the 1920s, are seen in an advertising card depicting a mother and child whose happiness is connected with alleviating the annoyance of normal toddler teething (the preparation contained codeine). Chromolithography was also extensively used on a large scale for advertising posters in the later nineteenth century (see pages 125–129).

A BALANCE SHEET OF REFORM

Early design reformers sought to identify standards for the application of art to manufactured commodities, based upon the study of nature, examples from history, and the art of other cultures. These efforts were in part political in nature, in that the reformers attempted to claim as universal a rather narrow set of criteria and felt a responsibility to educate, and hence convince manufacturers and a growing consumer public to accept such standards. The effort was epistemological as well, for it was grounded in a belief that laws underlie all spheres of human endeavor, from mathematics and the physical sciences to the application of ornament on household goods. Such views ignored the reality of free trade and a free enterprise economy, in which the harmony of utility and beauty was only one among many reasons that motivated consumers to buy clothing and manufactured commodities. Indeed, the tastes of manufacturers and new classes of consumers might be dictated by a different set of assumptions – particularly their relation to social aspirations, and to issues of identity and individuality. The reform agenda also did not sufficiently recognize the sheer excitement and flow of imagination stemming from experiments with new processes and the promise they held for personal expression. It has been argued that those who lamented the spectacle of decorative variety and ostentation among the middle class were seeking to perpetuate not only traditional tastes but also a conservative social system based upon the well-meaning but exclusive preferences of a small, dominant elite. While design reform and the harmony between utility and beauty formed a cornerstone in the narrative of a Modern "movement" in design as described by art historians such as Nicholas Pevsner, a more recent appreciation for eclecticism, popular culture, and the broader cultural context and commercial underpinnings of World's Fairs suggests that competing points of view are necessary to our historical understanding of design and of society in the nineteenth century.

The search for standards seems in many ways a natural tendency during any period of rapid change and the consequent erosion of traditional values and authority amid industrial and commercial expansion, and this certainly applies to the history of modern design. Whether they are standards for decoration, utility, performance, or safety, a desire for regulations and commonality has continued amid the commercial expansion of design and been part of the discourse of social, aesthetic, and technical issues relating to it. After all, as the Albert Memorial appears to demonstrate, reformers as well as manufacturers and consumers shared a belief in progress – the question was how to define and promote it.

CONCLUSION

So if one seeks to understand it [society], one must realize that it embodies at one and the same time everything that it has been, is, and will be in future; it is an accumulation over the long term of permanent features and successive inflections.

So wrote French historian Fernand Braudel in a three-volume study that examines the social and economic order in Europe roughly from the fifteenth to the eighteenth centuries. Braudel's words and his reference to "permanent" features of society sound a note of continuity that might be applied as well to the history of modern design: both what it had been and much of what it was to become are embedded in the complex interplay between changes in the technology of production and the social dynamics of consumption in the eighteenth and early to mid-nineteenth centuries.

Clearly the task of design, whether the contribution of patron, craftsman, artist, mercer, or merchant, was distinguished from, as well as related to, the work of artisans and laborers, and resulted from increasing complexity in the process of production and the expansion of demand. Consumption effectively blurred lines between social classes with increasing speed following the period of political revolution in the United States and in Europe, while novelty became a means for manufacturers to attract an expanding market with the promise of a better life and social distinction. In short, this phenomenon, seen increasingly with changes in production technology, is both an expression of the democratization of culture as well as the commodification of the Romantic cult of individualism amid rising materialism. These elements appear to some degree during the eighteenth century, and provide a useful basis for examining the full-blown expansion of the industrial revolution in the successive decades of the nineteenth century, and the calls for reform that would follow and seek to regulate that expansion.

Perhaps the central issue to emerge during the first half of the nineteenth century is the apparent conflict between technology, commercialization, and democratization on the one hand, all of which signify change and a state of flux, and the search for standards on the other, the desire to regulate change through the application of principles that might stand beyond the whims of fashion, the quest for profits, and the innovations of industry. It is in this context that early design reform can be analyzed. Although the forms and function of decoration may have been the battleground for the proponents of design reform, such debates were part of a broad effort on the part of a traditional group of designers, theorists, and politicians, to educate (or perhaps better, to indoctrinate) an expanding public and merchant class whose own interests might prove threatening to established authority.

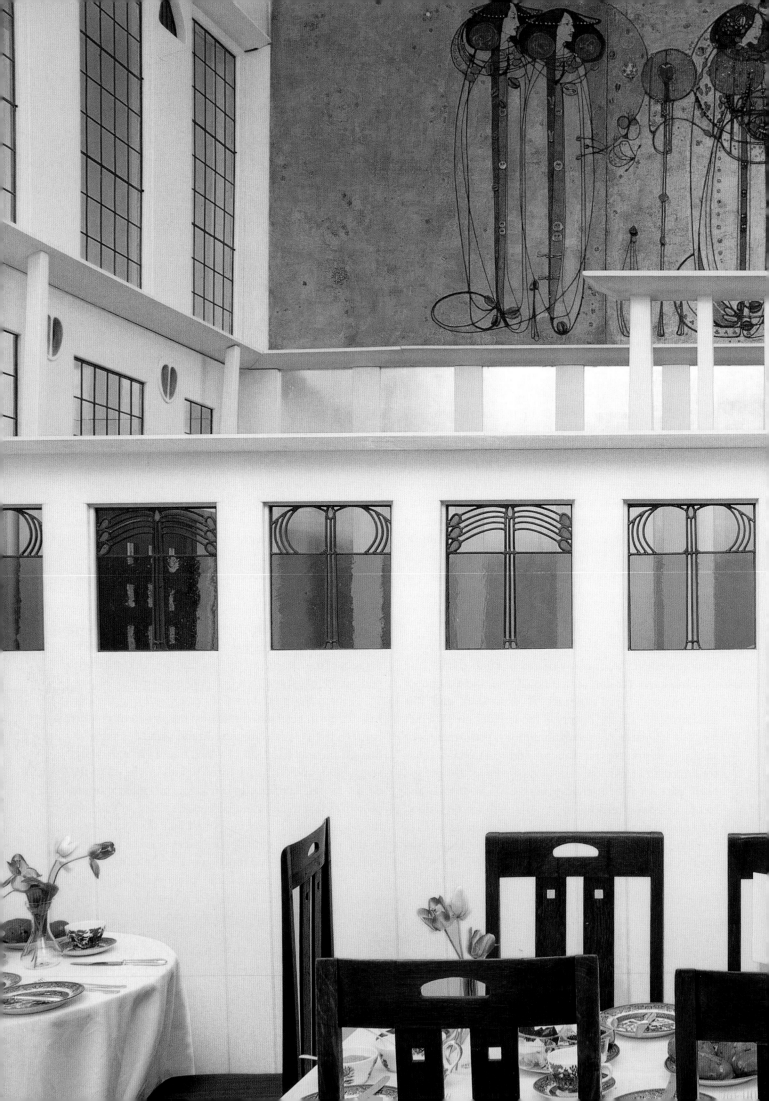

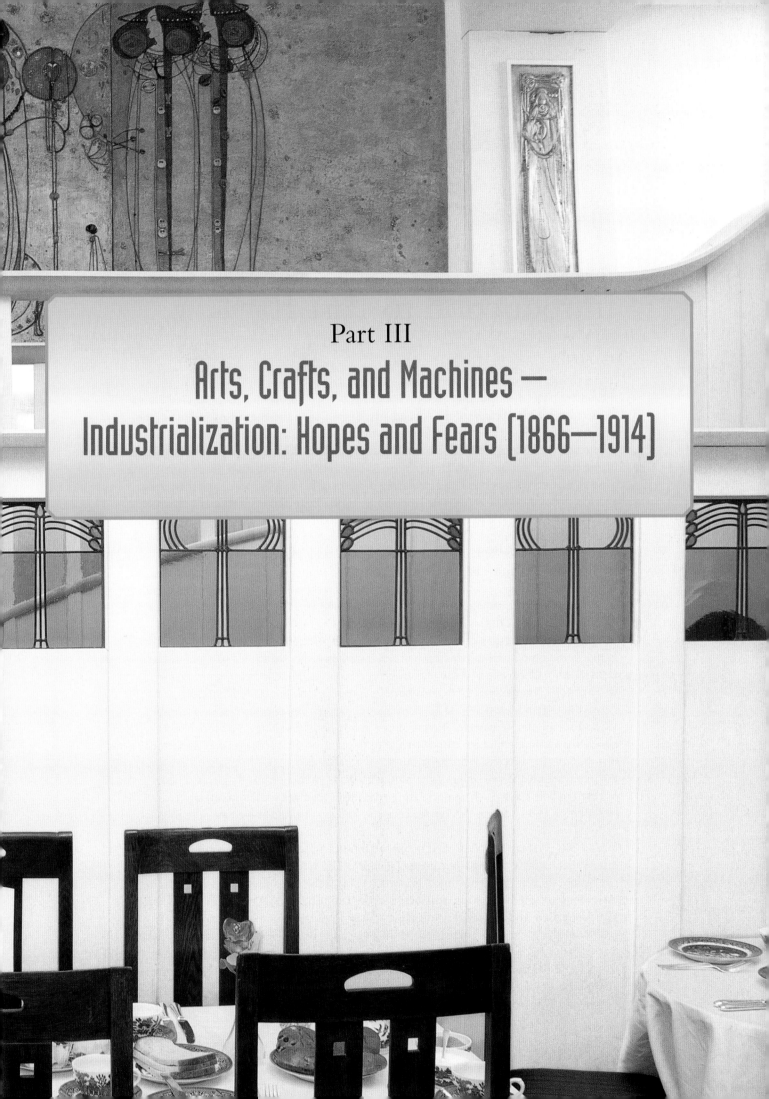

Part III
Arts, Crafts, and Machines —
Industrialization: Hopes and Fears (1866—1914)

Introduction to Part III

In the second half of the nineteenth century, the activities of the early design reform movement dovetailed with other reform initiatives both in Europe and in the United States in elevating the significance of the applied arts. Beginning in the later 1850s in Britain, the writings of John Ruskin and the activities of William Morris placed the issues of design and production within a new ethical framework based upon an almost religious attitude that united craft, art, social, and political reform. Ruskin and Morris criticized the dehumanizing aspects of mechanization and the increasing division of labor in factories, and their ideas provided inspiration and models for workshops, crafts organizations, and crafts communities on both sides of the Atlantic dedicated to the human and social benefits of handicraft as an antidote to the often alienating effects of the modern urban and industrialized world.

Only slightly later, both in the United States and throughout Europe, a number of architects and fine artists became increasingly involved in many aspects of interior design and decoration. Their activities called attention to the aesthetic and expressive character of the home and its furnishings as a total work of art, emphasizing originality and the unity and integration of all the visual arts. At the same time, a number of younger designers sought to consider issues of manufacturability and to form organizations and publish journals to promote improvement within the craft industries and the elevation of public taste. The broader scope of these initiatives found a place in the increasing number of well-attended international exhibitions both in Europe and in the United States.

In the United States, printed advertising and illustrated mail-order catalogues in the 1880s also spurred demand for manufactured goods and furnishings, accompanied by new initiatives in methods of rationalized and mechanized production as well as national distribution. The success of the department store beginning in the 1860s also stimulated the manufacture and marketing of the products of design to an expanding consumer-oriented middle class. Such democratizing tendencies involved a wide variety of historicizing styles such as the Renaissance and Rococo Revivals as well as more original or "modern" approaches to design recommended by tastemakers such as Charles Eastlake in his *Hints on Household Taste*, first published in 1868 and directed toward cultivating a discriminating taste among a female readership.

Finally, with Germany playing an important role, design organizations, schools, and exhibitions sought to reconcile what were seen as conflicting attitudes toward technology, standardization, and the scientific management of production on the one hand and individual identity and self-expression on the other, aimed at reforming the tastes of middle-class consumers by establishing and reinforcing more standardized and socially responsible forms for modern manufactured goods. Amid various debates and activities, the aesthetic, commercial, and social meanings of the applied arts enlarged the scope of the activity of design in the years leading up to World War I.

Chapter 5

The Joy of Work

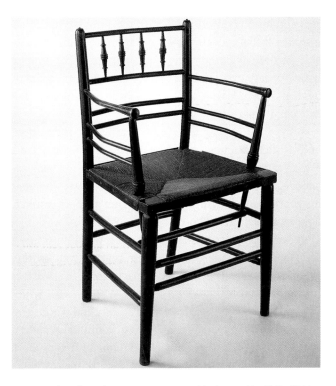

5.1 Armchair from the Sussex range, possibly designed by Philip Webb, ebonized beech with rush seat, 33 ¾ x 20 ½ x 17 in (86.6 x 52.4 x 43 cm), *c.* 1860, manufactured by Morris, Marshall, Faulkner & Co. Victoria and Albert Museum, London.

RUSKIN, MORRIS, AND THE ARTS AND CRAFTS MOVEMENT IN BRITAIN

The English writer and art critic John Ruskin (1819–1900) played an important role in shaping attitudes toward the decorative arts in the second half of the nineteenth century. Like A. W. N. Pugin, Ruskin admired the crafts of the Middle Ages and saw the decorative arts as a vehicle for enlightenment, both for the artisans who made goods and furnishings and the public who might purchase and appreciate them. The values he attached to the Gothic style, however, concerned the nature of work, an elevated view of labor, which he felt was fundamentally undermined by mechanization, the division of labor, and a capitalist system that increasingly alienated workers from the products of their efforts. For Ruskin, the specialization inherent in the division of labor, and a market that stimulated cheaper and faster production, deprived workers of

the satisfaction of making products from start to finish as he believed they were made in the guilds during the Middle Ages:

> We have much studied and much perfected, of late, the great civilized invention of the division of labour; only we give it a false name. It is not, truly speaking, the labour that is divided; but the men: divided into mere segments of men – broken into small fragments and crumbs of life; so that all the little piece of intelligence that is left in a man is not enough to make a pin, or a nail, but exhausts itself in making the point of a pin or the head of a nail.

Ruskin's views on art and design drew in part upon his own careful descriptions and drawings of architecture and decoration; the sensitivity he developed to working methods of craftsmen formed the basis for conclusions about the nature of craft and inspired sweeping solutions to the problems of an industrial society. In looking at carved architectural ornament from the Gothic period, Ruskin admired the dialogue between artisan and materials, the imperfections, the differences between one carved capital and another, the struggle to overcome the resistance of stone or wood with the tools at hand in the realization of an idea. The methods of the craftsman were, for Ruskin, the basis for joyful work and the equality among the arts in which craftsman and artist alike shared in the redeeming act of human labor. As a result Ruskin deplored the machine, because machines made work easy or just plain dull, and because they made things uniform and lacking in the individuality of their handmade counterparts:

> All the stamped metals, and artificial stones, and imitation woods and bronzes, over the invention of which we hear daily exultation – all the short, and cheap, and easy ways of doing that whose difficulty is its honour – are just so many new obstacles in our already encumbered road. They will not make one of us happier or wiser – they will extend neither the pride of judgement nor the privilege of enjoyment. They will only make us shallower in our understandings, colder in our hearts, and feebler in our wits.

It probably comes as no surprise that Ruskin was no admirer of Joseph Paxton's Crystal Palace, for no cast-iron structure, regardless of its grand proportions or economy of construction, could aspire to being "art" in the sense of having been the product of the direct manipulation of materials that Ruskin understood to be the essence of all artistic endeavor.

In addition to his analysis of art and architecture, Ruskin's views also stemmed from a renewed sense of urgency regarding social reform. The only child of a wealthy wine merchant and the beneficiary of a large inheritance, Ruskin was nevertheless sensitive to the levels of poverty, unemployment, and poor working conditions in Britain. He felt a sense of social conscience not uncommon among wealthy families of his day, which found outlets in political activism, philanthropy, and other private initiatives aimed at the well-being of the poor and working classes. Rather than applauding the economic expansion and material progress of his own time, he blamed industrialization and materialism for helping to create poverty, inequality, and misery, and saw the restoration of meaningful work as a means to alleviate them. Indeed, his exaltation of labor may be seen as a compensation for his own loss of faith, for if religion was of little comfort to humanity in the modern world, then it might perhaps be replaced by some substitute spirituality. For Ruskin, that substitute was the happiness provided by work, and thus the products of work acquired new levels of meaning. It follows, almost of necessity, that if labor was its own reward, then the technological and material progress of the nineteenth century represented for Ruskin only a kind of empty materialism that ignored the spiritual values that should inform an ideal society:

> the foundations of society were never yet shaken as they are at this day. It is not that men are ill-fed, but that they have no pleasure in the work by which they make their bread, and *therefore look to wealth as the only means of pleasure.* [Italics author's own]

Earlier in his career, Ruskin had championed the cause of the British landscape painter J. M. W. Turner (1775–1851) in his book *Modern Painters*, vol. 1, but Ruskin grew to question whether the uplifting qualities embodied in Turner's works would enrich the experience and add to the well-being of working people. Ruskin then focused his attention on architecture and the decorative arts because their cost as well as their utility might have a greater impact upon the workers who made and might enjoy them. Work was a common element in the lives of both the middle and working classes, a basis for social equality linked to mutual respect among people. Unlike Pugin or Owen Jones, it was joy rather than taste that governed Ruskin's attitudes:

> the right question to ask, respecting all ornament, is simply this: Was it done with enjoyment – was the carver happy while he was about it? It may be the hardest work possible, and the harder because so much pleasure was taken in it; but it must have been happy too, or it will not be living.

In other words, Ruskin advocated no particular style or set of rules for designers to follow other than that the work be a unique creation reflecting a craftsman's skill, pride, and effort. His views share an interest in individuality with designers of the Aesthetic Movement (see chapter 6), but Ruskin's overriding emphasis was upon the moral and spiritual benefits of handwork, that is, as much upon the "doing" as upon the designing.

While Ruskin remained primarily a writer and theorist commenting on issues concerning art and society, William Morris (1834–1896) was more interested in integrating theory with practice. Like Ruskin, Morris came from a wealthy middle-class background and benefited from an annual income from his family's investment in the lucrative copper-mining industry, yet he also possessed a strong sense of social responsibility characteristic of the

Victorian age. As a student at Oxford preparing for a career in the clergy, he was deeply moved by Ruskin's ideas concerning the relation between art and social reform, and also shared friendship and ideals with a group of young Romantic artists and poets who called themselves the Pre-Raphaelite Brotherhood (PRB). The group was critical of the materialism that accompanied modern industrialism and was committed to creating a closer relation between art and craft in reaction against the established policies of the Royal Academy in England and the elevated status it accorded the fine arts. It was his kinship with the PRB that led Morris to abandon his training for the ministry and pursue a career as an artist–craftsman. One can detect the echo of Ruskin in Morris's own writings, which have had a lasting effect upon designers in the later nineteenth and twentieth centuries:

> yet I cannot in my own mind quite sever them [the arts of architecture, painting, and sculpture] from those so-called Decorative Arts, which I have to speak about; it is only in latter times, and under the most intricate conditions of life, that they have fallen apart from one another; I hold that, when they are so parted, it is ill for the Arts altogether; the lesser ones become trivial, mechanical, unintelligent, incapable of resisting the changes pressed upon them by fashion or dishonesty; while the greater, however they may be practiced for a while by men of great minds and wonder-working hands, unhelped by the lesser, unhelped by each other, are sure to lose their dignity as popular arts, and become nothing but dull adjuncts to unmeaning pomp, or ingenious toys for a few rich and idle men...

In addition, Morris was a poet, novelist, publisher, socialist, translator, preservationist, and public speaker, whose myriad activities were influential both in Britain and in Germany, Belgium, France, and the United States (in fact, Morris's writings were influential even for those, such as Frank Lloyd Wright, who freely interpreted and "modernized" his views). The spiritualization of craft, its link to social reform, and skepticism toward the widely held view that industrialization and progress went hand in hand characterize Morris's attitudes and became the basis for a number of organizations and other initiatives that are known generally as the Arts and Crafts Movement.

Morris's interest in design emerged with the interior decoration of his home, Red House, in Kent, beginning in 1858, designed by his friend Philip Webb (1831–1915). The house eschewed the tendency toward superficial period styles as well as expensive (or expensive-looking) materials in favor of straightforward brick and wood, modest Gothic pointed arches, and a less formal, asymmetrical plan.

Rather than purchase furnishings from a showroom or manufacturer, Morris and his friends took on the task themselves. At the outset Morris's wife, Jane (1839–1914) took an interest in embroidery, while Webb, painter Edward Burne-Jones (1833–1898), and poet and artist Dante Gabriel Rossetti (1828–1882, a member of the PRB) designed furniture and stained-glass windows. The ideal of a more "natural" and self-sufficient lifestyle appealed to Morris, who later wrote, "If I were asked to say what is at once the most important production of Art and the thing most to be longed for I should answer, A beautiful House." In 1861 he formed Morris, Marshall, Faulkner & Co. with a showroom in London, for the design and manufacture of a wide variety of furnishings, including furniture, wall-papers, textiles, stained glass, tapestries, and ceramics. In 1875 Morris reorganized the venture as Morris & Co. The company, or "Firm," as it was called, put Morris's ideas into practice and might be seen as the beginning of the Arts and Crafts Movement. An example of the Firm's furniture is a type of chair with handwoven rush seats that used relatively simply tooled spindles for legs and backs. The chairs were based upon designs by Webb and Rossetti that derived from rustic country examples (fig. 5.1). Such furnishings established a link with pre-industrial craft traditions only minimally affected either by contemporary commercial considerations or by the use of more modern machine tools and techniques. Not all furniture manufactured by the firm was economical or even restrained in decoration – indeed individuality, the love of nature, and the joy of craft all found expression in design, especially in ornament. Where decoration appears, it provides an outlet for the skill and invention of the craftsman as well as the delight of the owner within the constraints of material and labor costs.

As a craftsman himself, Morris first relied upon his training as a painter in the design of windows and the painted decoration of wooden furniture; from the 1870s onward he primarily designed patterns that were used in the manufacture of ceramic tiles, embroideries, wall-papers, carpets, and printed fabrics. In many cases Morris relied upon craftsmen to execute his designs, but he also practiced techniques himself, installing equipment in his residence first in London then in the western suburb of Hammersmith after 1878. He also leased facilities for weaving at Merton Abbey, Surrey, where he experimented in the development of vegetable dyes for fabrics rather than commercially available aniline dyes, patented in 1856 and produced using coal tar. For ceramics he seems to have entrusted production to artist–craftsman William de Morgan (1839–1917), an independent potter who had worked previously for the Firm, and who also produced his own designs, including tiles for the home of Lord

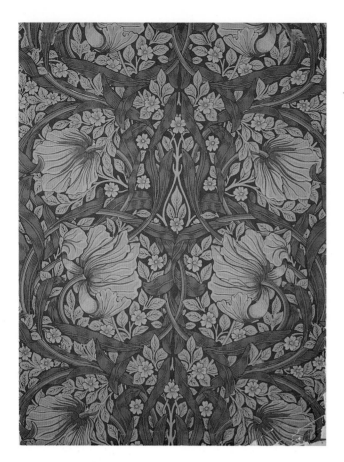

5.2 William Morris, *Pimpernel* design for wallpaper, block-printed, 26 ¾ x 20 ¾ in (68 x 52.5 cm), manufactured by Jeffrey & Co. for Morris & Co., 1876. Victoria and Albert Museum, London.

Frederic Leighton (see page 109 and fig. 6.8). Whether directly or indirectly involved in actual production, Morris advocated close collaboration between designer and craftsman and refused to use machines even for the manufacture of blocked wallpapers or printed fabrics: "it is not desirable to divide the labour between the artist and what is technically called the designer, and I think it desirable on the whole that the artist and designer should practically be one."

Morris's own pattern designs seem to follow the general tendency of earlier design reform to view decoration in the context of architecture, that is, as an embellishment to construction; it was the unity and implied collaboration in his understanding of architecture that guided his approach. He also believed in the importance of individual expression, and advocated original designs in addition to those inspired by the decorative patterns in medieval illuminated manuscripts.

Morris's patterns may be described as a dialogue, often tense, between a love of the beauty and richness of nature found in plants and flowers and the discipline needed to transform that appreciation into patterns

suitable for the embellishment of flat surfaces. An example is found in his *Pimpernel* wallpaper of 1876 (fig. 5.2). Against a dark green background, lighter green flowers are symmetrically arranged and repeated, but varied in their positions; each is framed by interlocking spiral vine tendrils in brown loosely entwined by thin green leaves. A secondary motif is defined by smaller and flatter green leaves with round blue morning glories placed at intervals on the stems. The naturalism is at its height with the windswept flowers and their undulating contours, slightly reduced for the thin leaf forms and becoming more regularized and schematic for the blue flowers, tendrils, and smaller oval leaves. The sense both of nature's luxuriant variety and life, and the care with which the designer preserves this freshness within the constraints of pattern for a two-dimensional surface is remarkable in much of Morris's best work, and prevents his designs from becoming stale or dry.

The firm of Morris & Co. was reasonably successful during the 1860s and 1870s, profiting from orders to design and execute stained-glass windows and other furnishings for churches, as well as commissions from wealthy clients for comprehensive furnishings for domestic interiors. These patrons could afford the labor costs of Morris's production methods and shared his vision for a society based upon meaningful and satisfying work. An 1866 example of a Morris & Co. interior is the Green Dining Room at the South Kensington (now Victoria and Albert) Museum in London, commissioned as a lunchroom for visitors and still in operation today (fig. 5.3). The interior is coordinated through a wall-treatment of painted vine-scroll patterns in molded and painted stucco relief, rug, stained glass, lighting, ceramic panels, painted panels with repeated figural and plant motifs, and painted furniture all provided by the firm, and all intended to convey the love of nature transformed through the artist's imagination and the appreciation of materials and labor. The Green Room, which opened to the working classes on Sundays when they were admitted free of charge to the South Kensington Museum, enabled Morris to unite his ideal of art as "man's pleasure in labor" with his hope of integrating art into life.

In addition to maintaining facilities at his residence and leasing separate facilities for production, a Morris & Co. storefront showroom was maintained on Oxford Street, London, where other fashionable retail establishments were located, and the Firm exhibited work at international exhibitions, for instance in London in 1862 and at the Philadelphia Centennial Exhibition in 1876. As a businessman, Morris had in some sense to compromise his earlier ideal of the self-sufficient community of craftspeople sharing in both the creation and appreciation of

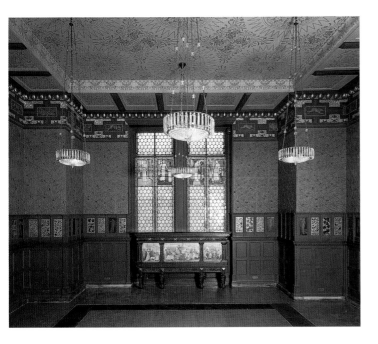

5.3 Morris & Co., the Green Dining Room, Victoria and Albert Museum, London, 1866.

handmade objects in the context of the domestic interior – instead his success depended upon his belief in the connection between manufactured objects and the values of honest labor that their forms communicated through the visible signs of process that were shared by mostly wealthy customers.

MORRIS AND SOCIALISM

Despite the success of the Firm, the founder became increasingly disillusioned by the inability of his efforts to effect broad social change and to reach his intended working-class audience. In the 1870s he was an outspoken critic of the British government's foreign policy in the Balkans (which he believed was motivated by economic rather than humanitarian interests), and in the 1880s he became actively involved with the Socialist movement in Britain in the hope of creating social equality and reducing the pressures for production and consumption that fueled the capitalist system:

> what I mean by Socialism is a condition of society in which there should be neither rich nor poor, neither master nor master's man, neither idle nor overworked, neither brain-sick brain workers nor heart-sick hand workers ... in which all men would be living in equality of condition, and would manage their affairs unwastefully and with the full consciousness that harm to one would mean harm to all – the realization at last of the meaning of the word COMMONWEALTH.

Another recurrent theme in his writings, echoing Ruskin, is the excessive self-interest that was created by competition:

> Manufacturers are so set on carrying out competition to its utmost, competition of cheapness, not of excellence, that they meet the bargain-hunters half way, and cheerfully furnish them with many wares at the cheap rate...

Morris was active in organized socialist activities in London, and his views, expressed in public speeches and in the journal he founded entitled *The Commonweal*, echo the themes of alienated labor, the concentration of wealth and growth of capital in partnership with industry, and the "fetishism" of commodities found in the writings of Karl Marx (1818–1883) and Friedrich Engels (1820–1895). Morris's political views were radical; he sensed that it was not enough merely to make and enjoy handmade objects as a craftsman and responsible businessman, and that real change could only come with working-class revolution. But while Morris's ideology was opposed to industrial capitalism in terms of the economic inequality it brought, he could not account for or effectively fight the increasing attraction of consumption (and shopping) across all classes of modern society. Ironically, the success of Morris & Co. depended almost entirely upon an exclusive market, thus in a sense supporting the same capitalist system he hoped to eliminate.

Morris did eventually acknowledge a role for mechanization in the production of goods and furnishings, particularly if it reduced drudgery. But his view of the role of the machine was narrowly circumscribed and he felt its products should never deprive a craftsman of the opportunity to find pleasure and satisfaction in work. Nevertheless his views appear to be, not without some irony, the basis for the later equation of machine-made goods with simple designs and smooth surfaces: "The more mechanical the process, the less direct should be the imitation of natural forms." Such an approach was espoused by American architect Frank Lloyd Wright (1869–1959), whose own attitudes toward the machine are considered below (see pages 99–101; 147–148).

MORRIS AS PUBLISHER

William Morris's last design venture was the founding of Kelmscott Press in 1890, which brought together his attitudes to art and design with his activities as poet and author. Morris produced an illustrated edition of his own poem "Story of the Glittering Plain" as well as a short volume containing Ruskin's "Nature of Gothic" chapter from *The Stones of Venice*, which eloquently stated his beliefs about the dignity of work. In Morris's introduction to the "Nature of Gothic," he wrote:

> For the lesson which Ruskin here teaches us is that art is the expression of man's pleasure in labour; that it is possible for man to rejoice in his work, for, strange as it may seem to us to-day, there have been times when he did rejoice in it; and lastly, that unless man's work once again becomes a pleasure to him, the token of which change will be that beauty is once again a natural and necessary accompaniment of productive labour, all but the worthless must toil in pain, and therefore live in pain. So that the result of the thousands of years of man's effort on the earth must be general unhappiness and universal degradation; unhappiness and degradation, the conscious burden of which will grow in proportion to the growth of man's intelligence, knowledge, and power over material nature.

Morris's close friend Edward Burne-Jones designed woodcut illustrations for *The Kelmscott Chaucer* (fig. 5.4), while Morris himself designed a series of border patterns used on pages with illustrations, as well as the typeface and block initials of various sizes. *The Kelmscott Chaucer* used a calligraphic type with characteristics of Gothic (Blackletter) letter forms that Morris designed and drew, and which he called "Troy," one of three faces used at the press. His Roman font, known as "Golden," was influenced by fifteenth-century printers working in Venice

such as Jacobus Rubeus and Nicholas Jenson, who were responsible for some of the very first Roman (as opposed to Blackletter) types beginning around 1470. Morris's Golden eschewed the mechanical precision of modern fonts (see figs. 1.14 and 1.15) for heavier forms with modulated transition from thick to thin strokes and the low x-height characteristic of fifteenth-century Venetian models. Morris's interest in these Venetian types, sometimes known as "humanistic," in turn stimulated a revival of letterpress printing sometimes known as the Private Press Movement. The richly decorated pages of *The Kelmscott Chaucer* fulfill Morris's objective to make the book itself an object of beauty, even if some historians find many of its more elaborate pages less well suited to reading, perhaps a result of the distraction of elements other than type. The Kelmscott Press was located at the artist's home in Hammersmith on the bank of the Thames river. The venture emerged at a time when photomechanical reproduction was transforming the character of illustration, and when steam presses were finally being introduced into the book-publishing industry. Inspired by the example of the nearby Chiswick Press (see page 71) and the independent efforts of printers and other craftsmen to maintain the quality and craft traditions of the printed book, Morris succeeded in revitalizing fine printing, even if the cost of such efforts limited their audience, generally attracting only a well-to-do clientele.

Morris's Kelmscott Press was one among several private publishing ventures that emerged during the last quarter of the nineteenth century. Illustrated books, art journals, and a burgeoning illustrated literature for children constituted the means by which the Arts and Crafts Movement communicated its ideas to different audiences.

Publishing is a collaborative enterprise, and a number of printers, founders, binders, and illustrators were involved in Morris's Kelmscott Press venture. Emery Walker (1851–1933), for instance, worked as a printer at the Chiswick Press not far from Hammersmith where Morris lived and began his own press. Prior to the initiation of the Kelmscott Press, Walker had contributed to the Century Guild's *The Hobby Horse* journal, whose quality and character had stimulated Morris's own interests in printing (see page 88). After Morris's death in 1896, Walker and the lawyer-turned-bookbinder T. J. Cobden-Sanderson (1840–1922) began their own publishing company known as the Doves Press also in Hammersmith (in fact, directly across the alley from Kelmscott on the Thames riverside). These efforts combined interrelated concerns for the quality of paper and ink, the aesthetics of calligraphy, as well as legibility in type, ample white space, harmonious relationships among borders, initials, and illustration, and the overall unity of the page or open double-page. Walker

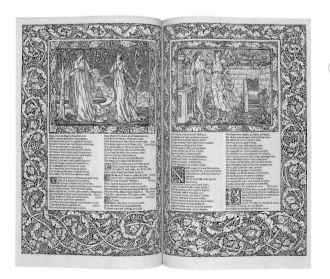

5.4 William Morris (wood-engraved illustrations after designs by Edward Burne-Jones), folio from *The Works of Geoffrey Chaucer*, 16 ¾ x 11 ½ in (42.5 x 29.2 cm), printed at the Kelmscott Press, London, 1896. Cheltenham Art Gallery and Museums.

designed a Roman font for the press (called Doves), while the calligrapher Edward Johnston (1872–1944) contributed initial designs, often printed in red, to enliven the page layouts. The results can be seen in a page of the *Doves Bible*, printed between 1903 and 1905 (fig. 5.5). The Doves Press embodies the idea of the book as a work of craft and beauty that is the result of the unity and interrelationship of its parts. Its margins are ample, the initials and title lettering fluid and elegant, and the typeface equally refined. It has a larger x-height to the lower-case letters and an ample use of white space not found in the darker and shorter forms of Morris's Golden font, but rather suggesting a purity and restraint that appears more "modern" in the practical or functional sense that begins to emerge at this time. A rift between the two partners resulted in the closing of the press in 1916. It must have been quite a disagreement; one day Cobden-Sanderson threw the Doves types (and matrices, presumably) off Hammersmith Bridge into the Thames so that Walker would never have them.

Toward the end of his career, Morris's vision for a better society took the form of utopian writings, often published first in serial form in the Socialist journal *Commonweal*. The romance *News from Nowhere* (1890) takes place in England in the twenty-second century, but

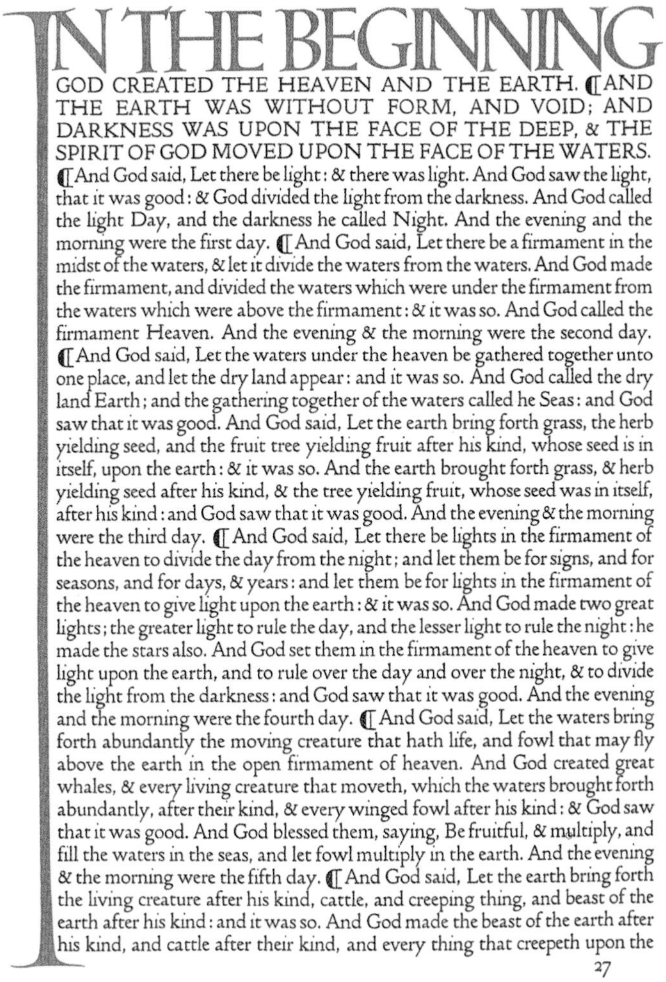

5.5 First page of the *Doves Bible*, 13 5/16 x 9 1/4 in (33.8 x 23.5 cm), Doves Press, Hammersmith, London, 1903–1905. Library of Congress.

its setting is reminiscent of the riverside village community of Hammersmith where Morris lived after 1878. The book's frontispiece illustrated the pathway leading to the country farmhouse known as Kelmscott Manor that Morris kept in the countryside of West Oxfordshire, near to where he is buried:

> ...*all* work is now pleasurable; either because of the hope of gain in honour and wealth with which the work is done, which causes pleasurable excitement, even when the actual work is not pleasant; or because it has grown into a pleasurable *habit*, as in the case with what you may call mechanical work; and lastly (and most of our work is of this kind) because there is conscious sensuous pleasure in the work itself; it is done, that is, by artists...

In the aftermath of World War I, Morris's equation of simple forms with machine production would yield views that linked the machine to the working class and newer, twentieth-century utopian dreams for social equality based upon defining human needs along more utilitarian and collective lines. But for Morris the joy and dignity of craft remained paramount in the attainment of human happiness; it was difficult to reconcile this attitude with mechanization and serial production except in a limited way, either from a social or an aesthetic standpoint. The inexpensive items of machine production also had costs of their own.

THE INFLUENCE OF WILLIAM MORRIS IN BRITAIN

William Morris's ideas and example found fertile ground for development in Britain, continental Europe, and in the United States, but his views at times underwent considerable transformation and interpretation. Arthur Heygate Mackmurdo (1851–1942) was born in Britain in the year of the Crystal Palace Exhibition. He was a friend of both Morris and Ruskin, and traveled with the latter to Italy in 1874. Like Morris, Mackmurdo was concerned with the preservation of historic buildings; he is perhaps best recognized for the woodcut title page of a book that he published privately in 1883 entitled *Wren's City Churches* (fig. 5.6), containing illustrations of churches designed by the English architect Sir Christopher Wren (1632–1723). An architect by training, Mackmurdo advocated an elevated status for craft and the abolition of the distinction between fine and applied art. He was a founding member of a group of artists known as the Century Guild, dedicated to the following goals:

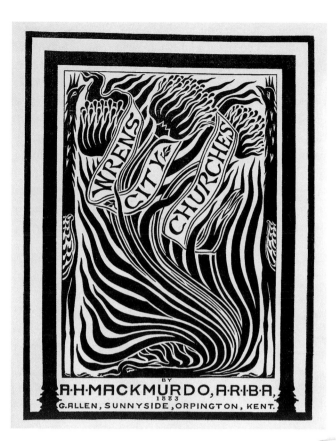

5.6 Arthur Heygate Mackmurdo, title page of his *Wren's City Churches*, woodcut on paper, 11 $^7/_{17}$ x 8 $^3/_4$ in (29.2 x 22.25 cm), printed by G. Allen, Orpington, Kent, 1883. Victoria and Albert Museum, London.

to render all branches of art the sphere no longer of the tradesman but of the artist, to restore building, decoration, glass painting, potter, wood-carving and metal to their rightful place beside painting and sculpture.

The flamelike shapes for the title page from *Wren's City Churches*, framed by two tall birds, are based upon a floral form but clearly are exaggerated and abstracted to suggest a heightened sense of movement and growth, enlivened by the strong contrast between figure and ground. Banners displaying the title (as well as the lettering of the words themselves) have the same sense of elasticity as the floral motif, and stand out only by being placed against a larger expanse of white ground. Mackmurdo used the same design for the back of a chair manufactured by the Century Guild in the same year (fig. 5.7). The abstract, subjective treatment of naturalistic forms seen in these examples by Mackmurdo may be compared to contemporary Post-Impressionist art in France, seen for instance in the more subjective approach to still life of Vincent van Gogh's *Irises* from 1890 (fig. 5.8), with their sinuous contours and emphasis upon the flatness of the picture plane. In this

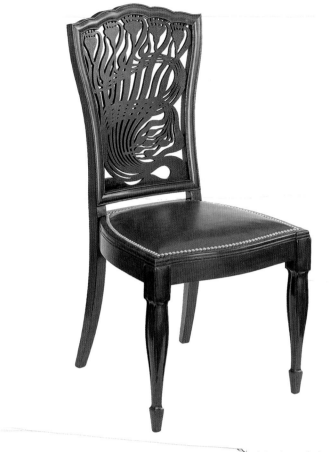

5.7 Arthur Heygate Mackmurdo, chair, mahogany with leather upholstery, 38 ¼ x 19 ½ x 18 ¹¹/₁₆ in (97.2 x 49.5 x 47.6 cm), manufactured by the Century Guild, 1883. Victoria and Albert Museum, London.

made book... Most simply and generally art may be thought of as the "well-doing of what needs doing;" every work of art shows that it was made by a human being for a human being.

Charles Ashbee (1863–1942) was another versatile designer and educator who shared Morris's desire to integrate art and life through the decorative arts and hand craftsmanship by establishing a community of workers living and working together in utopian harmony. After graduating from Cambridge University in 1886 Ashbee moved to Toynbee Hall, a residence for university graduates in a working-class section of London established to rebuild relationships between social classes and improve the lives of the working class. In 1888 Ashbee helped to found the Guild and School of Handicraft, based in London's East End (this section of the city was associated with high-volume piecework that supplied the furniture industry and that was condemned by social reformers and proponents of the Arts and Crafts Movement), employing as many as 50 workers. Ashbee's interest in the preservation of craft traditions stemmed from his own experience with materials and process as an artist and a belief that the applied arts provided the means for original work: "the education of the hand and eye are only fully achieved in the education of the individuality of the workman."

Ashbee's designs respect and explore the nature of handcrafted materials; his work possesses a striking originality in both decorative forms and a respect for the

case, the formal characteristics of Mackmurdo's approach to decoration approximate those of avant-garde painting in that the artist subjectively transforms a more naturalistic manner of working, suppressing illusionism in favor of expressive surface pattern. It seems as if Mackmurdo was intent upon demonstrating the transformative value of art, as well as defining a highly individual approach to ornament in the applied arts.

Other craft associations, both in Britain and in the United States (see page 91), followed Morris's efforts to link art and life by focusing upon craft. For instance, an Arts and Crafts Exhibition Society (the origin of the actual name of the movement) was founded in 1887 to organize annual shows of craft objects. The versatile designer William Lethaby (1857–1931) established a school in London based upon a close relationship between designer and maker and the practical value underlying and uniting all art:

...a work of art is first of all a well-made thing. It may be a well-made statue or a well-made chair, or a well-

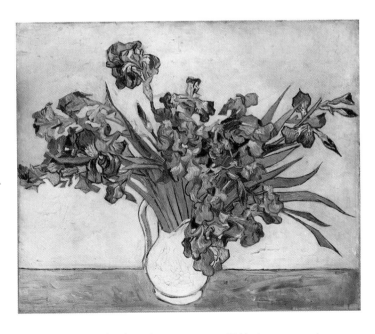

5.8 Vincent van Gogh, *Irises*, oil on canvas, 29 x 36 ¼ in (73.7 x 92.1 cm), 1890. Metropolitan Museum of Art, New York.

integration of ornament and function as seen in a silver bowl (fig. 5.9) of 1904. In this work the surface has been patiently worked by hand, and the symmetrical handles extend outward with a flowing, somewhat exaggerated curve, whose organic effect is enhanced by contrast with the simple and regular form of the bowl and its plain surface (Ashbee's inspiration may have been examples or representations of the ancient Greek drinking cup known as a kantharos). As early as 1902, Ashbee relocated his guild to a community in the Cotswolds in rural Gloucestershire (in the same general area as Morris's Kelmscott manor), a move suggesting that the ideals of the Arts and Crafts Movement were more compatible amid village rather than urban conditions; instead of posing a threat to the combined forces of capitalism, competition, and industrialization, the ideal of the craft guild became a retreat from or antidote for the ills of the modern world, directly for its practitioners and vicariously through those who shared their beliefs as consumers.

After meeting architect Frank Lloyd Wright on a visit to the United States in 1901 and following the economic failure of the Guild and School of Handicraft in 1908, Ashbee came to acknowledge and accept the role of machinery and the separation of design from production in the decorative arts, and to admire Wright's efforts to reconcile design, machine production, and social responsibility (see pages 99–101).

Parallel to the ideal of the Arts and Crafts community in the history of design was the Garden City Movement, initiated in England by the American-born reformer Ebenezer Howard (1850–1928). Like many of those individuals affiliated with the Arts and Crafts Movement, Howard sought to remedy the alienation and poor working-class living conditions that accompanied industrial development throughout the nineteenth century. His solution lay in the design of communities of single-family dwellings connected by rail to larger industrial cities. Here residents could cultivate gardens and thus preserve elements of self-sufficiency, independence, and the joy of work that characterized pre-industrial societies. The Garden City model provided for trees and central parks, and residential zoning that separated the office, retail shop, or factory from domestic life. In separating work from family, however, Howard's model also confined women to the private sphere, where their role was to create a comforting home environment. The first garden city, begun in 1903, was Letchworth in Hertfordshire north of London; its designers were the architects Barry Parker (1867–1947) and Raymond Unwin (1853–1941). Parker and Unwin were sympathetic to Arts and Crafts ideals, and an illustration from Parker's 1901 book *The Art of Building* shows a living room interior with its focus upon the hearth, exposed roof beams, natural materials such as brick, hammered copper and tile, and simply constructed as well as built-in (fitted) wooden furniture (fig. 5.10). Such interiors also imply a focus upon family life, wholesome and removed from the pace, distractions, and pretensions of urban life. Not all women found such a role satisfying, however, and other housing experiments emerged, especially in the United States, based upon a shared model of household work (see page 118).

Ambrose Heal (1872–1959) was a London-based furniture-maker whose use of oak and solid, simple designs shared the honest and natural appeal of the Arts and Crafts Movement and was sympathetic to the vision of the Garden City planners and architects. Heal's furniture was constructed using basic joinery (carpentry) techniques. He shared the vision of modest domestic comfort with the ideals of the Garden City Movement and its relationship to Arts and Crafts values of honesty and authenticity rather than luxury and implications of "conspicuous" consumption, but his attitude toward industry and the use of machines was more accepting than antagonistic. He advocated an accommodation to factory (rather than workshop) production, with "product" rather than "process" as paramount; the result was that the manufacturer remained responsible for improving the lives of workers *not* by maintaining craft skills and a closer relationship between designing and making, but by providing goods that defined and contributed to a modest but comfortable lifestyle. Heal's approach to furniture in England has parallels in the United States (see page 92). It also may be related to new models for design education known generally as

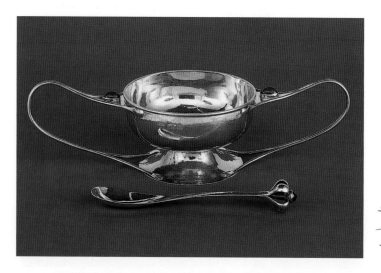

5.9 Charles Robert Ashbee, bowl and spoon, silver and chrysoprase, bowl: 3 x 10 ⅝ x 4 ¼ in (7.6 x 27.3 x 10.8 cm), 1904. Metropolitan Museum of Art, New York.

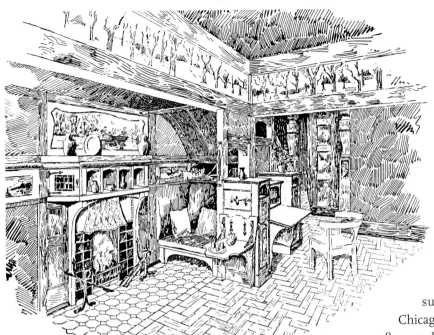

5.10 Barry Parker and Raymond Unwin, view of an interior from *The Art of Building*, London, 1901.

THE ARTS AND CRAFTS MOVEMENT IN THE UNITED STATES

A number of social critics, writers, and artists were sympathetic to John Ruskin's critique of industrialization and its negative effect upon the arts in the United States during the second half of the nineteenth century. In addition, examples of the decorative arts from Morris & Co. were on display at the Centennial Exposition of 1876 in Philadelphia, Pennsylvania. The influence of the Arts and Crafts Movement may be seen in the promotion and revival of craft societies and the initiation of craft education in cities such as Boston, Syracuse, Cincinnati, and Chicago. Reaching a peak in the decades between 1890 and 1910, Arts and Crafts initiatives stimulated considerable interest in the relation between design and social reform, and craft workshops, artisan communities, and journals addressed the challenges posed by mass production, mechanization, and advertising.

Gustav Stickley (1858–1942) is perhaps the best known of many American Arts and Crafts furniture manufacturers in the early twentieth century, in part because furniture bearing the Stickley name continues to be manufactured, and also because it has been featured in popular films such as *A River Runs Through It* (1992, directed by Robert Redford). Stickley learned furniture-making while serving as an apprentice at his uncle's chair factory in Massachusetts. He became familiar with Arts and Crafts ideology and practice through the writings of William Morris and the published designs of British architect M. H. Baillie Scott (1865–1945), which appeared in journals on the decorative arts on both sides of the Atlantic. In 1898 Stickley visited Britain and in 1900 he founded the Craftsman Workshops near Syracuse, New York, with himself as master craftsman. He published a journal called *The Craftsman* beginning in 1901 to promote his furniture along with the values of honesty, the personal satisfaction of handicraft, and reassuring ideas of comfort and simplicity connected with home and family. Stickley hoped his designs would appeal "strongly to the directness and common sense of the American people" with furniture that was solid, used simple materials such as oak and basic woodworking (joinery) techniques for construction, and avoided carved decoration and time-consuming marquetry as unnecessary and impractical for modern living. *The Craftsman* included plans for building your own house, essays on reformers such as Ruskin and Morris, and designs for furniture, textiles, and other crafts to encourage

"Industrial Art." The industrial art model acknowledged a balance between the skills and knowledge of the individual craftsman in an age when the craftsman and crafts workshop could not compete with the factory in terms of achieving the goal of a democratic art. Industrial arts education was a compromise, an effort to preserve elements of the doctrine of meaningful and satisfying work while acknowledging the advantages and inevitability of machines, rationalized production, and the promise they might hold for standards of living and the quality of life for middle- and working-class families. Yet while manufacturers and designers might control production, they could not always control reception and meaning for consumers. As noted by design historian Adrian Forty, simple undecorated furniture was often advertised and purchased by wealthy and middle-class families for servants' quarters, reinforcing class distinctions and the associations between decoration and more sophisticated tastes. Indeed, the afterlife of the Arts and Crafts Movement, especially in the early twentieth century, was full of contradictions as proponents sought to reconcile the cost and spiritual benefits of craftsmanship with the desire to bring "design" to the masses, whose own aspirations and desires often found an outlet in a wide range of associations between decoration and individual identity.

readers to engage directly in handicraft, hoping to "extend the principles established by Morris, in both the artistic and the socialistic sense," equating beauty with "simplicity, individuality, and dignity of effect." Other journals, such as the California-based *The Bungalow* illustrated interiors that embody the Arts and Crafts ideology. In the cover illustrated in figure 5.11, a family sits on matching built-in oak settees flanking a tiled floor and fireplace decorated with a mosaic landscape set into the wooden frame above on the wall. The woman occupies herself with embroidery, while the man, in business attire, relaxes with an issue of the journal; the home has become a place of rest for the family, restoring privacy, autonomy, and self-sufficiency in an increasingly interdependent and fragmented modern world – in short, as noted by historian Jackson Lears, the Arts and Crafts Movement in the United States was "therapeutic," a refuge that protected men and women against the often alienating experience of modernity and compensated for its anxieties and uncertainties.

Although he admired and promoted the virtues of hand craftsmanship, Stickley, like Ambrose Heal in

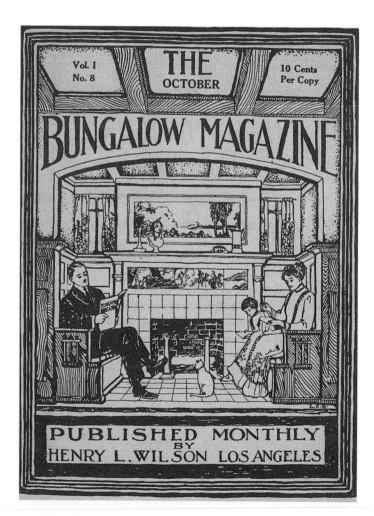

5.11 Cover illustration, *The Bungalow*, Los Angeles, California, October 1909. Library of Congress.

England (see page 90), acknowledged the reality of the market. In the Craftsman Workshops, machine tools were used to save production time in a competitive mid- and high-end market. Sometimes referred to as a "new" industrialist, Stickley accommodated his production methods to efficiency and machines, but also included vocational education for workers, maintaining at least some affiliation with the social reform ideology of the Arts and Crafts Movement. His small work cabinet from 1901 (fig. 5.12) is devoid of carved ornament: the plain surfaces and rectilinear shapes of the joinery, exposed mortise-and-tenon joints, and small pyramidal door handles exemplify the virtues of simple, honest craftsmanship, while the severity of the form is relieved by hammered copper hinges and irregularities of the sanded edges and surfaces. Stickley furniture shows great respect for the skill and intelligence of the craftsman in the selection and treatment of natural materials, and reveals care in the preparation of surfaces, as well as in the construction of joints and other fittings. The slats that appear in many examples of Craftsman furniture reduce the blocklike heaviness of the design and serve as a modest decorative feature integrated with function and construction techniques. Other furniture designed for Gustav Stickley has been attributed to the Rochester-born architect Harvey Ellis (1852–1904) and features taller proportions, thinner forms, and delicate inlay decoration reminiscent of Mackintosh and the Wiener Werkstätte (see page 131 and figs. 6.45 and 6.47). While some of Stickley's production methods deviated from the ideals of Ruskin and Morris, the style of his furniture embodied the virtues of clean, comfortable, natural, and modest living and gave expression to the longing for independence, honesty, and the dignity of labor in a world increasingly dominated by large, impersonal companies, nationally advertised brands rather than local products, and the interdependence of modern industrialized society.

The success of Stickley's enterprise encouraged him to move into new and larger headquarters in New York City in 1913. By that time he had numerous showrooms and distributors throughout the country, and participated in furniture exhibitions as a means of marketing his name and products. Despite expanding into the production of leathercraft and textiles, however, less expensive imitations and the waning of taste for the particular "Craftsman" style (his only product line) led Stickley to declare bankruptcy in 1915, and *The Craftsman* ceased publication the following year.

Self-contained craft communities were another expression of Arts and Crafts ideology in the United States. Among the most successful was the Roycrofters, founded by Elbert Hubbard (1856–1915) in 1893 and based in a suburb of Buffalo, New York. The Roycroft workshops

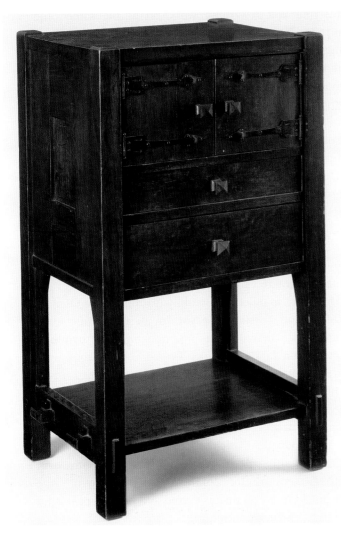

5.12 Gustav Stickley, work cabinet, oak and copper, 36 ⅛ x 21 x 15 in (91.9 x 53.3 x 38.1 cm), 1901. © American Decorative Art 1900 Foundation.

(the first volume was a biography of William Morris) in a small format. Hubbard used a heavy serifed typeface named Bookman, though with a taller x-height and shorter ascenders and descenders than Morris's Venetian-inspired Golden type (see page 86), and he included decorated title pages as well as hand-coloring for wood-engraved decorated borders and illustrations (fig. 5.13). The *Little Journeys* and other publications of the Roycroft Press attempted to reconcile the individuality and craftsmanship of the private press movement initiated by Morris with the effort to create a democratic design, if not for the masses, at least for a broader middle class. As a commercial endeavor, Hubbard built a hotel on the premises of the Roycroft village as a retreat for businessmen seeking the therapeutic benefits of the rustic and simple life as exemplified in Roycroft furnishings. Hubbard, formerly a successful salesman for the Larkin Soap Company in Buffalo, was a zealous and tenacious reformer. He was able to lower costs by printing books in a small format, but his success also depended upon a tight control of wages and autocratic authority to dictate the terms under which welfare was to be defined on behalf of his worker

concentrated primarily upon the printing press, publishing editions of the founder's periodical *The Philistine* and a series of small paperbound books entitled *Little Journeys*, as well as metalcraft, leather-making, and furniture resembling the Craftsman style. Some of the designers employed by Hubbard also worked independently as well as for other manufacturers, but the Roycroft community was based upon Hubbard's somewhat paternalistic concern with the physical, intellectual, and spiritual wellbeing of the workers. Like Stickley, he had visited Britain and became acquainted with the writings of Ruskin and Morris as well as the publications of Morris's Kelmscott Press. Early books of the Roycroft community were written by Hubbard but also contained verse by American poets such as Ralph Waldo Emerson (1803–1882) and Edgar Allan Poe (1809–1849). Among the most popular series of the Roycroft press were the *Little Journeys*, a series of short biographies of famous writers, teachers, and businessmen

The Roycroft Shop
G R E E T I N G

THE ROYCROFTERS are a community of workers who make beautiful Books and Things—making them as good as they can. The paper on which Roycroft books are printed is the best procurable, and some of the initials are illumined.
As a gift you probably cannot present anything at equal cost that would be more acceptable than a hand-illumined Roycroft book. Our work is the product of Hand & Brain in partnership. In things made by hand there are no duplicates; and further, there is a quality of sentiment attached to articles thus produced that never clings to fabrics made in vast quantities by steam. If you desire we will gladly send you " on suspicion " several volumes to choose from—a postal card from you will do it. We pay express both ways.

THE ROYCROFTERS
East Aurora
N. Y.

5.13 Elbert Hubbard, *The Roycroft Books. A Catalog and Some Comment Concerning the Shop at East Aurora, New York, and Its Workers, The Roycrofters*, 7 ½ x 5 ¹¹⁄₁₆ in (19 x 14.6 cm), 1902. Hagarty Library Archive, Drexel University, Philadelphia.

community. Not all of his workers reacted well to the nature of the communal enterprise as defined exclusively by Hubbard: some of his most original and gifted designers, including Karl Kipp (1882–1954) in the metal shop and the printer Dard Hunter (1883–1966), left the community intermittently to work independently.

The motto for the Roycrofters was "head, heart, and hand," and in addition to the practice of design and craftmanship in the workshops, the community lived together, participating in a Roycroft band and baseball team. Many products of the Roycroft copper workshop were designed by Karl Kipp, a former banker who worked at the community from 1908 to 1911 and again beginning in 1915 following Hubbard's death in the sinking of the *Lusitania*. The hammered copper surfaces and modest geometric decoration of a small tabletop jardinière dating to c. 1912–1915 by Kipp (fig. 5.14) demonstrate the simple and human quality of handcrafted goods produced at Roycroft. It is somewhat curious that Hubbard, and to a lesser extent Stickley, promoted the Arts and Crafts ideal of

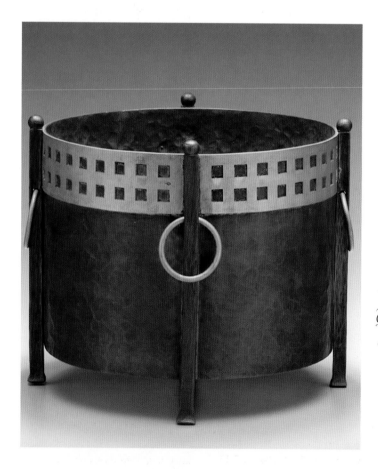

5.14 Karl Kipp, jardinière, copper and German silver, 5 ⅞ x 6 ⅞ in (15 x 17.5 cm), Roycrofters, East Aurora, New York, *c.* 1912–1915. © American Decorative Art 1900 Foundation.

satisfying and rewarding work yet at the same time borrowed from the practices of rationalized and specialized labor, industrialization, and benefited from advertising and branding in a rapidly expanding consumer culture, for whom "product" was more important than "process." Other craft communities, such as Rose Valley near Philadelphia, founded by architect Will Price (1861–1916), maintained the Ruskinian ideal in a purer form. Price coined the phrase "the art that is life" to characterize his experiment, hoping to unite artist and artisan in utopian harmony. But few could afford the cost of Rose Valley products, and the community ceased craft production in 1906, only five years after it began.

Artist colonies, such as Byrdcliffe near Woodstock in New York's Catskill Mountains, were also a product of emerging interest in both art and a return to nature, and were often founded by wealthy patrons committed to encouraging artistic endeavor in all media including metalwork, furniture-making, bookbinding, painting, pottery, and fabric printing. Byrdcliffe's founders were Ralph Whitehead (d. 1929) and his wife Jane (1861–1955). Whitehead was educated at Oxford and was familiar with the English Arts and Crafts Movement. Although never achieving its aim of being self-supporting through the sale of its products, Byrdcliffe sustained the efforts of a number of original artists working in the decorative arts, among them painter Zulma Steele (1881–1979), who designed pottery as well as carved and painted panels for simply constructed furniture.

More eccentric but indicative of a degree of creativity and inventiveness directed toward the decorative arts during this period is the work of Charles Rohlfs, who established a furniture workshop in Buffalo, New York, that was most active between 1898 and 1906. Rohlfs was trained as a designer of patterns for the decoration of cast-iron stoves, but was inspired to pursue a more artistic life first as an actor and then more successfully through the design and production of oak furniture. While the simple construction of many of his pieces recalls the honest workmanship associated with the Craftsman style of Gustav Stickley, his carved patterns display a highly original sensibility and outlet for creative energy. These take the form of asymmetrical spiral patterns inspired by Hiberno and other medieval decorative patterns as well as more unusual sources of inspiration. According to art historian Joe Cunningham, the open carving on the back of the oak desk chair of 1898–1899 (fig. 5.15) strongly resembles the structure of the oak molecule as seen through a microscope. Nature is the source of Rohlfs's invention but his approach is highly original in its attempt to reveal an underlying structure not visible to the human eye. While Rohlfs's work shares common elements with

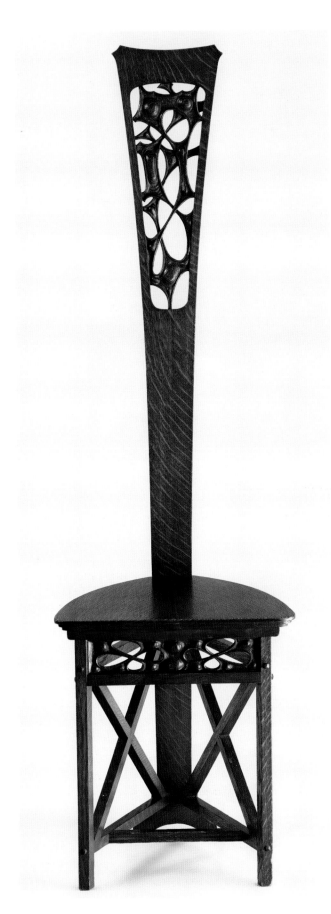

5.15 Charles Rohlfs, desk chair, oak (53 $^{15}/_{16}$ x 15 $^{15}/_{16}$ x 16 $^{7}/_{8}$ in (137 x 40.4 x 42.9 cm), Buffalo, New York, c. 1898–1899. © American Decorative Art 1900 Foundation.

Arts and Crafts attitudes, he did not espouse the social mission of others engaged in the movement: his workshop maintained a separation between designing and making, with a clearly implied hierarchy favoring the intellectual and spiritual component of the former.

The plain wood surfaces and understated decoration in much Craftsman furniture also appeared in other examples of design in the United States around the turn of the century that are sometimes known as the Mission style (the original meaning of the term is disputed: it may refer to the influence of Spanish mission architecture as a source of inspiration, but also of the missionary zeal of the Arts and Crafts Movement and its efforts to integrate art and life in harmony with nature). Brothers Charles Sumner Greene (1868–1957) and Henry Mather Greene (1870–1954), architects who also designed interior furnishings for a number of exclusive Eastern and Midwestern clients who enjoyed spending winters in southern California, combined an interest in natural materials and direct contact with nature with exquisite craftsmanship, often carried out by Swedish-born craftsmen John and Peter Hall, who translated Greene's subtle designs with skill and sensitivity. The homes of the Greene brothers show the integration of all aspects of interior design, elements inspired by Japanese architecture and furniture, an interest in natural materials, soft edges, and repeated motifs such as the cloud lift, as seen in as seen in the horizontal window moldings behind the built-in sideboard designed for the dining room of the Gamble House in Pasadena, echoed elsewhere in accents throughout the furniture and other carved details of the ensemble (fig. 5.16). In the work of the brothers, the Craftsman style was enhanced through inlay decoration, delicate relief carving to embellish surfaces, the combination of colored woods such as mahogany, walnut, or teak, and more sophisticated methods of construction than oak joinery. The result is an awareness of nature carefully cultivated and transformed by imagination and hand. While homes such as the Blacker House or nearby Gamble House were commissioned for wealthy clients, the wood shingles, exaggerated overhanging eaves, and low profiles of these homes became the basis for more modest "bungalow" houses that extended the idea of a contemporary architectural style more broadly, in Charles Sumner Greene's words, to "make common things beautiful." (See fig. 5.11.)

Certainly parallel but not always included in the literature on the Arts and Crafts Movement in the United States are the craft activities of the Shakers, a sect that emigrated to America in the late eighteenth century, settling in self-sufficient communities with the aim of uniting life and work and guided by beliefs in simplicity and humility.

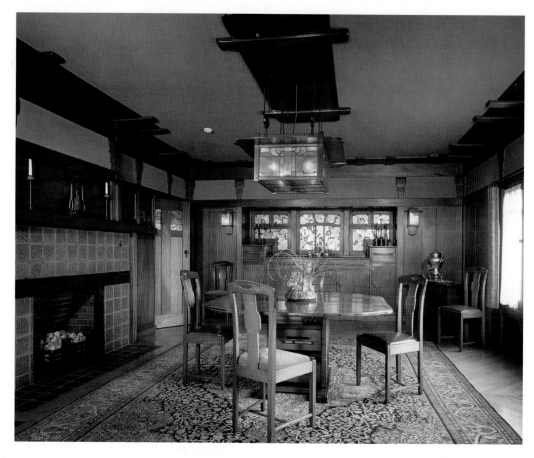

5.16 Charles Sumner and Henry Mather Greene, Gamble House, dining room with window showing cloud lift motif, Pasadena, California, 1908–1910.

Shaker furniture, like the ladderback chair (fig. 5.17), utilizes natural materials and certainly is an outgrowth of ethical conviction. Yet the Shaker concept of "meaningful" or "dignified" work lacks something of the element of individuality that not only united artist and craftsman, but also emphasized joy rather than drudgery for the maker, qualities frequently mentioned by Morris and Ruskin and embodied in the various expressions of Arts and Crafts in the United States such as the work of Charles Rohlfs. As a result, Shaker designs, while fashionable among Arts and Crafts consumers (and remaining popular with the buying public today) and even influential among other designers, were less subject to the innovation and change inherent in more individualistic conceptions of artistic activity, as well as to the commercial and competitive context for that activity.

Located in Doylestown in southeastern Pennsylvania, Henry Chapman Mercer (1856–1930) founded the Moravian Pottery and Tile Works around the turn of the century to produce molded ceramic tiles and mosaics for use primarily as architectural and mural decoration. Independently wealthy and well respected as an anthropologist and archeologist, Mercer lamented the decline

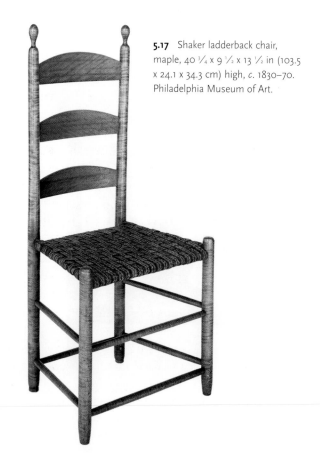

5.17 Shaker ladderback chair, maple, 40 ¾ x 9 ½ x 13 ½ in (103.5 x 24.1 x 34.3 cm) high, c. 1830–70. Philadelphia Museum of Art.

and disappearance of local, pre-industrial crafts in Pennsylvania. To preserve this endangered legacy, he began collecting tools and artifacts of the area and eventually built a museum (more like a warehouse today) to house the objects. He built his private residence and the museum using reinforced concrete with himself as amateur architect and hiring local laborers to help with construction. At the same time he founded a tile workshop and produced tiles using plaster molds with designs based upon historic models primarily from the Middle Ages but also from a variety of other sources. Mercer experimented with a process of two-coat glazing that varied the finish of each tile, and though hand-operated machines were used for shaping the slabs and pressing the tiles, each had an individual character from glazing and the many stages of the process that involved handwork. Although Mercer may not have been directly acquainted with the British Arts and Crafts Movement, his life's work and writings are entirely sympathetic to the attitudes of Morris and Ruskin. Perhaps the consummate "do-it-yourselfer," Mercer stated that the value of the products of the Moravian Pottery and Tile Works lay beyond the beauty of the colors and designs and had more to do with the dignity and usefulness of work. Perhaps the most well-known commission of the Moravian Pottery and Tile Works was for the floors of the State Capitol Building in Harrisburg, Pennsylvania, completed between 1902 and 1907. Even if only moderately successful or long-lived, Arts and Crafts workshops, communities, and publications in the United States demonstrate sensitivity to the impact of urbanization and industrialization and the threat that modernity posed to individuality, independence, and the meaning and value of work.

Ceramic ware was also an outlet for the Arts and Crafts ideal of achieving a closer relationship with nature through an appreciation of natural materials and the process of handmaking. As with furniture, the design and manufacture of ceramics ranged from the highly eccentric and individual work of George Ohr (1857–1918) of Biloxi, Mississippi, to the more production-oriented output of the Marblehead Pottery Company of Marblehead, Massachusetts. Ohr's pink vase (fig. 5.18) dating to around 1900 shows the irregular surface decoration associated with his hand-thrown and delicate, shell-like bodies. The Marblehead Pottery began in 1904 to provide therapy for patients recovering from tuberculosis. When the patients were unable to meet production schedules, the pottery shifted to a professionally run business. The simple, even heavy form, rough surface, and matte green glaze of the Panther vase illustrated in figure 5.19 suggest the natural qualities associated with the Arts and Crafts Movement. There is also a strong individual element: at the top of the vase the green glaze becomes a series of bands alternating

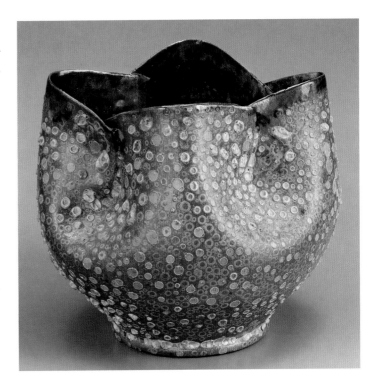

5.18 George Ohr, vase, glazed earthenware, 5 ¼ x 5 ½ in (13.2 x 14 cm), Biloxi, Mississippi, c. 1900. © American Decorative Art 1900 Foundation.

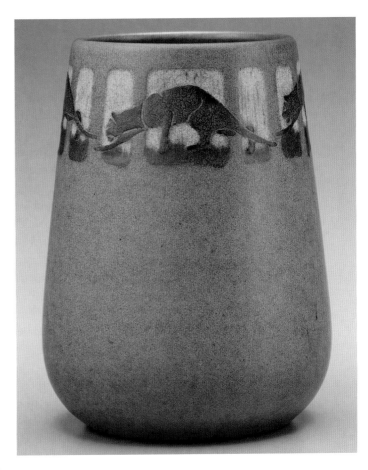

5.19 Marblehead Pottery, vase, glazed earthenware, 7 x 5 ¼ in (17.8 x 13.2 cm), Marblehead, Massachusetts, c. 1910–1911. © American Decorative Art 1900 Foundation.

with gold rectangles. This creates a border in which repeated panthers carved in low relief stride stealthily as if through shrubbery, with one rear leg behind and the other in front of the green bands.

PRINTING IN THE UNITED STATES

For his Kelmscott Press (see pages 85–87), William Morris drew three typefaces, all based upon earlier approaches to type design that he admired for their even stroke weight and the retention of calligraphic tendencies. His efforts, in effect, gave "new life to old faces," reviving interest in the Blackletter forms of the Middle Ages and suggesting variations to letterforms based upon Roman old-style faces of the later fifteenth century.

In the United States, two typographer–book designers based their work upon admiration for the Kelmscott fonts, and variations upon it that became widely used in more commercial settings. Both Frederic Goudy (1865–1947) and Bruce Rogers (1870–1956) were drawn to the beauty of Kelmscott books, which they encountered as young men, and embarked upon lifelong careers in type founding and book design. Their interests included type design and page design, and their careers testify to a respect for crafts-manship practiced in the broadest sense of the word as understood by Morris. The model set by Goudy and Rogers extended to others including William Dwiggins (1880–1956) and Morris Fuller Benton (1872–1948), both of whom developed influential typefaces used in modern book publishing. Dwiggins is remembered for having coined the term "graphic designer" to describe the varied professional activities that stemmed from craft origins in the printing industry and included typography, advertise-ments, and page design. Each of these designers studied historical typefaces and produced modern types suitable for text and titles. In addition to old-style (humanistic) faces by Caslon, Rogers produced a version of the Bodoni font for modern typesetting. Benton was employed as a punch-cutter for the American Type Founders Company (ATF), where he cut the type for Goudy fonts as well as developing his own typefaces. As noted by typographic historian Alexander Lawson, small variations in these historically inspired typefaces led to their wider use: by adjusting the height of ascenders and descenders, old-style typefaces could be more economically set without decreasing legibility. Will Bradley, whose advertising posters and illustrations are described below (see page 129) was also employed by ATF, which published *The American Chap-Book*. Along with other publications such as *Inland Printer*, *The American Chap-Book* introduced and dissemi-nated approaches to printing that emphasized new typefaces, lettering, and chromolithography.

Technology continued to affect the development of the printing industry in the later nineteenth century in a variety of ways. Among the most significant changes was the introduction of automatically setting type. As in the first half of the century, it was the newspaper industry, with its high-volume circulation and daily editions, that stimulated invention, leading to the introduction of a system known as Linotype at the *New York Herald* in 1886, and quickly spreading through Europe and the United States. The inventor of the Linotype machine was Ottmar Mergenthaler (1854–1899), who immigrated to the United States from Germany. His machine released negative impressions of letterforms through the operation of a keyboard, then cast each line of type in metal for the letter-press, eliminating the need for the hand-setting of type. As a result of this invention, the price of newspapers decreased and the number of pages printed increased, further increasing circulation and space for advertising. The Monotype machine, developed by Tolbert Lanston (1844–1913) in the 1880s and 1890s, offered an alternative to the Linotype. It produced multiple impressions of letters from a single matrix containing the entire alphabet, operated by a perforated tape that positioned the matrix to make molds for casting (the perforated tape resembled the "cards" used for Jacquard looms, see page 53). While developed for the newspaper industry, typesetting machinery such as the Monotype was also adopted for book printing. In both cases typographers wrestled with the challenges of maintaining consistency and legibility while adopting new and increasingly mechanized technologies. Achieving that balance led to increasing interest in the humanist roman letterforms of the later fifteenth and sixteenth centuries. This development was, in some sense, a reconciliation between respect for the highest achieve-ments of craft traditions and the inevitability of mechaniza-tion as the printing industry and the reading public expanded. Another invention of this period was the pantograph (also known as the "delineating machine"), developed by Linn Boyd Benton (1844–1932), who worked at ATF. The pantograph was a mechanical device that permitted variations of a single typeface to be produced as punches from a single set of drawings, both extending the range of a font (using extended and narrowed letterforms) as well as its point size with greater precision and speed.

Another technical development in printing was the mechanical reproduction of images using photographs. Translating a photographic plate into a mechanically produced image required the use of a screen to reproduce the tonal complexity of the image in a simpler form. Known as half-tone, the process made photography the basic tool of reporting and recording events for news-papers and magazines, and at the same time threatened

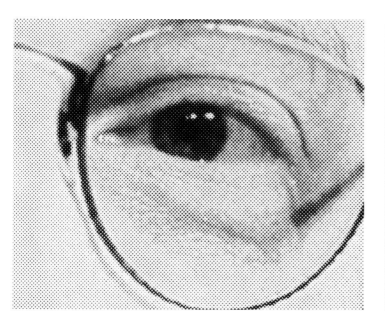

5.20 Enlarged photographic reproduction using half-tone printing process.

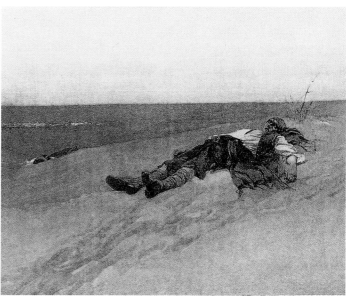

5.21 Howard Pyle, *On the Tortugas*, wood-engraving from original illustration for "Buccaneers and Marooners of the Spanish Main," *Harper's Magazine*, August 1887.

the jobs of those craftsmen who had met the expanding demand for images using the technique of wood engraving (fig. 5.20). The simplified shadows of the half-tone method of reproduction was adopted by graphic designers in the illustration of products in a larger format, for instance in the posters of Lucian Bernhard in Germany (see fig. 7.6).

Photographic reproduction was also used in the field of illustration. Yet while journalism shifted to photography as an eyewitness to faithfully record events, illustration still thrived in the realm of fiction, political and social commentary in the mass media, advertising, and in children's books, carrying on a tradition of narrative art outside of easel painting, where this tradition was challenged by Avant-garde ideas advocating the autonomy of art. *Scribner's Monthly, Harper's Magazine, Century*, and other publications were among the journals that provided a sphere of activity for illustrators. Howard Pyle (1853–1911) was one of several artists who worked at Harper Brothers under art editor Howard Parsons, providing illustrations to stories that were published serially. Early illustrations were wood-engraved from line drawings, while later examples were photographed and reproduced tonally and in four-color reproduction. Pyle brought to life stories of danger and adventure, taking readers to distant lands and places peopled by heroes and villains. Pyle lent immediacy to his scenes by often juxtaposing near and distant space and using strong contrast to heighten dramatic effect. An example is a tonal reproduction from Pyle's *Book of Pirates*, originally published in *Harper's Magazine* (August 1887), illustrating a shipwrecked sailor on a beach against a backdrop of empty sea and sky (fig. 5.21). The appeal of Pyle's illustrations was to escape and fantasy. The gap they filled in the lives of their vast readership was soon shared with a new medium, that of the moving picture, which introduced a new set of real-life heroes and heroines in the form of actors and actresses. While photography reduced the demand for illustrators in news reporting for newspapers and weekly journals, books and magazines continued to offer a creative outlet for illustrators' activities in the late nineteenth and early twentieth centuries. A new demand for narrative also arose during the same time through advertising, although not all illustrators were comfortable with the use of illustration techniques to sell products. To some degree a middle-ground was achieved in the late nineteenth-century advertising poster, which managed to appeal to audiences on different levels, that is, as the individual expression of the artist, as fostering a relationship between art and business in bringing high culture to the masses, and as generating appeal by linking products and services to a carefree or hedonistic lifestyle (see page 125 onward).

CHICAGO AND FRANK LLOYD WRIGHT

In 1896 and again in 1901 the British Arts and Crafts designer and advocate Charles Ashbee (see pages 89–90), founder of the Guild and School of Handicraft, visited the United States, traveling extensively and reporting on the contemporary design activities that he observed. Ashbee, who was a firm believer in hand craftsmanship, the well-being of workers, and a close relationship between designer and artisan, was impressed by a young American architect named Frank Lloyd Wright (1869–1959). Wright was one of a group of Midwestern architects and designers who created a "Prairie School" based in Chicago, Illinois. Many of Wright's early houses, such as the Ward Willits House in Highland Park, Illinois of 1900–1902 (fig. 5.22) shared a number of Arts and Crafts principles, for instance, in the effort to harmonize with their surroundings through low-hipped roofs and horizontal extension, in the attention to the use of natural materials, in a restraint toward the use of ornament and avoidance of overt historicism, and in an attempt to unify architecture, nature, and the elements of interior design and decoration to create a modern, democratic, and uniquely American version of the ideal home.

Significantly, however, Wright's approach to architecture and the decorative arts differed from Arts and Crafts ideology, particularly in regard to the relationship between designing, making, and handicraft. In a well-known lecture delivered in Chicago in 1901 at Hull House, a home founded in the city in 1889 by Jane Addams and Ellen Gates Starr to improve the lives of working-class women through a variety of social and educational services, Wright told his audience that the dream for a democratic architecture could only be achieved by embracing the machine, which saved time and reduced drudgery. He stated that the machine's ability to produce simple products of high quality and noble beauty had been obscured only by the greed of manufacturers and the ignorance of the public: "William Morris pleaded well for simplicity as the basis of all the art. Let us understand the significance to art of that word – SIMPLICITY – for it is vital to the art of the machine!" Indeed the invocation of William Morris recalls the British designer's own comments quoted earlier, that "the more mechanical the process, the less direct should be the imitation of natural forms," yet another instance of both the wide effects as well as the varied interpretations and applications of Morris's writings and example. Eventually Ashbee modified his own views to acknowledge a role for the machine along the lines envisioned by Wright, admiring the architect's courage in confronting the challenge of industrialization rather than ignoring its possible social benefits in improving the lives of a broader public.

Wright's linking of machine technology, aesthetic purity, and a democratic art provided a moral, ideological basis for approaches to modern design that emerged in the interwar period in Europe, although under different historical conditions and sometimes along universal and utopian lines; Wright's views and designs are also contemporary with initiatives in Germany to shape middle-class taste in relation to industrial manufacturing that also took place in the early twentieth century (see page 148 onward). For these designers and movements, decoration was viewed as being dishonest and vulgar if produced mechanically, and exclusive or elitist if made by hand: the modern designer should strive rather to create new and original forms designed for factory production to meet the needs and define the lifestyle of an expanding middle-class audience.

Wright's approach to design using restraint in decoration might be examined in connection with critiques of consumption by contemporary economists such as Thorsten Veblen (1857–1929), who criticized the purchasing habits of middle-class Americans as a form

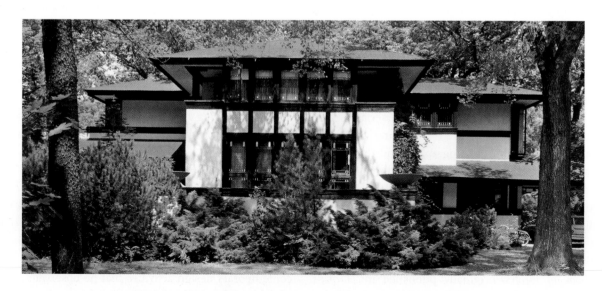

5.22 Frank Lloyd Wright, Ward Willits House, Highland Park, Illinois, 1900–1902.

of "conspicuous consumption," linking buying not with comfort and material progress but rather with the acquisition of social position that substituted the status acquired through buying with "real" status, formerly the result of honor and respect earned on the basis of action. For Veblen, fashion and consumption were menacing threats to the existing social order; for Wright, they were threats to the establishment of a true and natural "modern" taste, appropriate to its time and taking full advantage of new production technologies. Also contemporary with Wright's approach was the theory of Viennese architect Adolf Loos (1870–1933), another advocate of simplicity in design, who visited the United States in the 1890s and was familiar with the work and theories of the Prairie School. Loos equated decoration with cultural decline, and argued that modern urban life demanded an unpretentious style of living, in dress (where he favored the tailored black business suit worn by English men) as well as in architecture, where he advocated the use of modern materials such as reinforced concrete, flat roofs, and flat, unarticulated walls. His views were expressed in the essay "Ornament and Crime" dating to 1908–10 and reprinted in later publications.

Wright published some of his early designs for domestic architecture in illustrated mass-circulation magazines such as Edward W. Bok's (1863–1930) *Ladies' Home Journal* with the title, "A small house with lots of room in it" and a suggested cost of less than $6,000. But despite the simple elegance of Wright's designs in comparison with the more traditional preference for carved or molded ornament and adaptations of period styles ranging from Gothic to Baroque, Wright's homes were almost invariably custom-built for affluent clients, and his domestic furniture was neither mass-produced nor achieved broad appeal for consumers, who preferred more traditional expressions of comfort and beauty linked to richness of effect. Even the design published by Wright in the *Ladies' Home Journal* may be misleading for a modern reader, since comparative price indices suggest that a $6,000 home in 1901 would correspond more to a middle-class rather than working-class purchasing power today.

Another expression of Wright's preference for simple forms was the design of colored leaded glass windows, like the set of bay windows for the dining space of the Susan Dana house in Springfield, Illinois (completed 1904; fig 5.23). The windows are abstract interpretations of foliate forms and their rectilinear structure echoes the geometric relationships of the plan and elevation of Wright's architectural designs. The composition of these and other windows in Wright's Prairie houses suggests they might be assembled from prefabricated units or shapes, but their manufacture was still time-consuming, intricate, and ultimately craft-based. In other words, Wright seems to have created the converse of Morris's recommendation that machines should not imitate hand-work – the windows are handmade yet suggest how machines "should" make things. Despite the arguments presented in his writings and speeches that "the Machine is the great forerunner of democracy," Wright was hardly advocating democracy in the sense of "freedom of choice." Instead he equated an aesthetic preference based upon simplicity with a self-evident but entirely theoretical technical imperative, then assumed that the result shaped and elevated the taste of his intended middle-class audience, that is, design that the public should want. The concept of design unity not only applied to the open rather than enclosed interior spaces, but stimulated Wright to design ceramics, metalwork, windows, and lamps, all of which contributed to the warmth and harmony of the home, and also to the interrelationship between architecture and furnishings.

As noted above, Wright's career in Chicago should not be considered in a vacuum, for the city was a major metropolitan center, and his ideas took shape in an active artistic environment. After a disastrous fire of 1871 architects and artists were attracted to Chicago during an intense period of rebuilding and modernization that included the hosting of the Columbian Exposition of 1893, and the construction of an elevated mass transit system. A premium on office space in the city's center led to the design of several tall buildings, constructed from steel and utilizing motorized elevators. One of the most prominent architects during this period of artistic activity was Louis Sullivan (1856–1924). Sullivan was acquainted with the writings of Ruskin and with the Arts and Crafts

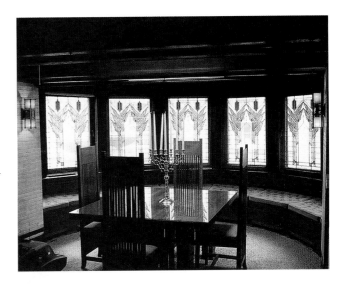

5.23 Frank Lloyd Wright, dining room furniture, Susan Dana House, Springfield, Illinois, completed 1904.

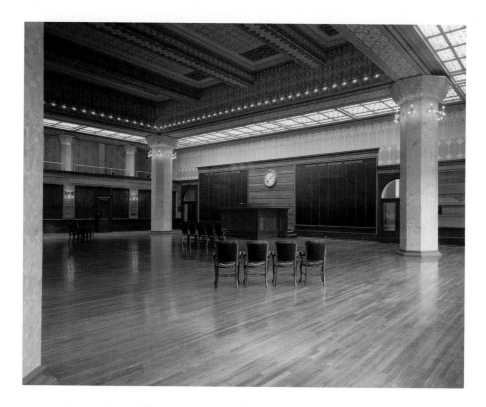

5.24 Louis Sullivan (and Dankmar Adler), trading room of the Chicago Stock Exchange, 1894, reconstructed 1977. Art Institute of Chicago.

Movement. Despite his well-known and often-quoted dictum "form follows function," Sullivan believed decoration to be an essential component of architecture. This elevated view was based upon an appreciation for nature and the spiritual energy embodied in natural forms as they were integrated into and contributed to the value of the built environment. He designed often intricate original patterns for architectural and interior decoration, used as framed panels (whether painted, molded in terracotta, or cast in iron) to balance and enliven the repetitive gridlike structure of tall buildings such as the Wainwright Building in St. Louis, Missouri, dating to 1890–1891. His interior of the Chicago Stock Exchange (fig. 5.24) from 1894 also featured complex interlace patterns, strongly linear and abstract, complementing the crisp contours of columns and other structural elements of the design. Similar curvilinear patterns appear in the windows, carpets, and other domestic furnishings designed by George Grant Elmslie (1871–1952) and George Washington Maher (1864–1926) for homes in the Midwest around the turn of the century. Elmslie, born in Scotland, worked for Sullivan and Frank Lloyd Wright. Maher's *Thistle* textile, for the Patten home in Evanston, Illinois (1901, fig. 5.25), is one of the more exuberant examples of his work, while window designs remained more restrained and geometric.

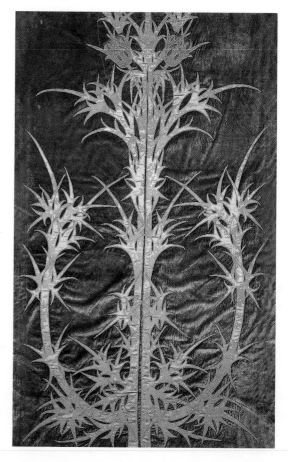

5.25 George Washington Maher, *Thistle* textile, silk velvet with appliqué of silk damask, 79 x 45 ⅝ in (200.7 x 115.6 cm), 1901. The Saint Louis Art Museum.

Chapter 6

The Equality of the Arts

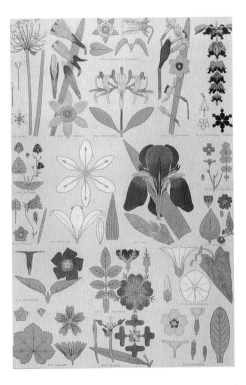

6.1 Christopher Dresser, *Leaves and Flowers from Nature, no. 8*, color lithograph, 13 ¼ x 8 ⅞ in (33.7 x 22.5 cm), from *The Grammar of Ornament* by Owen Jones, 1856.

DESIGN REFORM AND THE AESTHETIC MOVEMENT

New attitudes toward the decorative arts in England in the second half of the nineteenth century emerged in the career of designer Christopher Dresser (1834–1904). He contributed original plates to Owen Jones's *The Grammar of Ornament* featuring design motifs based upon leaf and floral forms in a style that simplified organic forms into flattened shapes defined by crisp contours (fig. 6.1). Dresser's background as a student at the London School of Design and his interest in the collaboration of designer and manufacturer demonstrate his strong ties to design reform and education, but the originality of his designs, early interest in promoting the craft traditions of Japan, and his views regarding the expressive meanings and associations of pattern and decoration, suggest an elevated attitude toward the profession of design that included a more active role for the designer in the process of manufacture.

Rather than concern with historicism or the appropriateness of representational decorative forms in relation to use, Dresser concentrated upon the transformation of naturalistic motifs into expressive pattern and on the integration of decoration with existing methods of workshop manufacture. A ceramic serving plate of 1872, manufactured by the Watcombe Pottery Company and attributed to Dresser (fig. 6.2) illustrates his approach to design. Its composition is a lively yet balanced play of triangular and circular shapes, related harmoniously to the form of the plate and abstracted from a variety of plant forms. The Watcombe plate follows Owen Jones's prescription for schematic or conventionalized natural forms to decorate flat surfaces, and the design conforms to the shape of the field to be decorated. It also emphasizes invention based upon a fascination with nature and its creative transformation into decoration. Indeed, Jones was one of the instructors at the London School of Design, and Richard Redgrave (see fig. 4.4) taught a course in Artistic Botany that encouraged students to carefully study the

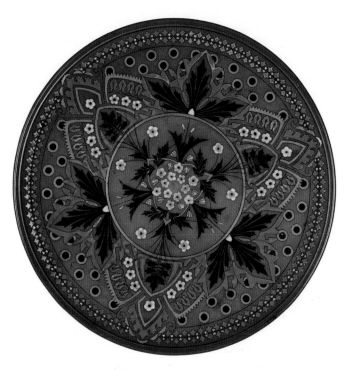

6.2 Christopher Dresser, earthenware plate with partial glazing, diameter 13 ½ in (34.3 cm), manufactured by Watcombe Pottery Company, Torquay, England, 1872.

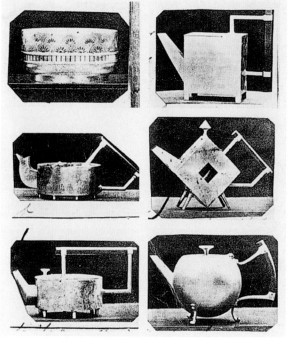

6.3 Christopher Dresser, silver-plate designs from the costing book of James Dixon and Sons Limited, Sheffield, England, *c.* 1879.

forms of nature in order to understand their underlying structure. Dresser established himself first as an "ornamentalist," providing patterns for wallpapers and useful goods. He considered design an intellectual and professional endeavor essential to elevating the quality and appeal of a wide variety of products, and worked with manufacturers to realize his designs in the most efficient way possible. Dresser created a motto and logo for his business: "knowledge is power." The phrase originated in the later Middle Ages, but in the nineteenth century it referred to the broad idea of progress: knowledge was something to be shared rather than kept private or secret. Expanding the audience for art through design for manufactures elevated ordinary useful objects and educated the public, contributing to the quality of life. Manufactures held the promise of the democratization of art, in which the role of designer was paramount.

Dresser designed numerous examples of metalwork, including tea sets, toast racks, and other serving dishes and utensils. The striking series of electroplated silver tea sets designed for the Dixon Company of Sheffield beginning in 1879 (fig. 6.3) emphasize the purity of the material's smooth surface, and include the use of identical parts for feet and brackets for handles. Dresser was inspired by examples of metalwork he had seen during a trip to Japan in 1866–1907, and his designs for metalwork were praised at the time for their originality in comparison with contemporary work featuring naturalistic relief decoration

produced by casting and other traditional craft techniques. Although the lack of decoration and elementary geometry of Dresser's work for the Dixon Company anticipates the early twentieth-century concern with product "types" designed for standardized mass-production, Dresser's work does not seem have been directed primarily towards standardized or "typical" forms and was aimed at a discerning middle-class audience (both the one that existed, and the one he hoped to create). The great variation of shapes, materials, decoration, and surfaces for his designs in silver suggest the potential for an original art applied to industrial production – for this reason a number of historians commonly refer to him as the "first industrial designer." Among his most intriguing works are the designs he created for the Ault Pottery Company in Swadlincote, England. While the vase illustrated in figure 6.4 and dating to 1892 suggests a spiraling asymmetrical form, Dresser designed this organic form to be made using a mold for ease of production rather than shaped by hand.

Dresser's interest in the decorative arts of Japan, and the originality of his designs and patterns also characterize the work of a number of artists and architects for whom the equality of the arts emerged as a provocative theme pointing to new directions and possibilities for their activities. The term Aesthetic Movement was often used to refer to these activities, which were labeled as such during the 1870s and 1880s and even satirized in the British periodical *Punch* and in forms of popular

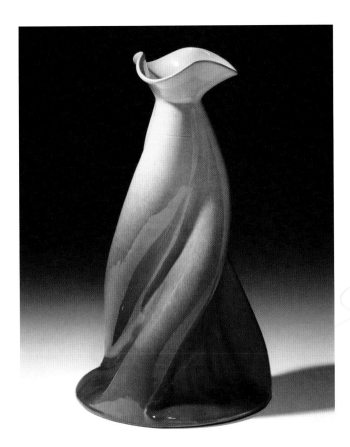

6.4 Christopher Dresser, vase, earthenware, height 12 ¼ in (31.1 cm), Ault Pottery, Swadlincote, England, 1892. Victoria and Albert Museum, London.

entertainment such as Gilbert and Sullivan's operetta *Patience* (1881). The importance of this movement to the history of modern design can hardly be underestimated, since it succeeded in shaping the attitudes of artists, manufacturers, and wealthy consumers and in elevating the status of the decorative arts. The Aesthetic Movement may be seen both as an outgrowth of early design reform while at the same time moving from a preoccupation with standards and paternalism toward a reconsideration of the sources of inspiration, materials, processes, and in particular the importance of subjective expression and meaning. Designers associated with the movement adopted a freer and more individual approach to historical styles, and greater freedom in their exploration of materials and approach to decoration. They advocated for equality and unity between the fine and applied arts, in particular as realized in the coordinated interior, in which every element contributed equally to the unified expressive or emotional effect of the whole. Interiors became "total works of art," imaginative spaces in which the barriers between art and life ceased to exist. Examples of aesthetic design were displayed at international exhibitions, including London (1862), Vienna (1873), Paris (1867, 1878, 1889, and 1900), Brussels (1897), Turin

(1902), and in the United States (Philadelphia in 1876, Chicago in 1893). They were also illustrated in journals and in showrooms and boutiques specializing in contemporary crafts and interior design. While important aesthetic designers of the period might specialize in a particular medium such as glass, ceramics, or furniture, many high-end manufacturers sought responsibility and control for all aspects of interior planning and decoration in order to achieve a coordinated effect that included fabrics, lighting, furniture, and furnishings.

The painter James Abbott McNeill Whistler (1834–1903) is regarded as one of the leading figures of the Aesthetic Movement in Britain. As an American-born painter who studied in Paris and resided in London beginning in 1859, Whistler's involvement with interior design asserted his belief in the equality and integration of the arts. This is seen in the painted decoration and easel painting he contributed to the design of the Peacock Room (fig. 6.5) in the London home of the Liverpool industrialist F. R. Leyland (1832–1892) in 1876 (now in the Freer Gallery in Washington, D.C.). The room was designed by architect Thomas Jeckyll (1827–1881) to display Mr Leyland's collection of Chinese porcelain. Its shelves, hanging globe lanterns, ceiling coffers and rectangular-backed chairs are unified through a shared rectilinear vocabulary consisting primarily of rectangles and hexagons. The severity of the décor was balanced by the collection of blue and white porcelain originally placed on the shelves. Leyland also purchased a painting by Whistler

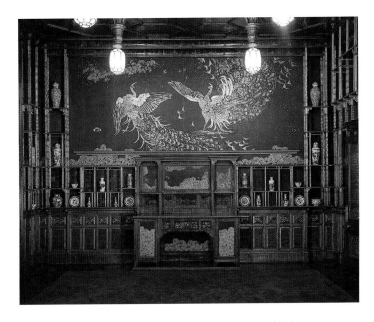

6.5 James Abbott McNeill Whistler, *Harmony in Blue and Gold: The Peacock Room* for the Frederic Leyland House, oil paint and metal leaf on canvas, leather, and wood, 1876. Courtesy of the Freer Gallery of Art, Smithsonian Institution, Washington, D.C.

for the room. Entitled *Princess in the Land of Porcelain*, the canvas depicted a young female figure wearing a Japanese kimono and was hung above the fireplace. The artist contributed to the elaborate design of the interior by painting delicate undulating, asymmetrical wavy lines in gold against the deep green of the paneled walls and cabinets. He also painted peacocks on the door screens on one side of the room, added without the owner's permission. Whistler demanded remuneration for the additional work, and Leyland's refusal to pay led to a dispute between the two men. In time Leyland agreed to pay one-half of Whistler's fee, but insulted the artist further by paying him with a check written for pounds, the currency of trade, rather than guineas, the currency generally exchanged for the work of artists and professionals.

The Irish-born writer and critic Oscar Wilde (1854–1900), a vocal proponent of the Aesthetic Movement, articulated the attitudes that informed the creation of such exotic and personal interior spaces as the Peacock Room. In a passage from his essay "The Artist as Critic" (1891), Wilde recognized the expressive content of abstract form in the decorative arts and acknowledged their elevated status:

> The art that is frankly decorative is the art to live with. It is, of all visible arts, the one art that creates in us both mood and temperament. Mere colour, unspoiled by meaning, and unallied with definite form, can speak to the soul in a thousand different ways. The harmony that resides in the delicate proportions of lines and masses becomes mirrored in the mind ... The marvels of design stir the imagination ... By its deliberate rejection of Nature as the ideal of beauty, as well as of the imitative method of the ordinary painter, decorative art not merely prepares the soul for the reception of true imaginative work, but develops in it that sense of form which is the basis of creative no less than of critical achievement.

Dresser's comments on the design for a pattern from his 1862 book *The Art of Decorative Design*, although written in more analytical prose, share some of the same spirit as Wilde's essay on the elevated and expressive content of the applied arts – both statements claim that design elevates the ordinary, but through expressive rather than representational form:

> I have sought to embody chiefly the idea of power, energy, force, or vigour; and in order to do this I have employed such lines as we see in the bursting buds of spring, when the energy of growth is at its maximum ... I have also availed myself of those forms to be seen in certain bones of birds which are associated with the

organs of flight, and which give us an impression of great strength.

The Peacock Room and other interiors of the period demonstrate an affinity for Japanese art shared by many adherents to the Aesthetic Movement in Britain. Dresser traveled to Japan (his visit was partially underwritten by Charles Tiffany in New York, who asked Dresser to return with examples of Japanese metalwork) and lectured widely on the art of that country, praising both the quality and character of Japanese craft as well as the religious significance of Japanese design. After the opening of trade with Japan in 1852, artistic and commercial interest in the country was stimulated by objects brought to Britain by its first official representative, Sir Rutherford Alcock, by a Japanese Court at the London International Exhibition of 1862, and by the acquisition of a collection of Japanese objects by the South Kensington Museum in the early 1870s. In 1875, collector and merchant Arthur Lazenby Liberty (1843–1917) opened a shop in London featuring Japanese craft, while further popular interest in Japan emerged with the success of the Gilbert and Sullivan operetta *The Mikado* (1885). Many of these activities influenced attitudes toward design and the decorative arts in Europe and in the United States. Japan offered collectors and European artists and designers a tradition that valued the decorative arts and the creativity of the artisan. In his book *The Traditional Arts and Crafts of Japan* (1882), Dresser wrote extensively on the practice of Japanese craft, and observed the esteem accorded to skilled artisans. The combination of skill with intelligence reveals Dresser's own interest in establishing the professional and creative status of designers:

> I cannot help thinking that the Japanese are right in regarding the man who can make a beautiful pot, a lovely cabinet, a charming fabric, or a perfect *netsuki* as a being superior to the mere buyer and seller of goods; for while the one denotes his best energies to mere money-making, the other ennobles matter by the impress of his mind, love, intelligence, and skill...

It was, at least in part, the high regard for Japanese decorative arts that allowed artists and artisans greater freedom in drawing, permitting them, in the words of art historian Ernst Gombrich, to "break the rules," for instance in the uneven spacing of motifs applied to surface decoration or in the irregular forms and textures of ceramic vessels. Designers such as E. W. Godwin (1833–1886) did not imitate Japanese furniture directly but used the lattice forms depicted in Japanese woodblock prints to create an "Anglo-Japanese" style, as in an intricately

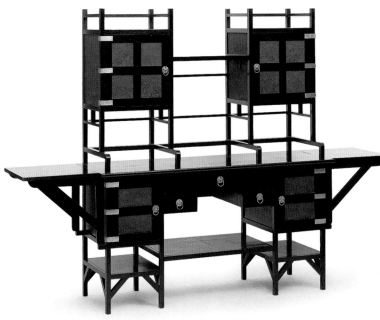

6.6 E. W. Godwin, buffet, ebonized mahogany and inset panels of embossed japanned leather paper, 102 ¼ x 157 in (260 x 399 cm), manufactured by William Watt, London, c. 1867. Victoria and Albert Museum, London.

constructed buffet dated c. 1867 (fig. 6.6) made of ebonized wood and intended for the display of ceramic wares. Godwin's buffet is severely geometric, lacks any carved decoration, and is composed of a variety of rectangular solids and voids relieved only by angled braces for shelves and legs and circular fittings of silver. Despite the plain surfaces, the materials and construction of Godwin's buffet were costly to produce and the simplicity, like that of Dresser's electroplated teapots, seems to represent a new appreciation of aesthetic purity rather than an overt effort to create inexpensive, functional designs.

Aesthetic Movement design included but was not limited to original adaptations of Japanese style or pattern decoration as seen in Godwin or Dresser. As we have seen, Dresser's overriding interest was in the expressive character and practical applications of a variety of botanical forms to manufactured goods. Godwin also drew freely from other traditions in creating original forms for a variety of interior furnishings. He collaborated, for instance, with Whistler on the interior design of the painter's apartment in London known as White House, and on a display for the furniture-maker William Watt (1834–1885) at the 1878 International Exposition in Paris. Watt eventually published an illustrated catalogue of Godwin's furniture designs in 1882, entitled *Art Furniture.*

Other designers linked to the movement, including Charles Eastlake and Bruce Talbert (1838–1881), turned to the Gothic style as advocated by Pugin or to the solid forms

of the seventeenth century in what is known as the Queen Anne revival, approaches that were also in keeping with the harmony of utility and beauty advocated by the early design reformers. Eastlake's designs achieved popularity through their publication in his *Hints on Household Taste* (1868): as mentioned in Part II, while Eastlake's standards in design were linked to reform and education, his concerns were more aesthetic and lacked the overt moral or political overtones of Pugin or Cole.

Eastlake acted as an advisor in matters of taste and his advice was not free from cultural assumptions about the role of design in society. His comments were directed toward female readers who were presumed to take responsibility for creating the ideal domestic environment, one that combined an appreciation for beauty as well as practical considerations such as a recommendation to avoid furniture with extensive carved decoration so as to reduce dust and promote healthy living. In this latter sense his and other tastemakers' advice books share the promotion of efficient and healthy living with the American writer Catherine Beecher (1800–1878), whose relationship to modern design is mentioned below (see page 118). A cabinet by Talbert (fig. 6.7), dating probably to the 1870s, is rectilinear in overall construction but allows ample opportunity for the decoration in the panels using complex techniques of marquetry rather than carving. With its self-conscious adaptation of historicism and interest in appropriate design for contemporary life, such

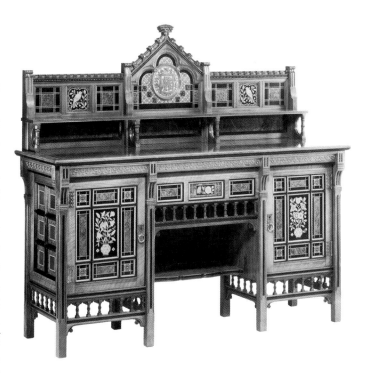

6.7 Bruce Talbert, cabinet, walnut with ebonized turnings, 58 ½ x 65 ½ x 20 ½ in (148.6 x 166.4 x 52.1 cm), manufactured by Gillow and Company, London, 1870s. Art Institute of Chicago.

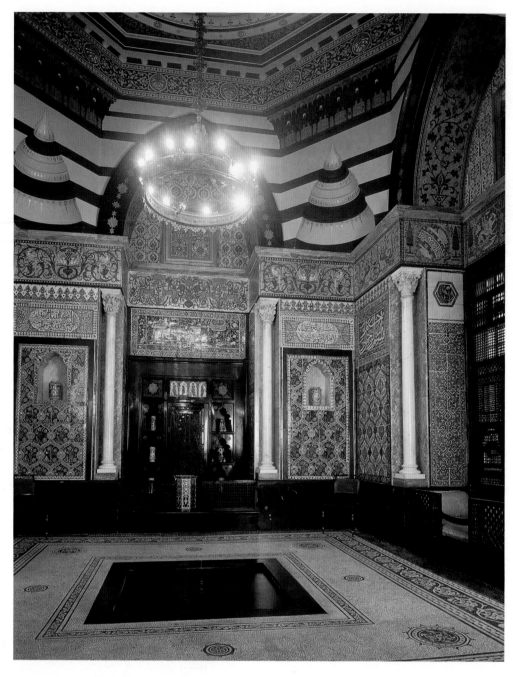

6.8 Walter Crane, frieze for the Arab Hall of Lord Leighton's house, mosaic, 1877–1879. Leighton House, London.

art furniture reinforced the individuality of the designer and exhibited the freedom and inventiveness associated with the original creative activity of fine artists. It also promoted a lifestyle that acknowledged modern circumstances of household maintenance, and placed the responsibility for domestic comfort and tranquillity upon women, not as producers, but rather as consumers of design. The appearance of turned spindles in much of this furniture may be related to changes in the furniture industry itself, where steam-powered lathes permitted the efficient manufacture of such elements, less expensive than the labor required for hand carving.

Recognizing increasingly commercial circumstances in their profession, artists were eager to enter the market for decorative arts as designers and broaden the sphere of their activities. Aesthetic furniture was directed toward a wealthy clientele. The manufacturers for these products, such as Watt, Gillows, Holland and Sons, or Collinson & Lock, were willing to produce items from artists' designs for display at international exhibitions in major European cities as well as in the United States, and art furniture was marketed as well through entrepreneurs and collectors such as Liberty in London, and later Siegfried "Samuel" Bing (1838–1905) and Julius Meier-Graefe (1867–1935) in

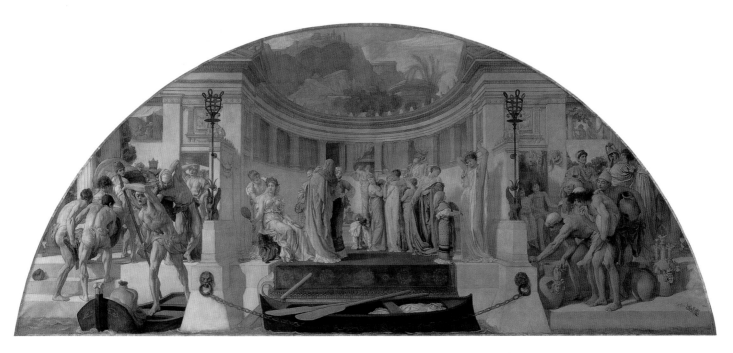

6.9 Lord Frederic Leighton, *The Industrial Arts as Applied to Peace*, cartoon for mural, 77 ¹⁄₂ x 177 ¹⁄₂ in (196.8 x 450.8 cm), 1872–83. Victoria and Albert Museum, London.

Paris (see pages 122 and 136, fig. 6.54). Where they exist, the business records of these firms show they provided comprehensive services for interior design on the basis of commission rather than retail sales of stock items.

Another form of marketing was the studio. Artists such as Whistler were known for the design of the interiors in their own homes and studios, at least in part to draw the attention of potential clients or patrons for their work. Another well-known fine artist with an interest in cultivating the importance of the decorative arts was Lord Frederic Leighton (1830–1896), a painter who served as President of the Royal Academy of Art and was made a peer in 1896. Leighton's house in Kensington was built from 1878 to 1880 and contains a two-story Arab Hall combining Islamic tiles with contemporary examples of tiles designed by Walter Crane (1845–1915) and William de Morgan (1839–1917). Both of these artists contributed to the flowering of the decorative arts in the later nineteenth century, Crane as a designer and illustrator, and de Morgan as a craftsman devoted to the art of ceramics (fig. 6.8). Leighton was also responsible for a large mural painting in one of the hallways of the South Kensington Museum (renamed the Victoria and Albert Museum in 1899), an endeavor that realized Sir Henry Cole's dream for a major building to house collections primarily devoted to the decorative arts and welcomed visitors from all social classes. The mural bears the title *The Industrial Arts as Applied to Peace* (a small sketch of the composition hangs in Leighton House). The title recalls the didactic aims of early design reform, but this idealizing work depicts a group of Athenian maidens trying on clothing and jewelry while muscular workmen transport ceramic containers and rolled-up woven carpets that have recently arrived by boat. The benefits of peace in this mural appear to be equated with the leisure time women spend adorning themselves with exquisitely crafted objects (fig. 6.9), with only the slightest reference to the industry and free trade that produces and brings such goods to market. Thus the value of the decorative arts is portrayed less in relation to productivity, labor, or general material progress than to an almost dreamlike cultivation of private aesthetic experience and personal transformation via luxury goods (one might compare this vision with that of Louis XIV inspecting the Gobelins Manufactory, fig. 1.1; see also fig. 8.1).

Clearly there were shared elements in the work of the Arts and Crafts Movement and the Aesthetic Movement, and some designers, such as de Morgan, Edward Burne-Jones (see Chapter 5), and Walter Crane, seemed to move comfortably between the two. Proponents of both movements believed that the decorative arts were important as vehicles of aesthetic experience and as the products of meaningful labor. But there were differences as well, at least in terms of emphasis. For Morris, artists with a social conscience could best direct their efforts by being craftsmen, where their products would most serve the needs of a troubled society. For the Aesthetic designer, the decorative arts were the vehicle for their subjective experience and expression. One might say that the Arts and Crafts Movement was directed toward process and in reducing the alienation between an artisan and the

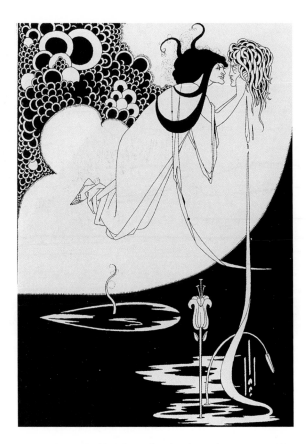

6.10 Aubrey Beardsley, design for *The Climax*, from Oscar Wilde's *Salomé*, print, 9 x 5 in (22.9 x 12.7 cm), 1893. Private collection.

the young English artist Aubrey Beardsley (1872–1898). Beardsley's *The Climax* (fig. 6.10), representing Salomé's embrace of the severed head of John the Baptist, is boldly calligraphic and simplified into broad shapes with strong contrast. The illustration makes use of the asymmetrical superimposed wave patterns in the upper left corner familiar from Japanese decoration, a motif borrowed as well by Whistler in his decoration of the cabinets in the Peacock Room. The drawing, in addition to its relation to sexual overtones in the themes of lust and violence, permits the artist considerable freedom and invention in the transformation of hair, plant forms, and the pool of liquid (perhaps blood) from which a thin flower grows at the bottom right of the composition.

Another prominent figure in the publication of books involving artists connected with aesthetic ideas was Charles Ricketts (1866–1931). Ricketts carefully considered the unity of page design involving typography, illustration, and decoration. He published a collaboration between Wilde and Beardsley, an illustrated poem entitled *The Sphinx*. Much lighter in overall effect than the books of Morris's Kelmscott Press, the pages of *The Sphinx* use blocks of text, decorated initials, and framed illustration to suggest the relationship among individual elements unified by shared qualities of weight and density. Ricketts worked with different printers to publish books under the name of the Vale Press. Other titles include a large but thin volume of *De Cupidinis et Psychis Amoribus Fabula Anilis*, an erotic Latin poem translated by Charles Holme (editor of *The Studio*) with woodcut illustrations, which appeared in 1901. Here the textured paper and ragged edges, Venetian-style humanistic typography, and varied width of columns to accommodate intimate scenes of lovers (fig. 6.11) are aspects of private and personal books meant for discriminating taste and requiring the skills of a designer sensitive to the page or double-page spread as a unified graphic composition of type and image.

Lucien Pissarro (1863–1944), son of the French Impressionist painter Camille Pissarro, pursued a career in private press publishing in London. Together with his wife Esther, Pissarro founded the Eragny Press in Hammersmith in the early 1890s and approached all the elements of book design, including typography, with equal interest. Early books used Ricketts Vale font, while later volumes employed a font drawn by Pissarro himself and called Brook type, much admired for its legibility. Borders were printed in color and constitute a distinctive characteristic of the Eragny Press (fig. 6.12).

Aesthetic attitudes and the Arts and Crafts Movement also had an impact upon the publication of illustrated books for other markets, including children. Interest in children's literature was strong among early design

products of his or her labor. In theory at least, manufacturers and buyers would support such an aim as an expression of sympathy with its skepticism toward the equation of industrialization with progress. Artists of the Aesthetic Movement identified with and gave visible form to subjective experience through the decorative art object or product, often in relation to an aesthetic view of life most often realized in the interior, where all elements were united by abstract, expressive qualities of color, shape, line, and texture.

BOOKS, ILLUSTRATION, AND TYPE

Aesthetic, expressive interests in printing emerged in Britain with the publication of the monthly journal *The Studio* in 1893. In addition to publishing illustrations of contemporary furniture and furnishings, *The Studio* included illustrations by artists with a highly subjective approach to the representation of nature and the human figure, related to contemporary Symbolist attitudes to art discussed above (see pages 88–89). For instance, the first issue of *The Studio* contained illustrations from Oscar Wilde's poem based upon the New Testament story of Salomé, published originally in French and designed by

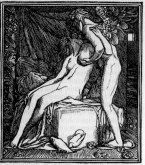

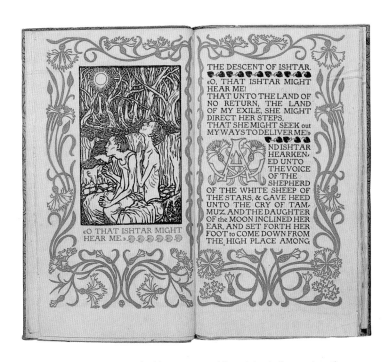

6.12 Lucien Pissarro, double-page spread from *Ishtar's Descent into the Nether World*, 7 ³/₁₆ x 4 ⁵/₁₆ in (18.3 x 11 cm), published by Eragny Press, London, 1903. Private collection.

6.11 Charles Ricketts, *De Cupidinis et Psychis Amoribus Fabula Anilis*, 11 ⁹/₁₆ x 7 ¹¹/₁₆ in (29.3 x 19.4 cm), London, 1901. Hagerty Library Archives, Drexel University, Philadelphia.

reformers such as Henry Cole, who saw these books as a means to cultivate taste and instill the values of work and moderation (see pages 62 and 71–72). In the later nineteenth century, attitudes about children's books changed to include a more innocent, playful, in short, a more childlike point of view, less didactic and allowing for greater experimentation with media and expression. In departing from illusionism and naturalism, children's illustrators shared an approach to imagery related to their Aesthetic Movement counterparts. In attempting to adopt the viewpoint of a child, they entered into an imaginative state of mind that was akin to other work in the fine and decorative arts at this time.

The embossed gold seal found on many well-known children's books today is named for a pioneer in the new approach to children's books, English illustrator Randolph Caldecott (1846–1886). Caldecott was a self-taught artist who became a professional illustrator only after moving to London from Manchester in the early 1870s. He served as a freelance illustrator for popular weekly news journals in London, and several of his illustrations were reproduced in *Harper's New Monthly Magazine* published in New York. Among his best-known works are a series of books published by George Routledge from color wood engravings

by Edmund Evans. The collaboration of illustrator and engraver is a significant one, for Evans's methods of reproduction preserved the simple, abbreviated quality of Caldecott's drawing, set off against broad unmodulated areas of lightly tinted color, and was a creative rather than mechanical approach that contributed to the success of Caldecott's work. Eliminating the more conventional detail and cross-hatching used in the wood-engraving process, picture-books such as *Hey Diddle Diddle* (1882; fig. 6.13) achieved wide popularity in both Britain and France. Caldecott also earned respect among noted designers such as Walter Crane and artists such as Van Gogh and Gauguin, both of whom owned copies of Caldecott's relatively inexpensive picture books. The recognition, in artistic as well as popular circles, of Caldecott's illustrations, along with the emergence of exhibitions and galleries devoted to the print media, is an example of the interrelationship among the arts that animated both artists and the public during the later nineteenth century, and that contributed to an emerging field of graphic design.

Contemporary with Caldecott's picture books were those of another British artist, Kate Greenaway (1846–1901). Greenaway's father was a freelance wood engraver who had worked with Edmund Evans for the publisher of the satirical illustrated journal *Punch*, and Evans was also responsible for the engraving and color printing of Greenaway's drawings. Greenaway's career and illustrations touch upon a number of attitudes toward the

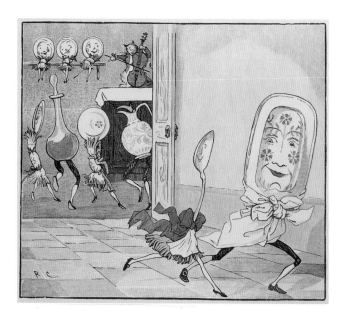

6.13 Randolph Caldecott, illustration from *Hey Diddle Diddle*, wood engraving, 7 3/8 x 8 7/8 in (18.8 x 22.4 cm), published by George Routledge & Sons, London, 1882.

that contributed so much to the contemporary Aesthetic Movement in Europe as well as in the United States.

The illustrations of Greenaway, Caldecott, as well as Walter Crane, were reproduced from these artists' original drawings rendered on wood for engraving, or in the case of Greenaway, later translated onto stone for chromolithographic reproduction as greeting cards for a mass audience. Black-and-white illustrations for more timely publications such as newspapers and weekly magazines used specialized labor to more quickly translate drawings into wood, and by the 1880s photomechanical methods of reproducing images were beginning to compete with and eventually to eclipse both relief and chromolithographic techniques for the reproduction of images we now take for granted. At first, photographs of original drawings were printed on wood for hand-engraving, eliminating either the artist's or engraver's role in this stage of production. A more significant development was the use of acid to engrave a wood or metal block printed with a photographic image, eliminating the need for any handwork at all except in the finishing stages. Direct methods of printing involving artists and craftsmen persisted, however, in the genre of book illustration, flourished in poster design, and in more editorial forms of imagery for political cartoons and caricatures in newspapers and magazines.

decorative arts in the later nineteenth century as they apply to printing. She received training at the government-sponsored design schools established around the middle of the century to prepare designers for industry, and Ruskin praised her work for its idyllic recreation of natural beauty in a pre-industrial era. The simplified drawing and frequent use of blank space in her compositions reveals an affinity to the graphic tendencies of Aesthetic design, and as a woman her creative energies found an outlet in the applied arts rather than in the male-dominated fine arts at this time.

Greenaway's first popular success was an illustrated book published by George Routledge in 1879 entitled *Under the Window*. A frontispiece for *Marigold Garden; Pictures and Rhymes* (first published 1885; fig. 6.14) features high-waisted dresses that recall the simpler fashions of the late eighteenth and earlier nineteenth centuries and a type of idealized child's face (it has been suggested that the artist derived the type from the collection of dolls she owned). Greenaway also used bands of flowers to frame the illustration and serve as a motif to suggest a landscape setting. In this case a garden twists around the playful composition of figures in various poses dancing in a circle. This component in her illustrations grew out of her own sketches from nature as well as the conventionalized approach to drawing she learned at the schools of design she attended and adapted to the genre of children's illustration. It has also been pointed out that the strong contours and areas of flat color found in Greenaway's as well as Caldecott's children's illustrations were derived from effects in Japanese woodblock prints

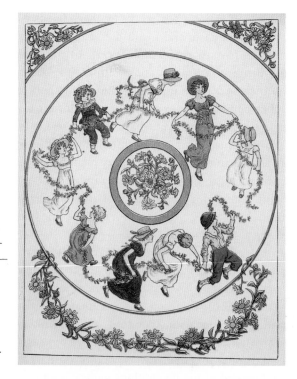

6.14 Kate Greenaway, illustration from *Marigold Garden; Pictures and Rhymes*, wood engraving, 9 5/16 x 6 13/16 in (23.7 x 17.3 cm), published by Frederick Warne & Co., London and New York, c. 1900 (first published 1885).

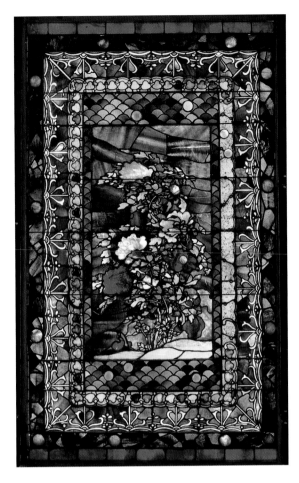

6.15 John La Farge, *Peonies Blown in the Wind*, leaded opalescent glass, 75 x 45 in (190.5 x 113.7 cm), from the Marquand House, Newport, Rhode Island, *c.* 1880. Metropolitan Museum of Art, New York.

their work – mostly from private patrons but also occasionally from public institutions. Both men received training in painting in Paris before turning to the decorative arts (La Farge studied and practiced law before becoming an artist). The new status of the decorative arts as well as the opportunities for commissions for all aspects of interior design influenced Tiffany, who wrote, "I believe there is more in it [i.e. the decorative arts] than in painting pictures." After establishing his own company for interior decoration in 1879, Tiffany became artistic director for the company founded by his father, Charles Tiffany, which manufactured objects in silver and other metals. Both Tiffany and La Farge experimented with new materials and techniques to achieve subtle coloristic effects in their works, Tiffany introducing Favrile glass in 1892 for bowls and vases, and La Farge developing "opalescent" glass for windows. The varied colors and surfaces of La Farge's opalescent glass enriched the iridescence of his windows, producing an effect that resembled the thick impasto of oil paint (fig. 6.15). Tiffany's windows achieve the same richness, but the designer also reached beyond unique commissions to produce a variety of vases and other objects aimed at a wider audience who might appreciate the rich aesthetic effects of a vase or lamp with cast bronze base. In an electric lamp (fig. 6.16) manufactured between 1904 and 1915, the rust and yellow colors of stalks and leaves dominate a few remaining touches of pale green suggesting an autumnal mood. This mood is echoed not only in the drooping curves of the stalks but also on the fallen leaves and petals casually strewn on the base. The subtlety of effect in color,

THE AESTHETIC MOVEMENT IN THE UNITED STATES

In the United States, numerous products of "Aesthetic" design, as well as a pavilion devoted to Japanese art, were displayed at the 1876 Centennial Exhibition in Philadelphia. Five years later, Oscar Wilde made a lecture tour of major American cities where he articulated new attitudes toward the decorative arts. Institutions such as the Metropolitan Museum of Art began to add examples of contemporary furniture and other decorative objects for the home to their collections in an effort to inform and elevate public taste, and schools of design and societies promoting the study and practice of the decorative arts thrived in a number of American cities. In the last quarter of the nineteenth century, American artists turned to the design and manufacture of stained glass and metalwork, achieving considerable success at home and gaining exposure abroad. In the field of stained glass especially, American painters John La Farge (1835–1910) and Louis Comfort Tiffany (1848–1933) received numerous commissions for

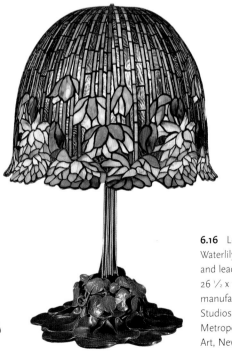

6.16 Louis Comfort Tiffany, Waterlily table lamp, bronze and leaded Favrile glass, 26 ½ x 18 ½ in (67 x 47 cm), manufactured by Tiffany Studios, 1904–15. Metropolitan Museum of Art, New York.

the close relationship between form, techniques of construction, and decoration, the lack of reference to "period" styles, as well as the mood and expressive unity of the whole, mark the high level of interest in the decorative arts in the United States during this time and express the aspirations of the movement to achieve equality among the arts. In addition to inventive experiments with techniques and materials, Tiffany was inspired by a variety of non-Western traditions. For example, he may have been influenced by glass flasks from Persia, both in terms of their translucence and their irregular and asymmetrical shapes (figs. 6.17 and 6.18). For his home near Oyster Bay, Long Island, known as Laurelton Hall (1902–1904 and after), Tiffany created an aesthetic interior in which it was difficult to discern the difference between art and nature: the dining room carpet, like the dome chandelier above the simple table and chairs, set an understated tone in blue and cream, while the transome of the picture window at the far end of the room was decorated with hanging wisteria in stained glass, looking out onto a terrace with hanging potted plants. Visitors remarked the panels looked "lifelike" in relation to the real garden beyond the room (fig. 6.19).

In 1895 Tiffany was asked to design and execute two large glass domes for the new Chicago Public Library on Michigan Avenue. The commission included a dome for the large reading room to the front of the building, as well as a second dome for a room serving as a memorial to soldiers who had died in the Civil War. The glass dome of the larger reading room rises on pendentives from white marble piers covered with mosaic tiles. The color scheme of green, gray, and white is cool, and the overall impression is bright and radiant. Tiffany seems to have been cognizant both of the role of the dome in providing the best use of natural light as well as the need to emphasize contrast and clarity through color and material. The memorial dome is more meditative: somber in color, utilizing mostly orange and brown tones, with foliate motifs filling the leaded glass panels as well as nine sections of frosted glass blocks set into the floor and emitting soft light from below (fig. 6.20). In both rooms Tiffany emphasized the ability of color and light to create a mood appropriate to the function of a designed space, expressing Wilde's statement, quoted above (see page 106), that "mere colour, unspoiled by meaning, and unallied with definite form, can speak to the soul in a thousand different ways. The harmony that resides in the delicate proportions of lines and masses becomes mirrored in the mind ... The marvels of design stir the imagination."

The influence of the Aesthetic Movement may also be seen in the highly individual approach to architecture by Philadelphia architect Frank Furness (1839–1912), who contributed furniture designs to a number of interiors for

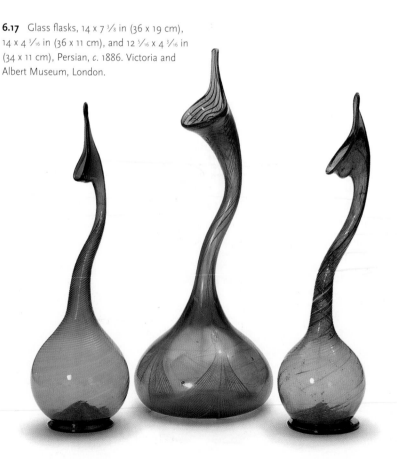

6.17 Glass flasks, 14 x 7 ⅜ in (36 x 19 cm), 14 x 4 ³⁄₁₆ in (36 x 11 cm), and 12 ⁵⁄₁₆ x 4 ³⁄₁₆ in (34 x 11 cm), Persian, c. 1886. Victoria and Albert Museum, London.

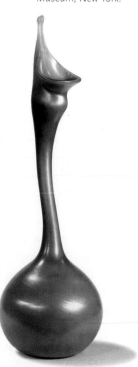

6.18 Louis Comfort Tiffany, Favrile glass vase, 13 ¾ x 3 in (35 x 8 cm), manufactured by Tiffany Studios, 1896–1900. Brooklyn Museum, New York.

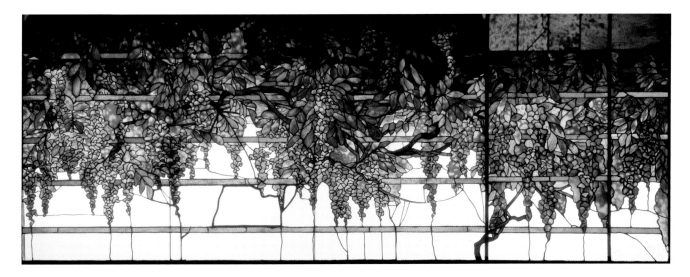

6.19 Louis Comfort Tiffany, Wisteria panel, dining room, Laurelton Hall, leaded Favrile glass, 36 ⁵⁄₁₆ x 47 ⁵⁄₁₆ x 1 in (92.2 x 120.2 x 2.5 cm), manufactured by Tiffany Studios, New York, 1910–1920. The Charles Hosmer Morse Museum of American Art, Winter Park, Florida.

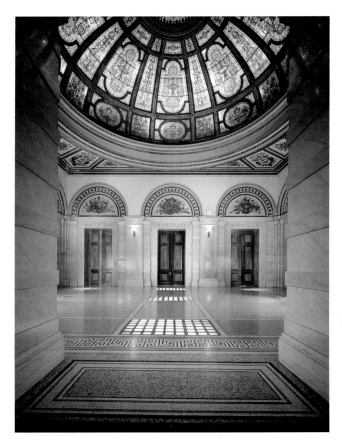

6.20 Louis Comfort Tiffany, War Memorial Room, interior with leaded glass dome and blocks of frosted glass flooring, 1896. Chicago Cultural Center (formerly Chicago Public Library).

plates of Owen's *The Grammar of Ornament* as well as Dresser's *The Art of Decorative Design*. Art furniture is also often associated with the Herter Brothers (Gustave and Christian), German immigrants who established a successful business in New York City that provided comprehensive interior design services in period and original styles featuring the highest levels of skilled craftsmanship and expensive materials for the apartments and mansions of wealthy industrialists such as Jay Gould and William Vanderbilt. An example is a low table with inlaid marquetry panels from the James Goodwin House in Hartford, Connecticut, dating to 1874–8 (fig. 6.21). Such homes were the subject of magazine articles with photographs during

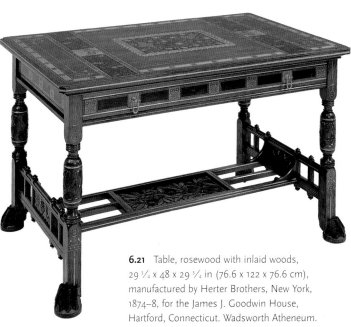

6.21 Table, rosewood with inlaid woods, 29 ¾ x 48 x 29 ¾ in (76.6 x 122 x 76.6 cm), manufactured by Herter Brothers, New York, 1874–8, for the James J. Goodwin House, Hartford, Connecticut. Wadsworth Atheneum.

the buildings he designed. His furniture displays a logical approach to the roles of construction and ornament, and also an original and eclectic combination of Gothic and Islamic features that may derive from familiarity with the

the 1870s and 1880s, in particular the collection entitled *Artistic Houses*, published in 1883, that served to demonstrate American awareness of and identification with current European design trends, stimulated by the displays at the Centennial Exhibition in Philadelphia in 1876.

Although designers such as Tiffany occasionally received important public commissions, the focus of the Aesthetic Movement, both in Europe and in the United States, was the cultivation of the domestic interior as a setting for individual and family life. Rather than the older concept of "household" where generations of parents and children lived or even worked under the same roof, the family home in the later nineteenth century provided a new ideal of comfort, intimacy, social, and self identity, increasingly distinguished from the anonymity and uniformity of the office and factory. Impersonal associations of the city and workplace might be balanced by thinking of the home as a refuge, a place for private and personal activity. The new climate of a consumer culture stimulated by store displays and illustrated advertisements reified these longings in goods and furnishings.

Within this private sphere, women were encouraged to participate in an expanded range of crafts and media traditionally practiced in and associated with the home, including embroidery, woodcarving, and the decoration of pottery. Local decorative arts societies and schools housed exhibitions and offered classes aimed primarily at middle-class women, who might engage in pursuits that were becoming more appreciated as "art," while at the same time maintaining their status and respectability in society and not threatening a traditionally male-dominated workforce. Involvement in the production of household furnishings opened up a sphere of creative activity to women. Candace Wheeler (1827–1923), for instance, founded the Society of Decorative Arts of New York in 1877, the aim of which was to cultivate art forms that were traditionally associated with women such as embroidery and other forms of needlework. Her designs frequently show the inspiration of Japan, and in addition to working in partnership with Tiffany in the early 1880s, she produced designs independently for manufacturers of machine-woven fabrics and wallpapers. Designs such as the textile sample in figure 6.22 use patterns based upon leaf and flower forms but treated in irregular and subjective ways reminiscent not only of Japanese decoration but also of Tiffany's own experiments in glass.

While critical interest in the decorative arts expanded women's range of activity as artists, at the same time the Aesthetic Movement tended to reinforce a type of gender inequality suggested below by the increasing polarization of women's from men's fashions. Despite an elevated status ascribed to the decorative arts as aesthetic expression,

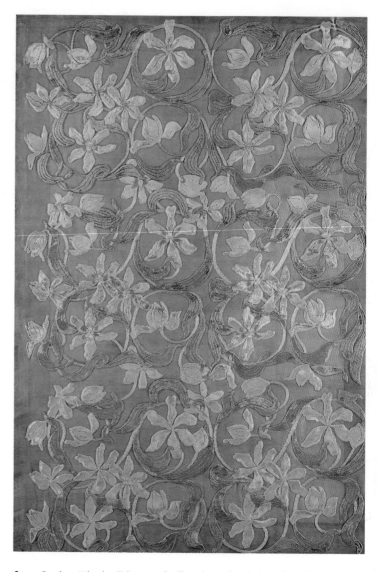

6.22 Candace Wheeler, Tulips panel, silk and metallic cloth appliquéd with silk velvet and embroidered with silk and metallic-wrapped cotton threads, 74 x 50 ½ in (188 x 128.3 cm), for Associated Artists, New York, 1883–1887. Metropolitan Museum of Art, New York.

women's creative activities continued to be associated with traditional domestic roles. Moreover, the women who painted pottery were rarely involved in its production or in the areas of sales or marketing. Such a separation of gender roles can be seen at the 1876 Centennial Exposition in Philadelphia, where women's decorative arts were displayed in a separate pavilion; in 1893, Candace Wheeler was invited to participate in the 1893 International (Columbian) Exposition in Chicago, as designer of the Women's Building.

Ceramic was one of the more prominent media for women's involvement in the Aesthetic Movement in the United States. Women took an active role in the development of art pottery, concentrated primarily in the Northeast and the Midwest. In Cincinnati, for instance,

Maria Longworth (1849–1932) became aware of the Aesthetic Movement through the efforts of British designers who were commissioned to decorate a number of homes for wealthy Cincinnati families. The list included her father's estate, called Rookwood, as well as the home she lived in with her first husband, George Nichols. Longworth studied ceramics at the University of Cincinnati's School of Design, and helped to organize the Cincinnati Pottery Club. With the backing of her father, she founded the Rookwood Pottery in 1880. Examples of Rookwood ceramics received medals at the 1889 Exposition Universelle in Paris and a number of them (fig. 6.23) show the assimilation of Japanese-inspired techniques in the use of irregular forms and asymmetrical arrangements of decorative motifs; indeed, the presence of Japanese ceramic artist Kataro Shirayamadani at Rookwood beginning in 1887 had an impact on the company's production. Rookwood Pottery and the work of other local ceramicists, such as Longworth's rival Mary Louise McLaughlin (1847–1939), made Cincinnati a center for the production of aesthetic ceramics, fostered as well through the publication of books and the training offered at the University of Cincinnati and private schools.

Adelaide Alsop Robineau (1865–1929) was another woman artist who explored new directions in ceramics around the turn of the century. Robineau worked in Minnesota, St. Louis, Missouri, and later in Syracuse, New York, and became aware of aesthetic tendencies in the decorative arts through international exhibitions, particularly the Columbian Exhibition in Chicago in 1893. Her Viking Ship vase from 1905 (fig. 6.24) combines carved

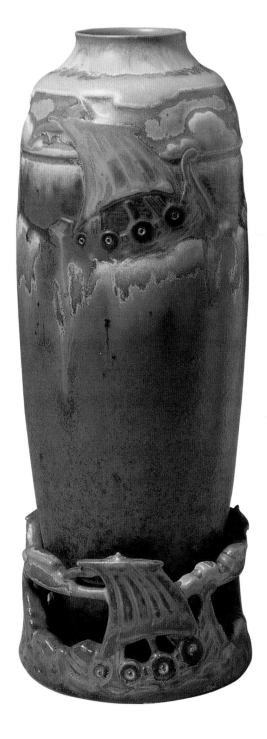

6.24 Adelaide Alsop Robineau, Viking Ship vase, porcelain, 7 ¼ x 2 ¾ in (18.4 x 7 cm), 1905. Everson Museum of Art, Syracuse, New York.

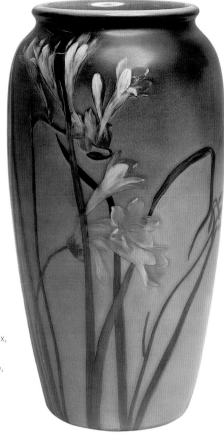

6.23 Harriet Elizabeth Wilcox, vase with sprays of freesia, earthenware with painted slip, height 22 ⅛ in (56.6 cm), manufactured by Rookwood Pottery, Cincinnati, 1900.

and molded decoration with smoother wheel-thrown shapes and attention to the irregularities of surface and overlapping glazes to suggest a wind-tossed sailboat in a seemingly unlikely medium. Robineau's work stretched the expressive possibilities of her medium in original directions more commonly associated with the arts of sculpture and painting.

Even with the professional limitations noted above, women's achievements in the decorative arts were considerable and their participation more common than in the fine arts. Despite the emphasis upon the equality of the arts in the Aesthetic Movement, women still moved less easily into the fine arts, and even painters such as Mary Cassatt (1844–1926), who studied in Philadelphia before settling in Paris in 1874, tended to be limited both in their choice of subject matter and of medium. Cassatt, for instance, worked extensively in pastel, which was thought to be a less demanding and more appropriate medium for women artists than oil.

Some women rebelled more radically against the restrictions implied by a domestic role. Gaining momentum in the early twentieth century, a group of early feminists looked to apply production technology toward liberating women from the drudgery of household work. While books such as Catherine Beecher's 1869 *The American Woman's Home* advocated a scientific approach to household management – in short a "domestic" economy or science that would enable women to organize household work more efficiently and provide opportunities for more creative pursuits – they did not question the underlying assumption that a woman's place was in the home. Other feminist writers and activists felt that a socialized approach to household management, where facilities for laundry, cooking, and childcare were maintained communally rather than within the family unit, promised greater freedom for women and could utilize technology more efficiently. Some feminists saw potential in machinery for dishwashing and laundry that might be maintained in separate facilities rather than in the home, while others felt that communal facilities for childcare also would contribute to integrating women into the workforce. Some of these ideas reached fruition in settlement houses and apartments, efforts to redefine living in response to industrialization and urbanization in the later nineteenth century. Such facilities, often open, spacious, and with a factorylike functionality, were meant to replace private kitchens and cooking areas in houses with more modern and efficient areas where working women would be able to pick up prepared meals for their families. Such experiments reveal the existence of alternatives to the nuclear family and the individual home that lie at the root of both the Arts and Crafts and the Aesthetic movements. In focusing upon the decorative arts, both movements recognized and even encouraged the creative participation of women, yet at the same time reinforced the identification of woman with the domestic sphere. On the other hand, material feminists sought a more radical gender equality based not upon the elevation of craft to fine art but rather upon a communal approach to modern living that questioned fundamental concepts of home and family and the gender roles they supported.

Dress

Attitudes toward women in the later nineteenth century may also be gleaned from a consideration of dress and fashion. Another indication of the wider diffusion of ideas about the equality of the arts and the new, elevated status surrounding the decorative arts is the emergence of high fashion or haute couture in Paris in the second half of the nineteenth century. The profession of fashion designer is almost synonymous with Charles Frederick Worth (1825–1895), who worked in London in the textile trade before moving to Paris with his wife and securing commissions for garments from the Empress Eugénie as well as other wealthy patrons beginning in the 1850s. Worth created the ideal image for aristocratic women in the later nineteenth century – in an age when some fashionable ladies rarely, if ever, wore the same garment twice, and when weekend parties might require several changes of clothing in a single day. Worth's wider success in Parisian society was made possible through the sewing machine, which accelerated the pace of constructing elaborate garments by the many seamstresses he employed. Worth also introduced more comfortable surroundings for buying and selling, invented fall and spring lines for fashion to stimulate consumer interest, and designed his clothing in closer relation to the human body, reducing if not eliminating some of the confining undergarments that characterized earlier formal dress. Certainly Worth's success grew from an emerging aesthetic interest in and appreciation for the varied textural and coloristic effects of fabrics, as seen for instance in the portraits of the French artist Jean-Auguste-Dominique Ingres (1780–1867), whose painstaking technique captured the nuances of light falling on the folds of the dress of his subject Mme. Moitessier in a painting from 1851 (fig. 6.25). Curiously, as interest in women's fashion grew in the mid-nineteenth century, fashions for men became both more practical as well as anonymous in the general adoption of trouser suits and a preference for black. While men and women competed for individual distinction in dress through the early nineteenth century, the increasing emphasis upon women's fashion in the later part of the century expresses portrait of Worth depicts the designer wearing a beret, reminiscent of a famous Rembrandt self-portrait.

While the products of the Aesthetic Movement were often made to order or sold in small shops and boutiques for an exclusive clientele, the experience of shopping for the middle class was revolutionized in the 1860s with the emergence of department stores both in Europe and in the United States. These large stores, with varied goods sold under the same roof, provided a permanent setting for the "spectacle of consumption" as witnessed in international exhibitions. Department stores such as the Bon Marché in Paris and John Wanamaker in Philadelphia endeavored to turn shopping into a pleasurable and transformative experience that encouraged shoppers to identify consumption with the fulfillment of an idealized dream of comfort, luxury, self-improvement, and self-realization.

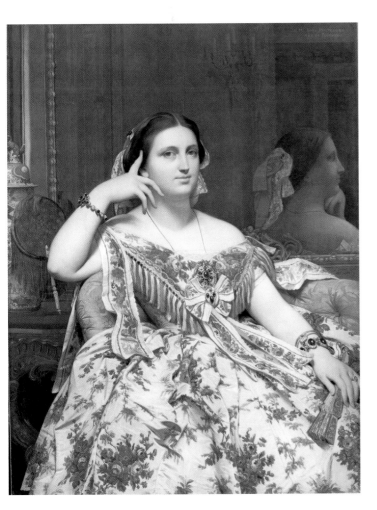

6.25 Jean-Auguste-Dominique Ingres, *Mme. Moitessier, seated*, oil on canvas, 47 ¼ x 42 ¼ in (120 x 107 cm), 1851. National Gallery, London.

gender discrimination: women's "preoccupation" with fashion signaled they had no need to work; indeed to do so would be to bring into question their husbands' ability to support them. Furthermore, married women were not encouraged to work, and the elaboration and complexity of much women's fashion suggests an impracticality that reinforces inactivity.

The unique place occupied by Worth is due to his sovereignty as an artist–designer, creating an individual and distinctive "look" for each patron, reflecting the patron's good "taste" and the designer's creativity and originality. Worth experimented with varieties of fabric for nuances of color, texture, and light, not unlike the interest of designers such as Tiffany or La Farge in the subtleties of reflection for colored leaded glass (see page 113). Such effects can be seen in the portrait of one of Worth's clients by the German portrait painter Franz Xavier Winterhalter (1805–1873), displaying the stiff folds and sparkling accents of gold thread in a garment made of silk tulle (fig. 6.26). Not surprisingly, the best-known photographic

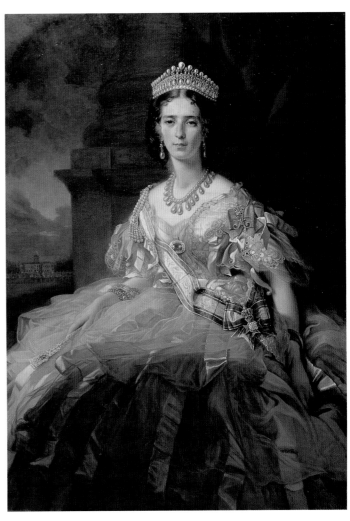

6.26 Franz Xavier Winterhalter, portrait of Princess Tatyana Alexandrovna Yusupova wearing a spangled tulle dress by Charles Worth, oil on canvas, 57 ⅞ x 40 ¹⁵⁄₁₆ in (147 x 104 cm), 1858. The Hermitage Museum, St. Petersburg.

Design, which elevated goods above utility and function, played an integral role in this commercial expansion engendered by the department store. These stores housed displays for furniture, fabrics and other home furnishings, as well as foods, all purchased in large quantities and sold at fixed prices (rather than by bartering between customer and vendor) with "specials" and seasonal sales to entice prospective buyers. Their success also depended upon quantity production of basic types of goods differentiated by a variety of styles of decoration, whether dresses with applied trims of different patterns of lace, or cabinets with decoration in a variety of historical period styles that had begun to emerge around the middle of the century. As an example we can illustrate two plates from a book of furniture designs published in England by furniture manufacturer Henry Whitaker in 1847 (fig. 6.27). The illustrations reveal the strong similarity among the sideboards, differentiated only by carved decoration in the "Elizabethan" and "Italian" styles. This is perhaps a far cry from the kind of furniture that aspired to be "art" in the sense envisioned by either Oscar Wilde or even William Morris, and yet it possessed "design," in that it rose above utility to some higher level of meaning, and thus signified progress and discriminating taste for the new middle-class retail market, forging some relationship between industry and art.

Advice books such as Eastlake's *Hints on Household Taste* and others demonstrate the close relationship between women, shopping, and self-identity. Rather than emphasizing the making of objects, either in terms of labor or design, this expansion of commerce focused instead upon the associations or connections between buyers and objects, as projections or extensions of their identity. By the end of the century, shoppers visiting department stores such as Harrods in Knightsbridge, London (only a short walk from the Victoria and Albert Museum) were treated to colorfully designed and brightly lit interiors with walls and ceilings that were covered with enamel-like patterned glazed tiles: an example is Harrods' Meat Hall, dating to 1902 (fig. 6.28). In addition to stimulating commercial activity, department stores offered free concerts and recitals that provided accepted, elevated forms of public entertainment – another demonstration of the link between design and generalized progress in an emerging consumer society.

DESIGN REFORM IN FRANCE: L'ART NOUVEAU

Although the image of "Art Nouveau" brings to mind the swirling linear style associated with posters, furniture, and applied decoration in the 1890s in France, the term is perhaps best understood in the broader context of later nineteenth-century ideas about aesthetic design and the unity of the arts as they took root on French soil.

As numerous Realist and Impressionist paintings of the period reveal, the 1860s and 1870s in Paris witnessed far-reaching changes in the character of urban life, beginning with the construction of grand boulevards, bridges, monuments, piazzas, and public gardens under Napoleon III (r. 1852–1870) and civic planner, Eugène-Georges Haussmann (1809–1891), and continuing with the building of the Paris Opèra and the emergence of other middle-class forms of entertainment. There was significant commercial expansion of the city as well, for instance in the opening of Bon Marché in 1862 and other department

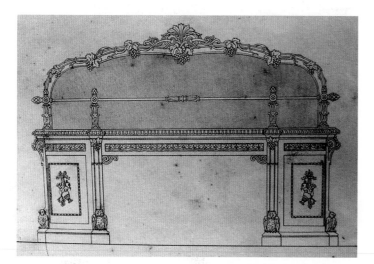 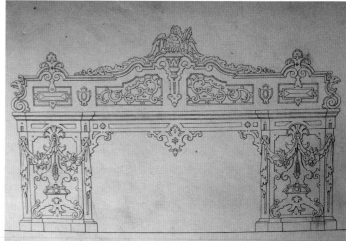

6.27 Henry Whitaker, two illustrations of sideboards in Elizabethan and Italian styles, from the furniture catalogue *Practical Cabinet Maker's Treasure*, London, 1847.

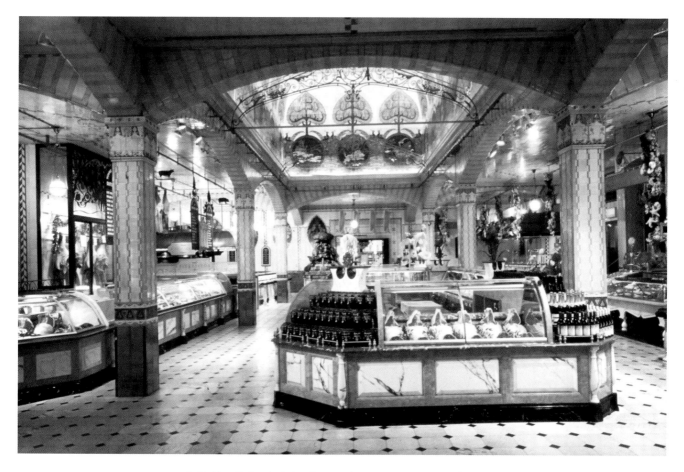

6.28 Meat Hall with tiled walls, Harrods Department Store, London, 1902.

stores that soon followed. Middle-class life was viewed as a "spectator sport," and writers used the term *flâneur* to describe that type of gentleman who delighted in strolling the avenues, window shopping, or meeting friends at a café. Casual slices of this new life of strolling and coffee breaks are captured in paintings such as Manet's *Corner in a Café Concert* (1878–9, fig. 6.29). International exhibitions of art and industry, modeled on the Crystal Palace, were also part of public life in Paris during the second half of the nineteenth century, being staged first in 1855, again in 1867 and repeated in 1878, 1889, and 1900.

The department stores' need for larger quantities of furniture placed inordinate pressures upon the system of workshop production, forcing artisans to increase production while receiving the same or even lower wages, leading to standardization, a decline in quality, and deterioration in working conditions. In part as a response to these circumstances, a private organization of manufacturers and skilled artisans known as the Central Union of Fine Art as Applied to Industry was created as early as 1864 to promote high standards in design based upon the harmony of beauty and utility, standards inherited from the design reform movement in Britain (see page 57

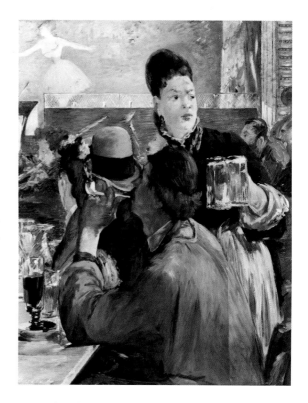

6.29 Edouard Manet, *Corner in a Café Concert*, oil on canvas, 39 ¼ x 30 ½ in (100 x 77.5 cm), 1878–9. National Gallery, London.

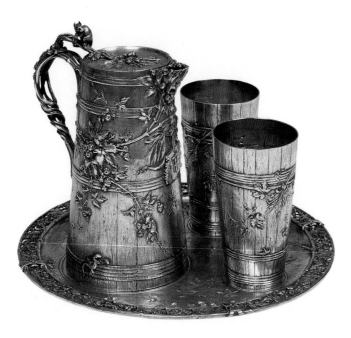

6.30 Fannière Frères, beer service, silver with gilt, pitcher 9 x 5 in (23 x 12.5 cm), 1865. Musée d'Orsay, Paris.

onward). The Central Union sponsored exhibitions and even created a "library" where artisans and manufacturers might consult drawings as models for production. The silver and gilt beer service (fig. 6.30) by Fannière Frères dating to 1865 illustrates the aims of the Central Union at this time. It features a naturalistic approach to decoration rather than a relationship with past styles, and the depiction of kegs exemplifies "fitness" of decoration to purpose also recalling aspects of design reform in Britain earlier in the century, where decoration might "illustrate" or at least allude to the purpose of an object (even though it hardly "improves" its function). Certainly the membership of the Central Union took an interest in elevating the quality of the applied arts in France and in educating consumers and manufacturers, but increasingly the efforts of this organization moved away from an involvement in the improvement of industrial production for a broader public toward both the restoration and renewal of the luxury crafts and the reputation they enjoyed during the eighteenth century. In fact, after 1889 the organization dropped the word "industrial" from its title, and concentrated instead upon promoting the strength of the country's artisanal heritage. Industrial production was increasingly associated with uniformity, poor quality, and unfavorable competition with other nations, and also was viewed as a betrayal of a significant cultural legacy. Such issues were contested among contemporary critics, often in relation to the displays at international exhibitions. Some critics praised the highest levels of technical skill and art as applied to manufacture, while others noted a movement away from concerns with elevating the taste of the middle classes through more practical products and furnishings.

In addition to reviving appreciation for the eighteenth century, advocates for design reform in France also encouraged contemporary approaches that displayed high levels of originality, and sophistication. German-born merchant Siegfried Bing (1838–1905) was involved in the activities of the Central Union. Bing collected and sold examples of Japanese decorative arts in Paris, published a journal devoted to his vision of Japanese art and culture (*Japon Artistique*), and helped to mount exhibitions of Japanese crafts that he admired for their refinement and the craftsmen's feeling for the nature of materials. Bing encouraged contemporary French designers to create new and original works, and visited the United States in 1893 where he saw and praised the work of Louis Comfort Tiffany in stained glass (see pages 113–114).

In 1895 Bing transformed his gallery of Japanese arts into showrooms with the name Le Maison de l'Art Nouveau featuring Japanese crafts as well as contemporary interiors designed by Tiffany and Belgian artist and designer Henry van de Velde (1863–1957; see fig. 6.54). Despite the eclectic and international character of Le Maison de l'Art Nouveau, Bing felt that the work was unified by its refinement and quality, demonstrating the kind of modern "renewal" of craft that would inspire artists and artisans and appeal to discriminating taste. Some critics, however, complained that the Le Maison de l'Art Nouveau showrooms lacked a more obvious stylistic coherence, and as a result Bing realized the necessity of appealing to a French audience with a more consistent and recognizable "French" style.

In this climate of strong national feeling, a number of French designers emerged whose works demonstrated respect for and continuity with the high levels of craftsmanship in eighteenth-century luxury goods and furnishings, yet without imitating their forms. This pride in the past merged with more modern concepts of artistic originality seen, for instance, in the works of French Symbolist artists, who saw the arts as the vehicle for subjective expression leading away from the more optical style of Impressionism in the 1870s and the early interest of those painters in the urban pastimes of the middle class. Such qualities emerge, for instance, in the glass objects designed and crafted by Émile Gallé (1846–1904), who trained as a glassmaker in the city of Nancy in northeast France. Gallé experimented with color, light, and texture in the medium of glass, exploring effects beyond the traditional associations with the material. Many works are highly individual, more like relief sculptures in glass than utilitarian objects. In his Waterlilies vase of 1901 (fig. 6.31), the flamelike shapes of the petals and leaves are lightly etched against an unevenly textured background with translucent colors ranging from lavender to blue to indigo. The irregular convex shapes of the surface not only accentuate the subtlety of the light but also suggest the reflections of clouds in a pond and imply their presence. Gallé's heightened sensitivity to nature and obsessive manipulation of materials to obtain the most delicate and subtle effects of light are contemporary with the series of studies of the same subject by Claude Monet (1840–1926) as well as the similar explorations of translucence and iridescence in glass by Tiffany and La Farge. Although perhaps less abstract, the feeling for growth, transformation, and juxtaposition in Gallé's works anticipate the automatic techniques of Surrealism in the 1920s, and in fact both movements were influenced by contemporary ideas about dreams and the unconscious. Gallé's work shares with Symbolist artists an interest in private, psychological experience, and the primacy of feeling and mood

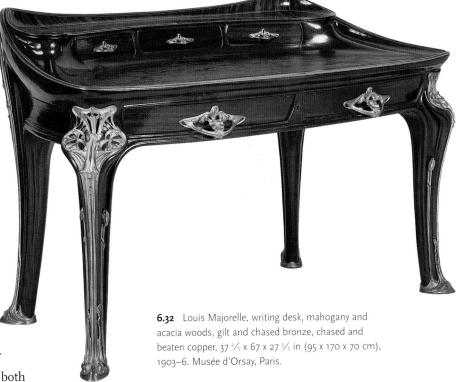

6.32 Louis Majorelle, writing desk, mahogany and acacia woods, gilt and chased bronze, chased and beaten copper, 37 ²/₅ x 67 x 27 ³/₅ in (95 x 170 x 70 cm), 1903–6. Musée d'Orsay, Paris.

over purely optical experience. Gallé was inspired by the Symbolist poets Charles Baudelaire (1821–1867) and Paul Verlaine (1844–1896), and phrases from their verse are sometimes etched directly in the glass surfaces of his objects. Such works achieve one of the aims of the later Central Union: to revitalize the arts by obliterating any boundary between them and restore the shared esteem in which French luxury products in several media were held in an increasingly competitive international market.

Like Tiffany, Gallé not only produced unique objects but was interested in the unified interior as a total work of art. He designed furniture for workshop production featuring carved forms but relying primarily upon elaborate marquetry for intricate linear and spatial effects. By employing more modern production techniques and woodworking machines, Louis Majorelle (1859–1926), who also worked in Nancy, made furniture in the Art Nouveau style available to a wider audience. His writing desk (fig. 6.32) includes gilt mounts that recall more directly the heritage of eighteenth-century Rococo furniture. Related desks by Majorelle include attached electric light fixtures in the shape of exotic orchids. Throughout the design of the desk, Majorelle conceives of decoration as something both expressive and more integral rather than interchangeable or "added on" to construction.

The boundary between sculpture and furniture is virtually eliminated in the highly original works of Rupert

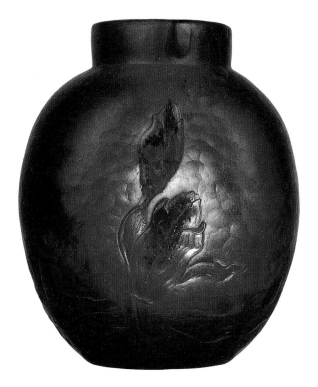

6.31 Emile Gallé, Waterlilies vase, glass, height 10 ½ in (26.7 cm), c. 1901. Private collection.

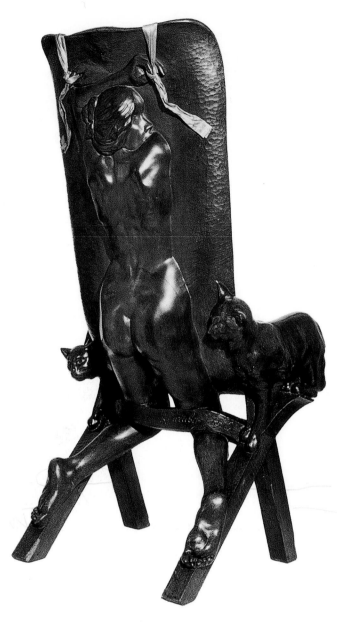

brushwork and surface among the Symbolist painters. Pierre-Adrien Dalpayrat (1844–1910) experimented with uneven or "unfinished" textures and irregular shapes, revealing a strong sense of process, suggestion, and the sensitive manipulation of materials by the artist (fig. 6.34). While this type of work does not have a stylistic similarity with the linear rhythms more commonly associated with French Art Nouveau, it nevertheless shares with other examples of the period the vision of craft as a vehicle for psychological expression through the exploration of original aesthetic effects. It is interesting to note that this emphasis upon the expressive possibilities of texture and overlays of glaze is parallel to the increasing autonomy of the artwork noted by artists such as Maurice Denis (1870–1943), who stated that a "picture, before being a battle horse, a nude, an anecdote or whatnot, is essentially a flat surface covered with colors assembled in a certain order."

In 1901, the Société des Artistes Décorateurs was established in France to protect the status of the applied arts against any encroachments by industry and to reinforce the unity and equality of the arts that Art Nouveau sought to achieve. During this period the decorative arts

6.33 Rupert Carabin, armchair, walnut, 43 ¹¹⁄₁₆ x 24 ³⁄₁₆ in (111 x 63 cm), 1898. Private collection.

Carabin (1862–1932), who worked in Paris beginning in the later 1870s. Carabin's one-of-a-kind pieces often sacrifice practicality to a highly original artistic vision that undermines traditional assumptions about furniture. A carved chair (fig. 6.33) dating to 1898 not only tests the limits of comfort, but surrounds the sitter with the unsettling feeling of a primeval forest inhabited by snakes and dryads.

In addition to glass and furniture, ceramics was another area of great vitality for French decorative artists. Asymmetrical forms, irregular surface textures, and the subtle overlaying of glazes suggest experiment and intuition in the manipulation of the medium, again parallel to the contemporary interest in expressive

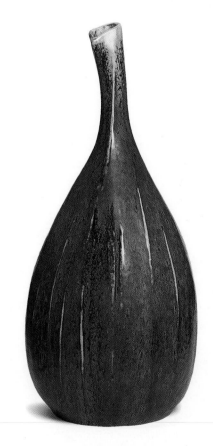

6.34 Pierre-Adrien Dalpayrat, gourd stoneware vase, 14 ½ x 6 ½ in (36.8 x 16.5 cm), 1893–1900. Victoria and Albert Museum, London.

acquired associations with originality and expression, while the fine arts were increasingly recognized for their autonomy from the imitation of nature and an appreciation for their "truth to materials" or medium. Artists freely crossed the increasingly permeable border between fine art and applied design, among them Odilon Redon (1840–1916), Pierre Bonnard (1867–1947), Maurice Denis, and Édouard Vuillard (1868–1940). These artists pursued associations of the word "decorative" that suggested personal and expressive possibilities in a variety of media beyond easel painting: working, for instance, in lithography, wallpaper design, and painted screens, though often for private commissions rather than more broadly commercial manufacture. Among their efforts might be included those of Lucien Pissarro (1863–1944), the son of Impressionist painter Camille Pissarro (1830–1903), who pursued a career in book publishing, but left France for London where an active private press movement held the promise of an even more receptive audience (see page 110 and fig. 6.12).

ART NOUVEAU IN PRINT AND IN PUBLIC

As mentioned above, strengthening the relationship between art and industry served many interests, for extending individual artistic activity beyond the fine arts, for elevating public taste, and for connecting products with the promise of individual progress and fulfillment. In the increasingly commercial conditions of metropolitan centers such as Paris, the new aesthetic sensibility seen in the decorative arts formed part of a more generalized modernity that extended to a broader and more heterogeneous public. At the Exposition Universelle held in Paris in 1900, l'Art Nouveau dominated the architectural constructions for the fair and interiors on display featured coordinated ensembles of decorative art in the new style. French architect and designer Hector Guimard (1867–1942) was particularly conspicuous in externalizing elements of l'Art Nouveau. Guimard adapted the elastic plantlike tendrils and flowers associated with many products of aesthetic crafts to the railings and entrances to the newly constructed Paris underground transportation system known as the Métro, a few of which are still in use (fig. 6.35). Cast iron was used for this vast project, integrating invention with modern industrial techniques of production in the public sphere. Guimard also used cast iron for the design of window grilles and a series of original numbers to mark the entrances to houses and buildings. In these ways the arts served a socially progressive role, beautifying the city, utilizing modern technology, attracting tourism and trade, and suggesting a cooperation rather than antithesis between art and industry.

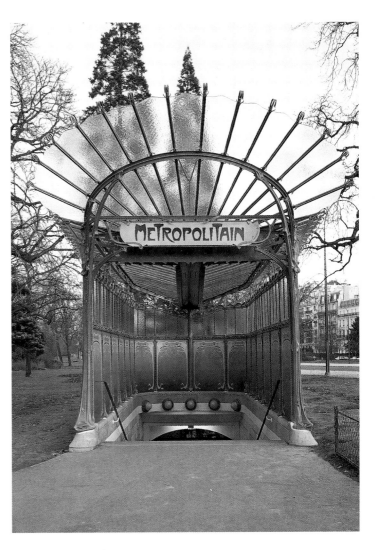

6.35 Hector Guimard, Métro station entrance, cast iron, Porte Dauphine, Paris, c. 1900.

Elements of Art Nouveau were also popularized via print media, chiefly in the design of posters, made possible through the technical development of chromolithography. Posters were an effective and, most importantly, a colorful means of advertising products, stores, nightclubs, and cafés, and were a ubiquitous presence in the city, enlivening walls, buildings, and kiosks along the grands boulevards. Among the most significant class of patrons for poster advertisement during this time were the providers of popular entertainment, as well as the printers themselves, who produced posters for sale to collectors as well as in larger sizes for public advertisements. The dance halls, circuses, and cabarets located in Parisian districts such as Montmartre served as a focus for middle-class leisure, in particular that element representing freer, less structured, and uninhibited public forms of self-expression. Whether as participants or spectators, this public found an outlet for playfulness, fantasy, and sensual pleasure in street traffic and nightlife.

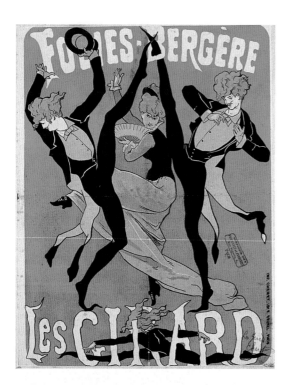

6.36 Jules Cheret, *Les Girard*, poster for the Folies-Bergère, color lithograph, 21 ¼ x 17 ⅛ in (54 x 44.5 cm), 1879. Musée de la Publicité, Paris.

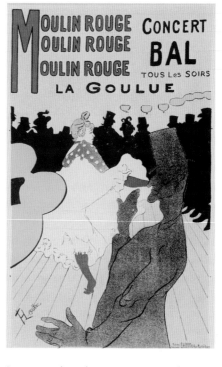

6.37 Henri de Toulouse-Lautrec, *La Goulue (Louise Weber) at the Moulin Rouge*, poster, color lithograph, 33 x 48 in (83.8 x 122 cm), 1891.

Jules Cheret (1836–1932) was an early master of poster design, beginning his career as an apprentice to a printer and spending time in England mastering the technique of chromolithography, which had been successfully developed in the printing of color images primarily for illustrated books (see page 68 and fig. 4.12). Cheret often approached the composition of the poster as an integration of text and image to create a unified design on a monumental scale, even if the actual size of the poster was not particularly large. In the poster advertising a group of acrobatic dancers known as *Les Girard* from 1879 (fig. 6.36), for example, areas of bold text at the top and bottom of the tall rectangular format announce the venue and particular act or time of the performance. The placement of the letters deviates from the strict horizontal format, and instead connects and interacts with the three silhouetted dancers in the center, almost like a prop for their elongated limbs. The sense of movement is strengthened by pinwheel-like shapes of arms, legs, and coat tails, and by the virtual elimination of detail and background. Cheret explored the medium of chromolithography in order to achieve these effects, in particular by working directly on the stone in an abbreviated, exaggerated manner in order to obtain the most spontaneous effects.

An expressive treatment of line, as well as simplified compositional elements derived from Japanese woodblock prints, can also be found in the lithographic posters of painter Henri de Toulouse-Lautrec (1864–1901), which often advertised the performances of popular Montmartre entertainers such as Löie Fuller and Louise Weber (known as La Goulue). The latter is featured in a poster of 1891 for the Moulin Rouge (fig. 6.37), printed in a large edition of 3,000 for public display throughout Paris. In this poster the illustration is simplified by strong contours for the foreground figures of Valentine le Désossé and La Goulue herself, while the silhouetted forms of the crowd and typography maintain the planarity of the image and unify the elements of the composition into a compact whole. For his posters Toulouse-Lautrec also worked directly on the lithographic stone, using strong contours as well as a technique known as "crachis" to splatter rather than to brush ink on broad areas of the lithographic stone. From this approach a vitality emerges to match the mood of gaiety and hedonistic abandon that generates appeal for an evening of casual and spontaneous entertainment. From their beginnings, the chromolithographic poster led a double life as advertisement and as artwork. Designers signed their work and printers issued them in separate, sometimes smaller format, for collectors. They provided the commercial sector with an added value as promotions for a new, reproducible form of public art, made popular entertainment appealing through associations with a carefree and uninhibited lifestyle, while at the same time enabled the expressive ideas of the aesthetic movement to

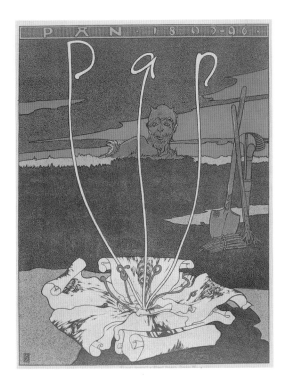

6.38 Joseph Sattler, cover for *Pan*, color lithograph, 15 ¹¹/₁₆ x 9 ⁵/₁₆ in (40 x 23.5 cm), 1895. Victoria and Albert Museum, London.

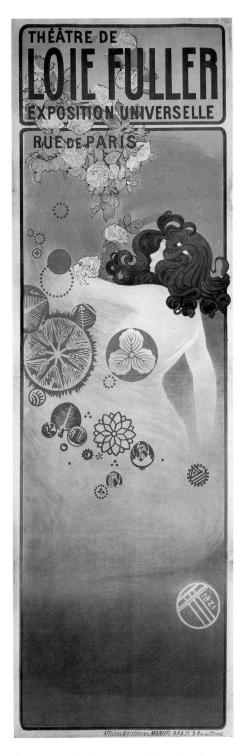

6.39 Manuel Orazi, poster for Löie Fuller, color lithograph, 78 ¼ x 25 ¼ in (198.7 x 64.1 cm), 1900.

extend beyond a narrow, exclusive circle of initiated viewers. They also demonstrated the power of simplified images to attract attention and identify performers such as La Goulue, Aristide Bruant, or Löie Fuller by particular gestures, attributes, or signs, to become familiar through their graphic image in advertising.

Although in a smaller format, another vehicle for graphic design of the period was illustrated covers for magazines. These were generally aimed at a more aesthetically minded audience. An example is the cover for the Berlin-based periodical *Pan*, designed by Joseph Sattler (1867–1931) in 1895 (fig. 6.38). The journal's founder and editor was Julius Meier-Graefe, who operated a boutique for modern decorative arts in Paris called the Maison Moderne and was a strong advocate for the unity of the arts. In the cover illustration for *Pan*, the mythological half-goat, half-man Greek god peeks out from behind the tendrils of elongated plant forms that happen to also be the extensions of the letters that make up the title (smaller red tendrils morph into the numbers "1895"). The tendrils in turn emerge from leaves of a plant that resembles rolled sheets of parchment or papyrus, suggesting that the vines that make up of the word "Pan" are also calligraphic strokes of a pen. Respecting the flatness of the page, Sattler was able to connect the various representational and typographic elements of the composition into a new, decidedly modern art form. In Sattler's example the

equality and interrelationship of the elements in the layout inspired both originality and experimentation in the medium of chromolithography.

Turning to the Chicago-born performance artist Löie Fuller (1862–1928), both Cheret and painter Manuel Orazi (1860–1934) designed advertising posters featuring this popular entertainer (fig. 6.39). Orazi hints at an erotic

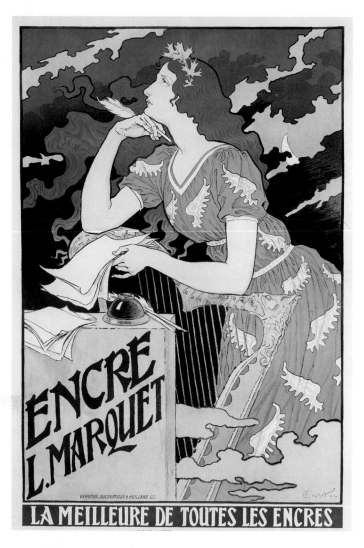

6.40 Eugène Samuel Grasset, advertisement for Marquet Ink, color lithograph, 47 ¹⁵/₁₆ x 31 ¹³/₁₆ in (121.8 x 80.8 cm), 1892.

into flames or pure decoration in the chromolithographic art poster, is here found in the human figure in movement. Historians have noted a relationship between artists' aesthetic fascination with this theme of transformation in nature and Darwin's theory of natural selection (first published in 1859), which revealed nature in a constant condition of flux rather than permanence, while at the same time guided by a process of selection toward perfection. The dancer's appeal certainly incorporated an abstract aesthetic dimension, but also extended to other audiences, who were attracted by the excitement of novelty, fantasy, sensuality, and the anticipation of the unexpected.

Eugène-Samuel Grasset (1841–1917) was an illustrator and advertising artist who developed a style for graphic images sometimes referred to as cloisonné. His approach uses strong black lines and figure–ground contrast to reinforce the planarity of the surface, while the linear treatment of drapery folds or strands of wavy hair create secondary patterns resembling the cells of leaded glass or jewelry, two media in which Grasset also worked. In an advertisement for Encre L. Marquet (Marquet Ink) the diagonal lettering runs parallel to wavy cloudlike shapes that balance the opposing diagonal direction of a woman who sits thoughtfully, pen in hand (fig. 6.40). Grasset's figures are often less spontaneous and abbreviated than those of Cheret or Toulouse-Lautrec. Nevertheless, female images dominate the art of the poster; they represent the "good life" when linked to the purchase of products and entertainment, and they offer new models for defining women in more active roles outside the home, as in American artist Will Bradley's advertising poster for Victor Bicycles (see fig. 6.42).

Alphonse Mucha (1860–1939) came to Paris from his home in Moravia (Czech Republic). His posters advertising the performances of actress Sarah Bernhardt were effective in promoting the actress's career in Paris. Many of Mucha's posters employ a severely vertical format in which figures are framed by arches or other more exotic architectural motifs that suggest the imagined world of the theater stage, and which also provide a frame for expressive lettering. In the 1895 *Gismonda* poster (fig. 6.41), the actress's costume features decorative brocade patterns that relate to the palm (referring to the play's final act in which Bernhardt is part of an Easter Day procession) and garlanded hair. The arch framing the actress's head, as well as a banner below the ground line, frame the text and link it to the image. Despite foreshortening and shadow, the simplified modeling emphasizes a heroic monumentality and the dreamlike space of the stage. Later posters are freer in the use of abstraction to suggest metamorphosis, especially in the kinds of abstract treatment of shape to suggest hair or lush plant forms.

component in the dancer's performance by outlining the partially nude body beneath a sheer garment. Orazi's poster also has a stronger sense of abstract and suggestive forms: hair, flowers, drapery become swirling and cascading shapes making it difficult to distinguish representation from more purely expressive, abstract decoration. Löie Fuller's dance was also the subject of a series of 15 ceramic figurines designed by Agathon Léonard (1841–1923) for the Sèvres manufactory in 1898 and displayed at the 1900 International Exhibition in Paris. In addition, Fuller's performance was captured on moving film in the early years of this new medium's development. On film there appears to be little if any suggestion of nudity. Rather we see the dancer's white scarf and circular arm movements combine to somehow transform her body into the form of a flower in bloom as if by magic. The theme of metamorphosis, seen in the transformation of letterforms into representation or hair

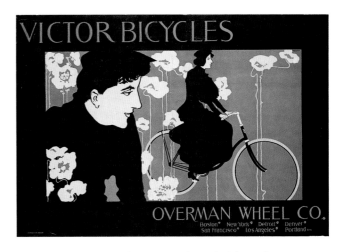

6.42 Will Bradley, poster for Victor Bicycles, color lithograph, 25 ¹³⁄₁₆ x 39 ¹⁄₁₆ in (64.4 x 99.7 cm), 1896. Victoria and Albert Museum, London.

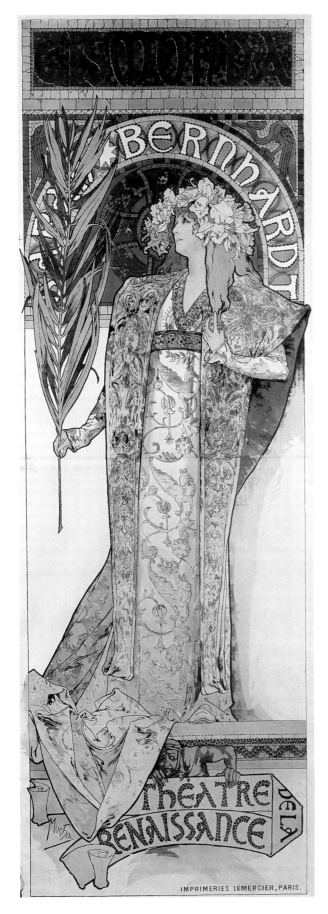

6.41 Alphonse Mucha, *Sarah Bernhardt in Gismonda*, poster, color lithograph, 84 ¼ x 30 in (216.3 x 76.2 cm), 1895.

In the United States, *Harper's Magazine* published cover illustrations by Eugène Grasset as well as by American designers such as Edward Penfield (1866–1925), while some of the boldest approaches to the medium can be seen in the oeuvre of Will Bradley (1868–1962). Bradley's early illustrations, influenced by Aubrey Beardsley (see page 110), had appeared in the British journal *The Studio*, and examples of his work were exhibited at the opening of Le Maison de l'Art Nouveau in 1895 at Siegfried Bing's invitation. In the United States Bradley was active in many areas of the expanding print media. He published illustrated books for his own private and short-lived Wayside Press in Springfield, Massachusetts, and also contributed to a magazine called *The American Chap-Book,* published by the American Type Founders Company (see page 98) as well as the trade journal *Inland Printer.* As seen in an 1896 advertising poster for Victor Bicycles (fig. 6.42), Bradley used four colors to create a strong and coherent image. Repetition in the black silhouettes of the riders and in the elongated floral decoration constitutes another form of simplification, while the use of black ties the border with its lettering to the image. Bradley's posters and illustration also create effective figure–ground reversal – for instance, in the negative shapes created between the arm and torso of the larger female rider.

The public and commercial expression of Art Nouveau also emerges in the design of interiors and displays related to fantasy and the experience of shopping. Jeweler Georges Fouquet collaborated with Alphonse Mucha on several brooches and

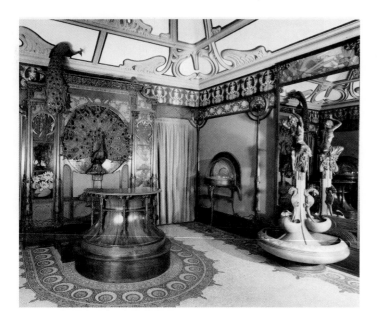

6.43 Alphonse Mucha, interior for boutique, Paris, for Georges Fouquet, jeweler, 1900. Photograph: Musée Carnavalet, Paris.

other pieces, and Mucha was responsible for designing Fouquet's new store on the rue Royale in Paris in 1900 (fig. 6.43). The boutique opened in time for the Paris World's Fair of the same year. Patterned tile floors and friezes, plantlike pilasters and other architectural details, relief sculptures of peacocks, and wall-mounted glass cases in the shape of bubbles unify wall, ceiling, and floor into a total work of art. Mirrors serve to make the space appear larger, indulging the fantasy of the spectator in creating an imaginative setting for effectively merchandising the exotic creations for sale in the bulbous glass cases. The merging of commercial and aesthetic interests is a feature of Art Nouveau; their relationship suggests the tensions between the private and individual concerns of artists on one hand and the broader goal, shared with manufacturers and entrepreneurs, of mobilizing a more diverse public. It is perhaps telling that Mucha left France to return to his native Moravia in 1910. There he spent the remainder of his career as a painter, engaged in a series of public murals narrating the history of his country, striving to create a "national" art free of more predictable commercial constraints. He donated the murals to the city of Prague.

GLASGOW: CHARLES RENNIE MACKINTOSH

The Scottish architect Charles Rennie Mackintosh (1868–1928) devoted much energy to the dialogue between the aesthetic and broader social issues relating to the visual arts. In his native Glasgow the construction and outfitting of ocean liners and locomotives dominated the local economy and demanded the widespread use of standardized methods of production for furniture and other elements of interior decoration. The Singer sewing machine company also operated a factory in Glasgow, and the city's population was proud of its growth, wealth, and reputation for modernization and industry.

While recognizing the importance of prefabrication and serial production in these industries, Mackintosh believed the role of the artist–designer was to integrate individual and local identity with the requirements of modern and efficient methods of production of designed furnishings. In his own architecture and interior design Mackintosh combined simple construction boldly stated through vertical and horizontal constructive forms expressing a clear relationship between weight and support, integrated with decorative elements that either played upon this geometry (as in the Library of the Glasgow School of Art, 1907–1909) or betray a debt to the tense linear rhythms of Celtic art and highly personal and abstract interpretations of floral and vegetal forms. In many of his projects Mackintosh collaborated with his wife, Margaret MacDonald (1864–1933), whose drawings and designs for tapestries, embroideries, and relief panels express sensuality and a delicate linear quality that appears in ornament carved in wooden furniture or molded in cast iron and other metals. The picture frame illustrated in figure 6.44, designed by Margaret MacDonald Mackintosh and her sister Frances (1873–1921), is made from

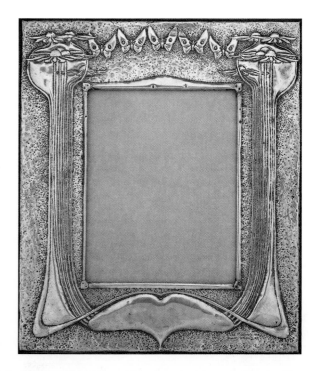

6.44 Margaret MacDonald Mackintosh and Frances MacDonald, picture frame, aluminum and oak, 27 3/16 x 12 3/4 in (69.2 x 32.4 cm), 1897. Carnegie Museum of Art, Pittsburgh.

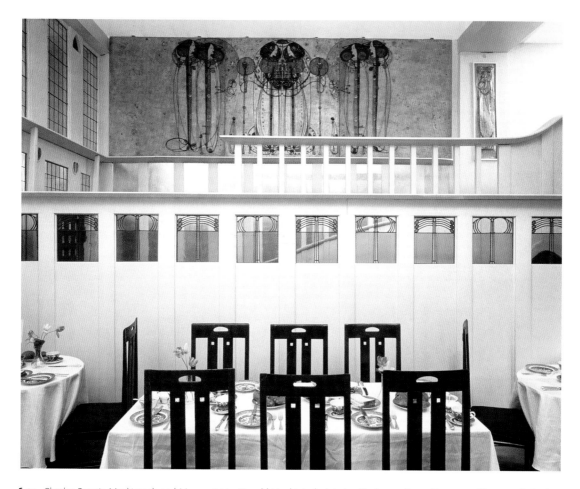

6.45 Charles Rennie Mackintosh and Margaret MacDonald Mackintosh, interior, Buchanan Street Tearooms, Glasgow, 1896–1897.

hammered aluminum on wood – an early use of the metal that was becoming more affordable due to cheaper methods of extraction. Moreover, aluminum was a local choice as well, since Scotland was a center for aluminum production in Britain beginning in the later 1890s.

The same vocabulary of an attenuated rectilinear framework forming borders for more organic floral and human forms can be seen in the murals MacDonald designed for Miss Kate Cranston's Buchanan Street Tearooms in 1896–1897 (fig. 6.45). The tearooms, which afforded a number of opportunities for Mackintosh and MacDonald to create unified, original interiors between 1895 and 1903, were a unique expression of Glasgow's modernity in design. Frequently owned and managed by women, Glasgow's tearooms attempted to introduce the kind of coordinated aesthetic character found in privately commissioned domestic furnishings and interiors into the public sphere. Mackintosh designed several tearooms for Miss Cranston from 1896 to 1902, where middle-class clientele might enjoy the ambience produced through the unity and equality of all the arts. Integrating decoration into his often austere interiors meant preserving the human and individual element in design. Mackintosh's

responsibility for design extended to flatware, dishes, glassware, and tablecloths, as well as furniture, windows, and lighting. Despite the control and coordination demanded by his design sensibility, Mackintosh believed that a modern and individual approach to design could be reconciled with industrial production. While craftsmanship does not appear to have been his priority (that is, design and production were more separate), Mackintosh believed that the decorative arts contributed to the quality of life, not just for the discerning few, but in competition with historicism and traditional associations between luxury and decorative richness.

AUSTRIA

The designs of Mackintosh, represented in illustrated journals and displayed at an international exhibition in Turin (1902; see fig. 6.68) stimulated the artistic efforts of a group of artists and architects in Vienna known as the Secession. These artists, like the Pre-Raphaelites in Britain and Les Vingt in Belgium (see page 136), rebelled against the rigidity and elitism of academic practice in the fine arts and sought both freedom of expression as well as active

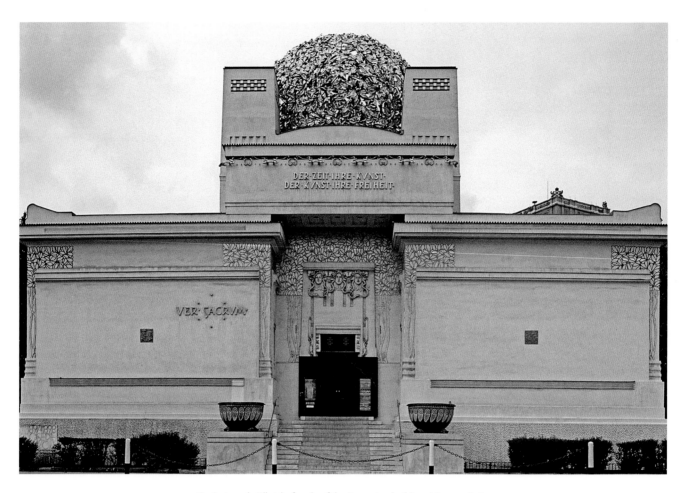

6.46 Joseph Olbrich, façade of the Secession building, Vienna, 1898.

involvement in the decorative arts. The attitudes of the Secession are revealed in the motto inscribed on their exhibition hall, designed by Joseph Olbrich in Vienna in 1898 (fig. 6.46): "Die Zeit ihre Kunst, Die Kunst ihre Freiheit" ("To every time its art, to every art its freedom"). Vienna proved fertile ground for elevated attitudes toward the decorative arts, where new ideas resonated with connoisseurs as well as a broader, open-minded public.

Josef Hoffmann (1870–1956), an architect and leading member of the Secession, and Koloman (Kolo) Moser (1868–1918) created an organization to link designers, craftsmen, and manufacturers in the shared hope of improving the quality and elevating the status of the decorative arts in Austria. The organization, known as the Wiener Werkstätte (Vienna Workshops), was founded in 1903. Hoffmann was deeply impressed by the example of Ashbee's Guild of Handicraft (see pages 89–90) as well as by Mackintosh, and wrote to the architect for advice. In his response, Mackintosh encouraged the Viennese efforts, sounding a note of optimistic liberal idealism in his plea for the role of the artist in improving the quality of everyday life through design:

If one wants to achieve an artistic success with your programme ... every object which you pass from your hand must carry an outspoken mark of individuality, beauty and most exact execution. From the outset your aim must be that every object which you produce is made for a certain purpose and place. Later ... you can emerge boldly into the full light of the world, attack the factory-trade on its own ground, and the greatest work that can be achieved in this century, you can achieve it: namely the production of objects of use in magnificent form and at such a price that they lie within the buying range of the poorest. First those who (look down at applied art) must be overcome and taught that the modern movement is not a silly hobby-horse of a few who wish to achieve fame comfortably through eccentricity, but that the modern movement is something living, something good, the only possible art – for all and for the highest phase of our time.

Products of the Werkstätte include a range of domestic items from clothing to glass and tableware, to wallpaper and individualized calling cards (given to servants when

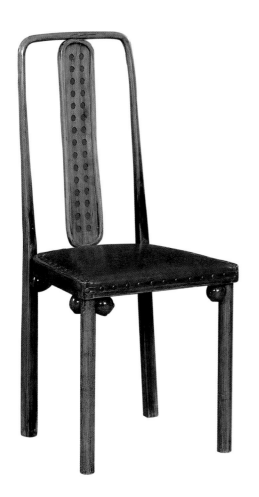

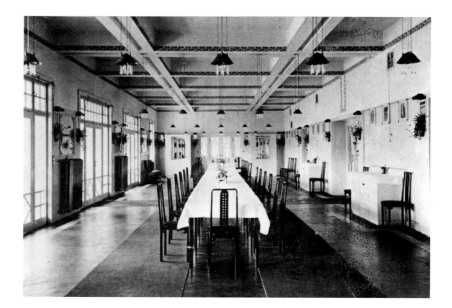

6.48 Josef Hoffmann, dining room of Purkersdorf Sanitarium, 1905.

6.47 Josef Hoffmann, chair, bentwood with leather seat, 38 ⅝ x 17 x 17 ½ in (98.4 x 43 x 44.5 cm), manufactured by Jacob and Josef Kohn, for the dining room of Purkersdorf Sanitarium, Vienna, 1905. Private collection.

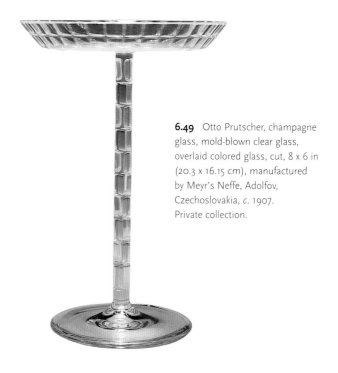

6.49 Otto Prutscher, champagne glass, mold-blown clear glass, overlaid colored glass, cut, 8 x 6 in (20.3 x 16.15 cm), manufactured by Meyr's Neffe, Adolfov, Czechoslovakia, c. 1907. Private collection.

paying a social visit), all of which were usually produced on commission from wealthy private clients. Each product bore the stamp of the artist, the manufacturer, and the distinctive interlocked "W" monogram, as an expression of individual responsibility and the spirit of collaboration between designer and manufacturer, that is, between art and industry. Designers varied in their approach, but all were committed to originality and an avoidance of historicism. Hoffmann's designs parallel the interests of Mackintosh in incorporating repeated geometric decorative patterns as a simple form of decoration on otherwise simple, even plain objects, as seen, for instance, in a chair manufactured for the exclusive Purkersdorf Sanitarium in 1905 that has a series of small circular perforations cut in its back (fig. 6.47). The absence of carved or molded decoration, as well as the light and open interior of the dining room, help to create not only an aesthetically coordinated interior but also a modern, hygienic one (fig. 6.48). Other examples of objects designed by members of the Werkstätte include a champagne glass manufactured

in 1907 in Czechoslovakia but sold in Austria by a Viennese retailer. The glass, based upon traditional techniques practiced in the region but treated here with great subtlety and sophistication, was designed by Otto Prutscher (1880–1949), and is made of clear mold-blown glass overlaid with colored glass and then cut to make the stem appear like links of a translucent chain (fig. 6.49).

Koloman (Kolo) Moser's (1868–1918) designs were no less original or ingenious, and also required painstaking craftsmanship and expensive materials. Moser preferred

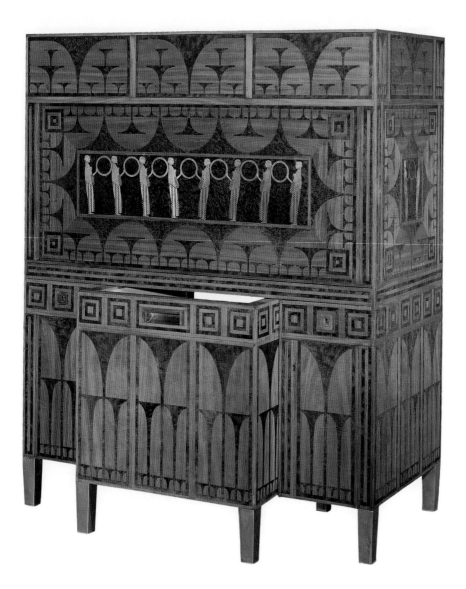

6.50 Koloman Moser, lady's writing desk, thuya wood, inlaid with satinwood and brass, engraved and inked, gilt-metal feet, 57 ¹¹/₁₆ x 47 x 23 ⅝ in (146.6 x 119.4 x 60.3 cm), manufactured by Caspar Hrazdil, 1903. Victoria and Albert Museum, London.

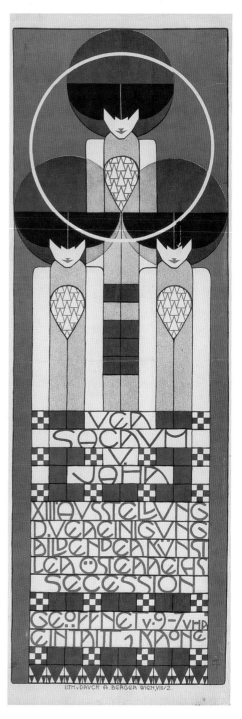

6.51 Koloman Moser, poster for 13th Exhibition of the Vienna Secession, color lithograph, 69 x 23 in (175.3 x 58.4 cm), 1902. Museum of Design, Zurich. Poster collection.

rectilinear shapes and forms and the dialogue between constructive and decorative elements in design. An example is a woman's pull-down writing desk and armchair, manufactured by Caspar Hrazdil and dating to 1903 (fig. 6.50), that come apart like interlocking pieces of a puzzle. Both elements employ a shared vocabulary of schematic papyrus patterns in inlaid wood. In the center of the desk panel is a frieze of standing maidens holding hoops inlaid in brass. Despite a debt to motifs derived from the ancient civilizations of Egypt and Greece, the design is free from conventional historical borrowings and original in its clever disguise of the pull-out chair as well as in Moser's apparent intention to save space with a compact form. Like many of the Wiener Werkstätte artists, Moser designed for many media including posters and journals.

His poster for a Secession art exhibition from 1902 (fig. 6.51) features three severely abstract bust-length female figures whose circular coiffures intersect a large central circle. Below almost illegible letterforms (note the odd upper-case "R") without word spacing inform the viewer, but clarity of information does not seem to be the primary purpose of Moser's visual communication. By comparison this example makes the Parisian posters of Cheret or Mucha seem almost like conventional illustration, suggesting the particular character of Viennese culture, where an appreciation of aesthetic ideas and accompanying artistic freedom were fairly widespread. And yet at the same time Moser's design might have held a more apparent meaning to a reasonably well-informed Viennese citizen of the time: the three women may refer to the three "arts" carved in relief above the doorway to the Secession Building, the circles above their heads to the gilt dome atop the building, and even the checkerboard designs at the end of lines of text find their counterpart in the patterns on the same edifice (fig. 6.46). Moser uses abbreviated signs rather than naturalism as identifying makers.

Perhaps the best-known work associated with the Wiener Werkstätte is the decoration of a home in Brussels for the wealthy Belgian banker Adolphe Stoclet, built between 1904/5 and 1911 by Josef Hoffmann with interior design and furnishings carried out and executed almost exclusively by designers and artisans associated with the workshops. No expense was spared for the materials and decoration of the Stoclet House, which include different varieties of rare marbles and an elaborate series of mural decorations in mosaic designed for the dining room by the Viennese Secession painter Gustav Klimt (1862–1918). Klimt's murals, based upon his color drawings, combined a number of materials such as marble inlay, enamel, gold, and ceramic tile. The brightness of the color, precision of contours, and expanses of geometric and curvilinear pattern consistently support the flatness of the marble walls containing the inlay decoration. Figural representations such as the embracing couple on each wall (fig. 6.52) are equally removed from naturalism or perspective and their garments are filled with patterns created from rich materials. In the dining room of the Stoclet House the abstract language of wall decoration imposes discipline but also allows freedom for the artist's personal vision of the intensity of human love as well as nature's abundance. These themes have a particular resonance in fin de siècle Vienna, where the topic of modern society's alienation from nature and the depths of emotional response and instinct were brought to light by Sigmund Freud (1856–1939), and through whom terms such as "repression" and "drive" have become part of our everyday vocabulary and culture.

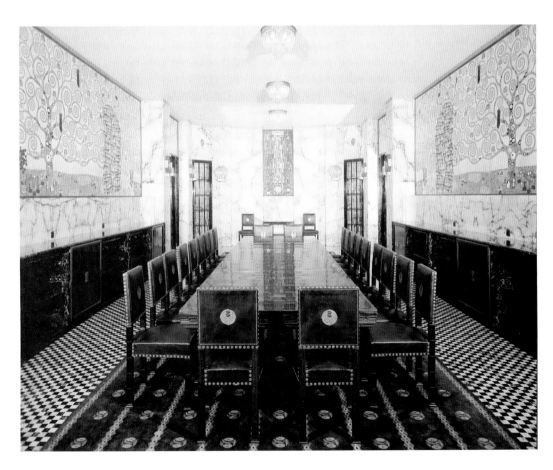

6.52 Josef Hoffmann, Palais Stoclet dining room, with murals designed by Gustav Klimt, Brussels, 1905–1911.

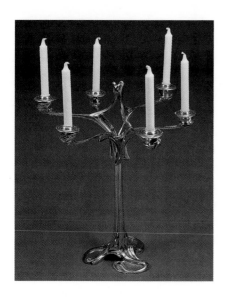

6.53 Henry van de Velde, candelabrum, electroplated bronze, 23 1/16 x 20 in (58.5 x 50.8 cm), 1902. Collection Musée Royaux d'Art et d'Histoire, Brussels.

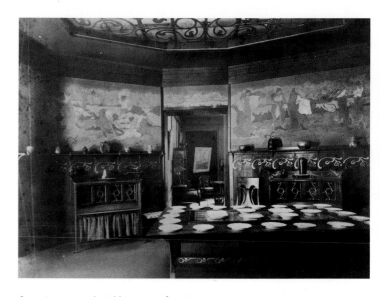

6.54 Henry van de Velde, interior from Bing's Maison de l'Art Nouveau showroom, Paris, 1895.

BELGIUM

Adolphe Stoclet's choice of the Wiener Werkstätte for the design of his Brussels home was not surprising, for the Belgian banker was familiar with Vienna and spent much time abroad. Yet artists in his native Belgium also had an interest in modern attitudes toward design. One of the country's most articulate spokesmen and practitioners for the unity and revitalization of the arts was Henry van de Velde. As a painter, Van de Velde was affiliated with the progressive Belgian modernist movement known as Les Vingt, but began to adapt a Symbolist style featuring abstract shapes and linear rhythms derived from organic forms to the design of furniture, books, and metalcraft. In almost all of his works the decorative elements, usually characterized by taut curvilinear contours invested with springlike energy, are integrated with structural elements such as the legs of a chair or the branches of a candelabrum (fig. 6.53). In works such as these Van de Velde unified decoration and construction, fusing aesthetic expression with an interest in production, as if the designer was thinking like a craftsman, or the craftsman as a designer; in either case, the goal was the unity and equality of the arts. The approach suggested the modern designer's active engagement with the elements and process of manufacture. Deeply concerned with the negative social consequences of industrialization and influenced by the ideas of the Arts and Crafts Movement, Van de Velde's designs exhibit a sense of decorative restraint to avoid the appearance of being luxurious or indulgent. Van de Velde was invited to install a showroom at Bing's Maison de l'Art Nouveau in Paris in 1895, where murals, fabrics, and furniture, much of it built-in, create a unified aesthetic effect in which all elements are equal and integrated (fig. 6.54).

Van de Velde also turned much of his attention to lettering and other forms of printing, producing announcements for his own domestic furnishings and advertisements for the German company Tropon, which manufactured powdered food products such as egg white and cocoa (fig. 6.55). In the Tropon advertising poster, Van de Velde developed original lettering, and the importance of the company name is reinforced with concentric outlines that frame it and suggest in a simplified and abstract way pools of poured liquid (compare a similar abstracted design of liquid in Beardsley's *The Climax*, fig. 6.10). Still, the reference to product is oblique at best; one of Tropon's best-known products was powdered egg whites, and the organic design below the company name may represent cracked eggs, though certainly not illustrated in a traditional manner. Used on packaging as well as in advertising, Van de Velde's abstract signs become a recognizable image for the company as well as an example of expressive abstract form. For Van de Velde, individual expression was compatible both with industry and with business practice. Van de Velde exhibited widely, contributed to publications on modern decorative arts, and was equally interested in the reform and elevation of craft education with stronger ties to the fine arts. In this latter role he was appointed in 1904 as director of a school of craft (Kunstgewerbeschule) in Weimar, Germany, a post he held until the outbreak of World War I. In 1919, following the war, the school was consolidated with Weimar's Academy of Fine Art to become the Bauhaus (see page 196 onward).

Van de Velde's originality in advertising design is matched by other Belgian artists whose posters experiment with imaginative letterforms and the transformations of

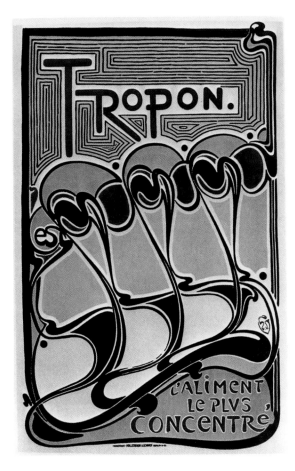

6.55 Henry van de Velde, poster for Tropon, color lithograph, 40 x 30 ⅛ in (101.6 x 77 cm), 1898. Private collection.

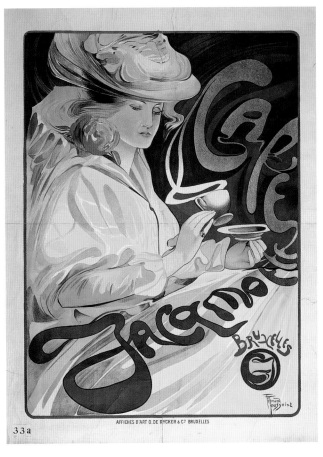

6.56 Fernand Toussaint, poster for Café Jacqmotte, color lithograph, 31 x 43 ⅛ in (78.7 x 110 cm), 1896. Museum für Kunst und Gewerbe, Hamburg.

representation and decoration in relation to large flat surfaces and unmodulated color. An example is the poster advertisement designed by Fernand Toussaint (1873–1955) for a brand of Belgian coffee (fig. 6.56). In this poster the hot steam from a cup of coffee held by a young, well-dressed female figure materializes in swirling rhythms that form the undulating letterforms of the words "Café Jacqmotte." On the bottom right is a circular monogram for the coffee containing elastic forms for the letters "C" and "J" making use of figure–ground reversal. Such manipulation and combination of letters into a single unit appears in artists' signatures (for Van de Velde, for instance, see the Tropon poster, fig. 6.55), as well as in monograms for organizations and companies such as the interlocked "W"s of the Wiener Werkstätte or the well known General Electric trademark, contained within a circle and dating to c. 1890.

Another designer associated with Belgian Art Nouveau was Gustave Serrurier-Bovy (1858–1910). Serrurier-Bovy designed expressive and original furniture featuring expensive woods, carving, and inventive approaches to materials. Beginning just after 1900, Serrurier-Bovy also

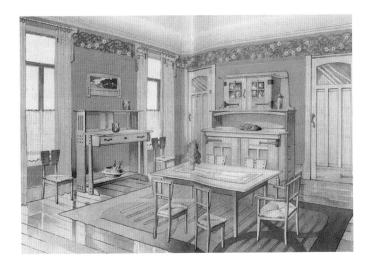

6.57 Gustave Serrurier-Bovy, scheme for an interior with Silex furniture, from *L'Art Décoratif*, Paris, 1904.

designed a line of more practical and inexpensive furniture under the name Silex. The design for a dining room in figure 6.57 was illustrated in a contemporary decorative arts magazine published in Paris in 1904, and features simply constructed furniture using light woods and simple abstract decoration. While individual and original expression remained important elements of design thinking in Belgium, the promise of integrating art into everyday life also remained a goal, realized in advertising art as well as in the unified interior. As art historian Amy Ogata has noted, this aim resonated both with conservative attitudes aimed at shaping middle-class values, and with socialist interests in reducing class difference.

MUNICH

The city of Munich in Germany had a strong heritage of public support for the arts in the nineteenth century. In addition to museums built in the first half of the century, the city sponsored construction of a large exhibition hall in 1854 inspired by London's Crystal Palace Exhibition Hall of 1851. A number of Munich-based artists felt constrained by traditional distinctions between the fine and applied arts in terms of education and the organization of exhibitions. Contemporary with debates of a similar kind in Britain, Vienna, Belgium, and elsewhere in Europe, artists took a keen interest in design and craft production, and an international art exhibition of 1897 in Munich included two rooms devoted to the decorative arts. In 1896 the journal *Jugend* ("youth") was launched in Munich to promote contemporary arts and entertainment, and its circulation reached 200,000 copies per week around the year 1900, acknowledging the strong role of art in contemporary life. The journal's title became the basis for the word Jugendstil ("youth style"), a reference to new ideas in art and design in Germany. A second Munich-based journal, *Simplicissimus*, was also founded in the same year. A key figure in the practice and promotion of new attitudes toward the equality of the arts was Otto Eckmann (1865–1902), who abandoned painting to pursue a career as a decorative artist. Eckmann designed woodcut illustrations for the periodicals *Jugend* (fig. 6.58) and *Pan* that depicted plants and flowers with strong outlines – gently undulating flattened shapes emphasizing strong figure–ground distinction that were based upon familiarity with Japanese woodblock prints. Decorative forms deriving from this approach were developed in furniture designs, tapestry, and other media, including lettering forms and even typography. Painter and illustrator Ludwig von Zumbusch (1861–1927) also dramatically transformed the abstract linear qualities that characterize Eckmann's oeuvre in an early cover for *Jugend* (1897; fig. 6.59) The chromolithograph illustrates two exuberant female dancers with wavelike hair floating against a simplified seaside landscape and framed by two attenuated elm trees into whose foliage the word "jugend" is cut using original

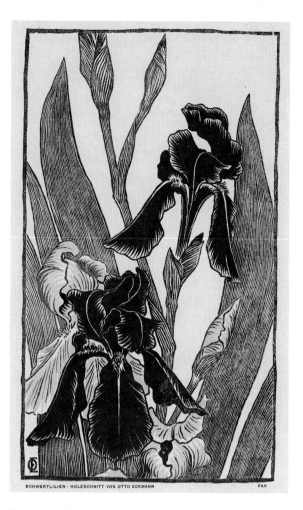

6.58 Otto Eckmann, *Iris*, cover for *Jugend* (Munich), color lithograph, 11 ²⁄₅ x 8 ⁴⁄₅ in (29 x 22.5 cm), 1901. Victoria and Albert Museum, London.

letterforms emphasizing related circular and spiral shapes. The floating letterforms of the title are an expressive part of the page design, and the integration of the lettering with the images, both in expression and in their flatness, demonstrate a new approach to type and image that emerges in the chromolithographic posters and cover art of the period.

Another figure who played an active role in the arts in Munich at this time was Richard Riemerschmid (1868–1957). His contributions are particularly noteworthy because of a later involvement in the Deutscher Werkbund, an organization formed in 1907 in Munich that inaugurated a discourse to establish a more practical and unified approach to design in Germany (see page 148). Riemerschmid was particularly versatile; he participated as a designer in the newly formed craft organization in Munich known as the Vereinigte Werkstätten für Kunst im Handwerk (United Workshops for Art in Handicraft) and later worked in Dresden, producing original designs for furniture, ceramics, and metalwork. Before his involve-

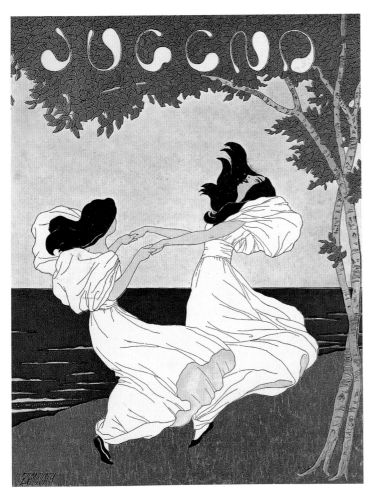

6.59 Ludwig von Zumbusch, cover for *Jugend*, vol. 40, color lithograph, 11 ²/₅ x 8 ⁴/₅ in (29 x 22.5 cm), 1897. Private collection.

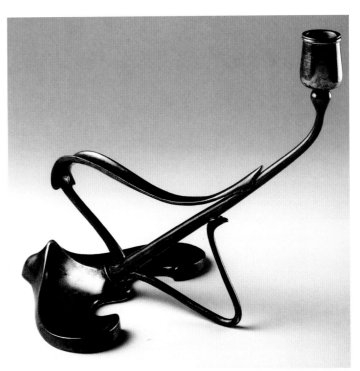

6.60 Richard Riemerschmid, candlestick, brass, 7 ⁷/₈ x 10 ⁵/₈ x 3 ¹/₁₆ in (20 x 27 x 7.8 cm), 1898. Private collection.

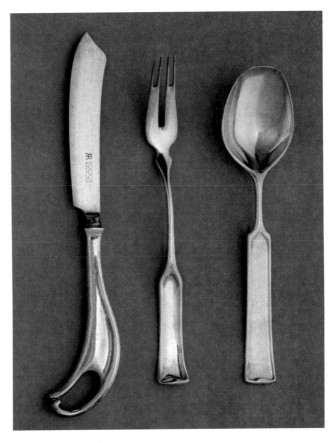

6.61 Richard Riemerschmid, cutlery, silver, knife length 9 ¹/₈ in (23.7 cm), manufactured by Werkstätten für Kunst im Handwerk, Munich, 1899–1900.

ment with the Werkbund, Riemerschmid's designs successfully combined expressive curvilinear decoration with constructive elements for a variety of furnishings, as seen in a brass candlestick of 1898, the asymmetrical vinelike arms of which function as handle and support (fig. 6.60). At the time, critics remarked that such work was austere in comparison with more historicizing examples of luxury metalwork. Likewise, a curved knife handle for a set of silver cutlery is not only a graceful decorative accent but also is efficient to use, even allowing an opening for the user's little finger (fig. 6.61).

Jugendstil in Munich certainly constituted a collaborative renewal of art and handicraft, based in part upon the ability of artists to elevate the everyday world of products and in so doing improve the general quality of life and the urban environment. Through the formation of workshops, the publication of journals that included design as a relevant contemporary subject, and the establishment of schools to educate designers and craftsmen, Jugendstil artists were interested in creating a "people's" art, even if the market for their products tended to remain exclusive. The integration of art and everyday life, however, remained elusive. The social benefit of Jugendstil was at times a target of satire, even within the movement itself, as evidenced by a short verse appearing in *Simplicissimus*:

The world will not be cured with blazing fire or knives,
But painlessly improved – by being "stylized."

SCANDINAVIA, EASTERN EUROPE, AND THE VERNACULAR

Aesthetic ideas helped to nurture and stimulate new developments in the decorative arts in the cities of Eastern Europe and Scandinavia beginning in the 1890s. Although they often assimilated ideas and forms from the British Isles, the United States, or Western Europe, Scandinavian and Eastern European artists added much to the modern development of the decorative arts, with contributions often based upon an appreciation for native folk traditions and the creation of a distinctive national style, often on view at international exhibitions. Their search for national identity was indeed a creative rather than historicist exercise, and was both highly selective and eclectic. Education or training outside of their homelands, the circulation of journals, and attendance or participation at international exhibitions all stimulated design activities in countries such as Denmark, Finland, Norway, Hungary, and Czechoslovakia, and added to the international scope of movements that championed the unity, equality, and cultural significance of the visual arts.

In Finland, the architect Eliel Saarinen (1873–1950) used native building materials such as granite to create a national artistic identity distinct from Russia (of which Finland was then a semi-autonomous province) or Germany, based upon a Romantic vision of Finnish history. Cultural identity was thus linked to political independence, international recognition, and a revitalization of the Finnish economy through manufacturing and international trade. Saarinen's Koti chair of 1897, designed for an exhibition, emphasizes simple, solid craftsmanship, with forms and simply carved decoration derived from indigenous architecture (fig. 6.62). Such designs may be seen as a visual counterpart to widespread interest in the oral folk traditions of Karelia (a region of Finland), whose poems and songs were first published in the second half of the nineteenth century. Historians sometimes refer to the concern with a primitive, authentic past as Romantic Nationalism.

The European-trained painter Akseli Gallén-Kallela (1865–1931) also contributed to the movement to create a Finnish art that included handicraft, designing a wool

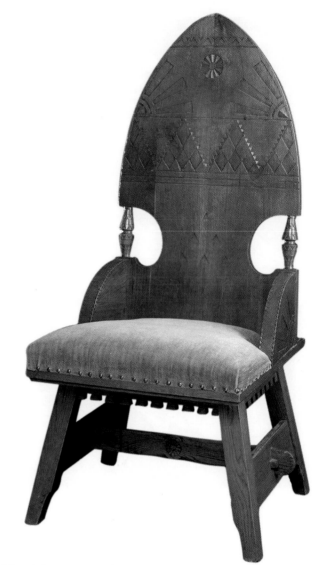

6.62 Eliel Saarinen, Koti chair, oak and reupholstered seat, 52 x 33 x 31 in (132 x 68 x 63 cm), designed 1897. Museum of Art and Design, Helsinki.

rug (fig. 6.63) that was woven using a rustic native technique known as *ryiji*. The asymmetrical curvilinear shapes seen in this example make their appearance in contemporary Finnish stoneware as well as in textile and wallpaper patterns. The similarity of these efforts to the products of aesthetic design in Belgium, France, and Britain demonstrates that a Finnish national style in the arts was less a recreation or revival of the past than an invention responding to modern economic conditions and nationalist sentiment and identity – one that involved an awareness of the role of design and manufacturing in contemporary life together with a nostalgia for native folk traditions. Both sources for late nineteenth-century Finnish design helped to foster an appreciation for the decorative arts, deriving from a connection to nature, the dignity of handicraft, and the creation of modern national

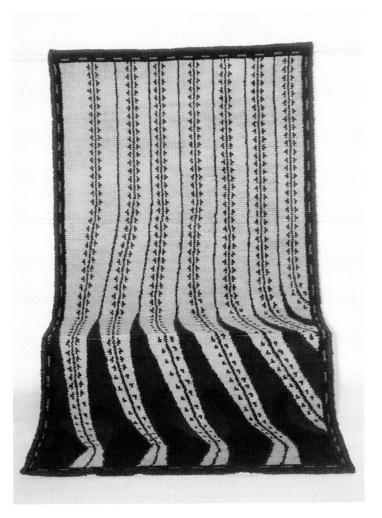

6.63 Akseli Gallén-Kallela, *The Flame, ryiji* rug, wool, 120 x 67 ¾ in (304.8 x 172 cm), 1899 (woven 1884). Gallén-Kallela Museum, Espoo, Finland.

bowl and pitcher is decorated with a swirling stem resembling the petals of a closed flower, imparting an organic quality to the ensemble through the curving ivory handles and swelling forms of the spouts. Delicate floral motifs also are seen in the ceramics of the Bing & Grøndahl Porcelain Manufactory, and were among those goods featured at international exhibitions in the late nineteenth and early twentieth centuries.

Czechoslovakia was another Eastern European country that took part in and helped to shape new approaches to the decorative arts in the later nineteenth century. The city of Prague was the focus for much design activity, directed both toward an expressive and original conception of decoration as well as integrating a range of aesthetic effects involving materials and process with simple forms for furniture, glass, and ceramic wares. Glass manufactories in Bohemia in the eastern region of the country, such as Loetz in the town of Klastersky Mlyn, experimented with new processes and effects based upon exaggerated linear interpretations of natural forms inspired by the success of Tiffany. Some of these manufactories produced designs by members of the Wiener Werkstätte. An integration of construction and decoration is also seen in the stained-glass doors and entrance with wrought-metal framed panels of the Novak Building in Prague dating to 1901–1904.

One of the more original Czech artists involved in the design of manufactured products was Jan Kotera (1871–1923). He designed interiors as well as a wide range of furnishings for several companies, studied in Vienna under the architect Otto Wagner, and held professorships in the School of Applied Art and Fine Art in Prague. Kotera's textiles often incorporate decorative motifs freely adapted from Czech folk traditions, but a number of his designs exhibit a strikingly simple monumentality in which the aesthetic effect seems to come from the character of the material and construction themselves

style. Finland was successful in sponsoring its own pavilion, separate from that of Russia, at the World's Fair held in Paris in 1900. The pavilion was designed primarily by Saarinen, with mural paintings by Gallén-Kallela, and featured carved cases with examples of Finnish handicraft.

Conscious of an increasingly international context and market for modern design after the end of World War I, Saarinen participated in design competitions abroad, and eventually emigrated to the United States in the early 1920s, becoming director for the Cranbrook Academy of Art in Bloomfield Hills, Michigan (see page 224 and fig. 10.1).

Original and aesthetic approaches to the decorative arts are also found in Denmark – for instance, in the studio established by Georg Jensen (1866–1935) in Copenhagen in 1904. Jensen's silver coffee and tea service (fig. 6.64) dates to 1905. The lid of each

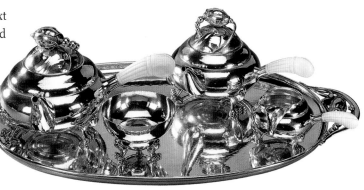

6.64 Georg Jensen, coffee and tea service, chased silver, ivory, height 2–9 in (6.3–23 cm), 1905. Private collection.

rather than from decorative detail. An example is a grand crystal glass punch bowl and glasses exhibited in 1904 at the World's Fair in St. Louis (fig. 6.65). The bowl's thick glass and simple columnar and circular forms eschew more conventional techniques for decorating crystal, while its regular series of carefully channeled surfaces produce unexpectedly brilliant patterns and reflections.

The region of the Czech Republic known as Moravia was also the birthplace of Alphonse Mucha, whose posters and interiors were discussed above (see pages 128–130). Mucha attended art schools in Vienna and in Paris, but later in his career he returned to Prague, where he worked on a large series of murals celebrating the folklore of his native country – another example of the attraction of artists at this time to ethnology and Romantic Nationalism.

The city of Budapest in Hungary had become one of Europe's larger urban centers by 1900, with a population of more than a million residents. Hungary was part of the Austrian empire, and decorative artists were inspired both by vernacular craft traditions and contemporary aesthetic ideas in the creation of a national Hungarian identity. The unique character of Hungarian design around the turn of the century is seen in the production of the Zsolnay Pottery in the city of Pécs, in the southern part of the country. Much of the glazed stoneware produced there,

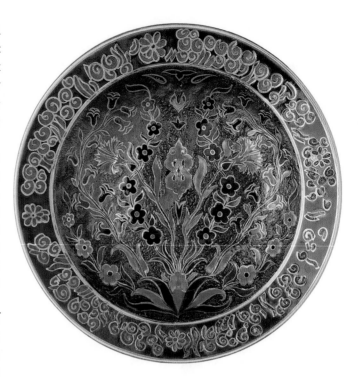

6.66 Jozsef Rippl-Ronai, decorated plate, Zsolnay earthenware pottery, diameter 9 ½ in (24.1 cm), 1889. Zsolnay Museum, Pécs.

beginning in 1862, incorporated decorative motifs based upon indigenous rustic folk traditions, whose flat, bright patterns were collected and published by ethnologists and were also used as the basis for architectural decoration in buildings designed by architect Ödön Lechner (1845–1914). Examples of this work were inspired by native Hungarian craft traditions, for example in a plate (fig. 6.66) designed by Jozsef Rippl-Ronai (1861–1927), a painter who devoted attention to the decorative arts, including pottery, weaving, and book illustration. The Zsolnay factory, employing as many as 1,000 workers by around 1900, also produced pottery with clearer associations to contemporary designs focusing upon elongated and asymmetrical organic forms and a wide variety of coloristic and textural variations (fig. 6.67). For businesses such as the Zsolnay Pottery, modern design was an essential component in fueling wider demand for artistic domestic furnishings. It was a clear example of the benefits of a close relationship between art and industry, the kind of enterprise that was celebrated at international exhibitions as a demonstration of cultural progress based upon international markets, improving taste, and increasing productivity.

Vernacular traditions are a rich aspect of the sources mined by artists in the later nineteenth century, as revealed in the countries of Eastern Europe and Scandinavia. The preceding pages provide only a sampling of the contribution of such traditions to modern design during this time.

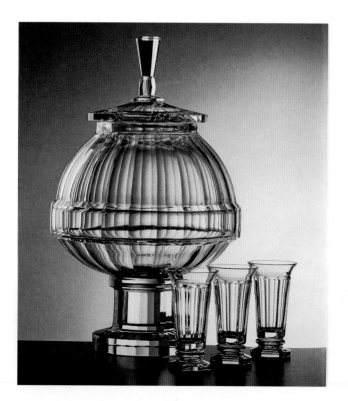

6.65 Jan Kotera, crystal glass punch bowl, diameter 12 ⅛ in (30.8 cm), manufactured by Harrachow Glassworks, Prague, 1904. UPM, Prague.

6.67 Vase, Zsolnay earthenware pottery, 9 ½ x 4 ⁹∕₁₆ x 4 ⅞ in (24.2 x 11.7 x 12.4 cm), 1898. Zsolnay Museum, Pécs.

Folk traditions and nationalism connected the fine and applied arts. In addition, folk traditions helped to create national identity and promote economic self-sufficiency at the turn of the century. Ironically, the interest in ethnography and nostalgia for pre-industrial societies were often adapted to an increasingly competitive, commercial, and international modern economy, involving the participation of artist–designers in the manufacturing industries.

ITALY AND SPAIN

In Italy, which was unified as a nation only after 1861, artists, craftsmen, and manufacturers consciously promoted the equality of the arts and the creation of a modern and original approach to design in the later nineteenth century. The city of Turin, in northern Italy, was the new nation's first capital and a center for design activity, hosting an important international exhibition in 1902 that included recent displays and interiors from Scotland, Vienna, and Paris. As in other countries, the economic benefit of competing in the international market for manufactured products was an incentive for design, stimulating new directions in a country where the classical past was such a strong part of craft traditions.

Leonardo Bistolfi's poster for the 1902 Turin Exposition (fig. 6.68) is animated by the linear energies found in contemporary posters and illustration in Paris and other metropolitan centers. There is a hint of conservatism, however, in the traditional modeling and foreshortening of the figures, in comparison, for instance, to Ludwig von Zumbusch's cover illustration for *Jugend*, which renders a similar theme with a stronger degree of abstraction (see fig. 6.59).

Despite instances of tentative or even derivative approaches to more abstract and expressive elements in late nineteenth-century design, the creative use and combination of materials and virtuoso craftsmanship are admirable, for instance, in the chimneypiece, made of walnut, brass, and ceramic tile, manufactured by Vittorio Valabrega (1861–1952) for the international exhibition in Paris in 1900 (fig. 6.69). On the panel directly above the tile border framing the fireplace is a carved motif

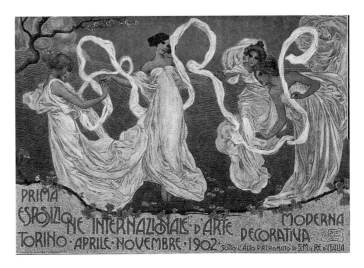

6.68 Leonardo Bistolfi, poster for International Exposition of Modern Decorative Arts in Turin, color lithograph, 43 ⁵∕₁₆ x 56 ⅞ in (110 x 144.1 cm), 1902. Museo Civico L. Bailo, Treviso.

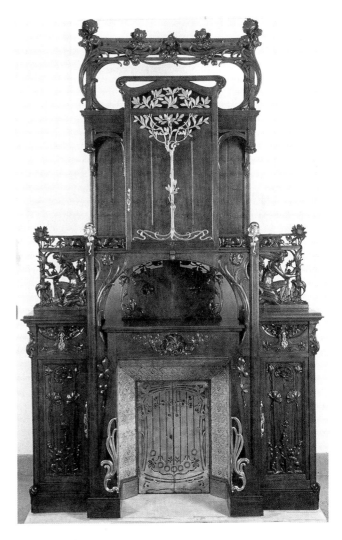

6.69 Vittorio Valabrega Company, chimneypiece, walnut, glazed ceramic, brass, and glass, 119 ¹¹∕₁₆ x 75 x 15 ¹³∕₁₆ in (304 x 190.5 x 40 cm), 1900. The Wolfsonian-Florida International University, Miami Beach, Florida, Mitchell Wolfson Collection.

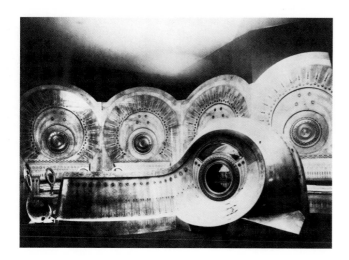

6.70 Carlo Bugatti, Snail Room, 1902. Photograph from the International Exposition of Modern Decorative Arts, Turin.

representing licks of flame carved in an impressionistic manner. At the same time they resemble both the strands of hair and elongated wind-swept vine scrolls that decorate other areas of the work. Despite these abstract aesthetic characteristics, the overall symmetry and kneeling female figures framing the central area demonstrate a connection with a strong nineteenth-century tradition of sculptural carving in luxury furniture practiced by Italian artists and often exhibited at World's Fairs during this period.

In Italy there are also examples of highly original, idiosyncratic approaches to the decorative arts, best seen in the furniture of Carlo Bugatti (1856–1940). Bugatti, father of the automobile maker Ettore Bugatti (1881–1947), was trained as a painter but began creating his own furniture in the later 1880s. An ensemble, known as the Snail Room, was featured at the International Exposition held in Turin in 1902 (fig. 6.70). Its furniture, including chairs, tables, and a massive, twisting bench, were constructed of wood transformed into elastically curved and stretched shapes, covered in vellum (sheepskin) with inlays of hammered copper. Despite the eclectic sources of inspiration for the decorative vocabulary employed in his furniture, Bugatti's designs are hardly derivative or historicist. Rather they exhibit a freedom from precedent and an inventiveness that

informs an important strain of late nineteenth and early twentieth design, namely the liberating effect of a closer relationship between artist and craftsman in producing highly individual, though often exclusive work.

Another city that undertook a revitalization in art and design in the later nineteenth and early twentieth centuries was Barcelona in the region of Catalonia in eastern Spain. Barcelona was the site for an international exhibition in 1888, and a group of the city's wealthy industrialists and professionals were avid art patrons, commissioning apartments, villas, and helping to underwrite the expense of public buildings and theaters as showcases of a vibrant and visually exciting urban culture. Designer Gaspar Homar (1870–1955) was trained as a furniture-maker, but the range of his work included integrated interior ensembles that produced a coordinated aesthetic effect. His Sofa-Display case from 1903 uses elaborate marquetry with the central panel (designed by Josep Pey) depicting a group of dancing nymphs as well as floral patterns repeated in two stained-glass panels (fig. 6.71). A sketch of an interior by Homar depicts an almost identical piece of furniture matched by wood paneling, wallpaper, and a

6.71 Gaspar Homar, Sofa-Display case with La Sardana marquetry panel, various woods with metal and bevel-edged glass appliqué, 95 ½ x 104 ⅜ x 27 ⁵⁄₁₆ in (240 x 256 x 70 cm), Barcelona, 1903. Ajuntament de Badalona, Spain.

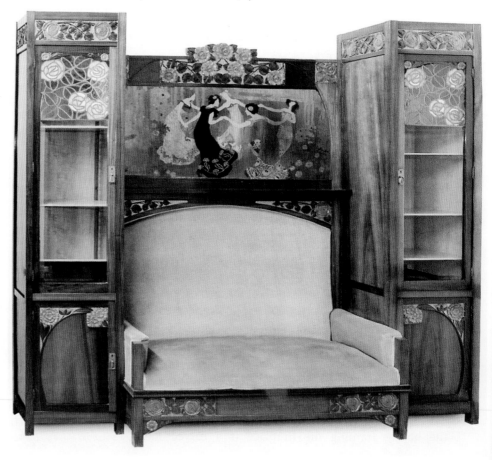

painted frieze. The integration of all components of the interior to create a unified expression emphasizes light structural elements and subdued patterns enlivened by a cheerful secondary color harmony of light green and orange. Josep Pey's panel illustrating the dance closely resembles Leonardo Bistolfi's 1902 poster for the International Exposition of Modern Decorative Arts in Turin (see fig. 6.68), and was entitled "La Sardana" after a popular dance in Catalonia. Homar also produced designs for wallpapers and fabrics both with floral motifs and more abstract linear patterns. It is interesting to note how frequently the theme or motif of popular dance appears in the posters and decorative patterns of design during this period, whether for Löie Fuller, La Goulue, "La Sardana," or Bistolfi's exposition poster.

The Catalan architect Antonio Gaudí (1852–1926) also worked in all aspects of the interior and exterior spaces he designed, including parks, apartments, and religious buildings. His oeuvre is characterized by ceaseless invention and materials explorations in pursuit of a highly individual and unified expression. Frequently the organic treatment of materials takes on an anthropomorphic character. Early furniture with Islamic-inspired decorative patterns gave way after 1900 to more abstract designs in which decorative and structural or functional forms are indistinguishable. Examples include a group of strongly

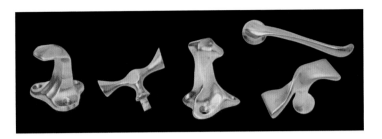

6.72 Antonio Gaudí, metal fittings from Casa Milà, brass, Mañach Smelting Works, knob 1 ⁷⁄₈ x 2 x 1 ¹³⁄₁₆ in (4.5 x 5.1 x 4.6 cm); spyhole bolt 1 ³⁄₈ x 2 x ⁵⁄₈ in (3.5 x 5 x 1.8 cm); knob 2 ³⁄₈ x 2 ³⁄₈ x 1 ⁷⁄₈ in (6 x 6 x 4.5 cm); door handles 4 ¹⁄₈ x ⁷⁄₈; 3 ¹⁄₂ x 4 ¹⁄₈ x ³⁄₄ in (10.5 x 2.5; 9 x 11 x 2 cm), Barcelona, *c.* 1910. Fundació Caixa Catalunya.

sculptural metal fittings from the Casa Milà in Barcelona, dating to around 1910; these are frequently asymmetrical and have twisting forms suggestive of natural rock formations or even strange inhabitants of Gaudí's vivid imagination (fig. 6.72). They almost prefigure the plastic furniture of Postmodern Italian designer Gaetano Pesce from the 1980s, whoalso used anthropomorphism to link design to the user, the natural and the artificial (see fig. 14.16).

The modernity of early twentieth-century Barcelona is also seen in the rich and integrated interior decoration of Lluís Domènech I Montaner's (1850–1923) Palace of Catalan Music dating 1905–1908 (fig. 6.73). Traditional

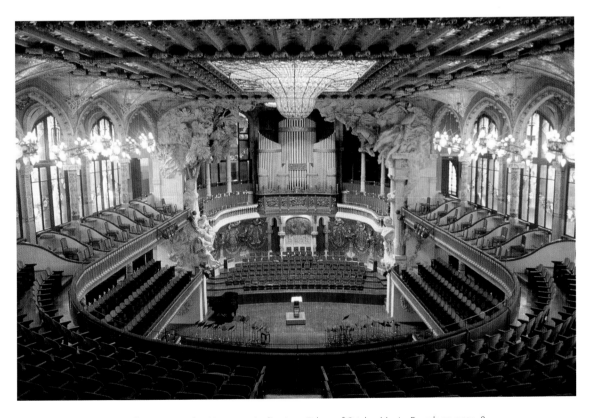

6.73 Lluís Domènech I Montaner, Auditorium, Palace of Catalan Music, Barcelona, 1905–8.

regional craft materials such as ceramic tile are given great expressive range through novel colors and shapes, and natural light comes from the blue windows at the sides of the auditorium as well as from a massive bell-shaped inverted dome, surrounded by busts of singing female choristers. Columns supporting the roof are reminiscent of Gothic fan vaults, a feature of later medieval religious as well as secular architecture in the city, here reinterpreted to resemble webbed plants with flowers that spill out into sculpted bosses carved in relief on the ceiling's horizontal beams. Montaner's concert hall has a celebratory quality, with designers being given great freedom of expression in creating a mood of excitement and optimism that accompanied urban and economic expansion.

As art historian Gabriel Weisberg noted in his review of the 2008 exhibition "Barcelona 1900", there was an underside to Barcelona's growth and revitalization at the turn of the century: Barcelona and other modern European and North American cities may have rivaled Paris in the material signs of progress, upward mobility, poster art, and the emergence of liberal democratic ideals, but urbanization and industrialization also created an unequal distribution of wealth and social tensions that occasionally led to outbursts of terrorism, police reprisals, calls for social justice, and solidarity among the disenfranchised. The dynamic forces of technology and capital that created wealth and nurtured opportunity also fed disaffection and seething tensions that could result in violence and anarchy. While it is unlikely to be able to gain a sense of social and political tension from advertising posters or home furnishings that are aligned with freedom of expression, promises of the good life, and liberal ideals, Toulouse-Lautrec's 1893 chromolithographic poster advertising the conservative newspaper *Le Matin* presents an unusually grim illustration of a public execution with a chained prisoner approaching the guillotine, silhouetted against an anonymous row of soldiers mounted on horseback (fig. 6.74). In some sense design is *always* political, but attitudes from the margins do not always find expression, especially if one relies upon advertising for evidence. Alternative approaches to redirecting the activities of design more broadly and redefining their meaning in relation to modern living emerged in the wake of World War I and the Russian Revolution and are treated in Part III.

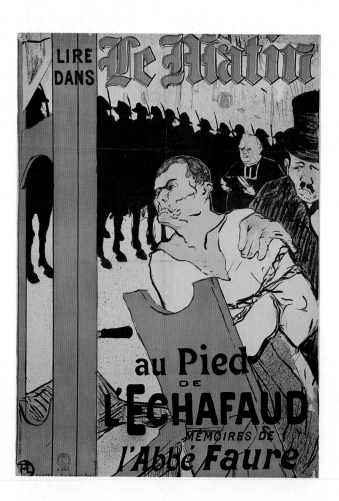

6.74 Henri de Toulouse-Lautrec, poster for *Le Matin*, color lithograph, 32 ½ x 23 ⅓ in (82.5 x 60 cm), 1893. Museum of Design, Zurich. Poster collection.

Chapter 7

Mechanization and Industry

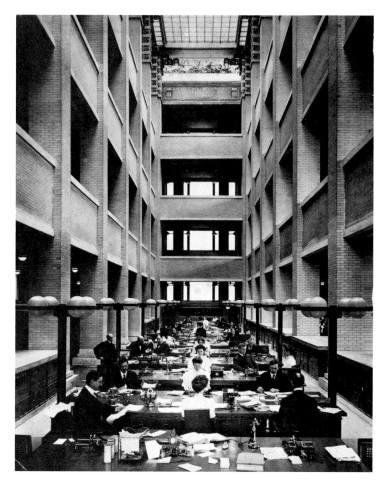

7.1 Frank Lloyd Wright, interior of Larkin Building, Buffalo, New York, 1906.

DESIGN AND THE WORKPLACE

Frank Lloyd Wright's views of a reformed approach to the machine production of furniture did not attract widespread interest among commercial manufacturers for the domestic market, where a variety of period styles appealing to heterogeneous tastes dominated the industry and could be ordered from illustrated mail order catalogues or purchased in department stores. The workplace, however, offered a new paradigm for design, distinct from the more individual and aesthetic associations of the private home. In Wright's Larkin Building in Buffalo, New York, the headquarters of a large and successful soap manufacturing company (1906), the architect addressed the design of the modern corporate office, housing and organizing the functions of the emerging white-collar professions who functioned as part of a complex business that manufactured, marketed, and distributed nationally branded products and services. In some ways the Larkin Building is the antithesis of Wright's Prairie Style houses, contrasting the horizontality and open flow of space in the former with the verticality and spatial insulation of the latter, with direct light entering only from the ends of the central rectangular workroom and high above the floor level. In this workroom, the clerks' sense of anonymity is established through the repetitive and regular arrangement of desks and a scale that dwarfs the individual or at least makes one aware of some larger presence (fig. 7.1). The uniformity and standardization certainly reinforces the efficiency and specialization required for the effective bureaucratized functions of the corporation, requiring workers to become conditioned to increasingly routinized and repetitive tasks. In exchange or as compensation for conformity and consent to these modern working conditions, Wright's design of the Larkin workroom offered both the security of feeling part of a larger whole as well as hope for advancement and the rewards of the sacrifice of individuality and self-determination: at the top of the workroom an inscribed motto, taken from the seventh chapter of Matthew's Gospel, reads: "Ask and it shall be given you; Seek and Ye Shall Find; Knock and it shall be opened unto you." Perhaps we'll never know if such words and communal spaces provided reassurance and incentive to the clerks and secretaries who toiled in the workroom of the Larkin Building, but its design offers a managerial point of view regarding the nature of labor and its wider business context of standardization in the early twentieth century.

GERMANY

In Germany similar attitudes, fueled in part by the interests of large companies in a more unified and functional approach to industrial design and production, took root in the early twentieth century. Reform initiatives advocating practicality rather than luxury and individual expression, found support in the formation of applied arts schools in Düsseldorf, Breslau, Weimar, and Berlin. German companies and workshops uniting designers with craftsmen also participated in international exhibitions in Paris (1900) and St. Louis (1904), and mounted an exhibition in Munich (1908) that received a positive critical response. Also included in these efforts was the formation of a large organization of artists and manufacturers in 1907 to promote the interests of the German applied arts, known as the Deutscher Werkbund (German Work Federation).

A significant figure in many of these activities was Hermann Muthesius (1861–1927), who visited Britain from 1896 to 1899 to study English architecture (published as *Das Englische Haus*), and subsequently became the Minister of Trade for the Prussian government. Like other advocates of design reform, Muthesius believed in the harmony of utility and beauty, but felt that individuality should be subservient to more practical, durable, and rational forms for manufactured products. Through the introduction of modularity, interchangeability, specialized, and mechanized production, Muthesius and his supporters argued that the benefits of efficiency in design and production outweighed individual expressive concerns; moreover, this not only included the cost benefits of standardization, but also the reform of consumer taste toward a more modest and

comfortable ideal for modern living. Such attitudes may be seen in Muthesius's criticism of contemporary Scottish design as being impractical in its degree of refinement and out of touch with the habits of modern middle-class living:

Once the interior attains the status of a work of art, that is, when it is intended to embody aesthetic values, the artistic effect must obviously be heightened to the utmost. The Mackintosh group does this and no-one will reproach them on this particular point. Whether such enhancement is appropriate to our everyday rooms is another question. Mackintosh's rooms are refined to a degree which the lives of even the artistically educated are still a long way from matching. The delicacy and austerity of their artistic atmosphere would tolerate no admixture of the ordinariness which fills our lives. Even a book in an unsuitable binding would disturb the atmosphere simply by lying on the table, indeed even the man or woman of today – especially the man in his unadorned working attire – treads like a stranger in this fairy-tale world. There is for the time being no possibility of our aesthetic cultivation playing so large a part in our lives that rooms like this could be general. But they are milestones placed by a genius far ahead of us to mark the way to excellence for mankind in the future.

The willingness of a number of artists and architects to work within the shared design ethos outlined by Muthesius and like-minded designers and businessmen is an important characteristic of German design in the decade leading up to the outbreak of World War I, stemming at least in part from a strong sense of nationalism in the wake of German unification (1871) and a willingness to compromise in the search for a common national identity through design. Although criticized by the Belgian architect–designer Henry van de Velde for its inhibition of artistic freedom and individuality, and opposed by a number of smaller manufacturers for being undemocratic, Muthesius had many adherents, especially among Germany's large industrialists and a number of leading artist–designers. Among these, Munich-based Richard Riemerschmid (see page 138–139) abandoned the tense, rhythmic curves of the Jugendstil for simple designs of furniture and other household consumer goods. His set of cutlery manufactured by Atelier Karl Weisshaupt in 1912 (fig. 7.2) features straight, mildly elongated handles and plain surfaces, contrasting with the engraved decoration and more asymmetrically curved handles of the Jugendstil (see fig. 6.61).

Another designer associated with the Werkbund and design reform in Germany was the architect Peter Behrens (1868–1940). Like Riemerschmid, Behrens abandoned

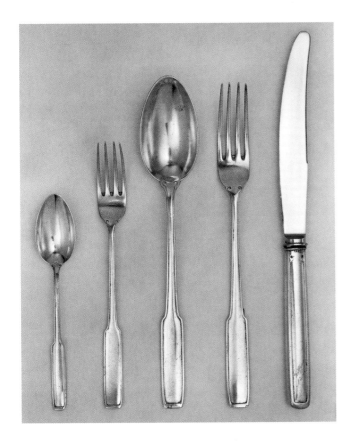

7.2 Richard Riemerschmid, cutlery, manufactured by Bruckmann, Heilbron, for Karl Weisshaupt, silver, length 5 ⁵⁄₁₆ to 6 ⅝ in (14.4 to 17.2 cm), Munich, 1912.

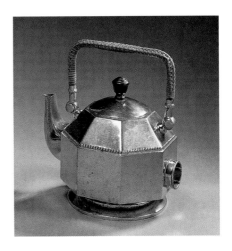

7.3 Peter Behrens, electric tea kettle, brass, chromium-plated metal, bakelite, and cane, 8 ¼ x 6 ⅜ in (21 x 16.5 cm), manufactured by Allgemeine Elektrizitäts-Gesellschaft (AEG), Berlin, *c.* 1908–1912.

the expressive rhythms of the Jugendstil for more sober forms, seen for instance in his turbine factory for the German General Electric Company (Allgemeine Elektrizitäts-Gesellschaft or AEG) of 1908–1909. From 1907 Behrens worked as a consultant for the AEG to develop promotional materials and to work with product engineers to design electrical appliances for industrial and domestic use. Promoting the use of electricity for cooking and other domestic purposes aside from lighting was a concern of companies such as AEG as they sought to maximize demand for electric power (in particular other than during rush hour when electric commuter trains required large amounts of power). Recognizing the advantage of standardized components in reducing labor costs, Behrens introduced variety into the line of electric tea kettles through the choice of material, finish, and handles. He also preserved associations with handicraft in the use of a molded exterior that resembled a hand-hammered surface (fig. 7.3). The visual unity among AEG electric products realized Muthesius's ideal of a coherent "style" for industrially manufactured goods at odds both with the teachings of the Arts and Crafts Movement as well as with the importance placed upon the individuality associated with the Aesthetic Movement. Although never a

national policy in Germany, this practical or "objective" approach to industrial design and production represents the outlook of large businesses and corporations who benefited not only from production economies that standardization brought, but also from products that achieved recognition in the marketplace by possessing a common visual vocabulary, along with a trademark that provided further identity and recognition.

Behrens's work for AEG also included the design of a consistent typeface (using Roman rather than Blackletter forms), trademark, and layout for all company products and printed materials. These characteristics in turn became a recognizable ethos communicating consistency and trust for the company; that is, a sense of permanence and stability in contrast with the confusion of varied styles and fashions. The hexagonal trademark designed by Behrens for AEG suggests, in its analogy to a beehive, the subordination of individual elements to a unified corporate image (the logo appears in fig. 7.4 in the lightbulb). The mark may also refer to the chemical compound benzene, represented visually as a ring or hexagon by the German chemist Friedrich Kekulé, and the applications and benefits of science to industry. Behrens was a well-known architect whose work for AEG helped to create as well as to legitimize the company's contemporary image and contribute to the recognition and associations of their products. The Behrens trademark appears in a 1912 illustration for a corporate prospectus that limits communication to a straightforward drawing of the AEG filament lightbulb above the bold Roman typeface designed by Behrens for all the company's materials (fig. 7.4). It is interesting to compare the blunt character of this

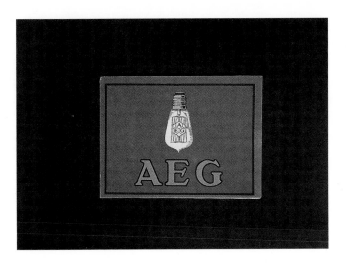

7.4 Peter Behrens, prospectus for AEG Lighting, color lithograph and letterpress printing, 4 ¼ x 6 in (11.2 x 16.5 cm), 1912. Klingspor Museum, Offenbach.

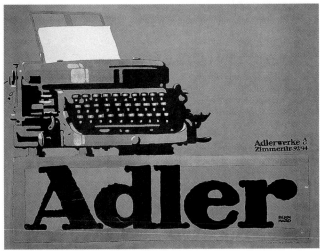

7.6 Lucian Bernhard, poster for Adler Typewriters, color lithograph, 27 ⅕ x 37 in (69 x 94 cm), Berlin, 1908.

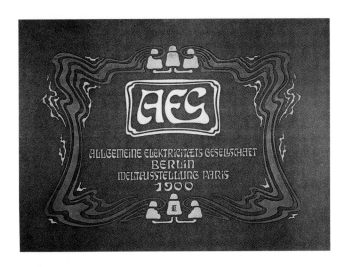

7.5 Otto Eckmann, cover for AEG catalog, Paris World Exhibition, color lithograph, 1900.

illustration to a catalogue illustration for the same corporation designed in 1900 by Munich artist Otto Eckmann (fig. 7.5). In the earlier poster, a fluid elasticity characterizes idiosyncratic lettering that merges paired letters and combines lower- and upper-case forms, while the rectangular frame abstractly visualizes the energy of an electrical current passing through bell-shaped transformers at the top and bottom. The expressive line and letterforms provide a graphic equivalent for electric current (as steam functions in an advertisement for coffee, or smoke for cigarettes and cigarette papers; see fig. 6.56), while Behrens's poster concentrates upon an identity between AEG's trademark and one of its most recognizable products, without reference to an expressive transformation of electric force or associations between product and

lifestyle. The art historian Frederic Schwartz has referred to this approach as "semantic restraint." Advocates of this type of design reform often referred to their approach to design for industry as "Typisierung," substituting the typical for the unique, and abiding, responsible standards of efficiency and practicality for varied consumer as well as designer preferences.

Behrens's graphic design for AEG shows an affinity to the posters of a young, self-taught Viennese artist named Lucian Bernhard (1883–1972), who was working in Munich in the first decade of the twentieth century and also had joined the Deutscher Werkbund. Bernhard produced a number of advertising posters of striking directness and simplicity, emphasizing bold company names linked to products in the most straightforward and effective way. An example is the 1908 poster for Adler Typewriters (fig. 7.6), where both the typewriter and its shadow are treated as equal partners in the presentation of the image. Although the presentation of the typewriter is in a three-quarter view, the simplified tone and justification of the image with the border at the left virtually negate recession and create a powerful presence for the product. Critics have suggested that such a treatment of shadow is the result of the influence of photography, where the halftone method of commercial reproduction (see page 125) reduced the tonal range of the original image, creating a more abstract effect. In Bernhard's posters rarely are the products themselves distinctive – whether matches or shoes or cigarettes, these national brands are represented by typical rather than by unique goods, with the letters of the name itself providing recognition and association, as a sign or image that could generate appeal and trust, almost *in place of* product differentiation or more persuasive advertising techniques employing illustration or slogans. Closer to our own time, clothing labels often serve the same function. For instance, casual clothing such as jeans or khakis are often differentiated as much by their labels as by their color or fit; the power of branding and trademark, is, in these examples, demonstrated most clearly, although aided in great measure by other advertising and media.

Behrens also designed furniture and interiors, such as a dining room featured in a display for the Wertheim Department Store in Berlin in 1906 (fig. 7.7). The rectangular and simply, solidly constructed furniture eschews carved decoration in favor of geometric motifs and metal inlays echoed in the lighting and stenciled wall treatment. The avoidance of overt displays of luxury in decoration or costly materials represents a sober, restrained ideal for modern living that equated industrialization with standardization rather than with the individual expression of designers in the middle-class market for consumer goods.

THE AMERICAN SYSTEM OF MANUFACTURE AND FORDISM

Standardization and the emergence of nationally branded (rather than local) products and services also contributed to new perspectives on design in the United States in the early twentieth century. The American System of Manufacture (see pages 54–56) continued to wrest control of production from workers in favor of factory owners and floor managers who determined production schedules that could be met only by increasing the division of labor and the use of interchangeable parts that required routine assembly rather than the skills of trained workers.

To reduce the cost of labor, Philadelphia-born Frederick W. Taylor (d. 1915) conducted experiments in the 1880s aimed at increasing productivity among workers. Taylor measured the amount of time taken by workers to perform a variety of routine tasks. In one experiment he demonstrated that a man shoveling coal would work at optimum efficiency with individual loads of 22 pounds, and even made drawings for the design of a shovel to best hold the load. Once determined, Taylor's recommendations were enforced in the workplace by managers and became the measure for labor productivity and rewards (wages), demanding higher levels of compliance and conformity on the factory floor. Taylor's analyses are described under the heading of scientific management. His findings reinforced the connection between the division of labor and efficiency as described in the eighteenth century by Adam Smith (see page 55), but extended the principle to studying and reducing the number of movements necessary to perform a given task

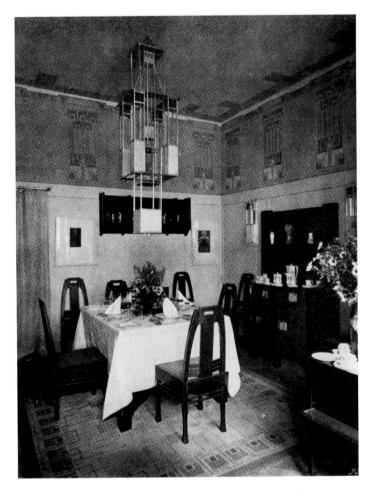

7.7 Peter Behrens, interior display for a dining room, Wertheim Department Store, Berlin, 1906.

in order to save more time and increase productivity. Taylor's system required a degree of conformity that might have made John Ruskin shudder, but the sacrifice was part of the bargain. As described by author Robert Kanigel,

> There it was, the Faustian bargain in embryonic form: You do it my way, by my standards, at the speed I mandate, and in so doing achieve a level of output I ordain, and I'll pay you handsomely for it, beyond anything you might have imagined. All you have to do is take orders, give up your way of doing the job for mine.

As in Germany, Taylor's approach to uniformity in production should perhaps be seen in the context of the critique of free-market capitalism at the time, which included government efforts of regulation as well as the growth of larger, monopolistic companies who sought to reduce competition through economies of scale in production. In terms of regulation, the United States government created uniform standards for the sizes of plumbing and electrical fittings, in order to help ensure compatibility without the

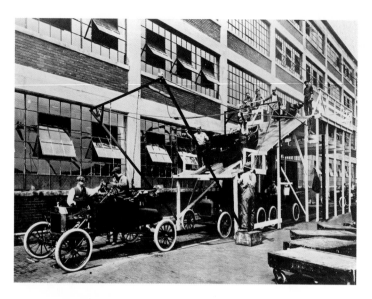

7.8 End of the line, Ford Motor Plant, Highland Park, Michigan, photograph, c. 1913. From the collections of Henry Ford Museum and Greenfield Village, Michigan.

confusion that might be caused by unfettered competition. Standards also applied to public utilities, for instance, in the telephone industry. The Bell Telephone Corporation had a monopoly on the manufacture of handsets, which as a result were only available in a limited number of models during the 1920s.

Industrialist Henry Ford expanded upon Taylor's scientific management. According to historian Peter Ling, rather than analyzing existing tasks, Ford and his managers saved time and increased productivity by rethinking the location of parts and the sequence of operations in manufacturing, eventually developing the moving assembly line. Through the assembly line, and Ford's decision to manufacture only a single model, labor was defined primarily as a factor of time rather than skill or thought, maximized by demanding production schedules dictated by floor managers, and humorously satirized by Charlie Chaplin in the 1936 film *Modern Times*. Ford's assembly line required an open and easily expandable interior factory space, made possible through the use of electric power to run machinery. Once up and running it marked a significant advance in quantity production. Through steel-frame construction, inexpensive building materials, and the use of a modular principle to facilitate expansion, Ford's architect Albert Kahn (1869–1942) created large, simple, well-lit factory spaces to serve the flexible needs of the moving assembly line, first at the Highland Park plant (fig. 7.8) in 1908 and later at the larger River Rouge facility.

Ford's production methods transformed the automobile from a luxury item requiring elements of fine, specialized craftsmanship for details of construction and finish to a middle-class form of personal transportation through complete uniformity, standardization, and interchangeable parts for ease of repair and replacement. Between 1907 and 1916 the price of Ford's Model T (Tin Lizzie) actually went down as demand increased. The car, available only in black, remained virtually unchanged and unchallenged in the market until the mid-1920s. The ability of the industry to produce an automobile within the means of many through the application of technology was almost universally admired and contributed to making mechanized mass production part of the ideology of economic progress in the United States and abroad in the period between the two World Wars. The human costs of this system of factory production were met in a variety of ways, including Ford's own "Five-dollar Day" in 1914 that compensated for the loss of worker independence with higher wages and the promise of saving for an automobile of their own, and through company efforts to build identity and compliance among workers through public and corporate relations (see also page 229). Eventually, labor unions helped to address these issues with threats of strikes as leverage for higher compensation and other benefits. Indeed, Ford's mechanized mass production demanded conformity, repetition, and strict control in the workplace, and such practices differed profoundly from the ideals of joyful and meaningful work that animated Arts and Crafts reform and various "aesthetic" movements in the nineteenth and early twentieth centuries. As discussed above, the crafts workshop founded by Elbert Hubbard's Roycroft community (see pages 92–94) was an attempt to humanize the workplace by creating a sense of cooperation among employees while incorporating more modern methods of production, provision of housing, and low wages for commercial viability. Oddly perhaps, Hubbard admired the success of Ford and other industrialists, whose biographies he published at Roycroft under the heading *Little Journeys to the Homes of Great Businessmen*. These and other pamphlets were printed in great quantities for corporations hoping to inspire loyalty among their own workers. Such efforts suggest a desire to reconcile Arts and Crafts ideology with market conditions profoundly affected by mass production – to its credit, the Roycroft community remained in business throughout most of the Great Depression, only declaring bankruptcy in 1938. It is also interesting to note that both Stickley and Hubbard opposed the modern labor reform movement. Deeply influenced by William Morris's attitudes toward craft, they felt that the concept of organized labor excluded a satisfying role for the individual beyond compensation in wages. Until the later 1920s, Ford did not invest heavily in advertising, as the appeal of affordable personal transportation offered by his Model T required little additional promotion.

In its purest form, the Model T, Fordism did not have a place for design in the way we've used the term in relation to craft and manufacture during the eighteenth and nineteenth centuries: decision-making was directed almost exlusively toward achieving maximum efficiency for production and minimum cost for labor. Only the pressures of competition made "design," in the sense of adding value to the utility of a product, an element in the company's approach. In 1927 Ford introduced its Model A in order to respond to competition that made design as well as advertising an integral component in the industrial manufacture of automobiles. After all, the Model T retained the basic carriage form inherited from horse-drawn transportation, and there was little artistic about its design in terms of harmonious proportions or a sense of a unified or simplified external form, as seen, for instance, in Behrens' product designs for AEG. But then again, Behrens was a "designer" responsible for providing both a distinctive trademark as well as recognizably tasteful and commercially viable product forms.

Following World War I, the moving assembly line, machine-production of interchangeable parts, and standardization achieved success in other American industries, most notably in the uniform mass production of household appliances such as refrigerators, vacuum cleaners, and washing machines. Many appliances were powered by electricity and strongly promoted by power companies hoping to increase domestic consumption of electric energy beyond its primary use for lighting in the home. The industrial-looking standardized forms of these new appliances suggested greater efficiency in the kitchen (also demonstrated by the reorganization of the room's workspace), while the use of white enamel paint connoted personal hygiene, making the ideal kitchen a combination of well-managed factory and laboratory (figs. 7.9 and 7.10). American author Christine Frederick (1883–1970) studied food preparation along the lines of Taylor's scientific management studies, and this extended into the overall coordination of kitchen tasks as well, all contributing to the reduction of drudgery. Frederick's *Scientific Management in the Home* (1912) contained diagrams demonstrating the most practical spatial relationship among various tasks in the kitchen in order to save time, and her efforts became the basis for domestic kitchen design in public housing developments in Frankfurt in the 1920s (see page 205). Frederick's book also emphasized personal satisfaction – choices in the arrangement of utensils or in the height of cabinets or sinks suggest an elevation of the mundane through design. Frederick's efforts, like those of Catherine Beecher, didn't question traditional gender attitudes towards women's role as homemaker (see page 118), but they did set the stage for

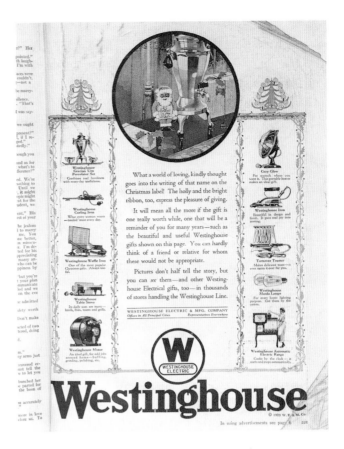

7.9 Advertisement for electric appliances manufactured by Westinghouse Electric & Manufacturing Company. *Good Housekeeping*, December 1923.

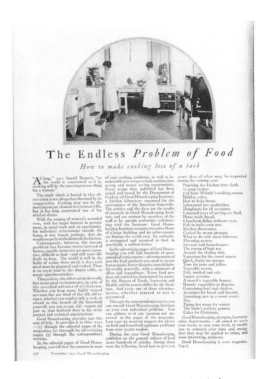

7.10 Modern kitchen and storage space. Article from *Good Housekeeping*, November 1923.

assigning to women a responsibility for a host of design-related issues, both in the form of household products and in the layout of the modern kitchen, with emphases upon hygiene as well as efficiency.

DEVELOPMENTS IN MERCHANDISING, PRINTING, AND ADVERTISING

Together with the success of the Ford Model T and the application of scientific management to the home in an effort to improve efficiency and reduce toil, the American System of Manufacture was also applied by manufacturers to a variety of household products with applied decoration that created variety and differentiation geared toward diverse consumer preferences. Here, as historian Regina Blasyczyk again explains, production economies and the division of labor produced flexibility in manufacturing that enabled a wider range of products to appeal to the desires of a heterogeneous market. Store owners and managers played an important role here, not as reformers or "tastemakers," but as observers who monitored consumer preferences and inventories, selecting among available styles as well as part of a feedback loop that was responsive to varied and changing styles.

The reality of the factory and office as primary locations of managed and increasingly routine work helped to create a stronger need to disassociate living space from workplace; if the factory turned men into

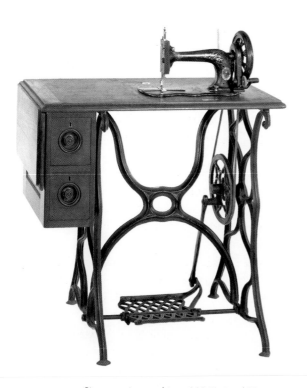

7.11 Singer sewing machine, 1866. National Museum of American History, the Smithsonian Institution.

machines and the kitchen into a "scientifically managed" space, for many consumers the other rooms of the home functioned as a refuge and antidote for the anonymity, uniformity, and repetition associated with the workplace. Mass communication through catalogues and mass-circulation magazines extended these attitudes to small town and rural areas as well. The distinction between home and work has been cited as the primary reason why manufacturers at first found it difficult to successfully market sewing machines for domestic use. Standardized models manufactured by Singer in the mid-nineteenth century were too reminiscent of the factory to appeal to consumers (the earliest models could be mounted on their wooden packing crates), and only by acquiring domestic associations through painted detailing in gold, a more tapered appearance, and a more traditionally carved table (fig. 7.11) did sewing machines successfully enter the home as a piece of artistic furniture rather than as an industrial "tool." In fact, they acquired "design." Rather than competing for work in the "public" world, women were encouraged to cultivate a comfortable and worry-free environment for their families. While this role might allow for their direct participation in handicraft, as the primary consumers of household goods and furnishings they were increasingly targeted by advertisers.

In addition to the need to distinguish home from office or factory through design, manufacturers were able to increase sales by creating different products for particular markets. Their efforts are evident in the mail-order catalogues published by national distributors such as Montgomery Ward (1872) and Sears, Roebuck and Company (1891), in monthly periodicals whose circulation increased dramatically through paid and often illustrated advertisements that covered the costs of production and reduced the price to readers, and in national retail chain stores such as F. W. Woolworths (1878). Leafing through the pages of mail-order catalogues, the reader confronts images of a seemingly limitless array of domestic products with minor variations meant to appeal to the desires of different groups of consumers. What these various outlets or intermediaries have in common, however, is their ability to negotiate social relations and individual identity that are expressed through consumption (fig. 7.12). While urban consumers found such variety in large department stores such as Macy's or Wanamaker's, mail-order catalogues catered mainly to rural populations whose range of options for consumer goods were previously limited to the local "general store."

The relationship among different applications of modern production technologies, branding strategies, and advertising, may be seen in the piano industry. At the Crystal Palace, piano manufacturers used design to

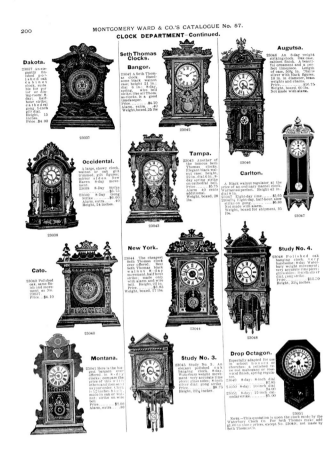

7.12 Catalogue page, clock department, Montgomery Ward catalogue, 1896.

connect their products with art and the associations between music and refined culture. Despite increasingly standardized soundboards and even sizes, cases were differentiated to reflect individual preferences and varying consumer aspirations. Yet the Steinway & Sons Company of New York (founded 1853) began to abandon this strategy and adopt an approach where piano cases were more typical yet branded both by trademark as well as advertising that used the personal endorsements of professional musicians and concert halls to help market their products. While advertisements continued to illustrate period cases into the early twentieth century, differentiation for some products yielded to strategies that moved in the direction of standardization.

Conclusion

The numerous individual, group, corporate, larger institutional, or even national design initiatives described in this chapter revolve in some way around the varied responses to industrialization and mechanized mass production during the late nineteenth and early twentieth centuries. These range from the protests of John Ruskin and William Morris to the aggressive pursuit of rapid uniform production by Henry Ford. Between these two extremes lie the varied approaches of aesthetic design and reform (whether "art" furniture, Jugendstil, or Art Nouveau), Werkstätten, Werkbund and other associations, and large commercial ventures such as department stores and retail chain stores described, that sought to balance the uniformity and rationalization demanded by an emerging system of industrial production with the individuality of the designer and the increasingly significant motivations of a growing consumer culture. Each phenomenon constitutes a particular reaction to the threat as well as the promise of industry, the dream of providing the many with what was once the privilege of the few, of elevating aesthetic awareness of household objects and interiors, of improving the standard of living and quality of life through design allied with manufacturing, of introducing "art" into everyday life. At the same time, technology threatened the very nature of craft production, depriving workmen of independence and increasing the disparity among social classes in competitive economic conditions. Various efforts toward creating an alliance of art and industry addressed these complex issues, including the well-being of workers, the role of designers, manufacturers, and consumers, all of whom held a stake in design. In France, as Debora Silverman and other historians have remarked, the political milieu in which design initiatives developed at this time was a conservative one in which the cultivation of a refined Art Nouveau style was expected to create economic opportunity as well as to reduce middle-class fears of unrest among an industrial working class. Design, as distinct from craft and manufacturing, greatly expanded during this period; artist–designers, craftsman–artists, tastemakers, the first professional industrial designers such as Christopher Dresser, and retailers such as Woolworth, all believed in the economic, social, and political significance of the decorative arts – all contested the uses and applications of technology, the role of labor, the functions of art, and even more importantly the meanings and definitions of progress. The social, economic, and political meanings brought to bear upon design activities in the period from the mid-nineteenth century until the beginning of World War I make this period one of great vitality, originality, and tension, in which there emerges a critical dialogue between art, craft, industry, social relations and reform, and an ever-expanding culture of commodity consumption.

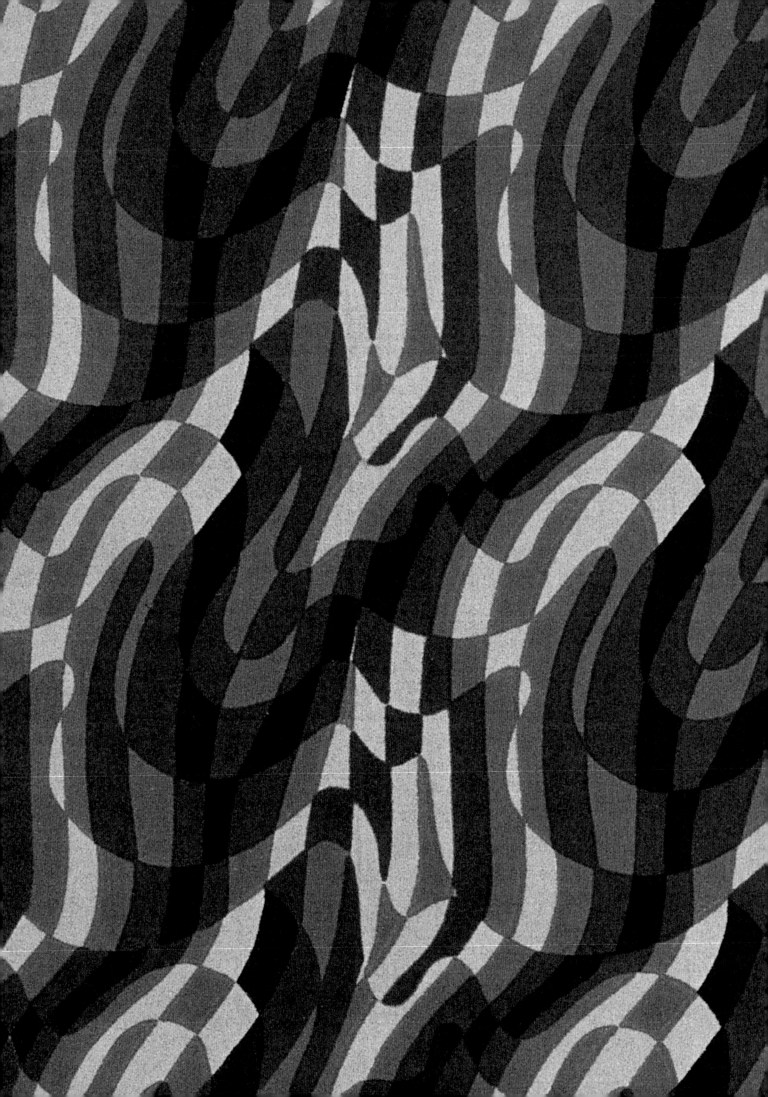

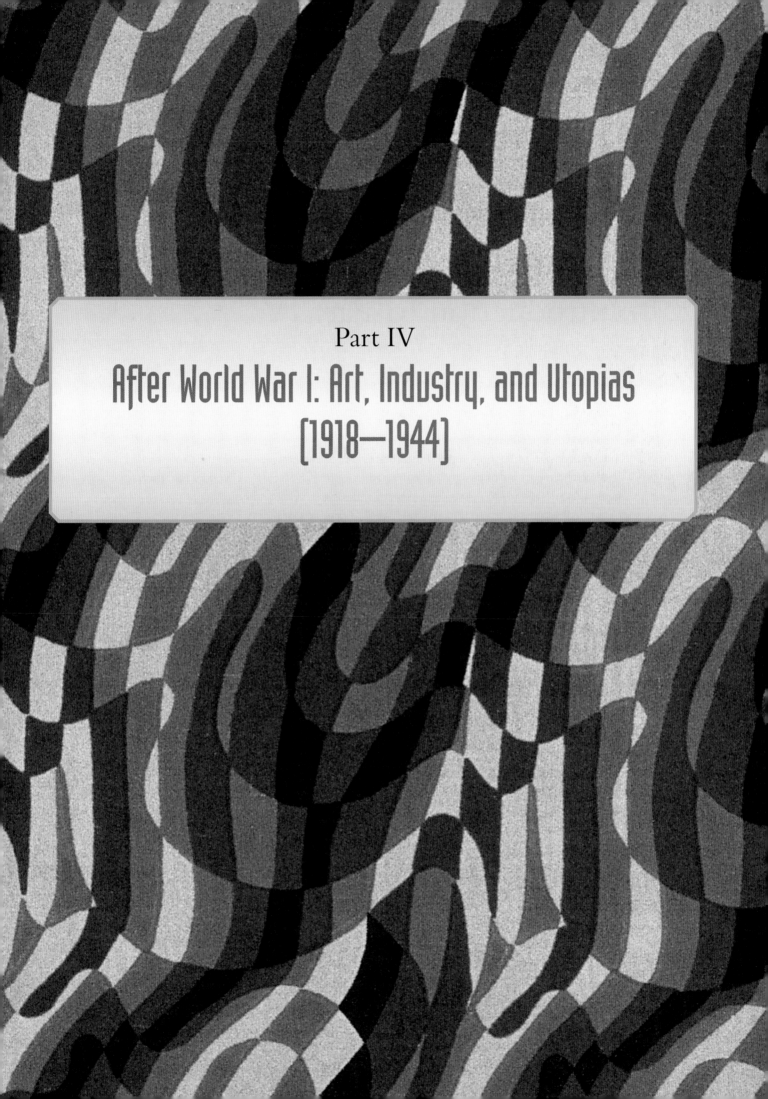

Part IV
After World War I: Art, Industry, and Utopias (1918—1944)

Introduction to Part IV

The period under review in this section, encompassing the years 1918 to 1944, includes three landmarks of modern design history: the long-awaited Exposition Internationale des Arts Décoratifs et Industriels Modernes in Paris (1925); the foundation of the German school for design education known as the Bauhaus (1919–1933); and the emergence of the industrial design profession in the United States, vacillating between aesthetic, commercial, and social dimensions of design, and culminating in the 1939 New York World's Fair. Each landmark corresponds to overlapping aspects of design thinking and practice during a period that witnessed the trauma of World War I, a crippling economic depression with accompanying social unrest and political turmoil, and the rise of totalitarian regimes in several European nations.

Each aspect of design during this period may be seen as a particular type of reaction to the tensions and aftermath of World War I (1914–1918). The origins of the style known as Art Moderne or Art Deco may be traced to the years just before the war. But the persistence of French organizers to house an international exhibition devoted to modern decorative and industrial arts in 1925, originally planned to take place in 1915, suggests the active promotion of French pre-eminence in the design and manufacture of modern furnishings and luxury commodities and a "modern" lifestyle that embraced travel and tourism, entertainment, and hygiene. The term "Art Deco" itself, though coined only in the 1960s, derives from the title of the 1925 Paris exhibition. The majority of Art Deco designers who took part in the exhibition saw themselves as artist–craftsmen, proud of the equality they shared with painters and sculptors and cognizant of an exclusive and discriminating international market for their goods. Advertising and promotion through posters, merchandising, and lifestyle magazines such as *Vogue*, expanded the market and commercial exposure of Art Deco.

The Bauhaus presents a complex and shifting institutional history. Its first director, architect Walter Gropius (1883–1969), was a veteran of World War I. The school's first home was the city of Weimar, and the Bauhaus manifesto (see pages 196–197) proclaimed a utopian faith in the unity of the arts as realized through the art of building, the exaltation of craft, and the integration of art and life. In the early 1920s the Bauhaus mission shifted its focus from workshop to factory, eliminating overt signs of handwork and adopting the theme "Art and Technology: A New Unity." The shift was apparent in the appointment of new faculty, in the construction of austere buildings for the school's new home in Dessau in 1926, and in the creation of prototypes for furnishings that eliminated decoration in favor of spare forms emphasizing an underlying, elementary geometric abstraction with universal aesthetic and social pretensions. The shift at the Bauhaus was contemporary with (and to

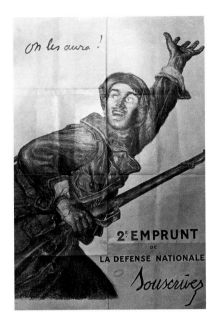

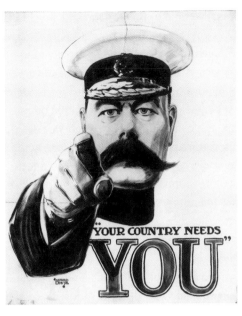

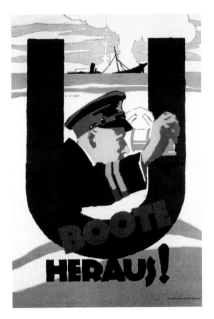

Jules Abel Faivre, *On les aura*, poster, 44 x 16 in (112 x 41 cm), France, 1916.

Alfred Leete, *Your Country Needs You*, poster, 30 x 20 in (76 x 51 cm), Britain, 1914. Imperial War Museum.

Hans Rudi Erdt, *U-Boats Heraus! (U-Boats Launch!)*, poster, 27 ¼ x 18 ⅜ in (69 x 46.7 cm), color lithograph, Germany, 1916. Deutsches Historisches Museum, Berlin.

an extent influenced by) international efforts of artist–designers in Soviet Russia and in other European countries, who, under banners such as Constructivism (Russia), l'Esprit Nouveau (France), and De Stijl (Holland), embraced mechanized mass production, and espoused the advantages of collective and objective standards as a basis for new attitudes toward design in a new, classless society. Such radical and utopian views, often subsumed under the term "Modernism" (with a capital "M"), were meant to replace outmoded individualistic values that were associated with luxury and viewed as contributing to the tensions, belligerence and destruction unleashed during World War I. The experimental use of modern industrial materials for furnishings, elimination of carved or molded ornament, and use of sans serif typography as well as photomechanical processes for printing are often associated with these movements, but were not limited to them or to their particular social and political ideologies. Simple, undecorated forms and the expressive use of typography and page layout in printing emerged in the 1930s in more broadly commercial contexts as well. Depending upon the specific historical context, "Modernism" could signify a variety of attitudes toward modern life, from austerity in the face of economic hardship, to a practical and efficient simplicity, to collective or communal lifestyles, to a lesson in the spiritualized experience of non-objectivity, or to a more casual, even "natural" lifestyle.

World War I mobilized artists and illustrators on both sides of the conflict to build broad public support through the mass media of posters and billboards. Governments sponsored such efforts as part of their campaign to enlist recruits, sell war bonds, and create a sense of shared national identity and purpose. The effort to use mass media to shape public opinion is a theme inherited from nineteenth-century reform (see pages 70–76) and was renewed during World War I with increasing emphasis upon the power and impact of visual images rather than text. At times there is a remarkable similarity among such war posters. Often aimed at a male audience, the combination of romantic idealism and monumentality identifies war with heroism, as seen in Jules Abel Faivre's (1867–1945) 1916 poster image of a young soldier with arm raised high in a plea to buy war bonds (above, left). The direct appeal of gesture and imperative tone of both image and slogan in Alfred Leete's (1882–1933) *Your Country Needs You* poster of 1914 in Britain (page 159, center) made for powerful rhetoric. Such images combined the contrast and simplicity found in German posters by artists such as Lucian Bernhard (see fig. 7.6) with a sense of viewer confrontation derived from the stock techniques of advertising copywriters exhorting potential customers with slogans to buy particular products. War posters blurred the boundaries between art, advertising, and patriotism, and contributed to the tremendous impact that the advertising industry and the art of illustration assumed during the 1920s and 1930s. In Germany poster artists sometimes explored more reductive and sophisticated techniques for engaging the viewer, approaches that laid the foundation for modern graphic design. Hans Rudi Erdt's 1916 *U-Boats Launch* poster (page 159, right) not only simplifies the representational elements of the composition, but also exploits scale contrasts with the sunken ship at the top, as well as integrating lettering and image, with the letter "U" becoming an exploded view of the hull of the submerged ship.

The United States emerged after World War I as a world leader in the mechanized mass production of automobiles and related products of industrial manufacturing such as kitchen appliances, due to the unparalleled success of Henry Ford's moving assembly line in the production of the standardized, unchanging Model T (see pages 151–153). After the mid-1920s, however, consumption levels needed to be sustained through advertising as well as through design innovation. The emergence of Art Deco in the United States was stimulated by the emigration of European designers after World War I in search of creative and economic opportunity, and by the application of modern art to industrial production through the efforts of a small group of artists, collectors, museums, manufacturers, and retail merchandisers. Out of this context developed an indigenous modern expression sometimes known as the Skyscraper Style, inspired by the excitement of urban experience and the rhythms and improvisational spontaneity of jazz music, and marketed through museum exhibitions, department stores, illustrated magazines, and the popular cinema.

The appearance of the professional industrial designer, beginning in the later 1920s and 1930s, was primarily a product of manufacturers' interest in stimulating consumption of industrially manufactured appliances through an appeal to novelty and fantasy in an increasingly competitive economic climate. The need to generate consumer desire, however, was often couched in terms of reform; that is, as a contribution to social progress, aesthetic improvement, hygiene, and the application of domestic science to everyday life, clearly expressed in the modern style known as Streamlining. The planners of the 1939 World's Fair in New York saw design as a component of economic growth and improved living standards for the middle class. Organizers and manufacturers hoped that the resulting reduction of social ills amid the hardships of the Depression would act as a bulwark against the possible lure of Fascist dictatorships in Europe and the attraction of socialism and its threat to capitalist free enterprise. On the eve of the United States's entry into World War II, these efforts hoped to demonstrate that modern industrial design, sponsored by large corporate manufacturers, could have broad consumer appeal through largely symbolic associations between new product designs, technology, progress, and values of efficiency, health, freedom, and comfort.

Purged of some of its threatening associations with collectivism and control, the promotion of modern industrial design reaped even larger rewards for designers, manufacturers, and retailers in the two decades following the end of World War II. And yet the vision of tomorrow on display at the New York World's Fair of 1939 was in some ways an appealing escape from the despair and hopelessness of the Depression, relating more easily to the claims of advertisers than to the grim reminders of poverty and uncertainty found in the photographs of Walker Evans and Dorothea Lange.

Chapter 8

Paris and Art Moderne (Art Deco) Before and After World War I

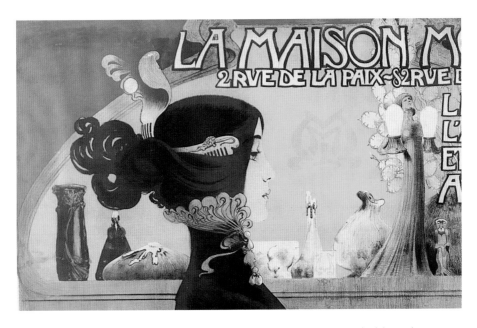

8.1 Manuel Orazi, poster for La Maison Moderne, 31 x 44 ½ in (79 x 113 cm), color lithograph, *c.* 1902.

By 1905 Siegfried Bing's La Maison de l'Art Nouveau showrooms had closed, following the fate of a similar design workshop venture under the direction of the German connoisseur Julius Meier-Graefe known as La Maison Moderne, which had folded during the previous year. There is no single cause for the demise of Art Nouveau. Scholars have argued that competition from antique dealers and manufacturers offering period furnishings for the luxury market may have reduced the market for Art Nouveau. It is also possible that department stores marketing less expensive imitations and reproductions of the style deprived the more exclusive audience for modern decorative arts of the social distinction and cultured sensibility and progressive ideals associated with modern goods and products. A sense of that refinement is found in Manuel Orazi's poster for La Maison Moderne from c. 1902, featuring a slender woman seated in a softly lit interior next to a display of contemporary handcrafted glass and ceramic objects (fig. 8.1). Another reason for the

demise of Art Nouveau could have been the emergence of more practical and efficient attitudes toward modern living, as seen in the Werkbund debates in Germany (see pages 148–151), in the writings on domestic science by Christine Frederick, or the recommendations of taste-makers such as Elsie de Wolfe (1865–1950), who advocated the cultivation of uncluttered interiors, light, and good ventilation in her 1913 book *The House in Good Taste*.

Despite the demise of Art Nouveau, many of the attitudes that nurtured Bing's and Meier-Graefe's showrooms remained, particularly a belief in elevated craft, a close relationship between fine and applied art, and the encouragement of self-expression and innovation in materials and original decoration. These values continued to be supported in France under the auspices of the Société des Artistes Décorateurs (S.A.D.) and the annual Salon d'Automne in which fine and decorative arts were exhibited together. In addition, the publication of periodicals devoted to design (*Art et Décoration*, for example)

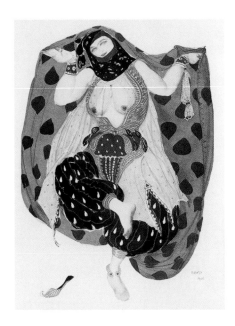

8.2 Léon Bakst, costume design (Odalisque) for *Schéhérazade*, 1910.

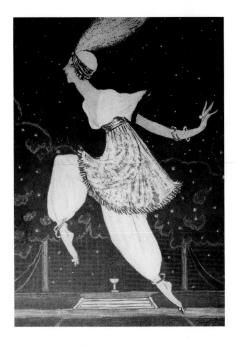

8.3 Georges Lepape, Mme. Poiret wearing "harem" pants designed by Paul Poiret, gouache, 1911.

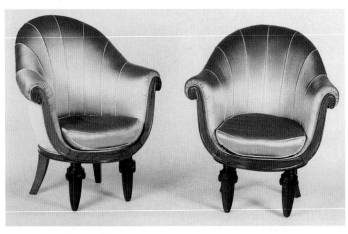

8.4 Maurice Dufrène, pair of chairs, mahogany and upholstery, 30 x 23 in (76.2 x 48.4 cm), (shown at the Salon d'Automne) Paris, 1913.

continued to promote the work of modern designers to a luxury market. French designers were not willing to relinquish the reputation for individuality and originality they had acquired through their association with fine art as well as continuity with a distinguished national legacy of craft excellence prior to as well as after the French Revolution. In this context designers explored new sources of inspiration, including contemporary painting and sculpture, original adaptations of late eighteenth-century Neoclassical furniture design and fashion, as well as sensational entertainments in Paris such the Ballets Russes, associated with an aggressive, spirited modernity.

As most students of early twentieth-century art are aware, bold, non-naturalistic color and a higher degree of abstraction distinguished the paintings of a group of artists at the 1905 Salon d'Automne who acquired the nickname "Fauves" (Wild Beasts), coined by critic Louis Vauxcelles. A similar boldness and intensity of expression characterized productions of the Ballets Russes in Paris, particularly the costumes and stage sets designed between 1909 and 1913 by Russian artists Alexandre Benois (1870–1960) and Léon Bakst (1866–1924) for productions of *Cléopatre* and *Schéhérazade*. These productions featured an element of eroticism and primitivism associated with Near and Middle Eastern cultures expressed in vibrant colors for sets and costumes. Such a shared milieu involving fine arts, entertainment, and fashion is also seen, for instance, by comparing a costume design by Léon Bakst for *Schéhérazade* (1910), and a costume featuring "harem" pants designed by French couturier Paul Poiret (1879–1944) from 1911, both aimed at an elite audience (figs. 8.2 and 8.3). A similar exoticism and sensuality is found in paintings and sketches of Henri Matisse (1869–1954) based upon visits to Morocco in 1911–1912.

FURNITURE AND MODERN ART

While reminiscent of the compact forms, refined crafts-manship, and restrained carved decoration of French later eighteenth-century Neoclassical furniture, there is little that is sober or subdued in the luxury French furniture that emerged during the early twentieth century. Taut curves and spirals, bold color contrasts created by lacquered surfaces and mother-of-pearl or ivory inlays, prancing stags, and luxurious vegetation create a sense of nature's vitality and abundance, only slightly muted by the discipline of symmetry and care taken in the integration of decorative and constructive forms. Maurice Dufrène's (1876–1955) pair of upholstered mahogany armchairs (fig. 8.4), based upon an eighteenth-century "type" known as a bergère (see page 23) and exhibited at the 1913 Salon d'Automne, exemplifies the new direction pursued by

French artist–designers in the years just before the outbreak of World War I. Dufrène began his career as a painter, worked as a furniture designer and manager at Julius Meier-Graefe's La Maison Moderne showrooms, which featured interiors in the Art Nouveau style, helped to found the Société des Artistes Décorateurs in 1901, and managed the retail design studio known as Maîtrise for the Parisian department store Galleries Lafayette beginning in 1922. Dufrène's furniture designs reveal an appreciation for craft and workshop production, and from the second decade of the twentieth century he embraced a robust yet controlled modern sensibility. In the pair of armchairs, for instance, the broad contours of both the back and seat are comfortably balanced and embellished by the carved spiral scroll at the termination of the armrests and the seams of the silk upholstery to create a design remarkable for its harmony and unity of structure and decoration. The broad, sweeping curves of Dufrène's designs recall the ripe fullness and energy in the paintings of Henri Matisse, and also bring to mind Matisse's analogy between painting and furniture in his 1908 essay "Notes of a Painter." In this essay, the artist compared the tranquil mood he hoped that his canvases would provide with the comfort of a good armchair:

> What I dream of is an art of balance, of purity and tranquillity, devoid of troubling subject matter, an art which could be, for every mental worker, for the businessman as well as for the man of letters, for example, a soothing balm, a mental calmative, something akin to a good armchair which eases his physical fatigue...

The acknowledgment that both paintings and furniture could bring relief from the pressures of work and the distractions of daily life (Matisse's remarks stem from a similar statement made by French writer Charles Baudelaire; 1821–1867), reinforces a shared milieu for modern artists and high-end artist-designed craft in common pursuit of original creative expression that contributes to the joy and sense of well-being found in the everyday acts of modern living for a discriminating audience with sufficient leisure to exercise imagination and rise above ordinary perception. Perhaps not surprisingly, Dufrène also designed patterns for woven textiles and upholstery inspired by nature.

Louis Süe (1875–1968) and André Mare (1887–1932) were also painters who pursued careers in the decorative arts beginning around 1910, though unlike Dufrène their backgrounds in design did not include a direct involvement with craft and production. The partners' black ebony cabinet (fig. 8.5 on the right), part of an ensemble dating to 1927, is based on a simple rectangular form, animated

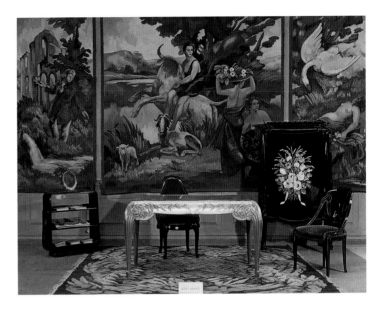

8.5 Louis Süe and André Mare, furniture ensemble (exhibited at the Société des Artistes Décorateurs), 1927.

by tapered legs, a scalloped lower edge to the cabinet doors, and rounded edges above with floral designs lightly carved in relief. The top of the cabinet flares outward to provide a kind of "rail" where objects may be safely placed. When closed, the cabinet doors reveal a lavishly decorated composition of flowers constructed of inlaid mother-of-pearl, balanced but not symmetrical, and brilliantly set off against the black lacquered ground. The ensemble includes a gilt table whose legs and relief decoration match that of the ebony cabinet. Each piece of the ensemble shares common elements but does not constitute a coordinated set in the same way that a late nineteenth-century interior is conceived as a "total work of art." As art historian Nancy Troy has observed, designers during this time seem to have consciously pursued a less integrated aesthetic in which the variety of color, texture, and shape mirror the fragmentation and discontinuity of modern urban life. Critic Gustave Kahn made such connections in his review of the 1912 Salon d'Automne (also known as La Maison Cubiste), noting the relationship between the interiors of the exhibition and the dislocations and changing viewpoints of early Cubism.

Although a Cubist aesthetic may have played a part in the critical reception of a new approach to interior design in the early twentieth century, and the style's angular facets and overlapping planes also contributed in the 1920s to the development of an emerging expression of the urban experience in poster and advertising design (see fig. 9.3), references to the decorative arts in the early Cubist paintings of Georges Braque (1882–1963) and Pablo Picasso (1881–1973) consist primarily of the incorporation

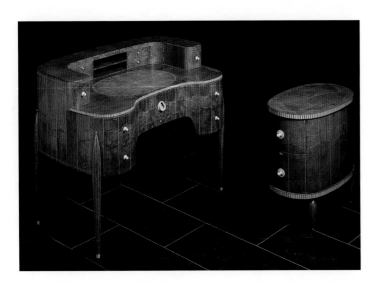

8.6 Jacques-Émile Ruhlmann, desk and tabouret, designed for David-Weill residence, Paris, beech, amboyna veneer, shagreen, and ivory, desk 37 x 47 ½ x 29 ½ in (94 x 121 x 75 cm), tabouret: 27 ½ x 16 ½ x 28 ¼ in (69.9 x 41.9 x 71.8 cm), *c.* 1919. Metropolitan Museum of Art, New York.

of cheap printed wallpaper and the borrowing of wall-painters' techniques for imitating wood grain. Such appropriations constitute encroachments from ordinary life upon the territory of high "Art," both in terms of their lower middle-class associations and the implied blurring between mechanical reproduction and the individual, original, and exclusive work of fine art. Thus while Cubist paintings appear to attack the exclusivity associated with fine art, early twentieth-century critics did not generally acknowledge this provocative crossing of boundaries. Instead, they found parallels for the abstract, compositional elements of Cubism in contemporary luxury craft such as those ensembles displayed at the 1912 Maison Cubiste that reinforced the elevated view of expressive formal composition promoted by the S.A.D.

Different interpretations of Cubism make the relation between this movement and twentieth-century decorative arts complex, raising issues ranging from abstraction, to conflicts between the realms of exclusive and vernacular design, to the definition and role of art in an age of mechanical reproduction. In a similar fashion, some of the experimental typography that emerged in literary works during these same years, treated in more detail below (see pages 208–211), borrowed techniques from newspaper advertisements, challenging expectations for the printed pages of a traditional book.

Like many of his contemporaries in the world of design, Frenchman Jacques-Émile Ruhlmann (1879–1933) studied to be a painter but turned to the decorative arts around 1910. His designs are free interpretations

of French Neoclassical or "Empire" furniture, upholding the French patrimony of virtuoso craftsmanship distinguished by expensive and rare materials and the most exact standards of quality. Yet, as seen in a desk from c. 1919 (fig. 8.6), his furniture is replete with invention and novelty, employing veneers of exotic woods such as amboyna imported from Laos and macassar ebony, from Indonesia (both were French colonial territories at the time), with drawer pullers of ivory attached by green silk thread accenting a grayish-green sharkskin writing surface (on cabinets other exotic materials were used for doors, such as crocodile skin). The desk is supported by thin legs that project outward from the desktop and are delicately tapered in a form known as "fuseau."

The new style emerging in these years was, of course, not limited to wood furniture and techniques that built upon the tradition of the great French *ébénistes* of the eighteenth century. New materials and techniques particularly challenged modern designers in many media, as in the interior furnishings of Armand-Albert Rateau (1882–1937), for instance a 1922 chaise longue of patinated bronze (fig. 8.7). In Rateau's work foliate forms are simplified into spirals or arabesques. Gracefully proportioned stags frequently appear, their forms simplified into crisp, athletic contours, quite unlike the freer, meandering curves of Art Nouveau. Rateau's chaise longue was commissioned for a terrace outside of the bedroom in the Paris apartment of couturier Jeanne Lanvin (1867–1946), and it is worthwhile to note the degree to which fashion designers themselves were patrons of the new style in French decorative arts, such as Lanvin or fellow couturier Paul Poiret. In fact, Poiret was a patron of the Salon d'Automne of 1911 and the Maison Cubiste of 1912, and employed the Fauve painter Raoul Dufy (1877–1953) to design textile patterns. Dufy's designs, whether woven for upholstery or block-printed for curtains or wallpaper, often include figures set amid foliage or stagelike props that lend themselves to repetition and reinforce two-dimensional

8.7 Armand-Albert Rateau, chaise longue, patinated bronze, 25 ³⁄₁₆ x 60 ¼ x 23 ⅜ in (64 x 153 x 59.5 cm), *c.* 1920–1922. Musée des Arts Décoratifs, Paris.

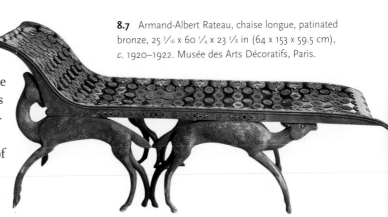

pattern. An example, from 1929, is a block-printed wallpaper design depicting paired ice skaters (fig. 8.8). The emphasis upon carefree leisure pastimes has much in common with the formal as well as thematic character of eighteenth-century tapestry and porcelain described in Part I (see fig. 1.9). Photographs of Dufy's wallpaper patterns appeared in a contemporary issue of the fashion magazine *Vogue* in a section devoted to the arts. In a later monumental mural painting, Dufy decorated an enormous hall for the 1937 World's Fair in Paris with hundreds of figures and motifs illustrating the history of electricity. Dufy emphasized the discovery and benefits of electricity in human terms, depicting the scientists who contributed to its development, along with railways, turbines, and outdoor lighting for evening concerts with orchestra and chorus, and might be contrasted with more abstract, graphic, and mechanical treatment of electricity-inspired themes in posters and other media (see fig. 10.43).

In 1911 Poiret opened Atelier Martine to produce and sell fabric designs and furnishings, employing a group of young girls from working-class neighborhoods to sketch floral patterns based upon visits to the city's botanical gardens. Poiret's own silk textile (fig. 8.9) possesses the characteristics seen in the designs of the workshop: here a simple pattern of pink and silvery-white radiating petal-like shapes explode against a black ground, restrained only by the discipline of the repetition of the simplified lozenge and circular shapes. As mentioned above, Poiret's own fashions made use of the bold and even discordant color combinations of the Ballets Russes after its appearance in 1910 and the staging of ballets based upon *Schéhérezade* and other themes taken from the lore of the Near and Middle East. He created the idea of "harem" pants for women (see fig. 8.3), and his fashion designs permitted more freedom of movement and a closer relationship between garment and body that was considered quite provocative for its time. Poiret's own celebrity contributed to his success, and his considerable promotional efforts stand within a late nineteenth-century tradition of artists' studios that were specifically designed as meeting places for potential clients (see pages 108–109). Such notoriety, however, was short-lived for Poiret, whose reputation was damaged at the outbreak of World War I, when the popularity of his designs in Germany led to false accusations by some critics that he was an enemy sympathizer. Nevertheless, Poiret benefited from links between fashion and fine art that he also nurtured through associations with fine artists such as Dufy, and that helped to maintain the aura of exclusivity surrounding original works of art while cultivating the public exposure that brought greater opportunities for wider sales, markets, and serial production.

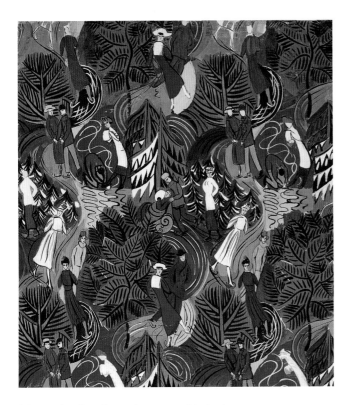

8.8 Raoul Dufy, wallpaper design, woodblock print, 1929. Private collection.

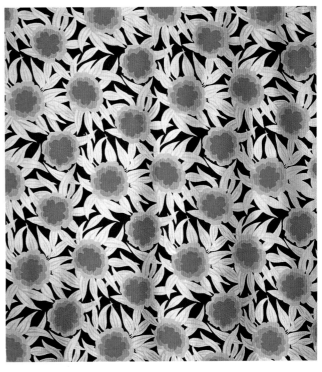

8.9 Paul Poiret, textile, printed silk, 70 ¼ x 50 ¼ in (180 x 129 cm), manufactured by Atelier Martine, c. 1919. Metropolitan Museum of Art, New York.

GLASS AND METAL

An examination of glass design in the period around 1910 reveals a lively interest in experimentation with a variety of techniques to permit individual and original expression in the medium. In many ways early twentieth-century French glassmakers drew inspiration from the example of Émile Gallé, and as with other designers, glass artists often began their careers as painters or sculptors. Perhaps as a result of Gallé's successful example and reputation, early twentieth-century glass does not always make a distinct break with Art Nouveau. The enameling technique known as pâte de verre, produced by refiring colored ground glass in molds, resulted in translucent surfaces of varied color whose rich effects were reminiscent of the earlier style, even if the technique, to be successful, required thick walls, more patient attention to the cooling process, and often resulted in smoother surfaces and more regular shapes than those of Gallé. An example is a pâte de verre bowl designed and produced by François Décorchemont (1880–1971; fig. 8.10). Other French designers directed their efforts to clear glass, often with thick walls pressed into molds to accentuate relief surfaces, or sometimes trapping bubbles in a technique known as "verre soufflé" or "bubble glass." The increasing emphasis upon working with clear rather than colored glass is seen in the oeuvre of Maurice Marinot (1882–1960), who abandoned an early career as a painter to work with the medium of glass. After experimenting with the process of pâte de verre, Marinot began exploring effects using transparent glass. Results were thick-walled and sculptural, incorporating bubbles and streaks produced in the process of making rather than as applied decoration, as seen in a bottle from 1924 (fig. 8.11).

Also identified with new explorations in the field of glass design in the early twentieth century was René Lalique (1860–1945), who operated his own facility near Paris for the manufacture of limited editions of his designs. Lalique was trained as a jeweler, and earlier in his career created some of the most celebrated examples of Art Nouveau jewelry using precious metals, stones, and enamel. Before the end of the first decade of the new century he began working with glass as an inexpensive industrial material rather than using precious gems, purchasing a lightbulb factory in 1911 to

8.10 François Décorchemont, bowl, pâte de verre, height 4 $^{13}/_{16}$ in (12.4 cm), 1909. Musée d'Orsay, Paris.

expand his knowledge of the medium. Like Marinot, Lalique explored glass primarily as a transparent rather than opaque medium, using etching with acid to achieve contrast and varied textures. Lalique's work was admired for its purity and brilliance, seen in the c. 1925 Firebird lamp (fig. 8.12), which took its name from a well-known production of the Ballets Russes that was staged in 1910 and again in 1926 with music by the Russian composer Igor Stravinsky (1882–1971). In this work the "ordinary," clear form of the material is rendered almost magically invisible, revealing an etched floating female figure whose feathered wings and plantlike tail echo the contour of an elaborate, fan-shaped shade. The reputation Lalique established before World War I continued after the Armistice in 1918. As early as 1907 he was asked by perfumer François Coty (1876–1934) to design labels for perfume bottles. The partnership grew to include the design of the glass bottles themselves, strengthening a link between art glass and the marketing of perfumes in the wake of the expansion of this industry with the introduction of synthetic perfumes in the early years of the twentieth century. Many Lalique perfume containers included glass stoppers that were an integral part of the design, and generated appeal through references to exotic plants whose extracts were the inspiration for the scents themselves.

Other early twentieth-century designers were also attracted to the idea of transforming ordinary and inexpensive materials into highly original designs through a reconsideration of their creative possibilities. For instance, Swiss-born Jean Dunand (1877–1942) came to Paris originally to study sculpture. His teacher, Jean Dampt (1854–1946), advocated egalitarian views toward the arts, and with his mentor's encouragement Dunand pursued and achieved critical success in the field of dinanderie, a term used to refer to small vases and utensils manufactured from

8.11 Maurice Marinot, bottle with stopper, blown glass with acid-etched decoration "verre soufflé," 10 $^1/_4$ in (27.3 cm) high, 1924. Philadelphia Museum of Art.

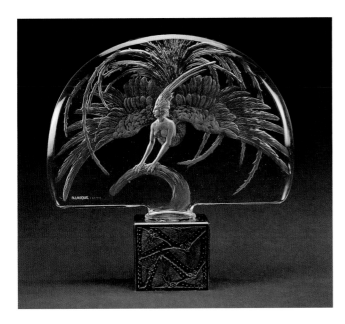

8.12 René Lalique, *Oiseau de Feu* (Firebird) glass lamp with bronze base, height 16 ⅞ in (43 cm), *c.* 1925. Private collection.

achieved with the medium (fig. 8.13). Dunand's obsessive dedication to craft is demonstrated in this description of the lacquering process for a wooden screen:

as many as forty coats of lacquer had to be applied and, as the lacquer in drying tended to contract and could thus twist the wooden panel of a screen out of shape, another coat had to be applied on the reverse side to counteract the tension: both coats drying simultaneously ensured that the base remained true. The drying process presented complications, taking any time between three and four days, and paradoxically could only be satisfactorily accomplished in a room kept perpetually damp by means of streams of water flowing down the walls. Further complications were added in that the drying process could only take place in a darkened room and for some mysterious reason was affected by the moon's influence, the best result occurring when the moon was full. After each coat a process of careful rubbing down and smoothing to a perfect surface had to be performed before another coat of lacquer could be applied.

non-precious metals such as copper and brass, using various kinds of patina for textures and colored surfaces as well as the technique of repoussé for introducing relief patterns based upon geometric and schematic floral forms. Occasionally the organic shapes of Dunand's early dinanderie vases recall the irregularity of Art Nouveau pottery or glass, but often his works exhibit a preference for more regular contours and classically-inspired shapes (such as the amphora), as well as spiral decorative motifs. Such works were shown at the exhibitions sponsored by the Société des Artistes Décorateurs and were illustrated in the publication *Art et Décoration*. In 1912 Dunand began learning the technique of applying lacquer to a variety of dinanderie from a well-known Japanese craftsman named Seizo Sugawara (d. 1940) who was living in Paris. Lacquer is a colored or transparent substance made from the sap of trees grown primarily in the Far East. A long process of refinement and purification is required to produce it, and its application to surfaces of wood or metal objects is equally painstaking. Although lacquer was used primarily as a protective coating to preserve and protect materials (with Dunand's assistance the French air force used lacquer to coat the surface of plywood propellers during World War I in order to prevent the dangerous deterioration of the material in wet or humid weather), Dunand became interested in lacquer's potential for design, which he developed more fully after the war. His exacting methods produced layered surfaces of great subtlety and brilliance on a variety of wooden screens, metal bowls, and furniture. An idea of the variety is seen in a composite photograph revealing the range of effects that might be

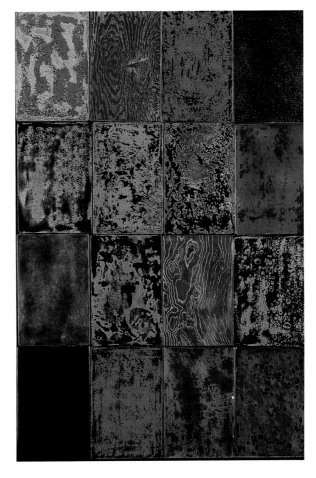

8.13 Jean Dunand, samples of decorative lacquers.

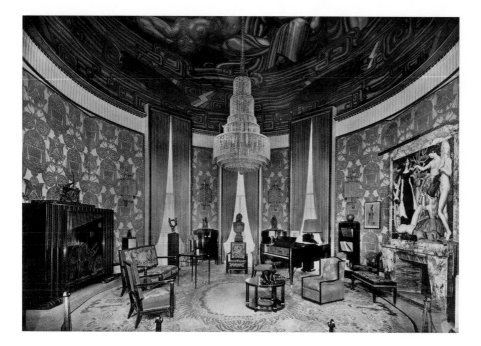

8.14 Jacques-Émile Ruhlmann, Grand Salon, Hôtel d'un Collectionneur, Exposition Internationale des Arts Décoratifs et Industriels Modernes, Paris, 1925, with black lacquer cabinet from the workshop of Jean Dunand on the left and Jean Dupas' painting *Les Perruches* (*The Songbirds* or *The Parakeets*) on the right.

Other examples of the technique include the large black cabinet incised with strips of silver in the simplified form of a hedgehog, a collaboration between Dunand, Polish-born painter Jean Lambert-Rucki (1888–1967), and metalsmith Jean Goulden (see below, page 175); this monumental cabinet, more than eight feet in length, was exhibited in 1925 in the interior of the Grand Salon of the Hôtel d'un Collectionneur for the Exposition Internationale des Arts Décoratifs et Industriels Modernes (figs. 8.14 and 8.15).

While many of the designers associated with the Art Moderne style were active in the years 1905–1915, others emerged more fully only after World War I. Metalsmith Edgar Brandt (1880–1960), who worked with wrought iron and experimented with combinations of metals and alloys, was an artist–craftsman who used new technologies, such as autogenous welding, which permitted the combination of different metals in the creation of furniture, lighting, plaques, doors, and screens. The projecting wrought-iron table with marble top from c. 1925

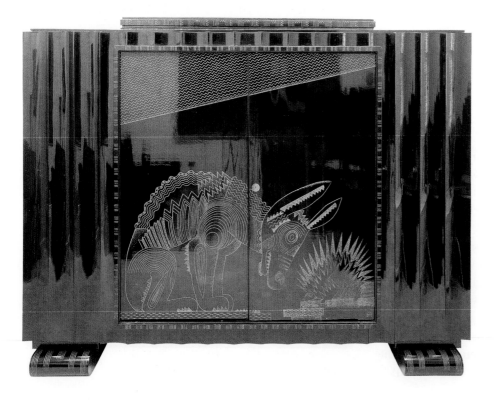

8.15 Jean Dunand and Jean Lambert-Rucki, cabinet, black lacquer with incised strips of silver, 77 x 98 x 29 in (195.5 x 248.9 x 73.6 cm), from Grand Salon, Hôtel d'un Collectionneur, Exposition Internationale des Arts Décoratifs et Industriels Modernes, Paris, 1925. Private collection.

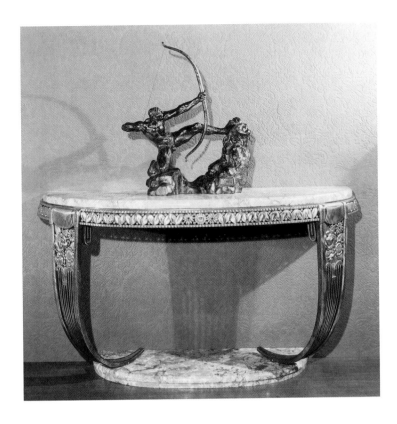

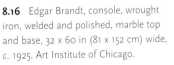

8.16 Edgar Brandt, console, wrought iron, welded and polished, marble top and base, 32 x 60 in (81 x 152 cm) wide, c. 1925. Art Institute of Chicago.

(fig. 8.16) is distinguished by the broad curves of its legs terminating in spirals. These contours are reminiscent of the sweeping lines of the inlaid mother-of-pearl bouquet in the cabinet of Süe et Mare (see fig. 8.5) or the amphora-shaped forms of lacquered vases by Jean Dunand. More original are the plaques and screens Brandt created for special commission, such as the *Cigognes d'Alsace* (fig. 8.17), a large grille in patinated wrought iron and tin. This design of 1922 was repeated, supported by a plywood surface, in a commission of 1928 for the interior wall panels of elevators in Selfridges department store in London (removed in 1971 to comply with new fire regulations and now relocated to the Museum of London with an additional example in the Victoria and Albert Museum). These large relief plaques rival the effects of an illusionistic ceiling from a Baroque church or palace, with circling birds hovering against an asymmetrically placed octagonal opening from which schematically rendered rays emanate outward. The composition is embellished with spiraling cloud forms in relief, repeated in smaller and more shallow variations throughout the large plaque. The *Cigognes* is a unique showpiece that tests the limits of a medium often associated with a limited vocabulary of stock motifs, textures, and patterns; in this example the inherent tensile strength of the wrought iron is maintained in the rodlike projections from the octagon containing the storks, while the varied textures of the cloud forms and the illusionism of the radiating composition itself suggest a softness or malleability that transcends the materials' usual associations through the artist's vision and virtuosity. Such dazzling technical displays found expression as well in the interior design of luxury ocean liners during the 1930s. A well-known example of interior decoration from the Grand Salon of the luxury liner SS *Normandie*, also evoking a Baroque theme, is *The Chariot of Aurora* lacquer and metal leaf on plaster

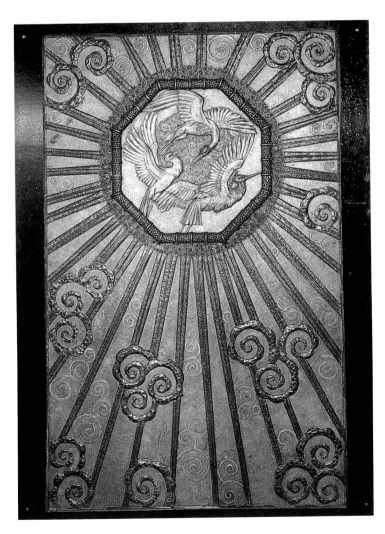

8.17 Edgar Brandt, detail of *Les Cigognes d'Alsace*, grille, patinated wrought iron and tin, 8 ft 2 ½ in x 6 ft 7 in x 3 ½ in (2.6 m x 2 m x 9 cm), exhibited at the Salon des Artistes Françaises, 1922. Victoria and Albert Museum, London.

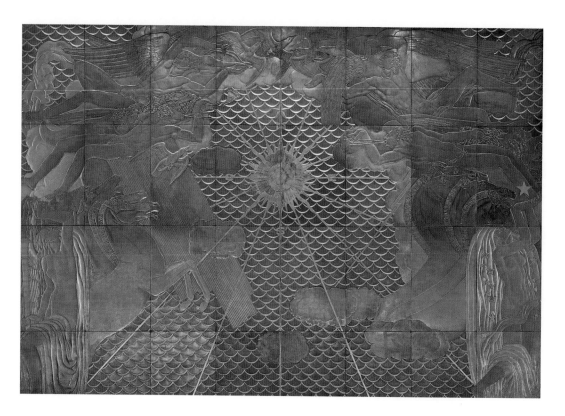

8.18 Jean Dupas and Jean Dunand, *The Chariot of Aurora*, detail, wall decoration, lacquer and metal leaf on plaster relief, 216 x 312 x 2 in (548.6 x 792.5 x 5.1 cm), 1935. Carnegie Museum of Art, Pittsburgh.

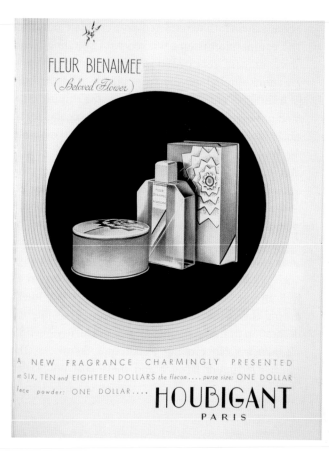

8.19 Perfume advertisement from American *Vogue*, November 10, 1930, page 97, Houbigant company.

relief, designed by the painter Jean Dupas (1882–1964) and executed by Jean Dunand in 1935 (fig. 8.18). *The Chariot of Aurora* (26 feet long) is one of four panels depicting mythological gods and goddesses in relation to the themes of travel and navigation. Sunrays emanate across clouds and schematic wavelike imbrications form a flaming disk. In this example, Aurora (the dawn) rises in a chariot accompanied by nude figures that are fused with representations of winds, rain, spring flowers, and the autumn harvest. Like extravagant hotels even today, such luxury interior design offered an appealing if ephemeral escape, at least for the wealthy, from the financial uncertainty following the New York stockmarket crash in October 1929 and its ensuing global economic repercussions. On the popular level, advertising and film brought similar relief in vicarious form, as the entertainment industry sought to attract viewers and manufacturers looked to designers, as well as celebrities, to market cosmetics and other less expensive fashion products as accessories to refined living. An example from a 1930 advertisement in American *Vogue* is illustrated in figure 8.19, featuring Houbigant perfume and face powder in packaging designed with Art Deco forms and decorative patterns.

Another metal designer to emerge after World War I was Jean Puiforcat (1897–1945), who came from a family of silversmiths in Paris. His father had directed

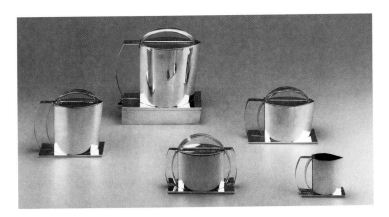

8.20 Jean Puiforcat, five-piece tea and coffee service, silver and crystal, tallest piece 9 1/8 x 9 x 3 5/8 in (23.2 x 22.9 x 9.2 cm), 1925. Minneapolis Institute of Art.

L'AMERIQUE DU SUD

A.M.CASSANDRE

PAR LE PAQUEBOT

"L'ATLANTIQUE"

(40000 T.)

COMPAGNIE DE NAVIGATION
SUD-ATLANTIQUE

8.21 A. M. Cassandre, poster for *L'Atlantique*, 24 3/8 x 39 in (62 x 99 cm), 1931. © Mouron Cassandre. All rights reserved.

the family business toward the luxury market, and also had acquired an impressive collection of antique silver objects for display in the workshop's showrooms. Throughout a career that began after his return from service in World War I, Puiforcat maintained an interest in both stone sculpture and silver, and was strongly influenced by the modern abstractions of the human figure in the sculptures of Aristide Maillol (1861–1944). Like the work of Maillol and that of Romanian-born sculptor Constantin Brancusi (1876–1957), Puiforcat's designs reduce naturalism in favor of more permanent underlying forms that reveal geometry and balance. In addition to his designs displaying affinity to contemporary sculpture for geometric abstraction, Puiforcat also admired the abstract geometric qualities and precision in the fields of engineering and transportation, particularly the great luxury ocean liners, whose smooth, tapered bows appear to be the inspiration for a tea and coffee service of 1925 (fig. 8.20).

A similar simplified abstraction of this basic form appears in the advertising posters of Russian-born artist Cassandre (born Adolphe Jean-Marie Mouron; 1901–1968), seen, for instance, in a travel poster for the luxury liner *L'Atlantique* in 1931 (fig. 8.21), in which the simplified shape of the hull is inscribed within a rectangle, again emphasizing its abstract geometric character and monumentality, further exaggerated by the contrast with the small tugboat to the lower left of the image. To further suggest the machinelike precision and geometric purity of the forms, Cassandre used a pneumatic airbrush to apply color to the lithographic stone, introducing an element of subtle and precise tonal control beyond the capability of more direct means of drawing or painting with brushes.

Cassandre likened his task as a poster artist to that of a telegrapher who was the instantaneous transmitter of condensed visual information rather than its author. Despite the matter-of-fact tone of this self-assessment, Cassandre's designs were highly original and recognizable, combining the tradition of the art poster with a relationship to graphic and reductive geometric abstraction seen in Cubist painting. He also incorporated sophisticated verbal as well as visual puns that helped to concentrate and integrate text and image. His work helped to define the profession of graphic design in the interwar years, eschewing more conventional narrative advertising illustration in favor of bolder ways of identifying products and creating

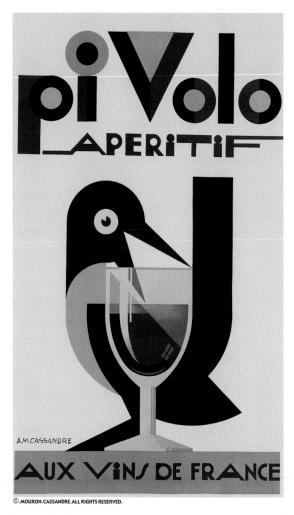

8.22 A. M. Cassandre, poster for PiVolo, 24 x 36 in (61 x 91.4 cm), color lithograph, 1925. © Mouron Cassandre. All rights reserved.

immediate and memorable visual impact. A 1925 poster for the aperitif PiVolo (fig. 8.22) not only creates an image out of the title lettering by repeating the circle for the lower-case "p" and "o" and the dot above the "i" (also note the bird's eye below), but also connects the wineglass with an upper-case "V," the left stem of which is formed from the contour of the bird itself. Indeed, Cassandre's symbols and letters had the ability, in a single or repeated image, to appeal with both immediacy and sophistication. They also allude to modern advertising techniques that stress transformation as a result of using a product, as in "before" and "after" comparisons. A similar sophistication, integrating fragmentary or pictographic images with blocks of text to create visual variety and interest, is found in books and high-end journals in Paris in the interwar period, as practiced by publisher Alfred Tolmer (d. 1957). In 1930, Tolmer published a book entitled *Mise en Page* that helped to define new techniques that explored creative approaches to visual communication in the publishing industry.

Following the end of World War I, economic reconstruction and a renewed sense of patriotism in France helped to expand the commercial scope of Art Deco. One element in this expansion was the growth of retail outlets for the marketing of modern design and decoration. In 1919 Süe et Mare founded the Compagnie des Arts Françaises to provide a showroom for their own products and those of their collaborators, and in the same year Ruhlmann established a storefront business as an addition to the private commissions that were virtually the sole basis of his earlier work. During the same period, metal craftsman René Joubert founded a company to market the works of modern designers, called Décoration Intérieure Moderne (D.I.M.), and the prominent French department stores also inaugurated special showrooms for the display of modern furnishings: Bon Marché opened Pomone in 1923 under the direction of furniture designer Paul Follot (1877–1941), and in 1921 Galleries Lafayette opened La Maîtrise directed by Maurice Dufrène. Many of these retail ventures supported an active engagement of art with industrial production to maintain and strengthen the French reputation for original designs of artist–craftsmen efficiently manufactured to compete internationally with historical styles through their connection both with modern art and with progressive contemporary living.

THE PARIS EXPOSITION OF 1925

As early as 1911, the French government began to plan for yet another large international exhibition of the decorative and industrial arts to take place in Paris, but the effort was delayed due to disagreements over the criteria for exhibitors and finally to the outbreak of World War I. Planning resumed after the war, resulting in the Exposition Internationale des Arts Décoratifs et Industriels Modernes of 1925. Due to lingering hostilities, Germany was not invited to exhibit, and the United States declined to participate, based upon a perceived inability to comply with the criteria established by the organizers that stipulated all designs be modern and not based upon historical period styles (see page 223 onward). Despite efforts on the part of the organizing body to encourage arrangements of furnishings that suggested real living and working spaces and visualized "new modes of life," most of the exhibits focused upon products and interiors aimed at an exclusive market, unique works and ensembles created by individual artist–designers.

The exhibition grounds featured temporary pavilions sponsored by the major Parisian department stores and associations of industries such as perfumes and decorative glass manufacturers, a Gallery of Boutiques exhibiting the works of individual designers, as well as pavilions sponsored by invited nations including Finland and the Soviet Union. Exhibition spaces were allotted to French design organizations, most prominently the Société des Artistes Décorateurs, as well as the more recently formed l'esprit nouveau, the latter featuring a model furnished apartment by the Swiss-born designer and architect Charles-Édouard Jeanneret (1887–1965), known since c. 1921 as Le Corbusier (see pages 176–177 and fig. 8.30). A number of members of the S.A.D. also contributed ensembles individually, and after much discussion this organization was asked to design a model French embassy with reception areas and living rooms assigned to different members.

Many of the interiors and furnishings at the exhibition featured the luxurious decoration and rare materials used by designers such as Ruhlmann and Süe and Mare. Ruhlmann's Hôtel d'un Collectionneur was a separate structure consisting of a number of interiors designed both for living and lavish entertaining. The Hôtel's Grand Salon (see fig. 8.14) was an oval-shaped room with ceilings over 20 feet (6 meters) high and a chandelier resembling a hanging fountain created by tiers of concentric circles hung with chains of clear glass beading. The monumental black lacquer cabinet, produced in the workshop of Jean Dunand (see fig. 8.15), was placed opposite the fireplace. The centerpiece of the room was a grand piano in macassar ebony, the S-curve of which was accentuated by Ruhlmann and echoed in its tapered legs. The piano's legs were inlaid in ivory and flared outward like the hooves of a fawn where they met the floor. Above the marble fireplace hung a large painting by painter Jean Dupas (1882–1964) entitled *Les Perruches* (*The Songbirds* or *The Parakeets*, see fig. 8.14), depicting a group of draped and nude women with elaborate coiffures, some clothed or partially clothed in heavy satin or silk brocaded fabrics, and set in a landscape of lush fruit, foliage, flowers, and plump birds. Photographs of the painting in situ reveal harmonies in color between the skin tones of the nudes and the light background of the fabric wall-covering as well as the grained marble of the fireplace. Dupas' image of abundance and sensual pleasure, both in nature and through the products of fashion, is a fitting counterpart to the comfort, grace, and luxury of Ruhlmann's Grand Salon. The ensemble reinforced the continued strength of craft traditions supported by modern workshop production and the close relationship between fine and applied arts.

Other interiors for the exhibition were distinguished by a preference for angles rather than curves, and by the use or imitation of industrial rather than natural materials such as smooth metal sheeting, expanses of plate glass, polished marble, or lacquer. Jean Dunand designed a smoking room (fig. 8.23) for the model French embassy

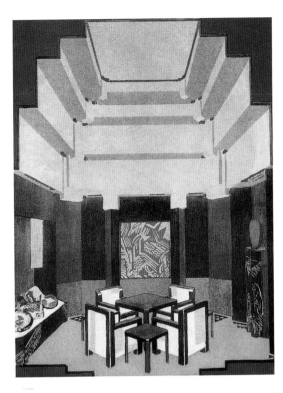

8.23 Jean Dunand, sketch for a smoking room, Ambassade Française, Exposition Internationale des Arts Décoratifs et Industriels Modernes, Paris, 1925.

constructed by members of S.A.D. The room was square with beveled corners creating an octagonal space, surmounted by a tiered ceiling resembling a stepped pyramid or ziggurat. The walls were covered with black lacquer panels and the ceiling painted silver with red accents in the corners. The same color scheme was repeated for a square table in the center of the room and four square armchairs with silver paneled sides. The geometric severity of the interior was relieved only by the abstract foliate textiles for cushions and pillows of the built-in sofa and the wall-hanging facing the entrance. Imagining the smoking room filled with a collection of diplomats in starched white collars and black evening attire increases the aesthetic effect of formal elegance Dunand may have envisioned. The relationship among architecture, decoration, and furnishings is as unified as Ruhlmann's Grand Salon, while the severity of the design suggests a source of inspiration based not upon the luxurious and sensual forms of nature but rather upon a heightened feeling for smooth textures and elementary geometric form found in early 20th century abstract sculpture (see above, page 171). Sophisticated and restrained in both color as well as form and decoration, the smoking room has an air of psychological distance, not unlike the aloof demeanor captured in contemporary advertisements and discussed below (see fig. 10.16).

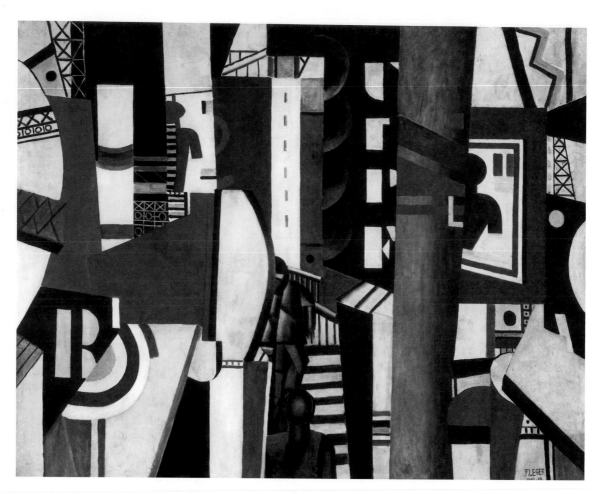

8.24 Fernand Léger, *The City*, oil on canvas, 7 ft 7 in x 9 ft ½ in (2.3 x 2.8 m), 1919. Philadelphia Museum of Art.

While nature and abundance remained a strong source of inspiration for Art Deco designers, the man-made environment of machines and construction was also a source of wonder and excitement in the early twentieth century. It emerges, for instance, in Cubist painting prior to World War I in the works of Fernand Léger (1881–1955). Léger incorporated bold stencil (rather than hand-drawn) lettering derived from nineteenth-century display typography used for signs and printed advertisements along with emphasizing the smooth surfaces of industrially manufactured cylindrical forms resembling pipes, iron rods, or artillery cannon barrels in explosive canvases such as *The City* from 1919 (fig. 8.24).

Until the second decade of the twentieth century, the attitude of many French artists and critics toward the machine and industrialization was ambivalent, as demonstrated by the virtual absence of the Eiffel Tower as a subject in contemporary painting for almost two decades after it was built as the showpiece for the Paris World's Fair of 1889. However, the tower appears as the inspiration for a series of works, entitled *Windows on the City*, devoted to the subject by Robert Delaunay (1885–1941) beginning around 1910. Delaunay completed many works based upon the

tower, increasingly employing abstraction to accentuate the sweeping energy of its tapered shape and open construction (fig. 8.25). He combined the Parisian landmark with airplanes and their spinning propellers to further celebrate the triumph of technology over nature, as in his *Homage to Blériot* of 1913, commemorating the French pilot's daring solo flight across the English Channel.

A tall painted mural by Robert Delaunay, featuring the Eiffel Tower, was included in one of the interiors for the model French embassy at the 1925 Exposition des Arts Décoratifs et Industriels Modernes, but a more persistent link between the fragmented and dynamic style of these works and the decorative arts was made by Delaunay's Ukrainian-born wife, Sonia Terk Delaunay (1885–1979). Sonia Delaunay used overlapping or interlocking abstract geometric shapes and prismatic color for the design of interiors, fabrics, clothing, and other furnishings. The Delaunays used the term "simultaneity" to describe the dynamism and transcendence of matter that emerged in the experience of modernity, and in 1925 a Boutique Simultanée was included as one of the Gallery of Boutiques featured at the Paris Exhibition. The following year, the Delaunays collaborated on the costumes and set

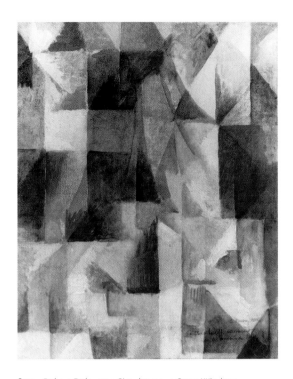

8.25 Robert Delaunay, *Simultaneous Open Windows*, oil on canvas, 18 x 14 ³⁄₄ in (45.5 x 37.5 cm), 1912. Tate Modern, London.

designs for a new production of *Cléopatre* performed by the Ballets Russes in Paris. A cover illustration by Georges Lepape in British *Vogue* from 1925 featured a model wearing a dress designed by Sonia Delaunay beside a roadster decorated with simultaneous patterns (fig. 8.26).

Cubist fragmentation also appears on a silvered bronze and enamel clock designed and crafted by Jean Goulden (1878–1946), a physician who learned the art of enamel (glass paste) while serving in the army in Greece during World War I and encountering Byzantine enamels at the monastery of Mount Athos (fig. 8.27). The simple circles and diamond shapes on the clock dial as well as the plain rectangular hands appear to tumble and splinter onto the asymmetrical base; without recourse to classical allegory (see fig. 1.12), Goulden nevertheless alludes to the often frantic and inexorable march of time.

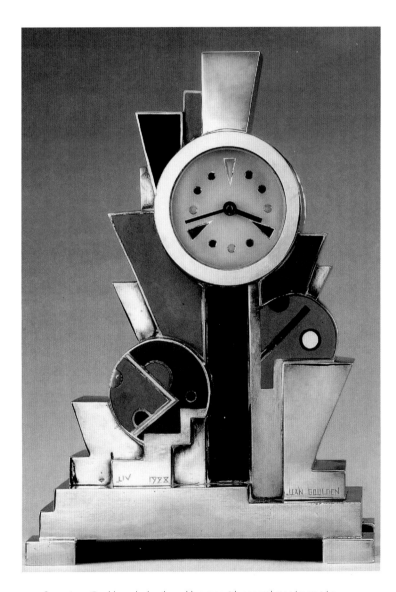

8.26 Georges Lepape, cover of British *Vogue*, January, 1925.

8.27 Jean Goulden, clock, silvered bronze with enamel, 14 ¹⁄₄ x 10 ²⁄₃ x 4 ³⁄₄ in (36.2 x 25.7 x 12.4 cm), 1928. Collection Stephen E. Kelly.

In addition to luxury, formal elegance and the exhilarating pace of modern urban life, Art Deco designers also helped to shape contemporary interest in athletics and exercise that found expression in simple, active sportswear, such as Elsa Schiaparelli's sketch for a wraparound dress dating to 1930 (fig. 8.28) or even earlier designs for tennis sweaters and outfits. Francis Jourdain's (1876–1958) Physical Culture Room and the adjoining Lounge designed by Pierre Chareau (1883–1950), also part of the S.A.D.'s French Embassy (fig. 8.29), employed smooth wood paneling attached to walls and ceiling to resemble riveted metal sheeting. A daybed in Chareau's Lounge was suspended from thin steel bars attached to the ceiling (rather than supported by legs) and covered with a bedspread, and the square clock, rectangular sliding screens, and simple, plaid patterns for curtains and fabrics repeated a geometric theme that further articulated the

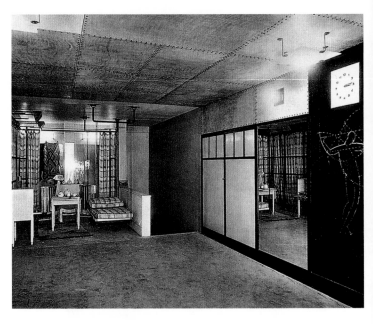

8.29 Francis Jourdain and Pierre Chareau, Physical Culture Room and Lounge, Ambassade Française, Exposition Internationale des Arts Décoratifs et Industriels Modernes, Paris, 1925.

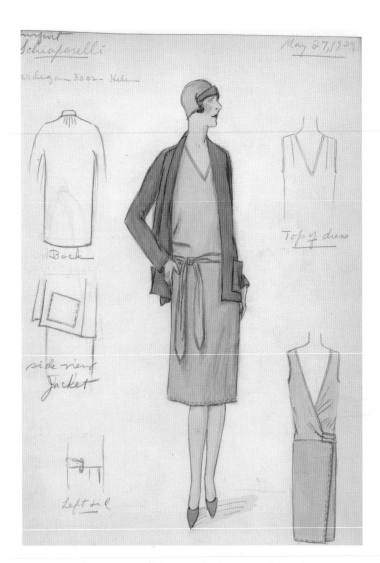

8.28 Elsa Schiaparelli, fashion sketch of wraparound dress for summer 1930. The Fashion Institute of Technology, New York.

rectilinear floor plan and elevation of the space. The interest in exercise seen in Jourdain's Physical Culture Room seems more appropriately to fulfill the hope of the organizers to offer examples of design that pointed to "new modes of life," in this case an emphasis upon personal health and hygiene. Such values also played a role in the design of kitchens based upon a more efficient arrangement of work and storage spaces, as well as the elimination of carved or molded decoration to reduce the accumulation of dust (requiring less cleaning in middle-class households without servants). Nonetheless, the Physical Culture Room is a private rather than public space, and suggests that exercise is understood here as both a modern and a fashionable form of leisure pursuit; indeed the silversmith Jean Puiforcat was a recognized athlete who competed for the French Olympic ice hockey team.

Even more spartan than Jourdain's and Chareau's rooms was a model housing unit known as the Pavillon de l'Esprit Nouveau, designed by Le Corbusier. This structure was perhaps the most radical French expression of new attitudes toward design emerging after World War I, embracing the use of standardized prefabricated building materials and rejecting decoration as a vestige of outmoded craft methods of production (fig. 8.30). The furnishings of the apartment included bentwood chairs, tables, and modular built-in storage units supported by thin dowel-like legs that divided an open rectangular space into connected living, dining, and study areas. Much of the furniture was available commercially through office-supply catalogues (although for the exhibition the pieces were custom-made to better conform to the proportions of the interior and the size of the doors), and the Thonet bentwood chairs were more commonly associated with cafés than with domestic living. Le Corbusier referred to such furniture as "type-objects," basic, anonymous, and permanent forms resulting from a process of gradual refinement based upon utility and economy. The architect used the term "mechanical selection" to refer to the process leading to these final forms for a variety of man-made products. Described as a "machine for living in" and compared to similar descriptions of automobiles as "machines for transportation" and airplanes as "machines for flying," Le Corbusier's Pavillon de l'Esprit Nouveau suggested that the basis of a design for modern living was to be found in the simple fulfillment of universal functional requirements for living rather than in the luxury and individuality of the traditional home or apartment. Satisfying those requirements depended more upon the skills of the engineer and the practical sensibility of the modern architect than those of the individual artist. Moreover, such a collective approach, developed in admiration of the accomplishments of engineering in the construction of bridges, airplanes, and other products of modern technology, was seen by Le Corbusier as essential to address pressing social and economic needs for housing that confronted the French nation in the aftermath of World War I. While some large building supply companies supported Le Corbusier's vision for modern design by underwriting the construction costs of the Pavillon de l'Esprit Nouveau, that vision conflicted with the traditional practice of design and its understanding by most manufacturers, retailers, and consumers in a competitive commercial context. Yet

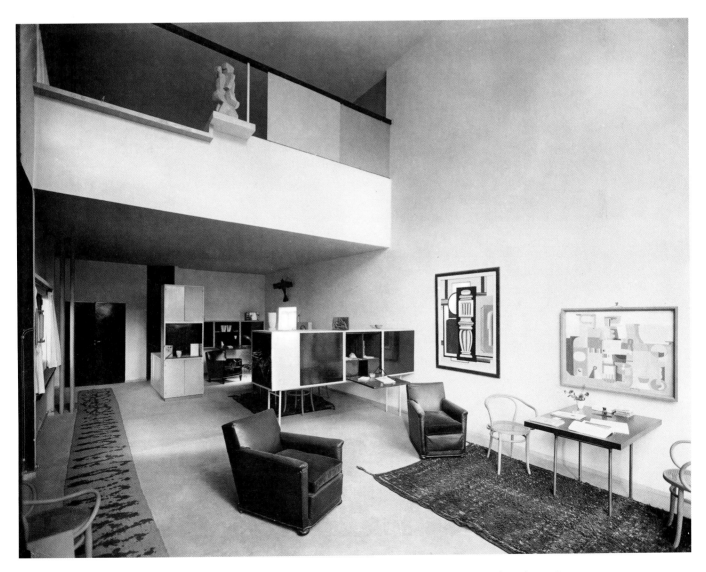

8.30 Le Corbusier, interior, Pavillon de l'Esprit Nouveau, Exposition Internationale des Arts Décoratifs et Industriels Modernes, Paris, 1925.

what Le Corbusier meant by design differed from the usual associations with rising above utility toward "art" as a measure of expression as well as technological and social progress; rather design had to do with the discovery of underlying, elementary forms based themselves upon objective principles not subject to the whims of fashion and decoration. Along these lines he and Jourdain had reprinted Adolf Loos's 1908 "Ornament and Crime" essay in a 1920 issue of their *L'esprit nouveau* journal (see page 101).

The inclusion of the Pavillon de l'Esprit Nouveau at the 1925 Paris International Exhibition reveals the coexistence of competing visions of a modern design that sought to shape the experience of modern living and that would be explored throughout the interwar period. In the hands and minds of designers, critics, manufacturers, and consumers, technology played a significant role in the definition and practice of design, whether in the application of mechanized production, or the introduction of new industrial materials, processes, or skills. Yet the connection between design and technology was quite varied; for instance, technology served as the vehicle for the mechanized mass production of standardized goods, or equally as a tool for the invention of original decoration. Both might be considered as "modern" applications of technology, and both were a matter of considerable debate during the interwar period.

The projects and ideas generated by Le Corbusier gained a number of adherents during the mid- and later 1920s. Le Corbusier and Amédée Ozenfant (1886–1966) coined the term Purism to refer to the paintings they produced beginning c. 1918, and Le Corbusier published essays about art, architecture, and design in *L'esprit nouveau*, edited with Ozenfant and the poet Paul Dermée (1886–1951). In their writings, Le Corbusier explored the relationship between pairs of polar concepts such as intuition and logic, the eye and the mind, the individual and the universal to argue for the existence of permanent standards for beauty in all forms of art, defined as harmony, proportion, and clarity, and independent of fashion. He claimed that manufactured goods, including architecture, were governed by universal principles of logic and economy, determined as it were by the "law" of mechanical selection analogous to the process of natural selection proposed in Darwin's theory of evolution:

From all this [previous discussion and observations] comes a fundamental conclusion: that respect for the laws of physics and of economy has in every age created highly selected objects; that these artificial objects obey the same laws as the products of natural selection and that, consequently, there thus reigns a total harmony,

bringing together the only two things that interest the human being: himself and what he makes.

Mechanical selection provided a basis for the design of both domestic architecture and machine-made consumer products, determined by underlying anonymous, inevitable, and universal principles rather than by individual expression or commercial motivation. Ornament and decoration only detracted and obscured the perfection of this underlying process of mechanical selection. *L'esprit nouveau* was subsidized by the French government, and advocated collective standards and standardized industrial production rather than individual approaches to design. The tone of *L'esprit nouveau* was urgent, suggesting that pressing economic and social needs following World War I demanded new approaches and solutions. This is the political context that informs Le Corbusier's model for low-cost housing at the Pavillon de l'Esprit Nouveau. Despite provocative illustrations of cylindrical grain silos, turbines, and airplanes that lent validity to the "law" of mechanical selection and the polemic, even apocalyptic tone of books such as Le Corbusier's *Vers une architecture* (*Towards a New Architecture*; 1923), the principle of mechanical selection was largely symbolic: aside from ship cabins, railway compartments, and office furniture ordered by Le Corbusier to furnish the Pavillon, neither Le Corbusier's logic nor claims of universality had much appeal beyond the office and private, custom commissions for wealthy clients. More applicable to modern design at the time were the realities of a market economy, the dynamics of which were explored more fully in Art Deco in Europe and the United States as well as in advertising.

After 1925, a group of designers including Le Corbusier, Jourdain, Chareau, and even Puiforcat (whose use of precious materials precluded his designs from reaching all but the very wealthy) quarreled with the S.A.D. over elitist attitudes that failed to consider the broader social benefits of industrial materials and standardized mass production. Indeed, Le Corbusier had admired the collaborative model of the Deutscher Werkbund and its attempts to synthesize design, production, and distribution, while the S.A.D. appeared to promote only unique works created for the luxury market. The polarization of attitudes and claims was more theoretical than actual in many ways, since the aims of department stores and other retail distributors of Art Deco were certainly to extend sales beyond an exclusive market. Nevertheless, in 1929 this group of dissenters split with the S.A.D. and formed their own design organization known as the Union des Artistes Modernes (U.A.M.). Examples of their work show a desire to link furnishings with factory assembly rather than

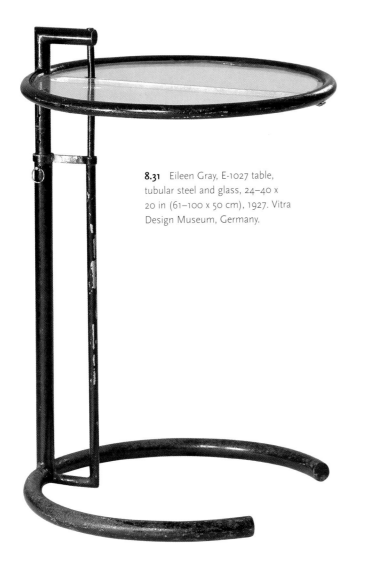

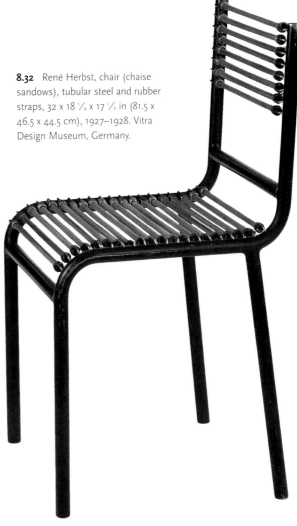

8.31 Eileen Gray, E-1027 table, tubular steel and glass, 24–40 x 20 in (61–100 x 50 cm), 1927. Vitra Design Museum, Germany.

8.32 René Herbst, chair (chaise sandows), tubular steel and rubber straps, 32 x 18 ¼ x 17 ½ in (81.5 x 46.5 x 44.5 cm), 1927–1928. Vitra Design Museum, Germany.

craft production, redefining the designer's role in creating elementary geometric forms as well as standardization and the use of interchangeable parts rather than craft manufacture. An example is the 1927 circular side table (entitled E-1027 after the name of her villa at Roquebrune on the Mediterranean coast) constructed of painted steel and glass by Irish-born designer Eileen Gray (1878–1976) and resting on a horseshoe-shaped base. The connection with the factory extends to the incorporation of working parts, in this case the set screw that enables the height of the table to be adjusted (fig. 8.31). Experimentation with industrial materials such as steel also characterizes the work of U.A.M. member René Herbst (1891–1983), whose metal chair dating to 1927–1928 is constructed of tubular steel connected at the seat and the back by elastic strips with hooked ends resembling today's bungee cords (fig. 8.32). In eschewing traditional decoration and upholstery and embracing industrial materials, such prototypes were intended to evoke parallels with building principles where

steel construction eliminated the need for load-bearing walls and defined architecture, in Le Corbusier's words, as the interplay of solid and void. Yet while the experimental use of industrial materials in furniture was bold and inventive, these models for assembled furniture proved marginal in the retail trade, failing to interest manufacturers or connect with consumers. The English writer George Orwell had little sympathy for this kind of modern design, referring condescendingly to tubular metal furniture as "gaspipe chairs" in his 1937 book of social criticism *The Road to Wigan Pier.*

Jean Prouvé (1901–1984) was also a member of the U.A.M. Trained as a blacksmith, he owned and operated a factory for metalwork production from 1927, and directed his efforts toward public commissions for schools, hospitals, and offices. Prouvé's direct knowledge of the structural properties of metal led him to experiment with sheet metal rather than tubular metal, which he thought was structurally weaker and required reinforcement for

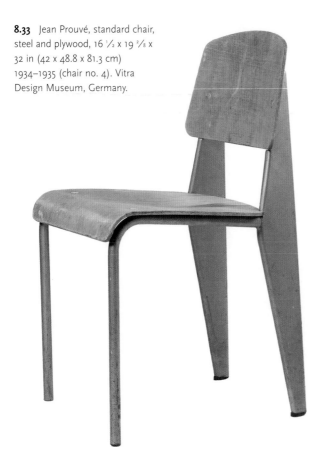

8.33 Jean Prouvé, standard chair, steel and plywood, 16 ½ x 19 ⅜ x 32 in (42 x 48.8 x 81.3 cm) 1934–1935 (chair no. 4). Vitra Design Museum, Germany.

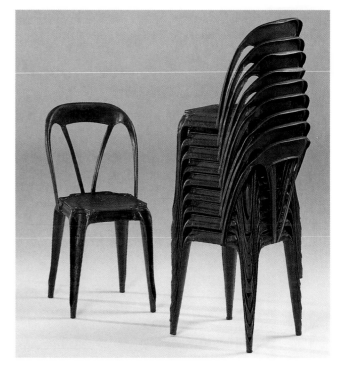

8.34 Anonymous, French terrace chair, varnished steel and wood veneer, 32 ½ x 17 x 18 ½ in (83 x 43.5 x 47.5 cm), 1926. Vitra Design Museum, Germany.

stability. Prouvé's "standard chair" of 1934–1935 (fig. 8.33) combined tubular with sheet metal and plywood and was featured in a catalogue of his factory's furniture published in 1936. Less "pure" or abstract than the prototypes of Herbst or Le Corbusier, Prouvé's furniture also shared these designers' belief in assembled rather than crafted furniture involving experimentation with industrial materials motivated by social concerns rather than individual expression. During World War II, Prouvé manufactured prefabricated army barracks, and after the war he designed and produced sturdy and durable furniture for schools and other public institutions.

Certainly there was a gap between the approach to design seen in the work of the U.A.M. and the outlook of many manufacturers and individual consumers in the 1920s. Industrial furniture in France, used for seating in sidewalk cafés or other outdoor settings, was often utilitarian but generally lacked the elementary geometric aesthetic preferences of U.A.M designers and their prototypes. More an equivalent in furniture to the Model T Ford, the anonymously designed French terrace chair (fig. 8.34), is constructed of a welded two-piece varnished steel frame, where the uneven surfaces created by the welding process are not disguised in any way. The seat is made of thin embossed plywood (imitating leather tooling)

riveted to the frame, and the splayed and grooved chair legs design permit convenient stacking. The chair was manufactured in Lyon from around 1926.

What is remarkable is that the design of such typical objects attracted the attention of a number of designers in the interwar period – their interest signals a shift in focus toward addressing ordinary and collective rather than individual need with solutions drawn both from applications of standardized industrial production as well as the identification of design with underlying laws and unchanging universal elementary geometric form. This approach suggests a relationship between modern design, industrial production, and the reduction or elimination not only of decoration but also of class difference. Rather than supporting an existing capitalist free-enterprise economic system, some modern designers looked to alternatives in socialism to best address social inequality. They also looked to engineering and problem-solving rather than to "art" as a paradigm for their approach. The emergence of such views should be seen as a response not simply to how to rebuild and reshape society after a catastrophic world war, but also how best to prevent international conflict in the future. Several international movements considered these concerns in the interwar period; their efforts are treated in Chapter 9.

Chapter 9

"Modernism": Design, Utopia, and Technology

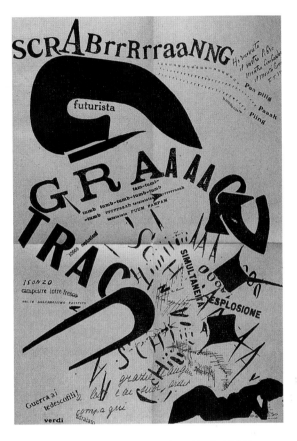

9.1 Filippo Tommaso Marinetti, "At Night in Her Bed," fold-out poem, 15 x 10 ⅛ in (38.1 x 25.9 cm), from *Les mots en liberté*, Milan, 1919.

World War I not only provides the background against which Art Moderne (Art Deco) flourished in the 1920s, but also stimulated more radical approaches to design. These approaches challenged an acknowledged framework among many designers, manufacturers, consumers, and critics that defined the decorative arts in relation to fine art, to industry, and in relation to social and economic progress. More radical approaches envisioned the decorative arts in relation to revolutionary utopian ideologies that aspired to create new social relations and a society free of greed, conflict, and social inequality. Art historians often use the term "Modernism" (with a capital "M," that is) to refer to the loose collection of ideas that included spiritualism, a faith in the machine as the vehicle for social change, and an emphasis upon perceived working class or universal needs. There were numerous points of contact between Art Deco and Modernism as well as differences among various Modernist theories and projects – but polemic was a Modernist strategy, and imparted a sense of a mission to efforts to reinvent society and redefine human values and ideals.

FUTURISM

In the years both preceding and immediately following World War I, a number of artist–designers were attracted less to the world of nature than to the machine-made environment as a source of inspiration for their work, developing a new language of form that embodied the dynamism of railroad and automobile transportation, and heroized the factory and industrial workers who operated machines and were engaged in building the modern industrial city.

There are, for instance, numerous references in the poetic writings of Italian poet Filipo Tommaso Marinetti (1876–1944) to the particular beauty of machinery as a symbol of speed, progress, and freedom, suggested in the following passage from his "Manifesto of Futurism," published in the French newspaper *Le Figaro* on February 20, 1909:

We declare that the splendor of the world has been enriched by a new beauty – the beauty of speed. A racing car with its bonnet draped with exhaust-pipes like fire-breathing serpents – a roaring racing car, rattling along like a machine gun, is more beautiful than the winged victory of Samothrace. We will sing of the stirring of great crowds – workers, pleasure-seekers, rioters – and the confused sea of color and sounds as revolution sweeps through a modern metropolis. We will sing the midnight fervor of arsenals and shipyards blazing with electric moons; insatiable stations swallowing the smoking of the smoke; bridges flashing like knives in the sun, giant gymnasts that leap over rivers; adventurous steamers that scent the horizon; deep chested locomotives that paw the ground with their wheels, like stallions harnessed with steel tubing; the easy flight of aeroplanes, their propellers beating the wind like banners, with a sound like the applause of a mighty crowd.

Futurist artists derived their means of visualizing the excitement of speed and change from the fragmentation and spatial dislocations of Cubism as well as the experiments of Jules Marey (1830–1904) and others with time-lapse or chronophotography, a technique that showed movement as a sequence of overlapping and abstracted linear patterns. In the medium of painting, results may be seen in the frenetic rhythms of works by Gino Severini (1883–1966), Giacomo Balla (1871–1958), and others, and were the inspiration for American artist Earl Horter's (1880–1940) painting *Rhapsody in Blue* (1927), incorporated into an advertisement and illustrated below (see fig. 10.15).

Crossing the boundary from fine to applied art was hardly a surprising development in Futurism. Marinetti used the popular press as a vehicle for communicating his ideas in print, and addressed the reader with an aggressive, imperative tone characteristic of the techniques of persuasion in print advertising. Electricity as a source of power for light, the internal combustion engine, and the airplane for travel suggested a spirit of liberation that removed limits to human potential in any number of areas of endeavor. Such developments in turn called forth new techniques of expression in art that dematerialized form and freed the artist from convention and tradition.

Marinetti hoped to move beyond the salon, the gallery, the museum, and the refuge of the bourgeois domestic interior, identifying with and appealing to an audience of industrial workers and youth in factories, on streets and athletic fields who themselves experienced the vitality of the urban environment and felt its constant state of flux. Such a public might be mobilized to tear down all that was traditional and static, both in art and in the status quo that maintained the political and social institutions and resisted rapid change and progress. The tone of Marinetti's Futurism was revolutionary, not only in artistic terms but in political terms as well.

Marinetti's medium for spreading the gospel of Futurism to the masses was the written word, not as phonetic symbol but as expressive image. In his poetry he followed the lead of Symbolist poet Stéphane Mallarmé (1842–1898) in arranging type on the page to visually convey the meaning of words or sensation of sounds. Different sizes of type within the same line, and different fonts within the same word, liberated the printed page from its usual directional order and standard spacing. An example is the poem "At Night in Her Bed" from a collection entitled *Les mots en liberté* (*Words in Liberty*) dating to 1919 (fig. 9.1), describing a letter from an artillery man to his girlfriend, who lies supine at the bottom right of the page. Fragments of handwritten words are interrupted by the sounds of gunfire, as well as abstract shapes and words such as "explosion" and "simultaneity." The reader's attention shifts from place to place without clear or prescribed organization aside from a tendency for the eye to wander downward. While earlier examples of Marinetti's Futurist poetry operate within the regularizing framework of parallel vertical and horizontal spacing of letterpress typography, the visual and calligraphic character of "At Night in Her Bed" appears to have been composed somewhat like a collage, with portions of cut-out text pasted on the page along with other cut-out shapes and handwritten words. The collage was then photographed and exposed as a negative on to a metal plate for offset printing. This technology permitted far greater freedom for typographic experiment, and emerges more prominently in the later 1920s (see page 207 onward). Just as painters in the early twentieth century were challenging the window as a paradigm for the art of painting, experimental poets such as Marinetti were challenging the grid of the printed page as a paradigm for poetry – in Marinetti's printed poetry, words and letters are not just the equivalent of spoken words but operate visually as images and symbols; they are meant to be "seen" rather than "read."

From 1912, the painter Giacomo Balla took an active interest in fashion (mainly men's fashion) and published treatises on the subject beginning in 1914. Asymmetrical geometric patterns printed on or applied to clothing mirrored the rhythms of urban life as seen in a vest with appliqué patterns designed by Balla made in 1915, or a drawing of the so-called anti-neutral suit of 1914, designed by Balla for the Futurist poet Francesco Cangiullo (1884–1977) to be worn at demonstrations supporting Italy's entry into World War I (fig. 9.2). This suit, as well as drawings of others designed by Balla, was decorated with asymmetrical circles, triangles, ellipses, cones, and spirals. According to the artist, modern clothing should avoid "faded and murky colors" and "symmetry," and strive to liberate emotion and action by being "aggressive," "agile," and "dynamic." It should also permit free movement. Balla and other Futurists appreciated the seasonal changes in the fashion world that provided continuous opportunities for creativity for designers and excitement for consumers. The attraction of consumer culture among Futurists differed from the condemnation of fashion by other Modernist designers and critics who sought more permanent forms (see pages 176–178 and 203).

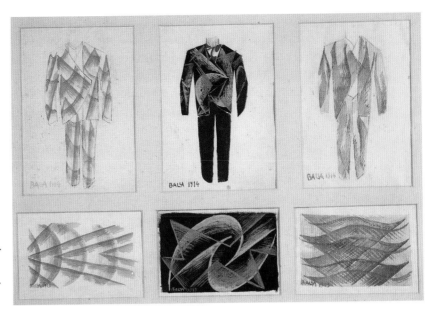

9.2 Giacomo Balla, illustration of the "anti-neutral suit," *Futurist Manifesto,* published in *Volantino della Direzione del Monumenti Futuristi,* 1914, Milan.

While perhaps not the call to political action envisioned by Marinetti, the expressive manipulation of letterforms and nervous energy generated by sharp contrasts and the rhythmic repetitions of geometric shapes associated with the Futurists found expression in advertising in the later 1920s, realizing in the mass media the hope of communicating a Futurist sensibility to a popular audience. Indeed, while the free association of word and image in Marinetti's explosive poetry may have signaled a new and more intense modern sensibility, its application to visual communication usually involved a stronger degree of simplification and order. For instance, Fortunato Depero (1892–1960) promoted his services as a graphic designer through the publishing company Dinamo Azari in Milan in the 1920s, and also designed advertising for the Italian distiller Campari, manufacturer of a refreshing rose-colored aperitif. Depero created a series of high-contrast black-and-white newspaper advertisements without advertising copy or product representation that made use of simplified angular shapes for typography, the cone-shaped drinking glass, and a mechanical, toylike figure (fig. 9.3). The product name in this example is composed of letters in descending size, resembling a megaphone and visually corresponding to the reverberating blare of a shouting vendor. Despite the playfulness and visual puns, there was a more broadly political and even utopian side to Depero's fascination

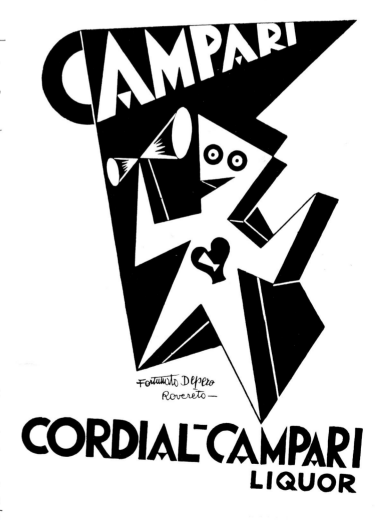

9.3 Fortunato Depero, advertisement for Campari, *c.* 1927.

with toys: he was the co-author, with Balla, of a treatise entitled the *Futurist Reconstruction of the Universe* (1915) arguing that Futurist-designed toys would foster imagination and spontaneity, and included the following advice for adults: "the Futurist toy will be very useful to adults too, keeping them young, agile, jubilant, spontaneous, ready for anything, untiring, instinctive and intuitive."

DE STIJL

De Stijl (*The Style*) was the title of a journal published in Holland, founded in 1917 by the painter–designer Theo van Doesburg (1883–1931). Contributors included the Dutch painters Piet Mondrian (1872–1944) and Vilmos Huszar (1884–1960), Belgian sculptor George Vantongerloo (1886–1965), Dutch furniture-maker and later architect Gerrit Rietveld (1888–1964), and architects Robert van 't Hoff (1887–1979), J. J. P. Oud (1890–1963) and Jan Wils (1891–1972). Although De Stijl designs were not exhibited in the Dutch pavilion at the 1925 Exposition des Arts Décoratifs et Industriels Modernes, Mondrian lived and worked in Paris both before and after World War I, and designs by Van Doesburg, Rietveld, and other artists associated with De Stijl were shown in 1923 at the Galerie de l'Effort Moderne owned by art collector and dealer Léonce Rosenberg (1879–1947), where they were seen by the French architect and Modernist Le Corbusier.

The term "movement" can only be used loosely in connection with De Stijl: no group exhibitions of De Stijl were ever held, and maintaining shared ideals and a spirit of collaboration among its various participants proved challenging, especially in light of Van Doesburg's strong personality: indeed, for one reason or another many of the contributors to early issues of *De Stijl* severed their relationship with the journal over differences with Van Doesburg during the course of its eleven-year history.

The manifesto printed in an early issue of *De Stijl* cites individualism as a cause of the conflicts that led to the outbreak of World War I, and proposed a new balance between individual and universal consciousness:

> There is an old and a new consciousness of time. The old is connected with the individual. The new is connected with the universal. The struggle of the individual against the universal is revealing itself in the world-war as well as in the art of the present day. The war is destroying the old world with its contents: individual domination in every state. The new art has brought forward what the new consciousness of time contains: a balance between the universal and the individual.

The De Stijl manifesto conveys revolutionary rhetorical tone, yet its translation into principles for design recalls the reform views found in the theories of Dutch architect Henrik Berlage (1856–1934), who had used the phrase "unity in diversity" to advocate a balance between unique and standardized elements in architecture and design. Another Dutch architect, J. L. Mathieu Lauweriks (1864–1932), promoted the reconciliation of unity and variety within the framework of geometric composition governed by mathematical relationships. Such views resonated with ideas advocated by members of the German Werkbund (see pages 148–150), who debated the relationship between standards and individual expression in manufacturing along economic, aesthetic, and social lines. As noted by Philip Meggs, Lauweriks's influence as a member of the faculty at the Düsseldorf School of Arts and Crafts may be seen in the consistent and standardized layouts for promotional material developed by Peter Behrens for the AEG (see fig. 7.4).

Berlage also admired the designs of Frank Lloyd Wright (see pages 100–101). The American architect's use of flat roofs and wide overhanging eaves explored the interpenetration of interior and exterior and were well-received by *De Stijl* contributors. Dutch designers used this idea as a basis for many of their own architectural projects. They extended the principle analogously to the equality between figure and ground in painting and solid and void in sculpture; that is, in each of these media they noted the active role of negative space as an aesthetic principle. Blurring the boundaries between fine and applied arts by suggesting their unity through underlying formal principles was a fundamental tenet of De Stijl, which included illustrations that demonstrated the ultimate unity of painting, sculpture, typography, furniture, interior ensembles, and architecture. For Van Doesburg, furniture was sculpture for the interior, and architecture a sort of walk-in painting, which placed the viewer "within painting instead of in front of it and thereby enable[d] him to participate in it," that is, to merge art and modern living. Similar ideas, in more utopian language, were expressed by Mondrian, who felt that architecture and the applied arts would more fully realize what painting had achieved in its more limited way, that is, the attainment of harmony and balance, based upon the rejection of representation and naturalism and an equilibrium among rectangular shapes of primary color created by the intersection of black strips of uniform width. Mondrian's numerous essays on this topic employ dualities similar to the writings of Ozenfant and Jeanneret (Le Corbusier) on Purism. Paired terms such as individual/universal, conscious/unconscious, subjective/objective, and mutable/immutable appear in a number of Mondrian's writings, in which he argues for "equilibration" between opposites, realized through the interplay of positive and negative space and the asymmetrical balance of rectilinear elements in walls, floors, furniture, and windows. Mondrian referred to his new conception of art as Neoplasticism or the "New Plastic," and anticipated its application to the built environment in essays published in *De Stijl* and elsewhere:

> the new spirit must be manifested in all the arts without exception ... As soon as one art becomes plastic expression of the abstract, the others can no longer remain plastic expressions of the natural. The two do not go together: from this comes their mutual hostility down to the present. The New Plastic abolishes this antagonism: it creates the unity of all the arts....
>
> Our age has reached the climax of individualism: the mature individual can now increasingly find equilibrium with the universal. When our mentality actually attains this equilibrium, it will also be clearly expressed in every aspect of outward life, just as it is expressed abstractly in the new plastic.

Mondrian also insisted that there should be no distinction between art and life, that the work of art should not be separate from living, an idea articulated in an essay of 1923. Before proceeding to develop the theme that both the machine and the urban environment are demonstrations of progress from the natural to the abstract, he writes:

> Indeed, the evolution of art consists in its achievement of a pure expression of harmony: art appears only outwardly, as an expression that (in time) reduces individual feeling. Thus art is both the expression and (involuntarily) the means of material evolution: the achievement of equilibrium between nature and non-nature – between what is in us and what is around us. Art will remain both expression and means of expression until (relative) equilibrium is reached. Then its task will be fulfilled and harmony will be realized in our outward surroundings and in our outward life.

The De Stijl principle of balance between universal and individual and the identification of the universal with an elemental geometric vocabulary of forms found expression in a variety of media. Gerrit Rietveld's armchair of 1918 (fig. 9.4), painted in 1923, was assembled from varied lengths of standard milled stock to which a rectangular plywood back and seat were added. In Rietveld's chair, joints extend beyond the point where right angles meet, accentuating the incorporation of negative space and a relationship to non-objective sculpture.

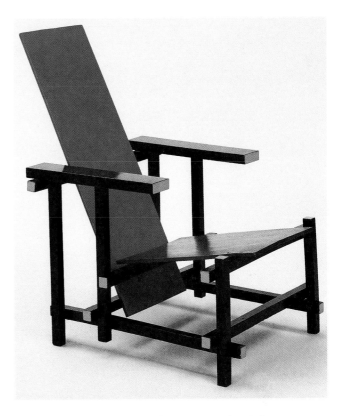

9.4 Gerrit Rietveld, red/blue armchair, 33 ⁷⁄₈ x 26 ³⁄₄ x 26 ³⁄₄ in (86 x 68 x 68 cm), 1918 (painted 1923). Stedelijk Museum, Amsterdam.

In 1920, Mondrian and Van Doesburg worked collaboratively to revise the cover for *De Stijl* that further provides a concrete illustration of "Neo-Plastic" ideas. In this simple cover, using a sans serif typeface (fig. 9.5), typographic elements are arranged as horizontal rectangular fields in a balanced, asymmetrical composition. The size of the sans serif letters and orientation of words

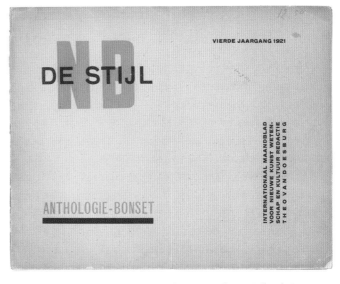

9.5 Piet Mondrian and Theo van Doesburg, cover for *De Stijl*, volume 4, 8 ¹⁄₁₆ x 10 ³⁄₁₆ in (20.5 x 26 cm), January 1921.

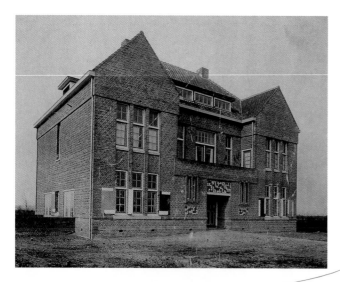

9.6 J. J. P. Oud, De Vonk residence, Noordwijkerhout, with colored tiles designed by Theo van Doesburg, 1918.

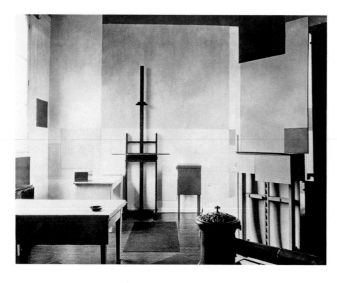

9.7 Piet Mondrian, studio of the artist, Paris, 1926. Documentation Archive, Gemeentemuseum, The Hague.

pages 208–210) as well as after World War II in Swiss graphic design (see pages 291–295).

Color was especially important to Van Doesburg for it served to activate spaces and surfaces so that they might be better understood and experienced as abstract form, as "realized" works of art. Often this transformation entailed collaboration, which signified not only the integration and unity of the arts, but also a working method that mirrored the balance of individual and group as opposed either to the hegemony of one art form over another or the egocentric model of the individual artist. Van Doesburg contributed patterns for colored brick tiles in a Dutch building known as De Vonk – a company-sponsored vacation residence for female workers – in Noordwijkerhout, designed by J. J. P. Oud in 1918 (fig. 9.6), Van Doesburg also designed windows composed of colored squares for other architectural projects. At De Vonk, the tile compositions above doorways or in hallway floors, although limited to these particular areas of the building, attempt to integrate architecture with abstract, non-objective painting.

Other examples of the "realized" work of art may be seen in photographs of the various studios used by Mondrian in Paris. In the studio illustrated in figure 9.7, framed paintings, painted rectangles tacked to walls, and the empty easels in the room form an abstract composition reminiscent of the artist's canvases, but extending into three dimensions, serving as a model for the experience of non-objectivity in the De Stijl interior.

Perhaps the best-known De Stijl project is the Schröder House in Utrecht, built in 1924–1925 for a widow and her three children, and designed by Gerritt Rietveld (figs. 9.8 and 9.9). Mrs Truus Schröder-Schräder contributed many suggestions to the design, such as the need to provide privacy in the otherwise open design of the first floor, achieved through the use of folding and sliding partitions. With its geometric areas of painted floor, painted furniture, projecting balconies with tubular steel railings, flat roof, expanses of square and rectangular glass even around the corner, rectangular "slab" construction (actually brick-faced with cement rather than standardized prefabricated units of concrete), the Schröder House fulfilled many of the principles embraced in De Stijl, in particular the attempt to create a "living" work of non-objective art, to extend the experience of non-objectivity, and its spiritual, antimaterialist connotations, to the built environment. The effort to use modern materials and standardized units of construction suggested that the design for the home might be seen as a modified or more customized version of a standardized design for public housing. Indeed, according to art historian Paul Overy, Mrs Schröder-Schräder was concerned that the furniture be simply constructed and that the décor specifically avoid associations with luxury.

determine a hierarchy of information, and even the overlapping of the letters spelling "De Stijl" with the bold letters "N B" (Nieuwe Beelding/New Plastic) suggests the visual equivalency of the two elements; moreover the vertical rather than usual horizontal orientation of words at the far right reinforces their relationship to the large "NB/DE STIJL" shape in the upper right, and color also functions in relationship to the hierarchy of information. Printers' rules, part of the typesetter's toolbox and used for spacing, are here used to reinforce information hierarchy and also create active diagonal eye movement rather than the conventional left-right and top-down of the traditional printed page. This approach appears both in the "New Typography" in Germany in the 1920s (see

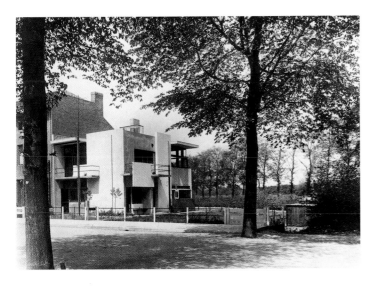

9.8 Gerrit Rietveld, Schröder House, Utrecht, 1924–1925, photographed *c.* 1925.

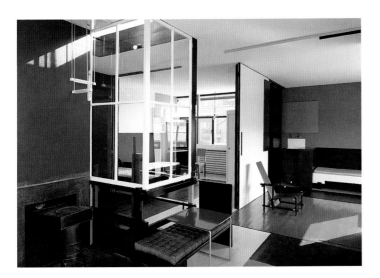

9.9 Gerrit Rietveld, first-floor interior of Schröder House, Utrecht, 1924–1925, restored 1985–1987, photographed 1987.

Throughout its publication, *De Stijl* sought to integrate aesthetic and universal considerations in design. The reconciliation between these goals remained difficult both in process and in result. Despite shared principles, individualistic preferences and differences persisted. While other approaches to Modernism stressed purely functional considerations in the design of furniture and interiors based upon the reduction of mass and a preference for types and standardization, these considerations did not emerge as overriding laws or principles in De Stijl. As Rietveld noted in commenting upon his furniture,

To me De Stijl represented a unit of construction which I considered of prime importance. A practical

realization was not always feasible. Function was for me a thing by itself which I never overlooked, it is true, but it did not come into play until the construction and spatial exercises in De Stijl had been completed.

In 1928–1929, Van Doesburg was asked to design a series of interiors for the Café L'Aubette in the center of Strasbourg, used for dining and public entertainments. Responsibility for the project was shared with Strasbourg native and artist Jean Arp (1887–1966) and his wife Sophie Täuber (1889–1943), who asked Van Doesburg to assist. The various rooms were designed independently with little collaboration, and Van Doesburg's participation confirms his receptivity to more individual and expressive tendencies of contemporary abstract art. Indeed, the Arps had been associated with the radical and anti-rational Dada movement in Zurich during the war and remained interested in incorporating the element of chance into their work. Perhaps the most striking design for the project was Van Doesburg's "Ciné-Dancing" intended both as a theater for film projection and as a cabaret (presumably akin to our own notions of multi-media performance). In this room the diagonals created by large, colored, diamond-shaped panels on the screening wall and ceiling created a dynamic tension with the rectangular, structural elements of the architecture in walls, windows, doorways, and balconies (fig. 9.10). When L'Aubette opened, Van Doesburg declared that the design was the result of "unbridled imagination," a phrase certainly at

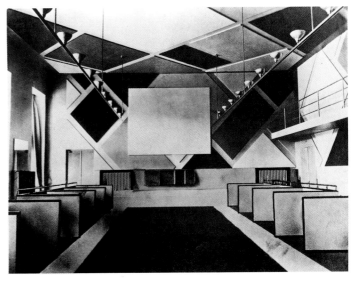

9.10 Theo van Doesburg, cinema-dance hall at the Café L'Aubette, Strasbourg, 1928–9. Documentation Archive, Musées Municipaux, Strasbourg.

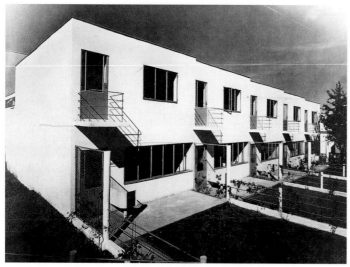

9.11 J. J. P. Oud, housing block, Weissenhof Colony, Stuttgart, 1927. Photograph: Nederlands Documentatiecentrum voor de Bouwkunst, Amsterdam.

compositions. The project offered an economical and modern solution to urban housing using prefabricated materials and industrial methods of construction (fig. 9.11) directed toward meeting housing shortages and defining essential living needs. Weissenhof continues to function as low-income housing in Stuttgart and is frequently cited among the early examples of a functional "International Style" emerging in the later 1920s (see page 237). Such an approach gained adherents in the later 1920s and 1930s as deteriorating economic conditions in industrialized nations seemed to support more sober, basic solutions to housing and other architectural projects. Other contemporary examples of low-cost housing include the Karl Marx Hof in Vienna designed by Karl Ehn and built in 1926, (fig. 9.13). These housing estates were built under a socialist government administration that subsidized rents for tenants. They also were important

some variance with the De Stijl manifesto's insistence upon a balance of universal and individual consciousness and with the more sober rectangular compositions of Mondrian. The introduction of the diagonal into Van Doesburg's work, beginning around 1923, alienated Mondrian from De Stijl, and from 1925 he stopped contributing to the journal.

In terms of projects on a civic scale, architects such as J. J. P. Oud also followed a course that increasingly moved away from the collaboration envisioned by Van Doesburg and the spiritual, anti-materialistic views of Mondrian. Already in 1921 Oud, who served as municipal housing architect for the city of Rotterdam, had rejected color designs supplied by Van Doesburg for the later housing blocks at Spangen (Rotterdam). Oud's approach to low-cost public housing leaned toward uniformity and an increasing emphasis upon efficiency, economic necessity, and social responsibility, precluding the incorporation of the more aesthetic and utopian De Stijl vision to create a "living work of art."

Oud's group of housing units constructed at Weissenhof (Stuttgart) in 1927 for an international exhibition (entitled Die Wohnung – The Dwelling) sponsored by the Deutscher Werkbund relied upon standardized dimensions for rectangular windows and doors set into flat expanses of plain white walls, but without color or three-dimensional effects characteristic of Café L'Aubette or the Schröder House. Oud's Weissenhof project eschewed for the most part the integration of painting and architecture seen in other De Stijl architectural projects, although the asymmetry and elementary rectilinear geometry of the elevation still recall Mondrian's abstract

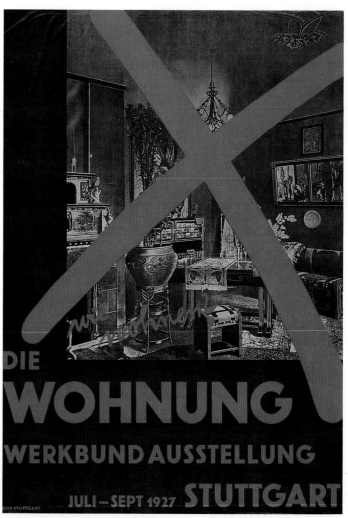

9.12 Willi Baumeister, *Die Wohnung* (*The Dwelling*), exhibition poster, lithograph, 45 x 32 ¹/₁₆ in (114.3 x 81.6 cm), Weissenhof, Stuttgart, 1927. Museum of Design, Zurich. Poster collection.

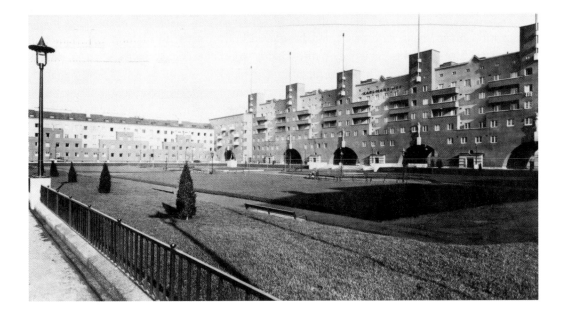

demonstrations of design aimed at collective rather than individual values: apartments at Karl Marx Hof were only provided with minimal space for kitchens and included communal services for cooking, playgrounds, kindergartens, and bathrooms (for an approach to functional kitchen design in Frankfurt, see page 205). The application of industrial technology to serve universal needs was an element of interwar Modernism with clear political ramifications at variance with the more common "art and industry" model that encompassed Art Deco or the more spiritual, utopian aspirations of early De Stijl. The polemic nature of the debate concerning the relationship between design and social progress is captured in a poster for the Weissenhof exhibition by graphic designer Willi Baumeister (1889–1955) (fig. 9.12). A broad red "X" slashes across a photograph of a middle-class living room at the upper right with ornately framed pictures, twisted columns, and upholstered Louis XV period furniture. The words "how to live?" written in cursive appear at the bottom of the photograph. Below to the left are bold sans serif capital letters, also in red, announcing the exhibition, and clearly critical of decoration, historicism, and luxury as elements in a vision of modern living. Meanwhile, the interiors of Van Doesburg's Café L'Aubette, despite the initial enthusiasm of the artists and press, became the object of indifference and the target of public criticism. Within a few years the interiors had been indiscriminately altered by the owners and no longer reflected the original designs. Van Doesburg's ideal of uniting art and life in the abstract environment proved a disappointment, where it was unable to effectively present practical solutions to social problems, or to shape a shared vision for the unity of modern art and a vision of contemporary life.

CONSTRUCTIVISM

Between March and June 1925, Russian artist and designer Aleksandr Rodchenko (1891–1956) was in Paris installing a furnished interior based upon his design for a Soviet Workers Club as well as assisting with other Russian exhibits for the Exposition des Arts Décoratifs et Industriels Modernes (fig. 9.14). The Workers Club was essentially a rectangular reading room. It contained two long wooden tables with hinged leaves that tilted to hold newspapers and journals and a series of chairs with rounded backs assembled from eight standardized components and lacking carved, painted, or inlaid decoration.

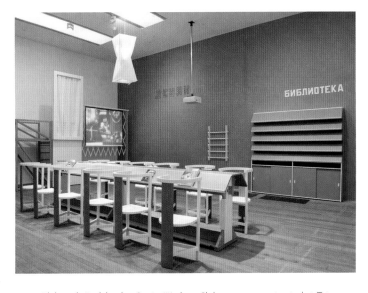

9.14 Aleksandr Rodchenko, Soviet Workers Club, 1925, reconstructed at Tate Modern, London, as part of the Defining Constructivism exhibition, 2009.

Rodchenko also designed and built a pair of armchairs, each with a shelf to the side that could be moved and attached to form a chess table when the chairs were placed facing one another. The room also contained a moveable platform with an elevated speaker's rostrum, folding table for displaying pamphlets and books, and folding screen for mounting posters or projecting films. Soviet publicity for Rodchenko's Workers Club contrasted its simplicity and communal purpose with the luxury and elitism they felt characterized the majority of interiors at the Paris exhibition, no doubt intended as a criticism of Ruhlmann's Hôtel d'un Collectionneur or the model French embassy designed by members of the Société des Artistes Décorateurs. Indeed the absence of decoration and emphasis upon simple standardized, interchangeable components for furniture, as well as the use of plain industrial materials such as plywood and sliding metal doors point to the replacement of the artist–craftsman with the newer paradigm of the artist–engineer as well as stressing public and communal rather than individual and private attitudes toward modern living. Rodchenko's model for working-class leisure included a prominent place for reading materials and posters as a means of mass communication for the shaping of socialist values following the Russian Revolution. While emphasizing standardization and elementary geometric forms as appropriate to industrial production, the austerity of the Workers Club was relieved by a lively and bright color scheme of red and gray that helped to create an active and dynamic interior space rather than a purely functional and practical one.

Rodchenko's Workers Club was a mature product of Constructivism, one of several evolving efforts on the part of artists who wished to participate directly in the reshaping of the Russian state following the revolutions of 1917 and the Bolshevik victory in the civil wars that ended in 1920. In 1918 the new communist Russian government established a ministry of culture known as the People's Commissariat of Enlightenment (Narkompros) under the direction of Anatoly Lunacharsky (1875–1933), a Communist Party official as well as playwright who was tolerant of radical and utopian artistic ideas as they applied to shaping public opinion. Narkompros and the various institutes and schools it formed replaced their more academic and conservative pre-revolutionary predecessors, permitting progressive artists a platform to put into practice utopian ideologies that linked non-objective abstract art to Socialist revolution. Many revolutionary artists shared a universal aim to liberate the masses from the tyranny of the past, and for a time they affirmed together the ability of art and design to radically transform the values and conditions of modern life.

The new abstract art played a significant role in the early formation of Constructivism. Abstraction's most articulate spokesman in Russia both before and after the revolution was Kasimir Malevich (1878–1935), who used the term Suprematism to refer to his non-objective style of painting. Malevich defined Suprematism as the expression of feeling in art, and noted the formal similarity between the simple geometric squares and rectangles of his canvases and the forms of modern technology and industry in their transcendence of organic naturalism. In this way he forged a symbolic link between the new art and the application of technology to socialist values. Malevich's paintings manipulated abstract geometric elements to suggest states of mind, as seen in titles for his works, such as *Suprematist Composition Expressing the Feeling of Movement and Restraint* or *Suprematist Composition Expressing Magnetic Attraction*. Malevich encouraged the integration of "art into life," and through his association with the art organization and school located in Vitebsk and renamed UNOVIS (Affirmers of the New Art) in 1920, he helped to coordinate efforts to use Suprematist decorations for signs and banners and the embellishment of temporary architectural constructions such as stages and speaker platforms. The expanded agenda led UNOVIS members such as Vasily Kandinsky (1866–1944), who had pioneered an expressive abstract non-objective style in Germany before World War I and returned to Russia after the revolution, to adopt a more precise geometric vocabulary in his paintings, and to approach abstraction analytically as well as intuitively, experimenting with the psychological effects of shapes and colors. According to art historian Christina Lodder, Kandinsky even conducted a survey of his colleagues to study their psychological responses to colors and other formal elements of design.

Malevich used the term "collective creative art" to emphasize the universal rather than individual aspects of Suprematism, and encouraged UNOVIS artists to exhibit works anonymously. The idea that a poster, banner, costume, or set design could function as both propaganda and as non-objective abstract "art," was not entirely new, for late nineteenth and early twentieth-century advertising posters served audiences in multiple, overlapping ways. One of the most daring experiments of this kind was the set and costumes for the play *The Magnanimous Cuckold* (written by the Belgian playwright Fernand Crommelnyk) designed by the painter Lyubov Popova (1889–1924) and performed in Russia in 1922 (fig. 9.15). The actors all wore blue overalls to suggest their collective rather than individual identity, and Popova used simple devices such as capes and aprons to distinguish prominent characters. Costumes as well as sets and the actors' movements and gestures had a mechanical character meant to be easily

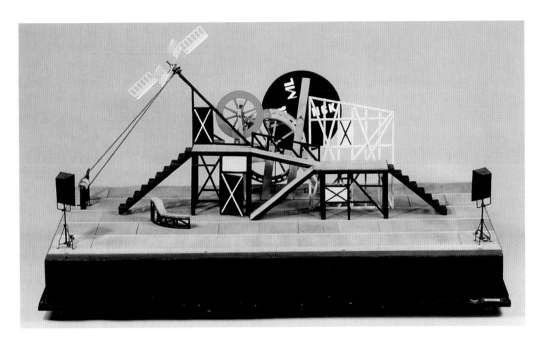

9.15 Lyubov Popova, set design (reconstruction) for *The Magnanimous Cuckold*, 22 ⁷/₈ x 44 ¹/₂ x 27 ⁵/₈ in (58 x 113 x 70 cm), 1922. Theaterwissenschaftliche Sammlung, Cologne University.

recognizable as well as easily learned to reduce the distance between the actors and the audience. Moreover, Popova's abstract costumes and set (which had moving parts) are themselves abstract compositions that convey movement and energy. Performance was an important element of Modernism in Soviet Russia; whether through the theater, demonstrations, or clothing, performance broke down barriers between art and life. Constructivists engaged movement and gesture to instill new, collective values among the proletariat, and transform older associations of artistic activity with fine art and elitism.

For El Lissitzky (born Lazar Markovich Lissitzky; 1890–1941), who studied architecture in Germany and later worked with Malevich at UNOVIS, the use of abstract art as a direct means to a political end found expression in a number of projects. El Lissitzky directed a short-lived program in architecture at UNOVIS, and later began to create his imaginative series of PROUNS (acronym signifying "for the new art"), a group of paintings and lithographs composed of abstract geometric shapes with an ambiguous suggestion of perspective and three-dimensional projection. Lissitzky referred to the PROUNS as "stations of interchange between architecture and painting," affirming the utilitarian possibilities of geometric abstraction. El Lissitzky's identification of artist with engineer and worker was almost a commonplace among Constructivists both in Russia and elsewhere in Europe. In an egalitarian society, everyone contributed in their own way to making the socialist dream a universal

reality. Some of El Lissitzky's best-known contributions to Constructivism were in graphic design, with its ability to communicate ideas visually and connect text with symbols and photographic images. His works include a book of poetry by the revolutionary poet Vladimir Mayakovsky (1893–1930) entitled *Dyla Golossa* (*For the Voice* or *To Be Read Out Loud*), designed for public performance and audience participation (fig. 9.16). In our example, from a poem entitled "Our March," the red square symbolizes the color of the Soviet flag as well as the blood of martyrs recalling the sacrifice of comrades made during the

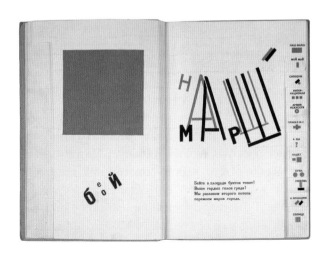

9.16 El Lissitzky, "Our March," from *For the Voice*, poems by Vladimir Mayakovsky, 7 ¹/₁₆ x 10 ¹/₄ in (19.5 x 26 cm), Berlin, 1923.

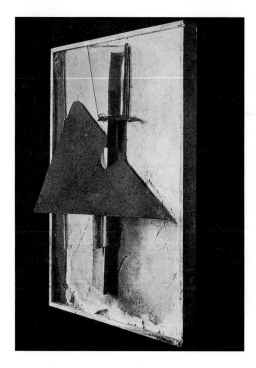

9.17 Vladimir Tatlin, *Selection of Materials: Iron, Stucco, Glass, Asphalt*, 1914. Whereabouts unknown.

revolution. The interrelationship of lettering, composition, and abstract symbol contains the elements out of which twentieth-century graphic design emerged in the context of experiment and challenging the traditional design of the printed page. As El Lissitzky said:

> The new art is formed, not on a subjective, but on an objective basis. This, like science, can be described with precision and is by nature constructive. It unites not only pure art but all those who stand at the frontier of the new culture. The artist is companion to the scholar, the engineer, and the worker.

While El Lissitzky's work represents a variety of possibilities for moving beyond the self-sufficiency of traditional art forms such as easel painting into the more utilitarian realms of architecture and visual communication, Vladimir Tatlin (1885–1953) was active in attempting to bridge the gap between abstract art and the masses in other ways. He used ordinary industrial and mass-produced materials in the creation of abstract collages, where works of art become "objects" and are grouped together with tools and other commodities as equal elements of the everyday environment of the proletariat. Strongly influenced by examples of Cubist collage seen by Tatlin in Paris as early as 1913, but animated as well by a desire to engage the arts in relation to Socialist revolution, works such as *Selection of Materials: Iron, Stucco, Glass,*

Asphalt, dated to 1914 (fig. 9.17), utilize ordinary materials such as wood, metal, and stucco as elements in an abstract relief composition. Although hardly functional, such experiments, sometimes referred to by their supporters as "laboratory work," were intended to provide a basis for the creation of future utilitarian products that incorporated a preference for simple geometric shapes and forms, and encouraged non-objective attitudes. The use of ordinary materials and collage technique emphasized the imagination of the "constructor" rather than sophisticated artistic skills, and suggested that the making of art could not only be appreciated widely, but could be made by everyone as an active participant in a new society.

In 1922 El Lissitzky began to publish an international journal of the new art entitled *Vesch/Objet/Gegenstand*. Translated simply as "Object" in English, the journal featured articles and photographs of works of fine art, decorative art, and industrial products, including projects by De Stijl artists as well as by Le Corbusier (work by El Lissitzky was featured in a 1922 issue of *De Stijl* as well). The use of half-tone photographic reproductions of illustrations rather than etchings or engraving conveys Lissitzky's interest in promoting the increased use of photomechanical images rather than craft-based techniques as a form of mass communication. The cover of one of the journal's issues from 1922 (fig. 9.18) reinforces the abstract relationships between bold sans serif typography, non-objective compositions of geometric shapes, and industrial forms, in this case a locomotive with a cowcatcher resembling

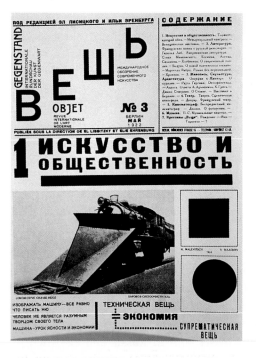

9.18 El Lissitzky, cover for *Vesch/Objet/Gegenstand*, 12 5/16 x 9 5/16 in (31.3 x 23.5 cm), Berlin, 1922.

Tatlin's abstract constructions and diagonally relating to the Russian word "Vesch." The vertically and diagonally oriented letters, horizontal and vertical printers' rules used as separation, and use of different letter sizes recall the typographical experimentation of the Futurist poet Marinetti (see fig. 9.1). But whereas Marinetti used such elements to make the page into a kind of poetic "image" to be experienced with a new sensibility characteristic of the dislocations and simultaneity of modern life, Lissitzky and other Russian Constructivists had to temper such explosive dynamism with a sense of discipline and order that permitted information to be communicated clearly, quickly, and dramatically. This implied a more visual approach to page layout, in which text, symbol, and image worked together to actively engage the viewer's attention.

Another Constructivist, Gustav Klutsis (1895–1938) used photomontage as a form of modern "assembly" in a series of political posters that promoted Communist Party initiatives and programs under Soviet leader Joseph Stalin. These often employed repeated images with dramatic changes in scale to conveying a strong sense of movement but also of progress, as in a poster for the development of transport from 1929 (fig. 9.19; and compare with fig. 8.21). Klutsis juxtaposes a diminutive figure on a camel in front of a modern locomotive to contrast past with future, with smaller locomotives suggesting stages in the progress of industrialization almost as a kind of growth chart. The red star and use of red behind the other engines refers to Russia, while the diagonal letter points to the future to reinforce the visual hierarchy in an asymmetrical arrangement. Constructivists saw photography as inherently modern because it was both reproducible and mechanical rather than being tied to illustration and art. Nevertheless, Klutsis's use of photomontage communicated both general meaning of dynamic progress in transportation as well as encouraging specific support or compliance with official policies, reinforced in the slogan "Transportation is One of the Most Important Tasks in the Fulfillment of the Five-Year Plan." On one level there is a connection to be made both with advertising slogans in the United States during the 1920s and 1930s as well as advertisements' juxtaposition of "before and after" results to proclaim the efficacy and desirability of products. On the other hand, one might compare Lester Beall's poster for the Rural Electrification Administration in 1937 in the United States (see fig. 10.43), where the emphasis seems to be less upon the overpowering machine than upon a single home illuminated by electric light or a faucet with water flowing from the spigot. Indeed, Klutsis's posters glorifying industrialization have more in common with Charles Sheeler's "Stamping Press" photograph for the Ford Corporation plant at River Rouge from 1927 (see fig.

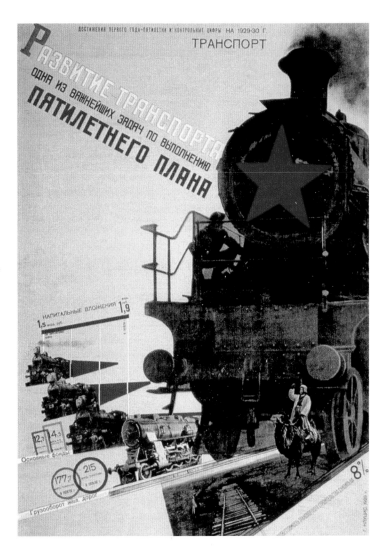

9.19 Gustav Klutsis, *Development of Transport, Five-Year Plan*, poster, intaglio, 27 ⅞ x 19 ⅞ in (73.3 x 50.5 cm), 1929.

10.19): in both cases, abrupt changes in scale communicate the power of machinery in the hands of the state or the corporation.

Stalin's increasing control of propaganda in the Soviet Union beginning in the later 1920s made it difficult for Constructivists to pursue their experimental and typographic approach to graphic design. While slogans proclaiming faith in the industrialized future remained, idealized illustrations of workers and peasants eventually replaced photography and dynamic asymmetrical compositions that closely related text and image more interactively. This so-called "Socialist Realism" also represented a form of communication designed to reach the Russian masses, but was decidedly *not* the kind of universal forms envisioned by the Constructivists, whose efforts were increasingly marginalized. In some cases they were seen as threats to the state: for unknown reasons, Gustav Klutsis was arrested in 1938 and executed three weeks later.

Among the examples of a lingering Constructivist sensibility is the sketch for a roller-printed textile illustrated in figure 9.20. One of several patterns designed in the later 1920s and early 1930s by a number of different artists working for the state-controlled industry, this example from 1930 by Sergei Burylin (1876–1942) has as its subject "Coal Recycling." It uses flat two-dimensional symbols for mountains of coal, scaffolds, conveyer belts, and pictograms of workers. The industrial theme and emphasis upon work demonstrates the desire to use even textiles as a means to reinforce the plans to collectivize Soviet industry. Yet such designs, despite the ideological aspirations to create a proletarian art and even the inclusion of figuration, were unpopular among consumers, who were familiar with pre-revolutionary floral and scenic Western designs (compare Raoul Dufy's wallpaper design, fig. 8.8). There was little room for resolving the conflict between Constructivist ideology and popular taste in the area of textile design. While Constructivist elements lingered somewhat longer in graphic design as effective techniques for propaganda, textiles, which involved personal preferences, did not prove a viable direction for Russian Modernism after the early 1930s.

Rodchenko was active among those artists who increasingly came to believe that it was necessary to take a more pragmatic and utilitarian direction in their activities, contributing directly to addressing collective social needs through design and justifying their endeavors in terms of their practical applications. His efforts were closely associated with an organization known as INKHUK (The Institute of Artistic Culture) in Moscow beginning in 1920, and with an exhibition that took place there in 1921 known as the Third Obmokhu, named for a group known as the Society of Young Artists. From these organizations a Working Group of Constructivist Artists was formed. These Constructivists viewed their efforts as being more in line with Marxist ideology that embraced a materialist view of culture (as opposed to a spiritual or aesthetic view) as the most appropriate to the collective needs of a new social order. The emphasis upon production and utility among the artists at INKHUK created a tension with those who felt that the imposition of practical considerations in design represented too strict an approach compared with earlier interpretations of Constructivism that focused upon the integration of art and life. As a result of this growing conflict concerning the role of artists and the functions of works of art in the new Communist state, a number of artists left Russia for the West, including Kandinsky and the sculptor Naum Gabo (1890–1977).

INKHUK members became actively involved in an institution known as the Higher State Technical Workshops, established by the Communist Party in 1920 to further integrate artists with production. By this time Rodchenko had come to question the compatibility of painting and sculpture with the practical aims of Constructivism. A number of INKHUK members envisioned the demise of traditional media associated with the fine arts such as painting and sculpture. Instead they promoted the training of "artist–constructors," a new kind of versatile and non-specialist creator who might apply universal principles of design to prototypes for clothing, furniture, lighting, architecture, and other basic goods and furnishings manufactured by machine.

It is to this period of Constructivism that Rodchenko's model for the 1925 Soviet Workers Club at the Paris exhibition belongs (fig. 9.14). Although the furnishings of the Workers Club were fabricated and assembled in a workshop setting, the concept of the "artist-constructor" was meant to apply to the design of prototypes for mechanized industrial production in collaboration with engineers, removed from the direct manipulation of materials by craftsmen. The designer's role was envisioned as more akin to the methods of a draftsman than those of the fine artist. The furnishings suggest the designer's adherence to a set of criteria based upon the needs of a collective and egalitarian socialist society, defined as the use of a minimum number of standardized parts, modern industrial materials, and adaptable, flexible construction. Together with the appeal to objectivity and anonymity, Rodchenko incorporated the precision of construction units based upon geometric rather than organic form, preserving a connection between "constructive" design

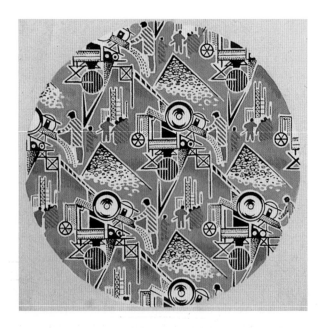

9.20 Sergei Burylin, sketch for "Coal Recycling" textile pattern, gouache, ink, and whiting, 5 1/2 x 5 5/8 in (14 x 14.6 cm), late 1920s or early 1930s. Ivanovo State Museum of History and the Revolution.

and the abstract compositions of the Suprematists, reinforced through areas of brightly painted color on the walls and floor that activated the space along non-objective lines.

While Rodchenko and other production-oriented Constructivists complained that earlier projects such as Tatlin's spiraling model for a *Monument of the Third International* (1920) were too utopian and unrealistic, their own designs in some ways were hardly more practical. The furnishings for the Workers Club were one-of-a-kind products and few if any prototypes were produced by industrial manufacturers, whose activities were hampered by a depressed economy and the lack of necessary investment and support to produce the new designs. It is unlikely that workers were able to spend time in the kind of club Rodchenko created for the 1925 Paris exhibition and that was intended to mold a new kind of socialist and collective society. To judge from the indifferent reaction to Rodchenko's project within Vkutemas and later attempts to replace traditional representational textile designs with decorative patterns based upon themes of industrialization (see fig. 9.20), the public (and eventually the official Party) reception of Constructivist design was equivocal. In addition a number of younger artists and former Constructivists during the early 1920s had turned to realism. These artists embraced easel painting and an idealized naturalistic style as appropriate to an art of mass persuasion capable of winning the endorsement of the Communist Party for whom the arts were a tool to build support for official policy along more traditional lines and employing techniques shared with narrative illustration and advertising.

Without clear public or Party support, Constructivist hopes to unify or at least to influence industrial production and further develop the potential contributions of the "artist–constructor" were dashed, and the activities of a Modernist "industrial design" in Russia were marginalized. Amid these circumstances Rodchenko and other Constructivists found the best outlet for their activities to be the production of posters, journals, and advertisements based upon the application of Constructivist principles to the mechanical reproduction of printed materials, incorporating photographs and photomontage rather than illustration to accommodate the revived interest in realism as a more effective form of mass communication and propaganda. An example is the cover for the journal *Novyi Lef* (*For the New Left*) from 1927, in which the profile head of a smiling worker extends to the left and right limits of the unframed page, and the square title at the upper right corner touches the figure's hat, creating a strong figure–ground equality (fig. 9.21). Through juxtaposition, overlap, and contrasts in scale, photographs also acquire a sense of drama on their own or in relation to the text and

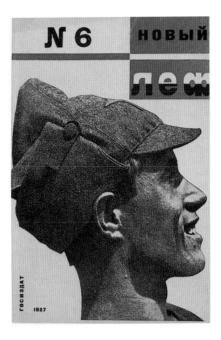

9.21 Aleksandr Rodchenko, cover for *Novyi Lef*, no. 6, 9 x 6 in (22.5 x 15 cm), Hoslow, 1927.

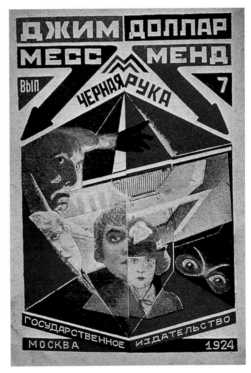

9.22 Aleksandr Rodchenko, book cover for the series *Mess Mend* by Dzhim Dollar (Marietta Shaginyan), 13 x 6 ¾ in (33 x 17 cm), St. Petersburg, 1924.

the bold contrasts of the composition. This can be seen, for instance, in one of a series of book covers designed by Rodchenko for the *Mess Mend* novels written by Dzhim Dollar (Marietta Shaginyan, 1888–1982). The *Mess Mend* covers (fig. 9.22) employed the same basic compositional formula amid variations, suggesting an analogy with interchangeability and efficient production. Critics have also noted similarities of the collage compositions in these and related cover designs with techniques of montage in filmmaking.

By the mid-1920s, tolerance for the universal pretensions of abstract art and Constructivism during the early years of Narkompros had eroded. The hope for defining a set of official collective standards and an art that contributed to the establishment of the Communist state began to be realized. But sadly for the Constructivists, such standards were not along abstract and non-objective lines. Soviet artists were increasingly made to comply with a policy demanding a heroic naturalism (or Socialist Realism) depicting working-class, athletic, or military activities and designed to provide persuasive and hopeful images to the Russian masses. An example that still owes something to the Constructivist principles of dynamic composition is Gustav Klutsis's poster (see also fig. 9.19) *We Shall Repay the Coal Debt to our Country!* from 1930 (fig. 9.23). In this more repressive environment, artists such as Rodchenko and El Lissitzky continued to produce graphic designs using photography that still permitted a measure of experimentation. One of the most striking examples is El Lissitzky's poster for an exhibition of Russian art that took place in Zurich in 1928, with a photograph depicting a male and a female youth in three-quarter view who share an eye as they peer into the distance (fig. 9.24). This image exemplifies the original approaches to photography undertaken by Russian Constructivists. It may also be seen as a metaphor for the collective ideal of social and gender equality under Communism.

THE BAUHAUS

The Soviet Workers Club was but one indication of the international scope of Constructivist activities: El Lissitzky's essays on modern design were published in issues of *De Stijl*, and the short-lived journal *Vesch/Objet/Gegenstand* contained texts by Van Doesburg, Mondrian, Le Corbusier, and other designers advocating utopian ideologies, the use of new industrial materials such as reinforced concrete and tubular metal, and mechanized industrial production. These ideas also found expression in a school of design located in Weimar, Germany, known as the Bauhaus.

The Bauhaus (from the German verb *bauen*; to build) opened in 1919 from the consolidation of Weimar's Academy of Fine Arts and the city's Arts and Craft School (Kunstgewerbeschule), both of which had closed during World War I. The school's first director was Walter Gropius (1883–1969), an architect who had worked in the office of Peter Behrens prior to the war. Gropius's architectural commissions included the well-known Fagus shoe-

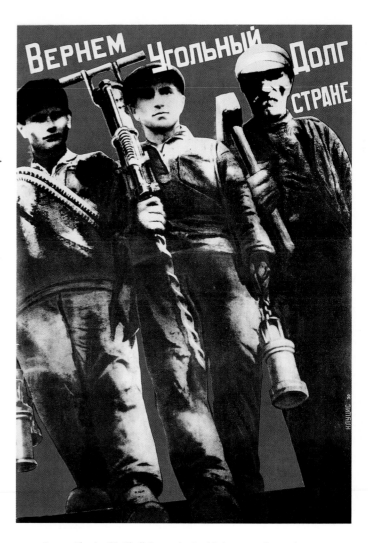

9.23 Gustav Klutsis, *We Shall Repay the Coal Debt to our Country!*, poster, lithograph, 40 x 28 in (101.6 x 71.2 cm), 1930. Private collection.

last factory at Alfeld an der Leine near Hildesheim, designed in 1911 in collaboration with Adolf Meyer (1881–1929), and often viewed as an early example of a modern approach to building with steel-frame construction, large expanses of plate-glass curtain walls, and an absence of traditional moldings and decoration. Gropius was also active in the Deutscher Werkbund and had designed railroad cars with efficiently furnished standardized compartments. Within the Werkbund, however, he supported artistic freedom and individuality rather than the imposition of typical forms as advocated by Hermann Muthesius (see pages 148–149).

The idealistic text of the Bauhaus manifesto (1919) shows little interest in either objective standards for design or industrial technology, but is concerned instead with ideas regarding the collaboration of artist and craftsman, pointing to the medieval building as a model to overcome the opposition between fine and applied art

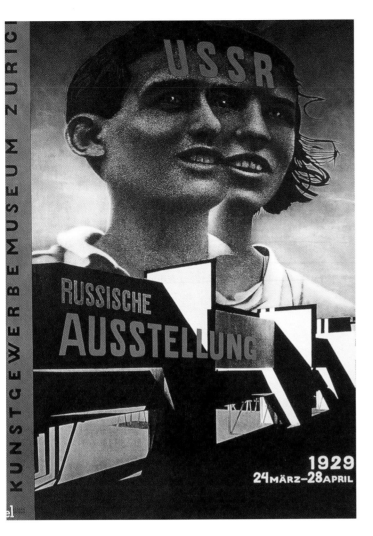

9.24 El Lissitzky, poster for Russian Art Exhibition, intaglio and lithography, 49 ¼ x 35 ½ in (126.5 x 90.5 cm), 1928. Private collection.

and to create a living art integrated into rather than separated from life:

> Architects, painters, sculptors, we must all return to crafts! For there is no such thing as "professional art." There is no essential difference between the artist and the craftsman. The artist is an exalted craftsman. By the grace of Heaven and in rare moments of inspiration which transcend the will, art may unconsciously blossom from the labor of his hand, but a foundation of handicraft is essential for every artist. It is there that the primary source of creativity lies.
>
> Let us therefore create a new guild of craftsmen without the class-distinctions that raise an arrogant barrier between craftsman and artist! Let us together desire, conceive and create the new building of the future, which will combine everything – architecture and sculpture and painting – all in a single form

which will one day rise towards the heavens from the hands of a million workers as the crystalline symbol of a new and coming faith.

The model of the medieval guild, and with it the egalitarian legacy of William Morris and the Arts and Crafts Movement, emerges in this strongly utopian passage in which the products and activities of design will transform both the visible and more broadly human conditions of society. The guild model also emerges in Gropius's practice of calling the Bauhaus faculty "masters" rather than professors, and in the manifesto's cover illustration for the school, from a woodcut by early faculty appointment Lyonel Feininger (1871–1956), depicting a church bathed in the light of three stars, symbolizing perhaps the collaboration and essential unity of painting, sculpture, and architecture in the Gothic cathedral. Such ideas formed the basis of the philosophy of education at the Bauhaus, even though architecture was not among the fields of study offered at the school during its existence at Weimar.

Although Gropius inherited a small number of faculty from the Weimar Academy of Fine Arts, many of them were hostile to the revamped curriculum for the Bauhaus and lobbied successfully to maintain their independence from the new school. As a result the director was able to hire a number of new "masters" for the Bauhaus over the first few years of the school's existence. The new appointments were almost exclusively fine artists, who embraced abstraction and subjective self-expression as the basis for art, but who at the same time were committed to a less elitist role for artists that encouraged contributing to the design of useful products and in the integration of art and life. What was envisioned seems to have been a healthy collaboration between artist and craftsman in educating new designers to reinvigorate the production of useful goods culminating in the construction and interior design of buildings, informed and conditioned by the discipline and unity implied in the architectural enterprise. Such ideas were shared among the faculty appointments in 1919, which included Johannes Itten (1888–1967), Gerhard Marcks (1889–1981), and Feininger, as well as the hiring of Paul Klee (1879–1940) in 1921 and Kandinsky (see page 190) in 1922. Kandinsky had worked as an artist and teacher in Russia after the revolution, but left for Germany late in 1921. Klee was born in Switzerland but studied painting in Munich, and it seems difficult to believe that he was unaware of or unaffected by the artistic milieu of that city in the heyday of Jugendstil (see pages 138–140). His views on the importance of the social role of the decorative arts in promoting a broad-based audience for aesthetic ideas is suggested in a letter he wrote to a fellow artist in 1919, revealing the charged political climate of the time:

Of course, exaggerated, individualist art is not suitable for the general public – it is a capitalist luxury. But I think we are more than just curiosities for wealthy snobs. And all that in us which is in some way or the other is striving for eternity would be more likely to be encouraged in a communist community...this new art would grasp craftsmanship and bring forth a great new flowering. For there would no longer be academies, but only art schools for craftsmen.

A key element in the curriculum of the Bauhaus was the common first semester of study (preliminary course or Vorkurs) before students selected one or more areas of specialization in the Bauhaus workshops (ceramics, glass painting, mural painting, furniture, metalwork, textiles). Georg Muche (1895–1987) assisted with the Vorkurs, and other mandatory but non-specialized courses in form and theory were taught by Klee and Kandinsky. The purpose of the Vorkurs, directed by Swiss-born artist and educator Johannes Itten, was to stimulate students' interest in materials, drawing techniques, and forms so that their innate creative ability might be best directed toward study in a particular workshop. Surviving examples of student work demonstrate contrasts of textures among different materials in an abstract composition, drawings from life that exaggerate a sense of rhythm in nature, and relationships among geometric shapes in the analysis of works of art. Despite the freedom of choice implied by the required Vorkurs, women were almost always directed toward the weaving workshop, which was viewed by the faculty as appropriate for female students (only with difficulty did Marianne Brandt obtain permission to pursue her apprenticeship in the metal workshop). In fact, so strict was the gender bias that a separate Vorkurs was taught to the women students at the Bauhaus.

One of the important elements of the Bauhaus Vorkurs was its role as a foundation for all of the workshops. Implied is the notion of an underlying basis for all of the arts that can be learned not from acquiring specific technical skills but from learning essential principles that might be applied to a variety of forms in architecture, ceramics, metalwork, furniture, or printing; principles that had their basis in elementary, abstract geometric forms. This "mental" or even spiritual part of the Bauhaus curriculum was balanced by later specialization in the workshops, but even then a "Form" master (fine artist) was paired with a technical master to provide guidance to students. Statements by Itten suggest not only the interrelationship and unity among the arts but also their contribution to giving a "visual character to modern life."

Scholars have been careful to point out that the early Vorkurs did not seek solely to familiarize students with the underlying elements of all the arts, but also to draw connections between artistic activity and the discovery of unconscious reality. It is in this context that Itten's mysticism and use of breathing and other synaesthetic exercises are best understood, as well as the connection between his teaching and Kandinsky's *Concerning the Spiritual in Art*, published in 1911. Despite the fact that a non-specialized preliminary course had been introduced in some form earlier in the Kunstgewerbeschule by Peter Behrens at Düsseldorf and also formed part of the curriculum in design education in Russia at INKHUK, the preliminary or foundation course tends to be associated with the Bauhaus. This is perhaps a result of the emigration of Bauhaus faculty and their students to the United States and Britain, where the concept became institutionalized as a cornerstone of design education after World War II. As noted above, in the workshops instruction was the shared responsibility of a technical master (*Lehrmeister*) skilled in the particular area of craft, and a master of form (*Formmeister*), in almost all cases a fine artist whose presence would contribute to the dialogue and creative effort aimed at renewing the essential unity and equality of the arts proclaimed in the Bauhaus manifesto.

The efforts of the Bauhaus in the early Weimar years are best summarized in the construction and interior design and decoration for the Sommerfeld House in Berlin, a residence (now destroyed) commissioned privately from Gropius but constructed with the collaboration of the Bauhaus workshops (fig. 9.25). The client was shipping industrialist Adolf Sommerfeld, who provided a large quantity of teak wood normally used in boat building; the project demonstrates the early Bauhaus emphasis upon craft techniques and the integration of construction and original abstract decoration. The horizontal emphasis of the elevation and the strongly projecting eaves of the roof of the Sommerfeld House recall the Prairie houses of Frank Lloyd Wright (see pages 100–101). The doorway and staircase of the entrance area are decorated with wooden relief panels that develop the angular construction of the teak paneling, exploring relations of geometric forms in two and three dimensions, as well as a variety of textures created by sanding and chiseling. These motifs, either in regular patterns or asymmetrically balanced compositions, are repeated in a series of leaded glass windows behind the staircase as well as in embroidered appliqué curtains, all produced in the Bauhaus workshops. Like Wright's Prairie houses, the Sommerfeld House remains strongly based on handicraft despite the emphasis upon abstract geometric shapes rather than organic forms in decoration. One might also compare the colored brick reliefs designed by Van Doesburg to articulate the doors and windows of Oud's De Vonk residence of 1918 (see fig. 9.6) with the Sommerfeld reliefs and windows in terms of the relation of ornamental to constructive elements. In the De Stijl example, the decoration relates more to standardized units of simple materials, requiring less of the time-consuming handwork of the early Bauhaus efforts. Moreover, decoration at the Sommerfeld House remains more subordinate to, rather than integrated with, construction, as in the more collaborative approach envisioned by Van Doesburg or Mondrian and realized in 1924–1925 in projects such as the Schröder House in Utrecht (see figs. 9.8 and 9.9). There Rietveld applied color to sliding panels, furniture, and walls to create a greater degree of identity between decorative and structural elements, forming a "living work of art" central to the aims of De Stijl.

Despite the collaborative effort on the Sommerfeld House and the limited commercial success of its weaving and ceramics workshops, the Bauhaus struggled for adequate resources from the Weimar government and battled local resistance to its unorthodox approach to instruction. In addition, the school was criticized by designers more aligned with Constructivism; they felt the school's methods and products were allied too closely to craft production and the fine arts, rather than with mechanized industrial production geared toward efficient modern living. As a result, claimed its detractors, the Bauhaus produced the kind of individual and indulgent art that was at variance with the social aims expressed in the 1919 manifesto. One of the most vehement of such attacks appeared in *De Stijl*. The journal's editor, Theo van Doesburg, moved to Weimar in 1921 and attended an International Congress of Constructivism held there in 1922. Although Van Doesburg never officially taught at the Bauhaus, he seems at one time to have been considered for a teaching position there, and was acquainted with Gropius.

Gropius appears to have been sensitive to criticisms of the school's shortcomings. He had already been in contact with Dutch architect J. J. P. Oud (associated at one time with De Stijl and employed by the housing authority of Rotterdam) and was interested in new developments in Dutch architecture related to standardization and newer prefabricated materials for government-sponsored housing. In response to financial, political, and ideological pressures upon the school, Gropius began to shift the focus of the Bauhaus mission and curriculum. One of the most important changes that took place during this time was Gropius's decision in 1923 to force the resignation of Itten and to hire Hungarian painter and Constructivist László Moholy-Nagy (1895–1946) as a replacement. The two men had met in Berlin, where Moholy-Nagy was living, having left Hungary following an unsuccessful socialist revolution. Moholy-Nagy became responsible for the Vorkurs and for the more industrial focus that began to

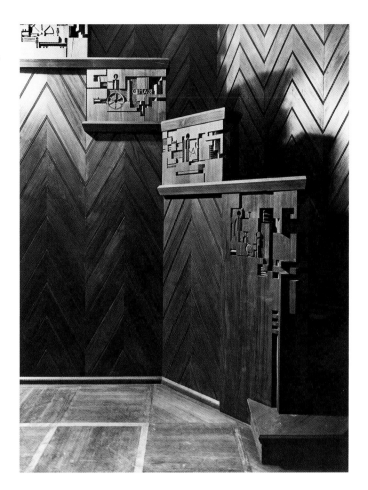

9.25 Joost Schmidt with students, wood carving for the staircase of Sommerfeld House, Berlin (now destroyed), photograph from 1921–1922.

inform Bauhaus education and activities. He brought with him a strong commitment to mechanized mass production and new material technology in design and reduced the importance of craft specialization and traditional workshop training. To emphasize the point, in what has become part of the canonical literature of Modernism, Moholy-Nagy designed a series of abstract geometric paintings and communicated instructions by telephone to assistants to have them produced. His efforts along these lines parallel Rodchenko's call for a new conception of the designer as the artist–constructor rather than artist–craftsman. Unconscious and spiritual associations with the creative process were de-emphasized. In their place, Moholy-Nagy identified the Modern artist with the proletariat, creating prototypes that provided solutions for efficient living, promoting an appreciation of the aesthetic potential of new industrial materials. Moholy-Nagy placed photography on an equal footing with the fine arts and experimented with kinetic sculpture. He praised the machine as a liberating force both in social and in creative terms: "Constructivism is not confined to the picture frame and the pedestal. It expands into industrial designs, into house, objects, forms. It is the socialism of vision – the common property of all men." In Moholy-Nagy's vision for the Bauhaus, students' familiarity with mechanical processes and industrial materials would enable them to apply their knowledge to a variety of fields rather than be limited only to specialized study of a particular material. Indeed, such versatility, implied in the general nature of the Vorkurs, seems in some way to have compensated for the loss of subjective expression and less direct handling of traditional materials implied by the use of standardized components and mechanized mass production.

When the Bauhaus mounted an exhibition of its work in 1923, Gropius proclaimed the shift in orientation in a speech entitled "Art and Technology: A New Unity." The poster (fig. 9.26) for the exhibition was designed by former Bauhaus student Joost Schmidt (1893–1948) and is composed of tilted rectangular and circular shapes, creating an "X"-like axis or grid. The grid imparts hierarchical and ordered relationships to the placement of the text for the words "State Bauhaus," "Exhibition" as well as location and date. The poster also contains the new logo for the Bauhaus designed by Oskar Schlemmer (1888–1943), a simplified pictogram of a profile head drawn with a ruler and built upon rectangular and circular shapes. The use of geometry to imply technical drawing and virtual absence of representation, along with the economy of means, were striking for the time and had a strong impact upon a number of yournger printers such as Jan Tschichold, who visited the Weimar exhibition (see pages 208–210).

The 1923 exhibition might best be summarized by a collaborative enterprise – the construction and decoration of the Haus-am-Horn (fig. 9.27), a model for low-cost single-family housing designed by Georg Muche and Adolf Meyer, who formerly had served as an assistant to Itten in the Vorkurs and continued to be Formmeister in the Bauhaus weaving workshop. The centrally planned Haus-am-Horn is designed with a large clerestory-lit living room surrounded on all sides by smaller rectangular rooms, each designed to efficiently meet a particular need for domestic living. The experimental design of the house was determined primarily by economic and objective functional considerations. It was constructed of prefabricated building materials (steel and concrete) and, like Le Corbusier's 1925 Pavillon de l'Esprit Nouveau, was intended as a prototype for public housing units that could be built cheaply and quickly.

Faculty and students in the Bauhaus workshops were responsible for the design and manufacture of furnishings for the interior spaces of the house. Photographs of the living room show furniture simply assembled from standardized lengths of wood, with chairs using overlapping joints; all are devoid of carved decoration or paint,

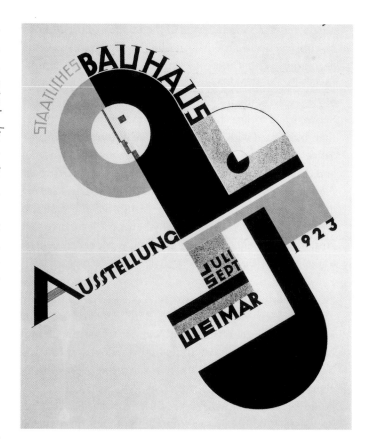

9.26 Joost Schmidt, poster for Bauhaus Exhibition, lithograph, 28 ¼ x 19 in (60.5 x 48 cm), Weimar, 1923.

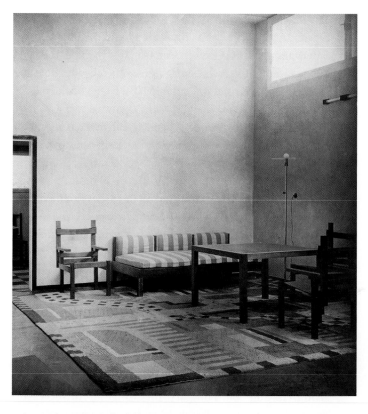

9.27 Georg Muche and Adolf Meyer with Bauhaus workshops, Haus-am-Horn, living room, 1923.

and are entirely rectilinear in form, recalling the 1918 chair designed by Gerrit Rietveld (see fig. 9.4). Lighting was designed by Moholy-Nagy and employed slender tubular metal forms emphasizing lightness, geometry, and the machine production of standardized parts. Textiles and carpets were also based upon abstract geometric designs and created a shared sense of geometric form, smooth, industrial surfaces, and the elimination of forms imitating nature. Features of the Haus-am-Horn kitchen were employed in the rational kitchen designs of the later 1920s and 1930s, associated with low-cost housing in the city of Frankfurt (see fig. 9.34). These also stemmed from studies of household efficiency that introduced a more scientific, objective approach to design stemming from the analysis of domestic work.

Renewing the Bauhaus commitment to educating a new type of designer for industry, Gropius hired a number of the school's own recent graduates as masters, replacing the former system of Formmeister and Lehrmeister in several workshops. Fine artists such as Klee and Kandinsky continued to exert an influence at the Bauhaus through required courses in form and theory, but their role in the workshops was reduced as the relationship between designers, materials, and production was re-examined in light of the importance of mechanized technology. The new direction, however, failed to please the Thuringian government that sponsored the school. In 1925 the Bauhaus in Weimar was closed and relocated to the industrial city of Dessau. With renewed local support, Gropius designed new facilities for the Bauhaus, renamed as the Bauhaus Höchschule für Gestaltung or "Institute for Design." At Dessau new facilities included modern printing presses and other equipment for the printing workshop and Jacquard looms for the weaving workshops. Gropius's studio building for the Bauhaus resembled a factory more than a traditional art school, with exposed steel construction and broad, uninterrupted expanses of plate glass that embodied Moholy-Nagy's identification of art with industry as well as designer and worker (rather than artist). Relocating the school to Dessau also provided the possibility for some faculty to acquire direct industrial experience, and faculty and students began to create prototypes for industrial production. Another change was the creation of a Bauhaus department of architecture.

Art historian John Heskett has emphasized that the effect of the Bauhaus upon industrial manufacturing in Germany was limited. Nevertheless some ties were forged, and Bauhaus designs were manufactured for a broad market, such as Marcel Breuer's tubular metal and wood chair with cane seating (fig. 9.28), manufactured by Thonet beginning in 1928. Breuer's design was based upon a novel cantilevered principle of support requiring

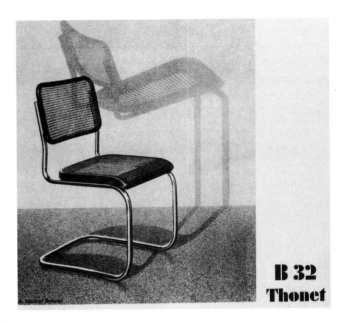

9.28 Marcel Breuer, tubular metal chair, chrome-plated steel and wood, and cane, 32 x 18 ¼ x 22 ½ in (81.3 x 46.4 x 57.2 cm), manufactured by Gebrüder Thonet, 1928.

two rather than the traditional four legs for support, a result of substituting applications of new materials and assembly to traditional craft-based techniques of furniture-making. Dutch Constructivist designer Mart Stam (1899–1986) also developed a similar cantilevered tubular metal chair as early as 1925, but that design was not manufactured in large quantities (a lawsuit ensued, and Thonet was forced to delete Breuer's name from its catalogue). In addition to Breuer's success with Thonet, lighting fixtures designed by a number of Bauhaus students were manufactured by Kortung and Mathieson, including those of Marianne Brandt (1893–1983) and Wilhelm Wagenfeld (1900–1990), who worked privately in Germany as an industrial designer during the 1930s after the close of the Bauhaus in 1933. Gunta Stölzl (1897–1983), who was a Bauhaus student in Weimar, became a professor in the weaving workshop, and was sent to the city of Krefeld to study industrial fiber and dyeing technology. Stölzl maintained a middle ground between early Weimar and Dessau, never abandoning handweaving and craft as a source of individual expression, while encouraging experimentation with newer industrial materials such as cellophane. She also focused attention upon other ideas, such as reversible fabrics and the relationship between fabric wall-coverings and acoustics, that went beyond aesthetics toward other factors augmenting use and value.

The printing workshop at the Bauhaus, with the support of Moholy-Nagy and under the direction of former student Herbert Bayer (1900–1985), introduced Constructivist approaches to visual communication including photomechanical reproduction and non-traditional approaches to letterpress printing. The workshop published a series of *Bauhausbücher*, exhibition and advertising posters, and displays, stationery, as well as a Bauhaus journal. In Dessau, Bayer created a series of "universal" sans serif typefaces based upon modular geometric shapes and a limited number of letterforms that decreased or even eliminated the vestiges of hand-lettering (fig. 9.29). He also eliminated capital letters, used in German for all nouns as well as at the beginning of sentences, creating regularized heights, a "bowl" rather than Roman "a," and in some cases a combination of lower- and upper-case forms, as in the "k." He introduced new possibilities for arranging text on the page outside of conventional centered layouts and hierarchies of information, all in the interest of a more simplified, efficient, and visual form of print communication. The printing workshop was able to introduce page layouts in which typography, photography, and heavy rules were all considered equal and complementary design elements, serving to attract and direct the viewer's attention and impart a new sense of active and asymmetrical order to the arrangement of information. An example is Moholy-Nagy's title page for the prospectus of the Weimar Bauhaus from 1923 (fig. 9.30), printed in red and black. Here, uniform sans serif typography is used in a variety of sizes to reflect a hierarchy of information and an asymmetrical balance of horizontal and vertical elements based upon an implied geometric grid. Decorative borders based upon plant or geometric patterns are purged, leaving large areas of white space that become part of the overall page layout, activated by rectangular shapes, even extending to the stem of large "B" to the left of the page. These plain black bars of different thicknesses, or "rules," are part of the printer's

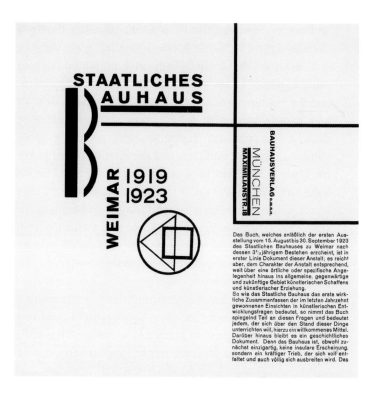

9.30 László Moholy-Nagy, title page of the Weimar Bauhaus prospectus, 10 x 10 in (25 x 25 cm), 1923.

type case used for spacing, but are employed here as part of typographic design: the vertical bar of the large "B" relates to the odd, vertically placed "WEIMAR" nearby. Moholy-Nagy's layouts promote a more broadly visual, "active," and *Modern* form of reading. While experimental in the use of novel letterforms and the orientation of words, they also display a strong sense of discipline and clarity, certainly in comparison with Futurist poetry, which also explored more expressive and symbolic approaches to letters and compositions (see fig. 9.1).

There is a strong parallel between the prominent role of such "empty" white space in Bauhaus page layouts and the furnished interior of the Haus-am-Horn and other experimental housing projects planned during the same years. In these projects, white walls dominated and space is "materialized" in relation to rectangular tables, chairs, and shelves (see fig. 9.27). In this way, mechanized mass production, involving standardization and uniformity, was, at least symbolically, linked to a universal and egalitarian vision for the society of the future. The machine thus held, for some artists, the promise of an international and enlightened democratic brotherhood, erasing distinctions of class, emphasizing modest, efficient living, and embracing a shared Modern aesthetic in which decoration and clutter had become outmoded and wasteful. This theme is echoed in Willi Baumeister's

9.29 Herbert Bayer, universal alphabet, 1926.

1927 polemic poster for the Weissenhof Exhibition in Stuttgart (see fig. 9.12).

In 1928 Gropius resigned as director of the Bauhaus, naming the Swiss-born Hannes Meyer (1889–1954), who served as professor of architecture, as his successor. Meyer was an unpopular choice at the outset, even though under his directorship the Bauhaus became more financially independent through commissions and sales of its prototypes. Meyer argued that design was synonymous with all man-made things and was a product of "function x economy." His views placed design solely in the service of universal working-class needs based upon objective standards of economy, brought to fruition through participation of the workshops in "real" projects for housing and utilitarian products. Moreover, Meyer tended to view design at the Bauhaus as a largely deterministic process, resulting more or less automatically from objective considerations of climate, hygiene, economics, and engineering. His approach marginalized the value of fine art in relation to design, and forced the resignation of several members of the faculty.

Although equally committed to technology and the social mission of the Bauhaus, Moholy-Nagy resigned quickly after Meyer's appointment as director. Moholy-Nagy held the position that modern design required an accommodation to standards and uniformity, but argued that versatility and more open-ended exploration of new technology and materials preserved the sense of intuition, creativity, and aesthetics in the design process. In Moholy-Nagy's view, versatility and experiment helped to relieve the fear of mindless and dehumanizing factory work and narrow specialization, as well as to combat a product-oriented, materialist view of design. To the end, he maintained the vision of a creative role for design and design education rather than the more pragmatic implications of strictly collective standards in design.

The differences between Meyer and Moholy demonstrate that Modernism was far from a monolithic movement, but was rather a loose collection of ideas with differences, contradictions, and strongly held opinions among its theorists and practitioners. Was the Modern designer an engineer? A worker? Or an artist? Today perhaps the need to choose among such options may appear overly zealous and polemic. Yet the stakeholders in these debates were often uncompromising, as the stakes themselves were felt to be high: shaping a future with little or no reference to the past, proposing solutions to social problems on a vast scale that seemed to require positions of firm and uncompromising authority. Despite inconsistencies and ambiguities, the term "Modernism" remains part of the literature and history of modern design, tied to many of the most familiar names and institutions of the first half of the twentieth century.

In time Meyer's position became untenable. Gropius had always attempted to avoid confrontation with government officials in the interests of the school's survival, but Meyer's politics were more revolutionary; under his directorship, political theory was taught as a classroom subject and a Communist student group was formed. After resigning in 1930, Meyer moved to Soviet Russia, where he hoped his activities and principles would find more ready acceptance. His place was taken by the well-established German architect Ludwig Mies van der Rohe (1886–1969), who had served as the director for the 1927 Weissenhof exhibition of modern housing projects in Stuttgart. Mies eventually moved the school from Dessau to facilities in Berlin.

In 1933, the National Socialist (Nazi) Party came to power in Germany. This government's strong nationalist and anti-Communist positions cast suspicion upon the international sympathies of the Bauhaus. The school's association with left-wing politics and radical ideas was linked to the influence of "foreigners" and conspired to bring about its demise, 14 years after its opening in Weimar in 1919.

The importance of the Bauhaus is not the result of its success in developing prototypes for industrial production, which was limited, but rather to the compelling nature of its original ideal of collaboration between art, craft, and industry in the education of designers, and the hope that modern design could reshape and unify art and life. This contribution is perhaps best exemplified in the career of Moholy-Nagy, who is remembered less for particular masterpieces of art or industrial products than for his embodiment of the new and versatile artist–worker-engineer, engaged in the creative process of design to address a broad range of human and social needs. It is also true that the emigration of Bauhaus faculty to other colleges and universities outside of Germany, respect for many of its faculty and students among institutions such as New York's fledgling Museum of Modern Art, have all added to the continuing power of a Bauhaus "image" that may vary somewhat from the institution's actual history. Nevertheless, the Bauhaus continues to exert an enormous influence upon post-secondary education in the visual arts and design, where many of its features still form the basis of art and design curricula. Despite the marginal, utopian, and occasionally esoteric element in Bauhaus ideology (which existed as well in those related international movements with which it came into contact), and despite the recognition that the school perhaps never realized the vision of its directors and spokespersons, the Bauhaus provided an environment in which designing for industry and in concert with technology became inspiring goals for a gifted and

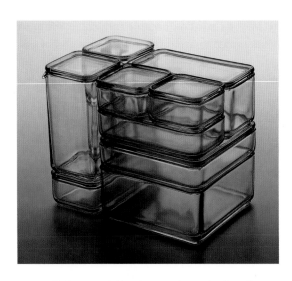

9.31 Wilhelm Wagenfeld, Kubus-Geschirr (cube-shaped dishware/storage containers), 3 ⅛ x 7 ⅛ x 7 ⅛ in (7.9 x 18.1 x 18.1 cm), manufactured by Lausitzer Glasverein, Weiswasser, Germany, *c.* 1938. Art Institute of Chicago.

committed body of faculty and students to pursue; the boldness of that effort remains a significant legacy.

BEYOND THE BAUHAUS

A small number of Bauhaus faculty remained in Germany after the school's closing in 1933 and designed products as consultants to industrial manufacturers. German industrial designer Wilhelm Wagenfeld, who had studied and taught at the Bauhaus, designed the line of Kubus glassware for the Lausitzer Glasverein in around 1938 (fig. 9.31). These inexpensive containers for kitchen use were made of a newly developed heat-resistant pressed glass, had interchangeable lids, and dimensions that permitted stacking for efficient storage. Wagenfeld remained in Germany and was successful throughout the 1930s as a

designer, and the leftist political leanings associated with the Bauhaus do not appear to have interfered with his practice. The absence of molded decoration in relief surely owes a debt to the Modernist elemental aesthetic, along with a relationship to efforts promoting standardization and efficiency in the design of offices and kitchens that took place in Germany during the later 1920s.

Trude Petri (1906–1998) studied ceramics in Hamburg (not at the Bauhaus) and designed the Urbino line of porcelain dinnerware for the Staatliche Porzellan-Manufaktur in Berlin, manufactured in 1930–1934 (fig. 9.32). The milk-white color, glasslike surfaces, and pure, circular forms of plates and serving platters, feet, and handles all suggest the abstract beauty of elemental geometric form. The gently tapering forms for tureens and lids introduce both an organic element and a sense of precision and elegance also found in the contemporary tubular metal furniture of the school's last director Mies van der Rohe (fig. 9.33). Both of these examples were produced in limited quantities by prestigious manufacturers for wealthy consumers by "star" designers, anticipating the international market for Modernist products and furniture after World War II related to formalist abstraction, and ideologically less compatible with the socialist attitudes of Moholy-Nagy or Hannes Meyer. Even the "Urbino" title of Petri's porcelain dinnerware recalls the Umbrian city famous for its renaissance court and patrons of such artists as Piero della Francesca, whose paintings also employ a stately geometric formality.

Initiatives to develop standards in the design of the workplace and in the home applied Frederick W. Taylor's theory of scientific management maximizing productivity in factory work through the study of movement in the performance of a variety of tasks (see page 151). Books such as American author Christine Frederick's *Scientific Management in the Home* (1915) proposed that the placement of sinks, cabinets, serving tables, ovens,

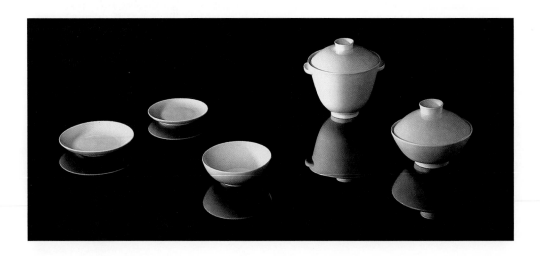

9.32 Trude Petri, Urbino dinnerware, porcelain, tureen, 6 x 11 ½ in (15 x 29 cm), manufactured by Staatliche Porzellan-Manufaktur, Berlin, 1930–1934. Metropolitan Museum of Art, New York.

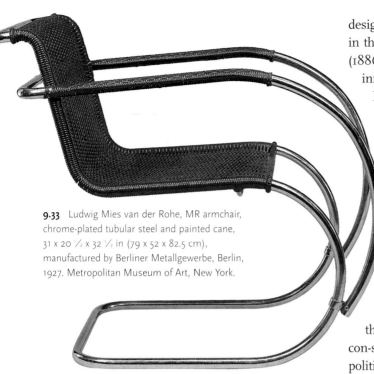

9.33 Ludwig Mies van der Rohe, MR armchair, chrome-plated tubular steel and painted cane, 31 x 20 ½ x 32 ½ in (79 x 52 x 82.5 cm), manufactured by Berliner Metallgewerbe, Berlin, 1927. Metropolitan Museum of Art, New York.

refrigerators, and work surfaces should derive from the rational study of food preparation, food service, and storage, defining a new dimension of research-based design for industrial production (see page 153). The ideas of Frederick parallel the efforts of Henry Ford to rationalize the assembly of automobiles at his Highland Park plant and also were particularly relevant in Germany. Housing shortages after World War I and a sluggish economy suggested to some that new construction should aim at efficiency and the fulfillment of minimum requirements for living, and that manufacturers should be encouraged to adopt standards based upon such. In an era when fewer families could afford servants, a rational approach to housework reduced its menial connotations and added an element of "science" and analysis to tasks and responsibilities usually assumed by women. Indeed, "home economics" was once a required subject for young women in junior high schools across the United States and still persists in many curricula as an elective, along with crafts and courses in wood-shop, metal-shop, or drafting for young men. In addition to efficiency, the designs for kitchens and office furnishings considered the effect of glare and brightness in lighting as well as posture in the design of furniture, maintaining some commitment to design standards based upon considerations of human factors. One of the goals of such research was to make objective criteria the basis for a "science" rather than an "art" of design, limiting the role of subjective expression.

The applications of such practical considerations for design often required the backing of local governments, as in the city of Frankfurt in the late 1920s, when Ernst May (1886–1970) held the position of City Architect. One influential result of these activities was the Frankfurt kitchen (fig. 9.34) designed under the direction of Grete Schütte-Lihotzky (1898–2000). The Frankfurt kitchen adopted the strategies devised by Christine Frederick and featured moveable "track" lighting and continuous work surfaces with built-in storage cabinets above. The contracts for low-cost, "minimum-existence" housing enabled designs for furniture and fittings to be mass-produced inexpensively in large quantities according to standard measurements. Smooth surfaces and the absence of decoration were warranted for ease of cleaning and hygiene, while government sponsorship of the project assured manufacturers of a ready market for the products without the need for variations to attract the con-sumer. As noted by John Heskett, the unique social, political, and economic circumstances in Frankfurt between 1925 and 1930 provided the basis for a rational and standardized approach to domestic design beyond the limits of office furniture or prototypes such as those used by Le Corbusier in the Pavillon de l'Esprit Nouveau.

The diversity of Modernist practices is also demonstrated by the career of Viennese architect and designer Josef Frank (1885–1967). Although he participated in the design of low-cost socialized housing in Vienna in the 1920s, Frank rejected a single, all-embracing elemental

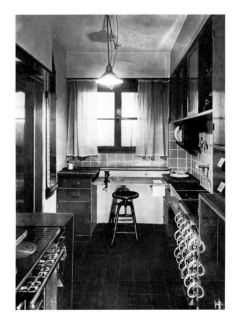

9.34 Grete Schütte-Lihotzky, the Frankfurt kitchen, 1924. Germanisches Nationalmuseum, Nuremberg.

approach to design that governed and united architecture, furniture, and furnishings. His flexible approach included dozens of textile patterns for curtains and upholstery that were contemporary interpretations of plant designs inspired by nature rather than by the machine or geometry, such as *Seaweed* (fig. 9.35) designed between 1925 and 1930. Meandering patterns of lines and leaf clusters suggest the movement of water and the beauty of organic forms. Such patterns, like the colored surfaces in Rietveld's Schröder House (see fig. 9.9) also relieve the austerity found in many Modernist architectural projects and proposals. Frank's remarks on interior design in the later 1920s reveal an appreciation both for the past and for nature:

> The goal...in designing an interior is not to make it as luxurious as possible or as simple as possible, but rather to make it as comfortable as possible...The most comfortable interiors have always been those that the occupant himself has put together over the course of time which betray no sense of intention or plan.

In a manner not unlike that of Matisse, who compared his paintings to comfortable armchairs (see page 163), Frank also wrote:

> the modern person who is increasingly more exhausted by his job requires a domicile cozier and more comfortable than those of the past. He has to obtain relaxation in more concentrated ways in a much shorter time. Therefore the domicile has to be the absolute opposite of the workplace. This applies not only to the...sitting and resting areas but to every visible object...; ornament and variety create peace and eliminate the pathos of the purely functional.

The emphasis upon the occupant, or "user" rather than an overriding doctrine is prescient in considering individual psychological rather than universal criteria in the design process. Historians have suggested that Frank's Swedish wife, Anna, may have influenced his less doctrinaire approach to Modernism, since Swedish as well as other Scandinavian designers in the interwar period tempered the more radical expressions of Modernism (see page 219 onward).

THE PRINTING INDUSTRY AND THE "NEW TYPOGRAPHY"

Sans serif typography and a new aesthetic sensibility toward graphic design reached beyond the limited circulation of books and journals such as *De Stijl*, the *Bauhausbücher*, and the short-lived *Vesch/Objet/Gegenstand*

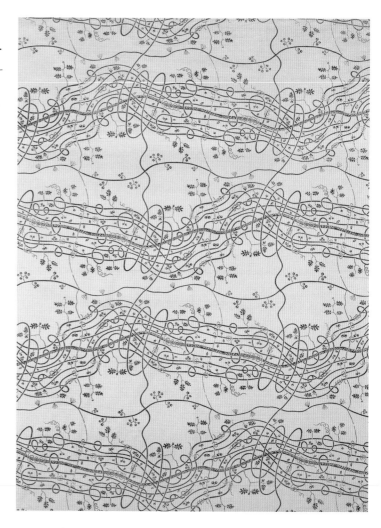

9.35 Josef Frank, *Seaweed* textile pattern, block-printed chintz cotton, repeat: 14 ¼ x 10 ¼ in (36.2 x 27.3 cm), 1925–1930. Victoria and Albert Museum, London.

during the later 1920s and 1930s. Large industrial type foundries in Europe and the United States were interested in expanding their range of typefaces in the interwar period, and also had the means to promote their efforts to the commercial printing industry. Lifestyle magazines such as *Vogue* (first published in 1892), incorporating photography and portraying contemporary fashion and leisure pastimes, also adopted experimental approaches to graphic design, meant to appear bold and independent of the past, but generally without relation to revolutionary social or political agendas.

The absence of serifs and other calligraphic features of typography, as well as the integration of type and image, and the reductive language of pictograms, all had a symbolic appeal to the movements associated with the Modernism in the interwar period. For instance, the sans serif typefaces designed at the Bauhaus by Bayer (see fig. 9.29) embodied the principle of generating a variety of letterforms from a limited number of related units as a metaphor for standardized mechanized production – they functioned as images of mass production as well as letterforms, but in so doing also sacrificed legibility.

The major foundries had introduced versions of sans serif faces primarily for newspaper printing and advertising around the turn of the century in response to a reform effort coinciding with the establishment of the Werkbund in Germany and the introduction of efficiency standards in other industries, for instance, in the sizes of pipefittings or electrical wiring, adapters, and sockets. In printing, this effort not only yielded the first twentieth-century sans serif fonts (see directly below), but also produced national standards for envelope and paper sizes, invoices, and other common business needs, including the dimensions of office filing cabinets. In Germany these were established under the auspices of the Institute for Standards, known as the DIN (Deutsches Institut für Normung), founded in Berlin in 1917.

Terminology in the field of typography is at times confusing, as the sans serif faces were known in Europe as "Grotesk" and in the United States as "Gothic." Franklin Gothic (fig. 9.36) was produced by the American Type Founders Company (ATF) and cut by Morris Benton between 1903 and 1905. Although it lacks serifs, Franklin Gothic retains Roman letterforms for the characters "a" and "g," and rounded letterforms narrow as they approach vertical stems rather than being of a single width (or weight) throughout. In Germany, the Berthold Foundry of Berlin introduced the closely related font known as Akzidenz Grotesk at about the same time. Both fonts were used primarily for titles and headlines in newspapers and advertisements rather than for body text.

Historically these Gothic or Grotesk fonts were designed for display, and developing them in the context of the printed page required control of letterforms, spacing, and weight. The commercial foundries addressed these practical concerns of legibility and precision to meet the varied printing needs of the market. Foundries developed large, extended "families" of fonts in a variety of weights as well as in expanded and condensed forms. Such efforts maintained continuity with traditions of expert craftsmanship established in the eighteenth century, and were often the result of

ABCDEFGHIJKLMN OPQRSTUVWXYZ? abcdefghijklm nopqrstuvwxyz! 1234567890

9.36 Morris Benton, Franklin Gothic typeface, 1903–1905.

a number of individuals working under contract for large companies whose resources enabled them to undertake such large-scale efforts. It is not surprising that ATF, which introduced Franklin Gothic around the turn of the century, was itself a product of the consolidation of a number of smaller foundries joining forces in response to competitive market conditions. A page from the 1923 ATF Catalogue demonstrates the quality and variety of letterpress printing produced by large foundries during this time, in this example the Caslon "family" of letterforms based upon the well-known English eighteenth-century printer (fig. 9.37). Business circumstances and new technologies for cutting and casting type promoted

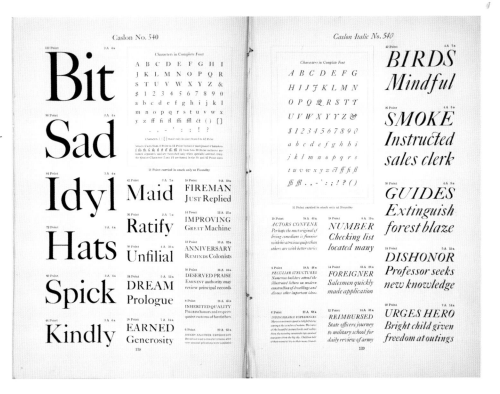

9.37 Caslon "family" typeface, from *American Type Founders Specimen Book*, double-page spread 10 1/8 x 13 in (25.7 x 33 cm), 1923.

ABCDEFGHIJKLMN OPQRSTUVWXYZ? abcdefghijklm nopqrstuvwxyz! 1234567890

9.38 Paul Renner, Futura typeface, 1927.

ABCDEFGHIJKLMN OPQRSTUVWXYZ? abcdefghijklm nopqrstuvwxyz! 1234567890

9.39 Rudolf Koch, Kabel typeface, 1927.

the development of new types and their "families," and permitted a healthy interaction between designers and printers. Collaborations involved artist–calligraphers such as Rudolf Koch in Germany and amateur experts such as Stanley Morison in England (see page 216), who designed or supervised the design of new typefaces as well as the revival or re-interpretation of older types utilizing new cutting and casting methods.

In 1927 Munich-based typographer and teacher Paul Renner (1878–1956) introduced the influential sans serif typeface known as Futura, including bold, light, condensed, and expanded variations demanded by the commercial printing industry (fig. 9.38). The font was produced by the Bauer Foundry in Frankfurt. Futura is known as a modular sans serif because several of its letter-forms share the same element, for instance, the circular lower-case "o" is used for the letters "a," "b," "d," "e," "p," and "q"), and "geometric" because all strokes are of a single width (also known as monoweight). The modular principle, implying interchangeability, is certainly inherent in earlier experimental typefaces but was applied with greater attention to legibility and the effects produced by modern automatic typesetting equipment. Other foundries followed with their own competitive versions of modular sans serifs typefaces in Germany; for instance, Rudolf Koch's Kabel for the Klingspor Foundry in 1927 (fig. 9.39). One difference between the Futura and Kabel typefaces was Koch's preservation of features of the Roman alphabet, for instance, the "a" as well as the slanted crossbar of the "e," a characteristic found in the earliest Venetian Roman fonts of the later fifteenth century. Despite the identification between sans serif and Modernism in typography, this type of letterform has a history going back to early nineteenth-century display

faces, renewed with expanded technology and the explosion of printed materials requiring headlines in the early twentieth century. While Koch agreed to introduce a "Modern" sans serif with Kabel, he is best known as a master calligrapher, knowledgeable in printing types as well as their traditions.

JAN TSCHICHOLD AND THE NEW TYPOGRAPHY

One of the strongest advocates and promoters of Constructivist principles for commercial printing during the later 1920s and early 1930s was Jan Tschichold (1902–1974). Tschichold was trained in lettering in Leipzig, Germany, and acquired a mastery of calligraphy, used at that time for display lettering in newspaper advertising and in developing brand names for products and services. As a young man he visited the Bauhaus exhibition in Weimar in 1923 (see fig. 9.26). Tschichold was enthusiastic about the printing on view at the exhibition, and saw sans serif typography and asymmetrical page design as means toward modern and direct communication of information to readers for a variety of printing applications, including advertising. He embraced a new approach and discipline for the composition of text and image without decorative borders and flourishes. The trademarks he developed from the later 1920s onward, often commissioned by publishing companies, appear somewhat conservative by present-day standards, but reveal an ability to combine letterforms and abbreviated, recognizable images into unified symbols, as seen in an example for the Bücherkreis (Book Circle) of Berlin (fig. 9.40).

Most of Tschichold's attention was directed to the varied tasks of commercial printing, ranging from posters to stationery, catalogues, and books. In a manifesto

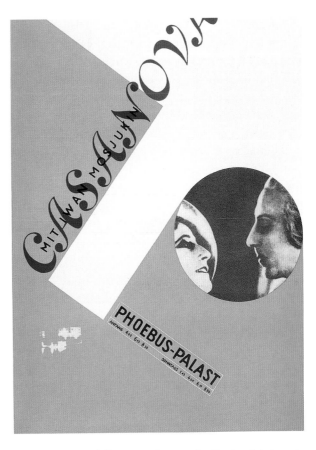

published in 1925 and again in his 1927 book entitled *The New Typography*, Tschichold articulated his approach, which strongly influenced Swiss graphic design after World War II. This included principles of clear and direct communication that favored the use of sans serif typography, half-tone reproduction of photographs rather than hand-drawn illustration, and asymmetrical layout. In *The New Typography*, Tschichold explained the Modern context for a disciplined approach that defined the emerging profession of graphic design:

> Every part of a text relates to every other part by a definite, logical relationship of emphasis and value, predetermined by content. It is up to the typographer to express this relationship clearly and visibly, through type sizes and weight, arrangement of lines, use of color, photography...

9.41 Jan Tschichold, film poster, *Casanova*, for Phoebus-Palast movie theater, letterpress, 47 ¹/₁₆ x 33 ³/₁₆ in (119.7 x 84.5 cm), Munich, 1927.

He also explained the rationale for asymmetry in light of stimulating eye movement for the modern viewer who is often too busy for leisurely reading and demands a more active engagement with printed material for effective communication:

9.42 Jan Tschichold, poster for a Constructivist exhibition in Basel, linocut and letterpress, 35 ¾ x 50 ¼ in (90.5 x 127.7 cm), 1937.

> Reading presupposes eye movement. The New Typography so designs text matter that the eye is led from one word and one group of words to the next. So a logical organization of the text is needed, through the use of different type-sizes, placing in relation to space, color, etc.

For posters, rectangular elements relating to the frame dominate, while the use of diagonal type and shapes, or other deviations from the strict discipline of the sans serif letters create tension and arouse interest (fig. 9.41). This example is one of several film posters produced not by the distributor but by the movie theater to provide a recognizable style and visual identity. Like his Constructivist contemporaries, Tschichold attached importance to white space, making it an integral element in composition. Its prominence conveyed a feeling for economy and purity, as in a poster illustrating the works of designers and artists associated with the Bauhaus, De Stijl, and Constructivism (fig. 9.42).

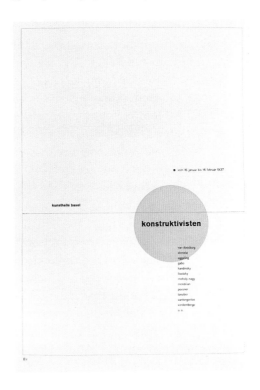

Tschichold's "New Typography" and related articles published in printing industry journals provided practical information for printers to adapt asymmetrical layout and an ordering of elements based upon content within the structure of a geometric grid to the needs of title pages, stationery, announcements, invitations, and other prosaic printing tasks, known as "jobbing." The grid, still based upon the process of letterpress printing, ensured precise relationships between parallel and perpendicular elements on the page. Elements of this approach became the basis for the so-called Swiss or International Typographic Style in many parts of Europe after World War II (see page 291 onward), as well as consistent identities developed for corporations working on an international scale. The New Typography imposed a certain degree of conformity upon the designer, but still required adjustments rather than simply the application of a formula. As a result, Tschichold's designs have an inherent sense of "rightness" in their abstract balance and in the feeling for the relationship among the various elements of the page as related to the hierarchy of information. The guidelines for the New Typography could be listed as rules or even described as laws, but they could not be programmed; in addition to the logical and effective communication of information, the abstract aesthetic pleasure of a New Typography poster also offered an independent level of appreciation to the viewer.

Tschichold actively promoted the use of half-tone photographs for modern printing. He wrote that photography was the "most obvious means of visual representation in our time," and embraced the interrelationship between the graded tonalities of photographs and blocks of text that provided unity and maintained the attention of the viewer. The reproduction of photographs opened up new possibilities for the printing industry and provided the basis for much experimentation. Like El Lissitzky and Moholy-Nagy, Tschichold was fascinated with the process of photography and its application to printing, and illustrated examples of photograms in *The New Typography*, where objects were exposed directly on light-sensitive plates in the darkroom. This technique, as well as photomontage, where photographic images were juxtaposed and related to lettering, opened up a variety of possibilities ranging from advertisements to covers for politically charged underground publications. German photographer and designer Max Burchartz (1887–1961) used photomontage to create a trade prospectus for the Bochumer Company, which manufactured industrial parts for machines and railway switching equipment (fig. 9.43). For Burchartz, the power of the photograph was its unmediated, truthful representation of the visible world in comparison with the more interpretive techniques of drawing and illustration. In addition to providing the viewer with an idea of the

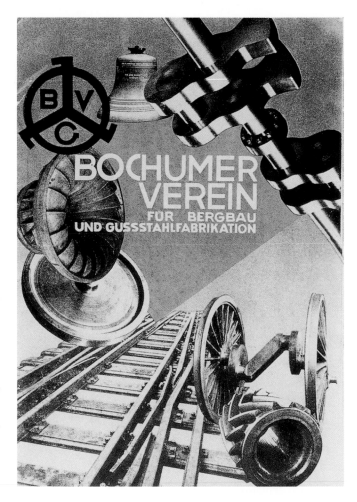

9.43 Max Burchartz and Johannes Canis, trade prospectus for Bochumer Verein fur Bergbau und Busstahlfabrikation (Bochum Association for Mining and Cast Iron Manufacture), 11 ¼ x 8 ¼ in (30 x 21 cm), Bochum, Germany, 1925. Private collection.

company's products, the Constructivist-inspired composition is asymmetrical and uses diagonal shapes to create a sense of drama and dynamism in reference to modern transportation. The prospectus cover is at least partially promotional, whereas the content of a company's catalogue was more strongly informational. For catalogues, Burchartz also used photography and layout effectively to familiarize readers with products along with printed descriptive information and consistency from product to product and page to page, using printers rules for spacing and visual continuity. The relationship between information and promotion was at times fluid; Tschichold believed that the New Typography had a role to play in all types of printed materials, including advertising and promotion, in which more graphic approaches to visual communication functioned with immediacy and effectiveness.

Dada artist and Communist activist John Heartfield (1891–1968) also used photography effectively in graphic design as an instrument of political commentary and agitation. Unlike the Constructivists in Russia who were part of a system of state-sponsored propaganda, Heartfield's oeuvre in Germany during the 1930s was an "outsider" effort meant to undermine existing political authority and appeal to workers. Many of his works appeared on the cover of the Communist journal *AIZ* (*Workers' Illustrated Newspaper*). Heartfield's posters and covers were often cut-and-pasted together, then re-photographed for printing, and the resulting quality is often grainy. The power of the composed images derives from the contradiction between an image with familiar, mass associations and an unfamiliar, even opposite meaning. The contrast between both visual statements is strengthened through the objective and impersonal qualities of photography. With increasing technical proficiency, the designer's manipulations of the medium became less readily apparent, and the power of juxtaposed images more provocative. This technique was common in Dada collage, but usually more open-ended, even humorous and playful, in its interpretation. There is little humor (except perhaps black humor) in Heartfield's manipulations: his image for an issue of *AIZ* in 1932 (fig. 9.44) is entitled "the meaning of Geneva." The image juxtaposes the League of Nations Building (forerunner to the United Nations) with the flag of Switzerland turning into the Nazi swastika, a sword, and dead dove. The "end of peace" seems to be the clear conclusion for the viewer to draw; in 1932 a demonstration in Geneva against the Nazi Party had resulted in the death of several activists, and in 1933 Germany withdrew from the League, as part of an effort to rearm despite restrictions imposed by the Versailles Treaty at the end of World War I. The emerging and experimental techniques of graphic design, including photography, were proving their worth in the interwar period, not only for advertising or as a form of public art, but speaking "louder than words" in a contentious political climate.

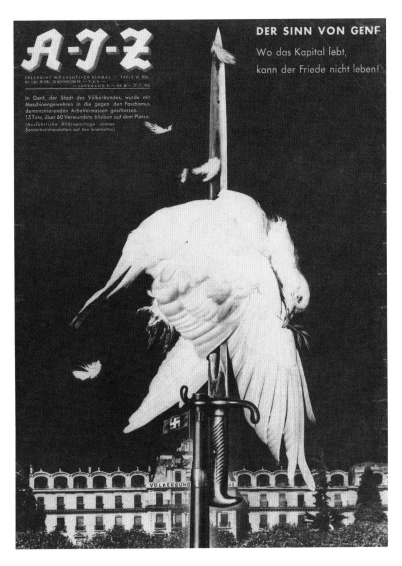

9.44 John Heartfield, *Der Sinn von Genf*, cover for *AIZ (Arbeiter Illustrierte Zeitung: das Illustrierte Volksblatt)*, 15 x 11 in (38 x 28 cm), November, 1932.

Whether for advertising or in the context of shaping public opinion, artists, as well as governments and businessmen, recognized that photography was a mass medium with great powers of persuasion. After departing the Bauhaus in 1928, Herbert Bayer worked for an advertising agency in Berlin and was art director for the German fashion magazine *die neue linie* (his typography for the magazine used all lower-case letters). Covers for this journal employed high-quality four-color printing technology. Bayer took advantage of the resources of this high-end commercial publication to utilize the techniques of montage and photomontage extensively, exploring expressive possibilities with more varied technical means at his disposal. Results were often startling and provocative juxtapositions of scale that triggered the viewer's associations with travel or to contemporary events. Aside from the monoweight sans serif used for the title, text was rarely used on cover art. The cover of an issue from 1930 is a study in reduction and contrasts (fig. 9.45). Bayer conveys an image of Mediterranean travel, suggested by a bright blue ground, and simplified and slightly oblique view of a sunlight-bathed Doric temple seen from below. A fashionably dressed woman with a knee-length skirt stands on the stereobate. Projecting from the entablature is the large head of a second female figure, also with fashionable cloche hat. Her heavy eyelids suggest a comparison with the so-called Severe style of Greek sculpture in the early fifth century BCE, adding to the juxtaposition of present and past.

Advocates of the New Typography found numerous commercial outlets for their modern approach to advertising and other forms of graphic communication. Magazine art direction, as practiced by Bayer and elsewhere in Europe and in the United States during the later 1920s was one outlet, in which photography and double-page spreads were creatively explored. Another outlet was the lithographic poster, such as figure 9.46, which promoted a large international exhibition devoted to the graphic arts held in Cologne in 1928. The poster betrays its debt to elements of the New Typography, and might be compared to Joost Schmidt's poster for the

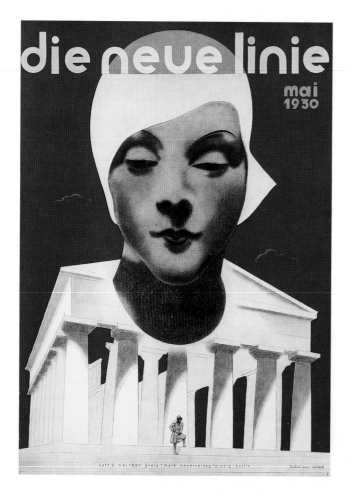

9.45 Herbert Bayer, cover for *die neue linie*, 14 ¼ x 10 ½ in (36.5 x 26.7 cm), Leipzig, 1930. The Wolfsonian Florida International University, Herbert Bayer Archive.

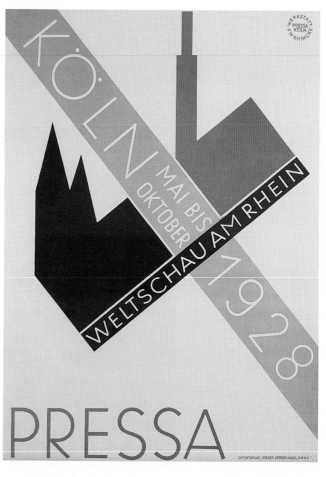

9.46 René Binder and Max Eichheim, *Köln, Mai bis Oktober, Weltschau am Rhein*, poster designed for Werkstatt F. H. Ehmcke, lithograph, 28 x 20 in (70.5 x 50 cm), 1928. The Wolfsonian Florida International University.

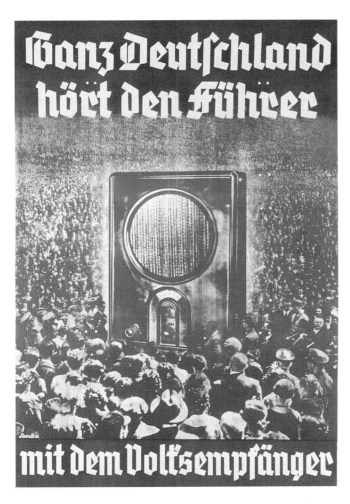

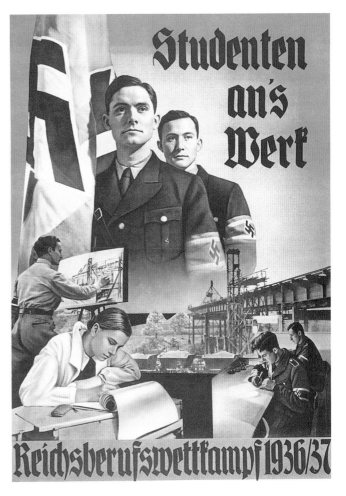

9.47 Leonid, *Ganz Deutschland hort den Führer mit dem Volksempfanger* (*All of Germany listens to the Führer with the People's receiver*), lithograph, 47 x 33 ½ in (119.4 x 84.8 cm), printed by Preussischer Druckerei und Verlgs AG, Berlin, 1936. The Wolfsonian Florida International University.

9.48 Anonymous, *Studenten an's Werk!* (*Students to Work!*), poster, color lithograph, 46 ½ x 32 ¼ in (117.8 x 83.2 cm), published by Deutschen GmbH, Berlin, 1937. The Wolfsonian Florida International University.

Bauhaus exhibition of 1923 (see fig. 9.26). Designed by René Binder and Max Eichheim for the Munich-based Ehmcke Workshop, the poster combines rectangular shapes of different colors intersecting at right angles and the use of monoweight upper-case sans serif lettering. In addition to strong contrast and establishing a hierarchy of information through the sizes and placement of typography with ample white space, the designers incorporated reductive abstract symbols for the twin towers of Cologne's Gothic cathedral and the tall modern tower built for the exhibition identifying the skyline of the city.

Even the National Socialist Party in Germany used techniques of photomontage as a way of mobilizing support and loyalty to the party and to their leader, Adolf Hitler. A poster from 1936 (fig. 9.47), by an artist known only as Leonid, superimposes the image of the plain, inexpensive "People's Radio" against a bird's-eye view of a vast crowd that bleeds to the edge of the paper. The radio was first manufactured in 1933 to encourage families to

purchase them to listen to Hitler's pubic addresses. They cost less than most radios of the period, and did not include short-wave capabilities to receive broadcasts from foreign nations. The juxtaposition combined with the bold text signifies radio as a substitute for actually being at a rally, reinforcing solidarity with the myth of a vast nation unified behind a single voice. The traditional, nationalistic German Blackletter type reads "All of Germany listens to the Führer with the People's receiver."

As in much contemporary poster art from the Soviet Union in the later 1920s and 1930s, the National Socialist government favored idealized monumental images of youthful workers and athletes to build a sense of identity with government initiatives. Both illustration and photography were used to promote a sense of duty on the part of all citizens toward the good of all, as seen, for instance, in an anonymous poster of 1937 (fig. 9.48). In this example, images of young workers against a background of factories are carefully placed below two clean-shaven soldiers with

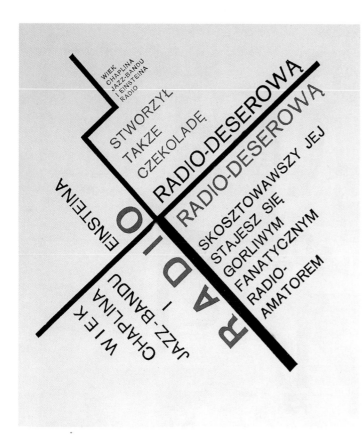

9.49 Henryk Berlewi, advertisement for radio station advertising, c. 1924, illustrated in Jacques Damase's *Révolution typographique depuis Stéphane Mallarmé*, Geneva, 1966.

swastikas on their arms, creating a stable pyramidal composition illustrating the phrase "Students to Work!" There also seems to be an identity between technical work, including construction and industrial production, and the German army. This theme is echoed in patriotic posters in Allied countries during World War II (see fig. 10.49).

Notwithstanding instances of the appropriation of New Typography techniques, the National Socialist Party in Germany was suspicious of the activities of the Bauhaus and other independent artists and designers sympathetic to Constructivism. Tschichold, as well as Paul Renner, fell victim to these suspicions, and after being arrested in 1933 Tschichold fled to Switzerland, where he continued to work as a freelance designer. Other graphic designers were not so lucky: the Dutch graphic designer H. N. Werkman (1882–1945), who had produced experimental typography in journals in Holland in the 1920s and 1930s, began publishing illustrated stories critical of the Nazis, who had invaded Holland in May 1940. He was arrested and exe-cuted by firing squad in 1945. At certain times, and in particularly authoritarian and repressive circumstances, printing, as well as graphic design, have been dangerous professions.

In time, Tschichold came to regret the polemic tone of his own early writings, recognizing that no single typeface or approach to layout can meet the varied demands for legibility and promotion required of every printing need or for every audience. In short, there were authoritarian and polemic implications of the New Typography that Tschichold came to reject, preferring instead to avoid ideology in favor of a more flexible dialogue between designer, text, publisher, and audience. As a tool of communication, he believed that creative modern graphic design should not be determined by a set of strict principles nor imposed upon every task or user. His initial enthusiasm for a new form of visual communication was tempered by an acknowledgment of and respect for difference and for history.

Outside of Germany, Switzerland, and the Soviet Union, several designers took an interest in the New Typography. Henryk Berlewi (1894–1967) established the advertising firm Reklama Mechano in Warsaw, Poland. His use of sans serif typography, asymmetrical layout, ample white space, and abstract geometric shapes for advertisement certainly are in sympathy with the guidelines of the New Typography, while a statement from 1924 appears both as a rejection of individualism and an embrace of the dynamism of modern life: "Art must break with the practices of the perfumed, perverse, hypersensitive, hysterical, romantic, individualistic, boudoir-type art of yesterday. It must create a new language of forms, available to all and in harmony with the rhythm of life." Both tendencies appear in his advertisements encouraging companies to use radio as a form of advertising. In figure 9.49, the printers' rules and diagonal type of different weights suggest not only the electronic communication of information but also the antennae of a radio tower.

BRITAIN AND MODERN DESIGN

In Britain, a number of artists with varied backgrounds took an interest in modern graphic visual communication. Edward Johnston (1872–1944), a master typographer and teacher who designed decorative initials for the Dove's Press established by Emery Walker and T. J. Cobden-Sanderson in Hammersmith (see page 87 and fig. 5.5), created a sans serif typeface for the London Underground in 1916 that remains in use to this day (fig. 9.50). The commission for this sans serif typeface for the expanding Underground system came from Frank Pick (1878–1941), who at that time held the title of Manager for Underground Electric Railways. Pick also commissioned posters from a number of younger artists to upgrade the appearance of Underground stations and advertise travel and public transportation.

JOHNSTON

This broadsheet is set in Johnston type. Edward Johnston (1872-1944) was one of the followers of William Morris (1834-1896) who took a leading part in reviving an interest in good lettering after the decadence of the late-Victorian fashions. In 1916 Johnston was commissioned by Frank Pick (1878-1941) to design a special fount for the exclusive use of London's Underground and its associated companies. The resulting Johnston sans-serif type was the fore-runner of many sans-serif founts both in England and abroad, including that of Eric Gill (1882-1940) who was Johnston's friend and pupil in this specialised field of design. Johnston is the standard type used for all official signs and notices throughout the London Transport system, and it is also used, where appropriate, for much of London Transport's general typographical publicity.

ABCDEFGHIJKLMNOPQRSTUVWXYZ1234567890
abcdefghijklmnopqrstuvwxyz &£.,:;'-""!?()*

9.50 Edward Johnston, Railway typeface,
1916. London Transport Museum.

ABCDEFGHIJKLMN OPQRSTUVWXYZ?
abcdefghijklm nopqrstuvwxyz!
1234567890

9.51 Eric Gill, Gill Sans typeface, 1928,
line drawing by John Langdon.

One of Johnston's students was Eric Gill (1882–1940), a sculptor who developed a family of typefaces known as Gill Sans (fig. 9.51) for the British Monotype Corporation in 1928. The London and North Eastern Railway used Gill Sans for all of their printed materials. Whether proprietary or not, designers and foundries were happy to oblige corporate customers who wanted to unify their printed materials through a distinctive typeface that formed part of a branding strategy. Historians generally find the British sans serif typefaces less mechanical and geometric than their Continental counterparts, though

they certainly rely more upon compass and straight edge than calligraphic faces based more directly upon the Roman alphabet.

Both Johnston and Gill, like Tschichold, wrote numerous essays and books on the subject of typography, generally intended for printers and dealing with a wide range of practical, aesthetic, scholarly, and social issues related to the subject. Many were published in the journals *The Fleuron* and *Signature*. Both men explored the advantages of sans serif typography and were inventive in expanding its application, particularly in the transportation industry, where clear signage and immediate recognition of information were primary considerations. At the same time, they continued to produce typefaces of great sophistication and subtlety based upon Roman letter-forms and the study of historic types for British Monotype and private presses. Eric Gill's Perpetua for British Monotype, for instance, released in 1929 and seen on the cover of a book of Gill's essays (fig. 9.52), has long ascenders and descenders in the lower case, as well as a gradual narrowing of the strokes of letters such as "d" or "p" toward their stems. Our example also includes Gill's woodcut illustration, whose graphic character is typical of private press publications of the period, respecting but not imitating the traditions of letterpress printing.

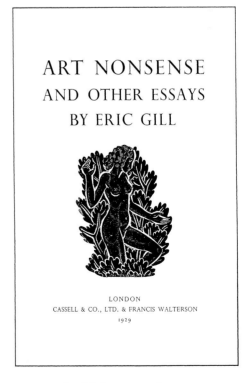

ART NONSENSE
AND OTHER ESSAYS
BY ERIC GILL

LONDON
CASSELL & CO., LTD. & FRANCIS WALTERSON
1929

9.52 Eric Gill, Perpetua typeface, 1929.

ABCDEFGHIJKLMN OPQRSTUVWXYZ? abcdefghijklm nopqrstuvwxyz! 1234567890

9.53 Stanley Morison, Times New Roman typeface, 1932, line drawing by John Langdon.

Stanley Morison (1889–1967) of British Monotype supervised the design of several typefaces derived from historical precedent but adapted to the requirements of modern printing technology. His best-known face was developed for the London *Times*, and known as Times New Roman (TNR; fig. 9.53). First printed in 1932, Times New Roman has been widely praised for its legibility combined with economical considerations such as shortened ascenders and descenders that reduce the space between lines in the text. Gill, Johnston, and Morison each invented or supervised the invention of fonts adapted to new production technologies and concentrating upon body text rather than titling or display uses. They explored the use of sans serif typography and were open-minded to its advantages, but their own training and experience prevented them from adopting it exclusively. Tschichold reached the same conclusion, probably for the same reason: in book design, serif typefaces and symmetrical layouts remained a direct and effective means of communication. Some of those principles may be seen in the work of Edward Young (1913–2003), who designed book covers for the series of paperback books published by Penguin. These books, issued first in 1935 and slightly modified by Tschichold in 1949, were certainly modern in the sense of being small, inexpensive, portable, geared to a more active lifestyle, as well as simply and economically designed. The paper covers used horizontal bands of bright color at top and bottom (color-coded for the type of literature), with the title set in sans serif against a white background. The design, along with the Penguin logo,

identified the book as part of a series, with the parent company (The Bodley Head) set vertically to each side of the bold black title, printed in Gill Sans Bold (fig. 9.54).

In many ways, book and type designers in England in the interwar period continued the tradition of great printer–typographers from the eighteenth century described above and revived by William Morris in the late nineteenth century. Certainly many aspects of the industry had changed. Commercial printing had expanded, the half-tone screen permitted the mechanical reproduction of photographs, and typographers had to take into consideration the way in which mechanical typesetting affected the look of a printed page. The design of new type required invention, a respect for tradition, knowledge of industrial process, and a feeling for the purposes of and audiences for printed communication. The collaboration and dialogue within these large typefounding companies among the viewpoints of consultants such as Morison, designers, and printers remains a vital part of the history of graphic design, as printed materials served increasingly varied roles in the modern world and vied with newer forms of media such as radio. One expression of that dialogue is a brief but famous essay published in 1930 by Beatrice Warde (1900–1969), who worked at the Monotype Corporation. In her essay "The Crystal Goblet," Warde uses the metaphor of a wine glass to describe the ideal typeface: like a crystal goblet, it should reveal rather than obscure its content, and otherwise be "invisible." Warde could not have been referring to advertising type or to the ways in

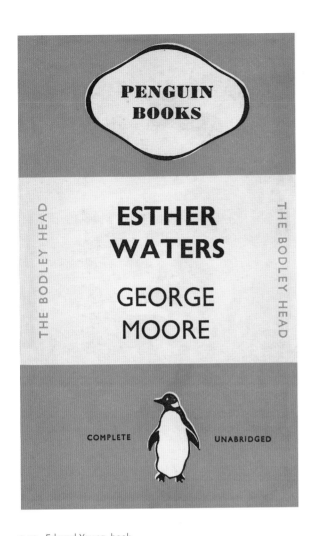

9.54 Edward Young, book cover for Penguin paperback, 7 ⅛ x 4 ¼ in (18 x 10.8 cm), London, 1936.

which graphic designers were loosening boundaries between type and image. Her subject was body text for book printing, and in that venerable but limited context, the metaphor resonated with her readership.

Penguin's inexpensive and portable paperbacks were geared to the modern lifestyles of commuters traveling by or waiting for trains, and a more casual form for storing those books was provided by the Isokon Company in England (founded in 1931) through their Donkey bookcase (fig. 9.55), designed by Vienna-trained architect Egon Riss (1901–1964) and manufactured beginning in 1939. Certainly non-traditional in form and making use of curved panels of thin plywood, the bookcase also was small and portable, and the dimensions of its asymmetrical shelves were designed to hold Penguin paperbacks stacked either upright or on their sides. The U-shaped form in the center was meant for folded newspapers, while the ends playfully resembled the ears of a donkey.

As Vice-President of the London Passenger Transport Board (established in 1933 through the merger of remaining independent service companies), Frank Pick again had the opportunity to apply skills of visual communication to issues of communication and identity in the public transportation industry. Through a design policy that encompassed architecture, interior design, furniture, and signage, Pick created a comprehensive and

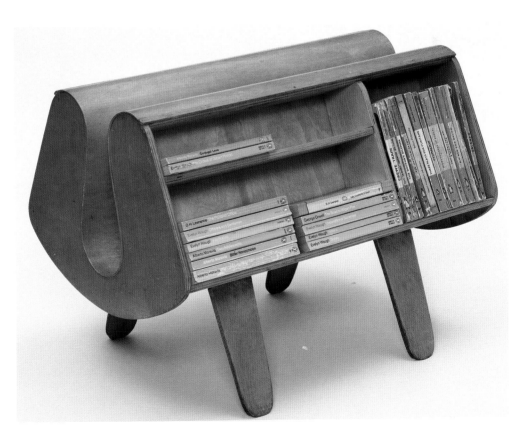

9.55 Egon Riss, bookcase ("Penguin Donkey"), plywood, 16 ½ x 23 ¼ x 17 ¼ in (41.9 x 59.1 x 43.8 cm), manufactured by Isokon Furniture, London, 1939. Victoria and Albert Museum, London.

cohesive visual identity for the London Underground transportation system (fig. 9.56). For the public, the unified identity system created the impression of order, reliability, compatibility, and control among the various lines and interchanges that comprise the Underground transit system. Colorful travel posters on station walls encouraged travelers to explore the attractions of urban and suburban London. An example is American-born McKnight Kauffer's (1890–1954) *Winter Sales* poster illustrated in figure 9.57. Here a group of women are swept into the vortex of a pattern of swirling lines and cool colors suggesting the unpleasant experience of shopping

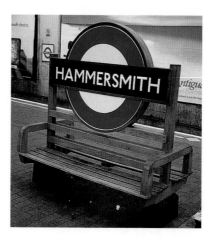

9.56 London Transport, combined bench and station sign, *c.* 1935.

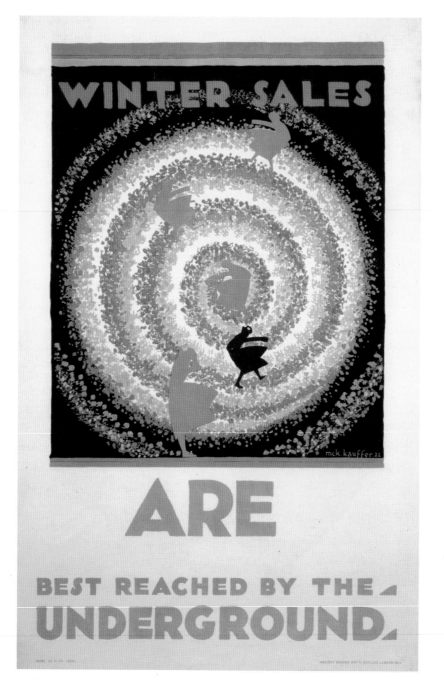

9.57 McKnight Kauffer, *Winter Sales* poster, 1922.

on a wet wintry day, and reminding us to avoid such discomfort by taking the Underground. The simplified forms and lack of consistent viewpoint contrast with more conventional illustrative techniques used in other contemporary travel and advertising posters. For the employees, visual identity created the sense of a single entity, while in fact the newly formed London Transport Board (LBT) was made up of dozens of competing private companies.

For a new map of the LTB's routes, Pick turned to an industrial draftsman named Henry Beck to reduce the confusion and uncertainty of navigating the vast interconnected routes of the public transportation system. The map (fig. 9.58) is a model of reduction for the efficient communication of information, based upon a geometric grid, and limiting the direction of routes to angles of 90 and 45 degrees. In this way the parallel lines not only make the system itself appear rational, but also make it easier for the traveler to locate stations and connections between routes when changes are necessary. The design, in a word, is "user-friendly," helping to break down barriers that inhibit the use of a service that might otherwise appear complicated. As a result of the map, the city itself became more manageable and accessible to the visitor. As noted by Adrian Forty, the simplicity of the London Underground map was not in every respect a virtue. The map had no uniform sense of scale to gauge distances between stops or a means of explaining the sometimes lengthy walking distances that accompany changing from one color-coded line to another. One result was that suburban locations often seemed far closer to the center of the city than they were. Such distortions might indeed make what looked like a simple trip from Piccadilly to Hampstead or Walthamstow into more of an adventure than a tourist had bargained for. Yet aside from the deception (and perhaps the weather), the trip still remains worth the while. Pick's strategies for London Transport engage several related approaches to design: posters advertised appealing activities or destinations related to Underground travel and were also works of art displayed in the midst of the everyday activities of commuters and other travelers; the signage used a combination of consistent lettering and distinctive symbols for easy recognition and familiarity, becoming mainstays of corporate identity; and the Underground map used a grid to make the complex appear simple and inviting, reducing the fear of getting lost or confused. More traditional ideas of design as a value added to utility (in this case getting from one place to another using public transportation) are combined with providing information to travelers simply and efficiently that makes them more likely than not to use the service.

This approach to design demonstrates that geometric abstraction can attain the level of an almost universal

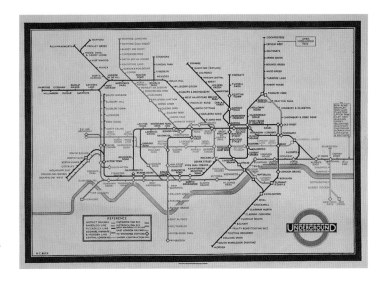

9.58 H. C. Beck, Map of the London Underground, chromolithograph, 6 ¼ x 9 in (15.7 x 22.6 cm), 1933. London Transport Museum.

visual communication that functions effectively for the traveler. Such an approach became the basis for transportation symbols designed in the early 1970s for airports and may be seen as a practical legacy of the visual strategies of the New Typography. Indeed, an Austrian sociologist named Otto Neurath (1882–1945) initiated the Isotype Movement in Vienna before moving to Holland in 1934. Neurath worked with artists to develop universal pictorial symbols to communicate statistics in a concise and direct manner intended to encourage the sharing of information on social and economic issues for the general public. Like the London Underground map, the Isotype Movement contributed to the developing profession of graphic design in the interwar period.

SCANDINAVIA AND MODERN DESIGN

In the interwar period, designers in Scandinavia developed an original approach to social and aesthetic issues raised by modern industrial technology. Steering a middle ground between standardization and efficiency on the one hand and psychological dimensions of modern living on the other, Scandinavia emerged in the 1930s as a model for international modern design after World War II (see pages 260–265). An overview of Scandinavian design in the interwar period might begin in Sweden with the hiring of artists such as Edward Hald (1883–1980) and Simon Gate (1883–1945) by large glass manufactories such as Orrefors in the production of art glass for a mostly luxury international market. Hald had studied painting with Matisse in Paris, and examples of his work in etched crystal glass, as well as those of Gate, were displayed at the

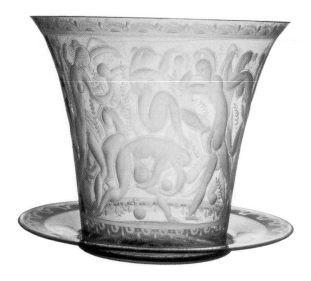

9.59 Edward Hald, "Girls Playing Ball" vase, blown glass, engraved with underplate, 9 ¼ x 11 ⅝ in (23.5 x 29.5 cm), Orrefors Glassworks, 1920. Orrefors Museum, Sweden.

1925 Paris Exposition Internationale des Arts Décoratifs et Industriels Modernes. Hald's designs resemble contemporary work being produced by Lalique in Paris and later by Steuben in the United States (see pages 167 and 224) and are seen in a 1920s blown glass vase depicting "Girls Playing Ball" (fig. 9.59).

At the same time, the Swedish organization known as the Svenska Slöjdföreningen, under the direction of art historian and critic Gregor Paulsson, advocated the adoption of standards based upon practicality, strongly influenced by the views of Hermann Muthesius at the German Werkbund (see pages 148–150). By the mid-1930s, an effective compromise between individuality and the perpetuation of craft traditions on the one hand and standardization and mechanized industrial manufacturing methods and materials on the other was already becoming identified as a specifically "Scandinavian" modernism, primarily through Swedish and Finnish participation in international exhibitions. Aspects of this approach can be seen in the work of a number of architects whose oeuvre included the design of furniture.

This Scandinavian synthesis of Modernism found expression in furniture designed by Swedish architect Gunnar Asplund (1885–1940), but is perhaps better associated with the molded plywood and laminated birch chair designs of the Finnish architect Alvar Aalto (1898–1976). Aalto's furniture was featured in an international exhibition in Paris in 1937, at a solo exhibition at the Museum of Modern Art in 1938, and at the 1939 New York World's Fair, for which he designed the Finnish pavilion. His armchairs (fig. 9.60), still manufactured by Artek, the company he established in Helsinki in 1935, were inspired

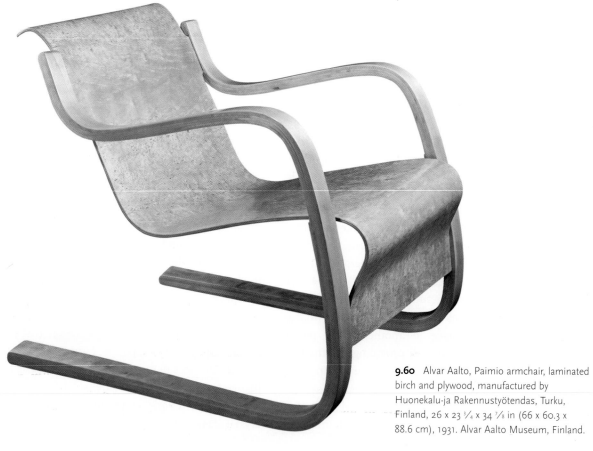

9.60 Alvar Aalto, Paimio armchair, laminated birch and plywood, manufactured by Huonekalu-ja Rakennustyötendas, Turku, Finland, 26 x 23 ¼ x 34 ⅞ in (66 x 60.3 x 88.6 cm), 1931. Alvar Aalto Museum, Finland.

by the light tubular metal furniture designed by Marcel Breuer at the Bauhaus (see fig. 9.28). While committed to the use of modern industrial processes of manufacture, Aalto preferred wood to tubular metal, and experimented with laminated birch (although bentwood chairs made of beech were also manufactured in Germany by Thonet). Aalto favored the use of native birch, an abundant natural resource in Finland, and adapted the technology of lightweight laminated wooden skis to the structural requirements of a variety of chair designs (including those based upon the cantilever principle). The armchair was first designed for use throughout the Paimio Tuberculosis Sanitarium in Finland, built between 1929 and 1932. Aalto minimized and even eliminated upholstery as well as carved or inlay decoration. Moreover, the quantity of furnishings needed for the commission allowed Aalto to give serious consideration to requirements for efficient serial production; in particular, the use of laminated rather than carved woods permitted uniformity and ease of assembly. Thus while making use of industrial materials and committed to their advantages in terms of serial production, Aalto's molded designs incorporated organic forms and the natural grain and finish of wood surfaces. As a result his experimentation in molded industrial furniture appears softer than the more geometric and often austere contemporary furniture in metal or wood constructed from standardized components (see, for instance, figs. 9.4 and 9.28). Aalto's furniture combines industrial materials and processes, as well as a consideration of factors such as comfort, psychology, and art that extend beyond utility and economy in the definition of modern living. Whether for individual residences or public buildings and institutions, Aalto's furniture reduces mass and is designed to maximize open space and flexible, informal arrangements. In place of geometric purity and to a certain extent the cool formality of contemporary European Modernist designers of the 1920s, his designs maintain a connection to nature, and his furnishings offer a closer analogy with the freer and more irregular abstract forms of Automatic Surrealism.

Aalto was able to explore such connections further in the design of glassware that also suggests analogies to the suggestive forms of Automatic Surrealism, particularly the sculptures of Belgian-born sculptor Jean Arp or the shapes in the paintings of Catalan artist Joan Miró. This can be seen in Aalto's so-called Savoy vase of 1936 (fig. 9.61), with its amoebalike forms and attempt to incorporate and activate negative space. Such considerations were also adapted to furniture by other Scandinavian designers, whose works are examined in the context of postwar design in Part IV. Aalto's approach emerges in the following excerpt from a speech he delivered to the Swedish Arts and

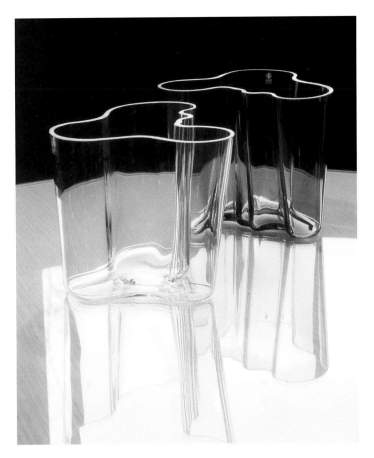

9.61 Alvar Aalto, Savoy vase, mold-blown glass, 5 ½ in (14 cm) high, manufactured by Karhula-Ittala, Finland, 1936. Alvar Aalto Museum, Finland.

Crafts Society in 1935. The expansion of the rational basis for design to include psychological and aesthetic considerations further distinguishes Aalto's understanding of modern design from earlier and other contemporary approaches to prefabrication and standardization in which industrial design was often viewed as a vehicle for solving social problems on a mass scale, tied to an ideology of collective need rather than individual expression:

we can say that one of the ways to arrive at a more and more humanely built environment is to expand the concept rational. We should rationally analyze more of the requirements connected with the object than we have to date ... A series of requirements that can be made of almost every object and that up to now has been given scant consideration surely belongs in the sphere of another science-psychology. As soon as we include psychological requirements, or, let us say, when we can do so, then we will have already expanded the rational method to an extent that, to a greater degree than previously, has the potential of excluding inhuman results.

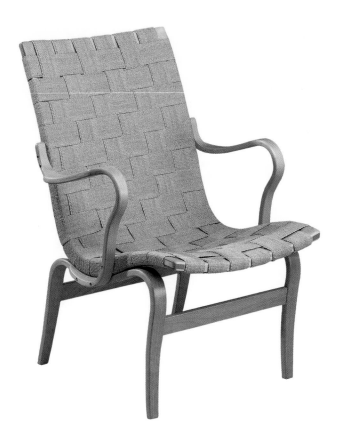

9.62 Bruno Mathsson, armchair, beech and birch plywood, hemp upholstery, 32 ¼ x 19 ¼ x 29 ⅛ in (83 x 49 x 74 cm), manufactured by Karl Mathsson, Vämamo, Sweden, 1934.

In Sweden, the use of laminated woods and organic forms was pioneered in the 1930s by Bruno Mathsson (1907–1988), who throughout his career manufactured original furniture designs in a family workshop. His 1934 armchair (fig. 9.62) consists of a broad curving seat with webbing rather than upholstery, the sculptural contour of which conforms to Mathsson's studies and measurements for ideal sitting positions for the human body for a variety of tasks, including simply "lounging." The legs of the chair repeat and balance the gently curving shape of the combined seat and back, while the arms provide additional structural support for the back.

Danish designers also contributed to the development of Scandinavian modern design both before and after World War II. Silversmith Georg Jensen (1866–1935) established an international reputation for original high-quality handcrafted designs for cutlery and tableware, and was represented at the Paris International Exhibition of 1925. At the same time, however, the interests of some artists in more rational and

permanent standards for design is found in the work of Kaare Klint (1888–1954). In addition to reducing or even eliminating carved ornament while retaining the beauty of natural wood surfaces, Klint based his furniture designs upon studies undertaken in the Furniture Department of the Royal Danish Academy of Arts, which he helped to found and where he served as an instructor. The sliding doors and dimensions of Klint's sideboard (fig. 9.63) were based upon the efficient storage of standard sizes of dishes, cups, saucers, and other dining-room utensils. Klint's furniture was handcrafted and employed a variety of woods selected for the appeal of grain and color. The simple geometric forms and absence of decoration in Klint's furniture bear some similarity to the elemental geometry of European Modernist designers, though a resemblance to examples of Chinese wooden cabinets has also been noted by historians. But Klint's motivation for a new and modern design was not primarily social or even industrial: his furniture was time-consuming to produce and expensive to buy. He believed that through the study of everyday household tasks like sitting or preparing a table for dining, designers could determine lasting solutions for the concerns of modern living. In turn, solid construction and attention to details of fittings and finish meant that Klint's furniture would not need to be replaced. Klint's modern designs were neither luxurious, abstract, nor purely functional; they offered a response to modern living that combined a variety of perspectives at the time – a problem-solving activity that involved intuition as well as logic; poetry as well as science.

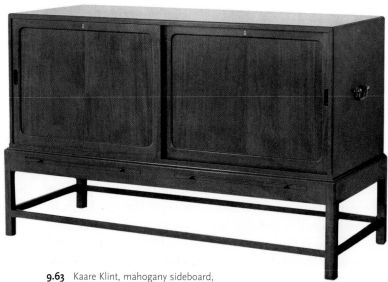

9.63 Kaare Klint, mahogany sideboard, 37 ⁹⁄₁₆ x 59 ¹³⁄₁₆ x 24 ½ in (95.4 x 152 x 62 cm), manufactured by Rudolf Rasmussens Snedkerier, Denmark, 1930. Danske Kunstindustrimuseu, Copenhagen.

Chapter 10

Design, Industry, and Advertising in the United States

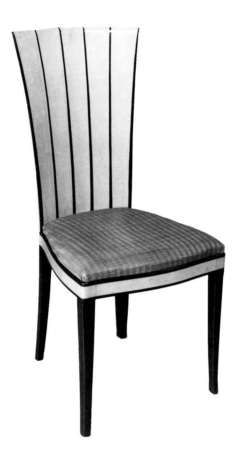

10.1 Eliel Saarinen, side chair, fir with black and ocher paint, red horse-hair upholstery, 37 ⅝ x 17 x 19 in (95.6 x 43.2 x 48.5 cm), upholstery fabric by Loja Saarinen, 1929–1930. Collection of Cranbrook Academy of Art Museum.

In the United States, craft-based industries tended to remain conservative in terms of design until the mid-1920s, unaffected by the self-consciously aesthetic approaches of Art Deco designers in France and elsewhere in Europe. On the recommendation of then Secretary of Commerce, Herbert Hoover, the United States declined to participate in the 1925 Exposition Internationale des Arts Décoratifs et Industriels Modernes in Paris because, in his opinion, designers were unable to comply with the criteria of submitting products that were modern and original. The United States did, however, dispatch a large

delegation to the exhibition, headed by the President of the American Association of Museums, Charles Richards, whose charge included organizing a traveling exhibition of works selected in Paris. This traveling exhibition, and others sponsored by institutions such as the Metropolitan Museum of Art in New York, stimulated public and commercial interest in newer designs, aimed mostly at a sophisticated audience. By the later 1920s, ensembles of interior furnishings by Jean Dunand and other French designers of modern luxury goods could be seen in the windows of New York department stores such as Lord and

Taylor and Macy's. Moreover, American retailers began to recognize the commercial benefit of supporting contemporary designs in a wide range of consumer goods. Museums promoted modern styles along broadly educational lines, emphasizing the integration of art into the lives of the middle class and the ability of the decorative arts to raise the level of public taste and contribute to cultural progress. In addition, magazines such as *Vogue* and *Vanity Fair* used photography and illustration to cultivate an idealized image of modern life associated with fashion, sport, travel, and other active leisure pursuits.

The Metropolitan Museum of Art was one of eight venues for the traveling exhibition from the 1925 Paris exhibition, and the museum continued to sponsor a series of annual exhibitions devoted to modern decorative and industrial arts throughout the 1920s. In such exhibitions a variety of new forms and new materials emerge. These include the wooden (fir) chairs with flared backs accentuated by black-painted vertical strips designed by Finnish architect Eliel Saarinen (1873–1950; fig. 10.1), as well as the etched crystal glass bowls designed by Massachusetts-born sculptor Sidney Waugh (1904–1963) for the Steuben Glass company (fig. 10.2). Steuben Glass was the "art-glass" branch of the Corning Glass Company in Corning, New York, and had changed from designs for colored glass to crystal beginning with a change of management in 1933.

Saarinen was named director of an artists' community founded in 1923 by newspaper publisher George Booth in Bloomfield Hills, Michigan, which later became the Cranbrook Academy of Art and focused upon both graduate-level fine and applied arts education. Saarinen's wife, Loja (1879–1968), was also trained as an artist in Finland and initiated the handweaving workshop at Cranbrook. Other American companies produced artists' designs for rugs and embroideries. California-born Marguerite Zorach (1887–1968) studied painting in Paris but returned to the United States with her husband, sculptor William Zorach, where they were part of an artist community in Massachusetts. Marguerite produced handhooked rugs featuring Fauve-inspired imagery and patterns. She also experimented with the Indonesian technique of fabric dyeing known as batik. Figure 10.3 is a Marguerite Zorach rug woven from wool and jute for the Crawford Shops in New York, dating to 1936. Entitled *Jungle*, the rug makes use of muted red-orange, gray, and brown hues arranged in a densely packed composition that achieves remarkable unity through consistent tone and abstract organic shapes based upon animal and landscape forms.

Following the 1925 Paris exhibition, several American manufacturers hired native as well as European-trained artists to design furniture and a variety of home furnishings in a contemporary style. Such work often involved a new new angular vocabulary of expressive decoration that echoed the great set-back profiles and sculpted decorative motifs of skyscrapers built between 1925 and 1930 in the United States. Indeed, the term Skyscraper Style is sometimes used to refer to the expressive decoration and furnishings of the era, whether William van Alen's Chrysler Building of 1927 or German-born Paul Frankl's

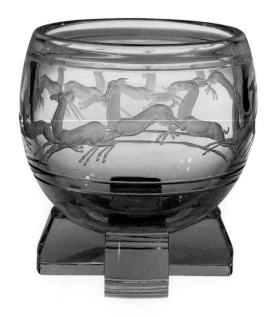

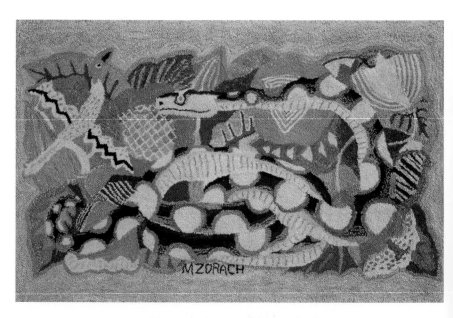

10.2 Sidney Waugh, Gazelle bowl, cut glass with engraving, 7 ¼ x 6 ½ in (18.4 x 16.5 cm), manufactured by Steuben Glass, New York, 1935. Toledo Museum of Art.

10.3 Marguerite Zorach, *Jungle*, handhooked rug, wool, jute, 42 x 60 in (106.7 x 152 cm), 1936. Museum of Modern Art, New York.

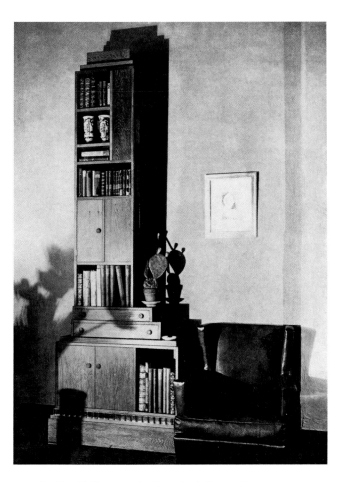

10.4 Paul Frankl, Skyscraper bookcase, birch, lacquer, 84 x 39 x 14 in (213 x 99 x 37 cm), 1926. Private collection.

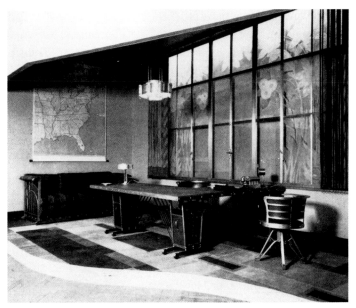

10.5 Raymond Hood, in collaboration with Henry V. K. Henderson, Business Executive's Office room setting designed for The Architect and the Industrial Arts: An Exhibition of Contemporary American Design, 1929. Metropolitan Museum of Art, New York.

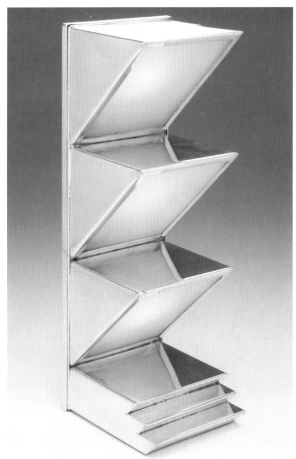

10.6 Donald Deskey, table lamp, chrome-plated metal and glass, 12 ⅛ x 4 ⁵⁄₁₆ x 5 ⁷⁄₁₆ in (31.1 x 11.1 x 14.3 cm), manufactured by Deskey-Vollmer, New York, 1927. Museum of Fine Arts, Boston.

series of Skyscraper bookcases (fig. 10.4) from 1926. Architects such as Raymond Hood (1881–1934), who designed the McGraw-Hill Building in Manhattan, and Ely-Jacques Kahn (1884–1972) played a leading role in creating furniture and interiors celebrating industrial materials such as aluminum and angular geometric decoration. Hood's approach to design is seen, for instance, in his Business Executive's Office for The Architect and the Industrial Arts exhibition at the Metropolitan Museum early in 1929 (fig. 10.5). The office features furniture whose aluminum structural elements relate to the aluminum mullions in the large glass picture window to the rear. Carpet and sofa use rectangular patterns, while the desk, curtains, and sofa frame display angular and tapered forms. Despite the smooth, industrial aluminum surfaces, some of the elements in Hood's model office have similarities to French Art Deco, as in the sunrays of Edgar Brandt's 1923 *Cigognes d'Alsace* panel (see fig. 8.17); while at times restrained, original and expressive decoration play a part in the American Skyscraper Style of the later 1920s, as in Donald Deskey's chrome-plated metal and glass table lamp of 1927 (fig. 10.6).

American artist Ruth Reeves (1892–1966), who had studied painting with Fernand Léger in Paris, designed textiles that featured the new vocabulary of Cubist-inspired forms. Her *Electric* design (fig. 10.7), manufactured by the Sloane Carpet Company from 1928 to 1930, uses zig-zag overlapping shapes to convey the speed and man-made power of electric energy, while Kneeland Green (1892–1956) used stenciled letterforms to create dense abstract patterns such as *Cheerio* in 1927 for printed fabrics and wall-coverings (fig. 10.8). Such admiration for the excitement and beauty of the present and an accelerated pace of life generated by technology and the metropolis are seen as well in the paintings of American artists such as Joseph Stella (1877–1946) and John Marin (1870–1953). Stella's series of works devoted to the Brooklyn Bridge, or Marin's watercolor interpretations of tall buildings in downtown Manhattan from the 1920s, are examples of the fascination with man-made rather than natural beauty. The works of these artists demonstrate a reverence for the exhilarating and heroic character of the modern metropolis. The aural equivalent of this sensibility is found in the jazz music that emerged in urban centers along the Mississippi River such as Kansas City, in Chicago, and also in the Harlem section of New York City. Textile designers also explored new processes and materials. British-born Henriette Reiss (1889–1992) produced textiles using the technique of screenprinting, as seen in her abstract *Rhythm Series* pattern of 1928 (fig. 10.9). Reiss's designs were applied directly or transferred

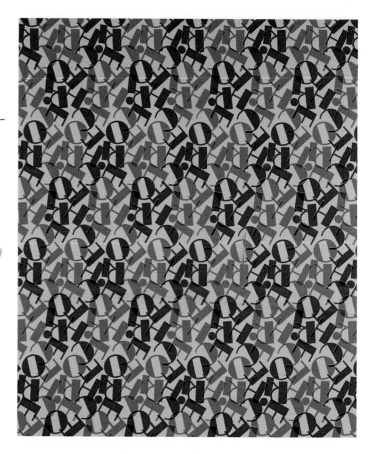

10.8 Kneeland Green, *Cheerio* textile, printed silk, 24 ³/₈ x 38 ¹/₂ in (62 x 98 cm), manufactured by Stehli Silks Corporation, New York. Metropolitan Museum of Art, New York, 1927.

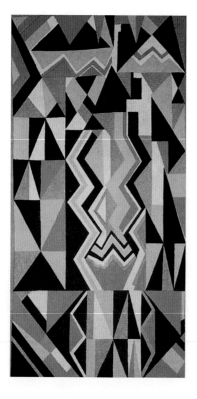

10.7 Ruth Reeves, *Electric*, hand-printed cotton, 74 ¹/₈ x 42 ¹/₈ in (188 x 107 cm), 1930. Sloane Carpet Company, New York. Collection of the estate of Ruth Reeves.

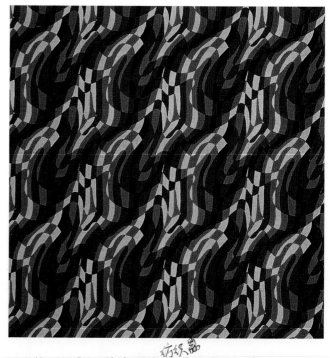

10.9 Henriette Reiss, *Rhythm Series*, textile, screenprinted on cotton, 51 ⁵/₈ x 50 ⁵/₈ in (131 x 128.6 cm), 1928. Goldstein Gallery, University of Minnesota.

to thin, porous screens of tightly woven silk. After the non-image areas of the design were blocked out, fabric was placed beneath the screens, through which ink was pressed using a squeegee. The ink only passes through the design and is resisted elsewhere, and the screen may be reused for printing in more than one color.

Modern design in the United States during the later 1920s was strongly promoted by museum exhibitions, upscale department stores, and in architecture through the design and interiors of skyscrapers. For the most part, American modern design appealed to an exclusive market despite a supposed alliance between art and industry. Certainly modern design reached a broader and more diverse public through illustrations and advertisements in mass-circulation magazines and in public entertainment through the constructed interior sets of the popular cinema. In the later 1920s, modern decorative motifs, derived from Cubism and Futurism, began to appear in less expensive products as well. Until the stockmarket crash in late 1929, industrial production was fueling an economic boom and lower-income householders were able to emulate the lifestyle of their wealthier countrymen and women by buying inexpensively manufactured personal and domestic products. Examples include Pittsburgh-born Reuben Haley's (1872–1933) Ruba Rombic line of sculptural and faceted frosted glass vases, designed for the Consolidated Lamp and Glass Company in the Pennsylvania town of Coraopolis, near Pittsburgh (fig. 10.10) and manufactured from 1928 until 1930.

In ceramics, modern shapes and patterns are seen in the work of brothers Victor (1906–2008) and Donald (1911–2001) Schreckengost. Victor's activities were not limited to ceramics, but both brothers worked as designers for small and larger ceramic manufactories in Ohio

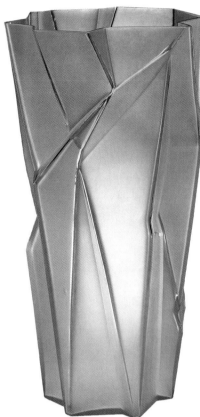

10.10 Reuben Haley, Ruba Rombic vase, glass, molded, blown, and acid-etched, 16 ½ x 8 ⅞ x 8 ⅞ in (42 x 22.5 x 22.5 cm), manufactured by Consolidated Lamp and Glass Company, Pittsburgh, 1928–1930. Toledo Museum of Art.

during the 1930s, producing a variety of original designs. An example is Donald Schreckengost's Tricorne tableware manufactured by the Salem China Company in Salem, Ohio, in 1933 (fig. 10.11). Large manufactories such as Salem supplied tableware to middle and working-class buyers through Woolworths and other low-end retail chain stores as well as grocery stores during the 1920s. While

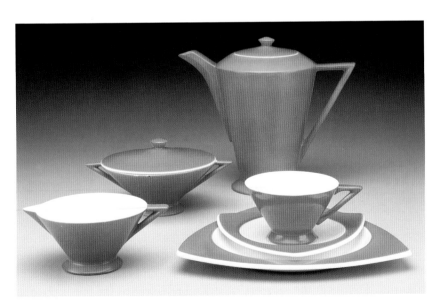

10.11 Donald Schreckengost, Tricorne tea and coffee service, earthenware, cup height: 2 ⅛ in (5.4 cm), diameter: 2 ⅝ in (6.67 cm), saucer diameter: 4 ½ in (11.43 cm), manufactured by Salem China Company, Ohio, 1933. Dallas Museum of Art.

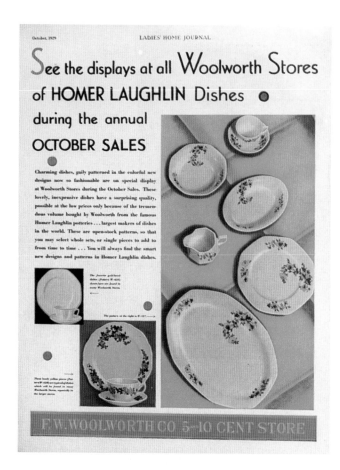

October, 1929   LADIES' HOME JOURNAL

See the displays at all Woolworth Stores of HOMER LAUGHLIN Dishes ●

during the annual

OCTOBER SALES

Charming dishes, gaily patterned in the colorful new designs now so fashionable are on special display at Woolworth Stores during the October Sales. These lovely, inexpensive dishes have a surprising quality, possible at the low prices only because of the tremendous volume bought by Woolworth from the famous Homer Laughlin potteries . . . largest makers of dishes in the world. These are open-stock patterns, so that you may select whole sets, or single pieces to add to from time to time . . . You will always find the smart new designs and patterns in Homer Laughlin dishes.

F.W. WOOLWORTH CO 5-10 CENT STORE

10.12 Yellowstone dinnerware, manufactured by Homer Laughlin China Company, Ohio and West Virginia, from *Ladies Home Journal*, October 1929.

large-production potteries introduced contemporary designs such as Tricorne with thin walls, smooth finishes, bright colors, and novel shapes with sharply angled handles, more traditional decorative patterns, often applied as printed decals rather than hand-painted, dominated the burgeoning, consumer-driven mass market. Even novelty tended to be less of a striking break with the past, as with the popular and widely imitated Yellowstone dinnerware introduced by the Homer Laughlin China Company of Ohio and West Virginia in the early 1920s (fig. 10.12). As noted by historian Regina Blaszczyk, department store and chain store buyers as well as store managers exercised an enormous influence upon design, observing shoppers' habits and selecting designs and shapes that appealed to the desire for attractive design that suited informal dining and a generally conservative taste.

Whether contemporary or traditional, consumers embraced design in the United States in the 1920s as proof of material and social progress, and the connection between design and modern life was strongly reinforced through advertising. In his 1922 novel of middle-class American life, *Babbitt*, Sinclair Lewis described the

"billboards with crimson goddesses nine feet tall advertising cinema films, pipe tobacco, and talcum powder." Chum Frink, one of George Babbitt's friends in the fictional city of Zenith, is a poet-turned-advertising copywriter. Just as the poetry of advertising slogans left an uplifting impression in the reader's mind, so design gave products like George's new electric alarm clock an aura that made him happy simply to own it. It is possible that our own innate desire to create categories and distinguish between "modern" and "traditional" are belied by the realities of the marketplace: Babbitt's alarm clock has a lighted phosphorescent dial but sounds like church bells, and Schreckengost's Tricorne design presents a novel shape for dinnerware yet is named for the eighteenth-century three-cornered hats associated in the United States with the American Revolution.

INDUSTRIAL DESIGN AND FORDISM

Design was slower to reach the mechanized industries that manufactured automobiles and electric or gas appliances for the home. Great advances in techniques of mass production, pioneered in the automobile industry by Henry Ford and concentrating upon the production of a single and virtually unchanging Model T, extended to the manufacture of household appliances in the 1920s, and were admired almost without reservation by capitalist as well as socialist governments in Europe. Standardized production vehicles such as the Model T Ford and electric appliances demonstrated the social benefits offered by the machine. They exemplified the democratization of culture and widespread improvement in the general standard of living. The Ford Company opened an automobile factory in Germany in 1924, and by 1929 the United States was responsible for more than 80 percent of automobile production worldwide. American industrialization was seen as the basis for prosperity and economic growth. Praise of business, the machine, and the assembly line had overtly religious overtones: skyscrapers were called "cathedrals of commerce," and Calvin Coolidge commented: "The factory is a temple – the worker worships there." In the Soviet Union, communist observers praised the assembly line but criticized private ownership of the means of production and the exploitation of workers and uneven distribution of wealth under capitalism.

The success of the Model T and other products of moving assembly line production stemmed from managing costs through more efficient machinery, standardized, interchangeable parts and the application of techniques of scientific management to labor. This represented a commitment to a combination of increasing both the speed of assembly as well as the precision and uniformity of manufactured parts. The revolutionary success of the Ford Motor Company took place within a decade, and until 1927, when its production halted, more than 15 million Model T Fords had rolled off the assembly line, virtually identical in their black lacquer finish and carriage-based body form. Sometimes dubbed "Fordism," this approach to industrial production was summarized by Henry Ford himself, with echoes of Adam Smith's encomium to the division of labor in a pin manufactory (see page 55): "the way to make automobiles is to make one automobile like another automobile, to make them all alike, to make them come from the factory all alike, just like one pin is like another when it comes from a pin factory."

The Model T suppressed elements of individual choice, artistic invention, and product differentiation associated with art and design – all effort concentrated upon the reduction of cost and the acceleration of routine and worker productivity in the plant. Capital investment in equipment and the rationalization of labor mitigated against variation in product; and, as pointed out by several observers, this combination of factors produced lower costs. In 1916 the Model T sold for $360 dollars, less than one-half its cost in 1910, and well below the cost of other domestic automobile manufacturers; in 1919 the cost for each model was $265! Without real competition in the marketplace, Fordism succeeded in delivering on the promise of producing standardized vehicles for personal transportation to an expanding middle and working-class market. To help offset the pressures of the assembly line and the unrest caused by accelerated production schedules and the repetitive routine of the assembly line, Ford introduced a profit-sharing plan labeled the "five-dollar day" for workers in 1914. In time, and through credit-purchase, factory workers were able to realize the dream of owning their own Model T, initiating turning workers into mass consumers.

As more Americans became owners of second cars and as the automobile became integrated into the leisure as well as work activities of the public, comfort, luxury, and styling became desirable to consumers and increasingly influenced the decision to purchase new vehicles. General Motors, formed in 1918 from the consolidation of a number of individual manufacturers under the leadership of its new president, Alfred P. Sloan (1875–1966), responded to these new consumer trends by establishing stronger ties to its retail dealers. In time their strategy was adopted by Ford, who could not fail to notice that market saturation had slowed new car purchases and that used car sales were

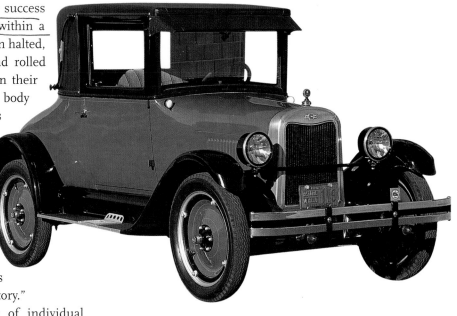

10.13 Chevrolet Superior, 1923. General Motors Corporation, Flint, Michigan.

beginning to outstrip demand for new cars (after all, older Fords were virtually identical with more recent models). General Motors began to distinguish their vehicles first through the introduction of variety in color, made possible by new enamel paints that dried almost as quickly as the traditional black lacquer. The company also introduced a series of minor styling changes and buyer options. These are first seen in the 1923 Chevrolet Superior (fig. 10.13), the contours of which appear more unified and compact than those of Ford's Model T. General Motors also invested more heavily in advertising as a means to stimulate sales, a strategy with important ramifications that are more thoroughly discussed below. In short, the production automobile became not simply a means of transportation but, like fashion and other goods for the home, a reflection of personal taste and a measure of self-improvement.

ADVERTISING, ART, AND THE SELLING OF MODERN DESIGN IN THE UNITED STATES

The history of modern design in the United States in the interwar period cannot be written without discussing the importance of advertising in the formation of a "culture of consumption." The overwhelming achievements of materials technology and mechanized mass production technologies could not be sustained without exciting desire and channeling it through the sale of products. Before the advent of television, the tools of advertising included illustration, photography, layout, and typography for effective, provocative visual communication.

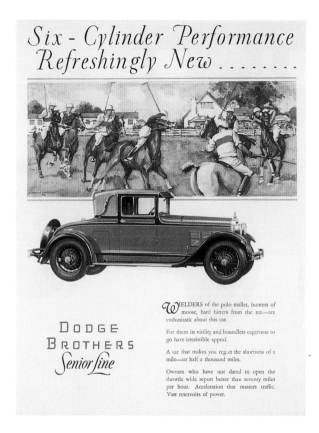

Six-Cylinder Performance Refreshingly New . . . .

DODGE
BROTHERS
Senior Line

WIELDERS of the polo mallet, hunters of moose, hard hitters from the tee—are enthusiastic about this car.

For them its virility and boundless eagerness to go have irresistible appeal.

A car that makes you regret the shortness of a mile—or half a thousand miles.

Owners who have not dared to open the throttle wide report better than seventy miles per hour. Acceleration that masters traffic. Vast reservoirs of power.

10.14 Advertisement for Dodge Brothers Senior Line, *Vogue*, 1923.

promote their products turned to artists and illustrators to provide suitable and often idealized images for products in magazines and even on large billboards that lined the boulevards and highways of a more mobile society. Fueled by the success of persuasive posters in public relations campaigns to enlist recruits and sell war bonds during World War I, advertising agencies saw illustration as a vehicle to shape the consumer values shared by an expanding and increasingly heterogeneous mass market.

Some companies promoted the use of art in advertising, part of an initiative to familiarize a broader audience with modern art and link companies with public improvement and education. These ads had little to do with products but rather established a paternalistic role for companies in support of values of quality, integrity, and culture. An example is an advertisement from 1927 by Philadelphia artist and illustrator Earl Horter (1881–1940), whose Futurist-inspired painting *Rhapsody in Blue* was reproduced in an advertisement for the renowned piano manufacturer Steinway (fig. 10.15). Advertising executive Elmo Calkins (1868–1968) supported such an approach to advertising, and employed artists such as Horter to demonstrate that an advertising "art" was in the public interest and enhanced the reputation of business.

Museum initiatives supporting modern decorative arts and a closer connection between fine and applied art dovetailed with the strategies of advertising agencies to build and strengthen the link between products and the hedonistic lifestyle of confident and energetic participants in the modern scene. In the 1920s, advertisements were decidedly upscale, promising charisma and success in exchange for the purchase of a wide variety of products ranging from toothpaste to toasters. An example is a 1923 advertisement from American *Vogue* for a Dodge Brothers automobile (fig. 10.14). The copy mentions the speed of the vehicle as well as the enthusiastic response of hunters, golfers, and polo players for the car: "Wielders of the polo mallet, hunters of the moose, hard hitters from the tee – are enthusiastic about this car. For them its virility and boundless eagerness to go have irresistible appeal."

Advertisers helped to define an emerging "good life," grounded in physical activity and experienced by an elite group of people engaged in an active and social life with whom an increasingly diverse audience could identify. The triumphs and conflicts of this group formed the subjects of popular fiction in mass-circulation magazines such as *True Story* and *Ladies' Home Journal*, and included color illustrations to augment the frequently serialized stories. Companies and the advertising agencies they hired to

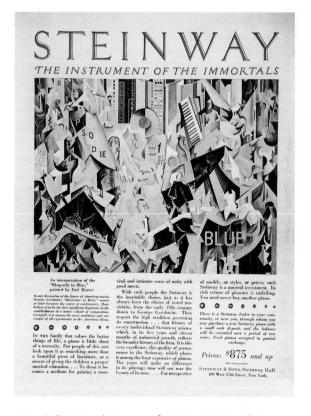

10.15 Earl Horter, advertisement for Steinway piano with reproduction of *Rhapsody in Blue*, watercolor and graphite on board, 21 7/16 x 27 in (54.5 x 68.6 cm), 1927. Private collection.

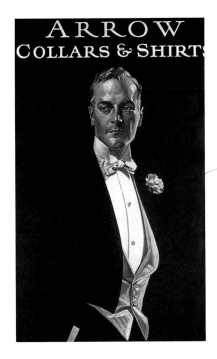

10.16 Joseph Leyendecker, poster advertisement for Arrow Shirt and Collar Company, 1920s.

Many advertising executives believed, however, that the purpose of advertisements was to sell products, and that references to individual artists or to works of art focused attention upon the ad as an "object," an end in itself, rather than as the vehicle for promoting a product. This had certainly been the case with the later nineteenth-century art poster, which functioned as public art as well as creating provocative associations with products and services. Art directors and consultants from the advertising industry recognized the importance of images in selling products, but also felt it was necessary, more often than not, to present familiar and recognizable images that could be easily grasped by a more heterogeneous public. Companies turned to illustrators to accomplish this task, creating the idealized types with whom buyers readily identified and connected with products. The blurring between illustration and advertising was felt as a constraint by some artists. On one hand it provided a steady and lucrative income for their work, while on the other it could lead to stale repetition of formulaic representations at the expense of the individual expression that often had formed the basis of their education and training at universities and academies. In general the advertising profession equated effective techniques of persuasion with naturalism rather than with more modern abstract styles. In the later 1920s and 1930s, art directors began to experiment with photography, typography, and layout in new ways that offered an alternative to illustration, particularly in fashion magazines, to excite viewer interest (see figs. 10.41 and 10.42).

In the early part of the century, Charles Dana Gibson's (1867–1954) "Gibson Girl" provided an ideal for the modern active woman on numerous magazine covers. As early as 1907, Joseph Leyendecker (1874–1951) created the "Arrow Collar Man" in a series of popular ads that drastically reduced the amount of text often used for magazine advertisements (fig. 10.16). Leyendecker's chiseled, confident ideal may have been removed from the lives of white-collar working men, but any threat to the reader's self-esteem created by the image offered at the same time its solution. Buying an Arrow shirt collar reduced the fear of not conforming to the modern urban culture of business. It is interesting to note that while tramps might not be tools for selling products, filmmaker and actor Charles Chaplin's (1889–1977) recognizable silent film anti-hero represents an alternative to popular advertisements of the period; often victim rather than hero, Chaplin, along with comic actor and film director Buster Keaton (1895–1966), revealed some of the challenges and uncertainties of modern working-class life. Another popular advertising image or ideal was McClelland Barclay's "Fisher Body Girl," appearing in advertisements for this manufacturer of automobile chassis to General Motors brands such as Cadillac, Buick, Oldsmobile, and Pontiac (fig. 10.17). This slender, well-dressed figure was usually found in the company of men in connection with cars, as well as on the covers of the *Saturday Evening Post* engaged in a variety of leisure pastimes.

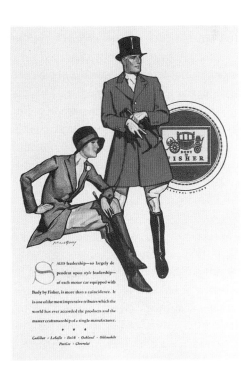

10.17 McClelland Barclay, Fisher Body advertisement, *American Magazine*, 1928.

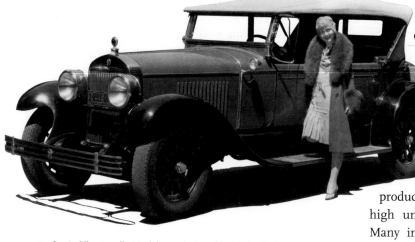

10.18 Cadillac Lasalle Model 303, designed by Harley Earl, 1927.

In 1927 General Motors hired Harley Earl (1893–1969) to head an Art and Color Section within the corporation, based upon Earl's success in redesigning the 1927 Cadillac Lasalle (fig. 10.18), a less expensive variation of the company's traditional luxury sedan. Earl came to GM as a designer of custom automobiles, in which lower profiles and a more unified approach to body design, found in expensive European automobiles such as the Hispano-Suiza, substituted for the traditional high chassis and collection of unrelated elements such as bumpers, wheel covers, and headlights of more standardized American cars. One of Earl's contributions as a designer for the automobile industry was to introduce new features that rarely required significant engineering changes or substantial capital investment in new machinery. Providing choice and variety in the automobile market without significantly raising production costs constituted an industrial design strategy that was in line with a consumer-oriented business and manufacturing practice. The competitive economic climate of the later 1920s made manufacturers recognize that Fordist uniformity and standardization in industrially manufactured goods were not sufficient to continue to guarantee profits, but rather that the need for change was a necessity for generating continued growth. Significantly, the Art and Color Section of General Motors was renamed the Styling Division in 1937: the new name appears to reflect the corporation's acknowledgment of its strategy for frequent model changes, as well as their understanding that this functioned to generate desire, and in effect was a branch of advertising. Later dubbed "planned obsolescence" (see page 307), the strategy encompassed the annual or seasonal introduction of new colors, patterns, or forms that made existing industrial products appear outmoded and encouraged consumers to purchase the latest, most "modern" item. It helped to reduce the risks of introducing substantively new products

and of keeping a graduated variety of products in continual production. Obsolescence was part of a new business model for manufacturers that used design as an investment to help stimulate consumer sales. Although some writers criticized this approach to design as a form of consumer manipulation, planned obsolescence operated on what Roland Marchand has called the new "consumer ethic," a recognition that consumption fueled production, putting people back to work in a period of high unemployment and restoring buyer confidence. Many industrial manufacturers began to think of this approach to design as an integral part of their business, and turned to advertisers, retailers, and designers to suggest new or modified products. Indeed, the incorporation of design into the business strategy sometimes spurred technical innovation: as explained by art historian Jeffrey Meikle, Earl's lower and more integrated, sculptural designs for automobile models of the later 1930s used newer and less time-intensive stamping processes that produced broader, curved, all-steel bodies, taking advantage of the availability of longer lengths of streel.

In 1927 Henry Ford succumbed to pressure to modify his stance on uniformity and standardization, introducing a new Model A together with a massive advertising campaign (virtually the first in the company's history) and the completion of a vast new production plant at the River Rouge near Dearborn, Michigan. The Ford Motor Corporation commissioned the painter and commercial photographer Charles Sheeler (1883–1965) to produce a series of photographs of the Ford Motors River Rouge facility that coincided with the introduction of the Model A, intended to communicate the inspiring grandeur and efficiency of the machine-dominated environment (fig. 10.19). Historians have noted that in these photographs, as well as in a series of paintings by Sheeler of the Rouge plant reproduced in the new business journal *Fortune* (first published in 1930), the human presence is often entirely absent or overwhelmed by the power of machinery. This in turn reflects the view that the progress guaranteed by mechanization, for better or worse, diminishes the agency of the individual worker, a telling indication of an inherent tension between man and machine as well as between labor and management in the factory system. Indeed, the success of Ford's moving assembly line was due to the replacement of skilled by unskilled labor, with increasing emphasis upon the performance of single tasks in required sequences measured against the clock and under the watchful eye of factory foremen. But while the focus of Sheeler's River Rouge photographs from the later 1920s was upon the power and productivity of machines, the

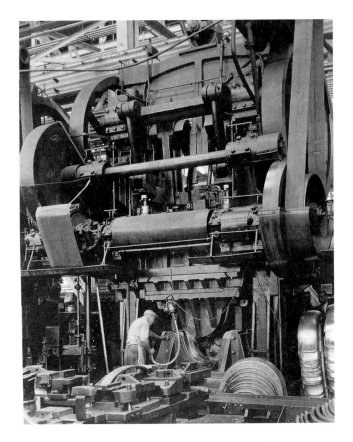

10.19 Charles Sheeler, *Stamping Press*, photograph of Ford Plant at River Rouge, Michigan, 1927. Library of Congress.

strategies of large manufacturing corporations, including Ford, were moving increasingly toward the consumer and the need to stimulate desire through promotion, advertising, and design. As noted above, the alienating effects of the assembly line and the general mechanization of the workplace were balanced by consumption in which workers now participated and the myths of personal and social progress that the purchase of commodities promised. The power of Sheeler's River Rouge photographs lies in the combination of documentary truth with the reinforcement of corporate authority.

While General Motors and Ford used in-house styling departments and advertising to create and promote design, some companies hired independent contract or consultant designers to modify and market their products. The phenomenon of the "consultant industrial designer" is significant in American manufacturing in the 1930s. It indicates that aside from the "styling" departments created by the automobile industry in the later 1920s, industrial manufacturing corporations were ill-equipped to introduce eye-catching design or respond creatively to surveys of consumer preference. Rather, they thought more in terms of product "engineering" than design, focusing upon what Jeffrey Meikle describes as the

"functional arrangement of a product's mechanical parts" instead of those features of a product that might generate consumer appeal. The stockmarket crash of October 1929 marked the beginning of an economic depression with high unemployment (reaching nearly 25 percent in 1933), falling domestic production, and an erosion of consumer confidence and spending. Within this context, more manufacturers turned to designers in an effort to bolster sales of their products. In the 1920s, advertising executive Elmo Calkins argued in business journals that design added appeal and value to products – during the 1930s this strategy was not only adopted but refined to produce a "consumer engineering" that sought to guarantee desire, and in which designers played a significant part. The emergence of a business model for stimulating consumption helped to define and promote industrial design during the 1930s in the United States.

Kem Weber (born Karl Emmanuel Martin; 1889–1963) opened an industrial design office in Los Angeles in the early 1930s. Weber was born in Germany and had studied in Berlin under designer Bruno Paul. He traveled to the United States in 1913 and remained there after the start of World War I. As a consultant for industry, Weber designed an electric clock with continuous numerical readout (rather than traditional dial) housed in a copper and aluminum case (fig. 10.20), manufactured by the Lawson Time Inc. of Alhambra, California in 1934. The rectangular form of the clock is swept back at the left edge in a curve rather than at a 90-degree angle to produce a smooth, streamlined look suggestive of flowing movement rather than the angles and abrupt staccato rhythms of Cubist or set-back Skyscraper-inspired forms of the 1920s. Historians have noted the use of such forms

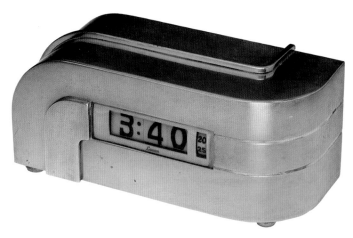

10.20 Kem Weber, Zephyr electric clock, brass, bakelite, 3 1/4 x 8 x 3 1/8 in (8.3 x 20.3 x 8 cm). Lawson Time Inc., Pasadena, California, 1934. Metropolitan Museum of Art, New York.

in the buildings and project designs of German architect Erich Mendelsohn (1887–1953), whose work was also admired by Frank Lloyd Wright. Such forms may also be seen in the lower stories of the 1932 Philadelphia Saving Fund Society Building designed by the firm of Howe and Lescaze. The electric numerical readout offered a sense of precision to the owner, and the flow of Weber's case suggested continuous uninterrupted movement.

A number of consultant industrial designers were artists who had worked directly in advertising or were successful in fields such as stage and set design for the theater. Often recommended to manufacturers by advertising agencies, industrial designers defined a middle ground between advertising's concerns for visual appeal and broadly humanistic concerns with progress through improved performance and the introduction of art into everyday life. Industrial design consultancies often employed large staffs, and in addition to redesigning products were responsible for package design, labels, advertising, and merchandising. Although the success of the profession in the 1930s was often based upon the value and marketability of individual names such as French-born Raymond Loewy (1893–1986), whose portrait appeared on the cover of a 1949 issue of *Time* magazine, industrial design office practice usually involved the contributions of many individuals working together as a team according to a division of labor and a dialogue between competing viewpoints and objectives. The team-based approach of industrial design offices approximated the existing conditions and complexities of the manufacturing industry more than the ambience of the artist's studio or the idealism of the academy, where isolation often produced compelling ideologies but few mass-produced goods. Designers such as Loewy and Geddes used their public image to promote the emerging profession and its value to consumers and manufacturers alike through books and magazine articles; articles and advertisements in journals such as *Fortune* mediated the advantages of design to the business community.

Studies of the projects of American industrial designers in the 1930s reveal the dynamic interrelationships between expressive, commercial, social, and manufacturing considerations. For example, Norman Bel Geddes (1893–1958) was hired by the Standard Gas Equipment Corporation in 1933 to redesign its kitchen ranges in the hope of stimulating consumer demand. Market research revealed that ease of cleaning was the primary consideration of housewives in their decision to purchase a new range. Geddes's response was to use large rectangular panels of enamel-coated sheet metal (including a panel to fit over the burners) rather than cast iron to create a more enclosed and unified, essentially

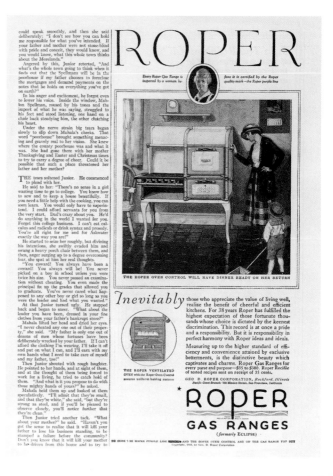

10.21 Advertisement for gas range, Geo. D. Roper Corporation, Rockford, Illinois, from *Good Housekeeping*, August 1923.

boxlike form, eliminating open areas that collected dust as well as the clutter of decorative handles and other hardware (fig. 10.21). Geddes hung the panels from a sturdy tubular metal frame. The new model presented a more integrated, unified housing or envelope, while advertising identified smooth surfaces and simple forms with improved hygiene as well as the promise of reduced housework. Many of these characteristics are also found in a 1933 stove manufactured under the brand name "Magic Chef" for the American Stove Company of St. Louis, Missouri, whose thin, tubular steel frame is left partially exposed (fig. 10.22). Bel Geddes' industrially redesigned stove demonstrated the commercial advantages of pressed metal production technology, with structural changes for strength, a smooth, unified, form, and a connection between modern design, efficiency, and the modern promise of reducing time spent cooking in the kitchen.

This approach, balancing new housing with mechanical or structural change for improved performance, appears to have been the ideal toward which many consultant industrial designers directed their efforts,

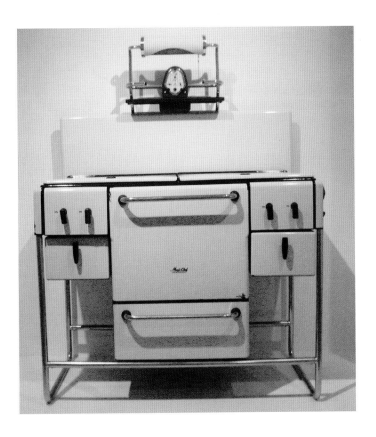

that is, to a point somewhere beyond mere "styling" or cosmetic change. It also helped to create some semblance of a partnership between designer and engineer, between art and the objectivity and problem-solving associations of an applied science. Another example is Raymond Loewy's design for British manufacturer Sigmund Gestetner's duplicating machine of 1929. Gestetner came to Loewy in New York for assistance in improving the appearance of his duplicating machine. Loewy's new design provided a unified housing that concealed many of the machine's working parts. Whether by intention or happy accident, the new shell reduced cost by making the nickel-plating of exposed mechanical parts unnecessary and improved performance by reducing the amount of space between parts where dust tended to accumulate and lead to malfunction.

Walter Dorwin Teague (1883–1960) worked as an artist for an advertising agency in New York before designing products for industrial production. Many of his designs were informed by a desire for simplicity and unity as well as a belief in the ability of design to improve the quality of life by promoting an awareness of taste and discrimination. He redesigned several cameras for the Kodak Company, including the entire line of Brownie models, introducing smooth plastic housing with vertical ribs to each model in the line, as well as the small 35-millimeter Bantam Special or "bullet" model of 1936 (fig.

10.23). Teague enclosed the lens in a unified shell with rounded sides and thin, horizontal metal ribs that covered the projecting lens. Teague explained that the ribs functioned to reduce the cracking of the black lacquer finish of the casing: thus ribbing was as much an element of design engineering as of modern styling, demonstrating Teague's desire for a balance between novelty and functional improvement.

In some designs, small improvements were made annually after a major innovation was introduced. For

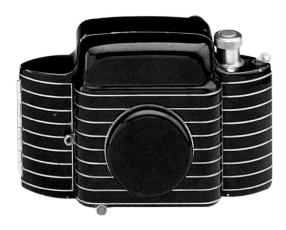

10.23 Walter Dorwin Teague, Bantam Special camera, painted brass, 3 ½ x 4 x 1 ¾ (9 x 10 x 4.4 cm), Eastman Kodak Company, Rochester, New York, 1936. Metropolitan Museum of Art, New York.

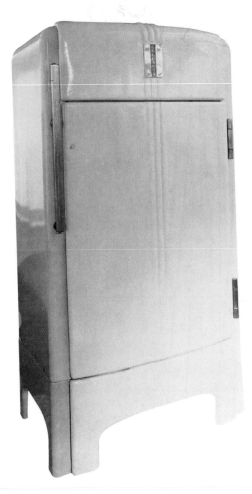

10.24 Raymond Loewy, Coldspot Super Six refrigerator, porcelain on steel and aluminum, 58 ³/₁₆ x 30 x 26 in (147.8 x 76 x 66 cm), Sears, Roebuck and Company, Chicago, 1935.

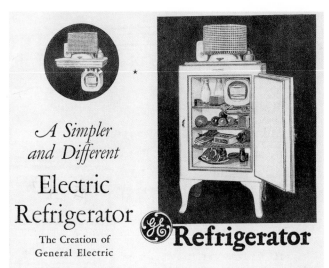

A Simpler and Different Electric Refrigerator

The Creation of General Electric

GE **Refrigerator**

HERE is a new development in electric refrigerators for the home that every person interested in a refrigerator will want to see —the creation of General Electric.

It marks an entirely new conception of electric refrigeration. It marks an entirely *new* type of icing unit—a type unlike any other you have ever seen.

The entire mechanism of the General Electric Icing Unit is housed on top of the cabinet in one hermetically sealed casing. (Note illustration.) That is *all* the mechanism—none below the box. None in the basement.' There are no pipes, no drains, no attachments.

All bulky machinery is eliminated

—virtually all servicing. Operating automatically, you need never touch it—never oil it. Current consumption is reduced to a minimum.

The result of fifteen years of intensive research

This new-day refrigerator embodies the best thought of the leading electrical research organization of the world.

It has reduced electric refrigeration to a point of *simplicity* which makes it almost as easy to operate as an electric fan—and almost as portable. You may place it anywhere—move it anywhere. Just plug it into any electric outlet and it starts.

The General Electric Refrigerator —designed to accommodate this revolutionary icing unit—has distinct advantages. It can be installed anywhere. It maintains a most uniform temperature. It needs no attention. It is unusually quiet. It is always clean because the circulation of air through the coils drives dust away—preventing it from settling.

You will want to see this refrigerator. But, meanwhile, send for booklet No. 7-G which tells all about it, including the various sizes which are available.

Electric Refrigeration Department
of General Electric Company
Hanna Building, Cleveland, Ohio

GENERAL ELECTRIC

In using advertisements see page 6   113

10.25 Advertisement for electric refrigerator, General Electric Company, Cleveland, Ohio, from *Good Housekeeping*, July 1927.

instance, Loewy's 1935 Coldspot refrigerator for Sears Corporation (fig. 10.24), as well as an earlier 1933 refrigerator designed for General Electric by Henry Dreyfuss, both integrated the condenser element into the body of the design. This created a unified shell or housing, unlike earlier models in which the unit appeared on top of the refrigerator (fig. 10.25). As Jeffrey Meikle has explained, Loewy added refinements each year to the Sears Coldspot, virtually eliminating protruding elements and accentuating vertical elements through the introduction of ribs both above and below the large refrigerator door. Such changes conformed to the strategy of obsolescence (see page 232) and made each year's model "new." The Coldspot broke records for sales, even though the economy was steadily approaching pre-Depression manufacturing levels in 1937. The title of Loewy's autobiography, *Never Leave Well Enough Alone*, characterizes his approach to design change and his acknowledgment of its relationship to marketing and advertising. The new sensitivity to consumer psychology is also found in the Loewy's acronym "MAYA," standing for "most advanced yet acceptable."

The combination of product improvement with commercial viability characterizes the design practice of Henry Dreyfuss (1904–1972). Dreyfuss shared with other industrial designers of the period a belief that successful and more or less "final" solutions to design problems for many products were possible. He defined a product's "survival" form as being simple and having a satisfying aesthetic that fulfilled its practical, production, and commercial requirements. This theory allowed for changes while retaining a memorable feature or form that created product identity. The Type 300 combined handset for the Bell Telephone Corporation, designed in 1937, is one of Dreyfuss's best-known pre-World War II projects (fig. 10.26). The combined handset had replaced earlier upright models with separate speakers and microphones in the later 1920s. Not subject to market pressures and competition, the design could be developed on the basis of ease of use, stability, cleaning, and durability. When Dreyfuss learned that he would be unable to consult with engineers when preparing a new telephone design for AT&T, he initially withdrew from the competition. After

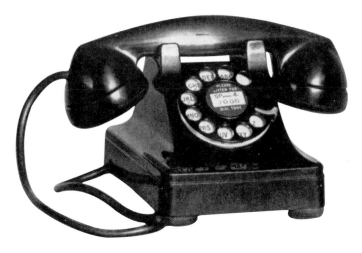

10.26 Henry Dreyfuss, Type 300, handset, black phenolic resin, Bell Telephone Corporation, 1937.

the company rejected proposals from other designers, Dreyfuss was given the commission for the new phone. The Type 300 was more cohesive than its predecessors, and indeed appears to adopt some of the basic ("survival") features from a combined handset phone designed by artist Jean Heiberg (1884–1976) for the L. M. Ericsson Company of Stockholm, Sweden, in 1930. After World War II, Dreyfuss made several small improvements to his design, switching from metal to lighter-weight plastic, and placing the numbers outside rather than inside the dialing mechanism for legibility. Perhaps the most important improvement to the postwar phone was its receiver, whose lightness and flattened form made it possible for the user to cradle it between ear and shoulder, freeing the hands to multi-task while talking on the phone.

THE UNITED STATES AND INTERNATIONAL MODERNISM

During the 1930s, the Museum of Modern Art in New York (founded in 1929) embraced and promoted a view of industrial design that incorporated elements of Constructivism, the Dessau Bauhaus, and the theories of Le Corbusier. The museum's approach to modern design derived from a preference for a more restrained functional architecture (referred to as the International Style and featured in a well-publicized exhibition in 1932), rejecting decoration and commercial styling. At the same time, MoMA was cognizant that a purely "scientific" or rational approach to modern living could appear cold and uninviting to consumers. In 1934, MoMA housed an exhibition entitled Machine Art, curated by architect Philip Johnson (fig. 10.27). This exhibition acknowledged the contributions of the Dessau Bauhaus and presented an anonymous approach to design for the modern world that

renounced handicraft in favor of machine production and elemental geometric form. The exhibition organizers argued for a universal machine aesthetic that promoted geometry, utility, new materials, and the rejection of ornament. In the museum's view, ornament was a vestige of craft and of privilege, unnecessary to the functional requirements of the new glass and steel architecture; not being necessary, decoration was therefore extravagant, even irresponsible in the context of widespread unemployment and hardship during the Depression.

Machine Art exhibited a variety of domestic, industrial, and even laboratory equipment to demonstrate, along Corbusian lines, the inevitability and underlying elemental and geometric beauty of particular objects, including machine parts like ball-bearings, tools and medical instruments, kitchen utensils, and tubular steel furniture. In promoting the relationship between geometric purity and the methods of industrial production, the Machine Art exhibition presented a reductive and somewhat limited interpretation of modern design and the role of the designer or "artist–engineer." Divorced from utility by being placed on pedestals and hung on walls with dramatic lighting, objects in the exhibition such as trays or pitchers were accompanied by price lists and could be appreciated for their abstract, geometric purity as machine age works of art for the home. Gradually an expanded International Style of modern industrial design, known generally as "good design," gained broader acceptance in the later 1930s and after the end of World War II, incorporating standards reminiscent of reform in their balance among individual expression, restraint, and practicality. The genesis of this approach to industrial design is a focus of Part IV.

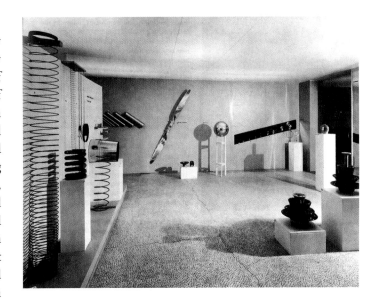

10.27 Machine Art exhibition at the Museum of Modern Art, New York, 1934.

More traditional craft-based industries, such as furniture and ceramics, hired contract or in-house designers to develop modern products for industrial manufacture during the 1930s based upon smooth forms, new materials, and restrained decoration. The career of Gilbert Rohde (1894–1944) offers an early example of industrial design in the American furniture industry. Rohde designed modern displays and furnished rooms for the 1933 World's Fair in Chicago, but is perhaps best known as the design consultant for the Herman Miller Furniture Company of Zeeland, Michigan, from 1932 until his death in 1944. Miller furniture was sold primarily through department stores such as Macy's in New York and John Wanamaker in Philadelphia, and on a contract basis to architects in the design of office and other public interior spaces. During the years he spent as consultant to Miller, Rohde developed a series of furniture designs based upon sectional or modular rectangular units for seating, storage, and shelving and a restrained use of decoration (fig. 10.28), broadly influenced by Constructivism and the

Dessau Bauhaus. D. J. DePree, the President of Herman Miller who hired Rohde, responded to the notion of a relationship between modern design and the promotion of ethical and egalitarian values of economy and efficiency, especially relevant as a response to the social unrest and the hardship of the Depression.

One popular domestic application for simple and practical modern design was in production ceramics, seen in the line of table service known as Fiestaware, designed in 1936 by British-born ceramicist Frederick Hurten Rhead (1880–1942) for the Homer Laughlin China Company in West Virginia, where he worked as artistic director during that time. Fiestaware (fig. 10.29) eschewed traditional connections with patterned decoration, sculptural contours, and relief decoration in favor of plain circular shapes with slightly raised concentric ribbing. Fiestaware's uniformity invoked the standardization of industrial manufacturing, but such anonymity was offset by a wide variety of brightly colored and highly durable glazes developed by Rhead. Fiestaware also retained some

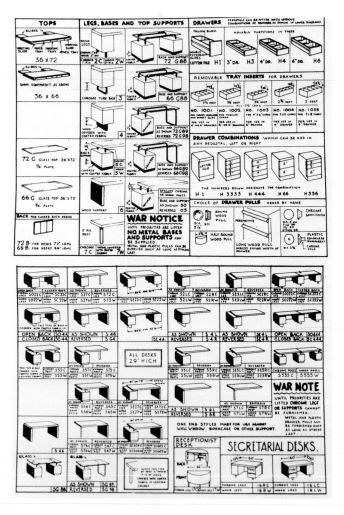

10.28 Diagram for modular desk units based upon designs of Gilbert Rohde, Herman Miller Company, Zeeland, Michigan, c. 1935.

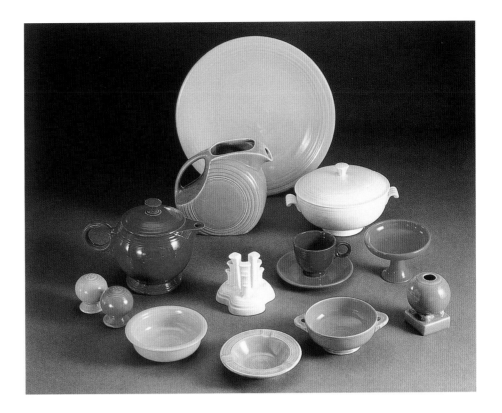

traditional elements such as the handles or feet for serving dishes and the concentric circles that suggest the technique of the potter's wheel. The service also introduced novel designs such as the "cutaway" pitcher, the handle of which is unified into its circular shape.

Modern approaches to ceramic design for utilitarian dinnerware also emerge in the work of American Russel Wright (1904–1976), whose career as an industrial designer included but was not limited to ceramics (D. J. DePree considered him as a designer for Herman Miller Furniture Company in 1944, following the death of Gilbert Rohde). Wright's American Modern dinnerware was designed in 1937 but not manufactured until 1939 by the Steubenville (Ohio) Pottery Company (fig. 10.30). It featured asymmetric, organic shapes for pitchers and dishes at a time when such ovoid forms were also being introduced for the manufacture of metals and plastics used in the production of automobiles and in appliance housings. The commercial success of American Modern came mostly after World War II, but Wright was active in the later 1930s promoting modern domestic products in connection with the idea of modest but comfortable, informal living. With his wife, Mary, Wright published a book entitled *Guide to Easier Living* (1950). Wright also

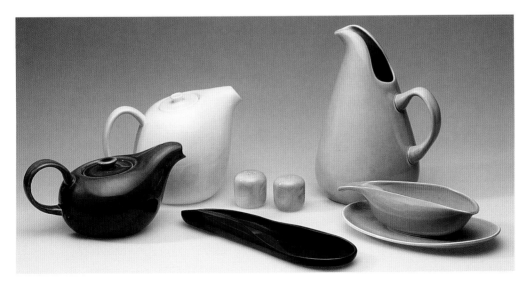

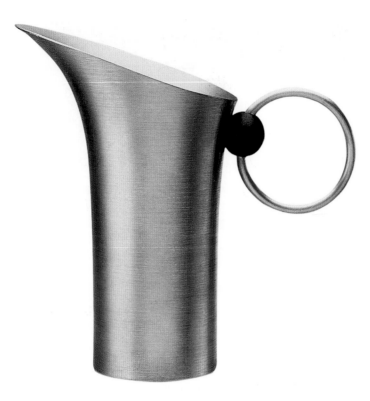

10.31 Russel Wright, spherical pitcher, spun aluminum, 5 x 6 ⅞ in (12.7 x 17.5 cm), 1932. Private collection.

was a pioneer in exploring new uses for aluminum, including modern designs for traditional household products. His pitcher of 1932 (fig. 10.31) uses the method of "spun" aluminum to create a smooth and swelling tubelike cylindrical form with no decoration. Wright's product line of spun aluminum servingware, however, included a concession to consumers' reticent attitudes toward modern design: the packages containing these wares contained a piece of emery cloth and instructions for housewives to rub the surface with the abrasive to produce the traditional look of handcrafted pewter.

STREAMLINING

Another area of American interwar industrial design covers the broad topic of Streamlining in the transportation industry. During the 1920s, wind-tunnel tests by engineers demonstrated that teardrop-shaped forms, rounded in front and tapering toward the rear, reduced wind resistance, enabling both faster speeds as well as improved fuel consumption for land-based as well as air travel. By 1930, these results were adopted in the aviation industry, where bullet-shaped noses, farings placed over landing gear, and wings molded to the body of aircraft appeared in airplanes such as the Douglas DC1 in 1933 or the earlier German Junkers F-13.

The American railroad industry also adopted Streamlining for locomotive design. Threatened with increasing competition from the automobile industry and commercial aviation, railway companies had seen a steady decline in passengers and profits since the 1920s. Early examples of Streamlined passenger trains were shown in the second year of the 1933 Century of Progress World's Fair in Chicago. They employed lighter construction materials such as corrugated steel (rather than heavier steel of a uniform thickness) combined with diesel engines to improve fuel efficiency. Broad curved front ends and reduced space between cars emphasized speed, and were features of the Budd Manufacturing Company's three-car commuter train for the Burlington Railway Company in 1934, appropriately named Zephyr. Bullet-shaped Streamlining also appears in the Union Pacific locomotive illustrated in figure 10.32 from 1934.

Applying the results of wind-tunnel research to the automobile industry proved elusive, but several prototypes and limited production vehicles emerged in Europe as well as in the United States. Hungarian designer Paul Jaray built a teardrop-shaped automobile as early as 1922, and in Britain A. E. Palmer designed a car in 1930 with a rear engine permitting lower ground clearance that also incorporated the new teardrop form. Inventor Richard Buckminster Fuller (1895–1983) designed a Streamlined three-wheel vehicle that achieved notoriety in the media and at the World's Fair in Chicago in 1933, but it was never put into production, while Streamlined prototypes for automobiles, boats, and aircraft were designed by Norman Bel Geddes and promoted in his journal *Horizons* beginning in 1932. While the teardrop may have promised efficiency for production automobiles on the basis of research and testing, the American automobile industry was hesitant to invest in such a radical retooling of its

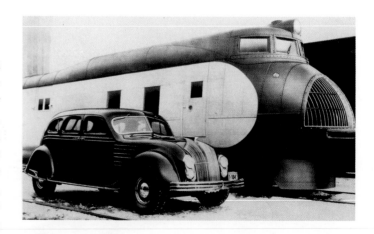

10.32 Airflow Imperial Coupe, manufactured by Chrysler Corporation, 1934, with Union Pacific Streamline Express, 1934.

factory equipment. Geddes did serve as a consultant to the Chrysler Corporation for the 1934 Airflow, which adapted a more unified approach to the construction of the grill, hood, and windshield to traditional front-engine production technology with flat sides. The advertising campaign for the Chrysler Airflow, featuring photographs of the auto alongside a Union Pacific locomotive (fig. 10.32) generated excitement and numerous orders, but negative publicity stemming from flaws in the first units to reach the market doomed the car, and manufacturing ceased in 1937.

In Germany, the "people's car," or Volkswagen, was designed by Ferdinand Porsche (1875–1951) and manufactured beginning in 1937 (fig. 10.33) with support from the Nazi government through a program called KdF (Strength through Joy). The Volkswagen also used an air-cooled rear engine found in earlier Streamlined prototypes and a simple, unified sloping body form. The design provided economical fuel consumption, adequate passenger and storage space, and incorporated the results of wind-tunnel testing. The Third Reich sponsored a program that encouraged workers to save five marks weekly toward the purchase of their own Volkswagen. Like the "People's Radio," the Volkswagen was a government-sponsored initiative aimed at providing the working class with, affordable, standardized manufactured goods that promoted modern forms of leisure activity and entertainment; at the same time, the Third Reich mobilized technology and forms of modern design, such as Streamlining, as part of a very public effort to unify its citizenry and promote loyalty toward its authority. The beginning of World War II halted production of the Volkswagen in 1939 as factories began producing military rather than domestic vehicles, and it was not mass-produced until after World War II. Nicknamed the "Beetle," the Volkswagen remained in production with few

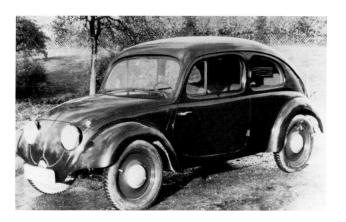

10.33 Ferdinand Porsche, Volkswagen, Wolfsburg, Germany, c. 1937.

changes well into the 1970s, and enjoyed renewed popularity in the United States during the 1960s in part as a reaction against the luxury styling and mass-marketing strategies of the large American automobile manufacturers General Motors, Ford, and Chrysler (see fig. 14.18).

While Streamlined automobiles in the United States remained experimental or limited to the custom market, the tapered forms and lightweight materials adopted in aircraft design during the 1930s found a popular expression in the Airstream trailer, first built in 1936 in Culver City, California, by Wally Byam (1896–1962). Intended for leisure travel, the Airstream Clipper featured a distinctive tapered bullet shape to lessen wind resistance and increase fuel efficiency, and lightweight aluminum construction with unified body and chassis (fig. 10.34). Production halted when the United States entered World War II in December 1941 and aluminum was needed for military production, but the success of the Airstream during the Depression in the later 1930s illustrates the popular commercial appeal of modern design.

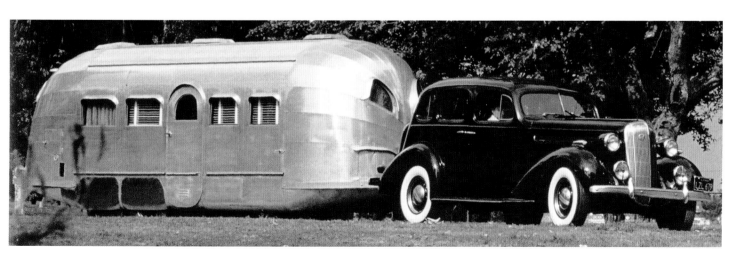

10.34 Airstream Clipper aluminum trailer, manufactured by Airstream Inc., California, 1936–1940.

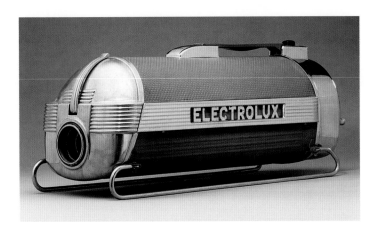

10.35 Lurelle Guild, Electrolux Model 30 vacuum cleaner, chrome-plated steel, aluminum, vinyl, rubber, 8 ½ x 23 x 7 ¼ in (21.6 x 58.4 x 19.7 cm), Electrolux Corporation, Dover, Delaware, 1937. Collection of John Waddell. Metropolitan Museum of Art, New York.

The appeal of Streamlining extended to a host of products unrelated to transportation. Kem Weber's electric table clock (see fig. 10.20) exhibits the smooth surfaces and swept-back contours of the style, while the Electrolux Model 30 vacuum cleaner designed by Lurelle Guild (1898–1985) beginning in 1937 (fig. 10.35) used lightweight aluminum for the body that rested on chrome-plated steel skids that slid along the carpet. Electrolux vacuum cleaners were manufactured in the United States in Dover, Delaware, though the company's origins were in Sweden before World War I. Whether a clock, vacuum cleaner, or pencil sharpener, Streamlined housings communicated an ideal of effortless movement, without tension or friction. In a complex world with mounting social tensions and economic challenges in the later 1930s, Streamlining provided manufacturers and consumers with a combination of hope and escape, fueled by imagination and the emerging awareness of consumer behavior.

THE 1939 NEW YORK WORLD'S FAIR

The 1939 New York World's Fair centered upon the theme of "Building the World of Tomorrow." Walter Dorwin Teague was on the planning board for the fair; Norman Bel Geddes designed the General Motors Corporation's popular Futurama exhibit and ride, where viewers on moving chairs experienced a vision for an American city in the year 1960, with suburbs connected to the city by networks of multi-lane highways, and automobiles defining the patterns of modern living. For both of these men, the World's Fair provided an opportunity to extend the range of their industrial design practice beyond products and appliances and to realize, if only ephemerally and in miniature, a unified conception for a future in which design transformed and improved upon the conditions of everyday life.

This vision was embodied in the centralized design of the fair, where several multi-colored avenues converged in a circular space that contained the fair's symbolic Trylon and Perisphere. Both the avenues to one side of the circle and the area to the other side were organized thematically for various activities such as transportation, international exhibits, and amusement and entertainment. Democracity, a miniature world of tomorrow, was contained within the large globe-shaped Perisphere, viewed from two rotating balconies and connected with the other symbol, the tall pyramidal Trylon by a walkway (fig. 10.36). Designed by Henry Dreyfuss, the buildings of Democracity were constructed in a single "Streamlined" style of architecture with smooth, concrete round-edged forms. Like the fairgrounds themselves, Democracity was separated into "zones" for business (in which tall towers dominated), for industry, and for living, where communities of houses permitted a closer relationship to the natural environment.

In Geddes's Futurama exhibit, traffic flow in the modern metropolis was managed by multi-lane highways and banked exit ramps, as well as by a radio-controlled system that monitored speed and distance between vehicles; the exhibit stressed the importance of highways, and paralleled the lobbying efforts of the automobile industry, tire manufacturers, and oil companies to expand government funding of the nation's road system and further stimulate the purchase of new cars. Conspicuously absent were mass-transit systems (other than buses), and pedestrian traffic in the city was kept separate from vehicular traffic by elevated platforms. Like the utopian vision of Le Corbusier's Voisin plan from the mid-1920s, a single style prevailed in Democracity and in the Futurama; it defined a controlled world that applied the efficiency and logic of large-scale modern technology and materials to erase differences, contradictions, conflicts, and irritants. Many contemporary historians have noted the contrast between this vision of tomorrow and the realities of unemployment and decay affecting the industrial cities in the United States, as well as noting the parallels to totalitarian regimes in Europe and in the Soviet Union that achieved political control and actively suppressed expressions of difference.

In addition to the utopian conceptions of the future in Democracity or Futurama, other manufacturers' displays commodified the vision of the planners through the display and demonstration of products and appliances, translating the clean, optimistic vision of Democracity and the Futurama into a present rather than distant reality, often with an emphasis upon the relationship of technology to leisure. Exhibits documented the steady and

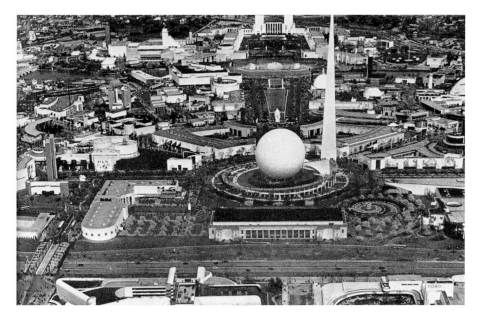

10.36 Aerial view of New York World's Fair, 1939–1940.

sure progress of "science," the attainment of frictionless speed in the transportation industry, for instance, and tested how machines reduced toil and increased comfort and the expansion of free time. In one exhibit for the Westinghouse Corporation, designed by Gilbert Rohde (see page 238), "Mrs Drudge" washed dishes by hand while her counterpart, "Mrs Modern," loaded an automatic dishwashing machine. Still in the wake of the Depression, aware of the hardship caused by high levels of unemployment, and fearful of mounting tension and conflict in Europe (already present in the exclusion of Nazi Germany from participation and the inability of a number of European nations to participate), the products and demonstrations of the fair exhibits provided some kind of tangible "proof" of improvement and sufficient hope for reduced toil through modern, efficient living.

Modern critics of the 1939 New York World's Fair have commented that its planners conditioned the experience of visitors, aiming through dramatic devices such as lighting and perspective to elicit a sequence of particular responses leading to a climax that gave substance to tomorrow's world today. Such devices were the stock in trade of architects and interior designers such as Morris Lapidus (1902–2001), who was a successful storefront designer during the interwar period. Lapidus employed techniques such as mirrors to create the effect of spaciousness and curving windows beckoning shoppers toward the entrance without sharp corners or barriers. He installed bright signs and lighting to create contrast or what he called a "moth" principle, intended to induce potential customers to enter a place of business. Such devices may be seen, for instance, in Lapidus's 1939 storefront for

Hoffritz for Cutlery in Manhattan (fig. 10.37). The mingling of utopian ideology and consumer engineering was characteristic of the 1939 World's Fair, representing the strategies of advertising agencies and the balancing of competing, even contradictory, priorities that characterized the profession of industrial design in American life as it emerged during the interwar period.

Planners and promoters expressed optimism that the provocative exhibits of the World of Tomorrow would last five years, but even with publicity in newsreels and other media, the exhibits closed before the end of 1940. Like

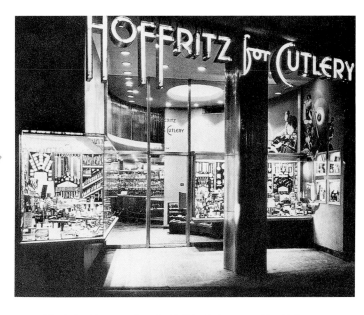

10.37 Morris Lapidus, storefront for Hoffritz Cutlery store, New York, 1939.

much popular entertainment, the 1939 World's Fair caused great excitement initially but failed to sustain interest beyond the fleeting impact of glitter and a sense of escape from harsher realities. While some of the organizers believed that the fair was educational in offering solutions and even proof of reduced hardship, alienation, and conflict, its longevity depended upon ticket sales from a public who appeared to see the fair as a short-lived collection of novelties with little meaning beyond the immediacy and excitement of their initial impact. As an experience based in part upon techniques derived from the advertising industry, it was, in a sense, a victim of the planned obsolescence that helped to shape it – without continued novelty and progressive change, the World of Tomorrow too quickly became yesterday's news. Interestingly, the idea of a more limited but nonetheless "progressive" fair resurfaced during the 1950s with the traveling Motorama showcases sponsored by General Motors (see pages 308–309). Nonetheless, the future as envisioned at the 1939 New York World's Fair by its many large corporate and government sponsors was indeed democratic, and focused upon the applications of modern technology to everyday living, promising ease of mobility through transportation, the elimination of drudgery by machines in the home, and new construction to replace deterioration and decay, rather than the luxurious displays of wealth and privilege that characterized the Paris Exposition in 1925.

PHOTOGRAPHY AND GRAPHIC DESIGN

In the mid-1930s, photography began to compete and gradually to eclipse illustration for advertising and for popular fiction. Illustration persisted, however, for magazine and book covers. Although advertisements formed part of his extensive oeuvre, Norman Rockwell (1894–1978) enjoyed a long relationship with the *Saturday Evening Post*. Rockwell's color illustrations for the *Post* lent themselves to narrative interpretation. They presented a variety of familiar themes drawn from common middle-class experience, frequently related to seasonal activities and holidays. Rockwell was familiar with the conventions of narrative art in the Western tradition, relying upon pyramidal composition to provide focus or climax as well as to guide the viewer. Frequently his covers and posters seem to suggest continuity with the sense of community and comfort provided by family and neighborhood, an antidote to the impersonal modernity of factory and city. The use of reassuring shared experiences and techniques of naturalistic illustration to communicate those values were the hallmarks of Rockwell's cover images. A *Post* cover from November, 1933 (fig. 10.38) illustrates a young mother spanking her child on a chair that is a simple design based

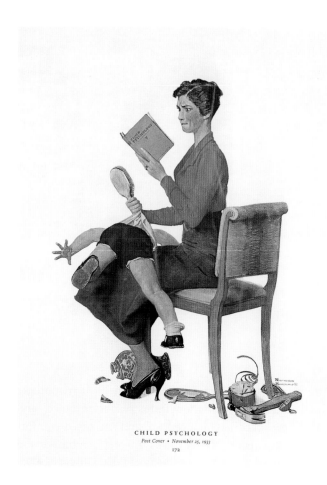

CHILD PSYCHOLOGY
Post Cover • November 25, 1933
172

10.38 Norman Rockwell, "Child Psychology" cover, *Saturday Evening Post*, November 25, 1933.

upon a Neoclassical model, and less frequent in Rockwell's illustrations than carved and more heavily upholstered furniture inspired by earlier eighteenth-century examples. Notwithstanding the political incorrectness of suggesting any form of physical abuse or threat in our own day, the story is clearly and simply told. The child has used a hammer to destroy a piece of fine decorative china, and the mother has responded with a traditional form of punishment. Her response, however, is not the result of an emotional outburst or of continuity with standard and inherited child-rearing practice. While the mother raises her hand, she holds a psychology book that has guided her actions. In fact, the "read" response is precisely the same as the inherited one, and modern psychology has recommended a solution with which we are already familiar. The illustration makes the reader feel more confident with some of the discomforting information that makes us feel insecure in dealing with everyday existence.

As Michele Bogart has suggested, Rockwell may have been ambivalent about his contributions, despite the success and celebrity he attained; his attempts to experiment with more expressionistic approaches to painting were rejected by his editors at the *Post*. It may also be helpful to view his illustrations in the context of mass images that seek at once to reflect as well as to shape common experience in periods of great social and political change. Rockwell's poster illustrating a festive family meal is one of four from a series entitled *The Four Freedoms*, in this case *Freedom from Want* (fig. 10.39). The composition suggests references to countless images of the Last Supper that lend formality, even solemnity, to the meal. Rockwell executed the series in 1942, in the midst of World War II, amid government-imposed rationing and shortages in support of the war effort. Like advertising illustrations connecting products with the good life, Rockwell's images steered away from troubling associations, and like advertising his illustrations indulge in escapism and fantasy as elements in the definition of mass culture. Minorities, for instance, find little place within Rockwell's oeuvre, and popular appeal seemed to preclude representing blacks or commenting on contemporary social problems.

Other examples of contemporary public art seemed to address more directly the hardship of many Americans during the Depression. The murals painted for the federally sponsored Work Progress Administration (WPA) presented artists with an opportunity both to work, and to work in a traditionally accessible naturalistic style. Thomas

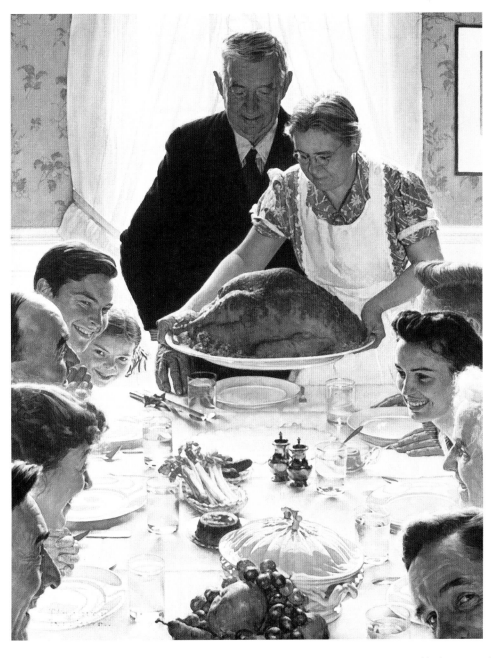

10.39 Norman Rockwell, *Freedom from Want*, oil painting, 1943. The Norman Rockwell Museum at Stockbridge, Massachusetts.

Hart Benton (1889–1975), for instance, was responsible for several murals in post offices and other public buildings during the 1930s. Benton used swelling shapes and sweeping curvilinear lines to invest his figures with energy and movement, often lending a heroic character to the depiction of ordinary everyday activities of traditional work and recreation during a time of high unemployment in the hope of building national unity and optimism (fig. 10.40).

Beyond Rockwell's appealing illustration and Benton's message of solidarity stood other artists whose realism moved in a wider variety of directions. The less narrative and more introspective realism of artists like Ben Shahn (1898–1969) and Edward Hopper (1882–1967) reveal an experience of alienation and loneliness in the modern world. Their work represents viewpoints on contemporary private life and is occasionally critical of both business and government. Only rarely, however, did their paintings reach the mass audience that read or subscribed to the *Saturday Evening Post* during the interwar period. After the war, progressive art editors such as William Golden and Cipe Pineles invited Shahn and other contemporary American artists to contribute illustrations for stories in journals such as *Seventeen* and in print advertisements for CBS radio and television.

While illustration continued to find a place on the covers of weeklies such as the *Saturday Evening Post*, the launching of *Life* magazine in 1936 and *Time* (first published in 1923) provides evidence of a gradual shift toward photography as the most compelling medium disseminating news, entertainment, and advertising. The term "photojournalism" refers to this shift in the print media. Even earlier in the 1930s, a number of art directors turned increasingly to photographic reproduction for its

sense of objective "truth," immediacy, and visual impact. Advertisers were attracted to the medium for the same reasons, as well as by the ability of commercial photographers to both simulate and manipulate narrative situations in order to make products irresistible. Instead of relying upon copy to sell products or report events, art directors and the advertising industry relied upon photographs to reach an expanding readership.

In addition to product advertisements (which often accounted for 50 percent of their content), mass-circulation magazines carried regular features on contemporary fashion, literature, travel, and entertainment. Photography played a key role in the presentation of such material, in particular the studio portraits by Edward Steichen, Charles Sheeler (see fig. 10.19), and other contemporary photographers. Through photography the pages of *Vogue*, *Vanity Fair*, *Fortune*, *Harper's Bazaar* and other monthly periodicals increasingly blurred the lines between advertising and art. With the hiring of European-trained artists to oversee art direction, monthly magazines began to acquire a more self-consciously modern, integrated presentation of photography, text, and titles in the later 1920s.

At *Vogue* and *Vanity Fair*, art director Dr Mehemed Fehmy Agha (1896–1978) adapted some of the distinctive asymmetrical experiments of the New Typography to cover design and page layout. Agha was born in the Ukraine of Turkish parents and was working as art director for German *Vogue* when he was asked by *Vogue*'s publisher, Condé Nast, to be the magazine's American art director in 1929. Nast hoped that Agha would bring a "new look" to American *Vogue*, a feeling for modernity seen at the 1925 Exposition des Arts Décoratifs et Industriels Modernes in Paris but generally absent in the pages of American mass-circulation magazines. Agha's art direction reveals a concern with the overall expressive arrangement of every element, often across a two-page spread, utilizing contrasts of shape and tone to create striking rhythms and vivid effects. The strong contrast and dramatic lighting employed by well-known photographers such as Edward Steichen were integral features of art direction in the pages of *Vogue* and *Vanity Fair*. The new look of such layouts can be seen in a two-page spread from a 1935 issue of *Vanity Fair*, featuring Steichen photographs of the fashions for that spring season (fig. 10.41). *Vogue*'s content throughout this period focused upon fashion and leisure activities of international celebrities including royalty, film stars, writers, musicians, and artists. Technically and creatively demanding as an art director, Agha brought to this lifestyle the sensation of change, excitement, and the drama of the unexpected in its visual presentation. Agha's association with Nast publications lasted until 1943. In his covers for *Vanity Fair*, Agha used simplified abstract forms together

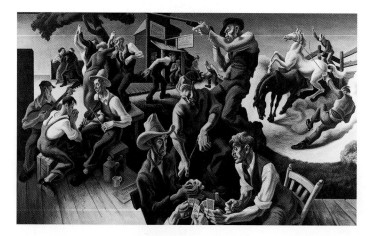

10.40 Thomas Hart Benton, *Arts of the West*, tempera, 7 ft 10 in x 13 ft 5 in (239 x 409 cm). The New Britain Museum of American Art, New Britain, Connecticut.

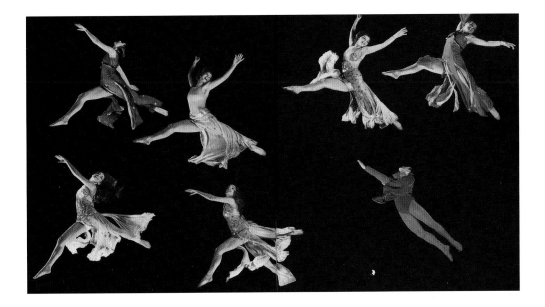

10.41 M. F. Agha (art director), Edward Steichen (photographer), two-page layout from *Vanity Fair*, 1935.

with text in subtle ways to convey meaning for content that included contemporary political and social issues. *Vanity Fair* introduced color photography and illustration in the early 1930s. An example is a 1933 cover designed by Cipe Pineles (fig. 10.42), using the technique of collage to portray two figures against a dark background that includes a mass of red ink. The figures, one bloated and smoking a cigar (1929), the other thin and rumpled (1933), are cut from newsprint from the stockmarket pages of the business section. The tall hat and goatee of the thin figure identifies the figure as Uncle Sam, whose profile appeared frequently on the covers of *Vanity Fair* throughout this period. Pineles's focus upon compositional unity among the elements of page design possessed both clarity and conciseness, and was initially compelling as well as sufficiently subtle to sustain visual and symbolic meaning.

In the 1930s, *Vogue* competitor *Harper's Bazaar* hired Alexey Brodovitch (1898–1971) as art director. Brodovitch had worked as a stage designer at the Ballets Russes in Paris prior to coming to the United States, and continued to oversee art direction at *Harper's Bazaar* well into the 1950s. The methods of expressively orchestrating text and image as abstract elements on a magazine page or cover describes the activity of graphic design as practiced by Agha and Brodovitch and that was increasingly acknowledged in the printing industry. Using photography and adapting the experimental strategies of the New Typography, interwar graphic designers set high technical and aesthetic standards for their publications. Characteristics such as the reinforcement of diagonal movement across the page, off-center layout, asymmetrical composition, unframed photographs that "bleed" to the edges of the page or blend completely with the white

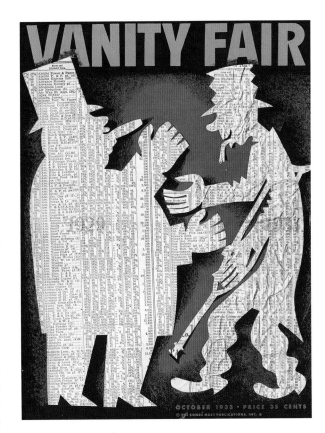

10.42 M. F. Agha (art director), Cipe Pineles (artist), cover for *Vanity Fair*, October 1933.

paper, and the juxtaposition of images helped to create visual interest in layouts and advertisements throughout the 1930s. Unlike Van Doesburg, art directors such as Agha and Brodovitch were neither publishers nor political activists. Their approach to visual communication was

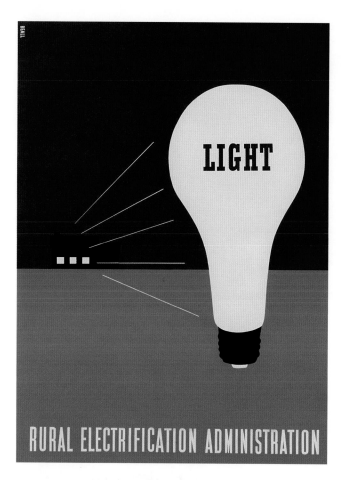

10.43 Lester Beall, *Light/Rural Electrification Administration*, poster, silkscreen, 40 x 30 in (101.6 x 76 cm), 1937. Metropolitan Museum of Art, New York.

information graphics and corporate identity that took shape during and after World War II.

Through illustration, photography, and graphic design, mass magazines and their advertising created a visual culture for the modern age in the United States. Advertising was a necessary corollary to sustaining the growth of an industrially based capitalist economy through focusing upon consumption. The advertising profession gained recognition and respectability through its connection with elevating public taste through art and reinforcing shared beliefs and values, and linking these public-minded interests to products. Sales, whether of magazine subscriptions or of the products advertised on their pages, came to depend upon seductive images and asymmetrical layouts to attract attention and create distinction. In this way, the New Typography found an outlet in the competitive commercial context of interwar America, in which the "new" and the "fashionable" were interchangeable, and where consumption was linked to status and self-improvement. Whether in illustrations or photographs, representations played a significant role in advertising and graphic design. As explained by Roland Marchand,

> Pictures surpassed copy not only in their ability to intensify emotion but also in their capacity to say several things at the same time. Visual imagery effectively reached the less literate portions of the population. It also conveyed dense messages. By setting up harmonics of atmosphere and imagery that resonated at a variety of levels, visual images also obscured problems of internal contradictions or irrational association. Such harmonics were exactly what gave style products their added value beyond pragmatic utility. Evocative pictures upped the consumption ante by inducing the customer to obtain the fullest satisfaction by "buying the ad" along with the product.

INDUSTRIAL DESIGN AND AUSTERITY

Alvar Aalto (see page 220) designed the Finnish Pavilion for the 1939 New York World's Fair, and in that same year the Museum of Modern Art sponsored an exhibition of Scandinavian design including a selection of Aalto's own furniture. MoMA reacted in the 1930s against the commercial motivations that influenced American industrial design, and advocated standards based upon "suitability to purpose, material, and process of manufacture." Such standards were implied in the 1934 Machine Art exhibition (see page 237) and were embodied in the household products chosen for a series of traveling exhibits entitled Useful Objects under Ten Dollars.

essentially aesthetic, and involved a recognition that attracting modern readers' attention demanded creative originality rather than cliché. They applied their awareness of modern art and the New Typography to serve the needs of the publishers who employed them, engaging the reader in a new awareness, appreciation, and identification with modern life that focused increasingly upon consumption as a vehicle for self-realization.

American artist Lester Beall (1903–1969) also employed characteristics of the New Typography and modern abstract art in a series of government-sponsored public-service posters promoting the use of electricity through the Rural Electrification Administration in the 1930s. Beall's approach is seen in a poster illustrating a lightbulb connected to a home by a series of white lines against a background divided into bands of highly saturated red and blue colors (fig. 10.43). The sense of contrast is strong and the imagery is striking for its simple, almost schematic and direct communication without need for text. Using flat shapes and schematic drawing to convey a message with minimal use of text, Beall's work anticipates the simplified elements of

In 1940, MoMA sponsored a competition entitled Organic Design in Home Furnishings. By "organic" the exhibition's curator, Eliot F. Noyes (1910–1977), an architect who later was responsible for formulating a unified design policy for the IBM corporation (see Part V), meant molded forms that were manufactured using industrial processes and materials such as laminated woods. Flexibility was also a consideration, and demanded "units" or "modules" for furniture and storage pieces that might be easily constructed, expanded, and configured in a variety of ways. Department stores agreed to display the winning designs and expressed a commitment to finding manufacturers to produce and market them.

One of the winning designs from the competition was a molded plywood chair upholstered in foam rubber covered with fabric, entered by Eero Saarinen (1910–1961) and Charles Eames (1907–1978), both of whom trained as architects (fig. 10.44). Saarinen was the son of the Finnish architect and president of the Cranbrook Academy of Art, Eliel Saarinen, and his wife, Loja (see page 224), and Eames had remained at Cranbrook following a fellowship there as instructor and head of a new department in industrial design. The originality of the Saarinen/Eames collaboration lay in the more contoured three-dimensional molding of the plywood, easily seen in comparison with the plywood seat and back of Aalto's armchair for the Paimio Tuberculosis Sanitarium from 1931 (see fig. 9.60). In other respects the industrial materials and processes as applied to furniture and an overall impression of lightness (the wooden legs were originally planned to be made from a thinner aluminum) recall basic aspects of Scandinavian modern design of the 1930s (see page 219 onward).

Organic Design in Home Furnishings hoped to demonstrate the ability of an industrially based design to meet the practical needs of modern living using technology and modern methods of manufacture and to replace the "weary" forms, materials, and methods of production in much traditional furniture. After the bombing of Pearl Harbor by the Japanese, and the United States's entry into World War II in December 1941, the emphasis upon usefulness was further seen as a proper and patriotic response to shortages, restrictions, and the retooling of industries to meet the demand for goods and materials to outfit and support the war effort. In this climate the German émigré Hans Knoll (1914–1955) manufactured and marketed the furniture of Danish-born and Scandinavian-trained designer Jens Risom (b. 1916) for the company Knoll had founded (Knoll Associates) in 1938. Risom's 1942 wood chair with cloth webbing (fig. 10.45) was originally manufactured using the synthetic material nylon purchased from US Army surplus and was constructed from a small number of standardized and undecorated parts.

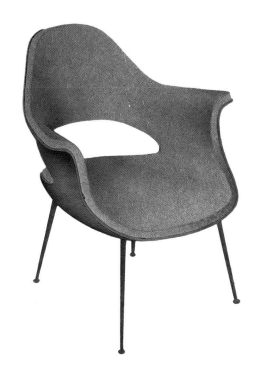

10.44 Eero Saarinen and Charles Eames, armchair, molded plywood and foam upholstery with fabric. Produced for MoMA's Organic Design in Home Furnishings exhibition, New York, 1940.

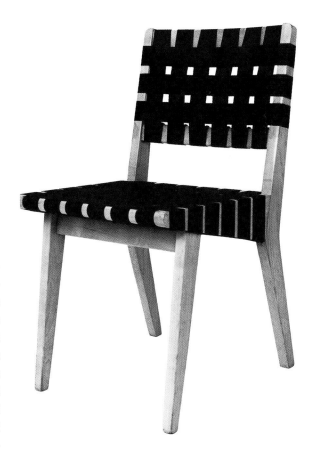

10.45 Jens Risom, chair, birch and cotton webbing, 30 ¹⁄₁₆ x 17 ½ x 20 ¼ in (77 x 44.5 x 51.4 cm), manufactured by Hans G. Knoll Furniture, 1942. Musée des Arts Décoratifs de Montreal.

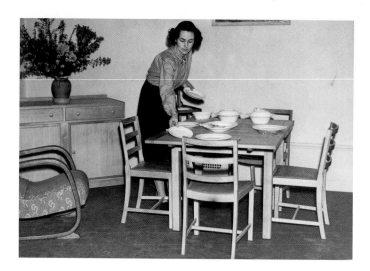

10.46 British utility dining room, 1945.

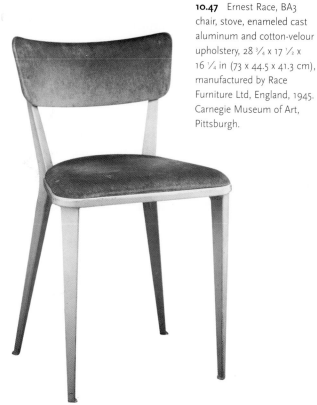

10.47 Ernest Race, BA3 chair, stove, enameled cast aluminum and cotton-velour upholstery, 28 ¾ x 17 ½ x 16 ¼ in (73 x 44.5 x 41.3 cm), manufactured by Race Furniture Ltd, England, 1945. Carnegie Museum of Art, Pittsburgh.

In Europe, particularly in Britain, civilian austerity within the context of patriotism in the war with Germany also provided conditions in which a utilitarian version of modern design found acceptance with the aid of government sponsorship. British designer Gordon Russell (1892–1980) was responsible for the design of "utility" furniture under the auspices of the British Board of Trade in the early 1940s. Designs embodied standards to ensure economy in the use of government-controlled raw materials such as timber as well as taking into account shortages in skilled labor. The utility dining room furniture seen in figure 10.46 dates to 1945 and met the standards of economy and solid construction required of British manufacturers in the 1940s. Rather than experimenting with new materials such as plywood, this table used solid woods and traditional craft-based construction. It was aimed to meet the needs of newlyweds setting up households and victims of bombing who had lost their possessions. The standards for the austere utilitarian furniture of the 1940s were motivated in part by the same paternalistic interest in influencing and educating the public as earlier standards of the nineteenth century, and also strongly recalled the honesty and moral socialist leanings seen in some manifestations of the Arts and Crafts Movement (see pages 90–91). They were imposed, however, in the national interest of conserving resources amid scarcity and appealed to patriotism and national unity rather than to a Modernist advocacy of new materials and production technologies.

More experimental in terms of materials is the BA aluminum chair designed by Ernest Race (1913–1964) in 1945 (fig. 10.47). Light in appearance, the aluminum legs required little bracing and were produced using methods of mold casting. This chair was displayed at the Britain

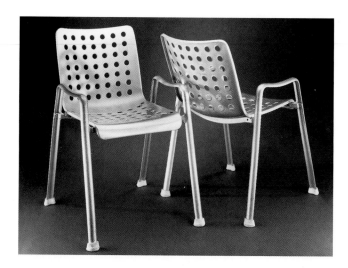

10.48 Hans Coray, Landi chair, molded, heat-treated, and stained aluminum, 30 ½ x 21 ½ x 22 ⅛ in (77.5 x 54.5 x 56.2 cm), manufactured by Blattmann Metallwarenfabrik AG, Switzerland, 1945 (first manufactured in 1939).

Can Make It exhibition held in 1946. Other aluminum furniture of the period includes the Landi chair (fig. 10.48), designed by Hans Coray (1906–1991) for the Swiss National Exhibition held in 1939. The perforated one-piece molded shell again takes advantage of the lightness and strength of the material, as well as permitting drainage for the chair's intended outdoor use.

While more conventionally representational posters using a naturalistic narrative style of illustration continued to be produced to support the war effort, a number of graphic designers began using the more direct and economical means of simplified text and visual image to serve a variety of public service purposes during World War II. French designer Jean Carlu (1900–1989) visited the United States in 1940 as an employee of the French Information Service and remained there during the Nazi occupation of France. While in America he designed his *Production* poster for the Office of Emergency Management using a clever combination of typography and image for the letter "o" that serves also as a hex nut, turned by a wrench tightly gripped by a powerful, gloved hand (fig. 10.49). Carlu connected industry with patriotism, emphasizing the worker's strong hand but also the alliance of government and industry for wartime production. The economy of means and symbolic use of letterforms signaled a shift away from illustration in the approach of the graphic design profession as it emerged after World War II.

Paul Rand (1914–1996) served as art director and designed covers for the cultural journal *Direction* between 1938 and 1945. Figure 10.50 illustrates a cover chronicling

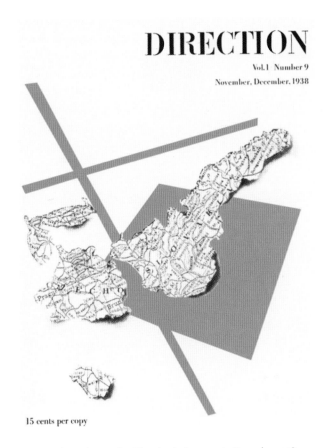

DIRECTION

Vol. 1 Number 9

November, December, 1938

15 cents per copy

10.50 Paul Rand, cover for *Direction* (vol. 1, no. 9), December 1938.

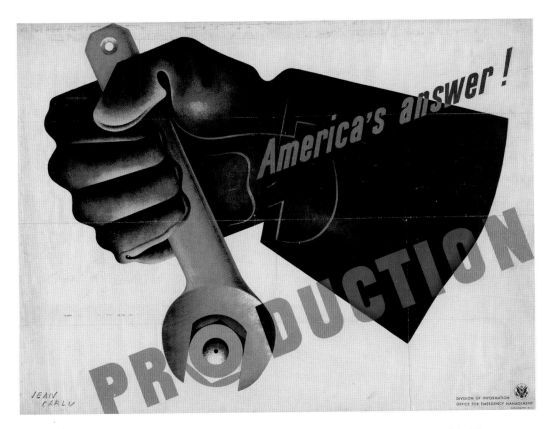

10.49 Jean Carlu, *America's Answer! Production*, lithograph, 29 ⅞ x 39 ⅝ in (76 x 100.6 cm), United States Government Printing Office, Washington, D. C., 1941. Museum of Modern Art, New York.

Nazi Germany's occupation of a portion of Czechoslovakia in the autumn of 1938. Rand's map, placed against diagonal lines and a square, alludes to the table of a military strategy room; the red cross and square provide bold and dramatic contrast to the neutral map, as well as connoting blood and possibly sacrifice. With an economy of means and absence of conventional narrative and representational techniques, Rand's open-ended juxtapositions possess a lingering power that seems to reside in provocative associations that are both immediate as well as thoughtful, obvious as well as subtle. After World War II, Rand became an articulate spokesman for the emerging profession of graphic design, emphasizing the varied skills that characterize the designer's role. In an essay from 1985, he wrote:

> Design is a way of life, a point of view. It involves the whole complex of visual communication; talent, creative ability, manual skill and technical knowledge. Aesthetics and economics, technology and psychology are intrinsically related to the process.

Graphic designers during World War II not only created posters for recruitment, public service, and influencing public opinion, but also designed training manuals in which the efficient and strongly visual communication of information proved especially effective. German-born Will Burtin (1908–1972) organized the presentation of visual and textual information in the design of instructions for the operation of aircraft gunnery. His approach was neither entirely as artist nor propagandist, but rather as problem-solver and analyst, devising the clearest method for combining words and images for the purposes of instruction. Burtin took in to consideration eye movement as well as the hierarchy and flow of information across two-page spreads (fig. 10.51). The design solution flowed from the requirements of the brief, and while not inevitable as the outcome of those requirements, the task of the designer was certainly akin to the methods of an engineer rather than the artist or advertiser. According to graphic designer and historian Richard Hollis, Burtin's training manual helped to reduce the training time for gunners from twelve to six weeks.

CONCLUSION

The interwar period produced two broad movements in design, Art Deco (or Moderne), and Modernism. While it may not be difficult to distinguish Ruhlmann's Grand Salon from Le Corbusier's Pavillon de l'Esprit Nouveau at the 1925 exhibition of decorative and industrial art in Paris as prescriptions for modern living, such comparisons do not convey the complex relationship among visions of modernity and modern living over the course of this period, nor the variations and differences among particular Modernist ideologies and practices. Many designers and movements rejected historicism yet also demonstrated continuity with the past, Art Deco with elements of progressive late nineteenth-century movements such as Art Nouveau, and Modernism with the German Werkbund and its search for more anonymous, practical standards for household goods and furnishings. Certainly World War I lent an urgency, polemic tone, and utopian character to Modernist practice, based upon an almost militant rejection of existing forms of authority, while the growth of advertising during this time sometimes made commercial motivations overshadow liberal ideologies and determine actual associations between art and industry.

A consistent element of Modernism was its focus upon working class or universal needs rather than upon luxury living, recognizing the ordinary rather than the exclusive and unique. While the role of "art" in Modernist design was a matter of difference among its advocates, the belief that technology in terms of materials and production promised a broader and brighter future was uncontested. Socialized housing, minimum requirements for living, or Le Corbusier's theory of mechanical selection, theories of elemental geometric forms underlying the varied branches of design activity, all discussed above, are expressions of this desire in the 1920s, while such ideas also gained broader currency in response to the worldwide economic depression of the 1930s. Even acknowledging the loose collection of ideas that comprises Modernism, it is important to recognize that the achievement of its utopian vision required more than the design and production of goods and furnishings in a competitive marketplace; behind the Modernist vision was the hope for a complete reorientation of living that required the education of the "New Man." Early expressions of this Modernist project often have an apocalyptic tone, forecasting the destruction of the old and the emergence of the entirely new. Soviet Russia and Socialist governments in parts of Europe provided political support for several experiments in the design and construction of socialized housing along Modernist lines. Yet at the same time designers such as Josef Frank in Austria and Alvar Aalto in Finland remained advocates of the frank use of industrial materials and modern techniques of production but took into consideration the individual and psycho-logical needs of consumers. During the 1930s, Modernism was not a strict set of design principles, nor a revolutionary social and political ideology, but an increasingly flexible approach to the advantages of modern industrial materials, eschewing conventional

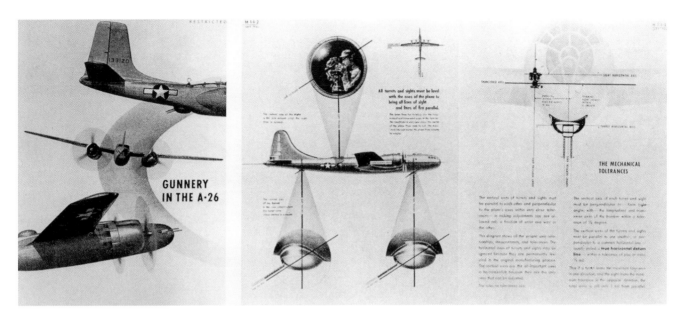

10.51 Will Burtin, training manual for A-26 Gunnery, United States Armed Forces, 1944.

associations with luxury and yet not entirely determined by scientific criteria.

Less revolutionary and utopian in vision, Art Deco designers reasserted the more traditional liberal belief in an alliance between art and manufacturing and the role of the decorative arts in elevating the taste and improving the quality of life through comfort, convenience, and enhanced possibilities for leisure activity. This movement gained momentum from post-World War I reconstruction, with the visual arts viewed as an expression of creative freedom, originality, and national pride. The style originated at the top, in the world of high fashion and hedonism, but mass-circulation magazines, department stores, cinema, and advertising expanded its market and associations with an active and fun-loving lifestyle.

In the United States advertising and modern design flourished in the expanding consumer economy of the 1920s, stimulated by exhibitions stemming from the Paris exhibition of decorative and industrial arts of 1925 and the emigration of European designers working independently or under contract to manufacturers. The extension of design to the utilitarian products of mechanized and standardized mass production such as kitchen appliances or assembly-line automobiles provided the basis for designers to work for large-scale industries in order to add consumer appeal to such products and stimulate sales. The phenomenon of Streamlining offers an insight into the complex relationship among competing commercial, scientific, and artistic interests in the expanding definition of design for industry in the 1930s.

In exhibitions and competitions, the Museum of Modern Art asserted a more narrow interpretation of modern design in the United States, focusing upon the application of technology to stricter standards of efficiency, economy, and geometric purity for manufactured products, which appeared to its defenders and promoters as appropriate and responsible in the depressed economy of the 1930s. After World War II and amid economic recovery, a relaxation of this austere interpretation of modern design permitted an expansion that included a greater degree of individual expression and greater tolerance and accommodation of commercial considerations. Such a synthesis, under the name of "Good Design," will occupy much of our attention in Part V.

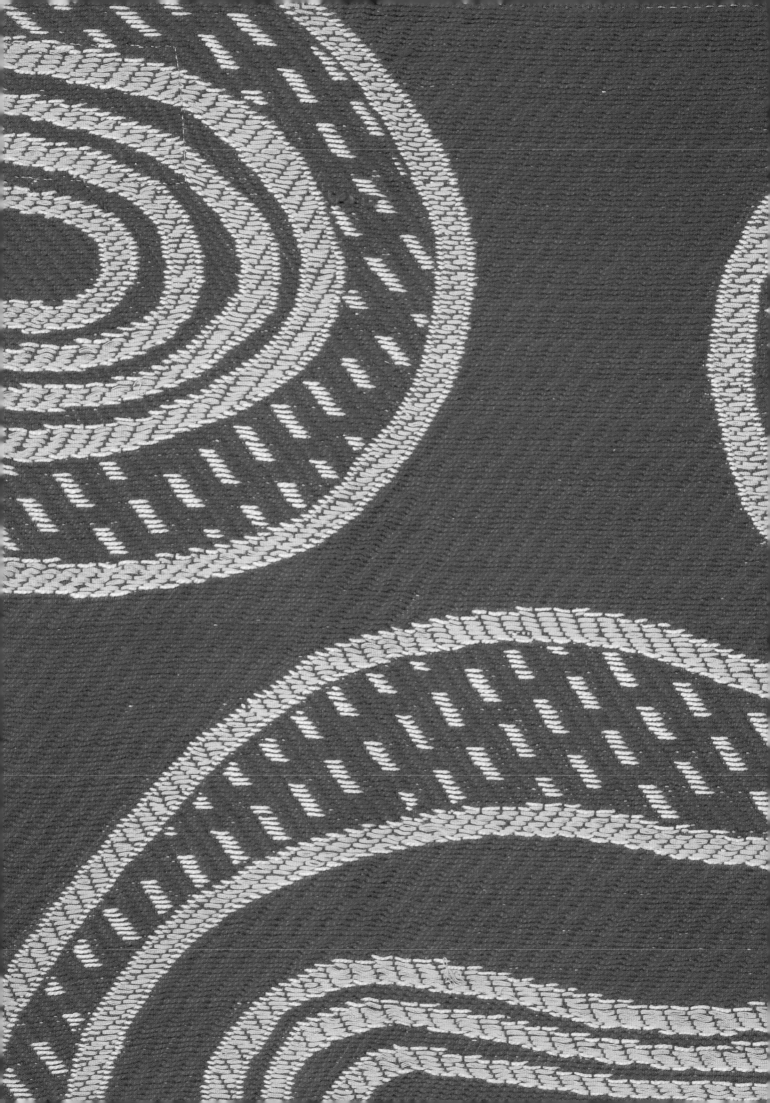

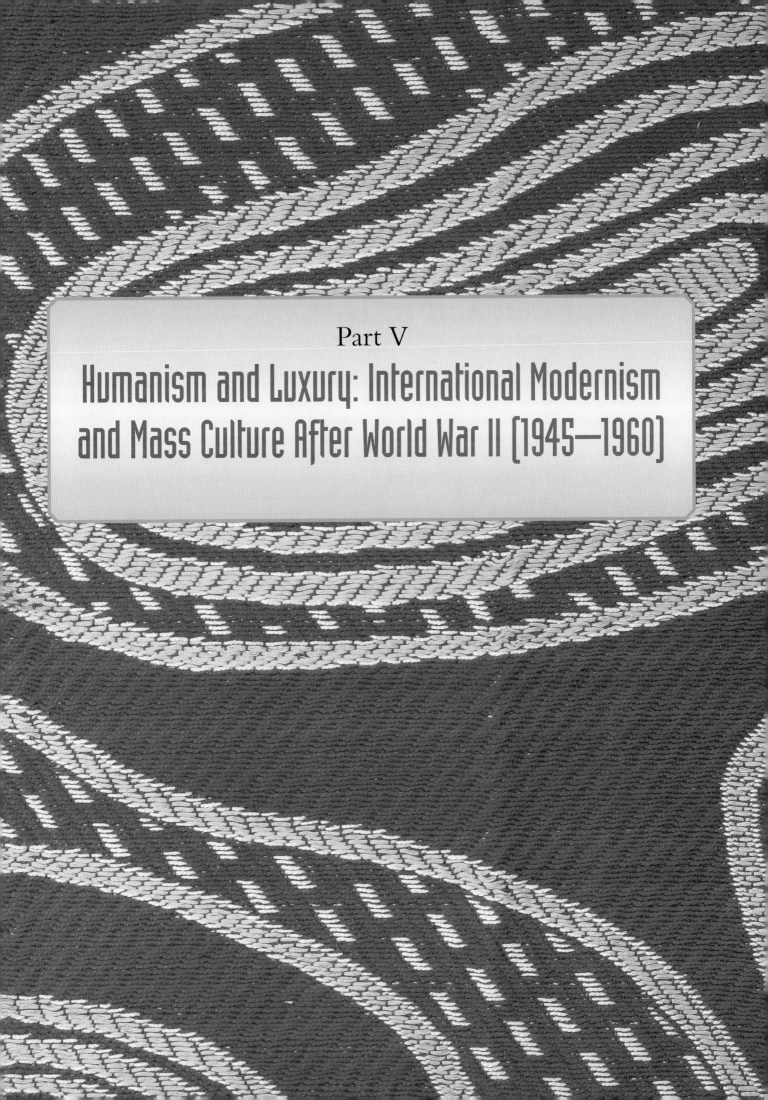

Part V

Humanism and Luxury: International Modernism and Mass Culture After World War II (1945—1960)

Introduction to Part V

Design initiatives took root internationally amid a cultural environment of reconstruction and strong economic recovery following the end of World War II. The role assumed by the United States in this expansion was paramount, both in terms of its own elastic market for manufactured goods as well as its national interest in stimulating the industrial production of European countries through rebuilding initiatives such as the Marshall Plan (1948–52). Such initiatives fostered capitalist enterprise in response to Soviet expansion into Eastern Europe and emerging Cold War tensions. Out of these particular economic and political conditions arose broader constituencies for the products of international modern designers as well as competing and sometimes overlapping visions for the role of design in contemporary life. Clients included large multi-national corporations such as IBM and CBS and their conscious development of prominent visual identity and image programs, as well as efforts to link their products and services with economic, social, and cultural progress through compelling and informative exhibitions and publications.

At times there was a didactic, even polemic tone accompanying the promotion of international design in the early postwar years. Advocates embraced familiar paternalistic themes of improving and educating the public to appreciate the aesthetic, social, and practical advantages of modern design and to embrace contemporary living that harmonized individualism with the self-imposed responsibility of citizens and businesses toward the wider community, in effect expressing what was referred to as a "new humanism." At other times criticism was leveled against a narrow and monolithic view of the commercialism of mass media and what designer Brooks Stevens termed planned obsolescence, both of which implied the absence of responsible standards and the exploitation of consumer desire. Standards for postwar design combined new industrial materials such as plastic, fiberglass, and plywood with production technologies such as molding to create furniture and furnishings that implied comfort, technological innovation, and the forms of modern abstract art. This is seen most clearly in the relationship between furniture and abstract sculpture associated with the movements of Automatic Surrealism and Constructivism, and in the international success of artists such as Henry Moore and Alexander Calder (1898–1976), whose sculptures appeared not only in museums but also as monuments in large urban public places and parks. Graphic designers in the United States such as Alvin Lustig and Paul Rand also adopted a sophisticated approach to advertising and magazine cover design that showed affinities with the symbolic associations of abstract art, while in Germany and Switzerland graphic designers often saw their task as simplifying and clarifying information using the discipline of a two-dimensional grid system.

Expanding beyond earlier design concerns with economy and efficiency in relation to minimum working-class needs, industrial designers and advocates in the postwar period often characterized their approach more broadly as "fitness to purpose." This term embraced ergonomics and anthropometry, defined as the science of designing for the ease and comfort of human use. Research of this kind attempted to place the profession of industrial design within an empirical, "problem-solving" context and to enumerate criteria, beyond profits and sales, by which products might be judged successful and innovative. Such views shifted the designer's role from that of mere "product stylist" whose intentions were subverted or compromised by fashion and commercialism to one whose focus was more on the product user, and upon meeting specific human needs. Advocates for modern design promoted the tenets or standards of modern international design as being in the public interest and distinct from the relativism and hedonism implied by fashion. Shared standards and limits to the expression of individual will, whether in product design, graphic design, or in political or moral attitudes, were viewed as bulwarks against manipulation by advertisers, especially in an age of mass communication and amid lingering fears of totalitarianism and propaganda. Indeed, mass media, whether as a vehicle for marketing products or for disseminating political views, permitted an unprecedented expansion of the ability of corporations and governments to influence public opinion. The pervasive power of totalitarian propaganda prior to and during World War II suggested that responsible standards went well beyond the issue of mere "taste," embracing politics and the role of design in shaping and strengthening shared cultural values and democratic ideals. As mentioned above, large and diverse corporations with global interests were among the strongest advocates and clients for modern design: their headquarters, office interiors, products, organization, and promotional materials both expressed and shaped shared values of efficiency, rationalism, progress, dependability, responsibility, and public education. A design policy, or "house style," not only informed the look of products, but bred familiarity and trust through a more generalized brand identity. It also reinforced loyalty and conformity among employees. At the same time, fears of manipulation and the concentration of power in the hands of too few emerged in United States President Dwight Eisenhower's farewell address in 1961, where he noted the connection between industrial technology and the arms race, also in the context of Cold War tensions between the competing superpowers of the United States and the Soviet Union.

Postwar design, promoted as "good design" or "Gute Form," was effectively marketed through museum exhibitions seeking to raise awareness and increase the level of public discrimination, and through international events such as the Milan Triennale, which included competitive awards. Postwar modern design also was the subject of articles and illustrations in journals such as *Domus*, *Industrial Design*, and *Design Quarterly*, and was supported by organizations such as the Council of Industrial Design (COID) in Britain and their counterparts in Japan and Scandinavia. Also important were schools such as the Hfg (Hochschule für Gestaltung) at Ulm in West Germany.

Yet for many consumers, the "good design" model was not understood as a universal set of standards that raised general cultural awareness or instilled responsible democratic values. Rather its products and promotion simply offered one among many possibilities for individual fulfillment in an age of increasing affluence and possibilities for leisure, a matter of "both ... and" rather than "either ... or." Perhaps seeking to escape the shortages and government-imposed restrictions on materials and manufacturing during the years of World War II, the expanding American middle class in particular responded enthusiastically to constant novelty, fantasy, and instant gratification, as manufacturers and advertisers of household goods recognized a seemingly insatiable appetite for products or gadgets that offered to reduce housework and expand leisure. In the early 1950s, photographs of modern interiors and advice for modern, suburban, informal living through design also appeared in mass-circulation magazines such as *House and Garden* and *Better Homes and Gardens.* In the course of this decade, however, this "mass" design (marketed through the mass media and in particular through the increasing role played by television) went considerably beyond the boundaries of a rational "new humanism" and its standards, which included the aesthetics of abstract art, technological development, cultural education, and ergonomics.

In terms of products, mass design is perhaps best exemplified in the popularity of the Detroit-manufactured automobiles of the 1950s and their prominence in Hollywood Technicolor films and in television, stimulating desire through the identification of materialism and consumer choice with freedom, leisure, luxury, power, and social mobility. Another medium that stimulated mass taste was popular magazines, whose images and product advertisements promised a better life for the American family and vicarious thrills for a generation of youthful consumers. Almost immediately such images were appropriated by the Pop Art movement in the United States, Britain, and elsewhere in Europe. The allure of mass culture for artists ranged from the pure visual excitement of bold aesthetics to a recognition of the seductive power of idealized mass-media images of beauty and fulfillment supplied by commercial artists, photographers, and illustrators.

Housing was also an area in which such attitudes toward modern design emerged. Architects and interior designers concentrated upon accommodating new and efficient patterns of family life through simple construction, central heating, open plans, large expanses of glass, and avoiding decorative moldings and other features of more traditional construction methods. Postwar suburban housing communities were another part of the broader idealism embodied in mass design, and a vision of life sometimes referred to as the American Dream. Many Americans moved from inner-city neighborhoods to newly created suburbs, where the availability of land for development and affordability of automobiles helped to define postwar lifestyles. Inexpensive gasoline prices, made possible by American-based corporate control of Middle East oilfields and refineries, made commuting affordable and reasonably comfortable. At the same time, mass-produced methods of construction for detached housing, initiated in communities such as Levittown, New York, offered alternatives to city apartment living and featured conveniences such as automatic washers, dryers, and modern kitchen appliances. For many Americans, individual home ownership brought with it the promise of leisure, green space, independence, security, and the freedom of personal mobility.

The emerging mass culture was criticized during and after World War II from a number of perspectives. Some commentators complained about consumers' lack of discrimination and questioned the morality of conspicuous consumption in encouraging submission to manufactured ideals of beauty and health, and in which superficial differences and consumer choice masked an underlying conservatism and conformity. Others viewed mass culture as a form of social control reinforcing traditional family and gender roles of the white middle class. Still others dismissed popular culture as "kitsch," debased mass-produced imitations of authentic culture standing at the lowest common denominator of taste, that is, of pure physical sensation renewed and manipulated by a commercial culture industry. In this view, culture is synonymous with leisure and entertainment rather than with more abiding values that contribute to well-being, enlightenment, self-realization, and active participation in a responsible democracy.

Eventually the monolithic view of mass culture derided by social critics and educators crumbled, as it was insufficiently narrow to embrace a strain of vitality, popular expression, subversion, and irrationality found in comic books, film noir, tailfins, and rock 'n' roll. At the same time, proponents of rational standards and research in design were less able to justify and defend the inflated claims for design as a vehicle for broad social progress and enlightenment. The dualism between "good" design and mass taste, between high design and popular culture, reflects a limited viewpoint that demands a broader and more nuanced cultural perspective. The attitudes and artifacts of both movements emerge as expressions of capitalist expansion emanating from Cold War tensions that made consumer goods one of the battlegrounds of competing ideologies for a democratic society.

In sum, despite an acknowledged critical dichotomy between the new humanism and mass taste, both strains of postwar design coexisted, and both came to express a form of democratic expression directed against the threat of Communism and state control of housing, manufacturing, as well as patterns of collective living. Whether conditioned by a new and broader set of criteria for a discriminating international audience or giving inventive form to popular images of power, dissent, freedom, and luxury for the American middle class, design thrived in the prosperity of the postwar period amid the emergence of new technologies, unprecedented increases in production, and escalating levels of consumption.

Chapter 11

Modernism After World War II: From Theory to Practice

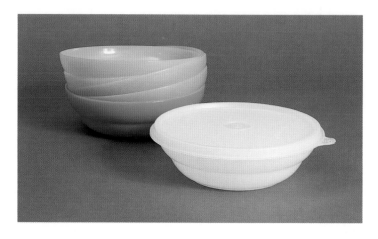

11.1 Earl Tupper, cereal bowls and seals, polyolefin, 6 ½ in (16.5 cm) in diameter, manufactured by Tupper, *c.* 1949. Philadelphia Museum of Art.

Although shortages, rationing, and austerity continued to affect the practice of design in the years immediately following the end of World War II, especially in Britain, economic recovery, optimism, and consumer confidence were stimulated by the example of the United States and by the staging of national and international exhibitions such as the Milan Triennale and the Festival of Britain (1951), the latter commemorating the centennial of the Crystal Palace Exhibition. The brighter European and American economic outlook permitted the transformation of largely theoretical attitudes toward modern design into more practical realities on an international scale. In the United States, a number of modern design initiatives undertaken in the years immediately following the end of World War II were based upon adapting new wartime materials and technologies to domestic consumption and efficiency, and some continue to be produced today. In 1947 Earl Tupper (1907–1983) began to market Tupperware (the company was founded in 1945), a line of flexible plastic storage and serving containers with self-sealing airtight lids to prevent spilling and preserve freshness (fig. 11.1). Tupperware utilized smooth, simple, often stackable forms and standardized sizes that permitted interchangeability for

lids. After being sold as conventional store-bought items, Tupperware was available after 1951 exclusively through catalogues supplied by neighborhood vendors who demonstrated the products in the home. Such merchandising emphasized an identity between buyer and user rather than the less personal connection between buyer and salesperson, and avoided comparisons and competition with related shelf products. It reduced consumer resistance to industrial materials being used in the home rather than products traditionally associated with craft such as ceramic storage items. Tupper's commercial success dated to the 1950s, but was based upon his invention of a new pliable plastic called Poly-T in 1942, manufactured by DuPont and other chemical companies as part of the war effort. This interest in harnessing wartime technologies and high-volume industrial production to improve domestic living through new, inexpensive, and practical products played a large role in shaping positive attitudes toward modern design in the decade following the end of World War II. It also helps to explain the leading role assumed by large chemical corporations in promoting modern design, as it enabled them to sustain, if not increase, production during peacetime. Chemical and pharmaceutical companies employed graphic designers who helped to explain and promote scientific concepts and their useful applications in visual terms to the public and to the business community through popular and professional magazines and journals.

In addition to Tupperware, a dazzling array of household domestic products were also being developed by designers after the war. A series of Bubble hanging lamps were designed by George Nelson Associates beginning in 1952 and manufactured by the Michigan-based Howard Miller Clock Company. The lamps were constructed from steel wire attached to rings (rather than welded) and sprayed with a plastic to create translucent shells in a variety of rounded shapes (fig. 11.2). The originality of non-traditional shapes for lighting and industrial production suggests creative applications of technology to modern living. In articles for the journal *Industrial Design*, Nelson cited the vitality of the industrial design profession in comparison with traditional forms and methods of production that were less relevant to modern living and could not take advantage of the emerging dynamic world of international business and markets.

Consultant designer Henry Dreyfuss (see pages 236–237) continued to emphasize practicality as a determinant in product housings for a variety of manufactured goods. For his redesigned combined handset for Bell Telephone in 1946, Dreyfuss introduced lightweight plastic and a receiver whose form could be cradled between ear and shoulder, freeing the hand and creating a more natural interface between product and user (see fig. 10.26 for the earlier model of 1937). He was a staunch advocate for the importance of measurement and research as determinants in the design process to contribute to safety and reduce fatigue whether at home or in the

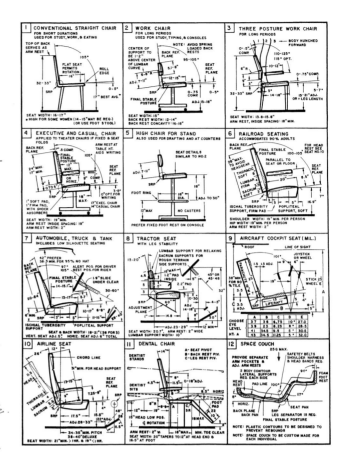

11.3   Henry Dreyfuss, illustration from *The Measure of Man: Human Factors in Design*, height 13 in (33 cm), New York, 1960.

workplace. Dreyfuss published his *The Measure of Man: Human Factors in Design* in 1960 (fig. 11.3), a manual of detailed drawings in which measurement forms the basis of design decisions. Using a series of average body sizes for men and for women that took into account differences, *The Measure of Man* used observation and measurement to determine heights of tables, distances between operators and machines or appliances, and the form and placement of knobs and controls on devices for ease-of-use, safety, and the reduction of error.

Another well-known, "classic" postwar example of his industrial design is the round, wall-mounted thermostat designed for the Honeywell Corporation (fig. 11.4). Honeywell dominated the market for thermostats to regulate temperature in homes and offices, but the idea of a round control was attractive to the company from a marketing standpoint as it would differentiate the company's product visually from its competitors. Although company records indicate some interest in a round model from the early 1940s, the new model did not appear until 1953. Adapting the thermostat mechanisms to a round housing necessitated significant invention, credited to the company engineer Carl Kronmiller (1889–1968), who

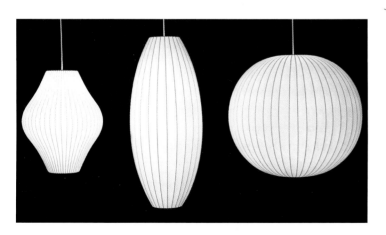

11.2   George Nelson Associates, Bubble hanging lamps, steel wire and sprayed plastic shell, height of largest lamp 33 in (84 cm), manufactured by Howard Miller Clock Company, Zeeland, Michigan, from 1952. Philadelphia Museum of Art.

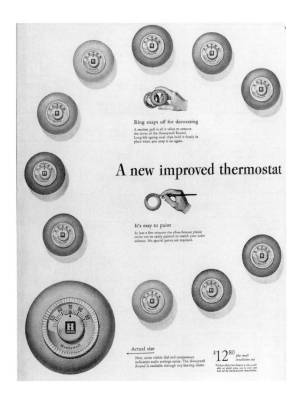
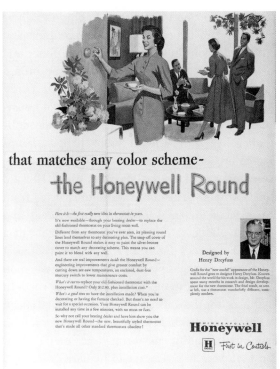

11.4 Henry Dreyfuss, Honeywell round thermostat, plastic and painted aluminum housing, 3 in (7.6 cm) diameter, manufactured by Honeywell Corporation, 1953. Advertisement in *Life*, November 9, 1953.

developed a spring coil to replace the conventional glass-enclosed mercury-filled thermometer that was difficult to manufacture in a curved form. While the costs of development were considerable, the final manufactured product was less expensive than earlier models. Dreyfuss liked the idea of the round control from the standpoint of mounting, that is, rectangular models almost always looked crooked when mounted on the wall. A further refinement that Dreyfuss developed was a concentric metal plate that fitted easily around the clear plastic readout and control. He was also responsible for suggesting that the concentric plate be manufactured in a variety of colors to match the wall. Dreyfuss's name was frequently mentioned in advertising campaigns, but the development process of this product began before he was hired and required considerable collaborative effort. Inexpensive, easy to operate, inconspicuous, and attractive in its simple and concentric forms, the Honeywell Round demonstrated the advantages of postwar industrial design, and companies often promoted the integral and creative role of the industrial designer as a marketing tactic.

American designers were eager to demonstrate the advantages of modern materials and methods of production for furniture that helped to create a contemporary, efficient, and comfortable standard of living accompanying the postwar boom in housing. Their clients also included corporations and businesses whose interior office design

projects an image of modern efficiency and sophisticated taste. As in the interwar period, original designs were manufactured and effectively promoted by the Herman Miller Company of Zeeland, Michigan (see fig. 10.28). Following the untimely death of Gilbert Rohde in 1944, Miller president D. J. DePree hired the architect and writer George Nelson (1908–1986) as chief designer for the company. In turn, Nelson seized the opportunity and encouraged DePree to manufacture and market the furniture of other designers, including Charles and Ray Eames. Charles Eames (1907–1978) studied architecture at Washington University in St. Louis, and was hired as artist-in-residence and instructor at the Cranbrook Academy of Art in Bloomfield Hills, Michigan, where he taught from 1938 until 1941. He met Ray (1912–1988) at Cranbrook, where she was a student in the weaving workshop, having first studied painting in New York. Charles Eames's design for a molded plywood chair, a collaboration with Eero Saarinen (1910–1961), son of Cranbrook's director Eliel Saarinen and his wife, Loja, won first prize at the Museum of Modern Art-sponsored competition for Organic Design in Home Furnishings in 1940 (see fig. 10.44). While working for the United States Navy, the Eameses experimented with plywood molding processes in the development of lightweight, flexible splints to treat wounded soldiers. At the end of the war they adapted this technology to the molding of forms for seating. Unlike earlier plywood

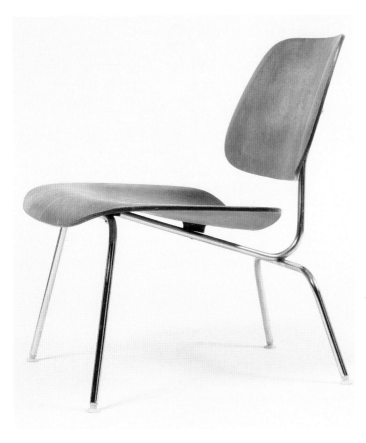

11.5 Charles and Ray Eames, Eames Low Chair: molded walnut veneered plywood, chrome-plated steel rods, and rubber shock mounts, 27 ³/₈ x 22 ¹/₄ x 25 ¹/₈ in (69.5 x 56.5 x 64.5 cm). Manufactured by Herman Miller Company, Zeeland, Michigan, 1946. Vitra Design Museum, Germany.

11.6 Charles and Ray Eames, lounge chair and ottoman, chair: 33 x 33 ³/₄ x 32 in (84 x 86 x 81 cm); ottoman: 24 ³/₄ x 17 x 21 ¹/₄ in (63 x 43 x 54 cm), laminated rosewood, aluminum, and leather upholstery, manufactured by Herman Miller Company, Zeeland, Michigan, 1956. Philadelphia Museum of Art.

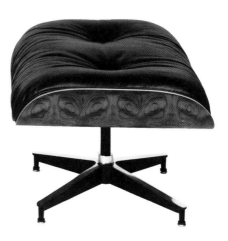

molding techniques used, for instance, by Alvar Aalto, the Eameses' approach to molding was three-dimensional – what design historian Peter Dormer has called "vessel and valley" forms as a reference to their more organic, sculptural character.

In 1946, the Eameses designed a molded plywood chair with separate seat and back supported by a thin, welded tubular steel frame and mounted with rubber shocks, eventually manufactured by Herman Miller (fig. 11.5). The couple continued to experiment with molded plywood and fiberglass for furniture in the later 1940s, and their unupholstered dining armchair of 1950, a single piece combining armrests, seat, and back, also mounted on a tubular metal frame, won another international competition sponsored by the Museum of Modern Art for "Low-Cost Furniture." In 1954, an armless, stacking version of the fiberglass chair was introduced by Miller, and became immensely successful for seating in schools and other institutions by virtue of its light weight and ability to be easily stored and moved. Like Tupper's Poly-T plastic, fiberglass was used as a lightweight and inexpensive material for aircraft extensively during World War II, and was developed for use in the home and office afterward, demonstrating the connections between military industrial technology and modern design, meeting domestic needs on the civilian front.

Mechanized production and industrial technology were not only the agents of improved efficiency but also of an emerging aesthetic of biomorphic sculptural forms. The Eameses, for instance, explored the organicism of molded plywood in his well-known lounge chair and footstool, designed for Herman Miller beginning in 1956 (fig. 11.6). This chair was constructed of three separate pieces of molded plywood, upholstered in leather, and supported by a five-legged metal pedestal base. The Eameses' lounge chair relates to individual comfort, abstract sculptural form, and expense beyond the earlier "low-cost" furniture, indicating motivations extending beyond efficiency.

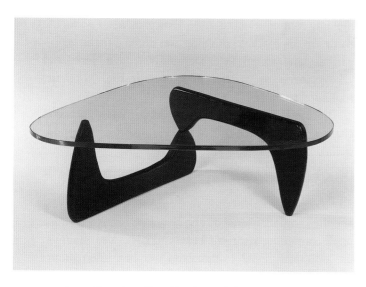

11.7 Isamu Noguchi, coffee table, glass and ebonized birch, 15 ⅝ x 50 x 36 in (40 x 127 x 91 cm), manufactured by Herman Miller Company, Zeeland, Michigan, c. 1947. Private collection.

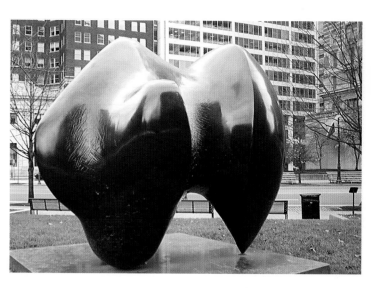

11.8 Henry Moore, *Three Way Piece Number 1*, bronze, height 76 in (193 cm), Philadelphia, 1964–1965.

Fueled by optimism stemming from faith in wartime technology, modern designers in the first postwar decade more expansively defined the relationship between their products and the quality of modern life, allowing for the self-expression of the designer and the comfort of the owner. It is not surprising that the context for postwar modern design was also shaped by manufacturers and marketing executives. In addition to a continuous supply of new designs with advantages to the consumer in terms of comfort, lightness, efficiency, or beauty, marketing strategies focused upon the individual designer, who lent uniqueness to serially manufactured goods. Herman Miller, for instance, manufactured abstract sculptural designs by Japanese-American artist Isamu Noguchi (1904–1988), such as his glass table (fig. 11.7), which is supported by an ebonized wood base consisting of two irregular forms, suggestive of Automatic Surrealism. Although elements of the egalitarian social ideology of the first machine age remained after World War II, it was the transformation of that ideology that often best exemplifies postwar modernism, especially in the 1950s. This transformation produced a benevolent "marriage of commerce and culture," in which an elevated taste merged with increasing production and economic prosperity. The organic furniture of the period also accompanied the increasing appearance of monumental abstract sculpture in public buildings such as Alexander Calder's mobiles or the bronze sculptures of Henry Moore (1898–1986), such as *Three Way Piece Number 1* in Philadelphia, dating to 1964 (fig. 11.8)

Another development of postwar modern design in furniture manufacturing was modularity, seen for instance in storage and shelving, which had appeared earlier in Eliot Noyes's vision of "organic design" for the Museum of Modern Art exhibition of 1940–1941 (see page 249). Eero Saarinen and Charles Eames designed a series of modular units for domestic interiors for the Red Lion Company in Pennsylvania, which were constructed of plywood with dowel-like legs and sliding doors for cabinets. The Eamess' small shelving units, known as the ESU system, designed for Miller (fig. 11.9), used light steel bracing for strength and support, as well as rectangular molded plywood sliding doors with embossed circular designs to create

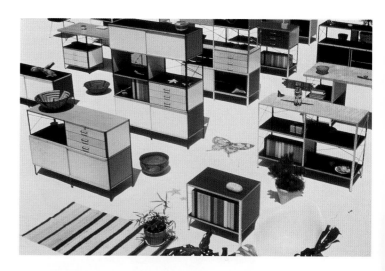

11.9 Charles and Ray Eames, Eames Storage Unit (ESU), plastic-coated plywood, lacquered masonite, and chrome-plated steel, 58 ½ x 47 x 16 ¾ in (148.6 x 119.4 x 42.5 cm). Manufactured by Herman Miller, Inc., Zeeland, Michigan, 1950.

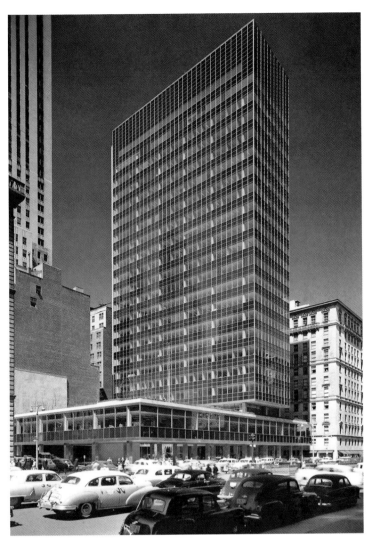

11.10 Skidmore, Owings, and Merrill, Lever House, Manhattan, 1952.

Associates in 1943. Knoll's wife and partner, Florence Schust Knoll (b. 1917), studied at the Cranbrook Academy in Bloomfield Hills, Michigan, and did much to establish the company's association with modern design after World War II. Knoll manufactured the furniture prototypes of architect and former director of the Bauhaus, Mies van der Rohe (see page 204), for instance, his steel and upholstered leather Barcelona chair designed for the German Pavilion at the 1929 international exhibition held in Spain. The company also produced designs by Cranbrook faculty and students such as the Italian-born sculptor Harry Bertoia (1915–1978). Bertoia's Diamond chair made of spot-welded steel (fig. 11.11) was manufactured by Knoll from 1952 and features the molded "vessel and valley" forms also seen in plywood and plastic designs for chairs by Saarinen and Eames (see page 263). Bertoia had worked with Eames on molded plywood designs in California. The chair's form approximates an abstract approach to the wingspan of a bird in flight, enhanced through the open and elastic weblike treatment of the welded steel wires.

bright and playful variations in color and texture. Moreover, Miller designs and other modular shelving units approximated in three dimensions the asymmetrical balance of paintings by Mondrian and the principles of De Stijl, as described earlier with Van Doesburg's desire to create "walk-in paintings" (see fig. 9.6). Their transparency and thin structural components also are contemporary with the abstract rectilinear character of steel and glass architecture in the postwar period, for instance, the Lever House office building on Park Avenue in Manhattan, designed by Skidmore, Owings, and Merrill, in 1951–1952 (fig. 11.10). The combination of standardized and industrial building components and geometric abstraction apply equally to the storage unit and the postwar office building.

The refinement of the Eameses' lounge chair and subsequent office chair designs in cast aluminum was also incorporated into furniture designs manufactured by German émigré Hans Knoll, who established Knoll

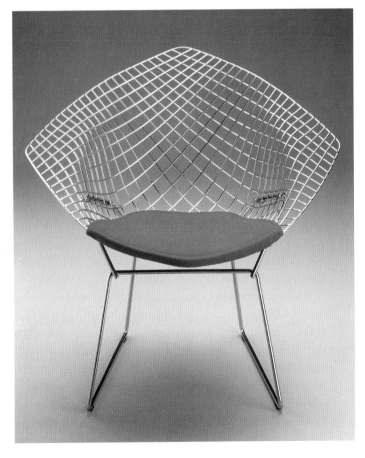

11.11 Harry Bertoia, Diamond chair, steel wire and upholstery, 30 ½ x 33 ¾ x 28 in (77.5 x 86 x 71 cm), manufactured by Knoll Associates, New York, 1952.

The Eameses' activities also included a trip to India in 1957, resulting in an "India Report" in 1958 at the invitation of the Indian government following independence from Great Britain in 1947. In their report, the Eameses steered a middle ground between the benefits and inevitability of industrial technology in the post-World War II period and a respect for local craft traditions that appealed to broader humanizing aspects of their practice and in the "primitive" objects they collected and displayed in their Los Angeles home. Rather than the rejection of the past and embrace of mechanized mass production often adopted by Modernist movements such as Constructivism, the Eameses' report on India recognized value in pre-industrial design and the need to accommodate local identity within the framework on modernism.

Eero Saarinen designed a modern furniture group using pedestals as support for Knoll, manufactured in 1956 (see fig. 11.15). Like Bertoia, Saarinen was interested in exploring the organic possibilities of modern industrial materials, in this case molded fiberglass, with chairs and tables supported by a painted aluminum base providing support as well as visual balance and harmony.

The growing taste for modern industrial materials treated with expressive individuality also helped to renew public appreciation for the designs of American architect Frank Lloyd Wright in the 1950s, thanks at least in part to articles written by George Nelson and published in the journal *Architectural Digest*. Wright's spiraling Guggenheim Museum in New York (opened 1959) used reinforced concrete to create a series of sweeping spiral interior ramps. Other related architectural designs featuring the aesthetic possibilities of reinforced concrete included Eero Saarinen's TWA Terminal at what is now John F. Kennedy International Airport in Long Island, New York, built between 1958 and 1962. The sculptural possibilities of new materials and production technologies for building continue to provide the basis for originality in architecture, for instance, in Frank Gehry's Guggenheim Museum in Bilbao, Spain (1997) or his Walt Disney Concert Hall in Los Angeles (2003).

A more restrained sculptural aesthetic is seen in the interior design of passenger airplanes, in particular Walter Teague's design for the Boeing 707 aircraft of 1955–1956 (fig. 11.12). Like Henry Dreyfuss, Teague established his reputation as a consultant industrial designer in the interwar period and was committed to a consideration of human factors and an understanding of manufacturing processes in products such as the 1936 Kodak Bantam camera (see fig. 10.23). Teague's airline interior demonstrates a preference for recessed indirect lighting and curving molded plastic surfaces without projections or intrusive patterned decoration; such features respected

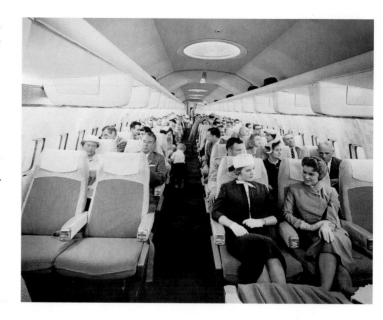

11.12 Walter Teague, full-scale model for interior, Boeing 707, published in *Interior*, 1955–1956.

concerns for safety and had a calming psychological effect, tested through the construction of a full-scale interior model to study and measure passenger reaction prior to manufacturing. Teague remained a vigorous spokesman for research and a range of determinants in design that moved beyond functional aesthetics toward observing and respecting the experience of users. Such an approach was articulated in books and in articles published in the journal *Industrial Design*; in a broad sense it reflects a designer's role in mediating between products and users, of considering options and making decisions that affect our relationship to complex technologies.

The use of molded surfaces, concave moldings around windows, and recessed indirect interior lighting in commercial airliners remain legacies of Teague's approach to industrial design. More recently headphones and personal movie screens provide added means of more comfortably occupying the traveler during longer flights as well as during delays. The same cannot be said of the industry's efforts to maximize profits by increasing the number of seats in coach class. It is interesting to note that when American Airlines began to advertise more leg room in coach class in 2000, the company based its claim on the measurement between the bolts that secure each row of seats to the floor of the aircraft known as "pitch." American had increased this measurement to 33 inches (83.8 cm) from the industry standard of 31 inches (78.7 cm). By comparison, in his 1960 book *The Measure of Man*, Henry Dreyfuss recommended the minimum pitch measurement for airline seating at between 34 and 35 inches (86 and 89 cm).

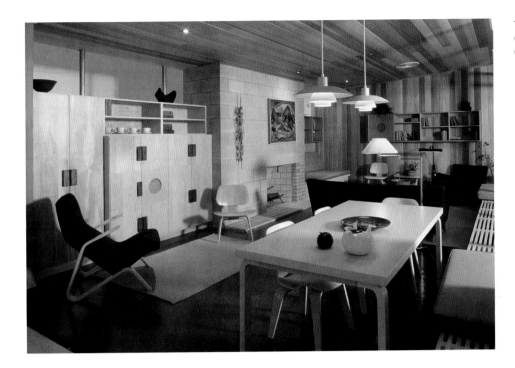

PROMOTING POSTWAR DESIGN: ART DIRECTION AND THE NEW ADVERTISING

In 1946, the Museum of Modern Art organized a solo exhibition of the Eameses' furniture designs. In 1949 the Detroit Institute of Arts also featured the Eameses' work as well as that of other modern designers in an exhibition entitled "For Modern Living." These exhibitions displayed the characteristics of organicism and flexibility as well as new materials and technologies directed toward redefining the practical and aesthetic character of modern offices and domestic living spaces. In addition to the Museum of Modern Art's exhibitions of Good Design and Useful Objects, the Walker Art Institute in Minneapolis, Minnesota, installed an "Idea House" in 1947 that utilized modern furniture and furnishings (fig. 11.13). It was intended as a public service in the immediate postwar years to encourage new home-owners to adopt the standards and values of modern design rather than more commercially motivated alternatives. The museum avoided endorsing particular manufacturers or products, but rather sought to act paternalistically to encourage consumers to recognize the advantages of modern design in terms of quality, comfort, convenience, and abstract aesthetics.

Modern designs also provided the setting for Hollywood films such as *The Man in the Grey Flannel Suit* (1956), and were visible in manufacturer showrooms and in department store windows in major cities across the United States. Features on the new designs appeared in journals such as *Art and Architecture*, *Industrial Design*, and *Architectural Digest*, whose readers included the architects and interior designers who served as consultants for corporate, professional, and individual clients. Modern interiors were also featured in mass-circulation magazines in the early 1950s, such as *Better Homes and Gardens* (fig. 11.14).

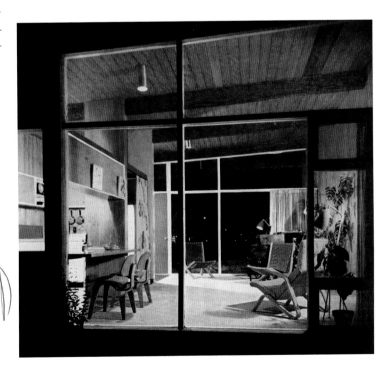

11.14 Modern interior, from *Better Homes and Gardens*, July, 1953, vol. 31, no. 7, page 49 ("Houses can be built for less money").

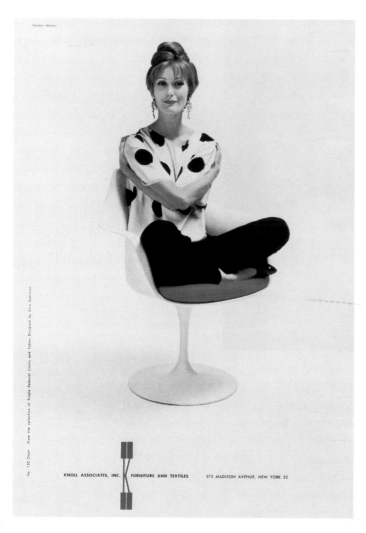

11.15 Herbert Matter, advertisement for Knoll Tulip chair, 1956.

Advertisements for new furniture and product designs were part of a tendency known as the "new advertising" that often favored the use of photography over illustration and simple copy over narrative. Graphic designer Herbert Matter used the inventive pedestal support for the Saarinen chair, labeled the Tulip chair, as the basis for surprise in a well-known advertisement on two successive pages for Knoll (fig. 11.15; the first page of the advertisement shows the pedestal with seat and back covered with brown wrapping paper). The advertisement's use of ample white space and minimal copy were elements of the "new advertising" that emphasized bold and immediate visual impact with little or no advertising copy. Moreover, the female model wears pants rather than a dress or skirt, and her informal pose suggests a casual, elegant ideal of modern living. Even the model's direct confrontation with the viewer plays a part in the surprise of the advertisement. The New York-based Art Directors Club featured examples of such advertising in yearly publications (the *Annual of*

Advertising and Editorial Art and Design) and also established awards in a variety of categories. These publications recognized achievements in the field judged by designers for creativity and innovation rather than focusing upon effective persuasion along strictly commercial criteria. This helped to locate the profession of graphic design within the world of art as well as of business, providing a degree of independence and authority for designers. The new advertising owed much of its power to the combined impact of word and abbreviated image, creating an interdependence that actively engaged the viewer. Visual metaphors and puns informed the approach, as did figurative typography. The more widespread use of photographic printing processes (rather than letterpress) stimulated experiment and the free use of a variety of techniques that could be combined to create a layout from which a flat printing plate could be produced. Newer agencies such as Doyle Dane Bernbach, founded in 1949, helped to introduce the more visually arresting approach to advertising, also seen in the work of Paul Rand (1914–1996), whose extensive work in advertising is sometimes overshadowed by his consultant work for corporations (see pages 303–304). Rand worked for the Weintraub Agency in New York, the same office where William Bernbach worked as a copy-editor before forming his own studio. Rand's *Thoughts on Design* (1947) is a short but well-illustrated book on the "new advertising," which discusses the enduring value of symbols, humor, and surprise to convey messages about products through a variety of pictorial means available to the designer. Intuition and experiment play a major role in the sensibility of the designer, and freshness of vision is both creative for the artist and persuasive, even educational, for the viewer. Rand's quotations from philosopher and educator John Dewey (1859–1952), and his invocation of "the integration of the beautiful and useful" to describe advertising and other forms of visual communication, suggest a link with standards and reform, the latter directed against the traditional visual and narrative conventions of advertising illustration:

> Visual statements such as illustrations which do not involve esthetic judgment and which are merely literal descriptions can be neither intellectually stimulating nor visually distinctive.... The visual statement, on the other hand, which seeks to express the essence of an idea, and which is based on function, fantasy, and analytic judgment, is likely to be not only unique but meaningful and memorable as well.

Rand's 1946 copy-less magazine advertisement for Coronet Brandy (fig. 11.16) features a collage of cocktail glasses being effortlessly juggled by a waiter whose head is

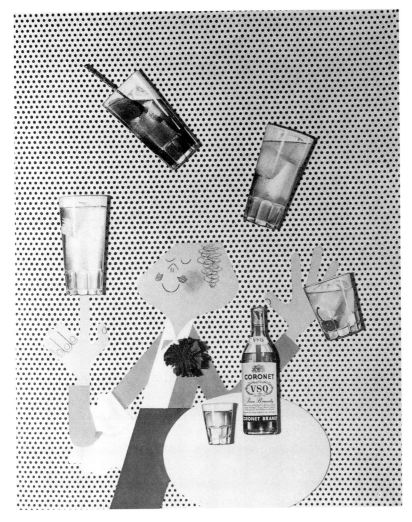

11.16 Paul Rand, advertisement for Coronet Brandy, reproduced in *Thoughts on Design*, Wittenborn, New York, 1947.

to advertisers (fig. 11.17). At the left, the sans serif "o" letters of "go" and "out" double as the lamps of a traffic signal. The signal faces the viewer along with the well-dressed mother and daughter in an automobile directly across the page, creating an identity between female reader, idealized model, and an active lifestyle that connects mobility with shopping. Again, simplicity, strong tonal contrast, and the unified, imaginative conception of photography and typography characterize the ad. The image was one of several double-page spreads for *New Yorker* set dramatically against gray or black backgrounds, whose repeated stylistic elements and format became familiar and identifiable from issue to issue.

The element of surprise, relationships with elements familiar from an exposure to contemporary fine art, and expressive use of typography also characterize much progressive postwar graphic design for book covers and record album covers. Alvin Lustig (1915–1955) harnessed these vehicles to create a number of original designs using a wide variety of techniques for covers published by New Directions Publishing in New York. Lustig employed a wide range of formal means, including photography, color, texture, and typography to convey a visual equivalent to content. Whether using montage or abstraction, Lustig's book jackets, magazine covers, and album covers, like Rand's advertisements, are suggestive rather than literal or illustrative in their approach to conveying the unified and

shaped like that of a brandy snifter. Rand explains that the dotted background suggests the effervescence of soda water used for mixed drinks. As an added element of surprise, Rand's flat cut-out shapes contrast with a photograph of a flower pinned to the waiter's lapel. Rand's approach to visual communication stressed creative solutions to the presentation of products in which the artist's originality and engagement of the viewer's interest through surprise, symbol, and humor were compatible and satisfying to the client.

Figurative typography is seen to great effect in a series of double-page spreads for the magazine *Woman's Day* designed by Gene Federico (1918–1999) and appearing in the *New Yorker* (1951–1954). Federico used routine, household errands as the basis for arresting advertisements that communicated the potential buying power of postwar-era housewives. The ads appealed both to would-be subscribers and

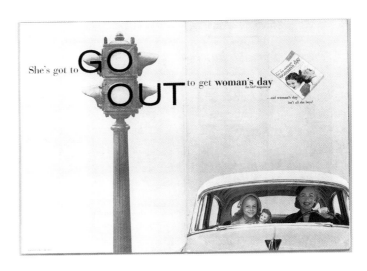

11.17 Gene Federico, advertisement for *Woman's Day* magazine, double-page spread in *New Yorker* magazine, 1953.

integrated relationship of word to image. A book cover by Lustig for Rimbaud's *A Season in Hell* from 1945 uses an asymmetrical arrangement of amorphous shapes reminiscent of Joan Miró's paintings against a fiery red background (fig. 11.18). The theme of duality is suggested by the division of the shapes into equal areas of black and white. While the red background may suggest an inferno, the lettering with its small circles as serifs resembles the star-filled heavens. The cover does not "illustrate" the title, but word and abstract image actively engage the viewer's attention. The application of a wide range of creative, open-ended solutions to design problems or challenges helps to define the individual character of postwar graphic design in a context that permitted artistic freedom. In an essay from 1954, Lustig characterized the "artistic" nature of the graphic designer:

11.18 Alvin Lustig, cover for Rimbaud's *A Season in Hell*, New Directions Publishing, New York, 1945.

The role of the designer and his most important "must" is to remain free, as free as he possibly can, from the prejudices and the ruts which affect so many others in the field of design. He must be constantly on guard, cleansing his mind of the tendency to relax into a routine format, ready to experiment, play, change, and alter forms. If he lacks the inherent ability, the insight, the intuitive selection of what is right for his time, he will not go far and will eventually be forced to enter another field. If he is equipped with these essential characteristics, he will lead the way to new and more effective approaches to design in all its forms.

Some of these characteristics were also apparent in the art-directed magazines that circulated widely in American households in the years after World War II. Dr M. F. Agha (see page 247) remained as art director for *Vogue, Vanity Fair*, and other Condé Nast publications during most of the war years. He was responsible for the modern and integrated approach to the layout of feature articles on fashion, travel, health, and other activities characterizing modern living aimed at a discriminating readership. Agha's approach to art direction stressed experiment and intuition in design decisions regarding typography, photography, illustration, margins, color, and composition. Such an approach demanded large staffs of copywriters and assistants, freelance photographers and illustrators, and also took advantage of the most up-to-date techniques for color reproduction and high-quality printing. Fashion or style magazines were large in format (*Vogue* and its rival *Harper's Bazaar* measured 9¾ × 12¼ inches; 25 × 32 cm) and replete with color. Their covers used striking compositions of photography and inventive uses of typography, while feature articles on fabrics or hair styling also used photography and color to advantage in conveying the vitality and excitement of contemporary life.

Such qualities are also found in new or revamped publications that appeared during and after the war, such as *Seventeen, Glamour*, and *Charm*. Cipe Pineles (1908–1991) served as art director for *Seventeen* and *Charm*, after working under Agha's direction at *Vogue* during the 1930s. Pineles, editor-in-chief Helen Valentine, and promotion editor Estelle Ellis were unique as a team of women in the male-dominated publishing industry, and Pineles became the first woman named as a member of the Art Directors Club in New York. *Seventeen* acknowledged the particular tastes, interests, and buying power of young women in the United States as distinct from their adult parents, and was specifically geared, through the choice of models and the editorial pages, to both reflect and shape their experience. Fiction articles were illustrated in full color by artists including Ben Shahn, who was often given wide latitude in interpretation for his images. An often-repeated story involving creative freedom and related by Pineles involves an illustration assignment for a short story:

> It (the story) concerned a 14-year-old boy, a keen tennis player, who is ashamed of his mother because she is very pregnant, and he is determined to keep this fact from his friends. To do this he keeps them from using the family tennis court, which up to the time of the pregnancy had been the center of social activity. I gave Ben a two-week deadline. He could do anything he pleased, in any shape and under any number of colors. There was only one restriction. The hero and his friends must be clearly recognizable as youngsters in their teens. Three days later the finished job came in and it was plenty clear. There was no hero. There were no friends to be seen. Instead, stretching across two pages in a long, thin picture, was the most deserted, clearest, biggest tennis court in a brilliant color, marked with the sharpest, neatest, traditional white lines. It was a breathtaking beautiful shock of a painting to go with that story.

Layout for *Seventeen* was generally asymmetrical but less varied than at *Vogue* or *Vanity Fair* under Agha. Photographs rarely employed bleeding and were usually arranged with parallel vertical edges. Typographically there was more experimentation, both in the sizes used for titles and in occasional integration of drawing for emphasis or visual puns. An example of the latter is a feature that appeared in a 1951 issue of *Seventeen* on rainwear, where a sequence of models was juxtaposed with the black vertical lines of musical staves symbolizing rain (fig. 11.19). The musical metaphor helps to connect rainwear with fashion, suggesting that inclement weather needn't be an impediment to an active lifestyle. It anticipates the association between precipitation, fun, and romance in the 1952 MGM film musical *Singin' in the Rain*.

Other magazines rivaled the innovations and technical excellence achieved by Condé Nast publications. *Esquire*, under the art direction of Henry Wolf (1925–2005) beginning in 1953, and *McCalls*, under Otto Storch (1913–1999), both provided numerous examples of expressive possibilities for layout using the integration of photography, illustration, color, and typography. The clever manipulation of type and use of photography helped to define the role of graphic design in communicating a mood or conveying an idea visually on a cover that was the subject of a feature article inside the journal. An example is Wolf's *Esquire* cover from 1958 illustrating a wine glass filled with water into which a packet of powdered "wine" has been sprinkled (fig. 11.20). Below the text reads "The Americanization of

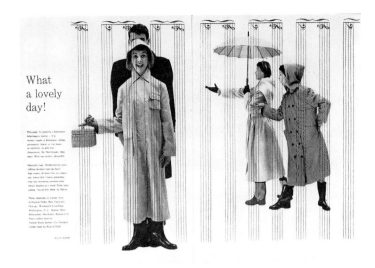

11.19 Cipe Pineles (art director), feature layout for *Seventeen*, July 1949.

Paris" in a bold sans serif mixing blue and red colors. The classic and simple wine glass (one may remember Beatrice Warde's essay "The Crystal Goblet," see pages 216–217) connotes a time-honored product associated with France, while the paper packet refers to the instant gratification that often characterized American culture at the time. The clash and interrelationship between two Western cultures are conveyed in the juxtaposition of symbols that are readily understood in connection with the text whose colors stand for the flags of both nations.

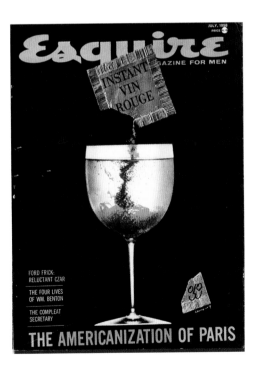

11.20 Henry Wolf (art director), cover for *Esquire*, "The Americanization of Paris," July, 1958.

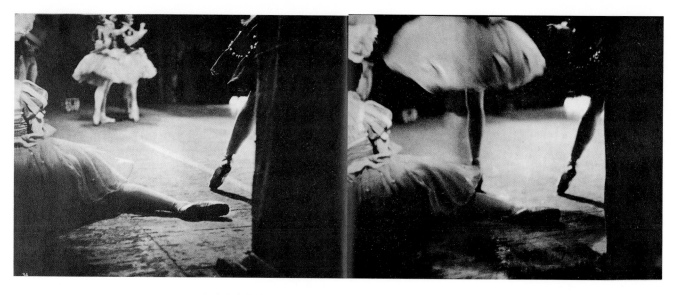

11.21 Alexey Brodovitch (photographs) and Edward Denby (text), *Ballet*, 8 ⅞ x 11 ⅛ in (22.5 x 28.5 cm), New York, J. J. Augustin, 1945.

The careful and expressive sequencing of images combined with text and titles emerged as well in *Ballet* (1945), a volume of black-and-white photographs by Alexey Brodovitch (fig. 11.21). Brodovitch (see page 247) used the blurred and bled images of dancers, often caught off-guard and cut by the edge of the page in an effect reminiscent of the paintings of Edgar Degas. The horizontal format, double-page spreads, and use of white space for the text portions convey the unique drama and excitement of the stage, taking full consideration of the range of graphic means at the designer's disposal. The striking aesthetic effect of Brodovitch's photojournalism continued in the work of many of his protégés and collaborators. Richard Avedon (1923–2004) worked with Brodovitch at *Harper's Bazaar*, where he served as art director until 1958. Avedon photographed the "New Look" in fashion design, introduced by couturier Christian Dior after World War II, using strong contrast to emphasize the contour of the model, the fullness of shapes and pinched waist. Figure 11.22 appeared in an issue of *Harper's Bazaar* in 1956.

Utilizing an increasingly broad array of techniques derived from modern art, elements of the New Typography, and creative latitude, advertising designers and magazine art directors brought visual excitement and intellectual sophistication to the presentation of products and to features focused upon the character of modern living as revealed in travel, fashion, entertainment, and cuisine. Editorial features also addressed contemporary political and social issues and permitted considerable freedom of expression. The combination of creative freedom with the effective visual communication of ideas provided an ethos that defined a progressive role for the graphic designer. That role echoed themes familiar from design reform, namely raising the level of public aware-ness of design and harmonizing individual freedom and expression with responsibility in visual communication. The glamorous world of *Harper's Bazaar*, *Vogue*, or *Esquire* may not always have corresponded to the social reality of these magazines' broad readership. Yet the thrill of imagining oneself in the

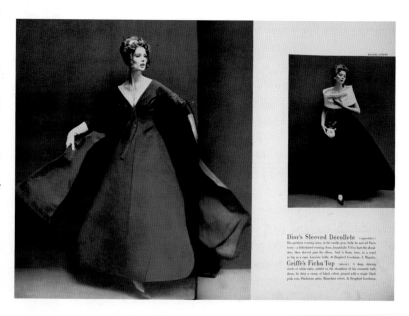

11.22 Suzy Parker, evening dress by Dior, Paris, August 1956, photographed by Richard Avedon for *Harper's Bazaar*, October 1956 issue, pages 144–5.

company of celebrities or dressed in haute couture fashion, or appreciating a clever visual pun, was pleasurable on many levels, and constituted a significant aspect of mid-century design – not necessarily the design of products, but the consumption of provocative *images* and the reality of vicarious experience. The enjoyment of that experience continues into our own time, where digital means of reproduction and manipulation provide today's designers with a wider range of options, allowing them to reach new levels of compelling visual engagement and expression.

GRAPHIC DESIGN AND TECHNICAL INFORMATION

During World War II, German-born graphic designer Will Burtin used the elements of graphic presentation to produce training manuals to teach airforce crewmen to understand and operate complex aerial guns (see page 252). After the war, the clear visual presentation of technical information became the focus of Burtin's long and distinguished career. His assignments covered a wide range of activities, from art direction for *Fortune* magazine (1945–1949) to design consultant for the Upjohn pharmaceutical company, and his work also included the design of three-dimensional exhibits. Guiding Burtin's varied projects was an abiding conviction that the increasingly complex and specialized scientific information upon which technological progress depended could be clearly and effectively communicated to a broader public through the means available to the graphic designer. Translating information into effective graphic design was a creative act of problem-solving as well as a form of public education and service. Burtin's success was testimony to his great powers of analysis and organization, as he searched for the underlying structure of complex processes. As art director both for Upjohn and its house journal, *Scope*, as well as for *Fortune*, Burtin frequently juxtaposed images that included diverse media, drawing with photography, color with black-and-white, precise line drawing with spontaneous brushwork. Cover designs were highly suggestive: juxtapositions between technical drawing, photography, and painting, with roots in Dada and Surrealist photomontage and collage in the interwar period, stimulated a creative, imaginative reading of medical research developments for an audience less familiar with particular technical knowledge of the field, while charts accompanying articles within the magazine clarified new research developments and their applications (fig. 11.23). Burtin's efforts for Upjohn were not limited to the printed page. He also explored information design in three dimensions, designing a 24-foot (7.3-meter)-wide working model of a human cell for Upjohn in 1958 (fig. 11.24) that was displayed at the annual convention of

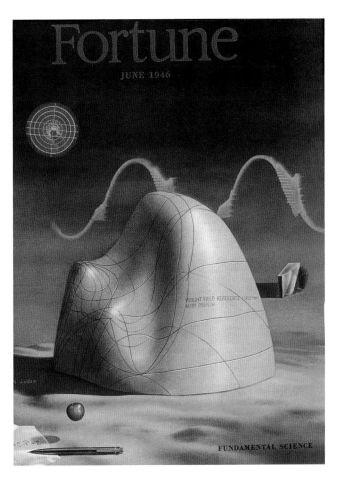

11.23 Will Burtin, cover design, *Fortune* magazine, June 1946. Rochester Institute of Technology, Archives and Special Collections, New York.

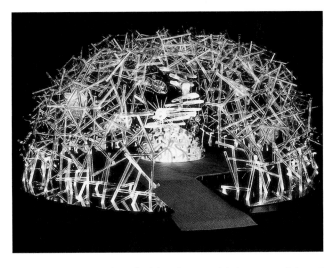

11.24 Will Burtin, Upjohn cell exhibit, plastic model, diameter 24 ft (7.3 m) diameter, 1958. Upjohn Pharmaceutical Company.

the Amerian Medical Association. A tour-de-force that included lights and circuits to show movement and arouse interest in the wonders of science, Burtin's work in this area expanded the boundaries of graphic presentation to include dramatic, interactive displays.

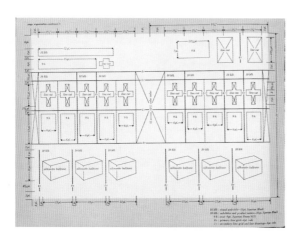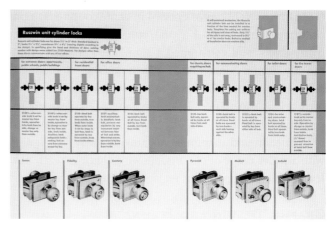

11.25 Page from K. Lönberg-Holm and Ladislav Sutnar's *Catalog Design Progress*, published by Sweet's Catalog Service (Division of F. W. Dodge Corporation), New York, 1950.

In 1959, the Eameses designed a multi-screen display for the American National Exhibition in Moscow that featured images of technology and everyday life with a running time of just over 12 minutes. Informational exhibits became an important part of the consultancy's design activities, which included a series of exhibits for the IBM Corporation (see fig. 11.86). Postwar designers such as Burtin and the Eameses saw themselves as contributing, through information design, to the shaping of a shared belief and public confidence in broad cultural progress through technology within the framework of corporate capitalism and government investment.

While book and magazine cover design afforded opportunities for designers to explore metaphors and juxtaposition to suggest content, the role of graphic designers in clarifying technical information was also an important contribution of the profession. Burtin occasionally used the services of the Czechoslovakian designer Ladislav Sutnar (1897–1976) for the presentation of charts and other quantitative information. Living in the United States from 1940 and committed to the principles of the New Typography as articulated by Jan Tschichold in the 1920s, Sutnar worked for Sweet's Catalog Service, a company specializing in visual systems to communicate information for products primarily serving the building industry and parts manufacturers. In books such as *Catalog Design Progress* (fig. 11.25), published in 1950, Sutnar and his collaborator K. Lönberg-Holm created standards for the graphic presentation of technical information based upon reduced use of text, visual clarity, and immediate impact. The authors cited signage for the transportation industry, such as road signs on highways, as examples of the necessity and importance of clarity and recognition as guiding principles of information graphics. They explained further in the introduction to their book that:

To many people, standards mean only uniformity and restriction, something negative and static. Opposed to this concept of the word is one which may be illustrated by a commonly used expression, like living standards. This may suggest variation, as among the living standards of different parts of the world, or progress, as from the time of the earliest American settlers to the present. In short, the word has potential for implying something dynamic, not static – something which is always changing, advancing.

Sutnar brought the same clarity and order to the creation of unified graphic standards for Carr's self-service department stores in New Jersey (1956–1957), and a system of easily recognized symbols for the Bell Telephone Company. Both projects are examples of the adoption of visual systems for identifying products and communicating a sense of organization through visual order and consistency. Such work made Sutnar a pioneer in the development of "house styles" for many large businesses in the postwar era.

Bauhaus student and instructor Herbert Bayer, who settled in the United States in 1938, produced one of the richest examples of information graphics, the *World Geographic Atlas*, published in 1953 by the Container Corporation of America (CCA). It featured technical information in a rich variety of subject areas related to geography, climate, and natural resources. An exercise in the effective visual presentation of information, it also fit within the humanistic framework of postwar design: figure 11.26 from the *World Geographic Atlas* used a human figure at the center of a series of overlapping concentric circles to illustrate the interrelationship between ourselves, our natural resources, and our economy. The book also exemplifies the often close relationship between corporations and the promotion of

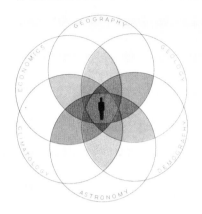

11.26 Herbert Bayer, *World Geographic Atlas*, Chicago, for Container Corporation of America, 1953.

modern design after World War II, the compatibility of technology, commerce, and democratic cultural values. During the 1960s, a number of graphic designers began to question the "marriage of commerce and culture" and sought alternative approaches to redefine the relationship between design and the business clients whose interests they served. The document "First Things First," which appeared in the British newspaper the *Guardian* in 1964 (see page 356) is one example of this emerging attitude.

Whether through cover art, advertising, art direction, or information design, designers such as Burtin, Brodovitch, Agha, Rand, Sutnar, Bayer, and Lustig expanded the vocabulary and techniques and awareness of graphic design in a variety of contexts in the decade following the end of World War II. These ranged from product advertisements to magazine covers and layouts, to logos and house styles, technical manuals, and the design of information for exhibits and displays. Design projects used high-quality color reproduction of illustrations and photographs, and solutions proceeded with technical freedom made possible through reduced reliance upon metal type. Large corporations and publishers helped to provide designers with a wealth of varied opportunities to develop original solutions to the challenges not only of selling products, but also of building public support for the promise of research and technology to a postwar audience.

SCANDINAVIA AND BRITAIN

Scandinavian designers contributed directly and indirectly to the expansion of postwar modern design, through the manufacture of domestic and institutional furniture as well as in the manufacture of glassware, ceramics, lighting, and metal. They consistently won prizes at the postwar triennial

exhibitions held in Milan, Italy, were represented in the Museum of Modern Art and other museum collections, and their work was manufactured by or influenced the production of furniture companies such as Herman Miller and Knoll. The Scandinavian reputation for both natural and new materials and production technologies, and the consideration of factors of comfort and fitness to purpose, combined with a respect for individual expression. Their work helped to define an international modernism that was successfully marketed for home furnishings as well as public buildings after World War II.

The continued influence of craft in the career of Alvar Aalto is seen in the persistence of materials such as brick or tile, explored for their effects of color and texture on the exterior or even the interior of buildings, and were brought into harmony with his sensitive and efficient use of wood in examples such as the Baker House dormitory at the Massachusetts Institute of Technology, built between 1946 and 1949 (fig. 11.27). The interiors feature exposed plumbing and maximize efficient storage utilizing the space beneath beds as well as built-in closets and cabinets (all designed by Aalto and manufactured by Artek), while the plan provides for rooms of varied and irregular shapes rather than uniform cell-like proportions.

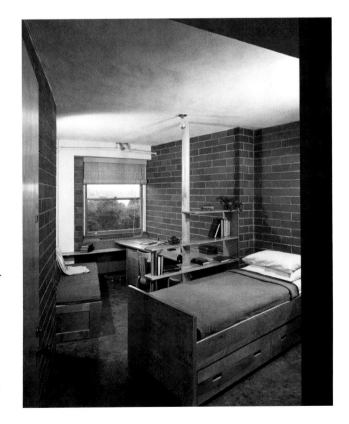

11.27 Alvar Aalto, student's room, Baker House, campus of the Massachusetts Institute of Technology, Cambridge, Massachusetts, 1946–1949.

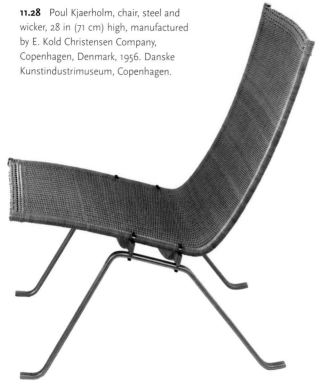

11.28 Poul Kjaerholm, chair, steel and wicker, 28 in (71 cm) high, manufactured by E. Kold Christensen Company, Copenhagen, Denmark, 1956. Danske Kunstindustrimuseum, Copenhagen.

rubber, covered in leather (as well as in a variety of other fabrics), and supported by a stainless steel pedestal base. The Egg chair and accompanying ottoman were designed for the Scandinavian Airlines System (SAS) hotel and terminal in Copenhagen. Jacobsen also served as the architect for these buildings, and designed their full range of furnishings from carpeting to cutlery. The organic forms of the Egg chair, with their deep cavities and winglike projections, go considerably beyond considerations of ergonomics and the psychology of comfort; they recall the abstract sculpture of Henry Moore or Jean Arp (see fig. 11.8). They demonstrate the sculptural possibilities of modern industrial materials such as fiberglass as a basis for individual expression. Jacobsen's designs are an intersection of technology and art rather than technology as a vehicle for social reform or the achievement of universal collective standards based primarily upon utility.

The combination of variety and standardization preserves a balance between individual and social considerations in design. It is not surprising that Aalto eulogized Henry van de Velde (see pages 136–137) after his death in 1957 with words of praise for the individual artistic and human qualities of his oeuvre.

Equally committed to industrial methods of production using lightweight materials and metals was the Danish designer Poul Kjaerholm (1929–1980). Kjaerholm was trained as a traditional furniture-maker, and his chair designs continued to use natural materials such as leather, cane, and wicker combined with steel construction. His steel and wicker chair (fig. 11.28) has a startlingly simple design based upon the balance of the opposing curves for the seat and one-piece footed legs, joined by clamps. Manufactured in Copenhagen by E. Kold Christensen in 1956, the chair combines an economical use of materials, industrial methods of production, as well as an emphasis upon factors of comfort and fluid linear refinement.

The furniture of Danish designer Arne Jacobsen (1902–1971) illustrates the more individual and sculptural character of Scandinavian design in the post-World War II period. Jacobsen's Egg chair of 1957 (fig. 11.29) was constructed of molded fiberglass, upholstered in foam

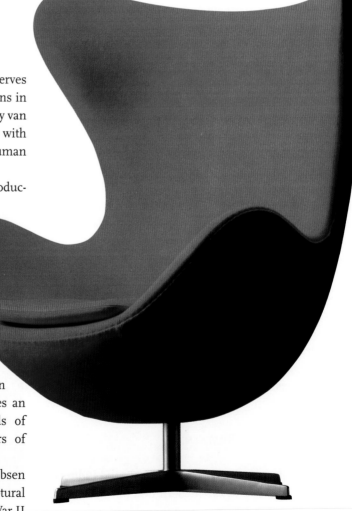

11.29 Arne Jacobsen, Egg chair, fiberglass and chromed steel with leather-covered foam rubber upholstery, 41 ⅞ in (106.4 cm) high, Fritz Hansen, Allerød, Denmark, 1957.

In addition to furniture, the Scandinavian approach to industrial design included other products with strong craft traditions behind them, such as glassware, ceramics, textiles, and metalwork. Aalto's glassware has already been mentioned (see fig. 9.61). An emphasis upon craft and the exploration of materials can be seen in the metalwork of Danish designer Henning Koppel (1918–1981). Koppel's designs in silver were exclusive products manufactured by Georg Jensen. His silver pitcher (fig. 11.30), although reminiscent of traditional, even utilitarian forms, suggests the smooth surfaces and exaggerations of abstract sculpture, particularly in the treatment of the curved handle that connects organically with the pitcher's base and lip, echoes its front curve, and accentuates the negative space between handle and pinched neck.

In Scandinavian glassware and ceramics, a more practical expression in the postwar period continued with the work of Finnish designer Kaj Franck (1911–1989). Franck served as artistic director for the Arabia Company in Helsinki, for whom he designed the Kilta earthenware table service beginning in 1952 (fig. 11.31). This tableware exhibits a preference for slightly tapered cylindrical forms in a small range of colors (originally white, black, yellow, and green) with undecorated surfaces. Handles and knobs are equally simple and unobtrusive, and the consistency of these elements surpasses in its purity and unified expression the equally utilitarian Fiestaware (see fig. 10.29), whose pieces retain molded and scalloped handles and bases.

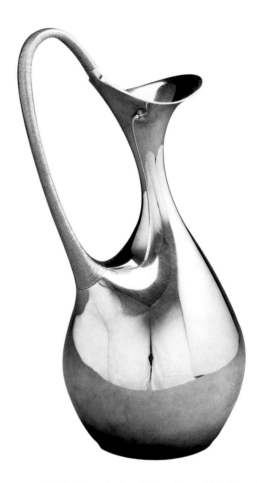

11.30 Henning Koppel, wine pitcher, silver, 13 ⅞ in (34 cm) high, manufactured by Georg Jensen Sølvsmedie (silversmiths), Copenhagen, Denmark, 1948. Musée des Arts Décoratifs de Montreal.

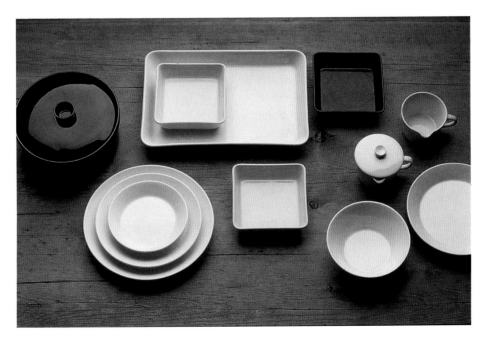

11.31 Kaj Franck, Kilta table service, glazed earthenware, diameter of largest plate 9 ⅛ in (23 cm), manufactured by Wärtsilä Arabia Company, Helsinki, Finland, 1952.

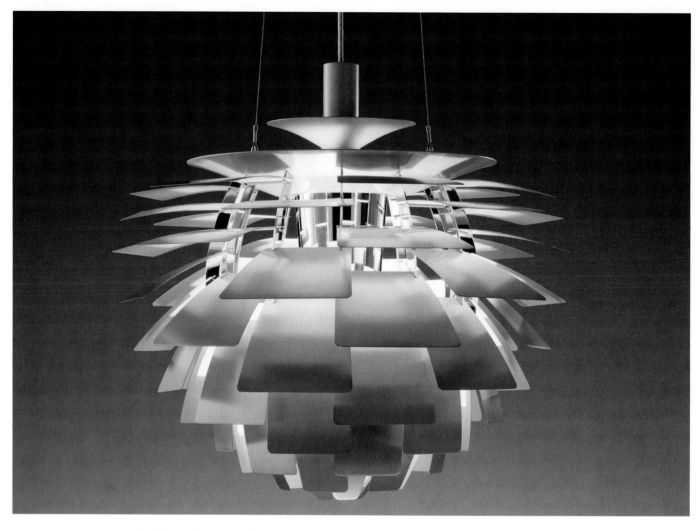

11.32 Poul Henningsen, Artichoke hanging lamp, copper, height 27 ⅛ in (69 cm), diameter 33 ⅛ in (84 cm), Louis Poulsen Company, Copenhagen, 1958.

In lighting, the hanging lamps of Poul Henningsen (1894–1967), manufactured by the Louis Poulsen Company in Copenhagen as early as 1926 (they were exhibited at the 1925 Exposition Internationale des Arts Décoratifs et Industriels Modernes in Paris), combine simple curved geometric forms in concentric and inverted arrangements to evenly diffuse interior light (fig. 11.33). After World War II, Henningsen expanded the vocabulary of elementary geometric components so characteristic of interwar modernism into more intricate and sculptural designs, such as the Artichoke hanging lamp of 1958 (fig. 11.32). The transformation is characteristic of an increasing artistic freedom in Scandinavian design, seen as part of an ideology stressing comfortable living as refuge from a cold climate, long distances between major cities, and consequently large amounts of time spent indoors.

Flexibility remained a principle of Scandinavian design. For instance, when designer and critic George Nelson praised the virtues of Scandinavian design in

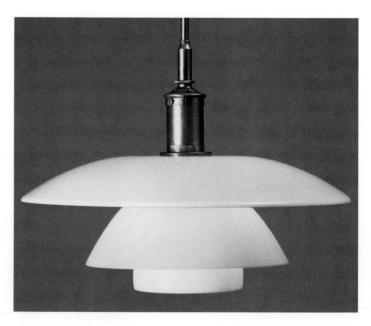

11.33 Poul Henningsen, hanging lamp, opal glass and brass, diameter 19 ⅝ in (50 cm), Louis Poulsen Company, Copenhagen, 1926.

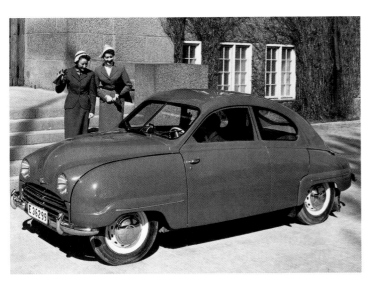

11.34 Saab 92 automobile, Svenska Aeroplan Aktiebolaget Company, Linköping, Sweden, 1950–1952.

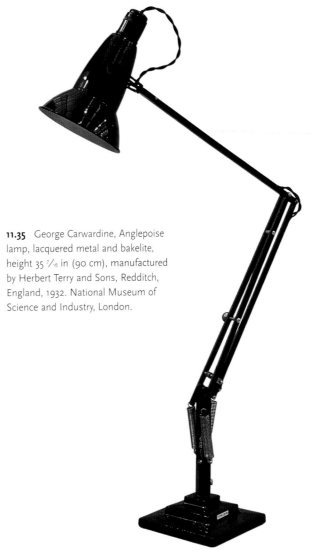

11.35 George Carwardine, Anglepoise lamp, lacquered metal and bakelite, height 35 ⁷/₁₆ in (90 cm), manufactured by Herbert Terry and Sons, Redditch, England, 1932. National Museum of Science and Industry, London.

urban housing, he also cited the efficiency of design planning for open, multi-purpose apartments filled with modular furniture. According to Nelson, such efficiency extended to the provision of social services for childcare and emphasis upon how a sense of community reduced the need for individual families to own large homes or purchase products to satisfy every need.

Qualities of comfort combined with fitness-to-purpose may also be seen in Scandinavian industrial design, particularly in the Saab 92 automobile manufactured in 1950–1952 by Svenska Aeroplan Aktiebolaget Company in Linköping, Sweden. As a consultant to the airline company that produced the original model, Swedish industrial designer Sixton Sason (1912–1967) contributed to the 1950 Saab 92 (fig. 11.34). With its swept-back hood and tapered body, the Saab is streamlined and strongly unified in appearance, and less geometric in form than the German Volkswagen. Perhaps owing to the aviation orientation of the company that produced it, the gauges and controls on the Saab 92 and Saab 93 were placed to ensure easy recognition and operation. As a result of meeting practical needs and integrating an aerodynamic approach to the form of the body, these early models underwent few changes, remaining in production for almost 30 years. The design of the dashboard and controls for the Saab 92 provides a model for later interest in user-centered design that incorporates a natural relationship between controls, the function or functions they perform, and the ease with which those functions and movements can be understood by those who operate them. These themes emerged in books by Donald Norman such as *The Design of Everyday Things*, published in 1988. The Saab

represented an alternative to the American automobile industry with its focus upon visual appeal, annual model changes, power, individual expression, and leisure.

The influence of Scandinavia, as well as a more gradual shift in modern industrial design from standardized and low-cost solutions toward more individual interpretations of modernism, also may be seen in Britain following World War II. Between the wars, British industrial designers followed a utilitarian and practical approach, seen, for instance, in the well-known Anglepoise desk lamp designed by George Carwardine (1887–1948) in 1932 (fig. 11.35). The exposure of the lamp's mechanical parts suggests a relation to technical equipment rather than domestic furnishings. Following the war, lingering austerity stemming from material shortages and rationing (not lifted until 1952) favored the continuation of an economical approach at the expense of aesthetic considerations. The liberal Labour Party government brought to

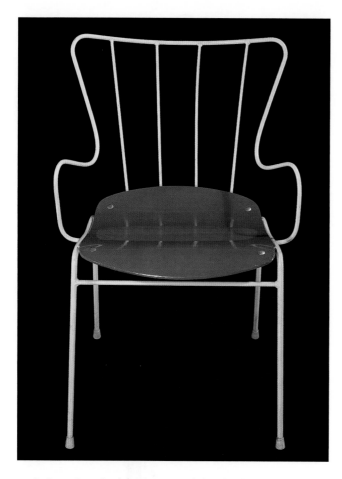

11.36 Ernest Race, Antelope chair, enameled steel and painted plywood, 31 ⅛ in (79 cm), manufactured by Race Furniture, England, 1951. Victoria and Albert Museum, London.

Scandinavian (chiefly Danish) models, focusing upon ease of assembly, lightness, industrial materials, and undecorated wooden components. British examples of postwar modern design include Ernest Race's (1913–1963) Antelope chair featuring the use of enameled metal wire (fig. 11.36). The chair was exhibited at the 1951 Festival of Britain. The timing of the Festival sounded a note of optimism, commemorating the 100th anniversary of the Crystal Palace Exhibition of 1851 (see pages 63–68).

Modern British interiors after World War II generally had white rather than papered walls, while upholstery fabric emphasized textural variety with muted earth tones rather than bright colors. A broad range of new surface designs was developed for the Festival of Britain, with patterns for curtains and ceramics often featuring delicate line drawing in an abbreviated, often childlike style with a variety of abstract organic shapes as well as simplified representational motifs. Examples include Viennese-born Marianne Mahler's (1911–1983) Bird and Bowl design from 1951, printed on the synthetic fabric rayon and manufactured by David Whitehead Ltd. (fig. 11.37). Another source of inspiration for abstract textile patterns was the microscopic world of molecular structures, revealed in the

power in 1945 favored nationalized services, including healthcare and subsidized "housing estates" built to meet minimum working-class needs. The legacy of Modernism was strong, favoring standardization, industrial materials and production, and modest, responsible modern living. Government regulation required that furniture designs be approved before they could be manufactured on the basis of economy and a sense of discrimination along modernist guidelines, as seen in photographs of a domestic interior from 1945 (see fig. 10.46). Such guidelines formed the basis of the 1946 exhibition Britain Can Make It. Such narrow parameters for postwar design in Britain broadened through the later 1940s, and began to incorporate the heritage of craft traditions and natural materials to give products a distinctively national identity in the hope of competing in the export market and appealing to popular taste. At the same time, government-sponsored design initiatives such as the Design Research Group emphasized testing and research to encourage manufacturers to hire industrial designers, while department stores such as Heals offered modern furniture designs inspired by

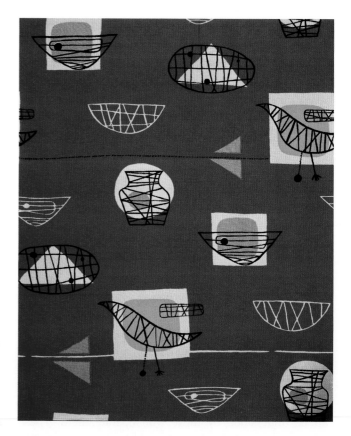

11.37 Marianne Mahler, Bird and Bowl pattern, roller-printed rayon, 18 in (46 cm), manufactured by David Whitehead Ltd., 1951.

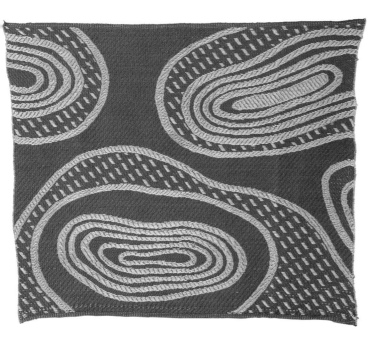

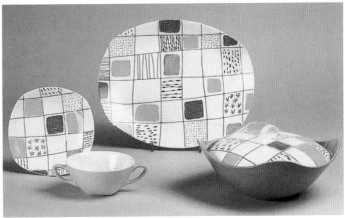

11.39 Sir Terence Conran, Chequers range, molded earthenware with printed and sponged decoration, for W. R. Midwinter Ltd., Burslem.

11.38 Marianne Straub, *Surrey*, wool and cotton tapestry, red, gold, and cream, manufactured by Warner & Sons Ltd. for the Festival Pattern Group Scheme and used for curtains in the Regatta Restaurant at the Royal Festival Hall, London, 1951.

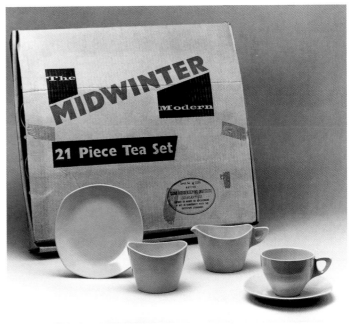

11.40 A. H. Woodfull, John Vale, and Roy Midwinter, Midwinter Modern tea set, melamine, cup height 3 in (7.6 cm), plate diameter 6 ¼ in (16 cm), sugar bowl height 3 in (7.6 cm), manufactured by Midwinter Modern Line, 1956.

woven fabric entitled *Surrey* designed by Marianne Straub (1909–1994) for Warner & Sons Ltd. in 1951 (fig. 11.38). In textile design, materials technology in home furnishings, and in marketing for the pharmaceutical industry, many initiatives in design internationally dealt with the applications and humanization of science, whether through decorative patterns, information graphics, or new materials for domestic products (see pages 273–274). Such efforts, at the Festival of Britain and elsewhere, are related in the promotion of common understanding in a complex, technological world of specialized scientific knowledge.

Industrial materials and methods of production were also applied to contemporary ceramics and interior furnishings from the early 1950s. Sir Terence Conran (b. 1931) designed earthenware dinnerware in square and rectangular forms with rounded edges, decorated with a hand-drawn checkerboard background filled with colored swatches and irregular patterns of lines, dots, and dashes (fig. 11.39). In many ways such examples are similar to the playful patterns seen in textile design from the same period (see fig. 11.37).

The 1950s also saw the introduction of new resins used as an alternative to ceramics for table service. A. H. Woodfull (b. 1912), together with John Vale and Roy Midwinter, designed a tea set in 1956 called Midwinter Modern (fig. 11.40). Marketed as "break-resistant" tableware, the white tea set was made of melamine, a form of hard industrial plastic. Midwinter Modern featured round-edged rectangular plates and sloping edges for the creamer and sugar bowl, emphasizing smooth but irregular organic forms. In the United States, Russel Wright also designed several comparable sets of dinnerware using plastics and intended for informal, festive home entertaining, with instructions for how to arrange plates and utensils for self-serving published by Wright in his 1950 book *Guide to Easier Living*.

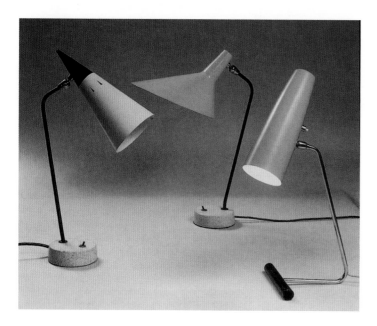

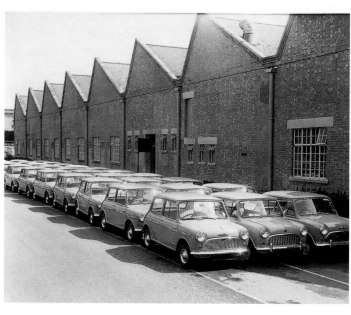

11.41 Anonymous, adjustable desk lamps, painted aluminum and brass, average height 20 in (51 cm), various manufacturers (Oswald Hollman Ltd., Beckenham, Troughton & Young Ltd.), London, c. 1955.

11.42 Alec Issigonis, Morris Mini, Morris Motor Company, Birmingham, UK, 1959.

This period also saw the introduction of metal in a variety of lighting fixtures, from desk lamps to standing lamps resembling microphone stands. Bulbs were enclosed in a variety of conical forms and the lamps were generally made of thin steel rods and painted aluminum, marketed for their adjustable height and direction (fig. 11.41). Aesthetically they possess thin, wiry forms favored for their lightness and harmony with built-in furniture, reduced upholstery, and more open interior spaces. As design historian Jonathan Woodham has argued, it is difficult to assess popular reaction to postwar modern design in Britain, since our main sources of information comes from groups such as the Council of Industrial Design (COID), which sponsored exhibitions and promoted shared standards and values. To judge from British receptivity to American popular culture, legislating taste was no easier in 1951 than efforts of design reformers a century earlier.

In London, maximizing available space led to new approaches to efficient housing, with more open plans and modern construction techniques using steel girders, permitting larger expanses of windows, and combined living and dining areas. Such design solutions stressed informal living geared to families and accommodating home entertainment in the form of stereo systems and television sets as well as wall units and other built-in furniture to create open and flexible floor space. This efficient, economical, and utilitarian approach was shaped by a desire for shared egalitarian values and parallels the introduction of government-sponsored socialized services

for medicine and welfare for the unemployed. More or less official views of design promoted a clear understanding of the distinction between needs and wants and an acceptance of the realities and restrictions of urban population density. Later in the decade, such values and the standards upon which they were based came under attack. The result was a renewed emphasis on one hand upon the importance of research and ergonomics in product development and on the other hand skepticism toward practicality and utility as the self-evident and abiding determinants of design, especially in competitive economic conditions. Yet despite growing fascination with American popular culture in Britain, and a search for alternatives to practical standards, the premises of economy and efficiency continued to inspire such successful products as the 1959 Mini automobile, designed for the British Motor Corporation by Alec Issigonis in 1959 (fig. 11.42). This efficient and space-saving vehicle was the British counterpart to the earlier Fiat 600 in Italy for inexpensive and basic personal transportation.

Also in Britain the legacy of craft and values associated with the dialogue between artisan and materials found expression in the oeuvre of Bernard Leach (1887–1979). Leach was active at least from the end of World War I, when he returned from Japan after having studied pottery with a well-known Japanese ceramic master. Leach practiced the technique of raku ceramics, fired at lower temperatures and modeled rather than thrown on a wheel. His designs, such as a stoneware bowl from 1957 (fig. 11.43), preserve and extend the vitality of handicraft

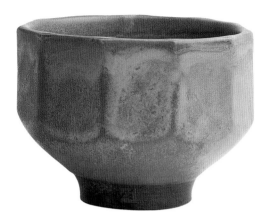

11.43 Bernard Leach, bowl, stoneware, diameter 6 in (15 cm), 1957. Victoria and Albert Museum, London.

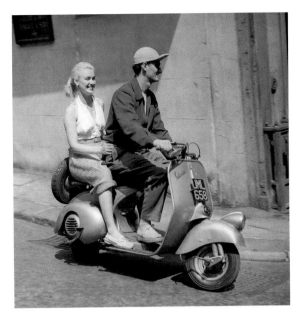

11.44 Corradino D'Ascanio, Vespa motor scooter, Piaggio Corporation, Pontedera (Pisa), Italy, 1946.

traditions as they were practiced in Japan and became a part of the Aesthetic and related movements in Europe and the United States in the later nineteenth century. Leach also designed teapots and other wares for serial production as an alternative to newer industrial materials. Less directly related to earlier movements of reform or utopian ideology, the persistence of craft continued to be a viable element of modern design history in Britain, the United States, Italy, and elsewhere.

ITALY

The conscious development of an international market and national image for modern Italian design was a phenomenon of the postwar era, and took place in a political climate of anxiety amid Cold War tensions between Communism and Capitalism in defining the nature of democratic values. Until 1948 Communists were the political majority in Italy, and sought to address pressing social needs for housing and affordable industrially designed goods and furnishings. One of the most potent symbols of industrial design to emerge in the immediate postwar years was the Vespa motor scooter, designed in 1946 by Corradino D'Ascanio (1891–1981) for the Piaggio Corporation (fig. 11.44). The Vespa was an efficient, practical, and inexpensive mode of personal transportation, but the emphasis upon streamlined housing, enclosure of mechanical parts, and cutaway profile of the seat introduced a graceful, expressive element to the design, connecting mobility with spontaneity and personal freedom in a period of economic reconstruction. Other standardized and affordable industrially manufactured products, for instance the tiny Fiat 600 of 1955 designed by Dante Giacosa, were more aligned with utilitarian and practical considerations in both economical production and performance, providing

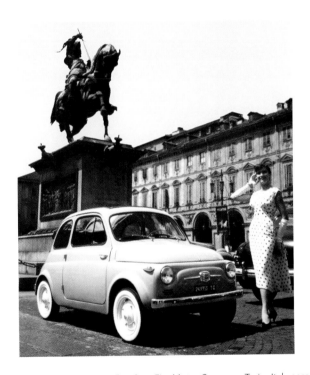

11.45 Dante Giacosa, Fiat 600, Fiat Motor Company, Turin, Italy, 1955.

four-wheel transportation and contributing to a tremendous domestic increase in automobile sales, estimated at 400 percent between 1950 and 1961 (fig. 11.45).

Following the American industrial design model of the 1930s, and strongly supported by the Marshall Plan and a more centrist government after elections in 1948, Italian companies adopting mechanized mass-production

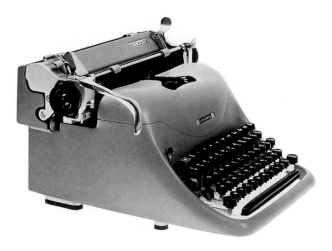

11.46 Marcello Nizzoli, Lexikon 80 typewriter, enameled aluminum housing, 9 x 15 x 15 in (22.8 x 38.1 x 38.1 cm), manufactured by Olivetti ING, Ivrea, Italy, 1948.

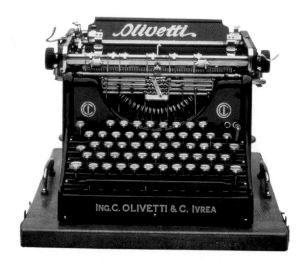

11.47 Camillo Olivetti, MI typewriter, metal, height 14 ¹⁵⁄₁₆ in (38 cm), Olivetti ING, Ivrea, Italy, c. 1911.

technology generally relied upon consultants to provide new designs, often for the export market. With a steady and inexpensive supply of labor, guaranteed by weak labor unions and government subsidies to industrial corporations, Italian manufacturers could justify the added cost of hiring designers in order to expand the international market for their products. The value of those products was in turn enhanced by an association with individual designers who left their unique mark upon manufactured goods.

The independence and contributions of the consultant designer was an acknowledged feature in Italian industrial manufacturing for corporations such as Olivetti after World War II. The designer was an integral member of a process that included marketing as well as engineering. The dialogue among participants was often distinguished

by a sense of drama and conflict rather than hierarchical directive. As described by Sybil Kircherer in her study of the Olivetti Corporation, the strategy resulted in creativity and a dynamic internal as well as external design identity. The Olivetti Corporation, for instance, relied upon painter and architect Marcello Nizzoli (1887–1969). Although hired in the later 1930s by Adriano Olivetti, son of the company's founder, Nizzoli assumed a more significant role in product design after World War II. An early example was the Lexikon 80 typewriter of 1948 (fig. 11.46), distinguished by its fluid, organic housing and integrated curved panel covering the mechanism, creating a sense of abstract sculptural form in comparison with the angular, black, standardized models manufactured earlier by Olivetti (fig. 11.47). Olivetti also employed graphic designer Giovanni Pintori for advertising and corporate communication. His colorful posters for the company's business machines use asymmetrical layouts and juxtapose the photograph of a product with a flat abstract design that suggests the dynamic action of the machine, whether a typewriter key or ribbon (fig. 11.48). Pintori's

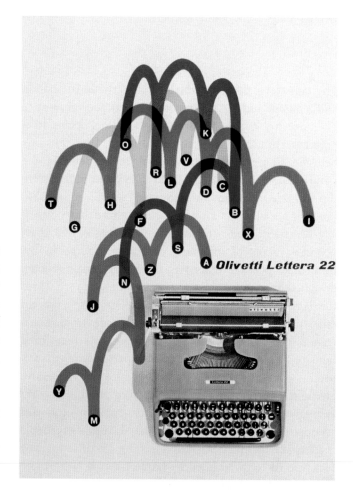

11.48 Giovanni Pintori, advertising poster for Olivetti, c. 1953.

store La Rinascente, for the integration of aesthetic and practical elements in the design of products for industrial production. The reputation of Italian design in an international context was also promoted in the journal *Domus*, particularly under the editorship first of Ernesto Rogers (1909–1969) and then Gio Ponti (beginning in 1947), which stressed the human and creative element in modern industrial design as well as its practical, economic, and social benefits.

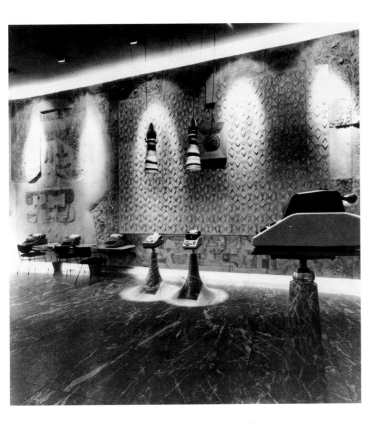

11.49 Ernesto Rogers, Lodovico Belgiojoso, and Enrico Peressutti, Olivetti Showroom, New York, 1954.

abstractions create a sense of dynamic mechanized movement, an aesthetic that extended to the company's showrooms as well, including the hanging lamp manufactured by Venini & Company for the Olivetti Showroom in New York in 1954 and designed by the architectural partners Ernesto Rogers, Lodovico Belgiojoso, and Enrico Peressutti (figs. 11.49). The dramatic presentation placed the business machines beyond of the context of the office, adding appeal and value in an international market.

Originality provided an aesthetic dimension for any number of otherwise ordinary standardized utilitarian products, for instance, Gio Ponti's (1891–1979) asymmetrically balanced commode and dramatically flared pedestal sink designed for Ideal Standard in 1953/4 (fig. 11.50). Ponti's bathroom fixtures received recognition at the 1957 Milan Triennale. These exhibitions, organized as early as the 1920s and revived after the war beginning in 1948, were responsible for increasing the visibility of Italian design in an international setting. Italian products were featured alongside those of Scandinavian, German, American, and British designers, aimed at the sophisticated, high-end market and often exhibited in response to a theme, such as the "Form of the Useful" (1951). The Triennale competition awarded prizes (known as the "golden compass"), sponsored by the Italian department

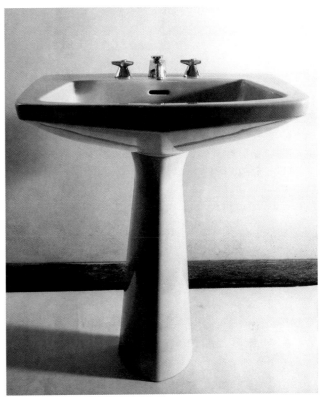

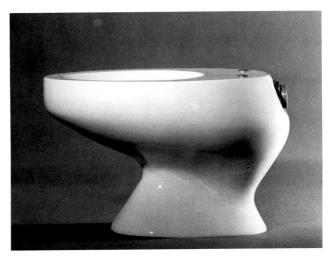

11.50 Gio Ponti, sink and commode, porcelain, sink height 31 ½ in (80 cm), and commode height 15 in (38 cm), manufactured by Ideal Standard, Milan, 1953/4.

At the same time, Ponti brought a humanizing factor into Italian design, emphasizing the persistence and continued transformation of traditional artisanal production. A case in point is his Superleggera chair of 1957 (fig. 11.51). This is a modern reinterpretation of a nineteenth-century wood and cane rush-seat design, emphasizing the light, tapered forms seen in plywood and metal, but also implying a relationship between design and the national heritage of craft skill in wood, glass, ceramics, and stone. An earlier version of this chair, known as the Leggera, which was produced for the Good Design exhibitions at the Museum of Modern Art in 1951, used cellophane rather than cane for the seat.

The Turinese manufacturer Cassina adopted mass-production technology for furniture in the years immediately after World War II. In the 1950s the firm emerged as an industrial leader, integrating the use of modern materials such as plywood and tubular steel with the tapered, organic forms featured in other products, and allowing freedom for individual designers to explore aesthetic possibilities of new techniques. In many ways the experiments of Italian designers parallel the interests of designers such as Charles and Ray Eames in molded industrial materials. Marco Zanuso (1916–2001) experimented with

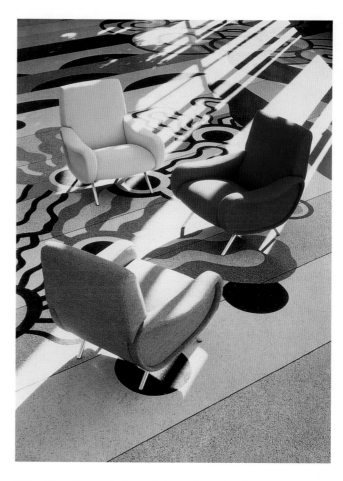

11.52 Marco Zanuso, Lady armchair, wood, metal, and elastic webbing, with fabric-covered foam-rubber upholstery, height 32 ¼ in (82 cm), manufactured by Arflex, Milan, 1951.

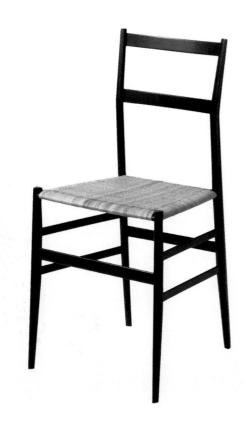

11.51 Gio Ponti, Superleggera chair, tinted ash and cane, height 32 in (81.3 cm), manufactured by Figli di Amedeo Cassina, Milan, 1957. Philadelphia Museum of Art.

the use of solid-colored fabric over a foam-rubber core to replace conventional upholstery in the design of his Lady chair for the Arflex Company in 1951 (a division of the Pirelli Corporation, otherwise known for rubber tire manufacturing, of which foam rubber was a byproduct). The chair (fig. 11.52) is composed of broad, regular curving forms supported by thin metal legs, and also received an award at the Milan Triennale of that year.

Equally inventive during the decade following the end of World War II were examples of lighting designed and manufactured in Italy. Simple and flexible, designs such as the 1949 Tubino by Achille (1918–2002) and Pier Giacomo Castiglioni (1913–1968) and manufactured by Arredoluce, eschewed conventional fabric shades and pedestal bases in favor of plastics, light metal, and thin tubing to conceal electric wiring (fig. 11.53). The simplicity of the Castiglioni's designs derives from the brothers' stated subordination of the fixture itself to the "effects of light it produces." Yet the remaining form, however negligible, retains an undeniable abstract linear character, akin to a delicate line drawing or to automatic writing.

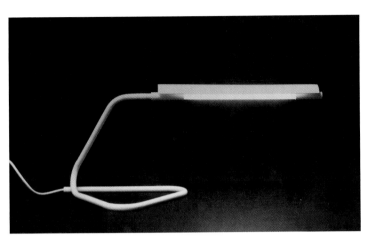

11.53 Achille and Pier Giacomo Castiglioni, Tubino desk lamp, enameled metal and aluminum, height 11 ¹¹⁄₁₆ in (28 cm), manufactured by Arredoluce, 1949.

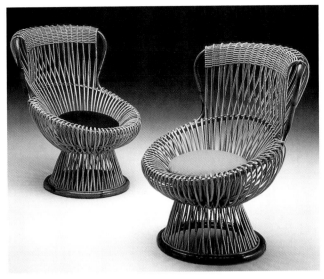

11.54 Franco Albini and Franca Helg, Margherita armchair, rattan and upholstery, 39 ⅛ in (99.4 cm) high, manufactured by Vittorio Bonacina, 1950.

The flexible plastics used for a number of Italian lighting designs in the 1950s also appear in domestic kitchenware pioneered by the Milan-based Kartell Company, whose in-house designer, Gino Colombini (b. 1915), developed an array of containers and simple kitchen machines with tapered forms that not only fulfilled functional requirements but also introduced a colorful and playful element into design. Bright colors and bold advertising combined to reduce the association of cooking and cleaning with demeaning labor or domestic science, making them instead part of a "modern" lifestyle linked to ease and a carefree atmosphere.

A number of design historians have pointed out that the Italian furniture industry did not entirely abandon its craft roots, despite the shift to industrial materials and other modern production technologies. It still maintained small workshops, primarily because they were capable of shorter production runs and were less reliant upon costly capital investment. These factors led to a combination of innovation and variety together with standardization in products that included the Superleggera as well as the Margherita armchair designed by Franco Albini (1905–1977) and Franca Helg (1920–1989). The latter was manufactured by the Bonacina Company in 1950, using traditional cane as well as a bentwood frame, in a design emphasizing the relationships of abstract curved and oval shapes (fig. 11.54). The craft element in Italian design surfaced as well in the growing reputation of leather goods and fashion in the postwar period, allied with "name" designers to lend distinction to products and accessories. While Fendi and Ferragamo are perhaps best associated internationally with this industry today, these designers inherited a postwar tradition initiated by Gucci leather accessories (named for Guccio Gucci).

Finally, while the Fiat models 500 and 600 dominated the domestic market for automobiles, accounting for 90 percent of sales in 1961, Italian car manufacturers also addressed the international high-end market with more streamlined, sculptural sports (rather than family) cars, where the legacy of custom coach-building and individuality expressed in graceful sculptural form continued. A well-known example is the 1946 Cisitalia sports car designed by Battista "Pinin" Farina (fig. 11.55), while models for industrial production included the more restrained Alfa Romeo Spider from the mid-1950s.

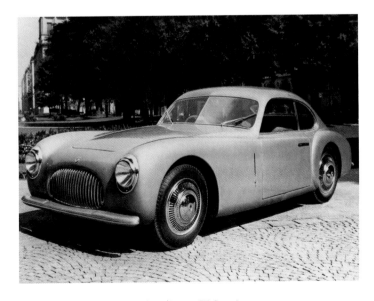

11.55 Battista "Pinin" Farina, Cisitalia 202 GT Coupé sports car, Pinin Farina, Torino, Italy, 1946.

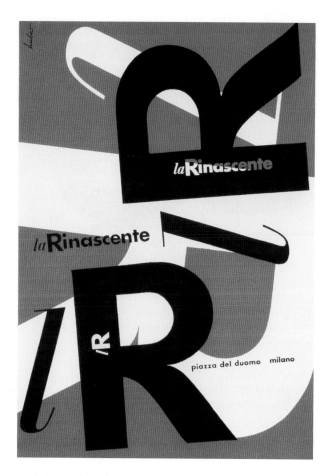

11.56 Max Huber, advertisement for La Rinascente department store, Milan, c. 1954–1958. M.A.X. Museum, Switzerland.

Rinascente department store designed by Max Huber (fig. 11.56). Huber's poster creates a playful, visually active typographic composition out of the letters "l" and "R." In addition to abrupt scale changes, overlapping, and inversions that recall the bold use of typography by the Futurists (see pages 181–183), Huber uses a combination of the sans serif "R" in Futura Bold with the more elegant Bodoni lower-case "l." According to graphic design historian Richard Hollis, the juxtaposition of the two typefaces may symbolize Milan's position between northern and Mediterranean cultural traditions.

GERMANY

Design played a large role in the economic reconstruction of West Germany following World War II. A number of examples of German industrially manufactured products demonstrate a kinship with the humanizing tendencies expressed through organic forms molded from modern materials, but more typically German industrial design is associated with objective standards based upon the systematic investigation of materials and processes. Precision and functional simplicity were factors in the international success of many electrical appliances in postwar Germany, associated foremost with the Braun Corporation of Frankfurt, founded in 1921 and rebuilt in 1945. The company established a connection with the newly founded Hochschule für Gestaltung at Ulm (1953) through Fritz Eichler (1911–1991), a member of the board of directors. Max Bill (1908–1994), the Hochschule's first director, was a graduate of the Bauhaus and sought to revive an approach to industrial design that emphasized studio practice and social responsibility in the design of prototypes for simple, practical, and efficiently produced furniture and objects of everyday use to improve the general standard of living in an increasingly technological age, and that equated technology with simplicity of appearance and function. In many ways Bill's approach to industrial design shared many elements not only with the Dessau Bauhaus but also with the practical, socially responsible standards for products and furnishings debated at the German Werkbund. This approach, known as "Gute Form," was the subject of an exhibition organized by Bill beginning in 1949 in Switzerland, which traveled in Germany and Austria during the 1950s. Such corporate and educational institutions tended to limit the role of individual expression and embraced a belief in research-based design solutions linked to performance and practicality. At the same time the establishment of a free market-based international economy in Germany also played a role in the relationship between design and manufacturing. All of these efforts were aided by the formation of

Contemporary with American and Scandinavian industrial designers, Italy helped to define the "new humanism" of the postwar era, embracing mechanized mass production and new materials technology while establishing a forceful role for the artist–designer within industry in the creation of useful, elegant products and an acknowledged aesthetic and individual element. Through periodicals such as *Domus*, the Milan Triennale and other exhibitions, Italian design achieved visibility and national identity within an expanding international market for consumer goods. Italian designers explored the creative use of modern materials and technology, individual expression parallel to modern abstract organic sculpture, and modern reinterpretations of enduring craft traditions. With the help of the Marshall Plan and the initiatives of companies such as Olivetti, postwar Italy exemplified the role of design in expanding industrial production, rebuilding national economies, and defining a modern, consumer-oriented lifestyle.

The character of postwar Italian design is also captured in advertising, for instance, in the posters, packaging, and window displays for the Milan-based La

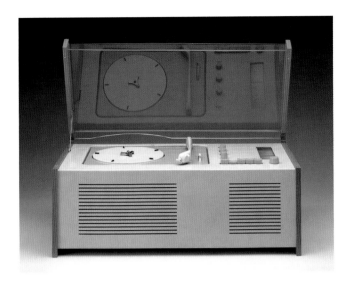

11.57 Max Braun, Dieter Rams, and Hans Gugelot, SK4 radio-phonograph, metal, wood, and Plexiglas, 9 ½ x 22 ⅞ x 11 ½ in (24 x 58 x 29 cm), Braun AG Kronberg, West Germany, 1956.

a German Design Council in 1949 and by the Marshall Plan to stimulate industrial production, economic recovery, and the restoration of consumer confidence.

Swiss-educated Hans Gugelot (1920–1965) and Dieter Rams (b. 1932), who worked as consultant designers for Braun, also served as faculty members at Ulm. They created a unified product identity for the corporation in response particularly to miniaturization, for instance with the use of transistors in electronics equipment, a technology that had emerged in the early 1940s. The SK4 radio-phonograph was designed by Max Braun, Rams, and Gugelot in 1956, and nicknamed "Snow White's Coffin" (fig. 11.57). The SK4 is a long rectangular box with hinged transparent plastic cover, housing controls, speaker grille, and other moving parts (tone-arm and turntable). All visible parts are reduced to circular or rectangular forms placed against smooth and flat surfaces. The arrangement of parts is controlled by a rectangular grid system for simple organization. The aesthetic purity and systematic approach to Braun design retain a relationship with the understated geometric abstraction of the period, seen for instance in Josef Albers' series of paintings entitled *Homage to the Square* (see below, figure 11.69), or to Max Bill's unexecuted project for a *Monument for the Unknown Political Prisoner* in Stuttgart in 1952, consisting of a connected series of boxlike structures set amid benches, far removed from traditional monumental heroic figural imagery. Such examples declared a belief in art as a life-affirming activity in the wake of World War II. Just as these minimalist approaches to fine art seem to demand a sophisticated and educated audience, so Braun products and design policy were not directed toward a mass market but rather to a discriminating audience with a more conscious awareness of abstract aesthetics and a belief in the connection between simple, undecorated forms and uncluttered, efficient modern living, rebuilding the German nation economically, socially, and spiritually.

Braun products emphasized enduring forms and determinants for design based upon considerations of production technology and fitness-to-purpose rather than upon rapid style change and obsolescence. In addition, products such as the Kitchen Machine of 1957 (fig. 11.58) possessed a sense of restraint, precision, and laboratorylike efficiency expressed through smooth white surfaces, qualities mentioned above in relation to contemporary abstract fine art and seen as well in the cool impersonality of buildings such as the Lever House (see fig. 11.10) or Mies van der Rohe's Seagram Building of 1954–1958. This approach to architecture dominated large public and corporate building projects in the decades after World War II, and was equally praised at the time for its beauty, efficiency, and responsible use of standardized and industrial methods of construction. The design of Braun products was not the inevitable outcome of a functional approach to industrial design, but rather the result of a combination of factors that included architectural and social theory, as well as a conscious and sophisticated aesthetic organization of geometrically abstract forms. The design program at Braun also reveals the increasing importance of corporate identity and branding as a commercial strategy in international business: house styles familiarized consumers with families of products and with logos and symbols that provided immediate recognition and differentiation among competitors. They also provided

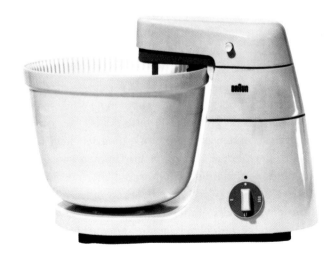

11.58 Gerd Alfred Müller, Kitchen Machine, polystyrol housing, 10 ¼ x 15 x 9 ½ in (26 x 38 x 24 cm), manufactured by Braun AG Kronberg, West Germany, 1957.

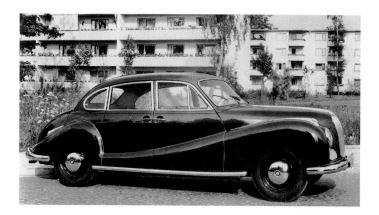

11.59 501 limousine, manufactured by BMW, AG Bayerische Motorenwerke Aktiengesellschaft, Munich, 1951.

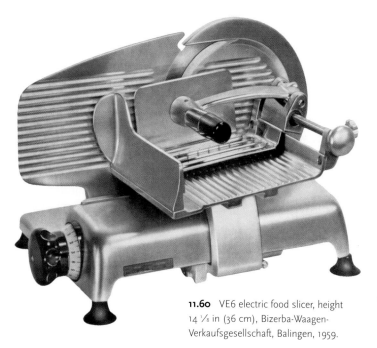

11.60 VE6 electric food slicer, height 14 ⅛ in (36 cm), Bizerba-Waagen-Verkaufsgesellschaft, Balingen, 1959.

designed by Ferdinand Porsche in 1937 as a "People's Car" and manufactured along Fordist lines to meet basic personal and family transportation needs primarily for the national market (see fig. 10.33). As in Italy, however, automobile manufacturing also extended to an international luxury market. Companies such as Daimler-Benz, Porsche, and BMW were receptive to combining fluid streamlined body housing with precision and a tradition of customized coach-building to produce high-performance vehicles in a higher price range, for instance the rear-engine streamlined 1952 Porsche 356 or the stately 1951 BMW 501 limousine model (fig. 11.59). An equally restrained sculptural approach to product housing may also be seen in the stainless steel VE6 electric food slicing machine dated to 1959 and manufactured by the Bizerba-Waagen-Verkaufsgesellschaft of Balingen (fig. 11.60).

We should not conclude this section without looking from West Germany toward the Communist East Germany, a division marked by the building of the Berlin wall in 1961 and a visible reminder of the Cold War. As recent exhibitions and scholarship have revealed, Eastern bloc countries soon after World War II adopted vernacular and traditional rather than Modernist approaches to architecture and design, which were viewed as "Western" and disconnected from popular taste in architecture and consumer goods. After the death of Joseph Stalin in 1953, urgent needs for housing led to greater receptivity toward Modernist design, demonstrating the domestic applications of new chemical technology. In East Germany, for instance, Albert Krause designed a set of hard plastic dishes in 1959 (fig. 11.61) in varied colors. Such efforts were similar to examples of postwar design in West Germany and elsewhere in the West and in Japan, even though some Communist officials continued to criticize modern design as "formalist" and removed from popular consumer tastes. While institutes were established to create prototypes for such goods, and

parameters and constraints for design that placed controls upon the process of change and emphasized design practice in the context of corporate communication. Designers not only gave form to products but also created an association between products and an image of efficient, uncluttered, technological modern living. While some designers criticized "Gute Form" for its failure to acknowledge diversity and playfulness, this approach helped to build an international reputation for German consumer goods and contributed to unprecedented economic reconstruction after World War II. As in other countries and in other fields of design, the 1960s witnessed challenges to the view of progress represented by modern postwar design, and resulted in alternatives to the practice and purposes of design activity (see page 355 onward).

Shortly after the war, Germany put into mass production the inexpensive and standardized Volkswagen Beetle

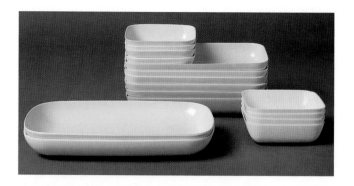

11.61 Albert Krause, set of dishes, plastic, long dishes 9 ⅛ x 5 ⅛ in (23.5 x 13.9 cm); square bowls 4 x 4 in (10.2 x 10.2 cm), manufactured by VEB Plast-Werke, Sonneberg, East Germany, 1959. The International Design Museum, Munich, Germany.

while designers visited the West for inspiration and models of how design functioned in industry, it was difficult for Soviet bloc countries to compete with free-market capitalism in the area of consumer products without adopting many of its forms and strategies, including an increasing emphasis upon consumption. At the same time, party leaders continued to believe in collective rather than individual need and in socialized rather than private services. Speaking in response to an exhibition of American automobiles in France in 1960, Soviet premier Nikita Khrushchev (1894–1971) proposed that the Soviet Union would develop a national system of rental cars to serve the needs of the Russian public rather than face the problems of too many cars caused by private ownership.

THE INTERNATIONAL TYPOGRAPHIC STYLE (DIE NEUE GRAFIK)

Also connected with Germany as well as Switzerland in the postwar period was the development of standards for graphic design and typography often referred to as the International Typographic Style or Die Neue Grafik. This approach to graphic communication for book design, posters, advertising, logos, and other business and organizational needs was promoted in journals such as *Graphis* and *Die Neue Grafik*, and formed the basis for the education of graphic designers at the Hochschule für Gestaltung at Ulm and the Kunstgewerbeschule in Basle. The combination of theoretical ideas, exploration of the visual components of graphic expression, and the use of those components for effective communication in an international context gave the movement a reputation for high standards and social responsibility in design. The hegemony of the International Typographic Style as the "voice" of modern graphic design was promoted in museum exhibitions and books, and was contemporary with a similar faith in the modern aesthetic and practical advantages of the tectonic steel-and-glass architecture of the "International Style."

Max Bill (see page 288), who lived and worked in Switzerland during and after World War II before accepting the directorship at the Hochschule für Gestaltung at Ulm, contributed to the development of the International Typographic Style. Along with several Swiss and other European artists and designers, Bill developed and worked within a framework of formal and ideological principles for graphic communication. These designers consciously moved away from illustration and were sparing in their use of both photography and color. Their shared interest was to communicate ideas universally and effectively with simple, reductive means. At the foundation of their approach were an acknowledgment of the

increasing complexity, fragmentation, and interdependence of knowledge, and a mistrust of the growing sophistication of the mechanical reproduction of images used to manipulate the public in mass advertising.

Bill's posters show a mastery of Jan Tschichold's New Typography (see pages 206–211), gained during the years he spent as a student at the Dessau Bauhaus from 1927 to 1929. Despite a commitment to modern, clear communication of ideas visually and simply, the abstract geometric relationships found in his exhibition posters and related print production also stem from his commitment to abstract art (called l'art concret) as an expression of imagination and creativity. Bill's 1945 poster for an exhibition of architecture (USA baut) presents a coordinated approach to abstract, photographic, and typographic elements (fig. 11.62). The poster is composed of nineteen diamond shapes of five different sizes, each containing photographic views of contemporary American buildings, urban complexes, and highways. The lower-case sans serif letterforms (Akzidenz Grotesk) and asymmetrical layout owe much to the principles of the New Typography, as does the careful attention to the relative "weight" and hierarchy of information. Bill balances, for instance, the

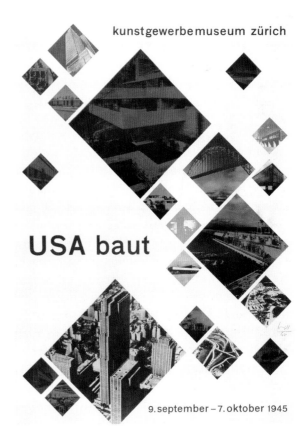

11.62 Max Bill, *USA Baut* exhibition poster, offset lithograph, 50 5/16 x 35 1/2 in (127.8 x 90.2 cm), 1945. Museum of Design, Zurich. Poster collection.

two larger diamonds right of center with the "USA baut" lettering to the left that gains visual strength from being isolated against a large area of white space. Beyond Bill's interest in eye movement as a basis for his approach to poster design, in this example the design is rich in other dimensions of visual communication: the blue and red tints applied to the photographs, along with the activation of white space, are, of course, the colors of the American flag, while the active arrangement of diamond shapes recalls the gridlike geometry of urban streets, intersections, and traffic as symbolized in the late "Boogie Woogie" series of paintings by Piet Mondrian, completed in the early 1940s while the artist lived in Manhattan.

One of the main features of the International Typographic Style developed by German and Swiss designers was the use of a grid system to govern layouts, subordinating all individual typographic elements to a system that maintained unity and governed relationships between those elements. The grid created modules as units of measurement to establish relationships for a hierarchy of information, and designers likened its standardized units to those of the units and industrial standards of modern architecture. Another poster by Bill for an exhibition of modern art from the collection of Peggy Guggenheim in Zurich in 1951 reveals the horizontal and vertical arrangement of text in an asymmetrical composition. The use of white space, vertical text, sans serif typography, and hierarchy of information based upon type sizes and placement incorporates the basic elements of the International Typographical Style and also demonstrates continuity with the New Typography.

Visual symbols also played an important role in the International Typographic movement. Armin Hofmann (b. 1920) and Anton Stankowski (1906–1998) are only two among a group of artists who used simple shapes together with sans serif typography to convey complex or mundane information with striking clarity and elegance. Swiss graphic designer and educator Hofmann was responsible for extensive series of posters for museums and other arts organizations in Switzerland, and used typography to convey the essence of a subject with utmost economy. His work reveals how much may be accomplished with an economy of means, as seen in the "Gute Form" exhibition poster of 1954 (fig. 11.63): the closely spaced, white, monoweight sans serif letterforms appear against the black ground as interchangeable mechanical parts. The viewer supplies each letter's missing parts while the words become an image of a clean, economical functional aesthetic. Bill's wall-mounted kitchen clock with timer (fig. 11.64) from 1956 is made of glass, ceramic, and plastic is an example of Gute Form: self-contained, free of decoration or expressive

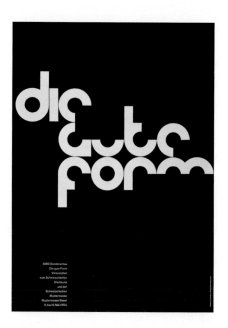

11.63 Armin Hofmann, *Gute Form* exhibition poster, offset lithograph, 11 x 35.4 in (28 x 90 cm), 1954. Museum of Design, Zurich. Poster collection.

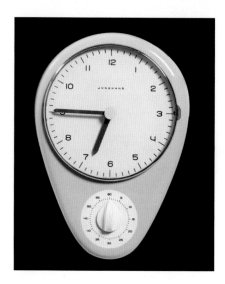

11.64 Max Bill (and Ernst Moecki), Kitchen clock with timer, metal, glass, ceramic, and plastic, 10 1/16 x 11 7/16 x 2 1/2 in (26 x 29 x 6.5 cm), manufactured by Gebrüder Junghans, Schramberg, Germany, 1956–1957. Victoria and Albert Museum, London.

associations, and contributing to a wholesome but modest lifestyle. Cultural institutions and exhibitions were among the strongest patrons of the Neue Grafik; dance, theater, film, and art contributed to the quality of life beyond the satisfaction of basic material needs, and were part of the optimistic outlook of many designers both in graphic as well as in industrial design. Moreover, journals such as *Neue Grafik* and *Graphis* promoted a serious consideration of the design profession and its social and political role, rather than its association with elitism, commercial advertising, and generating desire.

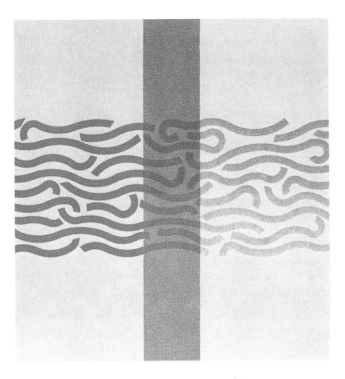

11.65 Anton Stankowski, diagram for the process of heat transfer, page from a calendar for Viessmann, 1957–1958.

Anton Stankowski demonstrated in a remarkable series of posters how complex technological processes might be given clear and comprehensible meaning through graphic design. This is seen, for instance, in the diagram illustrating the chemical transfer of heat using a series of broken undulating lines that change color from cool blue to warm red as they cross a barrier indicated by a heavy red vertical line (fig. 11.65). Stankowski's exploration of simple abstract form in relation to the design of information recalls the earlier and more intuitive research of Kandinsky to determine a systematic psychology of color while teaching in Russia in the early 1920s (see page 190). Both the artist and the designer shared an interest in research and experiment as part of the creative process, as well as an inclination to see abstract form as being universal in nature, but whereas Kandinsky used abstraction to communicate and liberate emotion, the interests of Neue Grafik designers was in creating a better-informed public. Such a public would in turn be more responsible participants in an ideal democracy. Designers such as Stankowski and Otl Aicher (see page 339) used their skills to forge a trust between the public and the corporations who contracted for their services. They do not, however, seem to have questioned whether businesses shared an abiding interest in improving living conditions through technology, products, and services. By the 1960s and even before in the debates that took place at Ulm and

elsewhere, the bond between business and design was beginning to fray (see page 353 onward).

An even more experimental approach within the parameters of the International Typographic Style characterizes the work of Josef Müller-Brockmann (1914–1996). His 1960 poster *Less Noise* (fig. 11.66) uses a sharply focused photographic image of a figure whose forearms create a viselike grip on a pained face viewed from below. The cropped image and heavy black areas further create a sense of claustrophobic space, and even the diagonal bold red letters adds to the feeling of tension. Here the photographic image and typography communicate like symbolic shapes in an abstract composition to convey a meaning.

The grid system and basic sans serif families of type were well suited to the consistent presentation of information and products for corporations. The repeated use of a "family" of graphic elements such as typography, logos, and elements in a layout ensured a uniform template that could be expanded while retaining subordination to overall

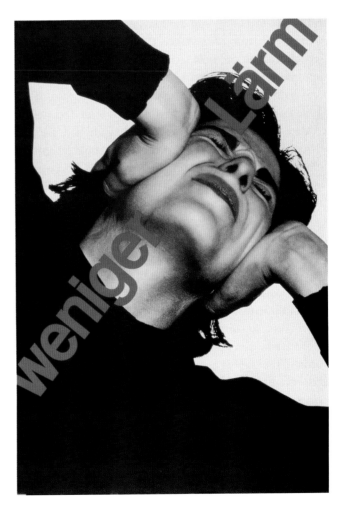

11.66 Josef Müller-Brockmann, *Less Noise* campaign poster, offset printing, 35 ²/₃ x 50 in (90 x 128 cm), 1960. Museum of Design, Zurich. Poster collection.

standards found in all permutations of corporate graphics. These could be disseminated in house-style manuals to insure the maintenance of standards and identity. An example is Stankowski's public graphics for the city of Berlin, all of which incorporated a thin horizontal line divided by a vertical line to symbolize the city's division into East and West in 1947 and the wall that was built in 1961 and remained until 1989. The interest of large municipal organizations and multi-national corporations in visual systems for products and publications during the postwar period created broad support for the International Typographic Style. Clean and recognizable systems of information reduced the visual "noise" and confusion of urban landscapes and enabled designers to create a sense of order and easy navigation in the manner of the London Underground maps two decades earlier (see fig. 9.58).

Examples of the International Typographic Style appeared in journals and were the subject of museum exhibitions in Europe and in the United States at the Museum of Modern Art. Many practitioners held teaching positions that enabled them to publish guides and exercises intended to encourage students to develop a formalist sensibility and responsible attitude to design. Armin Hofmann, for instance, taught at the Applied Arts School in Basle and held faculty positions at the School of the Philadelphia Museum of Art (now known as the University of the Arts) and at Yale University. Also in the United States, the Massachusetts Institute of Technology created a graphic design program that utilized a visual system for the institute and its press that could be applied to a variety of academic and public relations information and materials and that embodied the characteristics of the International Typographic Style.

In 1959, Swiss designer Karl Gerstner (b. 1930) published a trilingual history of modern graphic design entitled *Die Neue Graphik – The New Graphic Art – Le Nouvel Art Graphique*. This book presented the history of graphic design as the linear development toward clarity and simplicity as guidelines for the presentation of information to suit the needs of advertising and technical information. Gerstner illustrated canonical examples of chromolithographic posters from the later nineteenth and early twentieth centuries as "beginnings," and the more systematic use of asymmetric layout and vertical typography from the interwar period as "breakthroughs," all leading to "the present," in which system and the economy of means prevail. Gerstner illustrated numerous logos and reductive imagery, as well as photography of products. In one sequence of images he contrasted advertisements in which women's high-heeled shoes were photographed in profile and bird's-eye views for Lord & Taylor (1949) with an advertisement for I. Miller Shoe Company in which a

woman's leg is photographed wearing the shoe (1956) with the following caption, indicating the strong distinction that was drawn at times between the International Typographic Style and more illustrative and persuasive techniques of the advertising industry:

> One way of advertising shoes is to show a picture of them. Another is to make the picture promise the fulfillment of a wish: If you buy my shoes you will have beautiful legs (the shoe itself seems to have become a minor consideration). It is all rather like a fairy story and nobody troubles to check the truthfulness of such promises.

The efforts of Gerstner, Müller-Brockmann, and others presented graphic design as a creative and socially responsible professional activity, combining visual imagination and problem-solving skills, rather than as a branch of advertising whose role was primarily to stimulate consumer desire. Comparisons to modern art and the near universal application of the grid provided the combined subjective and objective parameters of modern graphic design practice and the higher, more professional purpose of educating the public and cleansing public spaces of clutter with clear, concise, and unified information systems.

Postwar designers in Switzerland and Germany favored sans serif typefaces for their simplicity and elimination of calligraphic or expressive embellishment. Until the 1950s designers such as Max Bill were comfortable using the early twentieth-century typeface Akzidenz Grotesk (see page 207). Then in 1957, Swiss designer Adrian Frutiger (b. 1928) developed the Univers typeface for the French foundry Deberny et Peignot (fig. 11.67). In addition to numerous variations of weight and width that were made available when it was introduced, Univers letterforms have slight variations in stroke width as compared with interwar sans serif faces, for example, in the slight tapering of the bowls of the lower-case "p" and "g" as they near the vertical strokes, or in the narrowing of the "o" at the top and bottom. Frutiger thought these changes made the face more versatile and better suited than monoweight sans serifs for reading as well as for display. In response, the Berthold Foundry in Berlin began working on a revision to its Akzidenz Grotesk font with a number of the same variations from monoweight stroke widths, also released in 1957. Originally named Neue Haas Grotesk, the name was changed to Helvetica, the Latin name for Switzerland (fig. 11.68). The development of postwar sans serif typefaces for use in International Typographic Style graphic design reveal the painstaking analysis of letterforms in terms of small variations in stroke and space, in response to printing techniques,

ABCDEFGHIJKL
MNOPQRSTUVW
XYZ   abcdefghijk
lmnopqrstuvwxyz
.,-;:!? 123456789

11.67 Adrian Frutiger, Univers typeface,
Deberny et Peignot Foundry, Paris, 1957.

ABCDEFGHIJKLMN
OPQRSTUVWXYZ?
abcdefghijklm
nopqrstuvwxyz!
1234567890

11.68 Helvetica typeface, Berthold Foundry,
Germany, 1957. Line drawing by John Langdon.

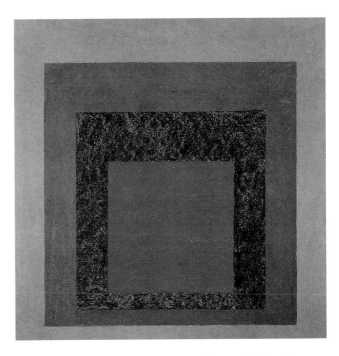

11.69 Josef Albers, *Homage to the Square*, oil on wood fiberboard,
23 ⅛ in (59 cm) square, 1961. National Gallery of Modern Art, Rome.

effects upon different kinds of paper, and an increase in the variety of printing jobs that required extended families of fonts. Although applications may have been less direct, design experiment and research into the means of expression in typography brings to mind Josef Albers' *Homage to the Square* series of paintings, where laboratorylike testing of color combinations reveal distinctions and variations in the formal perception of spatial relationships on a two-dimensional surface (fig. 11.69).

Not all graphic designers in Europe subscribed to the exclusive use of sans serif typography as did the practitioners of the International Typographic Style. Jan Tschichold became disillusioned with the dogmatism of his own New Typography, and his work after World War II shows a respect for tradition in both typography and layout in book printing (see page 217 and fig. 9.54). Respect for traditional typography is also seen in the new serif faces invented

by graphic designer Hermann Zapf (b. 1918). A self-taught calligrapher and art director for the Stempel type foundry in Frankfurt-am-Main, Germany, Zapf was strongly influenced by the example of Rudolf Koch (see page 208). Zapf developed several influential serif typefaces in the postwar period, including Palatino in 1948 (fig. 11.70). He was also responsible for the *Manuale Typographicum*, a compendium of material for typographers revealing a great understanding of both tradition and new principles of design. Palatino was designed for letterpress printing and was intended to maintain its legibility for printing on

ABCDEFGHIJKLMN
OPQRSTUVWXYZ?
abcdefghijklm
nopqrstuvwxyz!
1234567890

11.70 Hermann Zapf, Palatino typeface,
1948. Line drawing by John Langdon.

ABCDEFGHIJKLMN
OPQRSTUVWXYZ?
abcdefghijklm
nopqrstuvwxyz!
1234567890

11.71 Hermann Zapf, Optima typeface, 1952–1958. Line drawing by John Langdon.

inexpensive papers. Its letterforms show a smooth and controlled transition from thick to thin strokes, a characteristic that also identifies Optima (fig. 11.71), which Zapf developed between 1952 and 1958. Optima appears to lie somewhere between serif and sans serif typefaces. It possesses the boldness and close spacing of the latter and yet preserves some transition between thick and thin strokes of Roman letterforms. Some historians of typography praise Zapf for combining the best features of both traditions in the design of Optima.

MEANS AND ENDS

Advocates and practitioners of the International Typographic Style saw their work as inherently creative, objective, and socially responsible. Such work embodied a sense of restraint as well as reform, removed from the excesses of commercial art direction at one end and the indulgence of individual expression for a more exclusive audience at the other. As an example, Ulm faculty member Otl Aicher (1922–1991), developed corporate identity and advertising for the German airline Lufthansa in the early 1960s, with specifications that included grid layout, typography, and symbols (see fig. 13.22).

On a more theoretical level, the International Typographic Style is often mentioned in relation to semiotics, defined as the study or science of signs. Emerging first in the field of linguistics, semiotics holds that the meaning of language is the outcome of a process that involves both the "signifier" or means of communication (letters, words, images) and the "signified," that is, the way in which those means of communication are understood. Words, as well as images, do not have fixed meanings in relation to the objects or ideas they represent. Rather,

meaning is constructed or mediated socially in an active rather than passive process that involves both intention as well as reception. In the absence of objective communication, graphic designers focused attention upon controlling the range of meanings in the signs they constructed and establishing clearly, even universally understood information. Word, symbol, image, composition, and hierarchy of information constituted the elements of a responsible approach to graphic communication within the framework of semiotics.

The close relationship that developed between the International Typographic Style and corporate identity systems eventually complicated its claims of neutral communication. In 1955 Max Bill resigned as director of the Hochschule für Gestaltung (HfG), and Argentinean-born Tomás Maldonado (b. 1922) was appointed as his successor. Maldonado moved the curriculum of the school away from the experimentation with materials and visual practice toward a stronger involvement with social theory, reducing the emphasis upon studio work while concentrating upon redefining the role of design and the designer in a global context that was critical of materialism and commercialism. As a practicing designer, Maldonado served as a consultant to the Erbe medical equipment company in Tübingen, Germany, in the early 1960s, where his product housings employ geometric forms, simple manufacturing techniques, smooth surfaces to promote hygiene, and subordination to the impersonal architecture and furnishings of the laboratory (fig. 11.72).

Maldonado questioned the consumer orientation of postwar industrial design in the context of broader global considerations including hunger, disease, and pollution. He also questioned the alliance between design and business that limited the designer's role to stimulating desire

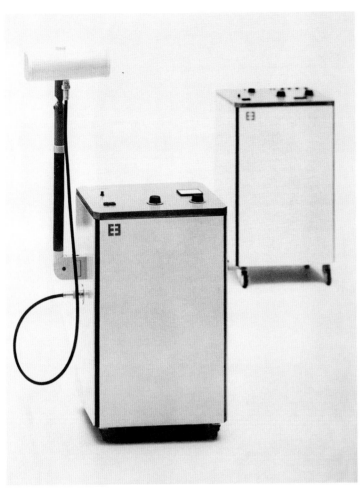

11.72 Tomás Maldonado, medical equipment, Erbe Company, Tübingen, Germany, 1961.

for consumer goods, and argued for design education that emphasized social consciousness and responsibility and an understanding of the economic and political structures that determined the practice of design. Difficulty in gaining unilateral support among faculty for his vision for the future of design and the education of designers led to tension at Ulm. Combined with financial problems that forced consolidation with a nearby vocational school, the Hochshule für Gestaltung closed in 1968.

Maldonado's interest in environmental design, however, was echoed by other contemporary theorists who were equally concerned with more radical possibilities of linking design with broader mandates for social change and individual responsibility. These views strayed farther from the more product-and-process-oriented mainstream of international modern industrial design into the realm of social and political activism. In fine art as well, contemporary artists such as Joseph Beuys (1888–1958) were less concerned with making objects (objects-as-commodities) than with reaching their audiences and provoking a

response alternatively through performance and demonstration, suggesting the possibility for a relevant public role for the arts outside the gallery or museum. Maldonado envisioned an expansion of the definition of design to include a wider range of activities that engaged users with technology, integrating information and other media to address broad human needs and social awareness. The paradigm for the designer went beyond form-giving and products to services and human interaction with technology and mass media, and is parallel to other efforts across disciplines that recognized design's increasing role in modern life. These issues are further explored in Part VI in relation to the counterculture (see page 354 onward) as well as to applications of digital technology to design (see page 378 onward).

The primacy of environmental rather than commercial or humanistic concerns also informed the theory and practice of other, more radical design practitioners and critics, including American architect and designer Buckminster Fuller (1895–1983) as well as Austrian-born architect Richard Neutra (1892–1970). In the 1940s, Fuller, inspired by the development of lightweight building materials, devised a technique for constructing "geodesic" domes using triangular components. Fuller advocated the new construction principle as a response to concerns about the efficient use of resources in a global society. Despite their relationship to the domestication of technology, Fuller's ideas were often couched in utopian terms, and the degree of prefabrication and uniformity implied a collective approach that did not resonate with manufacturers in an age of advertising and expanded materialism. Fuller's hopes for sponsorship of his building plans failed to materialize, perhaps as they were too far removed from the suburban ideal that was taking shape in Levittowns and other communities throughout the United States (see pages 317–320). Nevertheless, Fuller's message of social responsibility and the conservation of natural resources helped to make him something of a "cult" figure in the later 1960s in a more volatile political and social climate.

Neutra's response to postwar design was a book entitled *Survival Through Design*, published in 1954, an indictment of the commercial values inherent in postwar popular culture and a search for standards based upon basic human needs in a global setting. In his writing Neutra proposed the indivisibility of the man-made with the natural, and hoped that this thought would inform the future of architecture. He advocated stringent performance standards for industrially manufactured building materials, and the application of his ideas would have required a level of regulation and control of the building and manufacturing industries not possible in the expanding economic framework of developed capitalism.

Japan produced a vibrant interpretation of Art Deco during the interwar period seen in fashion accessories as well as in advertising, and even Jan Tschichold illustrated a page of advertisements from a Japanese newspaper as an example of the modernity of asymmetrical layouts in his *New Typography* of 1928. In the postwar period, attitudes toward design in Japan were strongly influenced by new government economic policy, actively promoted through the awarding of prizes such as the G-Mark and regulated by agencies that set and reinforced standards for quality and recognition in the international export market beginning in the mid-1950s. The process began with the investment in mechanized mass production of automobiles, trucks, and other durable products for reconstruction and rebuilding the economy following Japan's defeat in World War II and the period of American occupation that ended in 1952. During this early postwar period the phrase "made in Japan" connoted cheap toys and knock-off electronic products of often inferior quality, manufactured to the specifications of foreign buyers and merchandisers interested in marketing inexpensive goods for the mass public that lacked the reputation or quality of the original items they imitated.

With government support, a number of Japanese manufacturers began to make a conscious, pragmatic effort to enter the export market for the more sophisticated products of good design, focusing particularly upon electronic communications, motor scooters and motorcycles, and cameras, and eventually fashion design and furniture. Through sponsored prizes for original products of industrial design, Japanese manufacturers were encouraged to hire designers, and were also discouraged from pirating the original designs of other countries. Government initiatives brought American industrial designer Raymond Loewy to Japan, and a Japanese translation of his autobiography appeared in 1953. Related initiatives sent Japanese corporate leaders to the United States to observe business practice in industry. The role of government agencies in the success of Japanese industrial design emerges as a feature of the country's postwar development, contemporary with similarly sponsored efforts in Britain, Italy, and Germany. The Ministry of International Trade and Industry (MITI), Japan External Trade Organization (JETRO), the Good Design Selection System (responsible for the G-Mark), the Design Promotion Organization, and the Japan Design House, are only the most well-known of the agencies responsible for establishing standards for export products, for developing markets for Japanese goods, for promoting design through conferences, competitions, and integrating design as an

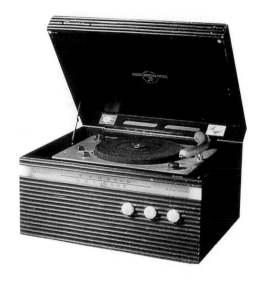

11.73 Sori Yanagi, radio-phonograph, wood, plastic, and metal, 16 ⅛ x 19 ¹¹⁄₁₆ x 12 ³⁄₁₆ in (41 x 50 x 31 cm), manufactured by Nihon-Columbia Corporation, Tokyo, 1952. Yanagi Product Design Institute, Tokyo.

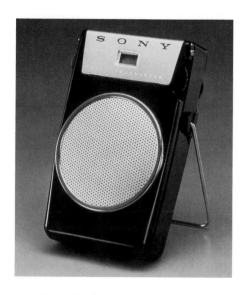

11.74 Sony radio, plastic housing, 4 ⅜ x 2 ½ x 1 in (11 x 16.4 x 2.5 cm), Tokyo Telecommunications Engineering Corporation, 1957.

element within corporate organization, and helping to sustain a system for design education. The results of this approach have been to transcend a particular look or identity for Japanese products, by demonstrating a willingness to absorb and build upon shared characteristics of practicality, individualism, human factors, indigenous craft traditions, as well as continual innovation in the design of modern appliances and electronic products with broad international market appeal.

Sori Yanagi's (b. 1915) radio-phonograph for Nihon-Columbia Corporation of Tokyo in 1952 (fig. 11.73) is an example of a modern practical approach to product design in comparison with the more self-conscious aesthetic considerations in similar Braun products (see fig. 11.57). The possibility for compact and even portable design for electronic products was pioneered by Akio Morita, founder of the Tokyo Telecommunications Engineering Corporation that later became known as Sony. Morita purchased the technology for the use of transistors from the American corporation Western Bell Laboratories in 1953, initiating its development for the domestic market in the production of small, portable radios, and acquiring a reputation for miniaturization in the manufacture of consumer electronics products (fig. 11.74). In the later 1950s miniaturization found expression in portable television sets, and the concept was applied to the Sony Walkman personal tape player of the 1970s. Such miniaturization was seen both as a convenience in defining more mobile lifestyles as well as contributing to flexibility and space-saving approaches to interior design, all elements subsumed under the term "organic design" as conceived by Eliot Noyes (see pages 249 and 267) and later known broadly as "good design."

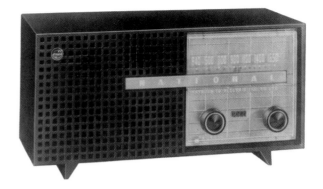

11.77 Zenichi Mano, National Radio, plastic, 7 x 14 x 5 ½ in (18 x 35.6 x 14 cm), manufactured by Matushita Electrical Industrial Company, Osaka, 1953.

In addition to the emerging reputation for the application of technology to the domestic market, Japanese companies Nikon and Canon successfully competed with German counterparts such as Hasselblad and Leica in the market for high-quality professional photographic equipment through refinements in design that appealed to the educated user. Nikon's 1957 SP3 single-lens reflex (SLR) camera (fig. 11.75) featured a wider horizontal viewing window than comparable models such as the Leica M3 of 1954 (fig. 11.76), demonstrating careful under-standing of user requirements for the highly technical and specialized equipment of professional photographers. The continuing success of this approach was demonstrated in later years by its extension, via increased automation, to 35-millimeter camera technology for a broader segment of the general public. While filmless, digital cameras can be even more compact and portable than their SLR predecessors, the comfort and familiar interface of the Japanese and German postwar cameras has to a great extent been adopted for the higher-end digital market. Whether to acknowledge the persistence of older habits as a marketing strategy to spur adoption of a new technology with the reassurance of compatibility with the familiar or to respect well-developed solutions to a combination of aesthetic and functional requirements, the digital camera demonstrates a varied response of industry to technological change.

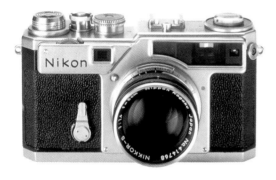

11.75 Nikon SP3 camera, metal, 3 ³/₁₆ x 5 ⅝ x 1 ⅝ in (8 x 14.3 x 4 cm), Nikon Inc., 1957.

Critics have noted the continuity between practicality and aesthetic simplicity in Japanese postwar industrial design and indigenous traditions of Japanese architecture and interior design. Zenichi Mano's (b. 1916) 1953 National Radio for the Matushita company of Osaka featured an asymmetrical composition of rectangular shapes subdivided into units inspired by the wooden shutters and sliding screens of traditional Japanese houses (fig. 11.77). Other references to Japanese architecture can be seen in the Butterfly stool designed by Sori Yanagi for the Tendo

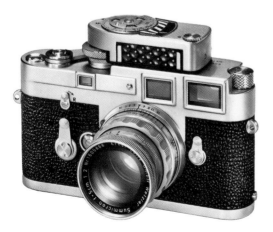

11.76 Ernst Leitz Gmbtt, Leica M3 camera, injection mold aluminum, brass, 5 ⅖ x 3 x 1 ⁵/₁₆ in (13.8 x 7.7 x 3.4 cm), Wetslar, Germany, 1954.

Mokko Company in 1956 and constructed of two identical curved molded plywood pieces easily assembled by a metal rod (fig. 11.78). The plywood technology was developed first in connection with industrial and wartime production for containers and aircraft requiring exact measurements and specification, but later was used extensively in furniture primarily for public buildings. Yanagi's stool has been compared to the roofline of Japanese buildings, but the abstract contour also recalls the fluid brushstrokes of Japanese calligraphy as well as examples of modern abstract organic sculpture.

The beauty of natural materials, sensitive craftsmanship, original designs, and simple construction also characterizes the furniture of designer George Nakashima (1905–1990). Nakashima was born in the United States but worked in Japan for an architectural firm after completing studies in architecture at M.I.T. After World War II (during which he spent a year in an internment camp for Japanese-Americans), Nakashima established a workshop for making his own furniture in New Hope, Pennsylvania (1946). Designs such as the Conoid Bench with back from 1961 (fig. 11.79) display an interest in preserving the irregular beauty of natural forms often combined with slightly irregular and uneven dowel-like supports or rails for chair backs. Nakashima's oeuvre relies upon a balance of modern and traditional approaches to furniture design. Although a small number of early designs for chairs were manufactured by Knoll, Nakashima preferred workshop production and direct contact between craftsmen, materials, and processes. The simplicity of his designs may also be appreciated in the bedroom furniture for the Japanese House built on the grounds of the Bloedel Nature Reserve on Bainbridge Island near Seattle in 1961. Set in quiet natural surroundings, the house and furnishings provide a refuge and sanctuary where the man-made appears not to intrude. Nakashima's approach to craft emphasized the workman's partnership with materials as related to Zen Buddhist philosophy and the connection between animate and inanimate nature.

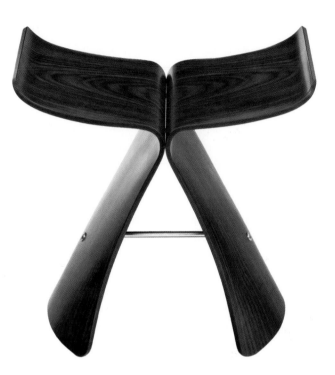

11.78 Sori Yanagi, Butterfly stool, plywood and metal, 15 ¹¹⁄₁₆ x 16 ⁹⁄₁₆ x 12 ³⁄₁₆ in (40 x 42 x 31 cm), manufactured by Tendo Mokko, Tendo, 1956. Philadelphia Museum of Art.

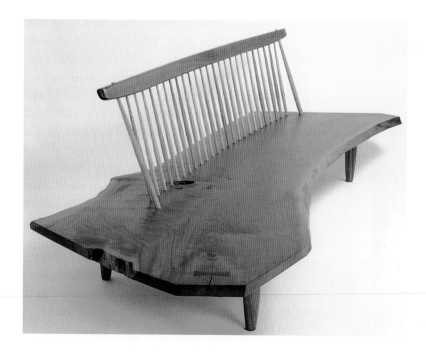

11.79 George Nakashima, Conoid Bench, walnut, 32 ½ x 84 ½ in (82.6 x 214.6 cm), Nakashima Studios, New Hope, Pennsylvania, 1961.

Unified standards, government initiatives and investment, international marketing, and the encouragement of innovation appear as elements of Japanese design after World War II. Moreover, for Japanese corporations there seems to be less of a dichotomy between standards, with their implication of socially responsible progress, and commercialism, where obsolescence is often associated pejoratively with conspicuous consumption and the exploitation of the mass market. The policies initiated through MITI and other design organizations in Japan were successful in revitalizing the Japanese economy, raising the income level and standard of living at home, and establishing a reputation for quality as well as technological and aesthetic innovation abroad. At the same time the products of Japanese industrial design made personal electronic products virtually a necessary accessory to a modern, mobile, active lifestyle, from transistor radios and portable television sets in the 1950s to pocket calculators and Walkmen in the 1960s and 1970s, Karaoke in the 1980s, and compact disc players (Discman) in the 1990s. Such a blurring between technological innovation, new products, and modern living is a phenomenon we will encounter internationally in the 1960s. Its emergence in Japanese design is prescient: it appears to signify a sometimes subtle but significant shift in business strategy from production to consumption, with the latter creating its own justification, requiring new markets and intensified advertising through the mass media. Sustaining postwar economic recovery offered many opportunities for Japanese industrial designers in an international market in which they played an integral role and their strategies proved effective throughout the second half of the twentieth century.

DESIGN AND CORPORATE CULTURE

A conscious connection between corporations and industries and the promotion of education and cultural awareness through information design may be seen in the advertising campaigns undertaken by the Columbia Broadcast System (CBS) under creative director William Golden (1911–1959) and the Container Corporation of America (CCA) under its president Walter Paepke (1896–1960). These executives sponsored fine artists and designers to develop posters and advertisements for company products and services as well as for more general advertisements that simply link the corporation to creative activities perceived by many to be an expression of democratic values. Golden was responsible for a massive campaign to attract attention and sponsors to CBS with a series of creative advertisements to demonstrate the power of radio and the newer medium of television to reach

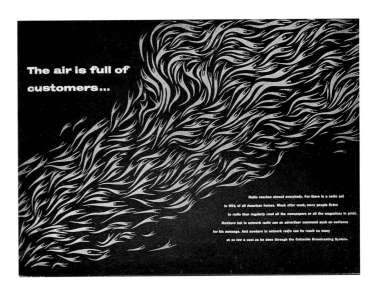

11.80 William Golden (art director), Nathan Polsky (artist), print advertisement for Columbia Broadcast System, thirtieth *Art Directors' Annual*, New York, 1950.

diverse audiences. In an advertisement intended for a trade periodical, Golden based his image upon an abstract drawing by artist Nathan Polsky that depicts small, white, ghostlike figures floating diagonally from left to right against a black background. In the manner of the "new advertising," brief copy appears to the lower right, while a heavier title reads "The air is full customers," referring to the medium of radio (fig. 11.80). A designer in his own right, Golden also developed the "eye" trademark for CBS.

Walter Paepke was another businessman who promoted the educational value of modern design through his large Chicago-based company, the Container Corporation of America. Paepke also sponsored a series of advertisements by modern artists including French painter Fernand Léger, helped to support the creation of the New Bauhaus in Chicago under the direction of László Moholy-Nagy, and established the Design Conference in Aspen, Colorado (where he owned a vacation home), beginning in 1951, to advance progressive thinking in design. Paepke saw the corporation as a participant in public education, identifying culture with high intellectual and creative pursuits, products of an enlightened democracy. As an example, CCA published the *World Geographical Atlas* designed by Herbert Bayer (see fig. 11.26). As explained by author James Sloan Allen, Paepke's interests were parallel to the efforts of University of Chicago president Robert Hutchins to establish educational standards based upon "great books" that contribute to the education of the individual in a democratic society. Like design reform in earlier periods, the view of culture promoted by CCA was paternalistic, reflecting the interests and biases of an educated and powerful class, and removed from the complex social and economic realities of the postwar period. Nevertheless, such endeavors and projects suggest the cultural climate of the postwar era, a time in which multi-national corporations aligned their activities with education, standards, and the promotion of shared cultural values.

TRADEMARKS AND BEYOND

Paul Rand, in his 1947 book *Thoughts on Design* (see pages 268–269), noted an almost "magical power" exerted by letterforms. This "aura" surrounding letters found expression in the postwar period, especially in the proliferation of memorable logos for corporations and organizations operating on a multi-national scale. The role of letters as a leitmotif of mid-twentieth-century industrial culture emerged in the United States Pavilion designed by graphic artists Tom Geismar (b. 1931) and Ivan Chermayeff (b. 1932) for the World's Fair held in Brussels in 1958 (fig. 11.81). These three-dimensional letterforms echoed other exhibits at the fair in promoting an American way of life through fashion and modern kitchens (rather than military technology). The exhibit acknowledged the ubiquity of signage and logos in everyday life, and their associations with technology, organization, commerce, and economic progress.

In the postwar period, many large multi-national corporations recognized the advantages of consistent policies toward design. Recalling the precepts of the Werkbund (see pages 148–151), standards of "good design" translated easily into corporate culture, subordinating the individual to the group whose shared ethos was guided by

dependability and consistent performance, and eventually by familiarity and trust. Corporations such as Olivetti in Italy, Braun and Lufthansa in West Germany, and Sony in Japan all drew upon consultant or in-house designers to create identity programs, implemented with the support of top levels of management. The increasingly international nature of business in many hi-tech industries such as pharmaceuticals, oil, transportation, and communications led naturally to a reliance upon letters or logos rather than lengthier company names for branding in a global market. The economic climate of aggressive growth through takeovers and mergers often created interest in maintaining a single image or company identity, and professional designers were able to meet these needs for both organizational behavior and marketing. Their activities included the development of logos, liveries, products, and packaging to establish and reinforce corporate organizational standards and ethos. Product design and logo development only form part of corporate identity. Many corporations rely upon slogans, packaging, architecture, signage, advertising, and exhibition design to create their image, particularly if their business is in soft drinks, energy transmission, or oil and gasoline products rather than in a line of consumer domestic wares such as coffeemakers, toasters, or cassette players. Even in these areas, packaging and prominent logos often create as much differentiation as product housings.

The corporate image of the Olivetti Corporation, as seen in showrooms throughout Italy in the later 1940s and in Manhattan from 1954 (see fig. 11.49), prompted

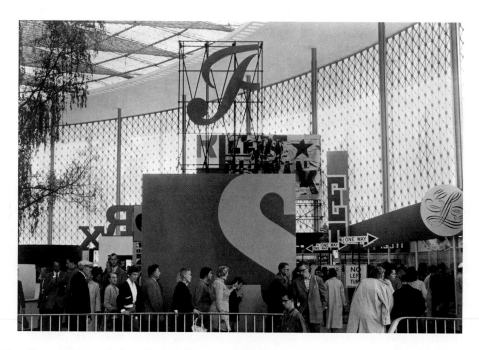

11.81 Tom Geismar and Ivan Chermayeff, exhibition design for United States Pavilion, Brussels World's Fair, Belgium, 1958.

IBM president Thomas Watson, Jr. (1914–1993) to pursue a unified corporate identity program. To direct this program Watson hired Eliot F. Noyes (1910–1977), an architect who previously was curator of industrial design at the Museum of Modern Art. IBM may serve as a paradigm of sorts for the corporate promotion of design under capitalism. IBM identity was not only related to the coherent design of products and promotional materials directed toward clients and investors, but also toward reinforcing community and exclusivity among employees, that is, in establishing visible signs and a framework for a unified corporate culture. Such a team-based approach had advantages in providing guidelines or standards not only for design but also for dress and behavior and their effect upon internal and external perception. Some observers noted a downside to the new corporate culture. As observed by sociologist David Riesman in his book *The Lonely Crowd* (1950), and seen earlier in the strategies of the advertising industry after World War I, a corporate "image" could have an alienating effect upon individuals, who felt that they had to "fit in" with the group in order to be successful. In Riesman's view, such corporate behavior was part of a shift from "inner-directed" to "other-directed" values that he saw emerging as the dominant form of conformity particularly in American society. The image of a unified corporate identity could be both comforting as well as disconcerting.

The IBM logo was designed in 1956 by Paul Rand (see pages 268–271), one of several specialists hired by Noyes (fig. 11.82). Like many global corporations, the success of the IBM logo depends upon simple recognition and the substitution of letters for longer, often complicated names. Rand used a slab-serif display face known as City Medium, introduced in Germany in 1930. Serif letters are less usual in corporate logos, but in this case contribute to strong figure–ground contrast through close spacing, creation of squared negative spaces between letters and in the counters for the upper-case "B" for added unity, and to the stability of the design. Subsequently Rand retained the

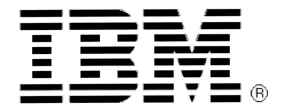

11.82 Paul Rand, redesign of trademark for IBM Corporation, 1972 (first designed 1956).

basic elements of his IBM logo, but expanded its treatment through repetition and color variation on packaging, introducing horizontal stripes that run through the heavy letterforms, and even playfully substituting an eye and a bee in place of the "I" and "B" letters. This last variation is indeed a testimony to the power of letters that he noted in *Thoughts on Design*. A similar use of serif faces in the later 1940s and early 1950s is found in the logo by Swiss designer Herbert Matter for the New Haven Railway in 1954 and for the Knoll Corporation around 1950 (fig. 11.83). These examples also create unified images out of letterforms, and the letters of the Knoll logo consist of connecting thin lines of uniform thickness ending in rectangular shapes.

Logos can be almost purely abstract, as is the case with "IBM," or can be related to the nature of company products or services, as seen in Rand's redesign of the Westinghouse "W," where abstract circles and lines construct the letter and symbolize electrical circuitry (fig. 11.84). More common in logo design, however, is sans serif typography, seen, for instance, in Rand's design for the American Broadcasting Corporation in 1962 (fig. 11.85). This trademark uses a variant of the Futura typeface with its bowl "a" rather than Roman lower-case "a," and a single weight for all letter strokes, resulting in an identity created among the shapes of the three letters. It is not surprising that graphic designers played so important a role in creating corporate identity. Earlier projects such as the London Underground in the 1930s (see fig. 9.58)

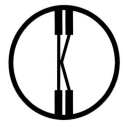

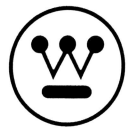

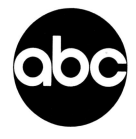

11.83 Herbert Matter, trademark "K" for Knoll Corporation, 1950. Line drawing by John Langdon.

11.84 Paul Rand, trademark for Westinghouse Corporation, 1960.

11.85 Paul Rand, trademark for the American Broadcasting Corporation (ABC), 1962.

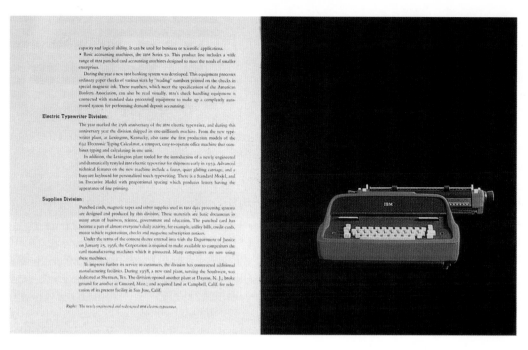

11.86 Paul Rand, IBM annual report, with photograph of IBM electric typewriter designed by Eliot Noyes, 1958.

demonstrated the importance of simplification and clarity in modern communication, reducing complexity and confusion and promoting understanding. It is not easy to differentiate between information and promotion: the "image" of unity brought about by logos reduced the distance between the public and the large private company, suggesting efficiency, order, and encouraging familiarity and trust. The same clarity and clean page design applies as well to Rand's annual investor reports for IBM (fig. 11.86).

As well as directing its corporate identity program, Eliot Noyes was responsible for the product design of typewriters for IBM. His success at IBM in building an identity system was based in part upon his close working relationship with company president Watson. Both men agreed that design could be a tool for greater cooperation among the various IBM divisions as well as communicating a coherent and consistent corporate structure. Noyes's efforts were an extension of the belief in the ability of design to shape shared attitudes and values. He believed that standards in product design should be based upon the adaptation of modern technology and considerations of fitness to purpose in which decoration and superficial change played little or no part. Noyes worked as a young architect for former Bauhaus masters Walter Gropius and Marcel Breuer after graduating from Harvard University and before his appointment as curator for industrial design at the Museum of Modern Art in New York. It is not surprising, given this familiarity with European-based interwar Modernism, that he extended to the multinational corporation the responsibility for setting high

standards of efficiency and taste in design. As a result, corporate identity provided visibility and respect for the design profession.

In the realm of corporate identity, the practice of design saw a merging of the efforts of graphic and industrial designers which extended far beyond merely giving form to products. It involved a broader and more complex discourse involving decisions that promoted understandings of large organizations and their constituencies both internally as well as externally. Design encompassed product forms, offices, showrooms, advertising, and myriad other public relations activities. In this context, design was a common denominator, its meaning linked increasingly to *information* and communicating with users or stakeholders. While "form" was one aspect of information, media and logos played an increasingly prominent role in design, especially in relation to business practice and new technologies. One outcome of this broader practice of design was Noyes's hiring of Charles and Ray Eames as consultant designers of exhibits and films for the corporation. The Eameses' work for IBM focused upon communicating technological and economic progress through images, in exhibits for the IBM Pavilion at the 1964 New York World's Fair and in the three-dimensional timeline for the exhibit "A Computer Perspective," held in the IBM corporate headquarters in New York in 1971 (fig. 11.87). The Eameses' exhibits, like those of Will Burtin's for the Upjohn pharmaceutical company (see fig. 11.24), expressed the postwar belief in the integration of business, government, and technology to affect living standards globally. We might see this development as the continuation of a tradition of versatility among modern industrial designers, who viewed their varied efforts as means toward serving human needs rather than as directed solely toward creating products for a market. Such a view emphasizes a broad, humanistic understanding of the profession. It also implies a sense of trust and shared purpose between designers and their clients that began to unravel in the later 1960s with debates and the search for alternatives, treated below (see page 353 onward).

In addition to his special consultant relationship with IBM, Noyes also worked for Mobil, Westinghouse, and other large multi-national corporations. His career documents the attempt to use design to form the basis of a consistent and responsible corporate image, even when technical and organizational considerations in such large businesses made uniformity and conformity difficult to achieve. His successes, featured in articles for *Industrial Design*, were based upon cooperation with executives whose authority helped to gain agreement and compliance with centralizing policies. The International Typographic Style provided the basis for the visual systems developed for many international companies. Other examples of the development of conscious policies toward design in a global market include the Philips Corporation of Eindhoven in the Netherlands. Recognizing competition and global markets for a variety of products ranging from lightbulbs to stereos, televisions, and medical equipment in the postwar period, Philips's management developed a consistent design policy and integrated design into the corporate decision-making process. For Philips, this did not result in a recognizable "look" for products as with Braun, but rather in a process of training and communication across a number of product divisions and brand names that had grown autonomously. While recognized as Philips for consumer electronics in Europe, in the United States Philips products were known by brand names such as Norelco, Sylvania, and Philco. There was no effort to create uniformity across products, but design was used to reinforce considerations of ergonomics, fitness-to-purpose, as well as target audiences in the development of a wide range of consumer electronic products.

Good design within the global corporation has been an effective marketing and organizational strategy emphasizing consistency, recognition, and technical standards through mass communication and mechanized mass production. It was not, however, the only corporate approach to design. Particularly in the United States, brand differentiation among products manufactured by a single company was another effective corporate strategy, giving the impression of variety and choice under the control of tight policies governing the parameters of change and the activities of industrial designers. Such strategies involved a close relation between design, market segmentation, and massive advertising investment (another instance of information); these were effective in limiting competition from smaller companies, and are explored below in chapter 12 on mass culture.

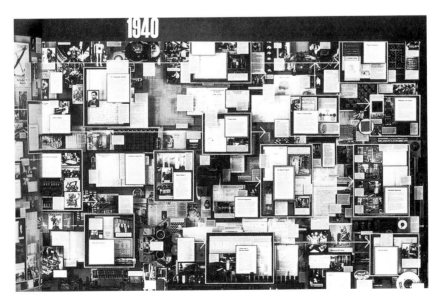

11.87 Charles and Ray Eames, panel from "A Computer Perspective" (History Wall or Timeline), one of six 8 ft (2.4 m) panels, 1971. Exhibit Design, IBM Corporate Exhibit Center, New York.

Chapter 12

Design and Mass Appeal: A Culture of Consumption

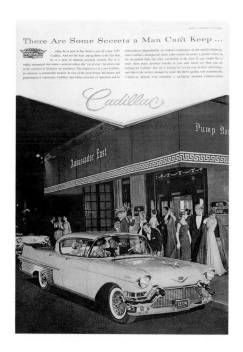

12.1 Advertisement for Cadillac Eldorado, from *Life*, September 9, 1957.

Standards of "good design," as described in Chapter 11, were embraced by private institutions such as the Museum of Modern Art in New York, and provided the framework for discourse at schools like the Hochschule für Gestaltung at Ulm. "Good design" formed the basis of policy and identity for corporations such as IBM and Braun, and was supported by government-sponsored agencies in countries like Britain, Japan, and Italy. It was marketed through international journals, books, and exhibitions, and informed the practices of industrial designers whose furniture and product prototypes were manufactured by Herman Miller or became part of the product line for companies like Olivetti. Through such efforts, as well as the United States's investment and incentives for peacetime economic recovery and growth in Europe and Japan, the products and accompanying ethos of progress through design reached a broader audience than ever before. "Good design" was the visible expression of a clear and socially responsible approach to change

motivated by technological progress and a shared commitment to improving the quality of life internationally under the embrace of capitalist free enterprise.

In the early 1950s in the United States, the middle class and a growing segment of an industrial working class reaping the benefits of increased production and higher wages entered the expanding and elastic market for residential housing, home furnishings, and other industrially manufactured products. The attitudes and expectations of this large and diverse consumer audience both incorporated and transcended the standards and paternalism of museums, identity systems, and a new humanism embracing social responsibility, aesthetic awareness, fitness-to-purpose, and comfort. New, broader needs were shaped not only by economic stability and postwar optimism but also by the unprecedented role assumed by mass media. The term mass culture may be used to describe the American market, especially after World War II. This term includes the designed products that reached this broad market, but approaching those products requires an appreciation of the ways in which mass media shaped and reflected the experience of post-war Americans.

The apparent indifference of the mass market to the standards of "good design" may be seen in the success of a wide variety of postwar products ranging from automobiles to kitchen appliances, portable electronics to furniture. In all of these examples there was a tremendous receptivity to the phenomenon of planned obsolescence; that is, the calculated efforts of manufacturers to generate demand with a seemingly unending supply of "new" products. In fact, the term was coined by the Milwaukee-based industrial designer Brooks Stevens (1911–1995) and acknowledges the connection between design, consumer desire, and continuous novelty. Obsolescence had the effect of making current products seem "old," conditioning the buying public to continual cycles of consumption and frequent replacement. In addition, while modern materials and methods of production were used, products made frequent references to the past, to the present, as well as to the future, replacing principles such as "fitness to purpose" with greater freedom of choice integrating expendability and a broad eclecticism. Indeed the phenomena of newness, an accelerated pace of change, and continual replacement tended to erode in some degree the very notion of fixed or timeless standards and the authority they imply. After all, standards suggest permanence and durability for products, while obsolescence and novelty imply a perpetual state of "becoming," of desire, where consumption itself becomes a way of life. British design historian and critic Reyner Banham (1922–1988) aptly described this phenomenon as a "throwaway culture."

Despite the commercial potential of novelty and obsolescence, the implementation of frequent product change entailed great economic risks: the retooling required for changes in the manufacturing process as well as the increased investment in the complex process of design translated either into higher, less competitive prices or lower profit margins for companies and their investors. Thus the successful implementation of obsolescence required corporations to manage risks of higher invest-ment costs, often by limiting the role of design to superfi-cial elements of product housing rather than integrating design with engineering, ergonomics, or other research-based considerations. Moreover, the success of this strategy also depended upon marketing the products of industrial design through a variety of media ranging from popular magazines and radio to the cinema and emerging medium of television. In many ways these media often employed similar strategies for the mass production of entertain-ment. An example is the form of serial programming,

utilizing the same familiar characters facing new conflicts or crises each week, or stereotypical Hollywood film heroes following the same plotline in an array of different settings. In these cases originality was limited to particular elements of the creative process in order to generate ever "new" products for consumers to watch or to buy while containing the costs of capital resources and investment. Also, popular design and entertainment were even more interrelated, since advertisement was sold to corporate sponsors of products and services on the basis of delivering an audience for the purposes of marketing.

Most historians acknowledge that the success of product obsolescence for the mass market could not have taken place without the stimulation of advertising and added incentives such as term and credit buying. Whether through illustration, photography, or the emerging medium of television, advertisements linked products to individual identity and social acceptance. On the basis of polls and other consumer studies, advertisers often targeted housewives and children, who played a large role in buying patterns in a majority of middle-class families. Such techniques extended Veblen's theory of conspicuous consumption to an age of industrial production and mass consumption. Manufacturing and new strategies for design, marketing, and advertising combined to create forms and associations that appealed to a diverse audience linked by a belief that consumption and materialism were the means to individual fulfillment. Such a seductive combination of forces was hard to resist. Strip malls, discount stores, promotions, and expanded distribution further reduced impediments to shopping for the products of mass culture. While the phenomenon of national brands may be traced to the early twentieth century, the postwar era accelerated the substitution of the national for the local and regional through chain stores, hotels and motels, and restaurants – their names includes Korvettes, Holiday Inn, and Colonel Sanders Kentucky Fried Chicken or McDonalds restaurants. The result was an emerging shared culture of consumption that extended to many areas of American life. Journalist Thomas Hine labeled the phenomenon "populuxe," a term that helps to define the dream of abundance and self-indulgence that exerted such appeal especially during the 1950s. The relationship between advertising and mass design reminds us that the interaction between products and users was mediated by images as seen in print and on television, with the latter assuming greater importance after the war, particularly in the United States. In addition to styling and obsolescence, the shift from production to consumption was also accompanied by an increasing focus upon the design of information, of an "age of information" that expanded the practice and understanding of design.

DETROIT: TRANSPORTATION AS SYMBOL

The Detroit-manufactured automobile illustrates the attitudes and practices governing mass design. The manufacture of new automobiles for the civilian market had ceased in 1942 as automobile makers contributed to meeting the material needs of the war effort. Although demand for new cars was strong in the years following the end of World War II and the resumption of manufacturing for the domestic market, there were signs of market saturation and a slowed rate of growth in automobile purchases in the early 1950s. Postwar automobiles resembled their pre-war counterparts, and the differentiating role of design was limited by the interest in meeting demand by increasing productivity and keeping the costs of capital investment at a minimum.

Stimulating sales through annual styling changes was not a new idea in the automobile industry, and it re-emerged with renewed vitality in the early 1950s. At General Motors, president Alfred Sloan renewed his plan for greater differentiation and more noticeable annual styling changes, minimizing costs through standardized parts for the chassis and other mechanical elements that could be shared among the company's numerous product lines. It was Sloan's dream to create a vehicle "for every purse," defining a series of gradations from efficiency to luxury in terms of visible differences in styling. Encompassing the ends as well as the broad middle of the market, General Motors effectively helped to equate car buying with social as well as personal mobility and to stimulate more frequent automobile purchases while remaining competitive with smaller manufacturers of both luxury and economy cars.

Harley Earl (see page 232), chief of General Motors' Styling Department since its inception in 1927 as the Art and Color Section, benefited from a close relationship with Sloan, and was able to carry out the president's corporate vision with great imagination. Earl preferred longer and lower bodies for GM cars and accentuated these characteristics by adding decoration in the form of chrome accents, wraparound bumpers, and introducing the tailfin. Earlier pre-war prototypes, such as the 1937 two-door Buick Y-Job, announced Earl's approach, and Sloan's embrace of planned obsolescence created the kind of sponsorship that gave designers greater freedom and influence within the corporation, provided the results could be measured in increased sales and profits.

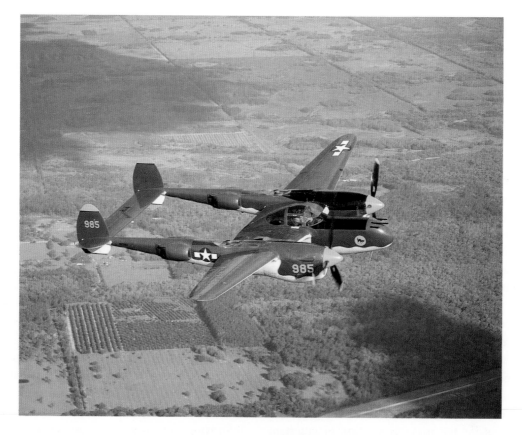

12.2 United States Air Force, P-38 fighter plane, 1941.

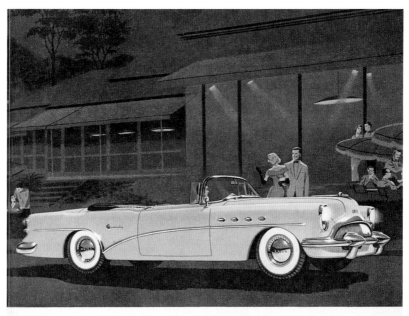

12.3 Advertisement for Buick Roadmaster, General Motors Corporation, Detroit, Michigan, 1954. *Better Homes and Gardens*, August 1954.

To approach the ideal of a longer and lower body, Earl favored flowing curvilinear forms and an integration of hoods, fenders, trunks, windshields, and roofs. As explained by Stephen Bayley, designers working for Earl made prototypes in clay rather than wood or metal to achieve more unified and modeled sculptural forms; in production, longer lengths of steel, available as early as 1934 (see page 232), reduced the gap between prototype and manufactured product. Earl introduced the tailfin first in the 1948 Cadillac, General Motors' high-end luxury car, and persisted with the feature despite an initial lukewarm reception by other company executives. The fins were a form of overt product symbolism, the result of Earl's fascination with the twin-body Lockheed P-38 fighter plane and its dual tailfins for increased stability (figs. 12.1 and 12.2). In Earl's estimation, the tailfin was a "visible receipt" for the consumer's

dollar. Its widespread success in the 1953 Cadillac encouraged Earl to include the feature in General Motors' lower-end models, where it appeared in the 1955 Chevrolet, thus making available to average customers a form of product association previously available only to wealthier buyers. The identification was encouraged through advertising, for instance, linking the potential buyer of the 1954 Buick Roadmaster with success and status (fig. 12.3). Interest in the tailfin and other features accentuating longer and lower bodies, for instance Buick's small bullet-shaped chrome "portholes," wraparound bumpers, or curved windshields, were often derived from GM's futuristic "dream cars." Dream cars were fantastic non-production models featured in traveling shows known as Motoramas or in dealer showrooms, related as well to a subculture of do-it-yourself car-buffs throughout the period who crafted customized

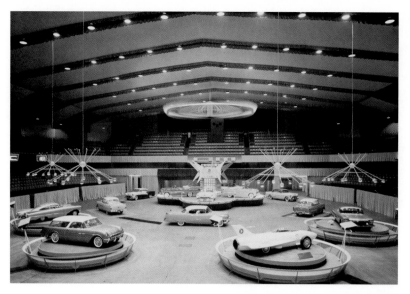

12.4 Motorama, General Motors, Flint, Michigan, 1954.

versions of standard production vehicles (fig. 12.4). The Motorama has sometimes been described as a traveling world's fair, encouraging the kinds of associations between buying, progress, and self-realization. Placing cars on pedestals only strengthened associations far beyond mere transportation, linking tailfins with the power of rocket engines and swelling forms and chrome protrusions with feminine sensuality.

The broad marketing strategy and financing of annual model changes across different brand names such as Oldsmobile, Pontiac, Buick, Chevrolet, and Cadillac, favored large companies such as General Motors and led to their increasing control of the market. In addition to their focus upon brand differentiation through styling, the large automobile manufacturers possessed the resources for advertising and other forms of marketing, such as the Motorama. Independent manufacturers like Hudson, Packard, Nash, and Kaiser either ceased production or became divisions of new conglomerates, gradually losing their independence. These smaller companies were unable to compete with or differentiate themselves from the larger companies and their comprehensive advertising, sales, and marketing strategies. Thus, despite the apparent variety and choice available to the consumer in terms of brands and models, American automobile manufacturing also became more homogeneous, controlled by a small number of large manufacturers with less room in the mass market for individual entrepreneurship. These large companies did not pursue a unified corporate image or identity but rather were successful in promoting "brand" identification with particular groups of consumers. Such a strategy seemed better suited to progressive obsolescence through

annual model changes and the introduction of new brands or sub-brands, for instance, "compact cars" such as the Chevrolet Corvair, introduced in 1960 (see pages 349–350).

The 1955 Chevrolet introduced not only the tailfin to the low end of its product line, but also the powerful, high-compression V-8 engine. For the average-income buyer, features such as styling, horsepower, air-conditioning, and motorized convertible-tops, all added a sense of individual expression and exhilaration to the experience of personal mobility also found in the popular weekly television series *Route 66* from the early 1960s (1960–1964). The continuing appeal of these associations was celebrated nostalgically in the 1973 film *American Graffiti* and the 1988 film *Rainmaker*, long after fuel prices, fears of gasoline shortages, pollution, foreign competition, and economic recession had taken their toll on the United States's "love affair" with the automobile. Advertisements for the American automobile of the later 1950s often combined references in the copy to practical advantages of roominess or advanced engineering with images that identified automobile ownership with luxurious living. These generally featured attractive, well-dressed couples returning home from an evening out or arriving in style at an upscale hotel (see figs. 12.1 and 12.3). Indeed, such product symbolism must be what Karl Gerstner had in mind in his endorsement of straight product photography rather than emotional promises in advertising (see page 294).

Contemporary cinema also featured the appeal of varied activities associated with personal mobility. Examples include the family outing of *Mr. Hobbs Takes a Vacation* (1962), the carefree spontaneity of *Two for the Road* (1967), or a reckless, self-destructive element in *Rebel Without a Cause* (1957). The automobile also formed part of the lyrics and pace of emerging rock 'n' roll music, for instance, Chuck Berry's "No Particular Place to Go":

> Riding along in my automobile
> My baby beside me at the wheel
> I stole a kiss at the turn of a mile
> My curiosity running wild
> Cruisin' and playin' the radio
> With no particular place to go.

The development of the powerful V-8 engine for regular production vehicles also took advantage of the inexpensive fuel prices in the United States, a result of favorable business agreements between American-based oil companies and refineries located in the Middle East. By the early 1970s, the oil-producing nations would assert their independence from Western oil companies, raise the price of fuel, and redefine the basis for automobile design as established by General Motors in the period under discussion. GM began to shed brands in 2004 with the elimination of Oldsmobile, followed by Pontiac in 2009 amid infusions of government investment and calls for massive restructuring. The rapport that GM had been able to establish with its customers eroded amid uncertain economic conditions and competition. When the once-mighty corporation declared bankruptcy and massive restructuring in May 2009, analysts cited a long list of miscalculations, perhaps none more significant than a failure to connect with consumers whose loyalty the company seemed to take for granted. But until that time, a large segment of the consuming public in the United States enjoyed the associations of styling, the anticipation of new annual models, and the varied associations and appeal of the open road.

A number of historians have noted an apparent irony between the products and images of indulgence, spontaneity, and self-expression in design and the generally conservative political climate of the period. This climate reinforced social conformity and threatened free speech through censorship in the Cold War fear of Communist expansion. In such circumstances an explosive popular design and its images in advertising exerted an especially strong appeal for consumers. On another level the distance between image and reality reached beyond irony. The combination of social accept-ance and individual expression that fueled consumption in the United States did not embrace all Americans; Black Americans were initially not permitted to buy homes in many suburban housing developments such as Levittown, and segregation for education, public services, and other opportunities was a fact of life in many parts of the country. The American Dream had racial as well as gender barriers;

while designers may not have been guilty of racism or gender bias, neither the design profession nor big business possessed sufficient diversity to fairly represent or serve the interests of a broader constituency. The 1960s would bring issues of free speech as well as racial and gender inequality into the foreground of public attention through protest and exposure in the mass media. These and related issues are treated more fully in Part VI (see page 354 onward).

General Motors was perhaps the largest but certainly not the only manufacturer to adopt styling and planned obsolescence in industrial design. The Ford Corporation introduced the Thunderbird sports car in 1954, a small two-seater appealing to the prospective buyer's personal indulgence rather than practical considerations of family space or comfort. The design, somewhat rectangular, seemed a restrained version of the more sculptural examples of Italian luxury coach-building (see page 287), but the Thunderbird was priced to appeal to a wider market of buyers who wished to indulge more overtly in the excitement of the open road. In 1952 Chrysler Corporation promoted Virgil Exner (1909–1973), a former associate both of Harley Earl at General Motors and of Raymond Loewy, to vice-president in charge of styling. Exner's designs for Chrysler emphasized longer and lower profiles, but minimized the rounded panels and swollen forms of General Motors cars in favor of more angular, tapered forms. In the industry this was known as the forward look, thought to be modeled upon the saber-nosed body and swept-back wings of jet fighter planes that appeared in the early 1950s. The effect was enhanced through decorative features such as overarching "eye-brows" above headlights, sweeping chrome strips reaching from front to rear and echoing the contour of the body, low and sloping rooflines, and tremendous tailfins with a pronounced upward sweep emphasizing length (fig. 12.5).

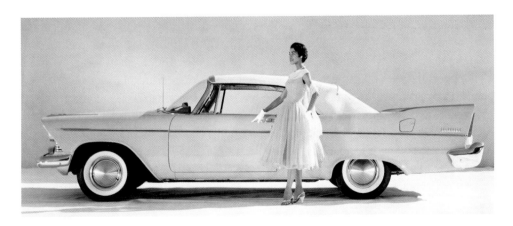

12.5 Virgil Exner, Plymouth coupé, Chrysler Corporation, Auburn Hills, Michigan, 1957.

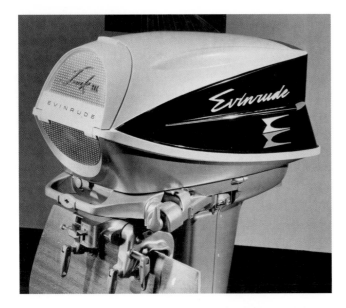
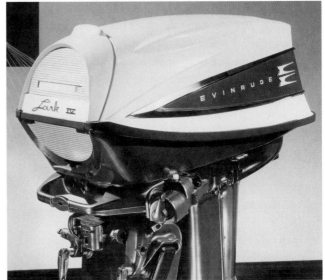
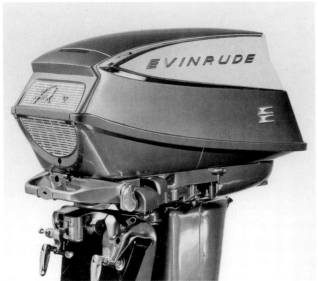
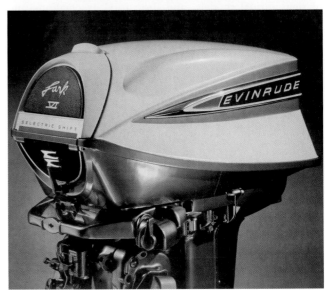

12.6 Brooks Stevens, Evinrude Lark outboard motors. Models III, IV, V, and VI styled for 1959–1962. Brooks Stevens Archive, Milwaukee Art Museum.

Consultant and in-house designers also were employed in areas outside of the automotive industry. Brooks Stevens was a successful consultant designer for several companies and products both before and after World War II. He anticipated the pent-up desire for eye-catching consumer goods following shortages and rationing during the war, and defended planned obsolescence on the basis of the joy and pride new designs gave their owners and the over-all economic benefits of increased levels of consumption. Stevens designed models for outboard recreational motor-boat engines produced by major manufacturers Evinrude and Johnson that featured cutaway housings and two-tone colors reminiscent of Chrysler's "forward look" in the later 1950s (fig. 12.6). Other designers worked in-house for companies manufacturing consumer electronics such as

Motorola, or Zenith, both based near Chicago, Illinois. These companies produced a wide range of portable and table transistor radios and phonographs. In contrast to Braun (see fig. 11.57), these their products were varied in form, color, and display (fig. 12.7), resembling automobile dashboards, grilles, and two-tone color combinations. American industrial designers for the mass market only rarely saw their role as educating consumers to appreciate modernist tastes; rather their designs acknowledged both a wide range of consumer preferences and motivations, as well as a sense of perpetual technical innovation and novelty in which the only constant was desire, as Stevens stated in his definition of planned obsolescence: "the desire to own something a little newer, a little better, a little sooner than is necessary."

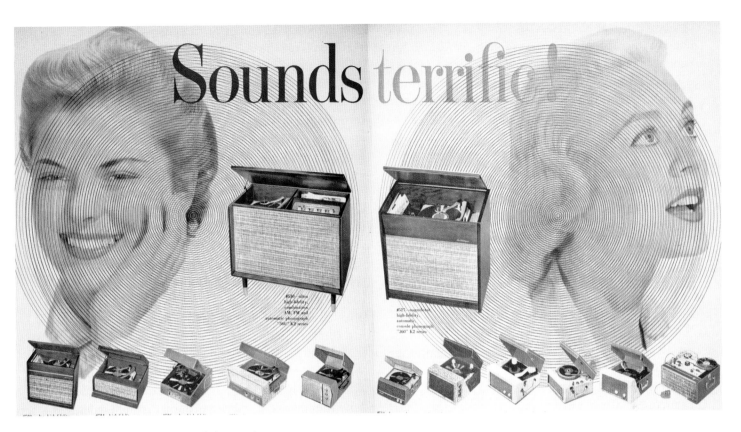

12.7 Feature on portable radios and phonographs, *Look*, vol. 20, no. 21, October 16, 1956.

CRITICS OF STYLING

By the later 1950s there was a tendency to criticize tailfins and other automobile styling features both as superfluous and tasteless. Raymond Loewy, for instance, who served as design consultant to the automobile manufacturer Studebaker, took aim at the American automobile industry in a speech of 1955, comparing that year's new designs to "gaudy merchandise" and "jukeboxes on wheels": even the author of *Never Leave Well Enough Alone*, who well understood the need to demonstrate the commercial advantages of design in industrial manufacturing, was offended by the degree to which styling had departed from a more substantive relation to the automobile's mechanical basis, or from broader considerations of performance and the ideal of beauty embodied in the characteristics of a unified streamlined modernism. Loewy's own designs for Studebaker were original and aerodynamic, pioneering the sloping roofline later introduced by former associate Virgil Exner for the 1957 Plymouth (fig. 12.8). But the Studebaker lacked the prominent symbolic jet-age tailfins of its General Motors, Ford, and Chrysler counterparts. In the end its appeal was more limited and it proved commercially unsuccessful.

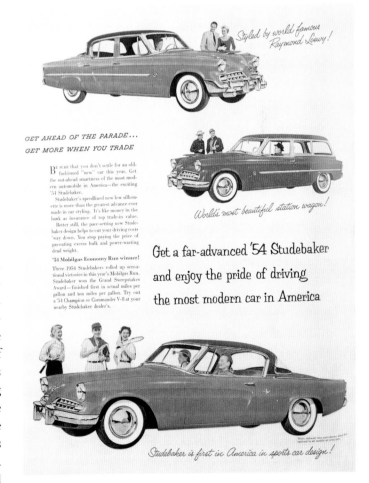

12.8 Raymond Loewy, advertisement for Studebaker, *Life*, June 1954.

For critics of the postwar American automobile industry, the manufacturer was often viewed as the manipulator of consumer desire: the manufacturer is seen as active and the consumer as passive, with the latter cast in the role of unwitting victim, conforming to social pressures and somehow "programmed" for shopping (see page 323). Perhaps it is naïve to equate freedom and self-improvement with consumer choice, but a look at the period shows that not all of the large auto-makers' styling initiatives were successful, that efforts to "manipulate" the public involved risks and often resulted in disaster (as easily observed in the high number of short-lived network television series produced each autumn). In other words, the phenomenon of mass design was and remains an unpredictable investment; its understanding demands careful study rather than the polemic and dismissive treatment that its critics often preferred.

One of the most widely known industry miscalculations of the mass market was Ford's introduction of the 1958 Edsel, a project that failed to attract consumer interest despite a heavy investment in styling and promotion. Historians have noted that family cars such as the Edsel were not attuned to consumer excitement at the time for luxury or sportier models. But as an exercise in design, the Edsel debacle reveals the complexity of predicting or manipulating public reaction in an economy dependent upon constant novelty and change. As a result, two viewpoints toward mass culture emerge. On one hand, mass design was seen as a form of exploitation manipulated as it were from above and masking the desire for corporate profit and power under the banner of freedom of choice and the democratization of luxury, heavily dependent upon advertising and product symbolism. On the other hand, mass culture was also viewed as being in touch with the everyday experience of ordinary folk, a popular expression of the desire for individuality for a diverse audience. In this view mass culture fulfills a basic desire to gratify material appetites, or to assert independence and even to resist both the efforts of corporations and advertisers alike. The elements of resistance, escape, self-expression, and difference within this popular culture emerges through products, fashion, and also through the medium of popular music, particularly rock 'n' roll, with its roots in African-American life and its rebellious challenge to conventional behavior and authority. Some of these latter attitudes linking popular music to grassroots expression may be seen in the career of rock musician and songwriter Bruce Springsteen (b. 1949). When Springsteen accepted the Oscar for Original Score at the 1993 Academy Awards for a song written for the film *Philadelphia* (1994; the movie dealt with AIDS and discrimination against its victims), he accepted the award

with the following comment: "You do your best and hope that it pulls out the best in your audience, and some piece of it spills over into the real world and people's everyday lives and allows us to recognize each other through our veil of differences." Thus popular culture reveals a paradox, for its expressions may be viewed both as a form of resistance to conformity on the one hand and as acceptance of the ephemeral criteria of mass appeal on the other. In either case, however, the status of commodities, their images in the mass media, and the economic system that creates and distributes them remain paramount, for even resistance most often takes the form of consumption rather than threatening social or political action. Moreover, whether owing to pent-up desire from rationing and shortages during World War II, or policies of Cold War containment that fostered conformity, designed consumer products may be seen as an outlet for personal expression in a climate of repressed individuality.

Author Thomas Hine noted that when United States Vice-President Richard Nixon met Soviet Premier Nikita Khrushchev in 1959 on the occasion of an exhibition of American goods in Moscow during a well-publicized meeting of the leaders of the global superpowers during the Cold War, the Vice-President proudly showed the Soviet leader an American washing machine as proof of the high standard of living enjoyed by American families. Nixon identified, in effect, materialism with the achievement of democratic ideals. While Americans might have feared the progress of the Soviets in space and weapons technology in the wake of the successful 1957 launch of the Sputnik satellite, there was little doubt that in translating technological advancement into domestic products the United States occupied a position of strength and confidence. Despite differences in regard to the issues of standards, proponents of "good design" and the products of mass culture in the later 1950s could both promote their approaches to design in terms that equated technology, leisure, and material prosperity with the achievement of democratic ideals under capitalism.

Resorts and Luxury

Together with the Detroit-manufactured automobile and the development of the new suburban tract home (see pages 317–320), popular design in postwar America was also defined by the resort hotel, first built in Miami Beach, Florida, and later in Las Vegas, Nevada. Miami Beach's Fontainebleau, built in 1954 and named for the sixteenth-century royal château outside of Paris, was one of several Florida beachfront hotels designed by Morris Lapidus. Trained as an architect in New York, Lapidus had spent much of his career prior to the war as a successful designer of retail storefronts and interiors (see fig. 10.37). Postwar affluence expanded the market for travel and leisure, providing Lapidus with the opportunity to design on a larger and more lavish scale, and to indulge the popular imagination for drama, escape, fantasy, and luxury gleaned from both the past and from a popular vision of a glamorous and indulgent future. Lapidus's resort hotels often displayed a preference for sweeping curves and recurves, for instance in the opposition of entranceway and façade at the Fontainebleau (fig. 12.9). Curving hallways rather than the repetitive rhythm of doorways and hall-lights created a sense of anticipation for the guest. Mezzanines, grand staircases, suspended ceilings with circular holes for chandeliers, and support beams hidden beneath sheathings of wood and textured materials were closer in experience to movie sets than to waiting and gathering areas. In art historical terms, Lapidus's designs tended toward the openness and grandeur of the Italian Baroque, and seemed to reduce the barrier separating Hollywood from the experience of Americans escaping cold winters for a week of vacation at the beach. Many of Lapidus's ideas derived from the expressive possibilities of shaping modern reinforced concrete. He admired the experimental architecture of German architect Erich Mendelsohn (1887–1953) and the organic forms and recesses of Surrealist art. Yet his hotels also featured decoration drawn from eighteenth-century French furniture and Italian Renaissance architecture, as in the coffee shop at the Fontainebleau from 1954 and the "Mona Lisa" room at the Eden Roc, also in Miami Beach and built in 1956 (figs. 12.10 and 12.11). It is no surprise that, paraphrasing Raymond Loewy's *Never Leave Well Enough Alone*, Lapidus entitled his own 1996 autobiography *Too Much is Never Enough*. The variety of Lapidus's

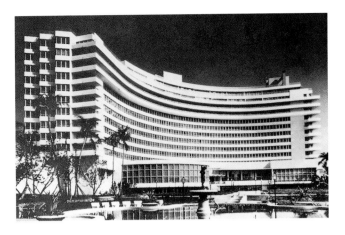

12.9 Morris Lapidus, garden façade, Fontainebleau Hotel, Miami Beach, Florida, 1954.

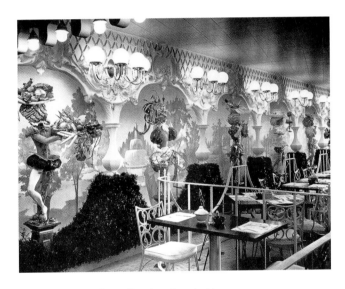

12.10 Morris Lapidus, coffee shop, Fontainebleau Hotel, Miami Beach, Florida, 1954.

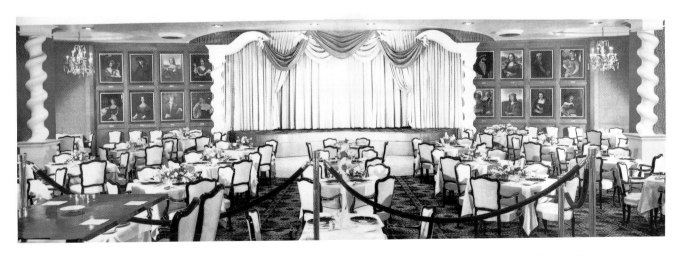

12.11 Morris Lapidus, "Mona Lisa" room, Eden Roc Hotel, Miami Beach, Florida, 1956.

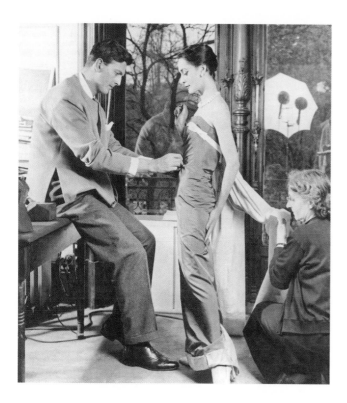

12.12 Hubert de Givenchy with model, 1952, photograph reprinted in *New Yorker*, February 19, 1996.

(1905–1957), Pierre Balmain (1914–1982), and Hubert de Givenchy (b. 1927; fig. 12.12), or designers working in France like the Spaniard Cristóbal Balenciaga (1895–1972). These couturiers maintained a reputation for elegance and the highest levels of craft and individual creativity seen earlier in French fashion, furniture, and the decorative arts from the period before and after World War I. Although exclusive, it came to the attention of a wider international audience through the medium of cinema, as well as via photography in the context of art-directed magazines such as *Vogue* and *Harper's Bazaar* (see fig. 11.22). The mass media created a cult of celebrity around movie stars, whose images provided models of ideal beauty. An example is film star Audrey Hepburn (1929–1993), known for her devotion to the designs of Givenchy. The haute-couture fashions of this period were varied and individuality was essential to the aura of the designer. But in general, eveningwear and daywear represented the first reaction against the austerity and severity of the war years. Called the "New Look" by the editor of *Harper's Bazaar* in 1947, postwar high fashion called attention, through ample use of fabric and contrasts between slim waistlines and full skirts and bodices, to an ideal of fullness and sensuality in the female form. Dior compared his creations to flowers, with stemlike waists and flowing, petal-like skirts. The hourglass was another apt metaphor for many postwar New Look fashions (see fig. 11.22).

The sensory excitement of Lapidus's Miami Beach resort hotels, enhanced by neon lights and the lure of gaming tables and slot machines in resort areas such as Las Vegas, Nevada, was captured by Tom Wolfe (b. 1931) in articles published first in *Esquire* in the early 1960s and in book form as The *Kandy-Kolored Tangerine-Flake Streamline Baby* in 1963. Wolfe likened the glitz and provocative sexuality of the Las Vegas strip to an image of paradise as a garden of delights for the senses above which humanity rarely rises. Indeed, modern popular culture offered almost unlimited delights for the senses, amplified through technology, available in fashion and vicariously through the cinema and magazine, or in reality through the vacation resort. These included movies in Technicolor for the eyes, stereo sound for the ears, processed foods for the palette, just to name a few.

Even earlier than Tom Wolfe in the United States, journalist and critic Reyner Banham (1922–1988) was questioning the elitism and paternalistic overtones of "good design" in a series of articles written for newspapers and periodicals in Britain. Banham recognized the appeal of mass culture's combination of fantasy, escapism, and healthy expression of the popular will in an abundant consumer culture dominated by large multinational industrial corporations rather than individual

conceptions, intended to satisfy his clients and appeal to the aspirations and fantasies of the hotel's clientele, characterized a "both ... and" rather than "either ... or" attitude toward design that fueled expectations of upward mobility. It was this broad eclecticism that was often criticized at the time for its commercialism and lack of discrimination between architecture and amusement parks, but later Lapidus began to gain critical acceptance and even praise for his imagination and sense of playfulness and fun. However indulgent or escapist, Lapidus's ideal of luxury gave to the many a glimpse of what had been the entitlement of the few, if only for a week or even a weekend. And if not experienced directly, the version of luxury embodied in the Fontainebleau and elsewhere was experienced vicariously in film, on television, and in the features and advertisements of magazines such as *Holiday*.

It is hardly surprising that one of Lapidus's sources of inspiration for luxury interiors was France. Following a trip to France in the mid-1950s, Lapidus commissioned dozens of copies of oil paintings after masterpieces in the Louvre, and even the name Eden Roc was inspired by a resort at Cap d'Antibes on the French Riviera. Indeed, the postwar period witnessed the resurgence of the association of France with the most cultivated tastes, particularly in regard to high fashion and especially with the emergence of French designers such as Christian Dior

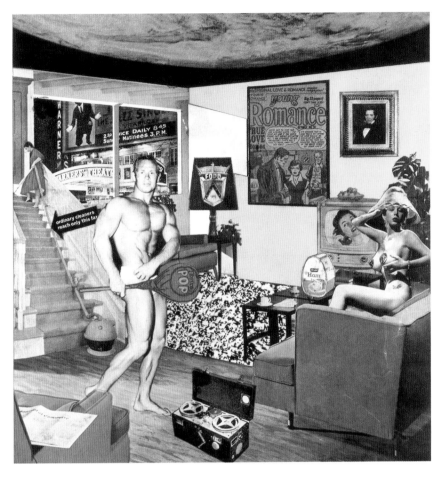

12.13 Richard Hamilton, *Just what is it that makes today's homes so different, so appealing?*, collage, 10 ½ x 9 ¾ in (27 x 25 cm), 1956. Kunsthalle, Tübingen.

producers. Such attitudes also help to account for the emergence of Pop Art both in Britain and in the United States, in part as a reaction to the stoicism of British design and the elitism and esoteric tendencies of avantgarde art. When Richard Hamilton (b. 1922) and Eduardo Paolozzi (1924–2005) created collage images such as Hamilton's *Just what is it that makes today's homes so different, so appealing?* (fig. 12.13), appropriating photographs and illustrations directly from American popular mass-circulation magazines, the images were less an indictment of materialism and commercialism than a celebration of the pleasures of the senses, a time-honored theme of the fine arts in earlier eras when the arts were indeed more approachable.

HOUSING: SUBURBIA, DOMESTICITY, AND CONFORMITY

The automobile stylings under Earl and Exner in the United States were also contemporary with the transformation of the housing construction industry and the emerging patterns of life in large suburban developments.

New approaches to home building were a response to a severe housing shortage for returning veterans coupled with slow growth in housing starts during the Depression. The elastic markets for housing and automobiles after the war were not unrelated. Indeed the growth of new suburban communities, constructed on inexpensive tracts of land located further from commuter rail lines, increased the dependence upon the automobile for commuting to the workplace. They also account for the commercial success of new shopping centers and later of malls, designed to bring dozens of businesses together in an area built with abundant space for vehicular parking. In fact, both industries supported and even lobbied successfully for government-funded interstate highway projects to help guarantee the success of their enterprise. Also contributing to the success of the suburban development was the ease of obtaining federally sponsored low-interest mortgage loans from agencies such as the Veterans Administration (VA) and the Federal Housing Administration (FHA), encouraging young couples and families to purchase new homes rather than rent apartments.

Builder William Levitt pioneered mass-production techniques in the housing industry after World War II in "Levittown" communities located in suburban New York, New Jersey, and Pennsylvania. Using pre-assembled parts and teams of specialized workers, each assigned to repeating a particular task in a rationalized approach to the home building process, Levitt became the "Henry Ford" of the housing industry. His methods enabled the construction of houses in less than six weeks on inexpensively purchased land beyond the limits of urban centers, and in communities with as many as 17,000 new houses, suburbia began to come into focus. Levitt's homes were built on concrete slabs rather than on foundations with basements, and his construction process quickly became the industry standard due to the affordability of the units, which began as low as $7,900. In addition, buyers could purchase homes with as little as a one-dollar down payment and federally guaranteed mortgages that minimized the builder's risk.

Postwar housing in the United States differed significantly from its European counterparts. Whereas dense, efficient, and uniform housing after World War II was normal in communities outside most large European cities, in the United States new building materials, inexpensive land, and mass-production techniques reinforced traditional associations between property, status, and independence. Individual home ownership implied stability and permanence, linked in the popular imagination with self-sufficiency and levels of comfort formerly available only to wealthier Americans. In lowering the economic threshold for ownership, the home became a realizable part of the American dream for a larger proportion of the working and middle classes, and was a clear measure of improvement in comparison with the apartments and row-houses in which many new home-owners had grown up. Within this appealing ideological framework it is not surprising that while the construction of early postwar suburban homes entailed new standardized methods of construction as well as new prefabricated materials such as drywall (as opposed to plaster), the design of these same homes recalled modest and traditional rather than contemporary housing types. Among the most common was the so-called "Cape Cod" style, rectangular in shape with a pitched roof sloping toward the front (fig. 12.14). Buyers were also attracted to the new homes by a number of practical modern features intended to make life more convenient and efficient. Kitchens, for instance, featured picture windows to allow parents to watch their children play in the yard, and attached garages that kept automobiles off the street and allowed entry directly into the home. The attraction of individual home ownership and the added convenience of appliances such as washing machines and even television sets, often included in the selling price, seemed to outweigh the drawbacks of a

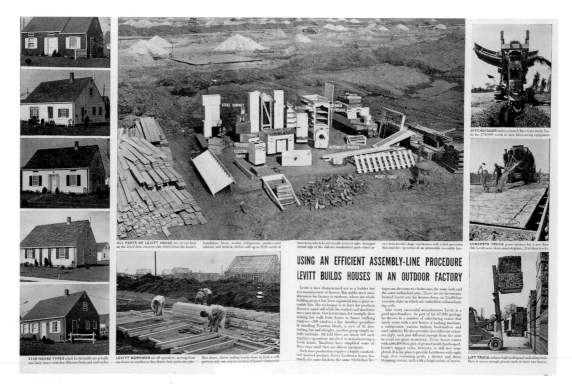

12.14 Levittown feature, *Life*, August 23, 1948.

conformity often noted by critics. Author Lewis Mumford (1895–1990) was one such critic, who saw few advantages to the postwar suburb in comparison with its more idyllic, villagelike predecessors, and predicted negative consequences should the trend continue:

> The ultimate outcome of the suburb's alienation from the city became visible only in the twentieth century, with the extension of the democratic ideal through the instrumentalities of manifolding and mass production. In the mass movement into suburban areas a new kind of community was produced, which caricatured both the historic city and the archetypal suburban refuge: a multitude of uniform, unidentifiable houses, lined up inflexibly, at uniform distances, on uniform roads, in a treeless communal waste, inhabited by people of the same class, the same income, the same tasteless pre-fabricated foods, from the same freezers, conforming in every outward and inward respect to a common mold, manufactured in the central metropolis. Thus the ultimate effect of the suburban escape in our time is ironically, a low-grade uniform environment from which escape is impossible.
>
> What has happened to the suburban exodus in the United States now threatens, through the same mechanical instrumentalities, to take place, at an equally accelerating rate, everywhere else.

The identification of home ownership with the lifestyle of the average family was also mirrored in the emerging television industry. Television families, such as the Nelsons of *Ozzie and Harriet* or the Cleavers of *Leave it to Beaver*, owned homes in suburban communities. Notable exceptions were the childless Cramdens of *The Honeymooners*, who suffered renters' frustrations of noise and lack of privacy found in urban apartment houses, or the family of nightclub entertainer Danny Thomas. Mr Thomas's career required that his own precocious children live in a spacious Manhattan apartment dominated by adults rather than by other children.

I remember a story from my grade-school reader written in the mid-1950s. In this illustrated story the child of a young family who recently moved into a new subdivision is troubled by an inability to distinguish his own home from the others on his block. The problem is solved when each family creates its own weather vane to add character and individual identity to otherwise bland and uniform surroundings. The housing industry also offered solutions to the practical as well as social desire for differentiation in the market. Attracting new buyers from the city to the suburb or encouraging suburbanites to "trade up" during the 1950s led to an expansion of the range of

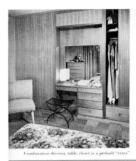
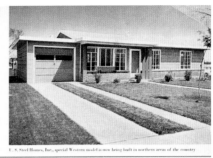
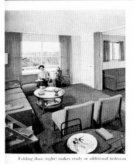
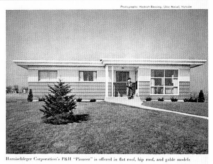
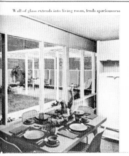
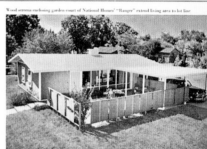

12.15 Feature on prefabricated homes from *Better Homes and Gardens*, August 1954.

housing types, featuring much inventiveness in introducing variations available for consumers to express preferences and "customize" their purchase. In addition to the standard "Cape Cod" home, builders began to include a wider variety of traditional types such as Colonial or Tudor, as well as modern Ranch models. The last included large expanses of windows and low single-story designs, or a "split level" with half-stories to either side of a central entrance (fig. 12.15). Informal family rooms and eat-in kitchens became ways to expand living space and move beyond basic housing needs toward comfort and entertainment, visible signs of success judged in comparison to one's neighbor, compensating for the conformity and alienation criticized by Mumford and others through ever-escalating levels of consumption.

The reduction of standardization in interior design and decoration resulted from new industrial materials whose potential for variation was exploited by manufacturers. Examples include Formica, a hard plastic available in a variety of patterns for use in kitchen surfaces to replace enameled metal or stainless steel, and Linoleum, a

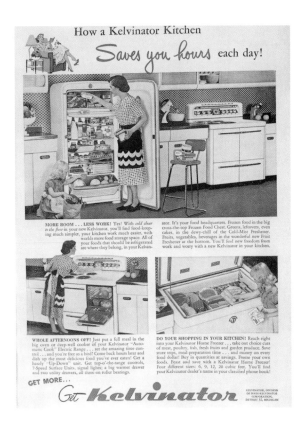

12.16 Advertisement, refrigerator, manufactured by Frigidaire Corporation, Dayton, Ohio, *Good Housekeeping*, January, 1950.

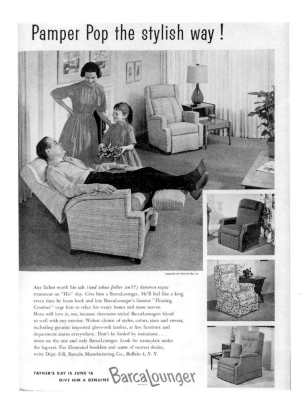

12.17 Advertisement, Barcalounger lounge chair with Naugahyde vinyl upholstery, manufactured by U.S. Naugahyde, illustrated in *Better Homes and Gardens*, June, 1951.

softer surface used for flooring in kitchens and recreation rooms. The more colorful and textured effects of Formica and Linoleum, as well as Naugahyde upholstery, made the kitchen less of a "laboratory" or workplace than a room for leisure and relaxation. The reduction of toil implied in this interpretation of the kitchen was to a great degree supported by advertising, in which appliances such as dishwashers as well as household cleaning products were viewed as improvements bringing new quantities of freedom and leisure. Fashionably dressed housewives were generally pictured along with the dishwasher or new dinette, marveling at the ease of loading the new appliance, admiring the sparkling cleanliness of the glassware, or enjoying time with family members (fig. 12.16). Comfort found expression less in the plywood and pedestal-based Eames lounge than in the more massive and heavily upholstered reclining chair known as the La-Z-boy or variations such as the Barcalounger and Stratolounger (fig. 12.17). Elements of the La-Z-boy derived from cushioned railway cars. Advertisements focused upon the variety of available fabrics and upholstery styles from which the buyer could choose, as well as upon the relaxed (mostly male) occupant resting after a long day at the office. The world of children's leisure was filled with a never-ending array of ephemeral fads and toys, from spinning tops to

butterfly yo-yos, hoola-hoops and frisbees, creating a market that is today augmented by videogames and their captivating virtual reality, all requiring the considerable contributions of a new generation of designers.

New domestic uses were also identified and successfully marketed for aluminum in the 1950s in an industry effort to maintain wartime production levels. The Alcoa Aluminum Company advertised creative uses of aluminum in mass-circulation magazines as part of a forecasting program using the word "imagineering." One of the more popular products to emerge in the early 1950s was sets of anodized aluminum tumblers in rainbow colors manufactured as Heller Hostess ware (fig. 12.18). Lightweight and certainly unbreakable, aluminum drinking cups were easily dented, especially around the lip, and their uniform weight created a high center of gravity that made them tip over easily when filled. Despite such shortcomings, the festive colors, novelty, and associations with the informality and pleasure of outdoor picnics and barbecues helped to make aluminum tumblers commercially successful. Such products might be contrasted with the use of heavier and more sober or "natural" stainless steel in Scandinavian dinnerware of the same period, characterized by a plain metallic finish and used for serving rather than eating or drinking (fig. 12.19). Another example

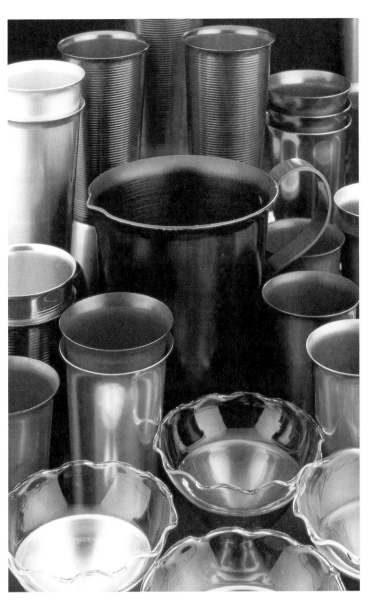

12.18 Tumblers, anodized aluminum, Heller Hostess ware, 5 ⅛ x 2 ⅞ in (13 x 7.3 cm), 1946–c. 1955.

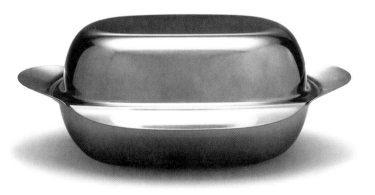

12.19 Sigurd Persson, vegetable dish, stainless steel, 8 ⁷⁄₁₆ in (21.4 cm) in length, manufactured by Silver & Stål, 1953. Philadelphia Museum of Art.

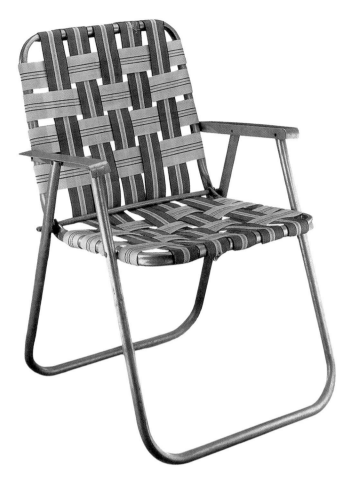

12.20 Folding chair, aluminum and nylon webbing, 31 ¾ x 22 ⅛ in (81 x 56 cm), America, late 1960s.

of "imagineering" in the 1950s was the folding aluminum chair, made of lightweight tubular aluminum (first developed for seating in the aircraft industry) and plastic webbing (fig. 12.20). There was nothing durable or particularly ergonomic about this anonymous outdoor chair. Unstable if placed on uneven ground and irreparable when the plastic webbing was torn or detached from the rivets that held it to the frame, the portable chairs were and remain the kind of expendable, replaceable, everyday product characteristic of mass culture, a paradigm of Banham's "Throwaway Culture." The ephemeral nature of such designs and other fads contrasted with some of the tenets of "good design" and international modernism, where research provided solutions to problems or an elevated aesthetic awareness. While museums' international exhibitions seemed to favor the latter over the former, it was perhaps popular design that better illustrated the realities of the postwar economy on a mass scale. Whether new products or variations of existing ones, design served to stimulate desire as part of an interdependent dialogue with advertising and branding strategies.

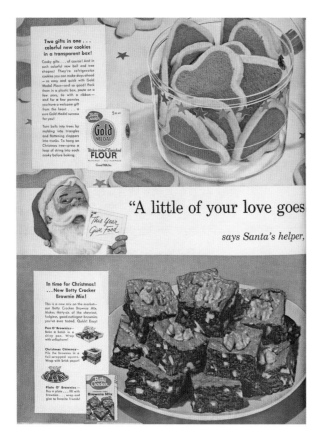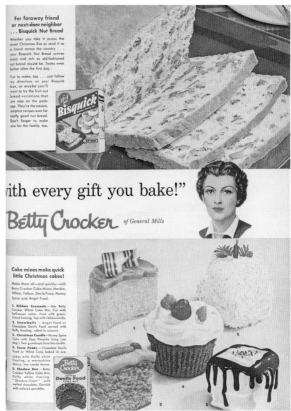

12.21 Advertisement for Betty Crocker products manufactured by General Mills Corporation, from *Better Homes and Gardens*, December, 1954.

The increased availability and popularity of packaged and processed foods was another component of postwar mass culture, a further instance of the equation of leisure with progress. Instead of baking from scratch, cake mixes included pre-measured ingredients to enable housewives to perform instant "miracles" in the kitchen. Such products were endorsed by the matronly Betty Crocker, a creation of the home services department at General Mills in 1921, whose immensely popular cookbook and advice helped to preserve the comforting sense of pride in being a traditional homemaker (fig. 12.21). As American studies scholar Karal Ann Marling relates, consultants to the General Mills Corporation (who manufactured and sold baking products) recommended that recipes call for using real eggs in cake mixes rather than powdered eggs to enable housewives to "make a creative contribution to the process." This combination of new goods with reassuring values of home and family is a characteristic often found in the products of mass culture. Processed foods such as cake mixes and "TV dinners" were modern in the sense of relating to contemporary lifestyles, and also in the technology of dehydration and packaging of meals for servicemen during World War II. The conflicting desires for both increased convenience and ease along with the satisfaction of being a responsible homemaker are addressed. The phenomenon of packaged foods exemplifies a shift from the commodity itself to the psychological motivation for its purchase, that is, from production to consumption. Packaging, from toothpaste to dishwashing liquids, was often bright and festive, with lettering in different colors and in different alignments, a playful, even carefree accent to bathroom or kitchen. Other products meant to reduce toil included Jiffy popcorn, where the fry pan itself could be disposed of after being used on top of the stove, and synthetic fabrics such as Dacron Permapress, which required no ironing.

BEYOND HIGH AND LOW ART: REVISITING THE CRITIQUE OF MASS CULTURE

While advertising outlined the applications of newly-found leisure in a variety of products and appliances, such leisure was at times problematic for the American housewife. Dissatisfaction with the suburban lifestyle and the ways in which it defined fulfillment found expression in Betty Friedan's *The Feminine Mystique* (1963), an outgrowth of the author's experience as a mother and housewife in the 1950s. Following the end of World War II, hundreds of thousands of women were displaced from jobs by returning soldiers, and found little opportunity to resume or begin careers. Mass media, in the form of women's magazines such as *Ladies' Home Journal*, *McCalls*, and *Redbook*, as well as most network television housewives, encouraged women to focus their energies upon the home, defining their role primarily as consumers while husbands went off to work. Friedan's experience demonstrated that the patterns of postwar suburban living and the ideals of beauty, comfort, luxury, and well-being advertised in magazines and on television did not always provide alternatives for women outside a range of activities some women found unrewarding. It is no wonder that surveys conducted at the time indicated less satisfaction with suburban life among women in comparison with men.

In addition to the sense of conformity described above, exclusivity was also an issue of the postwar suburban housing boom, and presented a different reality to the one imagined through the mass media and advertising. Conspicuously absent from these new suburban neighborhoods and their television counterparts were Black Americans and other minorities. Historians of the period such as Kenneth Jackson have noted that in addition to the uniformity implied by standardization, suburban housing communities tended to create economic as well as racial homogeneity. This occurred particularly through zoning laws that inhibited industrial building and prevented construction of housing for lower-income families, as well as overt policies by builders that denied access to black buyers. At the same time increasing numbers of black families were migrating from the rural south to the urban and industrial north, in search of higher-paying jobs or a new beginning after serving in the armed forces during the war. Equating American life with its image in advertising and through the mass media would present only a partial and imperfect picture that masks racial and gender inequality.

Other critics have argued that the link between technology, consumer goods, and an improving standard of living masked not only racial or gender discrimination, but also the connection between technology and the Cold War arms race; in other words, the focus upon peacetime consumption and affluence diverted public attention from the alliance between big business and government in contracts for military hardware and information technology. This alliance in turn leads to an increasing concentration of power in both capital and in government, and in the potential for international conflict. Popular opposition to American intervention in Vietnam and support for civil rights legislation in the later 1950s and throughout the 1960s expressed doubts about the relationship between technology and progress. Such opposition was expressed in design through underground posters

and artists' use of techniques of mass communication in new ways. This development is treated in Part VI.

Throughout the first two decades of the postwar period, a number of writers and critics condemned virtually every manifestation of the emerging mass culture and mass media on political, moral, and aesthetic grounds. Most criticism of popular culture was based upon the views of an educated and sophisticated elite seeking to universalize a set of criteria that itself preserved and extended a design discourse inherited from the very beginnings of industrialization and class conflict. Much criticism adopted a polemic tone and dismissive treatment of its target. In the immediate postwar years, commercially motivated mass culture and mass media were criticized for a lack of social responsibility. In part this was a response both to the exaggerated claims of early advertising as well as to the control of media and propaganda by Fascist regimes during the 1930s and 1940s. Common to both charges was the belief that the essentially passive "masses" could be easily manipulated with false promises. The tone of criticism of this kind can be sensed from the following remarks of Robert Hutchins, president of the University of Chicago, in 1940:

> In order to believe in democracy we must believe that there is a difference between truth and falsity, good and bad, right and wrong, and that truth, goodness, and right are objective standards even though they cannot be experimentally verified.... Political organization must be tested by conformity to ideals. Its basis is moral. Its end is the good for man.... These are the principles which we must defend if we are to defend democracy.
>
> Are we prepared to defend these principles? Of course not. For forty years and more our intellectual leaders have been telling us they are not true. They have been telling us in fact that nothing is true which cannot be subject to experimental verification. In the whole realm of social thought there can, therefore, be nothing but opinion. Since there is nothing but opinion, everybody is entitled to his own opinion.... If everything is a matter of opinion, force becomes the only way of settling differences of opinion. And, of course, if success is the test of rightness, right is on the side of the heavier battalions.

The warning against manipulation also appears in a 1957 book by Vance Packard entitled *The Hidden Persuaders*. The book dealt with sophisticated psychological techniques and motivational analysis by market researchers as well as advertising used to sell products to unaware consumers. Packard's analysis emphasized the role of insecurity in the promotion of consumption, for instance, in the need for men to feel "masculine" being met by cigarettes or aftershave lotions in a society where insecurity and conformity dictated the patterns and frustrations of everyday life. Packard quoted extensively from the heads of advertising agencies and marketing consultants, and used the terms "motivational research" (abbreviated as MR in the book) and "depth analysis" as labels for the persuasive techniques of selling derived from psychological surveys of consumers. Packard concluded that what motivates people to buy is not need but rather a desire to feel better about themselves. He was alarmed that such techniques of persuasion were being used not only for consumer goods but also in the political arena, and feared the consequences. Basic to Packard's rhetoric is the manipulation of the irresistible unconscious urges of the public by advertisers and those employed by them as consultants. *The Hidden Persuaders* saw advertising techniques as dehumanizing, suggesting that such techniques might be used to program our actions and thoughts:

> What the probers are looking for, of course, are the whys of our behavior, so that they can more effectively manipulate our habits and choices in their favor. This had led them to probe why we are afraid of banks; why we love those big fat cars; why housewives typically fall into a hypnoidal trance when they get into a supermarket; why men are drawn into auto showrooms by convertibles but end up buying sedans; why junior loves cereal that pops, snaps, and crackles.
>
> We move from the genial world of James Thurber into the chilling world of George Orwell and his Big Brother, however, as we explore some of the extreme attempts at probing and manipulating now going on.

Other critics took aim at the housing industry, echoing familiar concerns about the public interest and improving the level of public taste. In 1946 George Nelson published a book advocating modern designs over traditional ones and describing the modern suburban "Cape Cod" house as a sham reflection of its prototype, unsuited to the aesthetic and social conditions of contemporary life. Nelson echoed Lewis Mumford, who decried the uniformity of the suburban tract and the consequent decline of the quality of city life as resources were poured into roads rather than into the upkeep of urban residential neighborhoods, and as traffic congestion appeared to compromise the virtues of suburban living.

The criticism of mass culture was equally severe in European Marxist circles. Here issues of taste were combined with bitter disappointment and disillusionment

at the subversion of techniques of mass production and mass communication first to Fascist regimes in the interwar period and then after the war to capitalist enterprise and the fetishization of commodities rather than to the attainment of more enlightened socialist egalitarian ends. Part of the historical critique of capitalism in general focuses upon the need for large corporations to reap a return on their investment by guaranteeing a market for products of mechanized mass production through seductive advertising and marketing techniques. The result is the combination of design change and mass advertising that magnifies the symbolism of the product in a process often referred to as commodification or reification. While recognizing the much larger scale of mechanized mass production in the mid-twentieth century, the process nevertheless recalls the role of commodities as criticized by design reformers in Victorian England or social critics in turn-of-the-century America. The German critic Theodor Adorno (1903–1969), for instance, used the term "culture industry" to refer to the methods of mass media and the capitalist control of the means of production that underwrote the system of entertainment and related industries. By equating culture with leisure there was a tendency to devalue and corrupt the entire enterprise of design under capitalism. In this view one sees consumption as the reward of compliance within a system so pervasive as to eradicate even awareness of its power to compromise and subvert the freedom of the individual. Such a situation offers no escape aside from revolution or the pursuit of an alternative lifestyle akin perhaps to the Arts and Crafts communities of the late nineteenth century and their rejection of industrial society.

More recently the views of Adorno and other critics have been seen as being based upon a narrow and dismissive understanding of mass culture, one which presupposes a monolithic cultural homogeneity. Students of mass culture argue persuasively that even allowing for the manipulative, dehumanizing, and alienating associations described by critics, the phenomenon has a richness and complexity that earlier authors were unwilling to admit. As a result the facile dualism of many critics appears less tenable than was once believed.

The appreciation of mass culture is based upon a number of considerations, including a better understanding of the system of production, distribution, and consumption of cultural products, as well as a recognition of the various ways in which an audience responds to those products. Rather than a passive role for the consumer, students of mass culture suggest that the audience participates or is active in its response to the products of design – thus the product not only is created for an audience, but is also in effect created *by* its audience, and expresses that audience's preferences and values. One example of the rich and varied reaction to American popular culture was demonstrated during the later 1960s when it was embraced by German youth as a form of protest against government and corporate regulation of education and politics. Other observers have described the "sociability" of mass culture, that is, the way in which it appeals to a broad audience and communicates a variety of meanings.

The Marxist critique of popular culture has lost little of its ability to illuminate the underlying structures and mechanisms at work in our daily lives as citizens and consumers in a capitalist world, even if its political motivations have lost some of their credibility and if angry and revolutionary motivations tended to exaggerate their authors' polemic tone. In the end it is perhaps worthwhile to keep in mind the range of responses to popular culture and the dynamic relationship between the "culture industry" and an expanding, diverse new audience. The middle class found an array of outlets for consuming products, reacting to billboards and advertising images in weekly magazines, listening to the radio, going to the cinema, and watching television at home. As noted by author and literary critic Clive James (b. 1939), popular culture represented a "step up" for the working and middle classes, though perhaps not a step toward the culture envisioned by the advocates of "good design."

Curiously, while the proponents of "good design" defended their activities on the basis of noble aims that included the education of the masses, the fine arts generally retreated from pursuing a relation to the general public. Instead, the emerging New York art world sought a more rarefied atmosphere in which creativity was unfettered either by commercialism, the mass market, or the international standards of "good design" and its ideology of shared cultural values and social responsibility. The influential American art critic Clement Greenberg (1909–1994) neatly divided the post World War II art world into three groups. There were the avant-garde, advocates of high art who were the guardians of individualism and originality in the arts, seeking pure abstraction and autonomy as a field of interest. A second group consisted of practitioners of middlebrow art, who interpreted aspects of high art in more useful goods but undermined and compromised their aesthetic purity and independence. Finally there was low (mass) art, described

simply as "kitsch," catering to the uneducated masses with the appeal of the traditional and debased borrowings from more authentic forms of expression. Such distinctions began to erode in the 1960s with the growing phenomenon of Pop Art and the development of more pluralistic approaches to the study of culture.

CONCLUSION

The postwar period witnessed the expansion of industrial design involving the application of wartime technology to domestic products, fueled by the United States and its investment in the reconstruction of Western European and Japanese peacetime economies through support of industrial manufacturing. There was a broadening of the understanding of the industrial design profession to include ergonomics and a wider range of problem-solving skills pertaining to product development and information design. The emergence of mass communication also served to market and to affect the design of products to an ever-increasing audience through obsolescence and product symbolism. In the context of Cold War tensions in the later 1950s, consumption, technology, and materialism, whether motivated by social mobility or by social responsibility, became increasingly identified with democracy and freedom under a system of capitalist free enterprise. The result was a blurring of the distinction that critics had drawn between commercial styling and the more restrained and socially responsible approach once understood as "good design." Such critical awareness tended to provide justification for an appreciation and understanding of mass culture, while at the same time raised some doubts about the benevolent association between modern design and social and economic progress. An appreciation of the immediate postwar era includes thinking less in terms of a dichotomy between high and low art than in terms of a continuum in which commercial, aesthetic, reformist, scientific, and technological considerations operated in varied measure. At the same time the activity of design began to overlap into related fields of communication and information and expand the use and understanding of the term. Whether through corporate identity, complex systems for transportation, or advertising, design was seen increasingly as an interdependent rather than isolated activity within the larger context of connecting users of the designer's output with technology, products, and services.

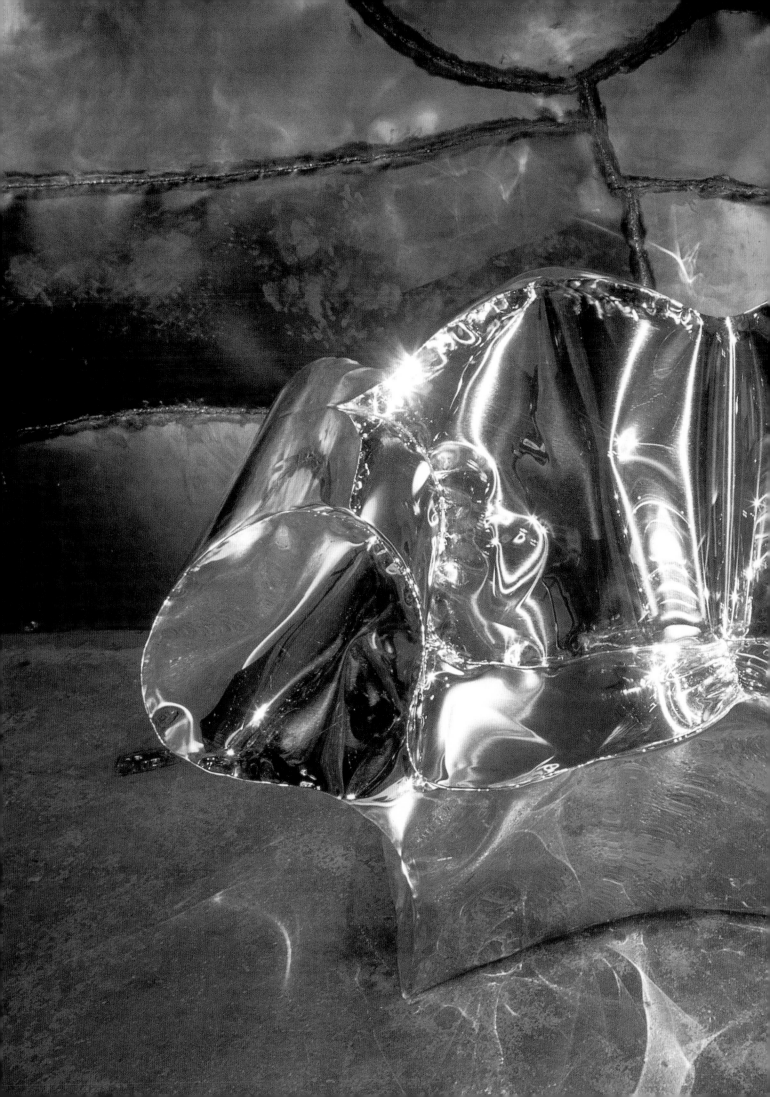

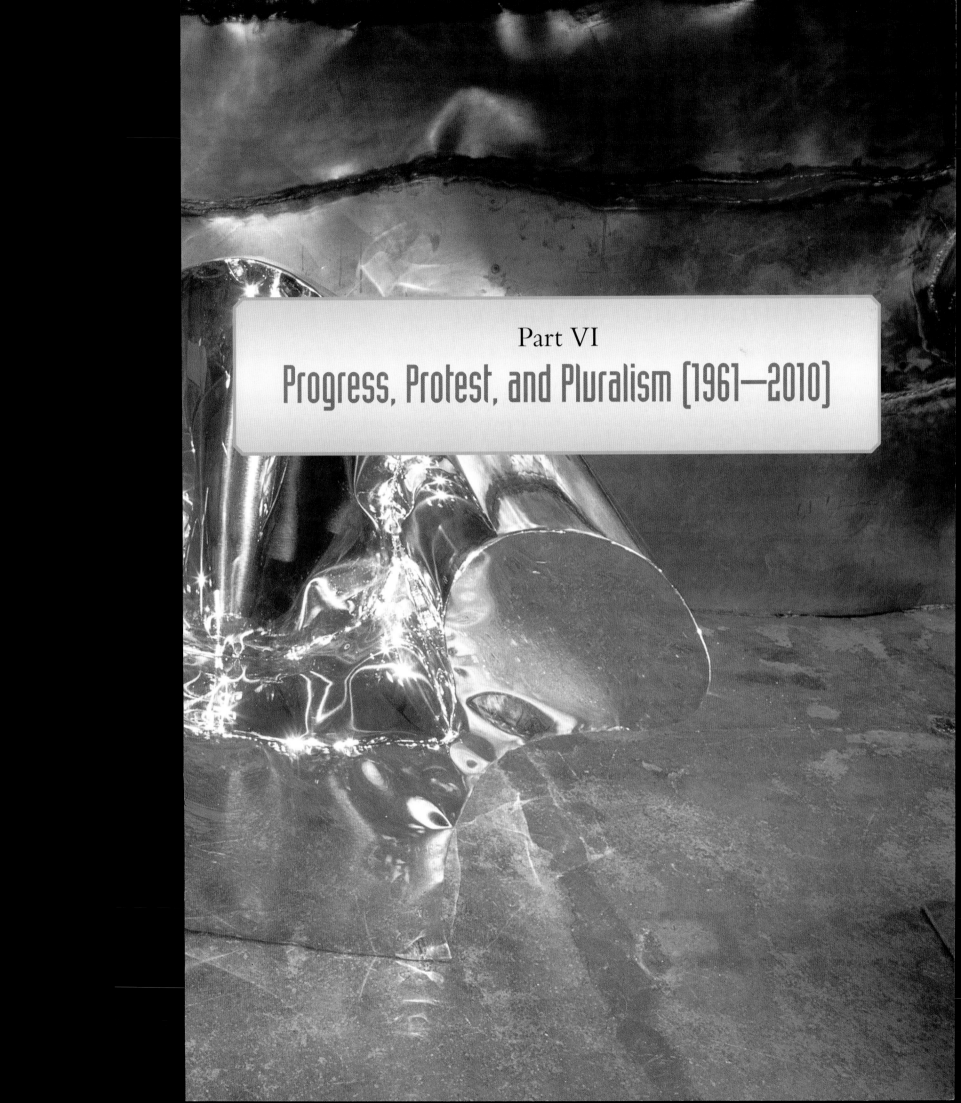

Part VI
Progress, Protest, and Pluralism (1961—2010)

Introduction to Part VI

Fulfilling the promise of the partnership between technology and progress through design in the postwar period has proven to be a challenging, often elusive goal, as the social, moral, economic, and political tensions that characterized the somewhat turbulent 1960s continue to be felt in the new century and millennium. Food processors, microwave ovens, compact disks, personal and handheld computers, MP3 players, interactive videogames, cellular phones, and global positioning systems are only among the most obvious examples of technologies affecting contemporary lifestyles, extending the range of our powers and redefining the relationship between work and leisure in the industrially developed nations of the world. Personal computers and the Internet have not only stimulated the marketing and merchandising of these and countless other products, but also have increased the emphasis upon design as an expanding sphere of activity that encompasses all fields of information and communication. The growth of the Internet is a clear indication of an emerging *post*-industrial age in which information, intellectual property, and a wide range of human services are increasingly the sources of economic power, and where manufacturing often takes place in the less developed nations of the world.

The expansion of markets for commodities has been further stimulated by the deregulation and privatization of communications industries, by the growth and sophistication of credit buying, by computerized techniques of product development and manufacturing, and by advertising, telemarketing, and electronic or e-commerce. The breakup of the Soviet Union in 1989 and the emerging independence of former Eastern Bloc countries have further extended the hegemony of market-based capitalist economies and their dependence upon innovation and expanding the production and consumption of commodities both domestically and internationally. China is the latest example of this movement, and the 2008 Summer Olympic Games in Beijing as well as the "Design China Now" exhibition (also in 2008) at the Victoria and Albert Museum in London and other venues attest to the role of design in promoting tourism and a modern image for the country.

While design consultancies such as Smart Design or IDEO are often identified by the products for which they are responsible, products only account for a relatively small percentage of their activity, which also includes corporate identity and organizational systems to facilitate communication. The visible form of products today is often the result of a lengthy process of dialogue and compromise among viewpoints representing client interest, user experience, development and production costs, aesthetics, materials, and market research. Design practice appears to be as much a model for non-hierarchical organizational behavior generally as a strategy directed toward producing physical objects.

This is certainly the case for the well-known Pentagram Design group (1972), founded in London and now operating with seventeen partners in five cities internationally. Primarily known for graphic design and high-profile corporate clients such as Citicorp, Pentagram's services also extend to products and architecture, involving teamwork and group rather than individual ownership of complex design projects.

Yet the connection between design and new or "improved" consumer goods continues to create an ever-increasing flood of products that appears at times to make us victims as well as beneficiaries of both technology and the information age, defining us perhaps too narrowly as little more than machines for programmed consumption, reducing the exercise of freedom to the choice between endless varieties of products that complicate and fragment our lives. At the same time, concerns with environmental as well as for social responsibility on a broader global scale undermine at least some of the confidence in the future we are designing. Sustainability has certainly shifted from the fringes to the mainstream, and is now the focus of corporate advertising strategies and interdisciplinary awareness in universities, presenting tremendous challenges to design that extend beyond innovation to rethinking basic assumptions about our relationship to the goods we produce and consume. Green design may have triggered a broad-based consciousness that informs shared attitudes toward new products in relationship to the environment, but to be effective that consciousness must extend to patterns of consumer behavior that are difficult to break or alter, especially when consumer spending remains a basic indicator of economic health. The specter of terrorism and cost of counter-terrorism in the wake of the attacks of September 11, 2001 threatens the safety we take for granted and often view as the bedrock of our freedom and confidence in shaping our future. Awareness of these contradictions and uncertainties, of the combination of hopes as well as fears for the future of design, form the basis for this final part of our study.

Chapter 13

New Materials, New Products

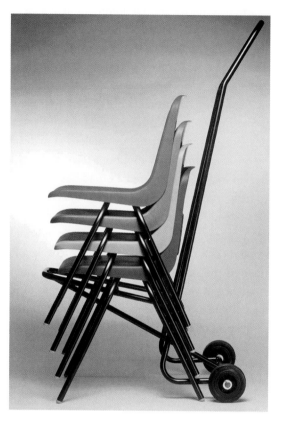

13.1 Robin Day, polyprop stacking chair, polypropylene and steel, height 29 in (74 cm), manufactured by Hille, 1964.

Material technology continued to stimulate a number of original product designs in the 1960s, reinforcing the forms and ideology of "good design" as it had emerged in the first postwar decade. Certainly a significant part of this growth revolved around developments in synthetic plastics and production processes. British industrial designer Robin Day (b. 1915) used a new flexible plastic known as polypropylene to compete with fiberglass in the design of seating. Day's 1963 polyprop chair (fig. 13.1), manufactured by Hille, shares much in common with the Eameses' and Saarinen's earlier examples of molded chairs (see figs. 11.5 and 11.15), but offered refinements in ease of assembly and a variety of thin steel supporting structures. Day's designs for Hille were successfully marketed internationally, while British designer and entrepreneur Sir Terence Conran (b. 1931; see page 281) expanded his contract furniture and fabric design business by opening a number of retail outlets in London under the name Habitat, beginning in 1964. Conran's Habitat stores expanded the marketing for international modern design beyond the scope of contract commissions from architects, corporations, and sophisticated clientele who constituted much of its audience in the immediate postwar decade. Habitat obtained rights to manufacture and distribute contemporary designs from Italy and Scandinavia and also offered simple and practical mass-produced furniture recalling period styles, as well as imported craft items such as traditional Japanese cookware and utensils.

Habitat's advertising and merchandising, featuring displays filled with home furnishing products and accessories, also were beginning to blur the lines that had distinguished "good design" from mass-marketed

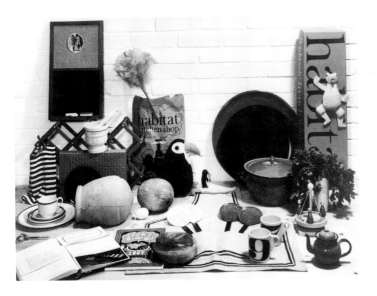

13.2 Counter display, Habitat store, London, *c.* 1965

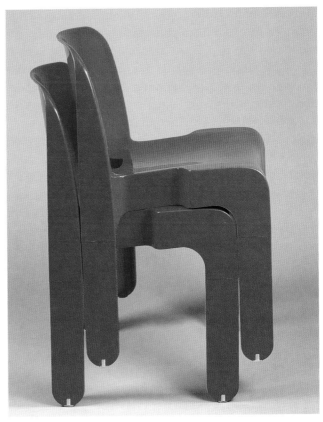

13.3 Joe Columbo, stacking chair, nylon and polypropylene (injection-mold plastic), height 28 in (71 cm), manufactured by Kartell, 1965. Photograph: Kartell USA, Easley, South Carolina.

13.4 Verner Panton, stacking chair, fiberglass-reinforced polyester, height 32 ¼ in (83.2 cm), manufactured by Herman Miller Company, 1960 (manufactured beginning 1967), Zeeland, Michigan. Philadelphia Museum of Art.

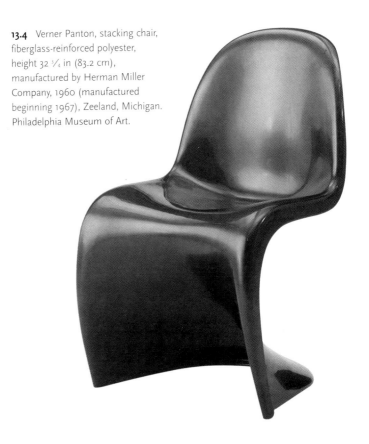

commodities during the 1950s (fig. 13.2). Inevitably the array of goods, changing displays, and variations of new but similar products resembled market-oriented design strategies such as obsolescence and emphasized increasing levels of consumer spending aimed at upwardly-mobile affluent consumers. The products and merchandising strategies of Habitat offered modern design as a lifestyle choice rather than to the more broadly humanistic or paternalistic motivations of "good design" in the immediate postwar years, obscuring the distinction between design and fashion, between needs and wants. In print media and on television, a similar blurring was taking place between journalism and advertising. Such directions continue and have been expanded in the warehouse approach of IKEA discussed below (page 381).

PLASTICS AND THEIR PROGENY

Also beginning in the 1960s, the process of injection-molding combined with stronger polymers further extended possibilities for furniture design using the plastics initiated by the Eameses and by Eero Saarinen (see fig. 11.15). Joe Columbo's (1930–1971) side chair of 1965, manufactured by the Italian company Kartell beginning in 1968, was designed as a molded seat and back into which plastic legs were inserted (fig. 13.3). Less organic than most of its predecessors, Columbo's plastic side chair was a unified design where legs, seat, and back were parallel or perpendicular to each other as well as to the walls, floors, and ceilings of the rooms they occupied. A single injection-molded form was Scandinavian designer Verner Panton's (1926–1998) stacking chair, designed in 1960 and manufactured by Herman Miller beginning in 1967 (fig. 13.4).

Unlike Columbo's side chair, Panton's unified design preserves an organic, sculptural quality reminiscent of the biomorphic forms of post-war furniture designers such as Isamo Noguchi, Eero Saarinen, or Arne Jacobsen, while the thin, concave base was designed to provide stability and permit interlocking. Both designs eliminated the need for steel, wooden, or aluminum supporting structures, making the chairs light and easy to move. Bright colors provided for consumer choice, suggesting yet another advantage of plastic in comparison to other materials.

Not every original design from the 1960s was inspired by the possibilities of newly developed materials or processes. Aluminum emerged in the interwar period as a constructive material for lightweight industrial furniture in aircraft as well as for outdoor use commercially; it was used after the war as well for the cone-shaped pedestals in Saarinen's Tulip furniture for Knoll in the mid-1950s (see fig. 11.15). Knoll also replaced steel with aluminum in manufacturing Mies van der Rohe's Barcelona chair, first designed for an exhibition in 1929 and re-released after World War II. In 1962, Charles and Ray Eames used aluminum construction for the Tandem Sling, manufactured by Herman Miller for seating that continues to be used in airport terminal gate areas (fig. 13.5). The design of the Tandem Sling responded to a variety of requirements. Easily assembled in flexible units from a small number of parts, with seats made from nylon (like plastic, another synthetic polymer) contoured to lessen pressure on the back of the legs, this seating system also facilitated maintenance by airport custodial staff, who could operate vacuum cleaners more easily to reach underneath the seats. As noted by designer and design historian Craig Vogel, armrests provided additional support for waiting passengers as they stood up, as well as preventing them from stretching out along the length of several units (airports and airlines felt this provoked negative associations of lengthy waiting times for departures or loitering). Less playful and organic than a number of earlier Eames chairs for the home or molded designs for public spaces, this aluminum and nylon seating exemplified continuity with the aesthetic, practical, and technological determinants of responsible industrial design, and was an example of creative problem-solving.

Furniture of the period, and in particular seating, was often closely allied to tendencies in the fine arts. While the biomorphic forms of the 1950s related to the improvisational forms of Automatic Surrealism, Columbo's side chair and other designs shared suggested similarities with the hard-edged abstraction and precision of New York artists such as Frank Stella (b. 1936) or Ellsworth Kelly (b. 1923). The audience for some of the most original examples appears to have been limited mostly to readers

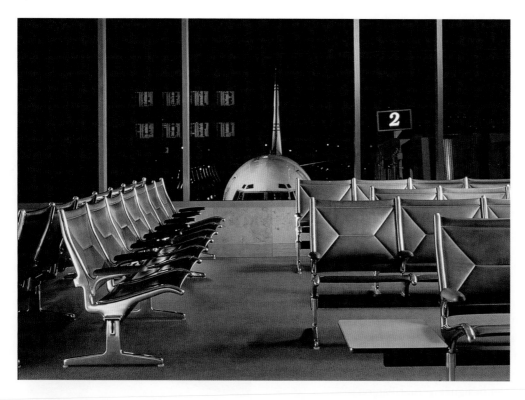

13.5 Charles and Ray Eames, Tandem Sling multiple seating (five-seat unit), aluminum, black steel bars, padded vinyl, 33 ¼ x 117 ¼ x 28 in (86 x 298 x 71 cm), manufactured by Herman Miller Company, Zeeland, Michigan, 1962.

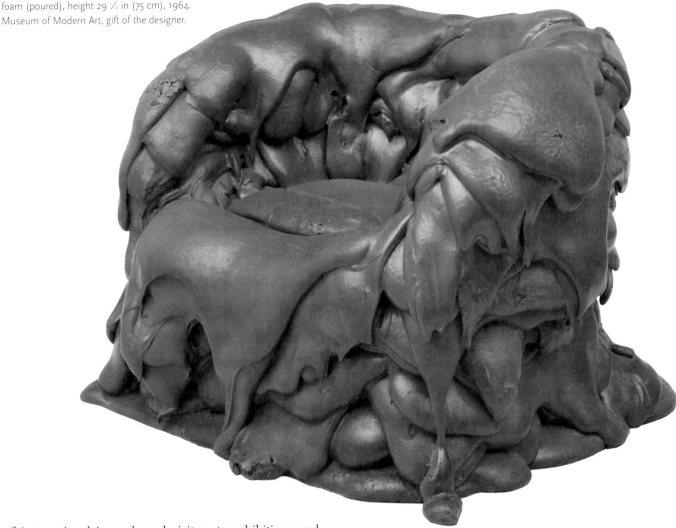

13.6 Gunnar Andersen, armchair, rubberized foam (poured), height 29 ½ in (75 cm), 1964. Museum of Modern Art, gift of the designer.

of international journals and visitors to exhibitions and museums rather than to the domestic or even the contract market catering to architects and interior design professionals. An example is Gunnar Andersen's (1919–1982) armchair dating to 1964, made from poured rather than molded rubberized foam, which explores the texture of a contemporary industrial material more generally used as a filling for fabric-covered upholstery (fig. 13.6). Andersen's design is certainly both sculpture and furniture, reminiscent in some ways of the installations of discarded tires or hanging strips of industrial felt by American conceptual artist Robert Morris (b. 1931). As a chair it seems alternatively to attract and to repel, but in either case exists more comfortably in a museum or art gallery than in a living room, better suited to reflections upon our relation to the industrial landscape we create and inhabit. Perhaps less rhetorical, other examples of foam rubber upholstered furniture of the 1960s operate within the framework of "applied design for art's sake." An example is French designer Pierre Paulin's (1927–2009) 1966 Ribbon chair manufactured by Artifort, made of upholstered rubber and wood on a metal base (fig. 13.7), or the Chilean Surrealist

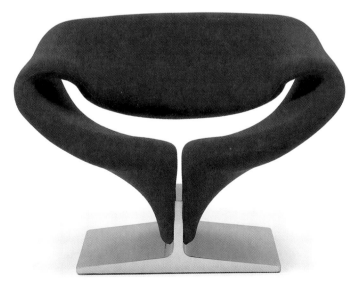

13.7 Pierre Paulin, Ribbon chair, metal, rubber, and lacquered wood with fabric-covered foam upholstery, 27 ⁹⁄₁₆ x 39 ³⁄₈ x 29 ⅛ in (70 x 100 x 74 cm), manufactured by Artifort, Maastricht, the Netherlands, 1966.

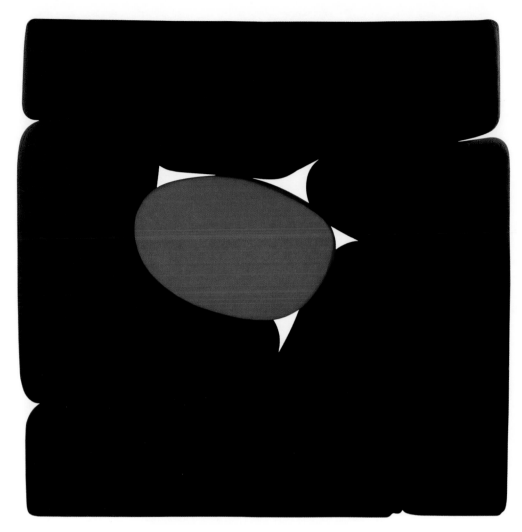

13.8 Sebastian Matta, Malitte multi-function seating system (closed), fabric-covered polyurethane foam, 63 in (160 cm) high when stacked, manufactured by Gavina (Italy), 1966.

painter Roberto Sebastian Matta's (1922–1990) Malitte seating system for Gavina, constructed of fabric-covered foam rubber beginning in 1966 (fig. 13.8). The work of both designers has much to do with originality and the appreciation of the restrained organicism of contemporary abstract painting and sculpture, and Matta's seating system also emphasizes an element of flexibility in the possibilities of alternative arrangements of its "components" as well as the ability to create in effect a kind of sculptural room divider or screen.

Similar hard-edged aesthetic qualities also apply to the Eclisse (Eclipse) lamp designed by Vico Magistretti (1920–2006) and manufactured by Artemide in 1966 (fig. 13.9) in a variety of colors. The lacquered aluminum lamp consists of two concentric semicircular shades attached to a semicircular base; the shades rotate to adjust the amount and direction of illumination. Again, the smooth shapes and compact design recall the purity of geometric abstraction, as well as its cool precision. Both the name and the forms allude to the solar system as well as to modern space exploration. In the 1960s, industrial designers played an important part in strengthening Italy's international reputation for original and sophisticated products, supplying new designs and name recognition for furniture, machines, lighting, and household products manufactured by numerous companies such as Venini (glass), Kartell (plastic), Pirelli (rubber), Flos, Arredoluce, and Artemide (lighting), and Gavina (furniture).

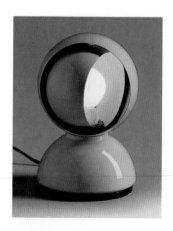

13.9 Vico Magistretti, Eclisse table lamp, lacquered aluminum, 7 x 4 ½ in (17.8 x 11.4 cm), manufactured by Artemide, Milan, Italy, 1966.

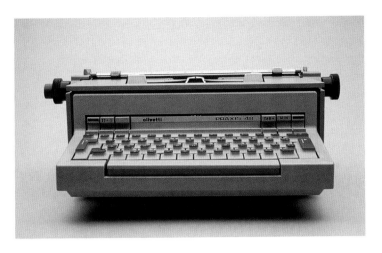

13.10 Hans von Klier and Ettore Sottsass, Jr., Praxis 48 electric typewriter, plastic housing, 6 7/16 x 17 5/8 x 13 5/16 in (16.5 x 44.5 x 33.8 cm), manufactured by Olivetti ING, Ivrea, Italy, 1964.

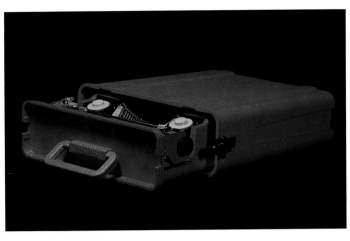

13.11 Ettore Sottsass, Jr., and Perry King, Valentine portable typewriter and case, ABS plastic housing, 13 1/4 x 12 in (34 x 30 cm), manufactured by Olivetti ING, Ivrea, Italy, 1969.

PRODUCT HOUSING

Housings, of course, constitute a broad category in industrial design, but generally refer to the shells enclosing mechanical products ranging from domestic appliances to office and laboratory machines and audiovisual equipment. During the 1960s, the bulbous and sculptural forms of many appliances and office machines in metal housings were generally replaced by more compact, rectangular shapes in both metal and plastic, while transistor and other electronics technologies also tended to produce small, portable products with simple unobtrusive forms.

A lead comparison might be between Marcello Nizzoli's 1948 Lexikon 80 typewriter for Olivetti (see fig. 11.46), and the tapered rectangular Praxis 48 electric typewriter (fig. 13.10) designed for Olivetti in 1964 by Ulm graduate Hans von Klier (1934–2000) and Ettore Sottsass, Jr. (1917–2007). Sottsass worked as a consultant to Olivetti to provide visual unity in the design of its Elea 9003 office computer. A further state of refinement and compact form may be observed in the sleek and rectangular manual portable typewriter known as the Valentine, also designed by Sottass and manufactured by Olivetti beginning in 1969 and housed in a smooth plastic sleeve (fig. 13.11). Its bright red color and product name also provided the machine with "personality" for added appeal directed toward an upscale and fashionable youth mar-ket, as seen in a poster advertisement by Egidio Bonfante (b. 1922; fig. 13.12). Sottsass later questioned some of the social implications of the designer's role in the corporation and became an important figure in Postmodern design. The conflict that began to emerge between design and big business produced a number of

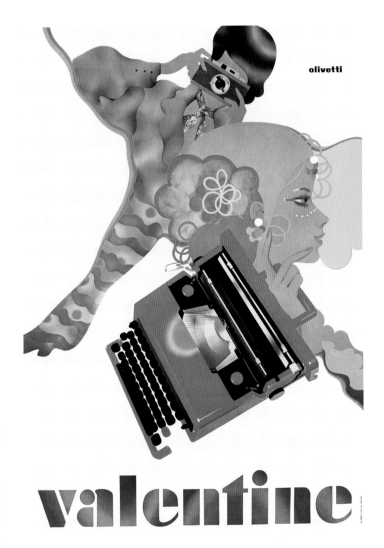

13.12 Egidio Bonfante, poster advertisement for Olivetti Valentine typewriter, 1969.

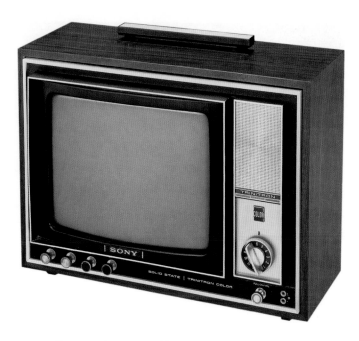

13.13 Trinitron television, metal housing with wood-grained finish, manufactured by the Sony Corporation, Tokyo, from 1965.

alternatives to postwar international modernism during the 1960s and will be treated in greater detail below (see page 355 onward).

Miniaturization continued to be a determining factor in the design of housings for a number of products such as televisions, tape recorders, and cameras. Sony pioneered the design of portable televisions using transistors as early as 1959, employing a thin metal casing around the irregular and slightly tapered picture tube, a carrying handle, and a steel track to support a visor that reduced glare. A similar design, with housing constructed of plastic, was introduced in 1962 in Italy by Brionvega, designed by Richard Sapper (b. 1932) and Marco Zanuso (see page 286), also emphasizing lightness and portability. These designs contrasted with more conventional, cabinetlike housings (often including hinged doors to hide the screen) constructed of wood in a variety of period furniture styles. Perhaps the most widely accepted compromise between the appeal of traditional wooden furniture and the advantages of portable television was the Sony Trinitron, which appeared in 1965. The Trinitron was rectangular in form, adaptable to a variety of shelves or moving stands, and had a wood-grained plastic laminate surface that harmonized more readily with wood furniture and paneling in the domestic interior (fig. 13.13). Further miniaturization of the speakers, picture tube, and the use of remote-control operation have led to even more compact and minimal designs, characterized by ever-thinner rectangular integrated housings in flat-screen televisions that can

be directly mounted on the wall (see fig. 16.38). Sony's approach to consumer electronics seemed to acknowledge that miniaturized technology dictated a degree of expressive restraint that was acceptable to consumers. Instead of cockpit or dashboardlike features, Sony electronic products favored attention to simple, transparent operation and frequent new models without significant changes in styling aside from color or lighter and more durable materials. The balance between novelty, innovation, and continuity reveals collaboration between competing perspectives that defined the expanding practice of design for many electronics and information technology-based companies. In this growing sector of the economy both for consumer goods, business needs, and government operations, design could be viewed as a form of strategic planning involving research, engineering, styling, marketing, and advertising. Whether in-house, as at Sony, or through consultancies working under contract, integrated and flexible services defined the role of design in competitive business practice that demanded innovation and responsiveness to a variety of considerations for the user.

Another example of miniaturization was in sound recording, where cassettes replaced reels for the consumer market resulting in greater ease of use in the 1970s. Handheld mini-cassette recorders appeared in Japan in the mid-1960s, while Sony's portable cassette player, known as the Walkman, was introduced in 1978 (fig. 13.14). The 1960s also saw the increased use of digital rather than analogue clocks, with numerical readouts that implied greater precision and accuracy (fig. 13.15) and fewer mechanical parts. They could reduce the digits of the Arabic numbers to a system using just seven dashes displayed electronically, as in the Visotronic tabletop clock manufactured by Braun in 1979 (fig. 13.16). In both cases, traditional clock hands and cases are abandoned in favor of more compact, space-saving housings. In lighting, the development of high-intensity bulbs spawned a generation of minimal designs for table lamps, including Michael Lax's (1929–1999) metal Lytegem table lamp of 1965 for Lightolier, which featured a collapsible, antennalike arm, making the lamp into little more than a 6-inch (15-centimeter) tall paperweight when not in use (fig. 13.17). Lightolier also developed systems featuring modular cylinder-shaped housings for lights, attached to ceiling tracks permitting lateral and rotational flexibility and reducing the need for table or floor lamps. Track lighting is compact, but still rather substantial in comparison with the more recent types of illumination using halogen lamps. Halogen technology for lighting has further reduced the size while increasing the intensity (as well as the heat) of illumination, and has created a variety of aesthetic possibilities as well. The almost weightless

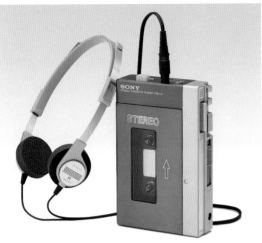

13.14 Walkman portable cassette player, anodized aluminum housing, height 5 ¼ in (13.3 cm), manufactured by the Sony Corporation, Tokyo, 1978.

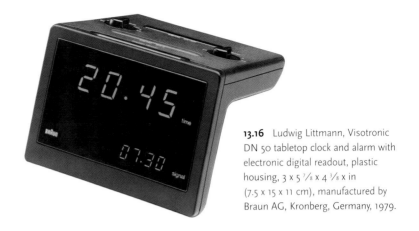

13.16 Ludwig Littmann, Visotronic DN 50 tabletop clock and alarm with electronic digital readout, plastic housing, 3 x 5 ⅞ x 4 ⅜ x in (7.5 x 15 x 11 cm), manufactured by Braun AG, Kronberg, Germany, 1979.

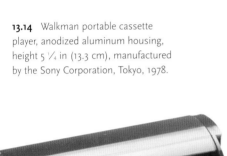

13.15 Gino Valle, Cifra 3, table clock, plastic case, 7 ⅙ x 3 ¾ in (18 x 9.5 cm), manufactured by Solari & C., Udine, Italy, 1966.

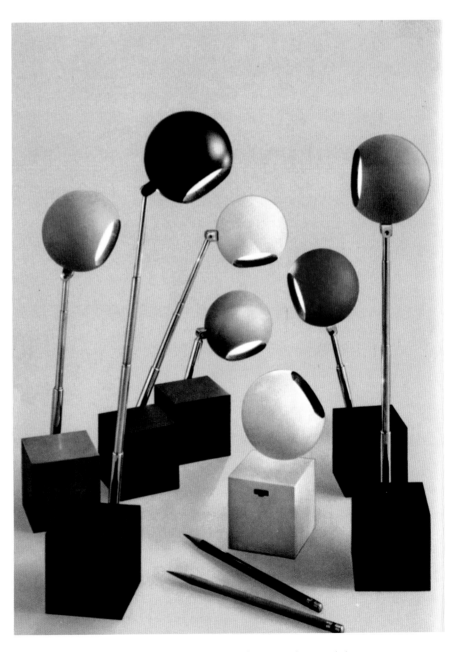

13.17 Michael Lax, Lytegem table lamp, zinc, brass, and aluminum, height 15 in (38 cm) when extended, manufactured by Lightolier, 1965.

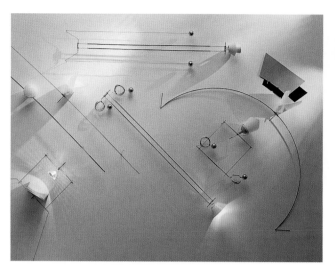

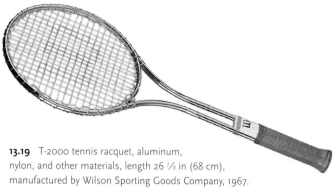

13.19 T-2000 tennis racquet, aluminum, nylon, and other materials, length 26 ⅞ in (68 cm), manufactured by Wilson Sporting Goods Company, 1967.

13.18 Ingo Maurer, YaYaHo lighting system, glass, ceramic, metal, and plastic, 19 ½ x 118 ⅛ in (49.5 x 300 cm), manufactured by Design M, Munich, Germany, 1981–1984.

appearance of halogen bulbs suspended from barely visible wires is seen, for instance, in Ingo Maurer's (b. 1932) YaYaHo lighting system from the early 1980s (fig. 13.18). This uses a vocabulary of standardized components to explore three-dimensional space, providing the experience of a work of installation art as well as interior illumination. More recently, Maurer's work has used LED (light-emitting diode) technology to illuminate interior spaces as well as to create exterior displays.

Sports Equipment and Progress

While it is not possible to include all areas of consumer products that emerge from or are transformed by new materials and technologies, sports equipment is one area that may serve as an example of tendencies in product design in relation to technology during the last 30 or 40 years. This is not simply because new materials may be linked to better performance, but also because small changes following the initial development of a product provide the basis for frequent replacement of existing models, blurring distinctions between progress, fashion, and company profits. A case study might be the tennis racquet industry, where metal racquets began to compete with traditionally crafted wood-framed racquets in the mid-1960s, with the T-2000 model aluminum racquet first introduced by the Wilson Sporting Goods Company in the United States in 1967 (fig. 13.19). The acceptance of the new racquets, first among younger audiences, was stimulated through endorsements by younger tennis professionals such as Jimmy Connors (b. 1952), and the increased exposure of professional tennis programming

on television. Wilson had used endorsements prior to the advent of television for its top-of-the-line Jack Kramer model – this model was still on sale long after Jack Kramer retired from active tennis in the early 1950s, an almost unthinkable circumstance with today's marketing emphasis upon technology, change, and the most current star athletes. A resulting tennis "boom," beginning in the later 1960s, produced a series of equipment improvements, such as lighter racquets with larger heads, followed by the replacement of steel consecutively by aluminum, graphite, lightweight ceramic materials, even lighter titanium, and more recently nanotubes combined with more traditional carbon fibers. It becomes difficult to separate the development of new technologies from their relation to the tennis "stars" who market particular brands or whose personalities, both on and off the court, are linked to the product and by extension to the consumer who purchases it. Once again, the complex nature of design during the 1960s makes it increasingly difficult to distinguish between technological progress, performance, and commercial competition, or more simply between improvement and novelty. Manufacturers and consumers alike acknowledge a permanent state of impermanence that forms the basis of sustained economic growth and characterizes our relation to the world of manufactured products around us.

Visual Identity, Information, and Art Direction

Rational graphics and coordinated corporate identity programs, as described in the postwar era in Part V, gained prominence in the 1960s. Paul Rand (see page 303), who was hired by Eliot Noyes to design the logo for IBM (1956), continued to develop a number of clear, bold logos for multi-national corporations, including the Westinghouse Corporation (1960; see fig. 11.84), and the American Broadcasting Company (ABC, 1962; see fig. 11.85). The

Mobil

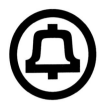

13.20 Tom Geismar of Chermayeff and Geismar Associates, trademark for Mobil oil, 1964–1965. Line drawing by John Langdon.

13.21 Saul Bass and Associates, AT&T trademark, 1969.

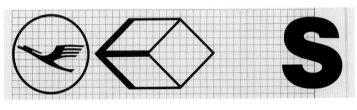

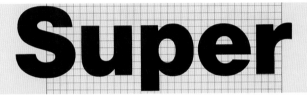

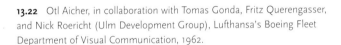

13.22 Otl Aicher, in collaboration with Tomas Gonda, Fritz Querengasser, and Nick Roericht (Ulm Development Group), Lufthansa's Boeing Fleet Department of Visual Communication, 1962.

New York-based firms of Chermayeff and Geismar (see above, page 302) as well as Saul Bass and Associates were also responsible for creating consistent and recognizable corporate identity systems, including Mobil Oil Corporation (1964; fig. 13.20), American Telephone and Telegraph Corporation (AT&T, 1969; fig. 13.21) and the Chase Manhattan Bank, all employing easily recognized symbols and bold sans serif typography. In Europe, a group of faculty at the Hochschule für Gestaltung at Ulm (see page 291), including Otl Aicher, developed the visual identity program for Lufthansa German National Airlines (1962), based upon a grid system and used for an entire range of labeling, scheduling, and advertising information (fig. 13.22).

Strategies for developing comprehensive visual systems for large organizations and corporations take into consideration the characteristics of the audience to be served, for instance, in terms of age and nationality. Banks use common elements of color and layout for identity in

series of brochures promoting their range of services. The National Park Service of the United States, whose audience includes visitors of all ages and nationalities, uses a related approach involving careful analysis of multiple areas of content and their combination in unified ways for each of its parks and monuments. The National Park Service identity system, developed from 1977 by a team of consultants including Massimo Vignelli (b. 1931), Vincent Gleason, and Dennis McLaughlin, consisted of a "Unigrid" system for the design of charts and brochures to provide consistent information for the nation's federally maintained sites. The system included bold white-on-black sans serif typography for bordered titles, photography, maps, short text, charts, symbols identifying services for parking, camping, restrooms, and information, as well as diagrams (fig. 13.23). Armed with foldout

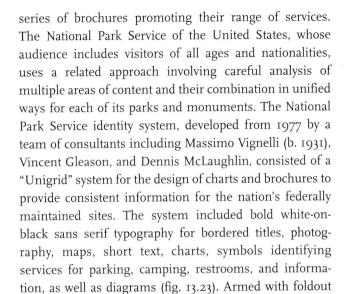

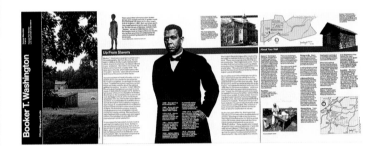

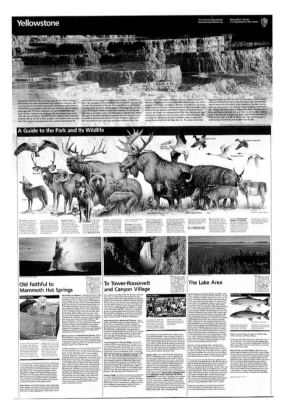

13.23 Massimo Vignelli and staff, "Unigrid" system for National Park Service brochures, from 1977.

brochures, travelers can be assured of basic information in simplified and consistent visual form that reduces the anxiety of navigating the park and facilitates the process of selecting and enjoying those areas one wants to visit. Recognizing the international attraction of such sites as the Grand Canyon and the Liberty Bell, the printed guides were translated into Japanese, German, French, and Spanish with the text treated as an "interchangeable part." Such systems produce artifacts in the form of signage and brochures, with emphasis upon reducing complexity and providing a sense of order and familiarity to information to promote the use of a service. Visual appeal, consistency, and ease of navigation are keys to effective information design, whether for wayfinding, product instructions, or in our interface with mechanical products such as calculators or cassette tape players.

Massimo Vignelli's career has encompassed a wide range of activities including the design of furniture and products. The firm Vignelli & Associates, with offices in New York and Milan, has also been responsible for visual systems that include brand recognition (American Airlines, 1967, Bloomingdales department store, 1972), information graphics (the New York Metropolitan Subway System, 1966), and creative freedom (Knoll International from 1966, where he succeeded Herbert Matter, see page 303). The solution to each client's brief requires an understanding of the market, the flexibility of a basic visual system in adapting to differing formats and future needs, and the careful manipulation and composition of a full range of technical graphic means including photography, drawings, diagrams, typography, and layout.

Complex identity systems emphasized the rational, problem-solving side of graphic design in the 1960s and beyond, with roots in Modernism, the New Typography and contributions in the design of information associated with the International Typographic Style and pioneers such as Otto Neurath and Ladislav Sutnar (see page 274). Such efforts often call attention to the role of the graphic design profession in simplifying the complex and bewildering nature of modern information through the use of accessible and reductive symbols, visual metaphors, and organization as well as the consideration of a multinational setting, whether for business or transportation.

Graphic identity for the Olympic Games is another example of visual systems designed for an international audience for clarity and attracting excitement for the location and for the events themselves. The use of reductive symbols based upon abstract shapes to convey universal messages was successfully employed in a series of pictograms for the 1964 Tokyo Olympic Games, designed by Yoshiro Yamashita (fig. 13.24). Like logos, these pictograms also use a simple series of related shapes

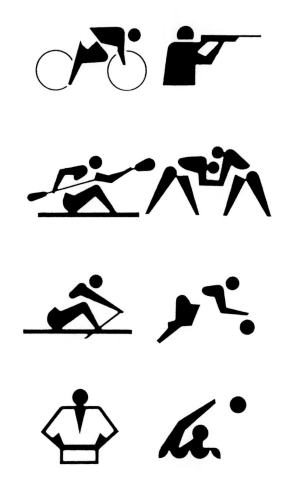

13.24 Yoshiro Yamashita, pictograms for eighteenth Olympic Games held in Tokyo, 1964.

to signify the parts of the human body and the field or equipment connected with a particular sport. Again in an international context, such an approach became common on packaging to encourage careful handling or later for graphics developed for airports – for instance, the series of pictograms designed by Roger Cook (b. 1930) and Don Shanosky in 1975 for the United States Department of Transportation (fig. 13.25). Similar reductionism in the transportation industry is seen in the cardboard tags used to mark luggage in airports, which are color-coded and display a code of three-letter abbreviations for the world's airport terminals in a bold sans serif typeface that can easily be read and separated by baggage handlers. The code was developed for the International Air Transportation Authority (IATA). Increasing globalization in a number of industries also encourages the use of self-evident (i.e. universal) abstract symbols in information graphics, for instance for the operation of tape decks, CD players, or MP3 players without the need for written instructions for commands such as "forward" or "fast forward."

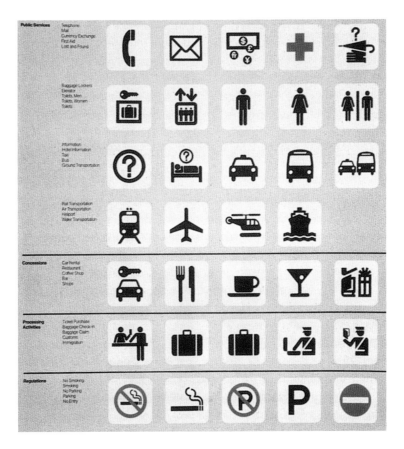

13.25 Roger Cook and Don Shanosky, signage symbol system for United States Department of Transportation, printed poster, 29 ¼ x 21 ½ in (76 x 55 cm), 1975. Private collection.

In addition to the generally rational methods used for information graphics and corporate identity systems, modern graphic design also encompasses more open-ended and often personal approaches to advertising and art direction. The expressive use of typography in relation to the meaning of words or phrases is seen in the work of American Herb Lubalin (1918–1981). Although Lubalin designed several eccentric typefaces combining elements from serif and sans serif families of type, his transformations of letters to convey the meaning of words visually demonstrates a fascination with the creative possibilities of type. In figure 13.26, for instance, Lubalin creates the illusion of torn paper breaking apart the word "cough" to suggest irritation and roughness in an advertisement for a pharmaceutical company. Whereas a biography of Eric Gill (see page 217) bears the title *The Man Who Loved Letters,* Lubalin's future biographer might be tempted to entitle his or her work *The Man Who Loved Words.* Taking liberties with letters in order to suggest their meaning without obscuring verbal recognition required intuition and experiment along with discipline and analysis. Both sensibilities are complementary aspects of the graphic design profession.

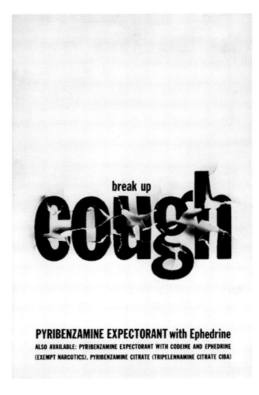

13.26 Herb Lubalin (of Sudler, Hennessey & Lubalin), advertisement for a pharmaceutical company.

While successful in commercial advertising, Lubalin also worked independently to promote experimentation and freedom of expression. He served as art director for several journals that challenged more conventional approaches to typography, photography, illustration, and layout, including *Avant Garde*, for which he also invented a sans serif typeface combining regular and forward-leaning italic forms for close spacing and a unified image (fig. 13.27). Lubalin also worked for the short-lived quarterly periodical *Eros* beginning in 1962. The magazine was both journalistically as well as graphically provocative, treating controversial political, racial, and sexual subjects; its publisher/editor, Ralph Ginzburg (1929–2006), was indicted and convicted on obscenity charges in a series of judicial proceedings that began in 1963. In a spread from *Eros* (1962), a photograph of embracing interracial lovers accompanies Aristophanes' play *Lysistrata* (also illustrated by Aubrey Beardsley in 1896), in which the women of late

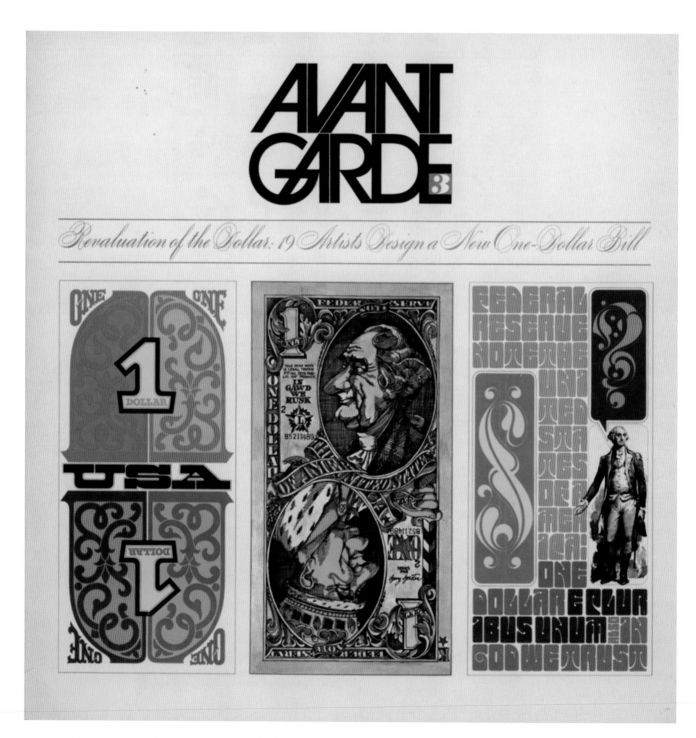

13.27 Herb Lubalin, cover for *Avant Garde*, issue no. 3, height 11 in (28 cm), New York, 1968.

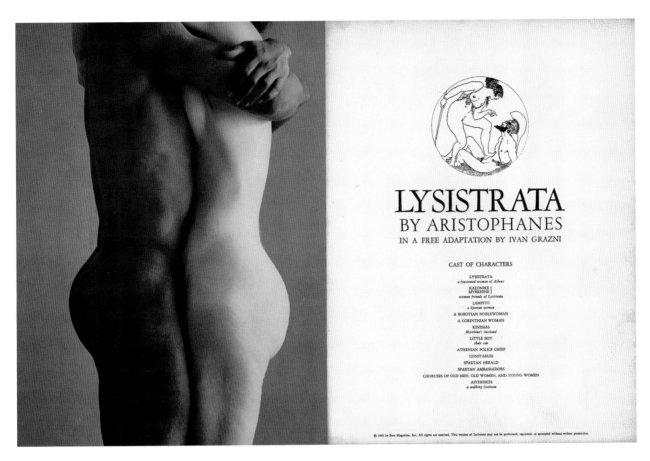

13.28 Herb Lubalin, spread from *Eros*, *Lysistrata*, vol. 1, no. 4, winter 1962, New York. Photography by Ralph M. Hattersley Jr.

fifth-century BCE Athens withhold sex from their husbands to force an end to the long Peloponnesian war between Athens and Sparta (fig. 13.28). The combination asserts the relevance of the play both for its sexual and racial content. Lubalin's creative expression was allied more generally with freedom of expression, even if that freedom conflicted with conservative attitudes politically and in the publishing industry. Journals such as *Avant Garde* and *Eros* were part of a broader movement affecting design, that placed individuals at odds with both larger businesses and government and that sought greater freedom of expression. Lubalin's efforts also produced the journal *U&lc* beginning in 1970, devoted to typographical experimentation through the technology of filmsetting. Filmsetting used photography rather than metal type to produce text in different sizes from drawn forms; negatives were exposed to thin metal plates for offset lithographic printing. *U&lc* promoted the International Typeface Corporation, founded in the same year by Lubalin, Aaron Burns, and Edward Rondthaler, which encouraged typographic invention. The shift to filmsetting, and eventually to computer-generated typefaces, gave more control to designers in developing new fonts to meet a wider range of personal and broadly political expressive

needs. While the graphic design profession gained stature and respectability through its service to government and business, practitioners beginning in the 1960s also sought alternatives that lay beyond mainstream channels of distribution for their activities, whether in underground publications or in other more active forms of protest. In these ways graphic designers were aligned with the counterculture movement of the period.

Milton Glaser (b. 1929) also exemplified the more intuitive aspects of graphic design during the 1960s and beyond, through perhaps with less controversy than Lubalin. His oeuvre owes much to testing the limits of traditional representational illustration through the use of a variety of techniques and media as well as reductive and subjective approaches to drawing and typography. Results are seen in posters, book jackets, logos, as well as in books of poetry and children's book illustration. A series of book covers for paperback editions of the plays and poetry of Shakespeare achieved unity through the use of ample white space, heavy black borders, and delicate wash drawings featuring a central character or grouping from each play. Abbreviating both technique and narrative promoted an active response from the viewer, and distinguishes the series from competitive editions. Suggestion and active response characterize

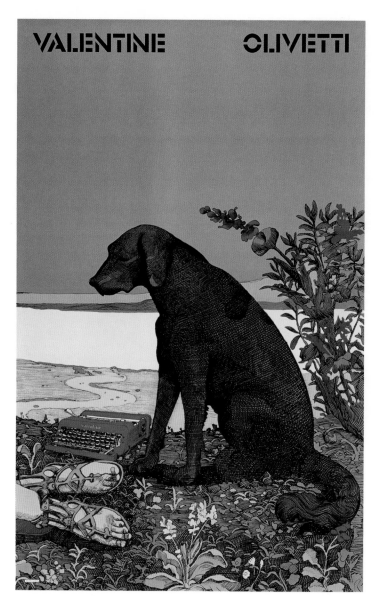

13.29 Milton Glaser, poster for Olivetti Valentine typewriter, 1969.

Glaser's children's illustrations, as well as his poster for the Olivetti Valentine in 1969 (fig. 13.29), in which the small red portable typewriter is juxtaposed against a verdant landscape. A seated dog presides over the typewriter while the sandaled feet of a reclining (or sleeping) figure suggest an idyllic past. The prominent canine may suggest the well-known "His Master's Voice" trademark for RCA Victor, with the typewriter replacing the phonograph speaker and alluding to the imagination of the written (typed) word rather than musical sounds. Glaser relied upon a wealth of imaginative associations familiar enough to supply meaning to his designs. His "I ❤ New York" logo, where the heart substitutes effortlessly for the word "love" is among his best-known designs and has spawned countless variations by virtue of the familiarity and recognition designers can assume.

Push Pin Studio, founded in 1954, included Glaser, along with graphic designers Seymour Chwast (b. 1931), Reynold Ruffins (b. 1930), and Edward Sorel (b. 1929). Chwast treated familiar visual symbols and associations in new and often ironic ways using caricature and odd juxtapositions to obtain new interpretations, not dissimilar from the collage techniques of Dada artists in the interwar period (see fig. 9.44). Chwast's work also could have a subversive edge – his designs protesting the United States involvement in Vietnam were contemporary with a competition for anti-war posters sponsored by the journal *Avant Garde* in 1968. The style (fig. 13.30) is reminiscent of early nineteenth-century wood-type posters with a centered layout and a variety of display lettering including sans and slab serif as well as shaded type, what appears to be a deliberately unsophisticated approach to design that

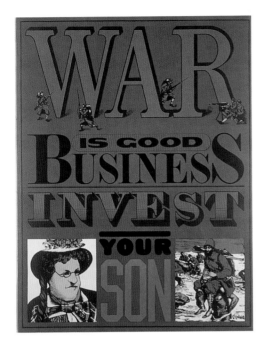

13.30 Seymour Chwast, *Graphic Statement about War*, 1967.

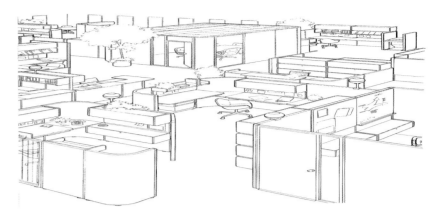

13.31 Robert Propst and George Nelson, Action Office system, manufactured by Herman Miller Company, Zeeland, Michigan, 1964.

borrows stock images for a seated soldier and matronly woman. The text, emphasizing the words "war," "business," and "invest," is a reference to the "military-industrial complex" that benefited from armament contracts and that was criticized by the anti-war movement for an indifference to the growing number of casualties and lack of resolution of the extended conflict. Both in content and in form, Chwast's poster mocks the political and the graphic design establishment.

LAMINATED MATERIALS

In addition to molded plastics, plywood and plastic laminates were also common materials for industrially designed furniture. In 1964, Robert Propst (1921–2000) and George Nelson (see page 262) introduced the Action Office system for modular office furniture, manufactured by Herman Miller (fig. 13.31). Available in a combination of surfaces including hygienic white laminated plastic, the Action Office system was meant to be adaptable to large areas of open floor space, with the possibility of flexible configuration for group clusters or individual offices. Dimensions were the result of determining average space needs and proximity between elements of individual components for the efficient and optimum performance of office-related tasks.

The plastic laminates of the Action Office system provided smooth and durable work surfaces that could be easily cleaned and maintained. The appeal of this material also extended to table and cabinet surfaces for kitchen, manufactured and widely marketed by the Formica Company. Originally developed as a form of plastic insulation and a coating for machine gears, the application of Formica as a laminate for furniture grew after World War II. The development of a variety of colors and pattern designs for Formica, like that of vinyl flooring, belongs more to the history of mass design and is treated accordingly below (see page 352).

Laminated plywood was also used for a variety of furniture designs in the 1960s. A good example from Japan is Reiko Tanabe's (b. 1934) teak plywood stool designed for Tendo Mokko in 1960 (fig. 13.32). The self-contained form is designed for efficient construction with three identical molded components that are glued together.

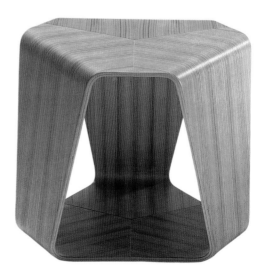

13.32 Reiko (Murai) Tanabe, stool, teak, plywood, 14 ³⁄₁₆ x 17 ¹¹⁄₁₆ x 17 ¹⁄₁₆ in (36 x 45 x 43 cm), manufactured by Tendo Mokko, Tendo Company Ltd., 1960.

In addition to new industrial materials and processes, the preservation and development of craft traditions aimed to further humanize design in the 1960s through the use of natural woods and fibers for furniture, curtains, rugs, and table-coverings. Occasionally, synthetic fibers such as polyester were introduced, for instance, with stretch upholstery, or to explore new textures or combinations of textures, as in Swiss textile designer Suzanne Huguenin's (b. 1930s) Nylon Homespun fabric manufactured by Knoll beginning in 1958 (fig. 13.33). Sheila Hicks's (b. 1934) Badagara fabric, dating to 1966–1967, is woven from cotton in horizontal bands of irregular diameter, one of several designs for the Kerala collection commissioned by a large manufacturing company in South India to stimulate interest in local craft production for an international market (fig. 13.34). Many of Hicks's works are monumental wall-hangings commissioned in public buildings throughout the world, employ-ing handweavers to assist with production but maintaining a strong link to fine art.

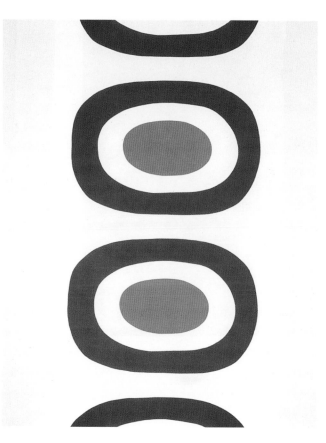

13.35 Maija Isola, Melooni fabric, screenprinted, width 54 in (137 cm), manufactured by Printex, Helsinki, for Marimekko Oy, 1963.

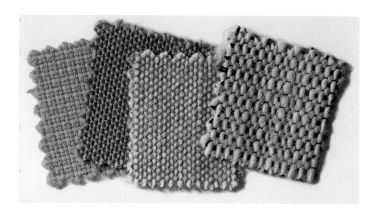

13.33 Suzanne Huguenin, Nylon Homespun fabric, nylon, width 50 in (127 cm), manufactured by Knoll International, New York, 1958.

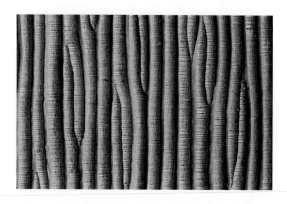

13.34 Sheila Hicks, Badagara fabric, cotton, 120 in (305 cm) wide, made by Commonwealth Trust, Calcutta, India, 1966, and still made today.

Scandinavia remained in the forefront of textile design internationally, and served as an inspiration to designers in the United States, particularly at the Cranbrook Academy in Bloomfield Hills, Michigan, where Finnish-born Eliel and Loja Saarinen had established a strong craft tradition beginning in 1923 (see page 224). In many cases woven and printed fabric designs were manufactured by Knoll and Herman Miller, as well as by Scandinavian companies such as Marimekko. Finnish designer Maija Isola's (1927–2001) bold printed cotton Melooni fabric, manufactured in Finland by Printex (which also introduced the Marimekko name), dates to 1963 and is reminiscent of the bold post-painterly abstract canvases of Ellsworth Kelly, Frank Stella, or Kenneth Noland (fig. 13.35). Simple woven patterns in cotton and wool continued to be produced by Scandinavian manufacturers as well as by the American-based Dansk Corporation beginning in the later 1950s. In Britain, potter Bernard Leach promoted an Arts and Crafts revival movement, encouraging designers' direct involvement with materials along psychological and aesthetic lines (see page 282).

The appreciation of abstract form in shapes and textures produced by experimentation with materials and processes also served to sustain an alliance between fine

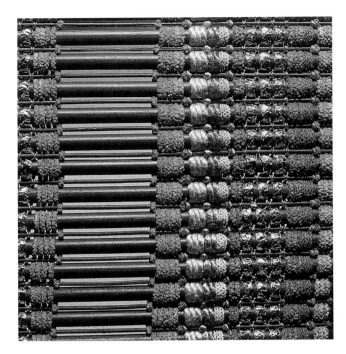

13.36 Dorothy Liebes, fabric, Orlon and metallics, width 50 in (127 cm), manufactured by Dorothy Liebes Design. Museum of Arts and Design (formerly American Craft Museum), New York.

13.37 Jack Lenor Larsen, Magnum fabric, wool, nylon, acrylic, and Mylar, 55 ½ x 53 ½ in (141 x 136 cm), manufactured by Jack Lenor Larsen Inc., New York, 1970. Metropolitan Museum of Art, New York.

art and craft, strengthened through museum and other international exhibitions, journals, and in education, including the foundation of the American Craft Museum in Manhattan in 1956 (the name was changed to the Museum of Arts and Design in 2003, along with its relocation from West 53rd Street to Columbus Circle).

Combinations of materials in textile design appear in the work of many designers, including a number of remarkable women such as Dorothy Liebes (1899–1972), Sheila Hicks (discussed above), and Anni Albers (1899–1994), wife of the painter and Bauhaus teacher Josef Albers. During the 1950s, Liebes made window blinds using a combination of fabrics binding wooden slats. In the 1960s she created fabrics for higher-quantity production using a variety of media, including synthetics such as Orlon and metal foils (fig. 13.36). Another American textile designer and manufacturer was Cranbook-trained Jack Lenor Larsen (b. 1927), whose Magnum fabric of 1970 is woven from a combination of wool, nylon, acrylic, and Mylar (fig. 13.37). Original forms involving craft rather than industrial production were designed by Philadelphia area sculptor and furniture-maker Wharton Esherick (1887–1970), whose music stand accentuates and unifies the abstract tension of an arched curve (fig. 13.38). Original craft-based furniture also characterizes the career of California-based Sam Maloof (1916–2009).

Craft revival was also an element of the 1960s counterculture. Borrowings from indigenous and non-Western

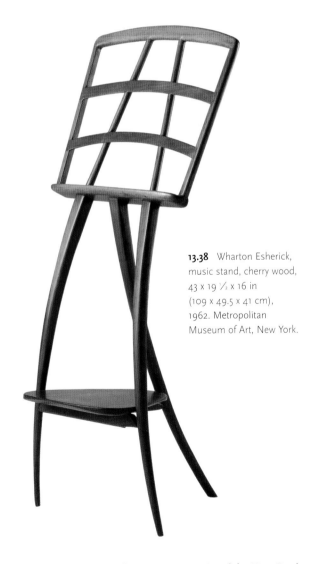

13.38 Wharton Esherick, music stand, cherry wood, 43 x 19 ½ x 16 in (109 x 49.5 x 41 cm), 1962. Metropolitan Museum of Art, New York.

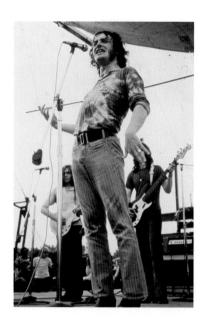

13.39 Joe Cocker wearing a tie-dyed T-shirt at Woodstock music festival, New York, 1969.

self-sufficiency, organic foods and gardening, and the use of natural rather than synthetic materials were choices that directed the daily patterns of life toward a closer relationship to nature rather than an acceptance and dependence upon the modern conveniences provided by industrial design and production.

Dale Chihuly (b. 1941), after studying architecture and design, pursued the craft of glass-blowing as a fine art, and today is celebrated both for his inventiveness and virtuosity. The molded and free-blown-glass *Deep Blue and Bronze Persian Set* is but one example, dating to 1999. Here a source for Chihuly was the suggestive organic forms of Persian glass, which also provided an inspiration for Louis Comfort Tiffany (see above, fig. 6.18) featuring a variety of organic forms, textures, and patterns (fig. 13.40). For Chihuly, large commissions and the celebrity deriving from being featured in mass magazines and on television have led to a separation between design and execution, with the majority of glass blowing now being carried out by assistants under Chihuly's supervision. Whether as an exploration of unmined sources for aesthetic effect, symbolism, or individual self-expression, handicraft emerged as a strain of both avant-garde as well as popular culture.

traditions were part of a sympathetic response to pre-industrial and communal lifestyles, with tie-dye designs on cotton T-shirts and tops, at first done in one's own washbasin and later available off-the-rack (fig. 13.39). Craft fairs often accompanied folk music and street festivals;

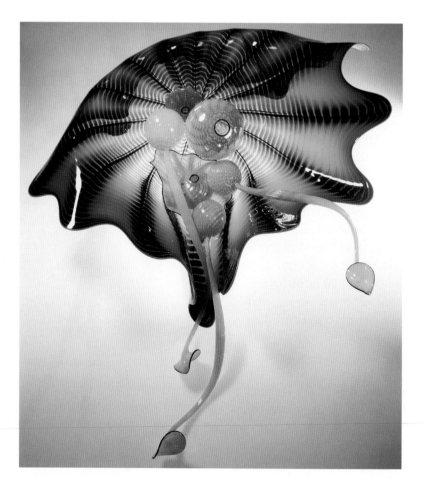

13.40 Dale Chihuly, *Deep Blue and Bronze Persian Set*, glass, with threading and twisted canes (filigree of various types), blown into an optic mold, free-blown, and handworked, width 34 9/16 in (89 cm), 1999. Overhead view. Victoria and Albert Museum, London.

Chapter 14

Dimensions of Mass Culture

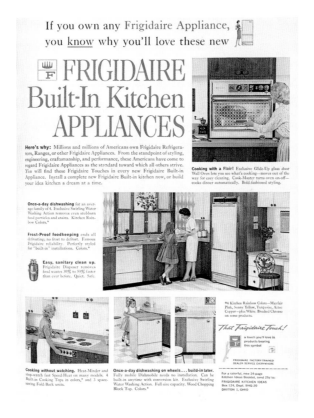

14.1 Advertisement for built-in kitchen appliances, Frigidaire company, Dayton, Ohio. *Better Homes and Gardens*, March, 1962.

Planned obsolescence remained a guiding principle in industrial design for the mass market, but during the 1960s many products relinquished flamboyance and playful novelty in favor of greater standardization and conformity. Appliances like washing machines, refrigerators, electric toasters, and clothes dryers abandoned earlier bulbous, or even streamlined housings for rectangular forms and sharp angles rather than rounded edges – an aesthetic change related at least in part to new developments in sheet metal fabrication. Dashboardlike controls and instrument panels yielded to less complex operation and customized features, following the lead of more restrained electronic products such as radios or televisions. As a result, appliances could also more readily appear built-in, part of a unified and space-saving ensemble for the laundry or kitchen (fig. 14.1). Color and accessories

offered variety and choice but added little to production cost; at the same time they reduced the form-giving role of the industrial designer in terms of styling and invention.

Perhaps even more noticeable during the 1960s was the homogeneity in the Detroit automobile industry. The vitality and variety provided by chrome detailing, flamelike tailfins and other jet-age features in the 1950s were toned down, replaced by more rectangular body designs and less variation among models and brands. Again color options and interior accessories (such as "bucket" seats and instrument consoles) still allowed consumers to customize or individualize their purchases, but body styling was more constrained by the consideration of cost and the fear of repeating failures such as the 1958 Ford Edsel (see page 313). The decade also produced a series of new compact cars such as the Ford Falcon, Plymouth Valiant, Chevrolet

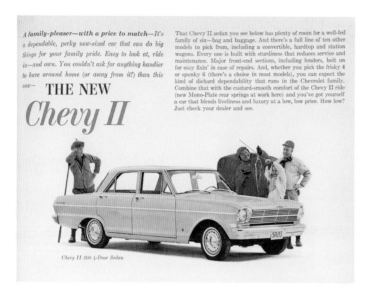

A family-pleaser—with a price to match—It's a dependable, perky new-sized car that can do big things for your family pride. Easy to look at, ride in—and own. You couldn't ask for anything handier to have around home (or away from it!) than this one—

THE NEW
Chevy II

That Chevy II sedan you see below has plenty of room for a well-fed family of six—bag and baggage. And there's a full line of ten other models to pick from, including a convertible, hardtop and station wagons. Every one is built with sturdiness that reduces service and maintenance. Major front-end sections, including fenders, bolt on for easy fixin' in case of repairs. And, whether you pick the frisky 4 or spunky 6 (there's a choice in most models), you can expect the kind of diehard dependability that runs in the Chevrolet family. Combine that with the custard-smooth comfort of the Chevy II ride (new Mono-Plate rear springs at work here) and you've got yourself a car that blends liveliness and luxury at a low, low price. How low? Just check your dealer and see.

Chevy II 300 4-Door Sedan

14.2 Advertisement for Chevrolet Compact automobiles, General Motors Corporation. *Better Homes and Gardens*, March, 1962.

Corvair, and Chevy II, often equally boxy in form along the lines of larger "family cars," and marketed primarily as "second" vehicles emphasizing economy and practicality (fig. 14.2).

More organic and tapered than many contemporary American automobiles of the 1960s, Raymond Loewy's design for the upscale 1963 Studebaker Avanti (fig. 14.3) received much critical acclaim for its sculpted contour and innovative fiberglass body, but did not find a niche in a luxury market dominated by the boatlike General Motors Cadillac of the early 1960s and its strong brand associations and loyalty. Despite the name-value of Loewy as a noted "personality" in industrial design, and the efforts to compete with lower-priced compact models by the introduction of its Lark model, the Studebaker

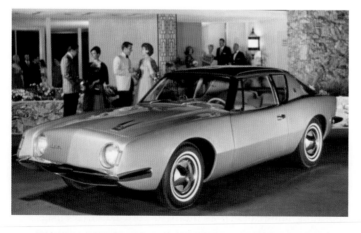

14.3 Raymond Loewy, Avanti, Studebaker Motor Company, South Bend, Indiana, 1962–1963.

Corporation finally went the way of Hudson, Kaiser, Packard, and other independent automobile manufacturers in 1964. As a result, even fewer North American competitors remained for the "Big Three" automobile giants: Chrysler, General Motors, and Ford.

At the 1964 New York World's Fair, the major automobile manufacturers were highly visible as in 1939, but the dream of suburban living and individual home ownership, personal mobility, and interstate highways had for many largely been realized. The future belonged to the promise of atomic energy, space exploration, and the dawning information age that would explore new horizons and bring about new benefits to humankind. These themes were symbolized by the Unisphere, a spherical stainless steel sculptural representation of the earth encircled by three rings evoking orbiting space satellites as well as electrons surrounding an atom. Corporations such as IBM presented not office typewriters and calculators, but promoted their mainframe computers in the context of amplifying human powers of understanding through multi-media displays designed by Charles and Ray Eames. Their goal was to humanize the computer to allay Cold War fears of the power of hi-tech missile systems for programmed destruction and a nuclear Armageddon. Presenting computers as sophisticated problem-solvers, the Eameses likened design to a series of informed decisions within an everyday context such as planning the seating arrangement of a dinner party (fig. 14.4) in their film, *Think*. The problem-solving metaphor of informed decision-making leading to a calculated and mathematical, predictable rather than random or whimsical outcome placed design in a rational framework that extended to a wide range of activities and produced desired results. As explained by architectural historian John Harwood, the Eameses emphasized in their exhibition display not only the rational aspects of problem-solving but their playful aspects as well, creating a circuslike atmosphere with multiple viewpoints to suggest both the magical as well as the natural aspects of computers. While computers have indeed become a very natural extension of our everyday lives within the past generation through miniaturization as well as increasingly portable and personal computing, their presentation at the IBM Pavilion in 1964 suggests a more ambivalent attitude not unlike present-day viewpoints regarding biological or genetic design. The idea of "thinking machines" (or in or our own time, "artificial" organisms) was greeted with both optimism and fear; whether through product housings, or promotional displays at World's Fairs, designers worked to connect computers to users, hiding their complex circuits in visually attractive and unintrusive forms, and communicating with a broader public via films suggesting that *artificial*

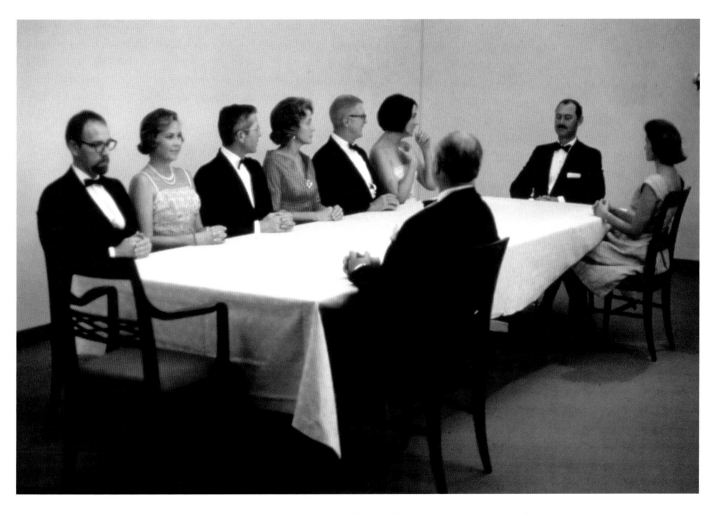

14.4 Charles and Ray Eames, still shot from the film *Think* showing the "design" of a dinner party, from the IBM Pavilion at the New York World's Fair, 1964.

intelligence was both natural and full of exciting promise. Such efforts supported positive attitudes toward the close relationships between government and business, not only in manufacturing but in the growing information and energy sectors of the economy. Through exhibitions and other forms of media, corporations engaged in public education and the promotion of pro-technology values: at the 1964 World's Fair, General Electric's space-age pavilion, for instance, featured moving theaters that presented the history and promise of a future of inexpensive electricity through the use of nuclear power. The 1964 New York World's Fair was contemporary with the first manned space missions and with corporate support of cultural programming on television as a form of public service. An early example of the latter was *General Electric Theater*, appearing first in 1954 and hosted by actor and future United States president Ronald Reagan (1911–2004). Mobil Oil Corporation's *Masterpiece Theater* premiered in 1971 through the Public Broadcasting System (PBS). Such sponsorship increased with the growth of multi-national corporations, which sought to minimize or offset possible areas of conflict between company self-interest, defense contracts, and the greater public good.

Mass Design and the Home

In addition to the promise of high-speed information processing in the emerging computer industry, other technologies inspired new domestic products aimed primarily at fulfilling the more immediate dream of reduced housework and better living through design for the mainstream mass market. At the 1964 New York World's Fair, the Formica Company, owned from 1957 by the giant chemical corporation American Cyanamid, created a series of model kitchens for a World's Fair House, including designs by Raymond Loewy. Formica, a form of hard plastic laminate attached to plywood backing for tables and countertops, was manufactured in an ever-increasing array of colors and patterns to suit every taste, including simulated natural and traditional finishes such

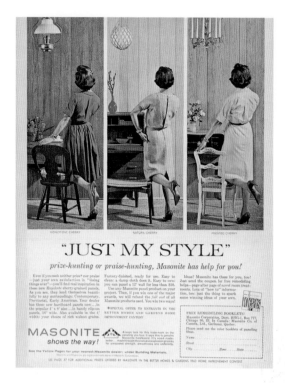

14.5 Advertisement for masonite wall paneling, Masonite Corporation, Chicago, Illinois. *Better Homes and Gardens*, January, 1962.

as wood, marble, and other types of stone. Its success was contemporary with a similar expansion of varied textures and patterns for vinyl flooring suitable for game rooms, kitchens, and enclosed patios. Moreover, products such as vinyl flooring, Formica, and plywood paneling appeared in popular magazine advertisements and continued to be featured in articles as prefabricated "do-it-yourself" products, manufactured in sizes to conform to the standardized dimensions of suburban housing construction for ease of installation, maintenance, and remodeling projects (fig. 14.5). More futuristic was the Monsanto House, built in 1957 in Disneyland and also on display at the New York World's Fair of 1964. The Monsanto House was constructed almost entirely of molded plastics, with curved walls and large windows, and the model home was elevated to accentuate the material's lightness and suggest a connection to the space-age future.

A backlash against synthetics in fabrics and products also emerged during the 1960s, part of a countercultural reaction to the environmental risks of pesticides and the use of chemical weapons (such as Agent Orange, also manufactured by Monsanto) during the Vietnam War. With at least some of the health and environmental risks of chemicals addressed and monitored through EPA standards and other regulatory agencies, the link between chemistry, new materials, and design remains strong. Today, synthetic products continue to fuel the mass home-

improvement and do-it-yourself markets, contributing to the nationwide success of large outlets such as Home Depot. Lowes, and other more specialized suppliers. Wall-coverings, paneling, cabinets, ceramic and lapidary tiles, and window blinds, are only a sample of the myriad products used in home remodeling and decorating that offer variety and a steady stream of new variations to stimulate consumer taste in home as well as other self-improvement industries involving design. As in the past, such products continue to be advertised in magazines such as *Better Homes and Gardens*, mail-order catalogues, and through the Internet. Expanded notions of comfort, convenience, privacy, and self-fulfillment, new materials and techniques of application that narrow the gap between professional and amateur, and the satisfaction of participating in the process of selection and installation combine to make home improvement an integral component of middle-class home-owning with the home as an extension and expression of oneself, and with the application of design to synthetic materials makes such aspirations available to the broader market. Former negative associations between synthetic products and kitsch tend not to apply so strictly to such products: to a degree, modernist taste has become less exclusive, and increasingly industrially manufactured marble or leather can simulate the natural varieties without obvious difference, undermining both the aesthetic and social distinctions between "real" and "fake," and rendering less obvious the meaning of "truth to materials."

The advertising for many of these products during the 1960s, almost exclusively featuring women either marveling at their new products or appropriately dressed to play hostess, or admiring remodeled domestic interiors (see fig. 14.5). This now seems naïve in its appeal to traditional gender stereotypes, and indeed the rejection of traditional role models was also a cultural phenomenon of the 1960s, emerging, for instance, in Betty Friedan's 1963 book *The Feminine Mystique* (see page 322) and later in the women's liberation movement. During the 1960s, women debated and protested sexual discrimination and actively rebelled against the gender stereotypes socialized and institutionalized through education and the mass media. Certainly the marketing of home products may be seen as a subtle form of social control, tied to familiar associations with women's roles in the nuclear family and fulfillment within rather than outside of the home.

At the same time the playful, democratic, and creative element in mainstream consumer culture was also being recognized, especially toward the end of the decade in books such as Robert Venturi, Denise Scott Brown, and Steven Izenour's *Learning from Las Vegas* (based upon travels and teaching beginning in 1966, published in book form in 1972). These authors, in addition to coining the phrase "less is a bore" (appropriating and refashioning Mies van der Rohe's Modernist dictum "less is more"), embraced the existing man-made, eclectic, artificial, and blatantly commercial architecture of billboards, neon signs, glitz, and historical references as evidenced in the sensory immediacy of the Las Vegas strip and its casinos. Limiting and even repressive in some ways, home-improvement products such as Formica, vinyl flooring and tile, avocado-colored electric frypans, and plywood paneling also provided a creative outlet and promised self-fulfillment for many middle-class homeowners, and represented a popular form of the democratization of leisure in postwar America. *Learning from Las Vegas* questioned the universal pretensions of Modernist design in the postwar period and argued for a more "sociable" approach to design that undermined the critical distinction between high and low culture.

Marxist critics have long pointed out that the increasing comfort and aestheticism associated with the domestic interior amounts to self-deception rather than liberation. In their view privacy and comfort do little more than hide an often empty, insecure, and unsettling existence, reinforcing social control and conformity by big business, all outgrowths of a capitalist system increasingly closed off to avenues for self-realization other than consumption and materialism (see pages 324–325). Even the family is not immune from such a skeptical attitude toward progress, since the hegemony of the nuclear family is a twentieth-century phenomenon (rather than a universal one) that creates a separation between work and leisure, of private and public, which is itself artificial and normative only within advanced capitalism. The advent of electronic media such as television and film, claimed Marxist critics, only erodes the ability of the public to discern the capitalist agenda at work in these increasingly seductive forms of communication and advertising, and the alliance of big business and government has consolidated rather than diffused political and economic power. For these reasons the apparent material and social progress of postwar western democracies as displayed at World's Fairs and in advertising concealed inequities in the distribution of wealth and economic opportunity.

But while a consumer culture certainly has its dangers and excesses, it has not precluded the emergence of alternative approaches and strategies for design, including efforts aimed at social and environmental responsibility and at resistance to quiescence and complicity. Indeed, many recent discussions of mass culture focus upon an inherent variety of response and reception, stressing an active rather than passive role for the consumer and a rethinking of the dynamics of production and consumption. Responses to popular culture cannot always be programmed, as noted by Venturi, Scott Brown, and Izenour in *Learning from Las Vegas*: "You can like billboards without approving of strip mining in Appalachia." Whether in the late nineteenth century or in the later twentieth century, and whether as a response to early or advanced industrialism, the appreciation for and creative use of materials and processes by designers, craftspeople, and ordinary renters or homeowners remains a tribute to the dynamism and diversity of popular consumer culture. Without this complex, multi-layered character, such design forms could not exert their mass appeal. Some of these alternative readings and interpretations of the phenomenon of mass culture are considered below.

MASS DESIGN: THE FRINGES

Stimulated by the mass media of television, radio, and film, European countries, and in particular Britain, first absorbed and then contributed to and even dominated the expanding youth market for commodities and music. The economic growth and resulting affluence of the later 1950s and 1960s in Europe challenged traditional class boundaries as well as social norms of behavior, which in turn found expression in clothing, dance, film, and music and emphasized freedom of expression predominantly through fashion and popular music. Such tendencies, particularly among youth, tested the limits of inherited values and norms of "proper" behavior, enacted through dress and leisure activities. Occasionally the new youth culture brought condemnation and even censorship, but such initial tension created by threats to established social norms was often followed by tolerance and wider imitation, acceptance, and commercial exploitation. Subgroups formed on the fringes of a generalized youth movement directed toward greater permissiveness and self-expression. As argued by British historian Arthur Marwick, an increasingly heterogeneous and diversified youth culture was joined by other marginal groups in the 1960s, including racial minorities, women, and the gay community, each with a strong desire for acknowledgment, recognition, and identity. Rebellions against inhibitions and prohibitions during this period ranged from skirt lengths and marijuana use to support for abortion, freedom of speech, lowering the voting age, and opposition to the death penalty, racial discrimination, and foreign policy – for instance the United States's participation in the Vietnam War. The acknowledgment in the media of several fringe or subcultures was a characteristic of the 1960s. Recognition of difference was not only applied to popular culture, but could also be seen in the fine arts, where the splintering of the avant-garde and the emergence of galleries on the American West Coast were easily contrasted with the

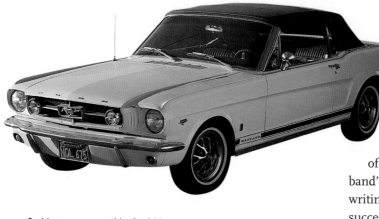

14.6 Mustang convertible, Ford Motor Company, Dearborn, Michigan, 1965.

international models such as Twiggy in the mid-1960s who exemplified a new style, as well as with influencing the trend toward more youthful approaches to fashion even among Parisian haute couture designers.

In music, the early recordings of the Liverpool-based band The Beatles demonstrate a complete assimilation and mastery of 1950s forms of rock 'n' roll music from the United States. The band's performance skills and gifts for original song-writing achieved an unprecedented degree of international success, in part through the marketing efforts of the group's manager, Brian Epstein (1934–1967). The Beatles' moplike hairstyles and modish clothing, live concerts, movies, newsreel and television interviews, were significant elements in the marketing not only of their music but of a lifestyle that also cultivated the mystique of mass media celebrity. By the mid-1960s, youth-oriented and American-inspired popular culture had not only become an international phenomenon, it had expanded beyond its youthful audience, as popular weekly television variety programs such as the prime-time Sunday evening *Ed*

identification of Modernism with abstract art and the dominance of the New York art world during most of the 1950s.

New attitudes and behaviors were easily commercially exploited or commodified as fashion products and accessories. Even in the increasingly conservative and homogeneous United States automobile industry there were some popular successes, for instance the Ford Mustang (fig. 14.6), first manufactured toward the end of 1964 and appealing to an expanding youth-oriented audience with features such as tapered concave cutaway door panels derived from earlier sports cars such as the Chevrolet Corvette. The legendary appeal of the Pontiac GTO, introduced in 1964, was based more upon a powerful V-8 engine than its conventional rectangular body, and the exhilaration of pushing the speed limit was much celebrated in popular youth culture, for instance in the rock music hit "Little GTO," recorded by Ronnie and the Daytonas in 1964. The song was a top 40 hit in the United States, complete with simulated motor sounds:

> Little GTO, you're really lookin' fine
> Three deuces and a four-speed and a 389
> Listen to her tachin' up now, listen to her
>   why-ee-eye-ine
> C'mon and turn it on, wind it up, blow it out GTO.

Other examples of the youth-oriented popular culture in the period came from the world of fashion and emerged early on in England. British designer and entrepreneur Mary Quant (b. 1934) designed and sold clothing aimed at young buyers, based upon simple, even traditional pinafore patterns but featuring higher hemlines, bold colors, and a series of fashion accessories ranging from dark fishnet stockings and knee-length leather boots, creating a look associated with an active, energetic, rebellious, and hedonistic lifestyle (fig. 14.7). Quant is credited with inventing the miniskirt and with helping to launch the careers of

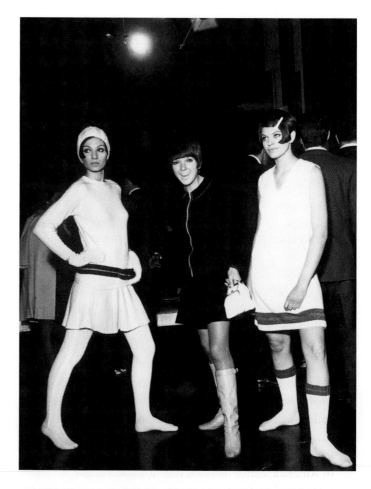

14.7 Mary Quant (center) and models presenting the "Viva Viva" line, Milan, 1967.

Sullivan Show began to feature rock 'n' roll groups as part of their regular entertainment features, broadcast from New York and targeting mainstream audiences more than the daily Philadelphia-based *American Bandstand*. In addition to the wave of British rock 'n' roll groups, the mid-1960s also witnessed the skyrocketing success of Detroit-based (Motown) black singing groups to a national audience extending far beyond racial barriers, including The Temptations, The Supremes, and The Four Tops. The acceptance of Soul music by a broad national audience via the mass media contrasted with the racial tension and increasing outbreaks of violence in American industrial cities and with the emergence of black separatist movements, who reacted impatiently to the slow pace of economic and social improvements for minorities, and who rejected the ideology of integration in favor of a more independent and often more threatening black identity.

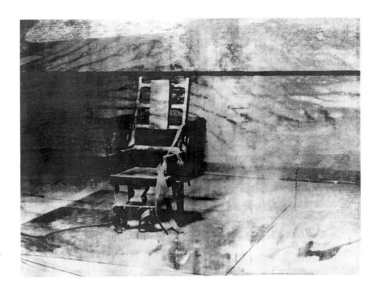

14.8 Andy Warhol, *Big Electric Chair*, silkscreen enamel and acrylic on canvas, 54 x 73 ⅛ in (137 x 186 cm), 1967. The Menil Collection, Houston.

POP, PROTEST, AND COUNTERCULTURE

The broad and varied role of rock music in the 1960s can hardly be overestimated, and emerges as a paradigm for the widespread interpenetration and relaxation of boundaries between traditional and underground behaviors, mainstream and fringe, pop and avant-garde. From general permissiveness and self-expression among youth and those older groups wishing to identify with a more open lifestyle, to non-conformism and rebelliousness by some subculture groups or advocacy for drugs by others, to political and social activism, this most accessible medium of rock music involved an active, engaging role for the audience. In short, the 1960s' maxim "do your own thing" did not mean the same thing to everyone.

In addition to rock music, social conservatism, conformity, the dangers of technology, violence, capital punishment, government foreign policy, and consumerism were all subjects of the expanding Pop Art movement in the early 1960s. Andy Warhol's series of stark, black-and-white silkscreen images taken from press photographs of suicide victims, fatal car accidents, and the electric chair chamber in a prison provide a grim commentary on violence in the United States, where the grainy quality of the image and its repetition also demonstrates a combination of sensationalism with the often numbing effect of mass media exposure (fig. 14.8). That such images still had a political edge in the early 1960s was demonstrated at the 1964 New York World's Fair when city officials whitewashed Warhol's monumental mural of the thirteen most-wanted criminals in America, commissioned for the façade of the New York State pavilion. Strategies employed by Pop artists used the familiar forms of commercial and news photography as well as other techniques of mass-produced imagery; like their counterparts in the rock music industry, they may be seen in part as an attempt to expand the political base of a new, vernacular art and audience. Integrating mass media imagery, cultivating celebrity and branding, Pop Art activities expanded beyond the rarefied space of the gallery and appear as the motivation behind Happenings, Performance Art, Earthworks, and other artistic efforts promoted activism in an effort to mobilize creative activity for a more broad-based audience. Like *Learning from Las Vegas*, Pop Art questioned the relationship between postwar Modernism and popular mass media culture.

Amid growing racial tensions in large American cities such as Los Angeles and Detroit, concern over escalation of the United States's involvement in the Vietnam War, worker strikes and student protests both in Europe and the United States, the political dimensions of Pop art and rock music appeared as part of a wider struggle of artists and designers to engage the mass media and public opinion in the interests of personal expression or wider political protest and social activism.

New artistic movements and design initiatives also seemed to demonstrate an unraveling of the partnership between art, business, government, and the promise of social as well as material progress that characterized more than a decade of expanded production, exhibition, and consumption following World War II. In 1964 graphic designer Ken Garland published the manifesto "First Things First" that was reprinted in the journal *Design* and received notice in the British newspaper the *Guardian*. Garland's text documents the self-examination and search for alternatives within the profession:

We, the undersigned, are graphic designers, photographers and students who have been brought up in a world in which the techniques and apparatus of advertising have persistently been presented to us as the most lucrative, effective and desirable means of using our talents. We have been bombarded with publications devoted to this belief, applauding the work of those who have flogged their skill and imagination to sell such things as: cat food, stomach powders, detergent, hair restorer, striped toothpaste, aftershave lotion, beforeshave lotion, slimming diets, fattening diets, deodorants, fizzy water, cigarettes, roll-ons, pull-ons, and slip-ons. By far the greatest efforts of those working in the advertising industry are wasted on these trivial purposes, which contribute little or nothing to our national prosperity. In common with an increasing number of the general public, we have reached a saturation point at which the high-pitched scream of consumer selling is no more than sheer noise. We think that there are other things more worth using our skill and experience on. There are signs for streets and buildings, books and periodicals, catalogues, instructional manuals, industrial photography, educational aids, films, television features, scientific and industrial publications and all the other media through which we promote our trade, our education, our culture and our greater awareness of the world. We do not advocate the abolition of high-pressure consumer advertising: this is not feasible. Nor do we want to take any of the fun out of life. But we are proposing a reversal of priorities in favour of the more useful and more lasting forms of communication. We hope that our society will tire of gimmick merchants, status salesmen and hidden persuaders, and that the prior call on our skills will be for worthwhile purposes. With this in mind we propose to share our experience and opinions, and to make them available to colleagues, students and others who may be interested.

signed: Edward Wright, Geoffrey White, William Slack, Caroline Rawlence, Ian McLaren, Sam Lambert, Ivor Kamlish, Gerald Jones, Bernard Higton, Brian Grimbly, John Garner, Ken Garland, Anthony Froshaug, Robin Fior, Germano Facetti, Ivan Dodd, Harriet Crowder, Anthony Clift, Gerry Cinamon, Robert Chapman, Ray Carpenter, Ken Briggs

"First Things First" was tame, even gentle, in comparison with later condemnations of industrial design by Victor Papanek and others (see page 364); nevertheless it suggests the presence of alternative voices within the design community, whether truly revolutionary or merely intent upon rethinking and redirecting the relationship between designers, technology, business, and progress.

GRAPHICS AND THE UNDERGROUND

In addition to rock music and happenings, protest movements created a number of distinctive cultural forms in the field of graphic design. The massive demonstrations and disruptive confrontations between police and students on college campuses over issues of free speech and the United States's involvement in Vietnam were media events whose tactics possessed elements of performance and provocation related to the extremes of art world happenings and rock concerts, a world where guitars were occasionally smashed and American flags burned, culminating in the 1969 gathering at Woodstock in upper-state New York and the currency of the term counter-culture. Posters were a part of popular protest in the later 1960s, accompanying the public sit-ins, demonstrations, and concerts on pedestrian-friendly university campuses throughout the United States and Europe. The poster forms were adopted as well for album covers for rock music groups (larger and more "posterlike" than today's compact disk packaging). Many poster designs eschewed precise, hard-edged letterforms in favor of a more calligraphic and elastic typography often derived from l'Art Nouveau and blurring distinctions between text, illustration, and decoration. An example is Robert Wesley (Wes) Wilson's (b. 1937) poster for the Otis Rush/Grateful Dead/Canned Heat concert held at San Francisco's Fillmore Auditorium in 1967 (fig. 14.9; see also fig. 13.27). Wilson's posters employed strong figure–ground reversals that reduced legibility and mirrored the experience of stroboscopic lightshows that

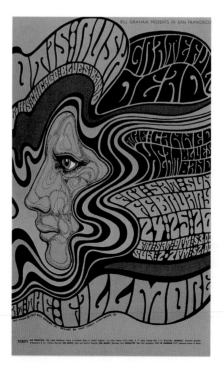

14.9 Wes Wilson, concert poster, silkscreen print, 1967.

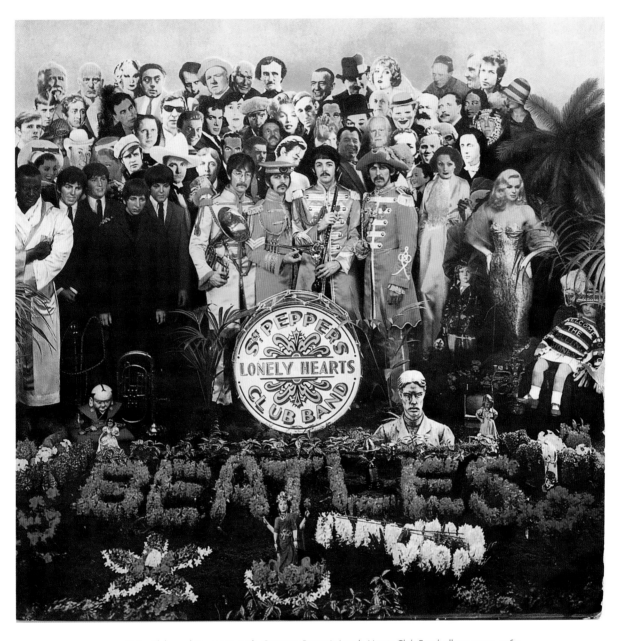

14.10 Peter Blake and Janna Haworth, *Sergeant Pepper's Lonely Hearts Club Band*, album cover, 1967

often accompanied concert performances. Whether in two or three dimensions, in still or moving images, such psychedelic effects were meant to intensify the underground drug experience popular among youth during the later 1960s and 1970s. Techniques referencing 1960s drug culture also appear on the cover of The Beatles' 1967 album *Sergeant Pepper's Lonely Hearts Club Band*, by Peter Blake and Janna Haworth (with photographer Michael Cooper), where elements of juxtaposition between past and present, reminiscent of Dada collage, provide a visual analogue for insider references to psychedelic drugs contained in the lyrics for a number of the tracks for the album, for instance the popular drug LSD in the track "Lucy in the Sky with Diamonds" (fig. 14.10).

On the other side of the Iron Curtain, posters constituted a significant popular art form in Poland after World War II during the establishment of communist rule. Amid occasional censorship, a generation of artists who remained in Poland after World War II produced posters for state-sponsored theaters, film houses, and other forms of public entertainment. Most of the designers were graduates of art schools rather than technical or industrial arts institutions, and they brought highly individual sensibilities to poster art. The Polish poster phenomenon reveals an interesting perspective for the study of design under communism. On the one hand designers eschewed conventional Hollywood poster conventions that focused upon the identity and celebrity of recognizable film stars

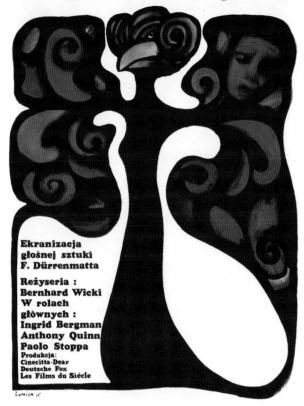

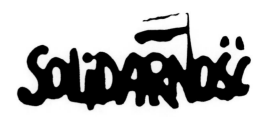

14.12 Jerzy Janiszewski, Solidarity logo, c. 1980.

14.11 Jan Lenica, *The Visit*, film poster, four-color offset print, 23 x 33 in (58.4 x 83.8 cm), 1964. Fine Arts Museum of San Francisco.

and were not forced to adopt similar illustrational approaches of socialist realism (see pages 213 and 231). Rather, artists were permitted to exercise considerable personal freedom without specific commercial pressures or political constraints. An example is Jan Lenica's (1928–2000) 1964 poster for the international film *The Visit* (fig. 14.11), in which a female figure appears to morph into a menacing monarch butterfly with wings, while a blurred face appears trapped in the right wing. The treatment of the wings resembles the colors and design of medieval stained glass, while the imagery and its varied associations echo the film's story, in which a wealthy woman returns to a village to seek revenge on the man who fathered her child.

While some artists left Poland for the West during the 1960s, in the 1970s the freedom of expression found in the Polish poster movement began to acquire political overtones as growing labor movements began to question and eventually rebelled against oppressive state control. Jerzy Janiszewski's (b. 1953) logo for the Solidarity labor

union (c. 1980, fig. 14.12) evokes in its sweeping and uneven strokes and drips the destructive and disruptive nature of public graffiti and suggests a banner-waving phalanx. Not all Polish poster artists were sensitive to typography in their work, but Janiszewski, representing a second generation of poster art, exploits the expressive and suggestive use of lettering as image.

ANTI-DESIGN IN ITALY

Protest was also a direction in design acknowledged in the exhibition Italy: The New Domestic Landscape held at the Museum of Modern Art in New York in 1972. In 1968, student protestors and workers staged demonstrations in Milan, disrupting the Fourteenth Milan Triennale and forcing an early closing of this major international showcase for industrial design in the postwar period. Protests, strikes, and sit-ins were prevalent in many Italian cities during that year: on university campuses student demonstrators rebelled against authoritarian administrations and biased admissions policies, and in factories workers organized for better wages as a response to frustrated expectations for higher standards of living. In solidarity with students and workers, a number of Italian industrial designers began to view their role in the creation of sophisticated domestic objects as part of a repressive collaboration between government and corporate management interests that reinforced class distinction and fueled commodity consumption for the wealthy. In sympathy with unrest on campuses and in factories (at Fiat and Pirelli, for instance), designers looked to alternative strategies that might redefine the relation of design to society.

Design curator Emilio Ambasz (b. 1943) organized the 1972 MoMA exhibition. It included both new and familiar examples of postwar modern Italian design in furniture, lighting, and product housings featuring molded plastics and abstract sculptural forms (see figs. 13.9, 13.15), as well as a section devoted to modular and flexible designs for seating and storage. An additional category, however, featured "objects selected for their socio-cultural implications," which Ambasz defined in the following way:

The second ... attitude is motivated by a profound concern for the designer's role in a society that fosters consumption as one means of inducing individual happiness, thereby ensuring social stability. Torn by the dilemma of having been trained as creators of objects, and yet being incapable of controlling either the significance or the ultimate uses of these objects, they find themselves unable to reconcile the conflicts between their social concerns and their professional practices. They have thus developed a rhetorical mode to cope with these contradictions. Convinced that there can be no renovation of design until structural changes have occurred in society, but not attempting to bring these about themselves, they do not invent substantially new forms; instead they engage in rhetorical operation of redesigning conventional objects with new, ironic, and sometimes self-deprecatory sociocultural and aesthetic references.

In addition to individual designers represented in this section of the exhibition, a number of design groups were included, such as Archizoom and Superstudio, both founded in the later 1960s and devoted to experimental ideas in architecture and design, with collaboration seen as being outside the usual relationship between individual "star" industrial designers and manufacturers.

Ambasz's definition of an experimental industrial design in the 1972 MoMA exhibition was tentative, although his essay suggests that the meaning of designed products lies not only in their physical form but in the relationship or interface between products and users; moreover, appropriating references to American popular culture emerges as an important characteristic of many of the objects selected for this category: the familiar symbols of American consumer culture engaged the critical debate between high and popular culture and were at the same time an affront to the refined international Modernist sensibility. Paolo Lomazzi, Donato D'Urbino, and Jonathan De Pas's Joe chair (1970/1), made of polyurethane foam covered in leather in the shape of a baseball mitt (fig. 14.13), eschewed the sophisticated abstraction of much contemporary Italian design and referenced images of everyday banal consumer products associated with postwar American affluence and leisure. According to Andrea Branzi (b. 1939), a founding member of Archizoom, one of the intentions of such objects was to appropriate and invert the message of popular culture, to create a design situation in which "consumption coincides with opposition." Blatantly anti-functional and garish furniture, with exaggerated elements drawn from luxurious Art Deco or American popular culture such as the model "dream" beds and interiors designed by Archizoom

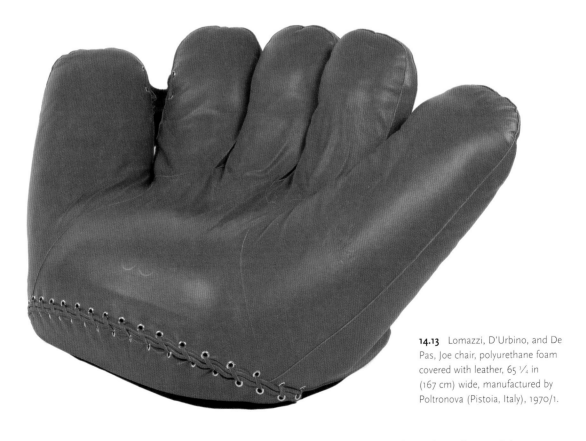

14.13 Lomazzi, D'Urbino, and De Pas, Joe chair, polyurethane foam covered with leather, 65 ¾ in (167 cm) wide, manufactured by Poltronova (Pistoia, Italy), 1970/1.

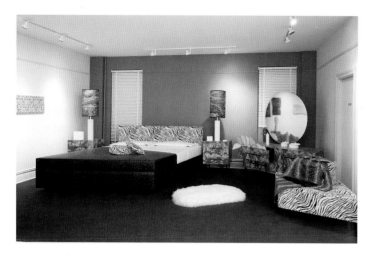

14.14 Claes Oldenburg, *Bedroom Ensemble*, Replica 1, installation, 303 x 512 x 845 in (770 x 1,300 x 2,146 cm), 1969. (Original installation 1963, Whitney Museum of American Art, New York.)

demonstrated the designer's liberation in moving outside of the accepted parameters for sophisticated contemporary industrial design. It is not difficult to see parallels for such subversive, political interpretations of banal objects as they appear in fine arts of the same period. For instance, Claes Oldenburg also produced installations or environments of everyday objects and furniture, a strategy employed in the contemporary art world to move outside the white walls of conventional New York galleries and to more actively engage the spectator. Such projects included his *Bedroom Ensemble* (1963; fig. 14.14), which featured diagonal rather than square furnishings such as beds and dressing tables, constructed of wood and covered in lively, clashing surface patterns of manufactured Formica, not unlike a walk-in Pop Art assemblage by Tom Wesselman (1931–2004; fig. 14.15). Again, the acceptance of popular culture and open-mindedness to heterogeneity, playfulness, and multiple

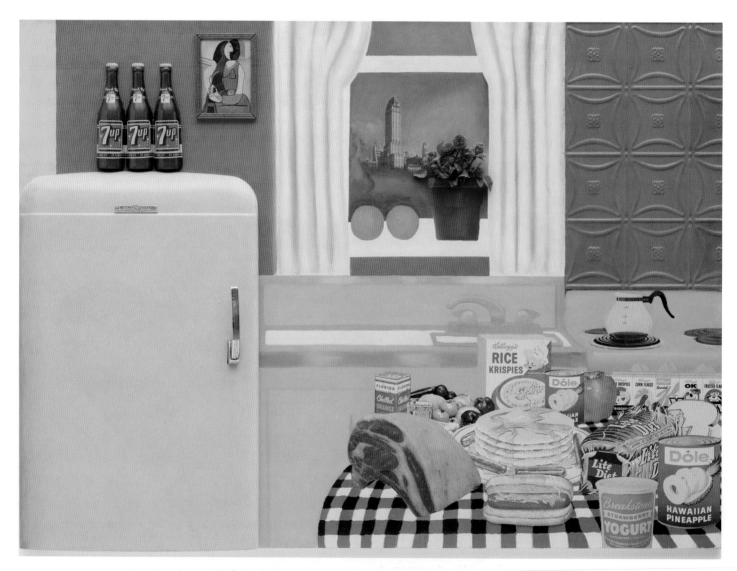

14.15 Tom Wesselman, *Still Life Number 30*, oil, enamel, and synthetic polymer paint on composition board with collage of printed advertisements, plastic flowers, refrigerator door, plastic replicas of 7-Up bottles, glazed and framed color reproduction, and stamped metal, 48 ½ x 66 x 4 in (122 x 167.5 x 10 cm), 1963. Museum of Modern Art, New York.

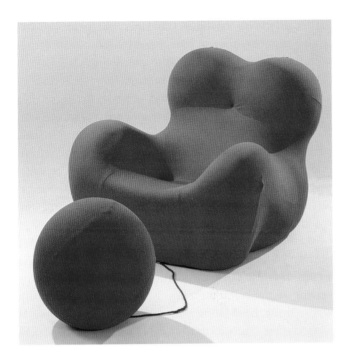

14.16 Gaetano Pesce, Donna chair, cold foam-molded polyurethane foam and nylon jersey fabric, 32 ¼ x 46 x 54 in (82 x 117 x 137 cm), 1969, manufactured by Cassina and Busnelli, Como, Italy, 1970–1973.

readings of cultural artifacts provide the basis for a new kind of artistic freedom involving greater participation on the part of the spectator. Flaunting elements of "kitsch" through decoration and imitation materials, Oldenburg's *Bedroom Ensemble* transgressed the notions of "good taste" and a single "modern" style in design.

Even where a dialogue or association with abstract sculpture might exist, such readings are subverted or opened to multiple interpretations. An example is Gaetano Pesce's (b. 1939) Donna chair, designed in 1969 and manufactured between 1970 and 1973 by Cassina and Busnelli (fig. 14.16). The Donna chair, constructed of polyurethane foam covered with a nylon jersey fabric, brings to mind earlier postwar chairs with female names by Italian designers, most notably Marco Zanuso's 1951 Lady chair (see fig. 11.52). Its concave and convex forms are suggestive of the female form as evoked in Neolithic fertility figures as well as in the contemporary abstract sculpture of Henry Moore and allusions to underlying human themes. Yet the round ottoman attached to the chair with a cord provokes alternative meanings, alluding to the women's liberation movement, introducing another level of reflectionean. As Pesce wrote:

In this design I have expressed my idea of women. A woman is always confined, a prisoner of herself against her will. For this reason I wanted to give this chair the shape of a woman with a ball chained to her foot to use the traditional image of a prisoner.

One also recognizes that the works Ambasz characterized as "sociocultural" in intent were often more rhetorical than practical. Some examples included theoretical tracts and drawings accompanying, for instance, a series of "counter design" environments commissioned for the MoMA's 1972 New Domestic Landscape exhibition, such as Ettore Sottsass, Jr.'s entry (fig. 14.17). In addition to the role of decoration in the patterns used for bedding and headboard or along the walls, there appears to be a conscious effort to create a total environment in which traditional distinctions between wall and floor or furniture and architecture are broken down. The brief for the visionary environments by Sottsass and others calls to mind the guidelines for contributors to the 1925 Exposition des Arts Décoratifs et Industriels Modernes, who also were encouraged to create "new modes of living" through design; indeed it was this brief that produced Le Corbusier's model apartment for the Pavillon de l'Esprit Nouveau, an alternative to the luxurious interiors of the Société des Artistes Décorateurs (see page 177).

Such anti-design activities were not intended primarily for consumption: generally designers wished to liberate themselves from a repressive system in which they felt their contributions were circumscribed and made efforts to provoke and undermine the practices of

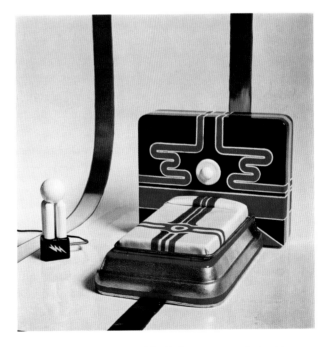

14.17 Ettore Sottsass, Jr., *Modular Environment*, manufactured by Kartell, Boffi, Ideal-Standard, for The New Domestic Landscape exhibition at the Museum of Modern Art, New York, 1972.

consumers and manufacturers alike. Some, such as Enzo Mari (b. 1932), were more interested in language than in products, and viewed inactivity itself as a political stance; Mari produced a polemic essay rather than a physical environment for MoMA's 1972 exhibition. While appropriating popular culture as subversion and advocating radical political change, the activities of this "anti-design" rarely extended beyond the boundaries of exhibition spaces, catalogues, and journals, with exceptions such as the amorphous and portable "Sacco" or beanbag chairs designed by the firm of Gatti, Paolini, Teodoro in 1968–1969. The relation of most "anti-design" experiments to workers' strikes, student protests, and contemporary lifestyles was often distant, rarely sharing the real-life dangers and confrontation on the front lines, although the boycott and demonstrations at the 1968 Triennale in Milan suggests that the militant spirit of the later 1960s in Italy did indeed have design practice as a target.

RADICAL REFORM: TECHNOLOGY, SAFETY, AND THE ENVIRONMENT

The 1960s marked the resurgence of several alternative strategies aimed at redirecting the practice of the corporate-based industrial design community along the lines of public and environmental responsibility, often in terms of global and safety perspectives that added urgency to the rhetoric of reform. Calls for reform ranged from consumer safety to considerations of a wider variety of technologies to improve living conditions in the Third World to futuristic, utopian visions based upon an awareness and more efficient use of the world's limited natural resources. The search for new principles or standards of design sometimes questioned the faith in the combination of industrial technology and unbridled individualism as endorsed by free-market capitalist enterprise and stimulated through the contributions of the industrial design profession. In some ways the voices of reform were not always in harmony with the hedonism that informed many expressions of the counterculture, though both movements shared a strong sense of countercultural idealism.

Criticism of design issued both from within and from outside the design community, often with the support of a public mobilized by articulate spokespeople and activists, advocating for the rights of consumers and minorities. The impact of grassroots movements remains part of our understanding of the 1960s, part of a perceived ability of ordinary citizens to "change the system" through strikes, sit-ins, rallies, boycotts, and engaging the cameras and microphones of the mass media. Although social activism was indeed a theme that engaged artists and designers, other design activities of the period recall in some ways

earlier efforts to establish standards and practices that would balance corporate profits and individual expression with social and environmental responsibility.

Unlike earlier efforts of reform, however, criticism directed at industrial design did not take the form of a single, unified theme or objective, nor did it originate with the endorsements or proclamations of organizations, museums, or government committees. In general, reform efforts resulted from an ideological confrontation between the optimism and affluence of the postwar "American Dream" and "European Economic Miracle" and the realities of lingering inequities and unfulfilled promise.

One form of industrial design criticism targeted a number of large corporations on behalf of the consumers whose interests the corporation was supposed to be serving. A pioneer in this effort was Ralph Nader (b. 1934), whose 1965 book *Unsafe at Any Speed: the designed-in dangers of the American automobile* attacked General Motors for neglecting significant safety issues in the design of the aluminum rear-engine compact Corvair, introduced by Chrevolet in 1960. Ironically, the Corvair was the magazine *Motor Trend*'s choice as "Car of the Year." According to Nader, GM had ignored evidence that this type of rear-engine vehicle had a tendency to spin out of control under certain road conditions, even though warnings of this and other design flaws during the model's development were brought to the attention of company management. The implication of Nader's book was that GM spent significant sums for styling to boost sales, while ignoring safety, product reliability, and public welfare. *Unsafe at Any Speed*, and the subsequent Senate investigation of GM efforts to silence Nader by conducting surveillance in the hope of uncovering damaging information about his character and background, made this lawyer and author a champion for the rights of individuals to question corporate power and practice and to assert their rights as private citizens through the mass media, boycotts, organized protest, and litigation. Nader extended his investigations of corporate business practice to include chemical food preservatives in popular American products such as hot dogs; in this and other cases the evidence was convincing and the result was to undermine consumer and public confidence in corporate responsibility. Such efforts also eroded confidence in the government that failed to regulate business and protect its citizens. Eventually such efforts produced legislation for more truthful and informative product labeling as a measure of consumer education and protection, as well as other regulatory requirements.

While Nader did not bring an end to the "big three" automakers' emphasis upon styling, his efforts did ignite a wave of consumer awareness and the initiation of legislation to monitor automobile safety. Another response to

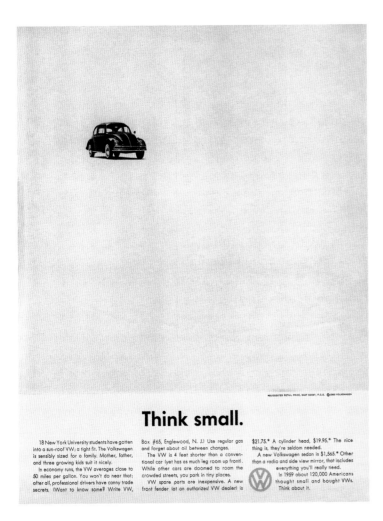

Think small.

18 New York University students have gotten into a sun-roof VW; a tight fit. The Volkswagen is sensibly sized for a family. Mother, father, and three growing kids suit it nicely.
In economy runs, the VW averages close to 50 miles per gallon. You won't do near that; after all, professional drivers have canny trade secrets. (Want to know some? Write VW,

Box #65, Englewood, N. J.) Use regular gas and forget about oil between changes.
The VW is 4 feet shorter than a conventional car (yet has as much leg room up front). While other cars are doomed to roam the crowded streets, you park in tiny places.
VW spare parts are inexpensive. A new front fender (at an authorized VW dealer) is

$21.75.* A cylinder head, $19.95.* The nice thing is, they're seldom needed.
A new Volkswagen sedan is $1,565.* Other than a radio and side view mirror, that includes everything you'll really need.
In 1959 about 120,000 Americans thought small and bought VWs. Think about it.

14.18 Doyle Dane Bernbach, "Think small" advertisement for Volkswagen, 1959.

corporate self-interest in the American automobile industry was a steady rise in the sales of imported cars more independent of the marketing practices of annual model changes by large American manufacturers. Rather than comply with the American strategy of planned obsolescence, buyers could exercise freedom of choice by opting not to buy an American car. Perhaps the best-known alternative of this sort was the small rear-engine air-cooled Volkswagen Beetle, designed in 1937 but not manufactured continuously in Germany until after the end of World War II (see pages 241 and 279). Sales of the Beetle increased during the 1960s mostly through popularity with younger buyers, while individual owners sometimes customized its standardized form through hand-painted designs rather than factory options and accessories. Volkswagen also benefited from an ad campaign by the New York agency Doyle Dane Bernbach (fig. 14.18), using the slogan "Think small." The large amount of white space in the 1959 ad functions as a design element to reinforce the theme of economy, but the power of the ad also resides

in its acknowledgment of alternative attitudes toward the automobile and its presumption of viewer familiarity with standard automobile advertisements (see figs. 12.1 and 12.3); even the lower-case "s" in the word "small" and sans serif type contribute to the appeal of being different rather than conforming to Detroit automobiles or their advertising strategies.

The appeal of smaller, standardized vehicles received another, stronger boost after 1973 when the oil-producing nations of the Middle East established a cartel (the Organization of the Petroleum Exporting Countries; OPEC) that fixed oil prices and eliminated concessions to multi-national oil companies for inexpensive oil prices in the United States. Within a year of the formation of OPEC, fuel prices in the United States rose from below 50 cents per gallon to over one dollar. Both in person and through television, the sight of filling stations with gas lines and the resulting public fear of shortages and dwindling natural reserves for oil also spelled disaster for the "big three" United States' auto manufacturers, locked into design strategies favoring large-engine vehicles, unconcerned with fuel efficiency and conservation, and unresponsive to changing consumer habits and attitudes.

As American automakers struggled to make fuel economy part of a new design strategy, foreign manufacturers became increasingly competitive. Perhaps the biggest winner in the automobile market was the Japanese manufacturer Honda, whose 1975 Civic met consumer expectations in a new era of fuel economy (fig. 14.19). The rival Japanese Nissan Motor Company Ltd. (under the brand name Datsun), as well as Toyota, also provided several economical alternatives to gas-guzzling Detroit models, earning a foothold in the large North American market that has not been relinquished.

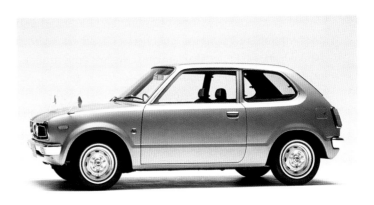

14.19 Honda Motor Company, Hamamatsu, Honda Civic automobile, 147 ¹³⁄₁₆ x 59 ¹⁄₄ x 52 ¹⁄₈ in (375 x 150.5 x 132 cm), American Honda Motor Company Inc., Torrance, California, 1975.

Amid skepticism toward corporate ideology linking design, technology, and progress, new alternative voices for reform sounded the battle cry for social responsibility, often with an added sense of urgency based upon the environmental costs of technology, consumption, and waste. The anger directed at industrial design in the 1960s is felt in the preface of a book written at the end of the era, Victor Papanek's *Design for the Real World*, published in 1971:

There are professions more harmful than industrial design, but only a very few of them. And possibly only one profession is phonier. Advertising design, in persuading people to buy things they don't need, with money they don't have, in order to impress others who don't care, is probably the phoniest field in existence today. Industrial design, by concocting the tawdry idiocies hawked by advertisers, comes a close second... By designing criminally unsafe automobiles that kill or maim nearly one million people around the world each year, by creating whole new species of permanent garbage to clutter up the landscape, and by choosing materials and processes that pollute the air we breathe, designers have become a dangerous breed. And the skills needed in these activities are taught carefully to young people.

The Austrian-born and British-educated Papanek (1926–1998) was an outspoken critic of styling and obsolescence in industrial design, advocating an approach that took account of limited natural resources and the satisfaction of needs as opposed to wants. Like R. Buckminster Fuller, who supplied the preface to *Design for the Real World*, Papanek was both utopian as well as apocalyptic: both designers envisioned a world in which individuals and grassroots organizations directed design projects for housing and products in the broad public interest for safety and the efficient use of resources, and warned of the global effects of unlimited production and consumption in terms of pollution and other environmental hazards. Fuller also lamented the lost opportunities for designers to play a more active role in meeting basic needs in developing countries. Papanek considered design as an inclusive and multi-faceted problem-solving activity that addresses considerations of materials, processes, and use in relation to issues of social and political urgency. The gravity, and the relevance, of his hope for design emerges again in this passage from *Design for the Real World*:

Isn't it too bad that so little design, so few products are really relevant to the needs of mankind? Watching the children of Biafra dying in living color while sipping a frost-beaded martini can be kicks for lots of people,

but only until *their* town starts burning down. To an engaged designer, this way of life, this lack of design, is not acceptable.

Papanek attempted to restore a sense of purpose to design as an activity integral to the survival of the planet in environmental as well as in social terms. Although less universal in his approach to the activity of design, Papanek's urgency reminds one of Le Corbusier's provocative question at the conclusion of *Towards a New Architecture:* "Architecture or Revolution?" Papanek also allows us to recognize that terms like "progress" are relative and invite alternative definitions and courses of action. Both designers believed in the ability of design to alter the conditions of life on a national or global scale; Le Corbusier believed that the machine and mechanized manufacturing held the key to realize his vision, whereas Papanek's efforts were directed more toward available or alternative applications of technology and a do-it-yourself approach that begins with individual commitment. He provided numerous examples of socially and environmentally directed projects that explored the problem-solving context of his approach to design and took into account local conditions and circumstances. As an example, he cited an anonymously designed low-cost stove constructed of reused automobile license plates for families in underprivileged communities, as well as a design he developed with James Hennessey for a cooling unit to keep food products fresh without the need for electricity (fig. 14.20). In addition to his own designs, Papanek directed student projects at a number of universities. In no sense was Papanek anti-technological; rather he advocated for the use of local materials and energy sources, and available

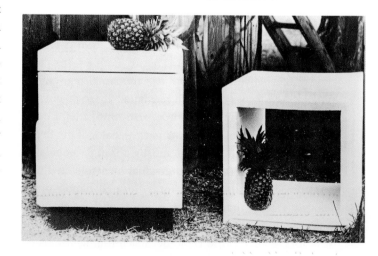

14.20 Victor Papanek and James Hennessey, drawing and prototype for cooling unit for perishable foods, using no electricity, from *Design for the Real World*, 1971.

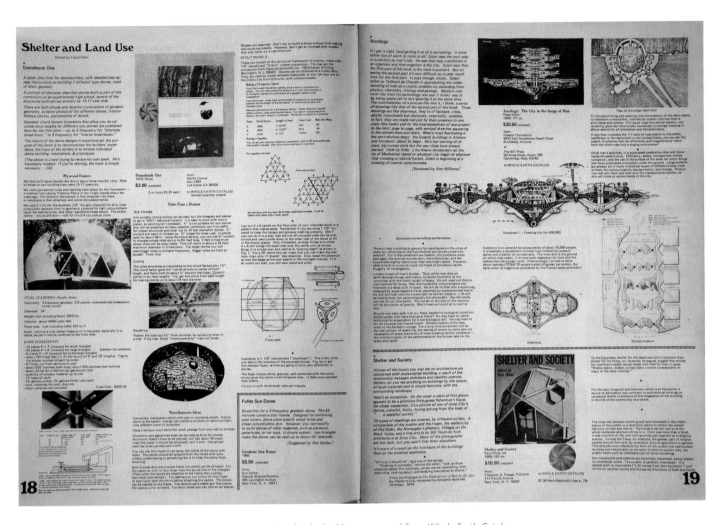

14.21 Stewart Brand, ed., double-page spread from *Whole Earth Catalog.*
Access to Tools, Menlo Park, California, spring 1970. Pages 18–19.

rather than high-tech solutions to design problems – solutions that enable people to help themselves rather than reinforce dependence upon massive external technological investment and the environmental, economic, and political consequences of such investment. His message is also found in the *Whole Earth Catalog* published by American-born activist Stewart Brand (b. 1938) and appearing regularly between 1968 and 1972 (fig. 14.21). The *Catalog* featured stories, diagrams, instructions, and products for simple living and an emphasis upon conservation. Sections included "Shelter and Land Use," "Industry and Craft," "Community," "Understanding Whole Systems," and "Learning." One might use the term "empowerment" to characterize the message of *WEC*: such efforts continue with organizations such as Design Without Borders and other service design organizations throughout the world (see pages 391–392).

The career of visionary designer R. Buckminster Fuller stretched over five decades, beginning with prototypes for a mass-produced Dymaxion house and the three-wheel streamlined Dymaxion automobile displayed at the 1933 Century of Progress World's Fair in Chicago (see page 240). Fuller believed that conservation of energy and materials were industrial design imperatives in the twentieth century. His lightweight geodesic domes, developed after World War II as a strategy to meet tremendous housing shortages, were fabricated from triangular units that could be made from a variety of materials; they could be used as a framework to support panels, windows, or even hang fabric to provide portable shelter. Like many of Fuller's projects, geodesic domes had limited commercial viability (see page 297); his design and promotional efforts had a utopian and visionary quality stemming from a belief in the ability of applied technology to solve global problems irrespective of markets and considerations of social and cultural difference. Fuller was an inspiration for the *Whole Earth Catalog,* and the apotheosis of the geodesic dome was its use for the United States Pavilion at the 1967 World Fair in Montreal, Canada, as a symbol of American technological innovation appropriate to the age of space exploration (fig. 14.22). Unlike the Unisphere for the 1964 World's Fair in New York, the spherical form was not just a sculptural symbol but a space-age architectural structure with a light monorail system connecting it with other fair pavilions. The possibilities of lightweight, portable, inflatable buildings also inspired a group of French architectural students to create alternatives to permanent building materials. They envisioned portable pneumatic architecture in projects with titles such as "Pneumo City," which suggested a closer relationship between nature, with "air as the primary element." Their efforts also inspired filmmaker British Graham Stevens's *Atmosfields and Desert Clouds* (1972) featuring amorphous billowing forms floating on water and moving rather than standing still. Despite the collectivist implications of his vision, Fuller's public appearances (lectures often lasting for hours on university campuses as well as television and news magazine interviews) attracted the interest of many youth counterculture groups, who embraced communal living as an alternative to either the suburban single-family dwelling or urban apartment. Fuller represents a point of connection between the romanticism associated with youth counterculture movements of the later 1960s and the radical views of those who wished to redirect technology away from materialism as well as business and military interests toward the elimination of human suffering. Both movements were motivated by idealism, but in fact the social implications of Fuller's utopia were quite removed from the unbridled sensory indulgence of the hippie counterculture of the 1970s. Yet both were in their own ways anti-establishment, part of a broad spectrum of subcultures with an alternative vision for a future society, rethinking the uses of technology, the relationship of individuals to nature, and the meaning of progress.

More mainstream efforts to address social problems might be seen in the low-cost, high-density housing projects and urban planning initiatives undertaken in the later 1950s and 1960s in a number of American cities. There is widespread agreement that these massive government-sponsored redevelopment projects deteriorated as physical structures and also failed to build a sense of community and shared responsibility among their residents. British historian David Harvey commented that the demolition of the 1955 Pruitt-Igoe development in St. Louis in 1972 signified the demise of the belief that a rational approach to modern design could help promote social or racial equality. As architectural critic and urban activist Jane Jacobs noted in her 1961 book *The Death and Life of Great American Cities*, housing standards based upon modernist aesthetic principles or social determinism do not seem to be able to effectively address the challenges of creating safe and self-supporting neighborhoods and

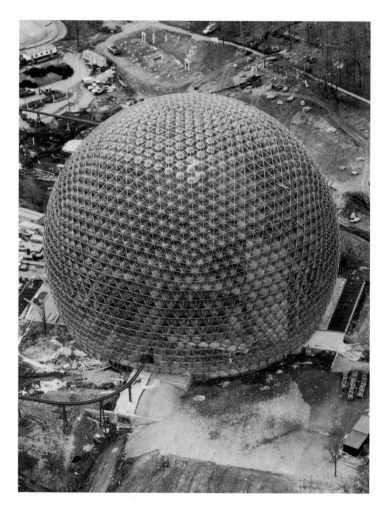

14.22 R. Buckminster Fuller, geodesic dome for United States Pavilion, Montreal, Canada, 1967.

communities. As a result, design solutions must take into account a variety of factors that include the perspectives of the population being served, the psychological effects of the environment, and zoning considerations that affect the nurturing of community. Despite progressive and democratic intentions of slum-clearance and the "war on poverty," modernist design was judged harshly by many critics as a solution for working-class urban living, representing the viewpoint of architects and planners without sufficient input from the users whose lives were affected.

Critical responses to modernist urban housing development provide the background for a shift in design thinking, seen throughout this chapter, from a focus upon products toward an interest upon users, with an acknowledgment that not all users (or stakeholders) are the same. Not only has this led to a rethinking of the practice of design in traditional fields like graphic, fashion, or product design, but also to an expansion of the field of design to include services as well as products. This expansion, its results and challenges, is examined below.

Chapter 15

Politics, Pluralism, and Postmodernism

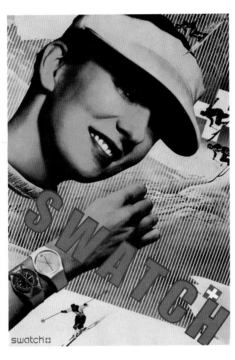

15.1 Paula Scher, Swatch advertising poster, offset print, 29 ⅛ x 20 ⅛ in
(76 x 51 cm), 1984. Museum of Design, Zurich. Poster collection.

The 1960s did not spark the social or political revolutions forecasted by campus riots in the United States and in Europe or the disruption of the 1968 Democratic Party National Convention in Chicago. As argued, however, by British historian and author Arthur Marwick, the challenge of new viewpoints stemming from minority groups, whether women, blacks, gays, or students, produced more open-minded attitudes toward difference and the protection of individual rights.

In the United States, federal enforcement of the 1964 Civil Rights Act and widely broadcast demonstrations such as Martin Luther King's 1963 March on Washington served to bring issues of racial equality to national attention. Government initiatives created the Environmental Protection Agency (EPA) in 1970, while the passage of laws aimed at reducing highway deaths through seatbelt laws and mandatory manufacturer recalls on defective parts and systems eventually resulted from Ralph Nader's spirited challenge to unquestioned faith in corporate power. For almost 20 years, the oil crisis of the early 1970s

and concerns for fuel efficiency and automobile safety produced lower speed limits (55 mph) on most of the nation's highways. Other legislation legalized abortion (Roe vs. Wade, 1973), required the reading of rights to criminal suspects placed under arrest (Miranda vs. Arizona, 1966), and made divorces easier to obtain. On campuses, quota systems for the admission of minorities were abolished and the percentage of students able to attend colleges and universities began to rise through need-based and merit-based scholarships and loans. And finally in 1976, though long-overdue for many Americans, broad-based pressure helped to bring an end to the drawn-out war in Vietnam, which had caused so much protest and anger both within the United States and hostilities directed toward the United States from its neighbors.

The 1960s also signaled the critical recognition of several coexisting cultural expressions in the areas of art and design, a situation sometimes referred to as Pluralism, in which no single approach to modernity dominated, and where the exchange value of all designed goods obscures former distinctions between "good," mass, and popular design. The situation accommodated, and even encouraged, diversity, but only within an acknowledged common culture of consumption, economic growth, and globalization. Perhaps late twentieth-century Pluralism may be understood simply as the commercialization of diversity: the margins do not exist without a dominant mainstream, but the mainstream also demands the margins to nurture innovation and penetrate new markets. Art historian Thomas Crow cogently summarized the situation: "The avant-garde is the research and development branch of the culture industry."

Capital investment in business following the breakup of the Soviet Union, and trade negotiations between the United States and the People's Republic of China, reveal that economic expansion consistently dominates politics in international relations, with human rights serving as a bargaining chip to ensure the political consent of governments on behalf of their broad-based constituencies. Scarcely more than a century ago, William Morris joined the Socialist League in protest over the British government's support of Turkish interests in the Balkans, despite evidence of atrocities by Turkish soldiers against Bulgarian citizens. For dissenters such as Morris, Britain's support was based upon economic self-interest rather than upon humanitarian concerns. Today, in general, the press and public it represents readily accept that the United States's foreign policy is governed by a convenient dovetailing involving the concern for human rights and the exploration of new markets for its goods and services. If in the end the interests of human rights are served through such compromise it is rarely due to the pressure exerted by fringe activism. This process tends to minimize differences between existing mainstream political parties, who continue to link, often uncritically, technology with economic growth (or more recently, recovery) and progress. Much design remains connected to this linkage.

Within this framework acknowledging the hegemony of capitalism and equating progress with technology and economic expansion, a variety of perspectives on modern design coexist, often symbiotically. This generally healthy heterogeneity reduces the dichotomy between a "cultural" modernism based upon standards and social responsibility, and an "economic" modernism governed by free enterprise and addressing the mass market that lent to the first two centuries of modern design history a particular kind of heroism, urgency, and vision. In the present context of inclusiveness and relativity, notions of reform, alienation, resistance, and subversion have relinquished a measure of their power to define what has been a vital current in the history of modern design. A more recent and general acknowledgment of global warming and its environmental impact in the past decade has renewed in some measure a shared sense of responsibility that is revealed in fringe as well as mainstream design efforts that include a wide range of products, services, advertising, and other forms of visual communication.

Toward the end of the 1970s, the pop and countercultural challenge to modern architecture and "good design" was becoming more widespread. The catalogue for the 1983 exhibition Design Since 1945, held at the Philadelphia Museum of Art and curated by Kathryn Hiesinger and George Marcus, included essays advocating rational standards and abstract aesthetics by Dieter Rams, Max Bill, and George Nelson, but also contained a contribution by sociologist Herbert Gans, who argued that postwar international Modern design was a "treasure trove of upper middle class culture," that is, a taste appealing to a particular class and reflecting particular rather than universal values.

At the same time, alternative design initiatives and protests began to relinquish the subversive and threatening political overtones they had in Italy and elsewhere in the later 1960s, acquiring an international high-end commercial cachet underwritten by manufacturers such as Alessi and Formica. In Milan, for instance, organizations espousing new directions were initiated in the later 1970s. Alchymia (1976) and Memphis (1981), for instance, included contributions of not only Italian but also Japanese and North and South American designers. The activities of Memphis and other groups or individuals designing ambiguous but less threatening appropriations of historical styles and popular culture are often described as being Postmodern, a term commonly used among critics and historians, and that has filtered into more general usage.

For design, Postmodernism encompasses projects and forms that signal an end to the polemic between aesthetically or socially directed design on the one hand and commercially motivated design on the other, an opposition that emerged as a strain of modernism in the early nineteenth century with the design reform movement and that continued to dominate design theory for much of the two decades following World War II. It may also be described even more broadly as an attitude through which various tendencies of modernism in design are deprived of their oppositional status or pretensions. Theoretically, Postmodernism shares with mass culture a user-oriented approach to design that emphasizes multiple interpretations and meanings and embraces ephemeral rather than permanent characteristics of the design enterprise, exemplified by connections with the improvisational, open-ended nature of performance art and the inclusiveness of popular forms of expression.

Design and Postmodernism

The term Postmodernism is often found in conjunction with others such as post-industrialism and late capitalism, all referring to a culture in which economic growth is the common subtext, emerging first in the early years of postwar affluence in the United States and spreading to Europe and other developed nations. Late capitalism signifies investment directed toward increasingly segmented audiences (rather than collective or a single shared taste), and a readiness of businesses to design, manufacture, and market products with increasing speed, responsiveness, and sophistication in a highly competitive environment. The design enterprise is also accelerated through the increased efficiency of batch rather than mass production, target marketing, and reduced material costs due to the shift from mechanical to digital components. Batch production focuses upon the assembly of limited quantities of varied products using similar components for flexible yet efficient manufacture. One example of batch production is in the fashion industry, where a limited number of "bodies" are expanded through variations in "trim" to permit more consumer choice. As another example, British design historian Nigel Whitely cites the success of the Swatch wristwatches first in Britain and then internationally in the 1980s, the result of inexpensive plastic materials and production, and an especially fashion-oriented approach to wristwatches to complement clothing styles (fig. 15.1). The ephemeral, virtually disposable Swatch (the name combines the words "Swiss" and "watch," but also brings to mind the word "switch"), manufactured by the Swiss company Eta beginning in 1983, targeted a young audience less likely to be influenced by the emotional attachments sometimes associated with personal objects and heirlooms. Graphic designer and Pentagram partner Paula Scher's 1984 Swatch poster advertisement appropriates elements of a Herbert Matter Swiss tourism poster from 1934, whose photomontage technique and juxtapositions suggest a broad range of associations between the two watches and Switzerland (mountains, skiing, an outline of the country's map, and the red Swiss emblem that is part of the company logo), with timepieces, leisure, and with Modernist design. The range of meanings here is open-ended, communicating at different levels to those with or without an insider knowledge of graphic design history.

Post-industrialism, seen in the design and manufacture of products such as the Swatch watch, is a broad and useful contemporary term signaling that the heroic age of industrial mass production has been surpassed by an increased emphasis upon the research, service, and communications sectors of economies and expanded efforts in fields such as product semantics rather than more traditional "form-making" previously associated with industrial design. In short, changes in the practice and perception of design have accompanied the shift from the mechanical age to the information age. In many traditional manufacturing industries, capital investment in robotics reduces the need for unskilled, assembly-line labor and demonstrates the increasing degree of sophisticated and intelligent interactivity between humans and machines, yet another theme in the contemporary discourse of design.

In some ways an extension of human factors into the realm of communication and information rather than physical interaction, the area of product semantics deals with the interface between products and users that breaks down barriers for understanding, use, and sales. Examples include the development of the mouse for desktop computers (see page 380), tracking devices for laptop computers, color-coding, and other instructions or diagrams for the wiring of electronic connections for the assembly of a wide range of consumer electronic products. Emphasis upon the user also extends to accelerating product change through the introduction of small differences in similar products to create consumer choice and faster rates of obsolescence and replacement. An instance of the blurring between technology, progress, and consumption is described below with reference to the telephone (see page 388), and the so-called "mutations"of the Apple iPod MP3 players connect obsolescence to users rather than manufacturers, where changes are a response to unplanned and unforeseen applications (such as podcasting) discovered independently by consumers who discover new ways of operating and personalizing such devices. The use of computers to generate patterns for machine-knit sweaters provides another instance of acceleration through a more direct relationship between design and production. If part of the history of modern design that we have been tracing depends upon examining the separation of design from manufacture from the eighteenth century onward through capital investment in technology and the growth of a consumer economy, the advent of computer-generated patterns and rapid-prototyping technology signals, at least in part, an about-face that uses machines to create unique products that are the direct, less mediated extension of the designer's imagination.

In the later twentieth century, theorists began to refer to contemporary design as being "soft," a term implying a number of related concepts, including the designer's manipulation of virtual and increasingly flexible rather than real materials and forms via computer imaging in a more dynamic and interactive process, emphasizing the interface between users, products, and services rather than the form of objects. Nevertheless, "soft" design, linked as well to *soft*ware and the information age, is also a metaphor for an aesthetic sensibility that combines nostalgia for science fiction, past and present, near and far, in an exciting, fast-paced, seamless (if fragmented) image characteristic of contemporary culture in the information age. It may refer to increasingly "soft" and pliable "user-friendly" materials, or to the complex layering and sensory richness that characterizes the work of a number of contemporary graphic designers.

POSTMODERN PRODUCTS

Postmodern design emerged in organizations such as Memphis, made up of industrial designers "liberated" from their contracts with particular companies, with the freedom to pursue directions beyond the parameters of "good design." Postmodernism or Pluralism also was the overriding theme of the exhibition Design Now: Industry or Art held at the German Architecture Museum in Frankfurt in 1989.

Ettore Sottsass, Jr., who worked under contract to Olivetti in the 1960s in the design of office machines, mainframe computer housings, and personal typewriters (see figs. 13.10 and 13.11), independently designed prototypes for furniture in the 1980s using commercial industrial materials such as plywood and plastic laminates in bright colors and patterns. These examples appropriated references to Hollywood-style historical set design, celebrating the sensory excitement of billboard advertising and rock music (Memphis is the home of rock icon Elvis Presley, immortalized in Warhol's silkscreen images and in the furnishings of the singer's own Graceland mansion). An example is Sottsass's 1981 Tartar table (fig. 15.2), whose

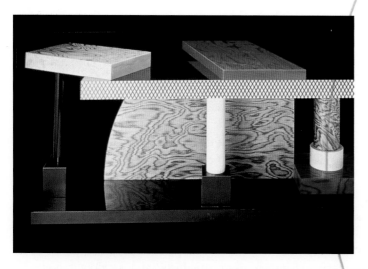

15.2 Ettore Sottsass, Jr., Tartar table, reconstituted veneer, lacquer, and plastic laminate, 30 x 75 ¾ x 32 ¼ in (76 x 192 x 82 cm), manufactured by Memphis, 1981.

laminated surfaces and juxtapositions of patterns recall Oldenburg's *Bedroom Ensemble* installation of 1963 or Wesselman's (1931–2004) *Still Life Number 30* assemblage (see figs. 14.14 and 14.15). Memphis organized group exhibitions in Milan, and the Formica Corporation invited members of the group to design furniture using its new ColorCore product, a solid variation of the material that could be molded and cut. The conflicting, overlapping interpretations are not atypical of Postmodern forms and their appropriation of the past in a reflective and complex way. Alessandro Mendini's (b. 1931) Proust armchair (1978; fig. 15.3), named for the introspective French writer Marcel Proust (1871–1922) and produced for Studio Alchymia, is another example: the Rococo Revival upholstered armchair references Victorian comfort and artisanal craftsmanship, while the brightly colored upholstery cover is a clear appropriation of French pointillism, a style of painting associated with Georges Seurat (1859–1891) concerned with reproducing the transient reflections of light in nature. The construction and carving assert mass, while the flickering upholstery patterns denies it: the chair both affirms and dematerializes physical form at the same time, as if to illustrate the coexistence of multiple, even opposite perspectives. Such dissonance among interpretations was characteristic of many Postmodern design initiatives; in addition to welcoming the return of decoration and historicism in objects as a jab at the hegemony of international modernism, such works also emphasize the shifting and complex relationship between objects and users that characterizes the late twentieth-century understanding of design thinking and practice.

While 1960s appropriations of popular culture took place outside of mainstream manufacturing practice, for instance, in Italy and were approached either rhetorically or with an eye toward a rebellious youth market in terms of style and price, Postmodernism of the early 1980s began to attract high-end commercial interest, seen in Robert Venturi's (b. 1925) series of chairs manufactured by Knoll. Venturi's Chippendale chair of 1984 (fig. 15.4) appears to mock or rebel against foundational tenets of modern furniture design, first in appropriating an eighteenth-century style, second in using an industrial material to imitate an original design in a natural material (here made even more obvious through painting), and third by flaunting decoration rather than eliminating it or treating it as subservient to function. Indeed Venturi, who encouraged architects and designers to think of themselves as "jesters," chose the chair as a focus, since it has been a paradigm of the very standards toward which contemporary designers direct their irony and through which they champion the "complexity and contradiction" of Postmodernism.

15.3 Alessandro Mendini, Proust armchair, painted wood with hand-painted upholstery, height 42 ⅛ in (107 cm), made by Studio Alchymia, Milan, 1978.

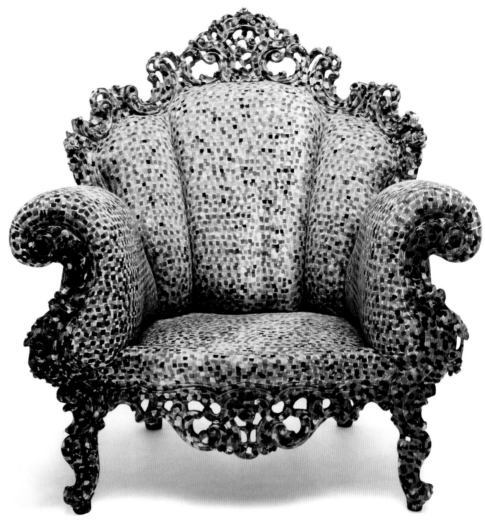

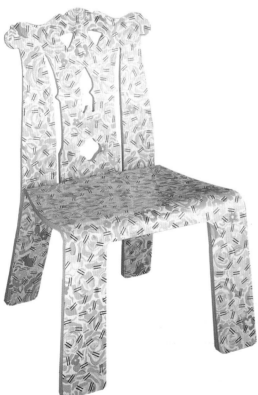

15.4 Robert Venturi, Chippendale chair, bent laminated yew and plastic laminate, 37 ⅛ x 25 ½ x 23 ¼ in (95 x 65 x 59 cm), manufactured by Knoll International, New York, 1984. Philadelphia Museum of Art.

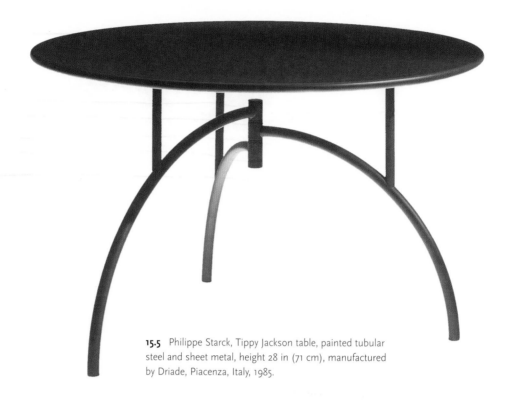

15.5 Philippe Starck, Tippy Jackson table, painted tubular steel and sheet metal, height 28 in (71 cm), manufactured by Driade, Piacenza, Italy, 1985.

French architect and designer Philippe Starck (b. 1949) emerged in the mid-1980s with original furniture for sophisticated clients such as fashion designer Pierre Cardin and French Prime Minister François Mitterrand. He is in this regard the heir to the luxury French Art Deco tradition of Émile-Jacques Ruhlmann (see page 164), but using assembled industrial materials, employing simple, often abstract geometric shapes with elegant solutions to support systems and collapsibility for storage, as in his tubular and sheet steel Tippy Jackson folding table manufactured in Italy by Driade in 1985 (fig. 15.5). The table's name may allude to Michael Jackson's 1982 album *Thriller*, and the MTV video featuring the performer's gravity-defying moonwalk dance step. There is also little that is "straightforward" about Tippy Jackson: there is no simple or logical explanation for the table's support system, with its bowed legs and struts of different lengths, and there are certainly more economical solutions to folding tables than the system Starck proposes.

In domestic wares, the Italian manufacturer Alessi has been active in promoting original design in silver. In the early 1980s American architect Michael Graves (b. 1934) designed the Art Deco-inspired tea and coffee service that featured polished ribbed surfaces, ebony feet, ivory handles, and non-functional blue knobs (fig. 15.6). The design appeared in a section of the 1989 Design Now exhibition entitled "Micro-architecture," a reference to the resurgence of decoration and popular symbolism in many Postmodern buildings. Many of the most popular appliances and furnishings were designed by major architects,

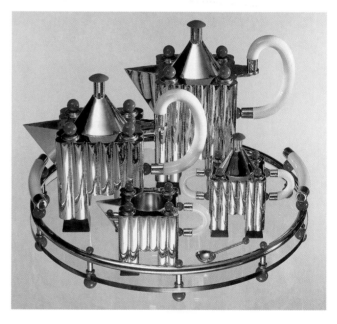

15.6 Michael Graves, tea and coffee service (prototype), silver, lacquered aluminum, mock ivory, and Bakelite, tray 3 ½ x 16 in (9 x 41 cm), manufactured by Alessi, New York and Italy, 1980–1983. Metropolitan Museum of Art, New York.

and their "micro-architecture" invites playful associations on the part of the viewer/user, making the dinner or coffee table into a kind of game board on which users engage imaginatively with objects that come to life, generating desire for high-end but more affordable Alessi products and associating the manufacturer with new directions in design and the experience of Postmodern living.

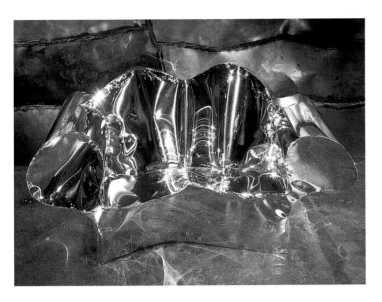

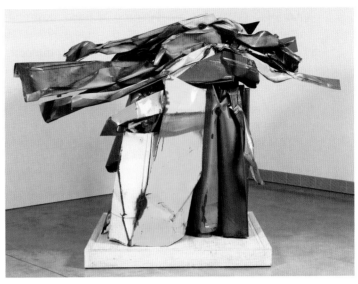

15.7 Ron Arad, Big Easy Volume 2 sofa, stainless steel and steel, height 34 ¼ in (87 cm), manufactured by One Off, London, 1988.

15.8 John Chamberlain, *Glossalia Adagio*, painted and chromium-plated steel, 77 x 87 x 124 in (210.8 x 221 x 315 cm), 1984. Philadelphia Museum of Art.

While the political activism of Memphis or Alchymia participants was subdued in comparison with earlier anti-design activities of the later 1960s, other contemporary designers continued to employ elements of popular culture to reflect issues of political and environmental awareness, albeit in a rhetorical way. One direction for such activity has been the reuse of materials, seen for instance in Ron Arad's (b. 1951) Rover chair of 1981, constructed from used automobile seats attached to a tubular metal frame, incorporating the socially conscious initiative of recycling. More complex in construction is Arad's asymmetrical Big Easy Volume 2 sofa of 1988 (fig. 15.7). This piece consists of sheets of industrial steel cut, shaped, and painstakingly welded to conform to the contours of a traditionally carved wooden seat and form of a heavily upholstered and well-worn sofa, bringing to the mind of the informed viewer the crushed metal sculpture of John Chamberlain (b. 1927), such as *Glossalia Adagio* (fig. 15.8), dating to 1984 and made from the wreckage common in automobile graveyards. Both examples focus attention upon the aesthetic qualities of an industrial material in a non-traditional form or setting. Nuances of decay appear in other examples of furniture with environmental or ecological overtones, indicative of new meanings of discarded or decomposing objects. Such objects demonstrate ambiguities of intention and interpretation. Clearly this kind of furniture is not intended for mass production. Often the results seem contrived and undermine any possible desire to reach beyond a sophisticated audience entirely prepared to view such objects aesthetically or as a form of sociopolitical commentary. Yet there remains an effort, in making references to banal materials and

everyday experience, to stimulate reflection in the viewer and to question some of the conventional associations of commodity consumption and materialism. Elements of these viewpoints also emerge in Punk graphics and its variations in other media, and will be treated below.

Despite museum exhibitions, commissions from companies such as Alessi or Formica to individual designers and groups such as Memphis, and the emergence of small galleries and boutiques that promoted interest in the self-conscious complexities that lend meaning to contemporary experiments in furniture and other household commodities, the majority of furniture and other domestic products in the broad mass market initially owed little to the clever ironies of much Postmodernism. Yet there was increasing evidence in the later 1990s that the forms of many Postmodern designers were reaching a wider market, such as Michael Graves's designs for Target (see pages 382–383). Much of this activity demonstrated the belief that Postmodernism's eclectic sources encouraged a healthy acceptance of diversity and difference in society, breaking down social boundaries in a tolerant, global society.

This view was not without its critics. Skepticism regarding the meaning of Postmodernism's inclusiveness was ongoing, and the issue of tolerance and liberation remained a matter of debate: Robert Hughes, in *Culture of Complaint: The Fraying of America* (1993) found little cause for optimism, seeing instead a Balkanization of subcultures in the products of a culture obsessed with the delineation of difference rather than with commonality or quality. Marxist critics lamented the lack of forms of art and design to nurture the seeds of resistance to capitalist hegemony. In *Postmodernism, or the Cultural Logic of Late*

Capitalism (1991), Fredric Jameson defined postmodernism as a "cultural dominant," the integration of a formerly autonomous aesthetic discourse with commodity production. For Jameson the result was an absence of true opposition in political terms and a demonstration of "depthlessness" in aesthetic terms, with mass media substituting for direct experience, producing an experience rich in immediacy and association but essentially alienating. Meanwhile, the growing gap between developed nations and the Third World continued to demonstrate, for some, the need for a more thorough sense of social responsibility in design on a global scale. Cultural and technological disparity remains an undercurrent in envisioning the role of design in the future: lobbying efforts for Internet access throughout the schools and households of the United States are typical of the ideology of progress, yet ignore the fact that a majority of the population in many underdeveloped countries lack the basic services many of us take for granted and call into question the meaning or reality of the Canadian educator and philosopher Marshall McLuhan's (1911–1980) term "global village" in the information age.

PLURALISM AND RESISTANCE: PUNK

Another challenging aspect of pluralism surfaced in the behaviors, dress, and accessories associated with the punk movement beginning in the later 1970s and early 1980s. Aggressive, destructive, and uninhibited, the expressions of punk culture in music, poetry, and the visual arts simultaneously attacked mainstream culture, celebrating practices such as graffiti and personal tattooing, and used highly commercialized products such as cosmetics and hair dyes to achieve exaggerated effects in personal appearance that provoked resentment and outrage. As in the 1960s, the punk movement had its origins in the combination of underground popular music, fashion/performance, and graphic design for rock bands such as the Sex Pistols. Jamie Reid's (b. 1947) cover for the single "God Save the Queen" (1977) featured the bust-length black-and-white image of Queen Elizabeth II, familiar from currency and postage in the UK, defaced with letters and words torn from newspapers in the manner of a ransom note (fig. 15.9). The technique here is pure Dada, irreverent and provocative for its time as a violation of the responsibility that many associate with freedom of speech, appropriating and subverting the usual meaning of both an image of respect as well as the title of Britain's national anthem (1977 also marked the Queen's Golden Jubilee). Appropriation, rebellion, and provocation not only applied to music and graphic design but also to clothing. Malcolm McLaren (1946–2010) who helped to form and promote

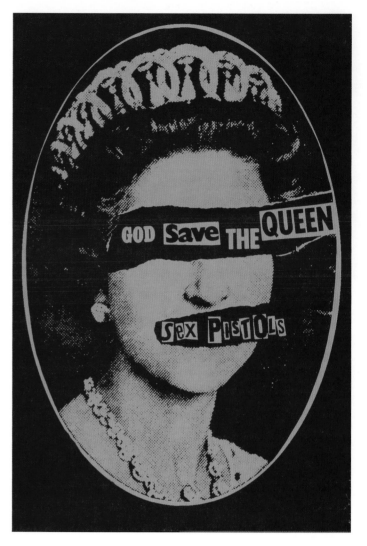

15.9 Jamie Reid, cover for the Sex Pistols' "God Save the Queen" single, 1977.

the Sex Pistols, was also an entrepreneur and part-owner of a clothing boutique with fashion designer Vivienne Westwood (b. 1941). The shop was originally named Let it Rock, and was rechristened Sex in 1975. Clothing invoked underground pornography and bondage with chains, tight-fitting elastic and shiny materials, and an unbridled freedom of expression intended to celebrate difference and test the boundaries of propriety (fig. 15.10). This "punk" movement also used media attention to create notoriety and scandal. Exploiting sensationalism, punk subverted mass media to gain attention and to assert legitimacy for its aggressive, self-destructive behaviors. But was punk a revolutionary social and political movement, a response to the repression of individual identity and decaying urban conditions in Britain and elsewhere? Was it more simply aimed at achieving greater inclusiveness in terms of lifestyle choices and providing a voice for new

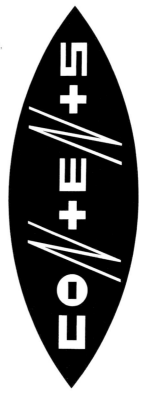

15.11 Neville Brody, "Kopf," hand-drawn logo for a hat company, London, 1985.

15.12 Neville Brody, Contents logo, *The Face*, no. 49, May, *c.* 1980.

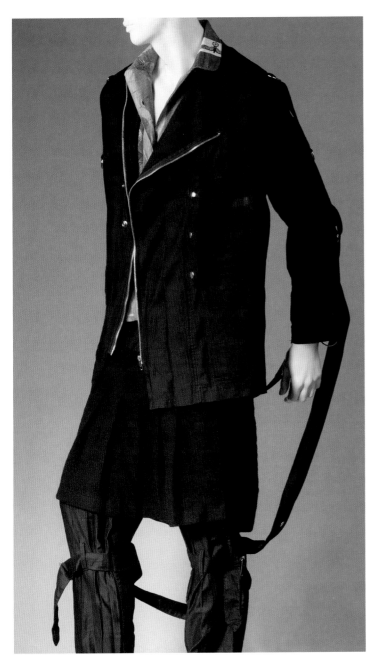

15.10 Vivienne Westwood, bondage suit, late 1970s. Metropolitan Museum of Art, New York.

underground subcultures? Perhaps part of the answer can be found in the career of McLaren himself, who once remarked, "Punk was just a way to sell trousers."

Punk culture found expression in the work of many artists, among them British-born Barney Bubbles (1942–1983) and Neville Brody (b. 1957). Brody experimented with original lettering and trademarks that seemed to parody the uniformity and consistency of corporate graphics, as in the 1985 logo for a London hat company (fig. 15.11). His typefaces, such as Industria (1984), reached print in magazines such as *The Face*, and were developed

to convey aggressive moods and attitudes beyond the range of fonts available from foundries (fig. 15.12). In addition to typography and lettering, Brody used record jackets and music posters as vehicles for evoking an emotional response in the viewer, accomplished through photographs, photocopies, typography, and video-generated images. He intended to relate his covers and posters in some way to the content of the music, rather than to follow the mainstream music industry's tendency to emphasize the celebrity of rock stars through photography. To this end he employed images suggested or even provided by the

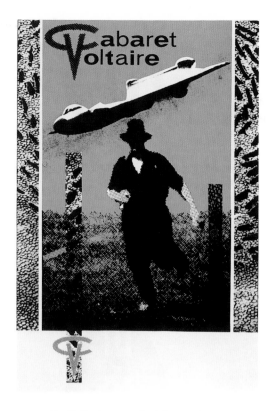

15.13 Neville Brody, poster for Cabaret Voltaire, 1980.

not serve, human interaction. Decay through process is also about repetition, and the loss of quality that you suffer when information is abstracted from its human origin....

Punk was about individual expression, and more than anything, it was a reaction against authority. It couldn't really describe itself as "independent" unless the authority was completely circumvented – which, for a very short time, it was. But as soon as the whole phenomenon was categorised as "the independent scene," this ensured that it would become exactly its opposite.

In many ways the punk phenomenon can be placed within the framework of Pluralism and Postmodernism, complex in its relationship to popular culture, appropriating rather than rejecting the multiple signs and meanings of our consumer culture. An example of adapting the rebellious counterculture aspects of the punk movement to advertising for products otherwise characterized by brand standardization was the Philips Tracer electric shaver, also sold in a variety of colors and targeting a youthful market (fig. 15.14).

musicians, and cultivated an array of techniques that avoided easy recognition or a consistent style. For a 1980 poster for the rock group Cabaret Voltaire (fig. 15.13), Brody juxtaposed a blurred image of a running man with a jet airplane against a blue background with black-and-white textured strips as lateral borders and within the central image. Photomontage, as well as the group's name (the Cabaret Voltaire, in Zurich, was a nightclub and meeting place for Dada artists and performers beginning in 1916), recalls the juxtaposed and manipulated images of Dada posters and covers (see pages 210–211) and the early influence of Dada on Brody's work. Yet the interlocking "CV" letters for the group is reminiscent of a corporate trademark and avoids a sense of direct borrowing from the past. In a similar fashion, Brody's imagery and comments about his work reveal the contradictory nature of the early 1980s in Britain. There is a desire to break away from the contemporary commodity culture that threatens freedom of expression, and yet the recognition that living within that culture forces compromises and acknowledges the limited and ephemeral ways in which artistic freedom functions:

> On every cover I have done for Cabaret Voltaire, the dominant theme is decay through process, the loss of human identity that results from communication being transmitted through machines that condition,

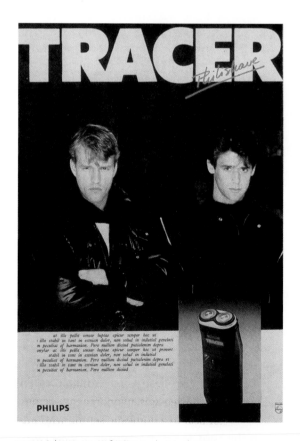

15.14 Advertisement for Tracer electric shaver, manufactured by Philips Corporation, Eindhoven, the Netherlands, c. 1983.

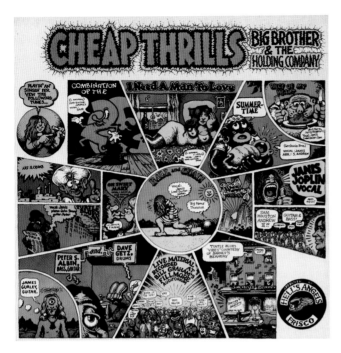

exemplifies aspects of the hi-tech aesthetic. Hi-tech interiors featured exposed ventilation ducts and riveted I-beams, pipe-railings, prefabricated industrial building materials, and perforated spiral staircases, seen for instance in the waiting room of the Occupational Health Center in Columbus, Indiana, designed by Hardy Holzman Pfeiffer Associates between 1974 and 1977 (fig. 15.16). Using color and emphasizing unfinished textures of concrete and metal, materials and spaces acquire an honest and earthy aesthetic as if industrial materials have become part of the natural environment. In a more celebratory tone, it appears in the loud and busy exterior of Richard Rogers and Renzo Piano's Pompidou Center in Paris (completed 1977). The hi-tech embrace of industrial materials and fittings extended into a wide variety of household accessories, including plastic-coated wire shelving units manufactured by the Elfa company in Sweden,

To the punk phenomenon in graphic design might be added illustrations for underground comic books by a number of artists including Robert Crumb (b. 1943). Many images, such as Crumb's well-known *Keep on Truckin'* (c. 1971) with its striding foreshortened foot, reached a broad popular audience via bumper stickers and decals. Their origins, however, were in the very private and often scurrilous world of underground comic books, from where they migrated to record jackets and the broader audience they served. An example is Crumb's 1968 *Cheap Thrills* (fig. 15.15), a cover for an album featuring rock singer Janis Joplin performing with Big Brother and the Holding Company; originally the album was to be called *Sex, Dope, and Cheap Thrills*", a title Columbia Records refused to allow.

Hi-Tech

The experiential context of Punk culture was the urban, industrial environment – metallic, raw, decaying, and cluttered. The reutilization of industrial products and materials for public and domestic spaces emerged under the term "hi-tech" in the later 1970s. The Castiglioni brothers' Mezzadro stool, first designed in 1954 and manufactured beginning in 1957, prefigured this phenomenon, reinterpreting a metal tractor seat in a domestic setting with little transformation of its utilitarian associations. Ron Arad's "Rover" chair (and other work, see page 373), made from tubular metal attached to a second-hand car seat also

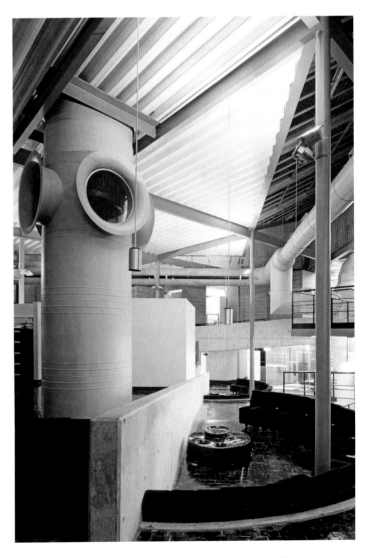

15.16 Hardy Holzman Pfeiffer Associates, interior, Occupational Health Center, Columbus, Indiana, 1974–1977.

also appearing first in the later 1970s (fig. 15.17). Furniture was a focus for hi-tech design, and a prime example is Japanese designer Shiro Kuramoto's (1934–1991) How High the Moon chair (fig. 15.18), dating to 1986 and manufactured in Switzerland by Vitra. Perhaps surprisingly, the metal mesh construction is both strong enough for support and flexible enough for comfortable sitting (its flexible mesh molds itself comfortably to the sitter's body).

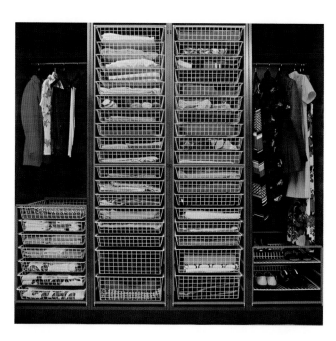

15.17 Wire shelving, plastic-coated wire, Elfa company, Sweden, late 1970s.

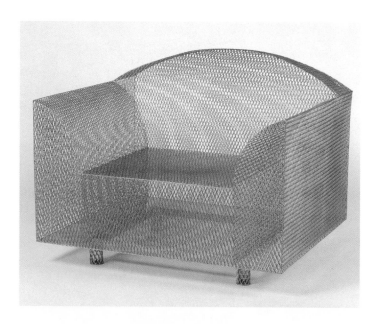

15.18 Shiro Kuramoto, How High the Moon armchair, nickel-plated steel, 28 ¼ x 37 ⅜ x 32 in (72 x 95 x 81 cm), manufactured by Vitra, Switzerland, 1986. Metropolitan Museum of Art, New York.

Yet How High the Moon does not seem to have been designed with sitting as its main or sole intention, as the lightness and transparency of its material, together with the precision of its curves and joints, exert an especially strong aesthetic appeal that allows us to experience the material independent from or in addition to its function.

THE EXPANDING DEFINITION AND ROLE OF DESIGN

Pressures for change both from within and outside the design profession, seen in the demonstrations held at the Fourteenth Milan Triennale in 1968, at the Aspen Design Conference in 1970, and in the formation of collaborative initiatives such as Archizoom or Superstudio in Italy, led to efforts to redefine the nature of design practice in increasingly holistic terms. Global markets spurred businesses to adjust to increased competition and acknowledge more sophisticated, knowledgeable consumers who demanded products differentiated less by superficial styling than by a broad range of considerations focusing upon how products and services communicated or interacted effectively with users. A human-centered design practice extended beyond products to services and business practice, with hierarchical structure and decision-making giving way to collaboration and interactivity.

In existing mechanical products, Jeffrey Meikle has pointed to the 1988 Ford Taurus as example of a successful design in the American automobile industry from this period. Design for the Taurus (fig. 15.19), which broke with industry practice by having designers, engineers, and marketing departments work together from the outset of the project, helped to ensure that different points of view were taken into consideration during development. Such practice permitted greater innovation and sophistication in styling, generated excitement for consumers, and resulted in increased sales for Ford's American division. Such an integrated approach has also been cited as an explanation for the success of the Japanese automobile industry, where factory workers are included in discussions of quality and efficiency. Inclusion gives workers a stake in an expanded design process, encouraging loyalty, responsibility, initiative, and innovation; qualities generally subsumed under the term "empowerment." The fact that many contemporary consultancies have group rather than individual names (e.g. Pentagram, Smart Design, IDEO, Frog, Droog, etc.) also suggests the effectiveness of this new paradigm.

Technology continued to play a role in expanding design practice. As noted above (page 336), miniaturization in the electronics industry reduced product differentiation in terms of styling, leading to increasingly standardized product forms. Under these circumstances, design's role

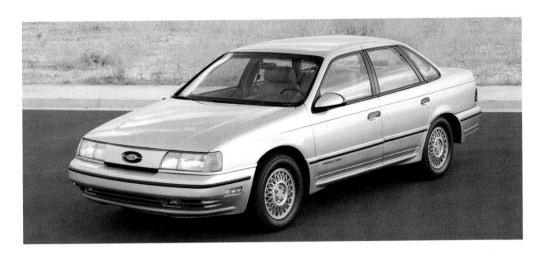

15.19 Ford Taurus, sedan or station wagon, Ford Motor Corporation, Dearborn, Michigan, 1988.

has been to create brand differentiation through establishing other approaches to creating a closer relationship between products and their users. Mario Bellini's design for the Divisumma 18 portable calculator for Olivetti in 1972 uses a soft synthetic rubber housing and keypad, enclosing the miniaturized components in a tactile, skinlike housing with rounded edges and a warm color that connected emotionally (and commercially) with consumers (fig. 15.20). This kind of soft, anthropomorphic approach to product design has only grown with newer materials and production technologies, and has been an essential component of the working methods of contemporary design consultancies – when the consultancy IDEO assembled examples of design from the collection of the Cooper-Hewitt National Design Museum for an exhibition in 2007, Bellini's Divisumma 18 was among those objects selected for display, exemplifying the consultancy's themes of intuition, inspiration, and empathy (see pages 406–407). The importance of the user not only applied to friendly materials and their ability to communicate positively with consumers, but also to a wider range of considerations in connecting consumers with technology. Here the issues had less to do with how to "make" something, which was in most cases taken for granted, but rather how to "design" products that fostered a natural relationship between human beings and a wide range of mechanical and electronic devices. As mentioned above (page 279), these themes emerge in books by Donald Norman such as *The Design of Everyday Things*, published in 1988. Using a wide range of examples drawn from personal but common experience, Norman described the often frustrating relationships we have with objects whose increased functionality comes at the expense of transparent controls and operation (such as programmable telephones with messaging and retrieval options), and argued the need

for taking user error into consideration as well as considering physical analogies in making products more natural to operate.

Design consultancies that emerged in the 1970s, such as Pentagram, which had offices first in London and then in other locations in the United States and Europe, offered a wide range of integrated services to corporate clients that transcended boundaries of product design in an expanded concept of branding, integrating typography, graphic design, office and retail interiors. This involved regular meetings among partners to present and receive feedback on concepts, in close communication with the client. Other international consultancies, such as Frog Design (founded 1969) market a similar approach, defining the company in the broadest possible terms on their 2009

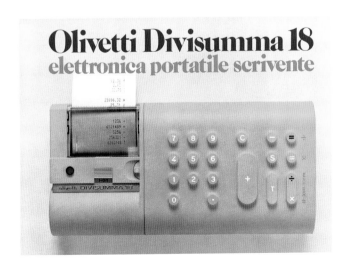

15.20 Mario Bellini, Divisumma 18 handheld calculator, ABS plastic, melamine, and rubber, 1 7/8 x 10 x 4 3/4 in (4.8 x 25.4 x 12.1 cm), Olivetti ING, Ivrea, Italy, 1972.

website as a "global innovation firm." Whether in consultancies, new technologies, or in response to environmental and social or economic need, the nature of the design enterprise became increasingly collaborative and interdisciplinary, recognizing the importance of Pluralism in a global and interdependent context.

While Bellini's Divisumma 18 remains within the historical framework of product housings and new materials, computer technology has introduced new dimensions and approaches to connecting products with users. Apple Corporation's Macintosh personal computer, introduced in 1984, offered a new portable and integrated "box" that combined monitor and hardware (fig. 15.21). More importantly, it included the company's Graphical User Interface (GUI), which used a small mouse that transformed the screen into a desktop and the cursor into a pointing device permitting users to access documents and folders. The distinguishing design feature of the Macintosh was not just its compact integrated form but the way in which the GUI created a direct link between personal computing and the familiar, reassuring physical act of arranging, manipulating, and accessing information visually and spatially, reducing the distance between machines and their users and making personal computers, indeed, more "personal" and an extension of our human capacities.

The expanded world of design in the information age is thus parallel and contemporary with the growing field of Artificial Intelligence. Herbert Simon (1916–2001), the Nobel prize-winning economist and computer scientist, offered an expanded definition of design in his 1969 book *Science of the Artificial*:

Everyone designs who devises courses of action aimed at changing existing situations into preferred ones. The intellectual activity that produces material artifacts is no different fundamentally from the one that prescribes remedies for a sick patient or the one that devises a new sales plan for a company or a social welfare policy for a state. Design, so construed, is the core of all professional training: it is the principal mark that distinguishes the professions from the sciences.

Simon's definition encompasses the act of form-giving but establishes new territories for design activity that emphasize the interface between technology and human beings with *information* as the common denominator of such activity; he also raises the possibility that the designed or artificial environment, in its responsiveness, becomes less and less distinguishable from nature itself. While Simon expresses his vision in a spirit of optimism and confidence in innovation and progress, others have expressed misgivings and doubts that the promise of digital information and technology is either benevolent or humanizing, especially in relation to surveillance and increased dependence upon mass media as the overriding source of public information. Just as the industrial age unleashed its share of discontent and upheaval, so has the information age produced its share of skeptics who reflect upon the limits and dangers of artificial intelligence – seen, for instance, in the 1982 film *Blade Runner*, directed by Ridley Scott. Similar misgivings have arisen in relation to global terrorism and the aftermath of the attacks of September 11, 2001, and are discussed in our final chapter.

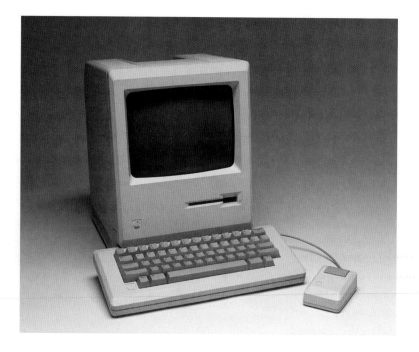

15.21 Macintosh computer, plastic housing, 13 ⅝ x 9 ⅝ x 10 ⅞ in (34.5 x 24.4 x 27.7 cm), Apple Corporation, Cupertino, California, 1984.

Chapter 16

Design in Context: An Act of Balance

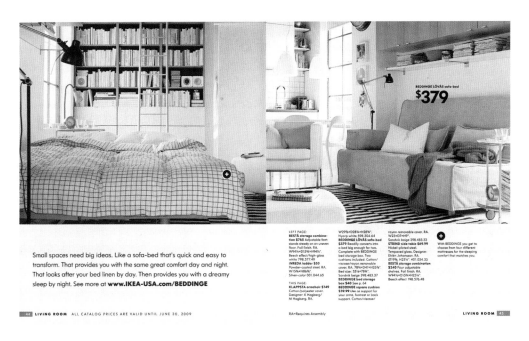

16.1 Beddinge interior, IKEA catalogue, 2009, pages 44–45.

Somewhere between universal standards based upon taste, safety, human factors, or environmental impact, and a democratic embrace of creativity and initiative in combination with technology and the seemingly insatiable desire for individual fulfillment through commodity consumption in a competitive global economy, there may lie a middle-ground that sustains hope for the future of design, a balance between permanent and ephemeral, between nature and the artificial, between individual and society. The shape of that future will indeed depend upon the manner in which a number of competing viewpoints and approaches to the expanding field of design continue to develop and also upon the degree to which such viewpoints and practices may be reconciled. These practices have emerged in relation to the broad history of modern design as described in each of the major parts of the present study. They include the role of technology and production and the political and economic circumstances in which they develop, consumption and commercialism, craft and aesthetics, as well as social and global responsibility. Each is increasingly interwoven and interdependent

with the others in a synthesis that may yet remain vital, dynamic, and enriching.

CONSUMERS

There is little doubt that for the past century consumption and economic growth have dominated the practice of design; whether a vision for an enlightened and sophisticated aesthetic taste or business strategy aimed at novelty and frequent replacement, capitalist free enterprise has shaped the role of design in increasing the supply of and demand for products as a guarantee of continued economic strength and expanding markets. Since the 1960s and the emergence of Pop Art and Pop-inspired industrial design, consumption has also played a large role in the theory of design, deconstructing a binary opposition that had existed between art and commodities. Meanwhile, broad international economic growth throughout much of the 1990s contributed to the belief that consumption is indeed self-justifying, fueling still further growth by creating jobs and stimulating the research and development of new technologies, products, services, and marketing tools on an increasingly global scale. Whether threatening or liberating, consumption has been a pervasive element motivating and affecting design as we enter the third millennium.

Consumer- or marketing-led design continues to present virtually limitless possibilities, and even the high-minded maxims of international modernism, such as "fitness to purpose" (see page 257), are increasingly subsumed under its banner. Habitat stores (see fig. 13.2), or more recently the international success of the IKEA Corporation of Sweden, originally founded in 1943, have successfully expanded and marketed a warehouse approach to Scandinavian design and international modernism in many large European cities as well as (since 1985) in affluent American suburbs. IKEA stores are presently found in more than 25 countries globally. Large color catalogues of merchandise, off-the-shelf availability, flat, carry-home packaging, as well as do-it-yourself assembly instructions and tools for fastening bolts all contribute to the appeal of IKEA and should be considered as integral the company's design policy, together with the affordability of products ranging from furniture and lighting to fabrics, household, and kitchen wares. IKEA offers a large variety of molded plywood furniture and modular units for shelving and using veneers attached to inexpensively manufactured pressed board, and many products are based upon the interwar and postwar furniture designed by Aalto or Klint (fig. 16.1). Other individual examples and ensembles include upholstered chairs and sofas, American Colonial designs, as well as craft-inspired furnishings in woven rattan or inexpensive cast metals with textured finishes. Furniture designed especially for children is heavily marketed at IKEA, as are desks and shelving for the apartments of young professionals and university-age students. In the catalogue and on the showroom floor prices appear in bold sans serif typography, and despite the odd-sounding (at least to American ears) names given to "families" of items, nowhere is the IKEA name linked to a specific country of origin. The overriding character of the merchandise and the shopping experience is *ease*, that is, ease of packing, shipping, transporting, assembling (some might argue this point, but one is saving the cost of assembly by doing it oneself), affording, and perhaps most importantly, ease of replacing. Planned obsolescence is here taken for granted in an industry whose products usually take longer to make and are at least generally intended to last longer as well. It also matches the transient lifestyles of students who would rather sell or leave the IKEA products than pay to move them from apartment to apartment. Beginning in the 1990s, it was easy for families with small children to shop at IKEA, as stores provided monitored playrooms that permitted parents to shop without distraction. Thus design for IKEA does not distinguish products from the way they are packaged, assembled, displayed, and sold. Stores combine displays with variations on standard types of chair, table, or bookshelf with furnished rooms complete with coordinated ensembles and accessories. For the most part, IKEA interiors emphasize ample and efficient storage and clean, bright colors and patterns for fabrics, all meant to maximize limited space and add comfort to smaller homes or apartments. Figure 16.1, for instance, shows an open studio-style apartment with combined living room, bedroom, and kitchen, efficient but permitting aesthetic coordination through a number of related IKEA systems; merchandising strategies also include showroom displays of individual items such as chairs that allow customers to select and substitute a particular item or replace a component in an interior with one that matches either cost or other features of individual preference. Indeed, expanded definitions of design make decisions for living spaces, clothing, or shopping in general a design activity, and bring to mind the Eameses' analogy between design and the seating arrangement for a dinner party (see above, page 350 and fig. 14.4). In other words, the consumer is not only the recipient of design, but enters into the design process itself.

Design has also become integral to the marketing strategy of the Target Corporation, with headquarters in Minneapolis, Minnesota. Target is not a manufacturer but a retail distributor, and markets the term "design," not as a "style" in the sense of a visual "look," but as a brand communicating better living in the broadest sense of the term. Their aim is to bring the benefits of "design," and "design-consciousness" to the discount-store shopper, with an array of designed and designer products, quite literally from "A" to "Z"; in fact, the Fall 2007 *Style* issue of the *New York Times Magazine* contained products for each letter of the alphabet in a multi-page spread. Acknowledging design is certainly related in this case to progress, via an awareness of beauty, function, as well as other kinds of product associations (and the educational association of the advertisement itself with a children's "ABC" book). On one page the letter "B" displays a stovetop espresso maker by the Italian company Bialetti first manufactured in the 1930s (fig. 16.2, left); under "X" appears the R*X*, a prescription labeling system designed by Deborah Adler (b. 1976) for multiple user groups, including pictograms for children, large type and color backgrounds for the elderly, and color-coding for different members of a family to more easily identify their prescriptions and prevent misuse (fig. 16.2, right). Target has launched an all-out assault upon "design," incorporating Postmodern elements such

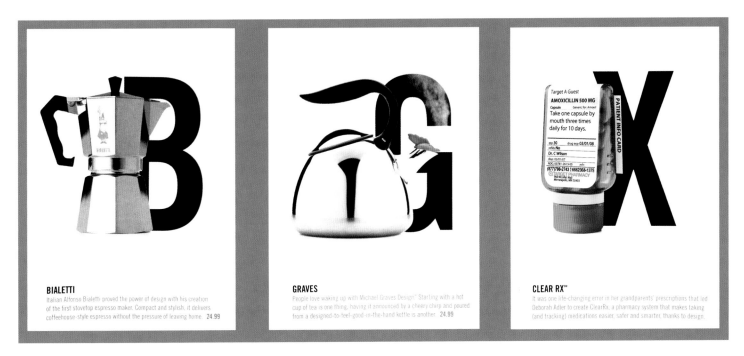

16.2 Advertisement for Target stores products, *New York Times Style Magazine*, Fall 2007, letters "B" (Bialetti espresso maker), "G" (Michael Graves tea kettle), and "X (Deborah Adler, Target ClearRx prescription system), Target Corporation, Minneapolis, Minnesota.

as nostalgia with functional information graphics; they've left few stones unturned in the design-product-progress equation. The texts accompanying the products reveal a fascination with the objects, their forms, and feel-good associations: here's the copy for the Michael Graves tea kettle illustrating the letter "G" (fig. 16.2, center): "people love waking up with Michael Graves Design; starting with a hot cup of tea is one thing, having it announced by a cheery chirp and poured from a designed-to-feel-good-in-the-hand kettle is another." In 1999, a Graves toaster for Target appeared in an advertisement with the phrase "finding the fun in functional". In an ad campaign from August 2005, Target monopolized the pages of *New Yorker* without including direct references to products. Lifestyle was the key: urban, youthful, provocative, even rebellious. It's as if shopping, Target, design, and fashionable living were indistinguishable from one another, all merging into a cutting-edge brand.

Environmental awareness has also become linked to consumption, for instance in the expanding industry of products promoting healthy living and ethically conscious shopping. Nigel Whitely has noted, for instance, the way in which Body Shop stores equate the purchase of their cosmetics with the protection of animal rights in carrying out product testing and the environment. Body Shop promotional materials assert that: "our future planning will be based upon achieving a balance between the need to limit the environmental impact of our business while not compromising our long-term commercial viability." Ethical consuming suggests an awareness of the broader consequences of consumption, but many critics remain unsatisfied, arguing that Body Shop products use mostly synthetic, non-renewable substances, and that the appropriate response to environmental concerns posed by the cosmetics industry lies in curbing consumption, not in making people feel better about the products they buy. Global responsibility is also an integral part of the mission of the Starbucks Coffee chain, originating in Seattle, Washington, in 1971 and now operating more than 17,000 stores internationally. Design communicates the mission of the company to support a sustainable environment, through its recyclable cups, preserving elements of the original structure in many of its stores, using natural colors of green and burlap brown, as well as the company's commitment to ethical and responsible growing and to fair trade in the interest of small-scale coffee farmers. It is not surprising that large companies like Body Shop or Starbucks promote environmental responsibility. Attaching values to their products through design helps to offset the impersonal nature of big businesses in comparison and in competition with locally owned shops offering similar products.

The celebration of playfulness and complexity, much-cited in Postmodern theory as the basis for irony and subversion, has also become part of accepted practice in industrial design for large corporations. Companies such as Philips maintain divisions responsible for developing product ideas independently from engineering or cost considerations, as a means of encouraging creativity and flexibility in the design process, a variation of the more integrated design approach used in the development of the Ford Taurus (see page 378). An example of such pure "concept design" is the brightly colored Beethoven radio developed by Philips in 1983 (fig. 16.3). These products are in some ways the progeny of the dream cars modeled in the styling sections of General Motors in the early 1950s under the direction of Harley Earl and previewed for marketing purposes at GM Motoramas (see fig. 12.4).

In the automobile industry of the 1990s, industrial design focused upon the high end of the market, less to inventive body styling than to the interior where comfort, quality sound, and individualized climate control were the focus. Author Peter Finch observes that the anxiety caused by traffic has contributed to this concentration upon making the automobile a refuge where design *protects* drivers from overcrowded streets, traffic lights, and noise, and the restrictions they place upon our freedom, enabling wealthy car owners to separate themselves from the frustrations of road congestion. The copy of an advertisement for a 1999 Lexus ES 300, for example, imagined the vehicle itself sporting an "attitude" and speaking to a red traffic light, in defiant refusal to acknowledge the constraints of the road: "Okay, fine. I'll just wait here. You think I care? I'll just wait here in my oh-so-comfortable car and stare you down. Until I get you to change your tiny, red mind." In such examples, the automobile is indeed an extension of the driver, to whom steering wheels and seats automatically adjust upon entering, creating a strong degree of personal responsiveness and interactivity between human and machine that is less dependent upon the kind of styling that General Motors pioneered and successfully implemented in the immediate post-World War II years. Although recognizable by insignia and "family" resemblances, only minor differences distinguish many of the vehicles at the high end of the luxury automobile market, which includes the Japanese Lexus, Infiniti, and Acura, the German BMW and Mercedes Benz, and the British Jaguar, Bentley, and Rolls Royce. The understated styling in the automotive industry is parallel in some ways to consumer taste in portable electronic devices in the 1960s, which also underwent a transformation toward greater uniformity in external appearance with less attention to expressive or symbolic references (see figs. 13.13 and 13.14).

At the lower end of the automobile market, one finds reinterpretations of older standard economical models such as the Morris Mini in the newer Mini Cooper, introduced in 2002 and manufactured by BMW (fig. 16.4; compare page 282 and fig. 11.82). Modernized with an array of bright and two-tone color combinations and accessories, the Mini Cooper is aimed at a generation of buyers too young to have experienced directly Issagonis's original design, and for whom it has become an image that may offset the self-indulgence and hedonism sometimes associated with consumer-oriented lifestyles. It is the issue of choice that most distinguishes the reinvented Mini Cooper from its forbear: the latter was virtually the only possibility for personal transportation at the low end of the automobile market when introduced in 1959, whereas its modern counterpart projects an owner's identification with an image of unpretentious, even responsible transportation. Comparing the retro Mini Cooper with earlier expressions of historicism can be an interesting exercise: in the later eighteenth and nineteenth centuries, the Neoclassical style (see pages 34–35) offered a vision of stability during a time of change and threat to an existing order. The popularity of the Mini Cooper also may project a nostalgic image associated in positive ways with simpler needs.

A more novel contemporary automobile design is the Smart Car, originating as a concept by the Swatch (wristwatch) Company in 1994 and produced in partnership with Daimler Benz beginning in 1998. The Smart

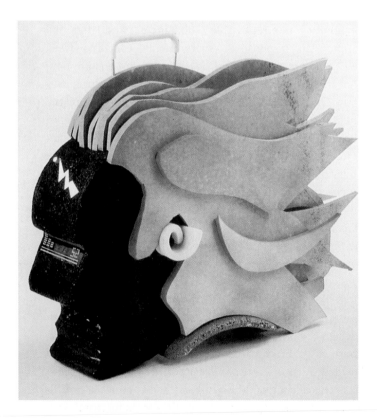

16.3 Beethoven radio product concept, Philips Corporation, Eindhoven, the Netherlands, 1983.

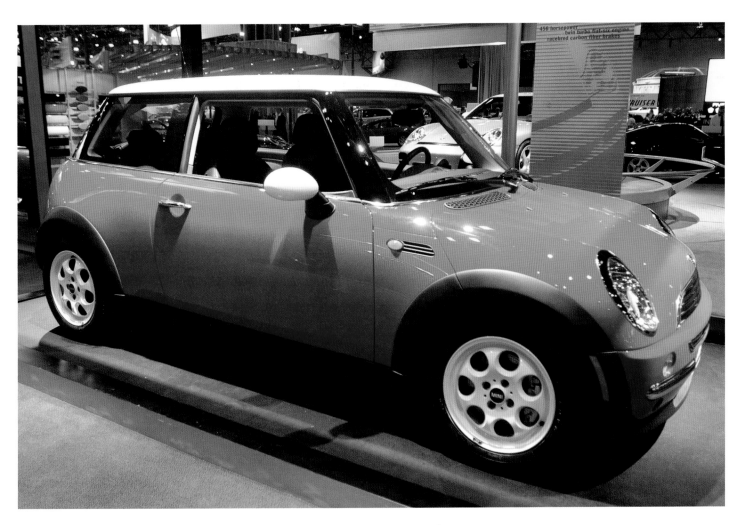

16.4 Mini Cooper, BMW Corporation, Munich, Germany, 2002.

Car was designed to allow parking with the front end toward the curb, in roughly one-third of the space needed to parallel-park a standard-sized vehicle. Its appeal lies both in fuel efficiency but perhaps more importantly in potentially reducing the often frustrating search for parking spaces in the modern city amid congestion and a variety of restrictions. Perhaps more pressing than parking in light of economic recession and rising oil prices is indeed fuel efficiency and hybrid technology that makes use of electricity as well as gasoline. Long-term cost savings must be weighed against the higher price of hybrid vehicles for consumers of mid-range vehicles such as the Toyota Prius (introduced worldwide in 2000), and the introduction of hybrid vehicles at the luxury end of the market suggests that the appeal to eco-responsible consumption may also play a role in future hybrid and all-electric initiatives for the automobile industry.

Planned obsolescence remains the cornerstone of consumer-led design, involving the stimulation of desire through novelty on one hand and the effective manage-ment of production costs on the other. Manufacturing similar products while projecting individual appeal are thus the goals. These ideals have become successful strategies for a number of corporations, perhaps most notably in the marketing of GAP clothing to a youth-oriented market attracted to an image of informal, fun-loving, and relaxed behavior easily recognized by fabrics such as khaki and cotton for pants and T-shirts. Here advertising helps to seamlessly merge standardized products with carefree, youthful behavior and rapid change with an enduring image.

GAP clothing continues to use color as a major component for the exercise of individual consumer prefer-ence, and this very basic strategy for introducing variety remains effective for merchandising. In 2000, the Heinz Corporation introduced its tomato ketchup in green rather than red (changing colors but not taste), combined with labeling for the original product that read "not green." The company reported more than a five percent increase in sales and a larger share of the market.

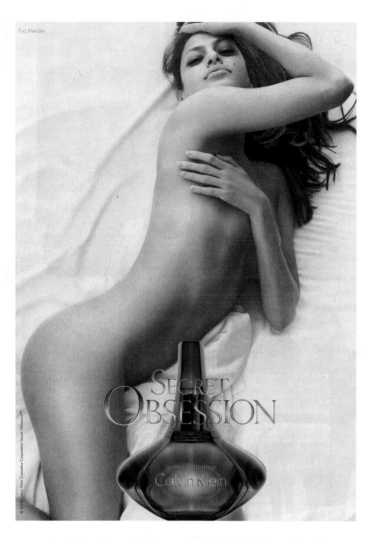

16.5 Fabien Baron, advertisement for Calvin Klein's Secret Obsession, photograph with fashion model Eva Mendes, 2008.

perfumes, engaging the imagination of male and female spectators by appealing to sexual fantasies, homoeroticism, and permissiveness, sometimes involving violence and sadomasochism. This is seen, for instance, in ads for the Calvin Klein fragrance Secret Obsession (fig. 16.5), where attention is drawn to the suggestive shape of the bottle through the contrast of color with the black-and-white photograph. The trend in such ads may have been triggered by earlier transgressions of accepted gender stereotypes pioneered in the Punk era, but it appears in contemporary fragrance or clothing in a provocative but less threatening way.

In the fashion industry, advertising, merchandising, celebrity, television and cinema, middle-class affluence, and the ability of manufacturers to respond quickly to trends and forecasts due to accelerated communications and the role of computer-assisted design (CAD), all transpire to stimulate production and consumption of clothing and clothing accessories. In addition to the broad economic impact of the fashion industry, dress also has attracted the attention of art historians and cultural critics within the Pluralistic framework of Postmodernism. As a significant element within consumer culture, women's apparel reveals a mixture of conformity and resistance that characterizes the Postmodern approach to popular culture, moving considerably beyond the usual theoretical framework of emulation. As targets of the advertising industry in the emerging culture of consumption of the later nineteenth and early twentieth centuries, the active as well as passive roles of women as consumers raise awareness of dress and female identity in our society. The cultural meanings of dress, however, need not be applied only to women's clothing. The popularity not only of tight-fitting clothes but also of clothes that appear to be "outgrown" (pants that do not reach to the ankle or jerseys that do not reach to the waist), for instance, beginning in the 1980s, is a phenomenon that appears both in men's and women's fashion. According to design historian Lee Wright, such clothing suggests a variety of often contradictory meanings. "Outgrown" clothing may call attention to particular parts of the body with strong sexual overtones. It may make the body appear larger and more powerful than normal (like the "Incredible Hulk" cartoon and film character), or at the same time imprison the body, as a child who uncomfortably wears clothes that are not just tight but simply too small.

Finally, we should keep in mind the marketing efforts that deliver products to the consumer and the expanding role of credit buying whether in malls, catalogue shopping by telephone, or via the Internet as e-commerce and its virtual shopping carts, rebates, free shipping, and other incentives to consumption. Sophisticated store merchandising

Outside of GAP and its competitors in the market for casual clothing, the business of fashion remains heavily dependent upon a more provocative novelty and strong ties to advertising in directing the consumer to associate clothing with alternative lifestyles, often exemplified by celebrity supermodels who serve as ideal paradigms for a particular look. Fabien Baron (b. 1959) has, since the early 1990s, been a successful art director for several fashion magazines, including *Harper's Bazaar*, *Interview*, and Italian *Vogue*. He has been responsible for a lean, simple approach to page layout in these journals, incorporating large areas of white space and dramatic black-and-white photography as well as combining different sizes of a single typeface on the page. In these practices he continues an expressive approach to layout pioneered by Alexey Brodovitch and M. F. Agha (see pages 270–272) both in Europe and in the United States beginning in the later 1920s. Baron is perhaps best known for using eroticism to sell clothing and fashion accessories such as

uses the analysis of the habits of shoppers to place particular products where they are more likely to attract attention
and sales. Such efforts demonstrate yet again the integration and extension of design into merchandising and
retailing. All of these efforts attest to the stimulation of
consumption in ever-creative ways, breaking down any
lingering resistance to shopping in terms of store hours or
even the necessity of stores themselves. The notion of a
permanent, omnipresent spectacle comes to mind, no
longer confined to material space but extending into the
uncharted realms of cyberspace with the click of a mouse
or touch of a screen.

Industry expos and conventions bring individual
consumers and store buyers into contact with recently
manufactured merchandise or prototypes of future
products. Their booths in convention centers, such as the
Consumer Electronics Show in Las Vegas, Nevada (fig.
16.6), or the International Housewares Association Show
in Chicago, Illinois, resemble a specialized version of the
nineteenth-century World's Fair. Essentially their message
echoes familiar historical themes – technology, imagination, progress, economic growth through free enterprise,
and self-fulfillment via new and improved designed
products. Trade opens markets, competition guarantees
affordability, investment spurs research and development
of new technologies, and advertising amplifies and
encourages the fulfillment and emulation we attain
through consumption, enhancing further the symbolic
meanings of the products themselves. Thus the trade
show offers a lively and popular contemporary perspective
on design, truly the offspring of the World's Fairs and the
rise of manufacturing and capitalism in the nineteenth
century, spearheaded by government and the captains of
industry. Such meanings help to form the popular
understanding of design as it appeared on the cover of
Time magazine in 2000 with the text, "Function is out.
Form is in. From radios to cars to toothbrushes, America
is bowled over by Style" (see Introduction, page 11).
Behind the emphasis upon products lies a broader and
highly sophisticated understanding of design that involves
decisions connecting products and services to users and
engaging interdependent fields of study and research.
While the relationship between design and products will
always be strong and accessible, the activity of design from
within the profession emphasizes the interface between
products and users as the focus of design activity.

REFORM AND SOCIAL RESPONSIBILITY

Mistrust of consumer-led design and commercialism in
design has a long history, stretching back at least as far as
Pugin and reformers such as Henry Cole in the mid-

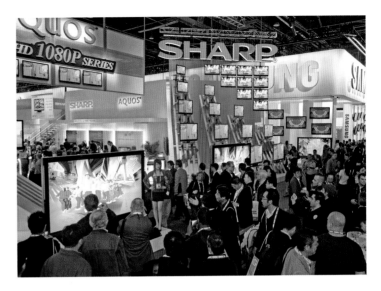

16.6 Consumer Electronics Show, Las Vegas, Nevada, 2008.

nineteenth century. Fears of declining aesthetic or moral
standards, of conspicuous consumption, or the democratization of consumption as a threat to an established social
order and cohesive cultural values, of commodity consumption as a form of unwitting political consent and
conformism, all are elements of this history. Yet universal
standards governing aesthetic or practical aspects of
product design have rarely been either successful or
popular outside of certain contexts such as information
graphics and the imposed manufacturing restrictions in
Britain during and immediately after World War II; even in
the nineteenth century, the paternalism of Pugin and Cole
appeared elitist and reactionary to writers like Charles
Dickens. As noted above (page 67), Herbert Gans, in an
essay for the Philadelphia Museum of Art's 1983 retrospec-
tive exhibition Design Since 1945, characterized the exhibition as a "treasure trove of progressive upper-middle
culture"; that is, the taste of a particular class rather than a
set of rational standards and universal aesthetic principles.
Today the postwar warnings of manipulation by authors
such as Vance Packard seem alarmist. Even the bare
mention of standards begs the question of "whose
standards?" and is construed as a needless impediment to
self-fulfillment in an age preoccupied with diversity and
difference, an age that acknowledges rather than worries
about the relation between advertising and conformism,
between mass consumption, insecurity, and manipulation.

Still, one wonders whether we are indeed at the
threshold of self-realization. One case in point is the
telephone. Before 1984, when the United States government broke up the American Telephone and Telegraph
Corporation (AT&T) into smaller companies, telephones
were relatively standardized products available only through

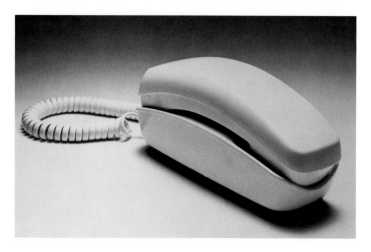

16.7 Henry Dreyfuss Associates, Trimline telephone, plastic housing, length 8 7/16 in (21 cm), manufactured by Western Electric for Bell Telephone Company, New York, 1965. Philadelphia Museum of Art.

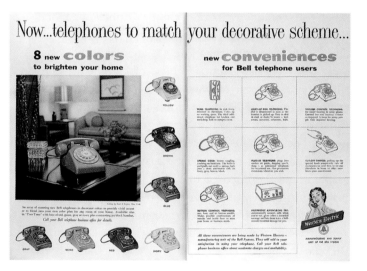

16.8 Advertisement for Bell Telephone Company telephones. *Better Homes and Gardens*, November, 1954.

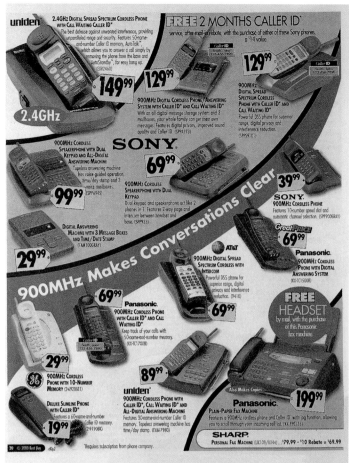

16.9 Advertisement for telephones at Best Buy stores. *Philadelphia Inquirer*, 2000.

a small number of outlets operated by subsidiary Bell Telephone. A standard desk or table handset unit was designed by Henry Dreyfuss in 1937 (see fig. 10.26) and redesigned in 1946. New models, such as the compact Trimline of 1965 (fig. 16.7) appeared, and features such as touch-tone rather than rotary dialing were added beginning in the 1970s. Color also provided an element for individual consumer choice (fig. 16.8). Since industry deregulation, telephones have been sold in a variety of hardware, electronics, and discount stores, and are available in ever-increasing variations of shape, color, and weight. They are constructed of different materials, ring with different, often personalized tones, and have become cordless and portable,

spurring yet more variations and possibilities for consumers, including prices so low as to make some models suitable as giveaway and promotional items. Like so many contemporary products, phones have become lifestyle accessories, styled to suit our age and help us achieve the image of who we'd like to be, and with names and services such as "I-phone" and "my Verizon," they become part of our very identity. Yet one wonders whether the result of deregulation has been an advantage to consumers: how many types of telephone are "too many" (fig. 16.9)? Does telephone communication require so many choices? Is phone shopping an area of the market that demands such dizzying possibilities for self-expression? Is this indeed an instance of real choice, or has the reduced durability of materials and components combined with variety made it instead another vehicle for planned obsolescence in an increasingly "throwaway" culture, where discarding old phones, and buying new ones rather than repairing them, is more often than not the case, as elsewhere in the electronics industry? In addition, corporate control is enforced when inexpensive mobile phone replacement usually requires purchasing extended contracts accompanied by high fees for early termination. Is there not a part of ourselves that actually longs for standards to assist us in making choices so that we may use our time in ways other than comparison shopping for items that last less than six months? What in the end is liberating, and what inhibits freedom? There are, it seems, legitimate issues to be addressed by considering the meaning of choice: consumers seem to accept the idea of standards in matters of product safety, and for the compatibility of components in communications and utilities industries, for instance in matters of computer cable connectors, operating systems, sizes of outlets, fuses, plugs, and plumbing and gas pipe fittings, to name just a few areas where regulation persists. Whether government- or industry-regulated, however, standards may be viewed as promoting a shared language of product semantics reinforcing basic guidelines for use and dependability in the market. Thus standards might indeed serve, together with diversity, as partners in promoting tolerance and understanding for the consuming public: it is not so much that consumption is dangerous or that it obscures values, but that it seems worthwhile to reserve a place for alternatives within a system of capitalist free enterprise for approaches to design that offer perhaps less choice, but for generally acceptable reasons. Graphic design also plays a role in the area of standards, developing appropriate labels for hazardous materials or recognizable symbols to designate inappropriate reading or viewing materials for children.

While regulation and standards affect fewer types of products, social responsibility continues to impact design through attention to the needs of special populations such as those with disabilities through research, determining for instance new forms and materials in the design of many everyday products and transportation systems. Government and foundation sponsorship helps to address special needs through design, while occasionally such markets also attract private, for-profit investment. One of the best-known organizations of this kind is Ergonomi Design Gruppen, established in Bomma, Sweden in 1979 as a collective of smaller groups, whose aim is to design solutions for special needs while at the same time appealing to broader markets through attention to aesthetics and commercial possibilities. The designers working for collectives such as Ergonomi conduct studies, for instance, to determine the strength needed for holding and gripping of objects and test the design of products like knives or cutlery to see which forms are best suited to their purpose, primarily but not exclusively from the standpoint of disabled users. Successful designs of this type include the knife and cutting frame designed in 1974 by Maria Benktzon and Sven-Eric Juhlin, made of Propene plastic

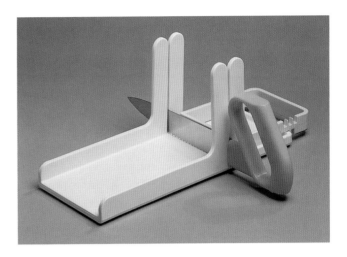

16.10 Maria Benktzon and Sven-Eric Juhlin, Ergonomi Design Gruppen, knife and cutting frame, Propene plastic and steel, width 13 ¾ in (35 cm), manufactured by Gustavsberg AB, Gustavsberg, Sweden, 1974. Statens Konstmuseer, Stockholm.

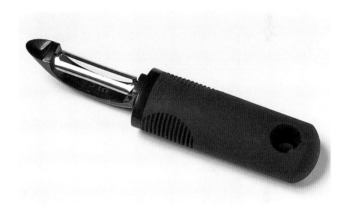

16.11 Smart Design, Good Grips peeler, rubber and stainless steel, lenght 6 in (15 cm), manufactured by Oxo, England, 2000.

and stainless steel and manufactured in Sweden by Gustavsberg (fig. 16.10). This design, based upon the principle of a mitre box, not only accomplished the specific purpose for which it was intended by safely guiding the knife and protecting the user, but also attracted wider popularity through its simple and clear statement of use and practicality. Marketed even more widely beyond an audience with special needs are the soft, rubber-handled kitchen utensils manufactured by the Oxo corporation and designed to be easy to hold and grip with less pressure (fig. 16.11). Oxo products exemplify the criteria of "Universal Design," embraced by a number of institutes and organizations and addressing the broad design needs of the disabled, the ageing, and children. Supported by corporations and foundations, Universal Design groups study and develop solutions to problems ranging from transportation, parks and playgrounds, housing, and kitchens. Universal Design is defined as "the design of products and environments to be usable by all people, to the greatest extent possible, without the need for adaptation or specialized design." Their principles include equitable use, flexibility in use, simple and intuitive use, perceptible information, tolerance for error, low physical effort, and size and space for approach and use. While initially designed to address the needs of special populations, the wider public appeal of Oxo products addresses the issue of how products communicate with different groups of users and satisfy needs beyond those originally targeted.

Another area outside the usual framework of market-led product design mechanisms is addressing the needs of developing nations. Victor Papanek (see pages 364–365) considered this area in the 1970s in developing ideas about appropriate technology, advocating an approach that included working within existing conditions, using local materials, revitalizing vernacular traditions, and involving the local population rather than only adopting paternalistic or hi-tech solutions. Penny Sparke has described such a varied, "multi-level" approach to addressing design needs in India, ranging from industrial technology for an international market to investing in the promotion of local craft production, to seeking efficient solutions to everyday problems by introducing low-cost products like plastic pails and monsoon shoes using industrial materials. In

Africa, industrial materials are reused in a variety of inventive ways, for instance, the use of old motorcycle and automobile tires for sandals (fig. 16.12) sold in local markets in Tanzania and other nations.

Social responsibility in design has also found an outlet in environmental awareness and reform. Often known as Green Design, environmentally conscious approaches to design range from the use of recyclable materials by manufacturers and the conservation of natural resources, to more radical efforts that make environmental impact the overriding consideration in the design process and promote the reduction in consumption and materialism as the only responsible directions for a future industrial design. A measure of changing attitudes and green awareness in design is the colorful 1977 disposable plastic picnic ware by Jean-Paul Vitrac (b. 1944) for Diam. What might have seemed a good example of efficiently manufactured, easily stored, and easy-to-use eating utensils in the 1970s now appears at least in part as wasteful and environmentally hazardous. While much green ideology once appeared unrealistically dualistic (polemic) and even apocalyptic, it stands in the tradition of reform advocating for shared standards based upon considerations beyond the perspective of the individual and toward the interrelationship between people and the environment we often take for granted. Environmentalist and writer Jonathon Porritt outlines this view:

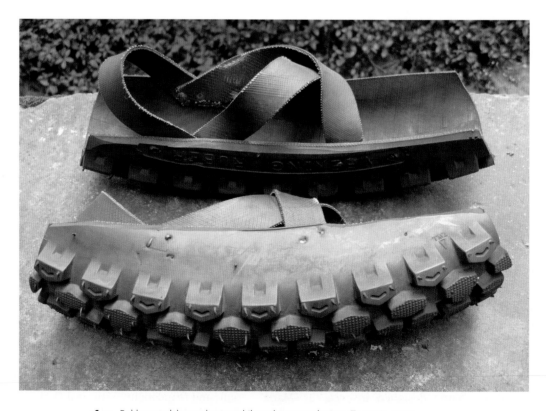

16.12 Rubber sandals, used automobile and motorcycle tires, Tanzania, 2009.

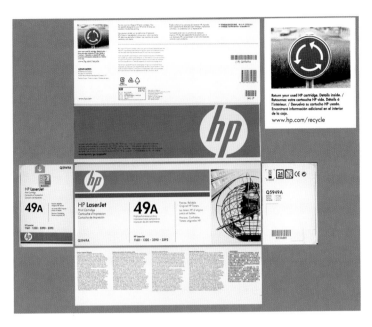

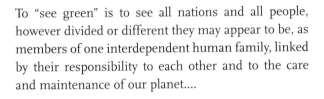

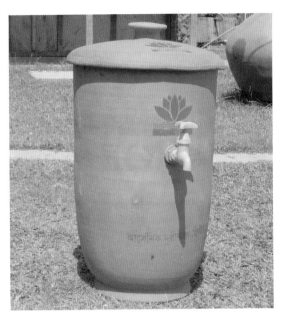

16.13 Hewlett Packard packaging for model 49A laser printer cartridges, cardboard, 15 x 6 ½ x 4 ½ in (38.1 x 16.5 x 11.4 cm), 2009.

16.14 Fakhrul Islam and the International Development Enterprises, Shapla arsenic removal filter, clay, plastic, cloth, and ferrous sulfate, 22 x 25 in (56 x 63.5 cm), Bangladesh, 2001.

To "see green" is to see all nations and all people, however divided or different they may appear to be, as members of one interdependent human family, linked by their responsibility to each other and to the care and maintenance of our planet....

And:

From our side of the divide it's clear that all nations are pursuing an unsustainable path. Every time we opt for the "conventional" solution, we merely create new problems, new threats. Every time we count on some new technological miracle, we merely put off the day of reckoning. Sheer common sense suggests alternative remedies, yet vested economic interests and traditional political responses ensure that the necessary steps are never taken. The old system endures, dominated by competition between various groups struggling for power so as to be able to promote the interest of a particular class, clique, or ideology.

Advocates of green or sustainable design express concern about the afterlife of manufactured products, and encourage designers to make such considerations part of their process. Degradable, reusable, and recyclable materials certainly belong on a list of considerations for green designers, and play a part in many corporate strategies, including Hewlett Packard's packaging for laser-printer cartridges, which can be used easily and at no charge to the consumer to mail back the used plastic cartridge for

safe disposal (fig. 16.13). Like reform efforts in the past, awareness about sustainability requires education and the recognition of shared responsibility to our environment. It is not surprising that such shared recognition has come about in response to crisis, which often serves to reduce differences and create community. Such efforts often can begin on a small scale without advanced technology: in the 2005–2006 Safe: Design Takes On Risk exhibition at the Museum of Modern Art in New York, among hi-tech surveillance and other devices intended to detect dangers to our personal safety stood a large roughly turned ceramic vessel with a green plastic spigot used in Bangladeshi villages to slowly filter water and remove dangerous levels of arsenic in the local water supply (fig. 16.14). Though somewhat out of place in the exhibition, this lo-tech filtering system demonstrated that safety and a consciousness of the preciousness of resources are a natural response of societies to environmental risk, and that solutions can be put into practice at the local level, and are a natural expression of our interdependence with the environment all human beings share.

DESIGN, SAFETY, AND TERROR

Safety may be considered as an extension of traditional ergonomic concerns with preventing injury in the design of equipment and accessories for the factory, home, or office. In focusing upon the experience of the user, safety concerns not only the form of objects (see fig. 16.10) but also information design such as the pictograms used for labeling prescription drugs or household products – seen above, for instance, in Deborah Adler's development of plastic bottles, labels, and her color-coding for the Target Corporation in 2005 (see fig. 16.2, right).

Government regulations and standards help to ensure compliance with building codes intended to minimize damage from natural disaster. Their absence or their lack of enforcement often has tragic consequences, whether in the wake of hurricanes such as Katrina in New Orleans in 2005 or in earthquakes in China in 2008. The dialogue between free enterprise, economic development, and legitimate safety concerns in construction lie outside the scope of this survey, but responses to disaster help to highlight aspects of contemporary design practice in relation to technology as well as to collaboration. In the wake of natural or even man-made disaster, recovery may demand temporary rather than permanent solutions in the short term. Shigeru Ban (b. 1957) developed an approach to temporary shelter using discarded cardboard carpet tubes glued together and covered with plastic sheeting. Cameron Sinclair (b. 1973) has headed an organization called Architecture for Humanity since 1999, coordinating design efforts directed toward providing basic human needs globally, and has completed more than a hundred projects worldwide. His approach to design addresses community needs by involving members of displaced communities in the design process. Projects have as their goal the building of community rather than the building of structures; that is, the emphasis is upon how people interact with forms rather than the forms themselves. Sinclair's projects certainly relate to the concerns of pioneers such as Victor Papanek (see page 364), and experience helps to determine the possibility and the limits of design initiatives, carried on a larger community scale. The inclusive approach to the design process is one of Architecture for Humanity's most basic features, one that offers a more participatory relationship between designer and client and blurs the lines among stakeholders. Figure 16.15 illustrates the front entrance to the Nadukuppam Vangala Women's Center located in Tamil Nadu, India, an area affected by a tsunami in 2005. The Women's Center's design, as well as its construction, involved the participation of local groups, village leaders, and other members of the community along with Architecture for Community staff, and locally made earth bricks were chosen as the main material for the structure. The design includes metal grills for windows inspired by lotus blooms in a nearby pond; the floral designs also relate to the names of the women's groups who make use of the facility. In addition to evening meetings and events for women and children, young women use the facility during the day for stitching and tailoring to generate income for the village.

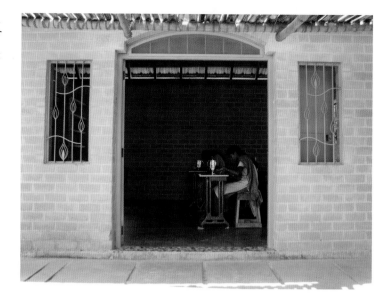

16.15 Cameron Sinclair, Architecture for Humanity, and local women's self-help group, entrance, Nadukuppam Vangala Women's Center, Tamil Nadu, India, 2008.

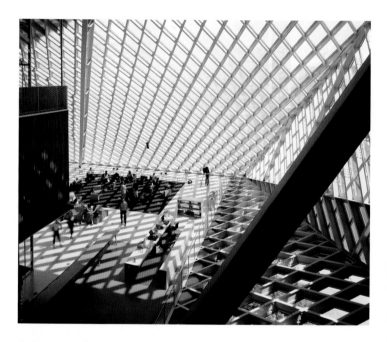

16.16 Rem Koolhaas, interior, Seattle Public Library, Seattle, Washington, 2004.

Giving up ownership of design is often challenging, but a number of designers are committed to such a process-oriented approach. An example of such an approach beyond the realm of disaster response is Rem Koolhaas's (b. 1944) Seattle Public Library (completed 2004; fig. 16.16). This large steel and glass structure, located on an entire city block, lacks the unified profile of much modern architecture; moreover, the design of its interior was based upon suggestions from different

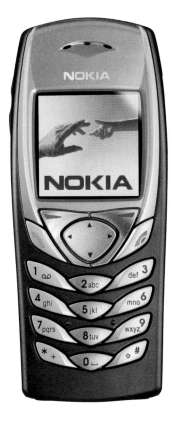

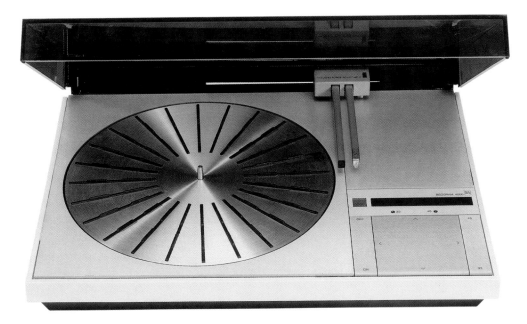

16.18 Jacob Jensen, Beogram 4000 turntable, wood, aluminum, and stainless steel housing, width 18 ⅞ in (48 cm), manufactured by Bang & Olufsen A/S, Struer, Denmark, 1972.

16.17 Cellular phone, plastic housing, length 4 in (10 cm), manufactured by Nokia, Finland, 2000.

groups of users to facilitate services rather than an overriding scheme or single idea or system. Relinquishing ownership can be difficult, but critics have applauded the building's ability to cater to different types of users, and the library has generally been welcomed by Seattle residents, who feel they had a share in its design. Koolhaas has seen a parallel for his approach to design not in traditional urban planning but in the haphazard growth of megacities with populations of upward of ten million such as Lagos (Nigeria) or Bombay (India). While such chaos conflicts with many traditional associations of design with unity and order, Koolhaas finds the fragmented aesthetic energizing and navigable for many of those who live and work in such places.

PRODUCTION TECHNOLOGY: MEANINGS OF MINIATURIZATION

New technologies during the past three decades continue to make miniaturization a significant consideration in industrial design. Integrated circuits, for instance, using silicon chips for industrial or domestic electronic equipment reduce the size requirements for many products, from portable handheld calculators and telephones

such as the Finnish-manufactured Nokia portable cellular model (fig. 16.17). Lightweight and compact, such products employ minimal and unified housings and a harmonious relationship among parts. Miniaturization in electronic products has led to a certain conformity among several manufacturers, though there is considerable creativity in devising solutions to reducing clutter, hiding dials and buttons, devising smooth and transparent interfaces with controls, and achieving a high degree of geometric aesthetic purity. Early examples include thin components for stereo equipment such as the Beogram 4000 turntable designed by Jacob Jensen (b. 1926) for the Bang & Olufsen Company of Denmark in 1972 (fig. 16.18), as with the Beogram 4000 turntable. Here the tone arm can be activated without lifting the cover by lightly touching the side of the unit, a feature that creates a smooth and uninterrupted external surface. The expense of portable and home electronic products often stems more from the cost of research, capital equipment for mechanically manufactured components, and the expense of consultant designers rather than from the materials themselves. Despite mechanization in manufacturing, labor is often still required for assembly. Increasingly this manual labor is carried out wherever it can be purchased cheaply, often in China, Indonesia, and in areas of Latin America. In many sectors of the fashion industry similar circumstances prevail. For clothing manufacturing, consumer activism operates to police the regulation of workers' ages,

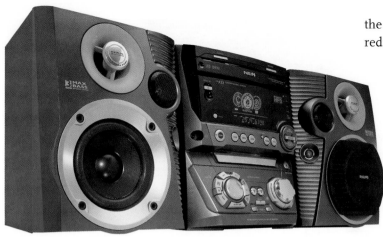

16.19 Portable stereo system with compact disk player, plastic housing, Philips, 2002.

hours, and factory conditions, backed by the fear of media exposure and the threat of consumer boycotts.

For sound, digital technology, in which audio information is transmitted as electrical impulses and recorded as a sequence or code of binary numbers, is used to produce the small, circular 5-in (12.7-cm) compact disk and CD players. Beginning in the early 1980s, these devices replaced both long-playing records and cassette tapes and players for recording and listening to music. The small CDs are resistant to wear and damage, and the devices that play them are compact, available for installation in computers, automobiles, and as part of integrated home stereo systems. Divided into discrete tracks, the listener is able to program a CD in a sequence of selections without lifting a tone arm or pressing rewind or fast-forward buttons, thus personalizing the listening experience. CD players are also easily activated through remote control devices. Maintaining them is easier than caring for cassette players or turntables, and requires less cleaning or attention to mechanical parts. Housings from the late twentieth and early twenty-first centuries were generally compatible with the other rectangular boxlike components of a home stereo system, and often permitted the user to access several CDs at once (fig. 16.19). The CD's miniature size also produced an endless variety of individual and expandable storage units for the home, from variations on traditional bookshelves to anthropomorphic wire sculptures that house dozens of CDs. Even as this second edition appears in print, CD players have given way to MP3 players such as the Apple iPod that reduce or eliminate the need for storage space, and manufacturers offer "docking stations" to move from personal to more public listening.

Digital technology also paved the way for the advent of personal computers, including desktop, laptop, and handheld units. Pioneered by the Intel Company in 1971,

the processing of digital information on microchips reduced the mechanical and space requirements of earlier computers. Since the mid-1980s, personal computers eclipsed and eventually replaced typewriters for business, research, and home use. They have also expanded the possibilities of information processing and organization to include databases, charts, and spreadsheets.

Industrial design for cellular phones and computers, as well as portable cellular and wireless telephones, may be studied from a number of viewpoints. Designers develop the most efficient, lightweight, and compact plastic or aluminum housing given the space requirements of the various integrated circuits, speakers, microphones, keys, and screens. They consider human factors involving the final form and location of speakers, buttons, and keys, both in terms of how easy they are to operate and how well they communicate their function to the user. An example of an ergonomic approach to computer design is an alternative keyboard for personal computers, designed using curves to conform to the more natural position of the wrists of operators to reduce fatigue as well as prevent injury and nerve damage. Designers also determine possible novelties in color, form, and even texture that might attract consumer attention in a competitive market through establishing a more personal relationship with the user. Even in housing for computers and cellular phones, the combination of miniaturized equipment and commercial considerations rarely results in stable "type" forms. Computer hard-drive components may be horizontal and located beneath the monitor, or vertical and more commonly placed on the floor or held in place by metal straps, creating more work space on the surface of a table or desk. An example of such variety is the Apple Macintosh iMac desktop computer (1998), which featured a translucent housing, more rounded, sculptural form, and choices of vibrant colors with names such as tangerine, strawberry, and lime that seem more suited to flavors of water ice (fig. 16.20).

For cellular phones, manufacturers advertised interchangeable plastic plates to personalize the product, featuring a wide variety of patterns, colors, and simulated textures. More recently, customization pertains less to visible features than to programmed features connecting users with information. For instance, figure 16.21 illustrates a phone that offers users a feature to indicate the direction of Mecca (Qibla direction) and remind Muslims of the correct times for prayer with alarms.

User-centered approaches to design also include the field of product semantics or the varied dimensions of interface between technology and the user, particularly in the field of personal computing, as described above for the

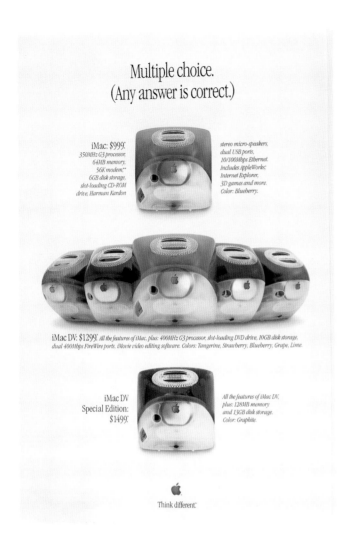

Multiple choice.
(Any answer is correct.)

iMac: $999:
350MHz G3 processor,
64MB memory,
56K modem:**
6GB disk storage,
slot-loading CD-ROM
drive, Harman Kardon

stereo micro-speakers,
dual USB ports,
10/100Mbps Ethernet.
Includes AppleWorks,
Internet Explorer,
3D games and more.
Color: Blueberry.

iMac DV: $1299: All the features of iMac, plus: 400MHz G3 processor, slot-loading DVD drive, 10GB disk storage,
dual 400Mbps FireWire ports, iMovie video editing software. Colors: Tangerine, Strawberry, Blueberry, Grape, Lime.

iMac DV
Special Edition:
$1499:

All the features of iMac DV,
plus: 128MB memory
and 13GB disk storage.
Color: Graphite.

Think different:

16.20 Advertisement for iMac desktop computer manufactured by Macintosh Corporation, Cupertino, California, 1998.

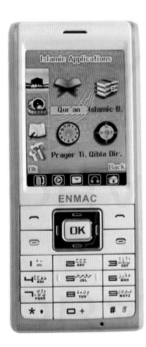

16.21 MQ9200 GSM phone with prayer times and Qibla direction, plastic housing, Enmac Engineering Ltd., Hong Kong, 2006.

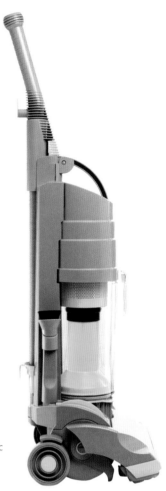

16.22 Dyson, Dual Cyclone DC 24 vacuum cleaner, plastic housing, 43 $\frac{1}{3}$ x 11 x 13 $\frac{7}{10}$ in (110 x 28 x 34.8 cm), c. 1998.

Apple Macintosh computer (see fig. 15.21). Designer and critic Guy Julier has described the Dyson electric vacuum cleaner along the lines of product semantics. The Dyson vacuum cleaner (introduced 1993) uses clear plastic to demonstrate with visual immediacy the effectiveness of the dust collection as well as mudguards and fins to evoke efficiency, all to psychologically suggest the capturing of dirt and reduce resistance to a new and more expensive design (fig. 16.22). The underlying concept of product semantics is the breaking down of barriers between ourselves and the products or services we use, *and* of course the products and services we may consider purchasing. Even James Dyson himself is part of the product semantics equation – he presents himself as part of the lore of invention itself, an appeal to identify with the tinkerer in each of us who has the capacity to think of something better, to create a preferred condition out of an existing one through imagination and questioning the status quo. In this light, it is not surprising that while we still may identify design with products, contemporary design consultancies report that only about eight percent of their business involves the design of products, while the majority is in communications and expanded concepts of branding.

Design and Softness

As mentioned above (pages 379–380), the term "soft" refers to the ways in which designers are able to modify ideas quickly in a virtual environment so that solutions are rarely final and exist more naturally in a state of flux. Implicit in Herbert Simon's 1969 definition of design (see page 380), "soft" approaches to design often focus upon the intellectual in addition to physical or aesthetic aspects of design. In this view both the computer and the notion of information have become the new common denominators of design activity. In our present "post-industrial" age of electronic information and imagery, the term "soft" encompasses not only the digital manipulation of virtual and easily modified images so prominent in many areas of design, but also the complex task of creating information systems or instructions (software) to facilitate the process of manipulation itself. In this way the boundaries between design, information science, and artificial intelligence have become more fluid, and collaboration in academic and industry settings suggests that the relationship between technology and the existing training and practice of modern design is indeed changing. As software becomes more sophisticated, a greater understanding of human psychology and thought makes traditional disciplinary boundaries permeable, not just boundaries between machines and craft production, but also boundaries between machines and the creative process itself.

Materials Technology and Softness

New synthetic materials and new uses for older industrial materials relate to obvious connotations of softness. Soft materials can replace traditionally "hard" ones, for instance in appliance design, as seen in Argentinian designer Roberto Pezzetta's (b. 1946) 1996 built-in oven for Zanotta, the curved surface of which eliminates the need for a projecting handle (fig. 16.23). The concept also suggests a closer relationship between products and users, where surfaces become like skins or membranes or objects move and react to their environment like bodies; where in short, the artificial mimics the natural. Another example is Marta Sansoni's (b. 1963) "Folpo" soft plastic hand mixer (1998) manufactured by Alessi (fig. 16.24), the blades of which resemble tentacles rather than rigid metal beaters. In the traditional hand mixer the action is mechanical and automatic, while in Sansoni's version the metaphor is that of a biological organism. The interface in such products is personal rather than impersonal, with the result of creating higher degrees of interactivity with users. As a result a number of contemporary designers have been commissioned to design new and more flexible

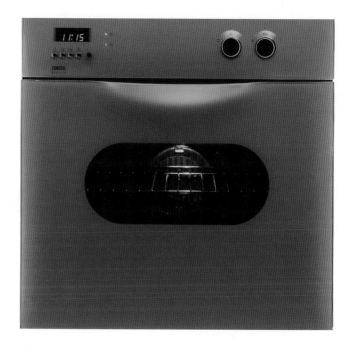

16.23 Roberto Pezzetta, soft-tech oven, front: 3-D deformed tempered glass, 23 5/8 x 23 5/8 x 21 1/4 in (60 x 60 x 54 cm), manufactured by Zanotta, Milan, Italy, 1996.

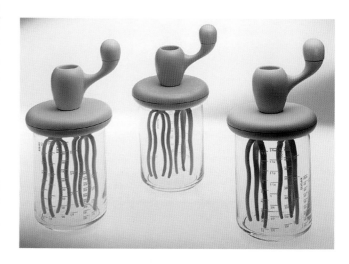

16.24 Marta Sansoni, "Folpo" hand mixer, plastic, height 9 9/16 in (25 cm), manufactured by Alessi, New York and Italy, 2001.

furnishings using older synthetic materials such as DuPont's Corian polymer, developed first in 1967.

The Cooper Hewitt National Design Museum's Triennial in 2006/7 was entitled Design Life Now, and explored relationships between design, biomimicry, and mutation. New materials were highlighted, such as Abhinand Lath's "SensiTile," which uses technology based upon fiberoptics to create movement in response to the light in a given room, in turn affected by the human presence (fig. 16.25). SensiTile can be embedded in materials for flooring as well as walls to create interactive spaces. The

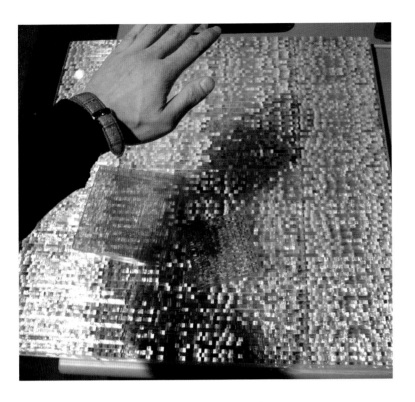

16.25 Abhinand Lath, Scintilla, cast PMMA acrylic, manufactured by SensiTile Systems, 2005.

theme of design and life relates to robotic devices such as the Roomba Scheduler Vacuuming Robot, manufactured beginning in 2002 by the iRobot Corporation in Burlington, Massachusetts (fig. 16.26). Here too the automated, "intelligent" device, despite its neutral appearance, not only reduces or eliminates a time-consuming household chore (theoretically at least), but also takes on the character of a family pet; owners can provide names and customize their Roombas with distinguishing stickers or painted decoration.

Design Life Now also included web-based information as an acknowledged form of design, featuring Google and the interactive Google Earth global position-ing system (GPS) among its displays to suggest expanded ways of thinking about design in relation to information and interactivity, where the responsive interface resembles a dialogue with an intelligent being rather than a pro-grammed machine. When such systems are installed in personal, handheld devices such as the Apple iPhone (first introduced in 2007) (fig. 16.27), the device becomes not simply personal but an extension of ourselves and our powers. In all of these variations, user input and choice transform

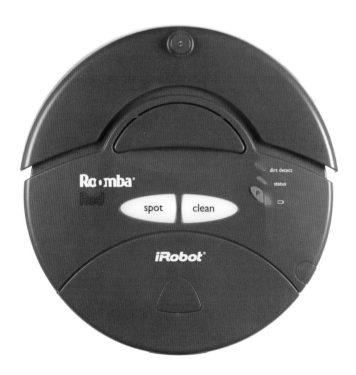

16.26 iRobot Roomba Scheduler Vacuuming Robot, plastic housing, AWARE™ Robot Intelligence System, 18 ⅓ x 14 ⁷⁄₁₀ x 4 ⁷⁄₁₀ in (46.5 x 37.3 x 11.9 cm), manufactured by iRobot Corporation, Burlington, Massachusetts, 2002.

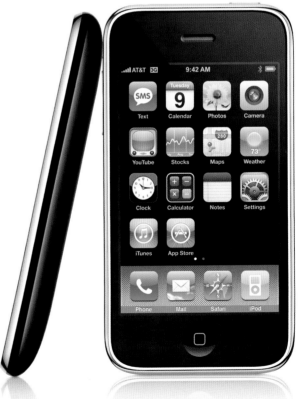

16.27 iPhone (3G), plastic, scratch-resistant glass, 4.5 x 2.4 x ¹²⁄₂₅ in (11.5 x 6.2 x 1.2 cm), Apple Corporation, Cupertino, California, 2008.

the inanimate into the animate, breaking down barriers between our-selves and technology, and expanding our understanding of contemporary design practice.

Another example illustrating the importance of information as the focus of design in relation to digital technology is the miniature MP3 player that has increasingly replaced the compact disk as a vehicle for storing music for portable players. The Apple iPod, introduced in 2001, has dominated the MP3 player market, outdistancing Sony, whose transistor radios, cassette players, and compact disk players formerly were the acknowledged industry leader. In a *New Yorker* article from 2006 profiling Sony Corporation CEO Howard Stringer, the subject of the interview turned to Apple's lead in the MP3 market. While Stringer and others have acknowledged the Apple iPod's sleek minimalist design, marketing strategy emphasizing individual expression, and attractive features such as the responsive wheel used for scrolling that make it fast and easy to use, the more significant consideration in its design was not the ease of operation, but the ease with which users could access or download content for the iPod. Unlike the cumbersome security required to download music for Sony's MP3 player, which pre-dated Apple's entry into the market, the iPod much more easily connected the product to musical content. In the words of the *New Yorker* writer, "Sony approached proprietary digital-rights management as if it were guarding nuclear secrets; Apple built a security-lite system that could download music from the Internet to a computer to an iPod so simply that your grandmother could get the hang of it while brewing tea." It was the interface that explains the success of the product, not the interface with the wheel, but with the music.

Other materials also remain the basis for design change. Sporting goods manufacturers continue to introduce strong but lightweight materials like titanium for bicycles and tennis racquets, while graphite is now used commonly for the shafts of golf clubs. Clothing is another area in which new fabrics stimulate new products. An example is the iridescent fabric woven from metallic yarns developed by Japanese designer Reiko Sudo (b. 1953) for the Numo Manufacturing Corporation in 1991 (fig. 16.28).

In furniture and household furniture there is considerable variety in contemporary directions in design. The Brazilian-born Campana brothers' (Humberto, b. 1953; Fernando, b. 1961) Anemone chair (fig. 16.29) uses a metal frame strewn with flexible transparent plastic tubing. In this example several elements of contemporary design emerge: the creative use or reuse of industrial material, exploration of the unexpected aesthetic properties of materials not usually associated with furniture, elimination of mass and emphasis upon lightness and

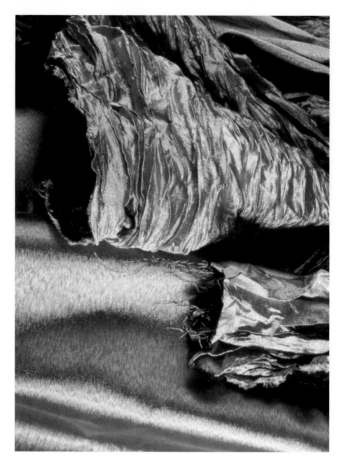

16.28 Reiko Sudo, Rusted Silver Washer fabric, cotton, polyester and aluminum lamé, 259 x 41 in (658 x 104 cm), manufactured by Numo Manufacturing Corporation, 1991.

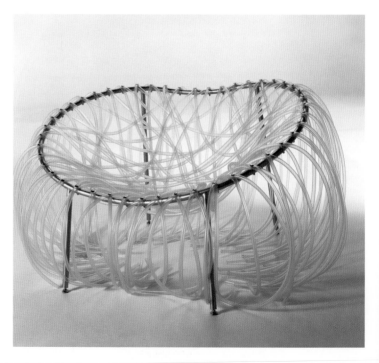

16.29 Fernando and Humberto Campana, Anemone chair, PVC tubing on stainless steel frame, 47 ³/₁₆ x 35 ⁷/₁₆ x 26 in (120 x 90 x 66 cm), manufactured by Edra, Perignano, Italy, 2001.

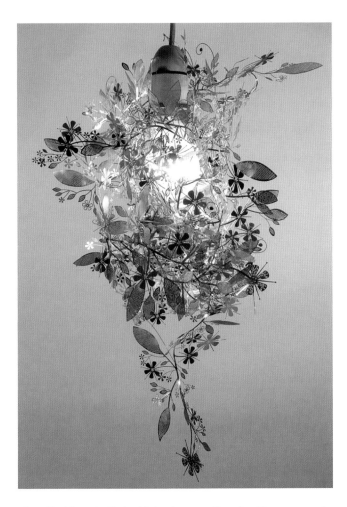

16.30 Tord Boontje, Garland lights, laser-cut silver-plated brass wrapped around hanging halogen light, laser-cut sheet, 28 x 16 in (71.1 x 40.6 cm), manufactured by Artecnica, Los Angeles, California, 2002–2003.

transparency, and the acknowledgment of expendability in design as a stimulus for replacement and further innovation.

The Postmodern rediscovery of ornament (see pages 370–372) has helped to create renewed interest in pattern and decoration and is now aided by newer technologies such as laser cutting and rapid prototyping, also known as 3-D printing. Rather than imitate craftsmanship at the highest levels of skill and direct manipulation of materials, laser cutting allows designers to create new levels of delicacy and aesthetic exploration, seen for instance, in the work of the Dutch designer Tord Boontje (b. 1968). Boontje's 2002 series of Garland Lights, manufactured by Artecnica (fig. 16.30), use ordinary hanging lightbulbs to explore light filtered through intricately and asymmetrically cut paper-thin silver-plated brass (other examples are cut from the synthetic polyethelene fabric Tyvek, manufactured by DuPont), something almost inconceivable with hand-operated machines. Equally exciting is the development of rapid prototyping equipment that produces three-dimensional designs directly from sketches. On view at the experimental MoMA exhibition of 2007 entitled Design and the Elastic Mind, curated by Paola Antonelli, was a video demonstrating such technology for Sketch furniture by Swedish designers Sofia Lagerkvist (b. 1976), Charlotte von der Lancken (b. 1977), and Katja Savström (b. 1976) (fig. 16.31). Using video cameras and 3-D printing, the designers' ideas, traced using a stylus in space like the baton of an orchestra conductor, are immediately translated into a unique piece of furniture made of

16.31 Sofia Lagerkvist, Charlotte von der Lancken, and Katja Savström, Sketch Furniture, Acron Formservice AB, Sweden, 2005.

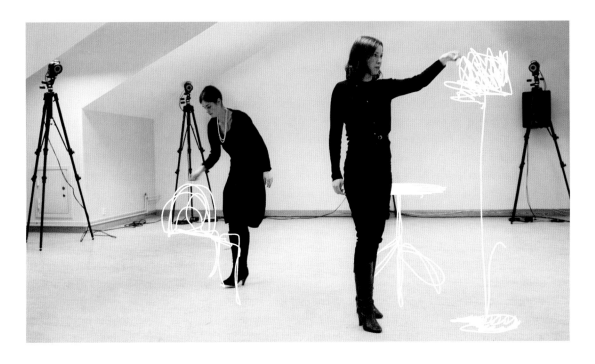

polyamide resin. Design and manufacture, whose separation has been an integral part of the history of modern design we have traced from the late seventeenth century and rationalized through mechanized mass production, have here become reunited. The interface is seamless, and only time will demonstrate how such discoveries may relate to themes of professionalization and democratization within design. One can imagine "do-it-yourself" facilities where consumers would "buy" time to fashion and customize their own furnishings or clothing, a more personal version of the do-it-yourself glazing and firing of ceramic blanks rather than purchasing available finished pieces. Nanotechnology takes this process one step further. Among the many ramifications of this technology, using subatomic particles measuring one-billionth of a meter, is the possibility of recombining materials into a variety of configurations for multiple use; the ultimate realization of Modernist flexibility and user interaction, by which, for instance, particles could be assembled and reassembled for different functions. Apart from the relationship between nanotechnology and new materials, nanotechnologists working with molecular structures to heal wounds, create prosthetics, or fight disease, and those scientists working to create more efficient semiconductors to store solar energy, often describe themselves as "designers," seeking on the one hand to understand the underlying rules of nature at the nano-level, and then to create possible structures that alter our experience.

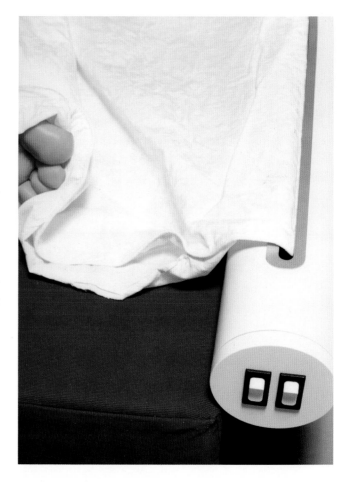

16.32 Noam Toran, Sheet Thief, aluminum, plastic, and electronics, from *Accessories for Lonely Men* models, 2001.

LIFESTYLE

The humanization of technology, making machines more intelligent and more of an extension of our bodies, may also have an effect upon our relationships with other human beings, seen for instance in new patterns of everyday life. One development has been an acknowledgment of single rather than couple or family lifestyles, reflecting societal patterns in developed countries, lower birth rates, and the rising age at which couples marry. At the Design and the Elastic Mind exhibition (see page 399), the needs of singles were addressed by American-born British designer Noam Toran (b. 1975) in a series of objects called *Accessories for Lonely Men* (2001). One device, the Sheet Thief (fig. 16.32), consists of an electrical mechanism that reels the sheet onto the other side of the bed, cleverly substituting for a partner's habit whose presence it implies. Curiously, the same theme appeared at the 2008 Venice Biennale in a display entitled *Singletown* by the Dutch consultancy Droog Design in collaboration with the advertising firm KesselsKramer. *Singletown*, seeks to combat loneliness and alienation in a variety of ways, including a book on display entitled *Love+Sex_with Robots* and an "instant

balcony" – a metal loungechair, designed by Jan and Tim Edier, that extends like an arm from an apartment window to bring the hi-rise inhabitant closer to nature. *Singletown* also was featured in Design and the Elastic Mind. Elsewhere at the Biennale, the term "alienated domesticity" appeared as a description of permanent "singleness."

POLITICS, TECHNOLOGY, AND THE MEDIA

There are voices critical of fundamental aspects of the information age, which seems for many to hold out such promise for humanizing technology, improving the quality of life, and making design more inclusive and far-reaching. A part of this criticism directs us to the structural level; that is, the interactive digital technology that powers our iPhones, guides us with reasonable confidence by global positioning technology to unfamiliar places, and allows us to program and personalize our MP3 players, may also be used for unauthorized surveillance and for remote, destructive military strikes. Such uses raise questions about the risks that technology poses to safety, and makes us think about whether the progress we associate with digital information does in fact mask more dangerous relationships between political authority and those businesses that design and provide information technology. It is hardly surprising that skepticism about the information age has been stimulated by global terrorism and responses to the attacks of September 11, 2001, when the Pentagon and World Trade Center towers became powerful symbols and targets for destruction, an extreme response on the part of the attackers and their supporters to fears of global hegemony and loss of identity.

While advocates of Postmodernism related the movement to Pluralism and tolerance, 9/11 and the war on terror have introduced a renewed and destructive ideological dualism. The media presentation of those events elicited strong patriotic feeling in the United States and a shared sense of sympathy for human suffering worldwide; yet the attacks also demonstrated that spectacular violence and destruction attract media attention and give voice to marginal groups whose threatening acts move quickly to a national and global center stage. Such strategies, on a smaller and usually far less violent scale, were appropriated during the protests of the 1960s as part of an effort to encourage reform. The relationship of such acts to the history of modern design as presented in this book is hardly direct, and yet in addition to renewed devices to promote personal security or respond promptly to victims of violence, the underlying political and economic structures that provide the context for design in the information age also have sown seeds of violent and threatening reaction.

GRAPHIC DESIGN IN A DIGITAL AGE

Digital technology has had a major impact upon the practice of graphic design. As the varied methods of graphic designers extend into the virtual space of the computer monitor, the experience of the user shifts from turning pages or unfolding pamphlets to clicking links triggering animations and revealing multiple windows filled with information that is seen, read, and heard, often simultaneously. The result is thus more interactive than traditional print media. While adapting to the new media seems almost natural for younger generations who were educated with computers, the interface with older populations can be overwhelming. The rapidly evolving technologies that make such new explorations possible provide designers with flexibility beyond that of photomechanical processes which allows them to produce typography and manipulate images with increased speed, employing an expanding range of experimental practices. Graphic processing and manipulation with the computer provide opportunities for

designers to unite photography, filmmaking, and more traditional graphic design and illustration. While the term "digital media" is sometimes used to refer to such activities, the degree of overlap in education and in practice makes discipline-based thinking appear narrow and out of touch with the graphic design industry practice. Such media convergence was at the root of the Media Lab developed at the Massachusetts Institute of Technology beginning in 1984, which continues to explore inter-relationships and interactivity in the digital realm. At the same time, the new tools that equip the designer with converging and overlapping means for communicating information require an ability to balance versatility with the specialized nature of sophisticated technology; these remain challenges for universities and professionals alike.

Using computers to generate digital type and manipulate digital images for graphic presentation began in 1984 with the operating system and user interface developed by the Apple Corporation for its Macintosh computers. The translation of type and images into electronic code on a low-resolution computer screen was not entirely new. However, creating and controlling those impulses with a computer mouse on a virtual desktop with pull-down windows rather than programming them with instructions on a keyboard was unique at that time to the Apple Corporation. This graphic interface used terms like "cut and paste" for functions familiar to graphic designers and amateurs alike. Amateurs used the new interface to democratize the printing and graphic design industries through desktop publishing. Manipulating fonts with a range of effects with the click of a mouse became commonplace, and office assistants could produce and edit reports and other communications with logos, borders, and images, generating a wide variety of materials formerly produced by professional printers and graphic designers. In completing these tasks, amateur designers borrowed from among thousands of symbols and popular graphics or "clip art" stored on five-inch compact disks or searched and downloaded from the Web.

The Macintosh also appealed to a small group of enthusiastic professional graphic designers, not as a "tool" to replace existing camera-ready design or printed output, but as a distinct form of communication offering new possibilities for expressing a contemporary sensibility. A pioneer in these explorations was the German-born and trained typesetter and graphic designer Wolfgang Weingart (b. 1941), who taught typography at the Basel School of Applied Art beginning in the early 1960s. Weingart expanded (and subverted) the techniques of letterpress and offset lithography through complex layering of photographic images and an ambiguous and suggestive use of symbols and letterforms, as seen in his

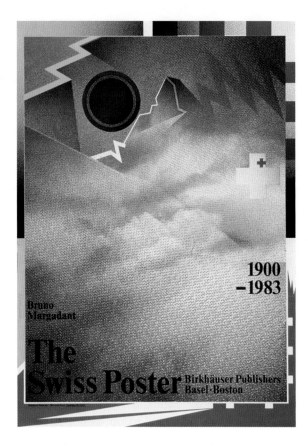

16.33 Wolfgang Weingart, *Schweizer Plakat* (The Swiss Poster), poster, offset lithography, 47 x 33 ⅛ in (119.4 x 84.3 cm), 1984. Museum of Design, Zurich. Poster collection.

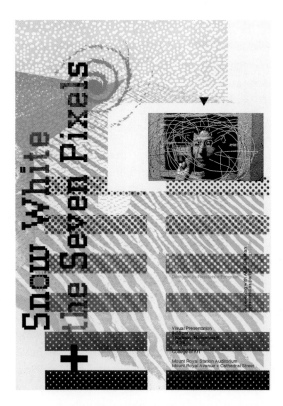

16.34 April Greiman, poster for "Snow White + the Seven Pixels" presentation at the Maryland Institute College of Art, Baltimore, Maryland, 1986.

poster announcing an exhibition of Swiss posters in 1984 (fig. 16.33). Los Angeles-based graphic designer April Greiman (b. 1948), who studied both with Armin Hofmann and Weingart in the 1970s, was receptive to layering and other experiments with type and image, and the graphical user interface of the Macintosh computer facilitated their introduction into her practice.

Early computer-generated digital images and text appeared primitive in comparison with letterpress or photomechanical typography. A most recognizable aspect of computer-generated fonts during this time was the distinctive effect of enlarged letters that revealed origins in coordinates based upon square pixels, resulting in "jaggy" transitions from vertical to horizontal elements of letterforms rather than smooth, curved ones. Another early use of digital output was through patterns and textures, generated both as "tools" by programs such as MacDraw or by digitized photographs that produced simplified, abstracted images. All three digital techniques are seen in a Greiman poster from 1986 (fig. 16.34). At the same time, Dutch-born Rudy VanderLans (b. 1955) launched the first issue of the magazine *Emigre* in San Francisco in 1984. In later issues of the journal, VanderLans worked with Czechoslovakian-born Zuzana Licko (b. 1961) and other designers. *Emigre* published work by international artists in a variety of media, and explored new territories in graphic design including the Macintosh as well as other desktop technologies like xerography. Licko, for instance, created modular typefaces on the Macintosh for *Emigre*, taking into account the "jaggy" corners of letterforms that resulted from the low-resolution capabilities of the computer, but with the freedom of an inexpensive alternative to costly equipment for typesetting (fig. 16.35). These typefaces, such as Emperor, employ modularity where possible to construct forms economically from a limited number of elements, similar to the strategy used by Herbert Bayer for his "universal alphabet" (see fig. 9.29). New software and higher resolution eliminated the "jaggy" edges of earlier digital typefaces and led to the variety of new fonts that were published in *Emigre* in the 1990s, including Barry Deck's Template Gothic (fig. 16.36). This typeface breaks down the traditional distinctions between sans serif and serif, mechanical and calligraphic, impersonal and expressive. Licko's sentiments were democratic and alternative in nature, as revealed in the following remarks:

> For centuries the design of typefaces has existed as an exclusive discipline reserved for specialists; today the personal computer provides the opportunity to create customized alphabets with an increased potential for personalization and expression. The design and manufacture of fonts can now be

Emperor

OAKLAND

Emigre

16.35 Zuzana Licko, digital fonts reproduced in *Emigre, c.* 1988.

Template Gothic:
AaBbCcDd
EeFfGgHhIiJjKkLlM
mNnOoPpQqRrSsTt
UuVvWwXxYyZz
(1234567890)

16.36 Barry Deck, Template Gothic typeface, 1990.

integrated into a single medium allowing for a more interactive design approach.... Digital technology has advanced the state of graphic art by a quantum leap into the future, thereby turning designers back to the most primitive of graphic ideas. Integrating design and production, the computer has reintroduced craft as a source of inspiration.

Licko's analogy between computer and craft seems not to refer to the manual drawing of fonts or the cutting of punches, but to the digital designer's independence and versatility rather than specialization. In addition, the excitement of experiment recalls the explosion of display types in the early nineteenth century. Just as the uses of typography expanded beyond the limited market for expensive printed books during that time, desktop publishing represented the late twentieth century incarnation of this phenomenon, in which more individualized expression for projects such as invitations, catalogues, or even student term papers became desirable. In addition to

Emigre, new digital fonts now appear in a wider variety of publications such as *U&lc*.

Typography underwent tremendous expansion as a result of digitization, with the invention of new typefaces and experimentation with a seemingly endless array of effects.

Among the most inventive and challenging experiments with the virtual workspace took place at the Cranbrook Academy of Art beginning in the 1970s under its graphic design director Katherine McCoy (b. 1945). In this laboratory-like environment, a good deal of experimentation took place exploring the possibilities of image and text manipulation, producing posters such as that illustrated in figure 16.37 (from 1990), promoting the academy's program with a suggestive but confusing array of unevenly set words, overlapping images encouraging multiple readings and individual interpretations.

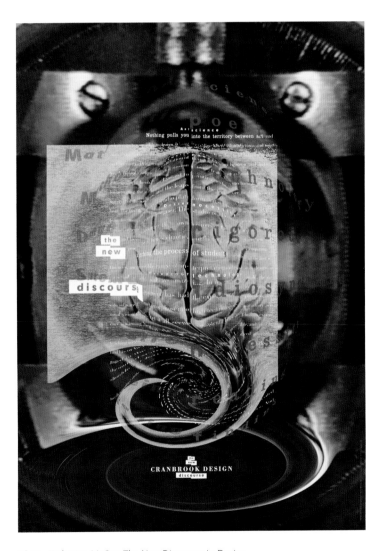

16.37 Katherine McCoy, The New Discourse in Design, poster for Cranbook Academy of Art, offset lithography, 27 x 22 in (59.9 x 55.9 cm), 1990.

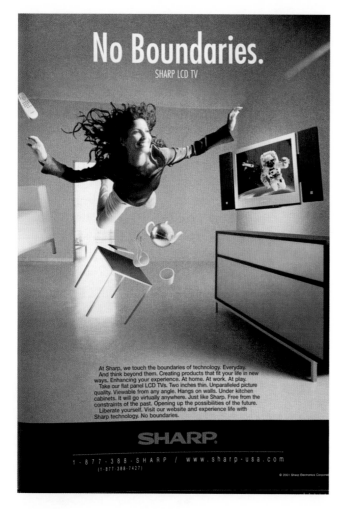

16.38 Advertisement for flat-screen television, manufactured by Sharp Corporation, *New Yorker*, September 2001.

Developments in technology during the 1990s made the computer the industry and educational standard for the graphic design profession. Students entering the field began to generate projects using software packages such as QuarkXpress and Adobe Photoshop, and universities replaced drafting tables and light tables (the latter used to cut and paste images and type for photographic reproduction) with computer workstations, scanners, and high-resolution printers. Hand-drawn calligraphy gave way to computer-generated typography on the Macintosh operating system, many of whose features were incorporated into the Windows system, developed by the Microsoft Corporation for IBM and IBM-compatible personal computers. Students began to carry packages of floppy disks (now Flash or keychain devices) in addition to (or rather than) toolboxes filled with X-Acto knives and felt-tipped markers, while administrators looked to the computer industry to help underwrite the tremendous cost of software licensing and workstations as a form of research

and marketing. Higher-resolution monitors and printers and an expanding desktop toolbox allowed designers to achieve exacting standards on a par with the most technically advanced art-directed magazines, including a wide range of colors and subtle tonal effects, and seamless manipulations of images and complex layering. Computer-generated images blur boundaries between animation and photography and create imagined worlds with a tremendous capacity to persuade and transport the viewer, especially in connection with advertising. An example is a 2001 advertisement for Sharp Electronics, which connects the high-quality resolution of a flat-screen television with the immediacy of the viewer's experience (fig. 16.38). With the rapid expansion of product and service marketing via the Internet, web page design emerged as a new virtual space not only for hi-tech layering, but for movement, time, and extensive multi-media communication beyond the limitations of the static two-dimensional surface of a page, poster, or cover. Graphic designer Chip Kidd (b. 1964), for example, began to explore typography creatively in hundreds of book covers that engage the reader's imagination but are generally less "layered" than the experimental poster work at Cranbrook. Kidd's book cover for the novel *Dry. A Memoir.* by Augusten Burroughs (2003) appeared in the Cooper Hewitt's Design Life Now exhibition. It featured ink bleeding from the letters of the title word "Dry," resonating with the obvious simulation of "wetness" of the letters themselves (fig. 16.39).

Computer-generated graphic design began almost as an "underground" movement by young artists experimenting outside mainstream professional channels with novel but unsophisticated, intentionally amateur production techniques utilizing the Macintosh computer. Within a decade, the field developed into the ultimate high-end technology of professional multi-media communication, with limitless possibilities both for the manipulation of images by designers (and interactive capabilities for users), the seduction of consumers, and endless tweaking by software developers and personal computer manufacturers that accelerated the range of the effects and encouraged the purchase of upgrades.

Computer preparation of type and layout now dominates the printing industry, although much printing continues to be done on offset presses from photographic plates rather than directly from the computer to the press. Beginning in the early 1980s, daily newspapers such as *USA Today* began to rival weekly magazines in color reproduction of photographs and advertisements, and daily rather than only Sunday editions use color for the comics pages. Art direction in many magazines reveals sophisticated approaches to layout for feature stories with integrated pictures, illustrations, titles, and text to interest the reader. Before the attack on the World Trade Center and the Pentagon in September 2001 focused the attention of the United States on its own security, the dominant story of the summer news dealt with the extramarital affairs of Washington's lawmakers (popular attention to this phenomenon has hardly abated). The *New York Times Magazine* featured an article on the subject with the title "Sex and This City," in a direct reference to the popular television show with a similar name (fig. 16.40) in one of a regular series of features devoted to current news topics. A centered title at the top gives only the date in arabic numerals (a repeated element in the series), while below, a cropped and off-center photograph shows a man's hand reaching toward the viewer across the thigh of a young seated woman wearing a short skirt. The photograph cuts into the text column at the right of the page. The asymmetrical layout, irregular column width, and secondary title below with the word "Sex," all generate visual and emotional interest. Art direction for fashion magazines remains more dramatic and immediate, geared to strong contrast and stronger emotional appeal, as in the work of Fabien Baron (see fig. 16.5).

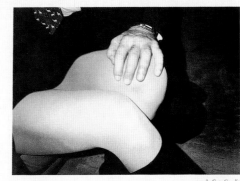

16.40 Page layout, *New York Times Magazine*, July, 2001. Photograph by Jessica Craig Martin.

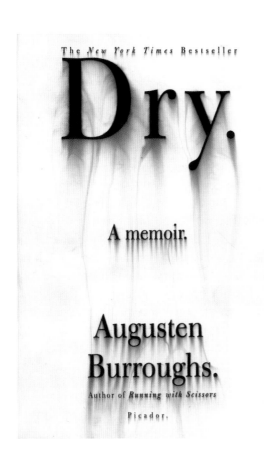

6.39 Chip Kidd, book cover design for Augusten Burroughs's *Dry. A Memoir.*, published by Picador (Macmillan), New York, 2003.

Alternative lifestyle magazines are venues for rebelling against convention both in expressive fashion features and in original art direction. David Carson (b. 1952) published his own magazines celebrating the carefree lifestyle of surfers and skateboarders, and exploring new popular music, beginning in the later 1980s with *Beach Culture* and *Ray Gun*. Design historian Michael Golec has noted the sources of Carson's imagery in the visual complexity of the modern urban environment, not so much its "newness" as its layered quality, for instance in decaying concrete walls that reveal traces of earlier posters or painted murals, creating a palimpsest in which a single image contains both past and present. Fittingly, the software tools of Adobe Photoshop allowed Carson to re-create and intensify this world as the visual counterpart of a complex and disjointed Postmodern experience. Some critics find Carson's work a triumph of style over substance, while students (mine at least) admire the designer as a rule-breaker with a highly personal and commercially successful practice. A monograph of Carson's work published in 1997 was titled *The End of Print*. The phrase is a provocative one, recalling the

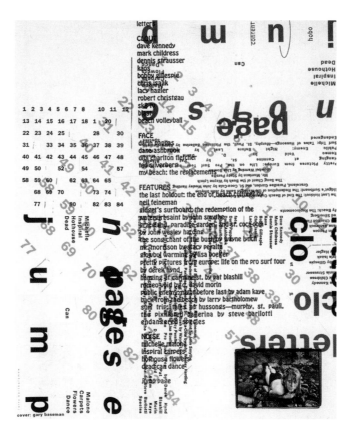

16.41 David Carson, table of contents from *Beach Culture*, Fall 1991.

Futurist manifestoes that heralded destruction as a prelude to a revolutionary modern spirit and new modes of life (see page 182). This may be a hard case to make. Carson's journals continue the tradition of art direction from the interwar period onward and are strongly backed by advertising aimed at the youth market. Figure 16.41, a contents page from *Beach Culture* (1991), was hardly designed to be read in any conventional sense. Words (content) and numbers (page numbers) appear, but seem to be arranged for expressive appeal rather than to identify or inform the magazine's readers. By comparison, Neville Brody's *The Face* from 1980 seems tame (see fig. 15.12).

CRAFT: THE PERSISTENCE OF PROCESS

While electronic imagery and software extend the possibilities of image manipulation and projection, it has often not been possible, nor even desirable, to eliminate skills in drawing, model-building, draping and tailoring, and a host of other more traditional techniques common in most design professions. Increasingly, computer interface also permits a great deal of experimentation, emphasizing the playfulness inherent in process rather than forming a shortcut to a predetermined result, as with 3-D printing and rapid prototyping and the flexibility they introduce into mechanical production. Experimentation, tinkering,

and intuition often exist in the very nature of the craft process, and even in front of the computer screen. It was fear of the elimination of this aspect of process that aroused the indignation of Ruskin and Morris more than a century ago. Despite the sophistication of an expanded, collaborative design process as practiced in modern consultancies, it is interesting to note that when the IDEO design consultancy selected objects from the permanent collection of the Cooper Hewitt National Design Museum for a small exhibition in 2007, the themes of the exhibition were intuition, empathy, and inspiration, rather than, for instance, research, analysis, testing, or even interface.

Despite an acknowledgment that its artifacts rarely occupy the same critical space as the products of the contemporary art scene, craft remains a vehicle for aesthetic exploration and individual expression, with a growing number of opportunities for exhibition in museums and galleries, and renewed interest in its cultural meaning. Despite a market limited at times by high costs and criticism of the commercial exploitation of star names, craft continues to chart new territory for expression and materials exploration, often without the burden of theoretical and historical knowledge and background placed upon the audience for contemporary fine art. Craft also often includes the contributions of women, who are less represented in many areas of

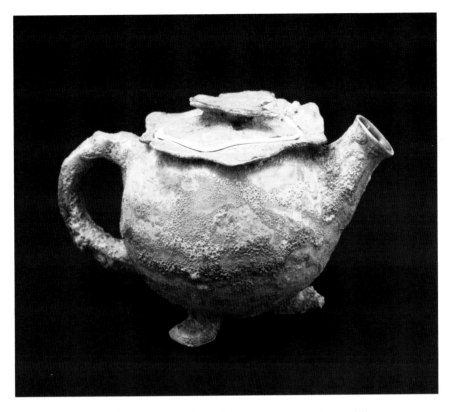

16.42 Sally Bowen Prange, Barnacle Teapot, stoneware, silicon carbide, 6 x 11 x 6 ½ in (15 x 28 x 16 cm), 1991.

industrial design. In ceramics, for instance, Sally Bowen Prange's (1927–2008) stoneware Barnacle Teapot of 1991 experiments with a variety of textures to simulate the effects of time and seawater upon human-made products, wearing them away while at the same time transforming them into new, almost animate, creations (fig. 16.42). While Prange's teapot remains within a tradition of utilitarian products, weaver Olga de Amaral (b. 1937) focuses more on exploring aesthetic effects of new combinations of materials, as in her *Alquimia XIII* wall-hanging of 1984, woven from cotton, linen, rice paper, gesso, paint, and gold leaf (fig. 16.43). In this work, strands of thread hover in front of rectangles of linen painted tarnished silver at the bottom and gold as the eye moves upward. The texture and color of the materials suggest a mysterious transformation or purification. Modern weavings also provide continuity with local traditions throughout the world, preserving and extending the varied role of craft in non-Western and pre-industrial societies.

The desire for freedom of expression, the enjoyment of working with materials, and the excitement of discovering the richness of effect, all combine to continually renew the inherent challenge and satisfaction of the craft process, and deserve to be included in any present or future understanding of design. Craft exhibitions range

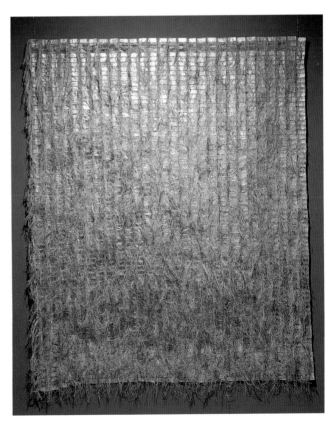

16.43 Olga de Amaral, *Alquimia XIII*, wall-hanging, cotton, linen, rice paper, gesso, paint, gold leaf, 71 x 29 ½ in (180 x 75 cm), 1984. Metropolitan Museum of Art, New York.

from the local to the national and international, and provide a venue for direct sales to the public or purchase prizes from major museums. The range of media at most craft exhibitions is broad and is organized as a combination of folk and guild traditions. Categories include, for instance, baskets and handmade fibers, as well as glass, furniture, leather, and ceramics. In many cases, however, work is highly individual rather than utilitarian. Statements by makers occasionally include references to keeping alive self-sufficient, pre-industrial patterns of life, and using craft to humanize the impersonal character of contemporary existence dominated by technology. While theoretical assessments note that craft does not easily approach the critical discourse of contemporary art practice (art historian Glenn Adamson refers to craft's "inferiority complex"), it enriches our understanding of the meaning of materials, skill, and encourages our reflection upon the human condition.

DESIGN AND CONTINUITY: CREATIVITY, RESPONSIBILITY, AND RESILIENCE

Design's strength lies in its breadth, its interaction with so many sources of inspiration and expanded areas of practice. Through technology, designers are in constant contact with new materials and processes that stimulate ideas for original products or transformations in existing products. Through production, designers work with manufacturers, investors, and must take account of markets, costs, and sales. As artists, designers are able to integrate an interest in aesthetics as well as self-expression and experimentation. With consumers in mind, designers increasingly work to incorporate human factors, user-friendly and appealing forms and interfaces, along with a wide range of possible meanings and interpretations. In today's world, design can be team-based, anonymous, or individual and heroic; ephemeral and self-indulgent or universal and relatively unchanging; negligent, amoral, or fueled by social and global consciousness and commitment. Throughout this history, with its dynamic range of possibilities, designers remain actively engaged with the world of nature and the man-made environment in all its excitement, complexity, and ambiguity. While the increasing range and variety of the design enterprise can be overwhelming in its scope, its history helps us to unite what design has been with what it might be, revealing relationships that provide continuity and a context for an ongoing shared discourse. Moreover, design continues to be responsive to those who use its myriad and ever-expanding products and services, to all of us whose lives it transforms, hopefully for the better.

Timeline

1650–Present

Seventeenth century
1650–1700

1654   Louis XIV crowned king of France at Reims
1656   French Academy for Painting established in Rome
1666   Charles Le Brun opens Royal Tapestry Manufactory at Gobelins
1666   Isaac Newton experiments in gravitation, optics, mathematics, astronomy
1672   Clarendon Press founded at Oxford
1675   Royal Observatory established at Greenwich
1682   Versailles becomes French royal residence
1692   Imprimérie Royale commissions "King's Roman" typeface

Composers active: Johann Sebastian Bach, Arcangelo Corelli, Jean-Baptiste Lully, Johann Pachelbel, Henry Purcell

Eighteenth century
1701–1750

André-Charles Boulle, cabinet-maker (1642–1732)
1702   Queen Anne becomes British monarch; succeeded by George I in 1714
1710   Meissen porcelain manufactory founded
1714   Daniel Gabriel Fahrenheit constructs mercury thermometer with temperature scale
1719   Daniel Defoe's *Robinson Crusoe*
1732   Benjamin Franklin begins publishing *Poor Richard's Almanac*
1734   tapestry manufactory at Beauvais appoints painter Jean-Baptiste Oudry as director
1736   glass manufacture at Murano, near Venice, Italy
1738   Vincennes porcelain manufactory founded

1751–1775

1754   Thomas Chippendale's *The Gentleman and Cabinet-maker's Director* published
1756   Vincennes porcelain manufactory moved to Sèvres
1760   Kew Gardens opens in London
Robert Adam designs homes in Neoclassical style in Britain 1760–1770
c.1764 James Watt's early experiments leading to development of steam engine

1767   Denis Diderot and Jean le Rond d'Alembert's *Encyclopédie* completed
1769   Wedgwood manufactory established at Etruria
1770   Captain James Cook discovers Botany Bay, Australia
1773   first cast-iron bridge completed at Coalbrookdale, Shropshire

1776–1800

Ébénistes Adam Weisweiler (1744–1820) and Jean-Henri Riesener (1734–1806) active in Paris
American Revolution 1775–1783
1776   Adam Smith's *Wealth of Nations*
1783   copper cylinder printing for calico fabric
1786   Wolfgang Amadeus Mozart's *Marriage of Figaro*
1792   French Republic proclaimed
1798   Aloys Senefelder invents lithography

"Modern" typefaces developed by printing families of Didot in Paris, Bodoni in Parma

Nineteenth century
1801–1825

1801   Jacquard loom
1804   Napoleon becomes emperor of France
1804   Thomas Bewick publishes complete color printing of *History of English Birds*
1807   gas lights for London streets
1807   Thomas Hope's *Household Furniture and Interior Decoration*
c.1813 Rudolph Ackermann's *Repository of the Arts* published
1814   steam-operated press at *The Times*, London
1814   Jane Austen's *Mansfield Park*
1816   Gioacchino Antonio Rossini's *Barber of Seville*
1823   Charles Macintosh invents waterproof fabric
Early development of steam locomotives and railways 1804–1830

1826–1850

1827   Publication of *Baedecker* travel guides
1829   Louis Daguerre and Joseph Niépce begin development of photography
1830   revolution in France

1830   first bentwood chairs manufactured by
        Michael Thonet
1830   Honoré de Balzac begins *La comédie humaine*
1830s   beginnings of chromolithography
        (Godefroy Engelmann)
c.1830 Figgins and Thorowgood's typographic
        specimen books
1834   National Industrial Fair, Paris
1837   London Schools of Design
1838   Queen Victoria crowned
1838   National Gallery in London opens
1840   Augustus Welby Northmore Pugin and Sir
        Charles Barry begin design of Houses of
        Parliament (completed 1860)
1844   Friedrich Keller invents wood-pulp paper
1845   Friedrich Engels' *Condition of the Working Class
        in England*
1848   European revolutions starting in Paris,
        spreading to other cities including Vienna,
        Venice, Berlin
1848   Karl Marx's *Communist Manifesto*
c.1850 papier-mâché used for furniture
c.1820 block-printed wallpaper manufactured widely

1851–1875

1851   London's Great Exhibition at the Crystal Palace
1851   sewing machine improved by Isaac Singer
1852   Japan opens to trade with West
        Paris World's Fair 1855 and 1867
1856   William Perkin develops first aniline (chemical)
        dyes
1856   Owen Jones's *Grammar of Ornament*
1857   Victoria and Albert Museum opened as Museum
        of Ornamental Art
1859   Charles Darwin's *Origin of Species*
        Guiseppe Garibaldi forms association for
        unification in Italy 1859–1861
c.1860 couturier Charles Worth active in Paris
1861   outbreak of Civil War in the USA
1862   World's Fair in London
1862   department store Le Bon Marché opens in Paris
1864   Union Central des Arts Décoratifs et Industriels
        established in France
1865   Louis Pasteur cures silkworm disease in France,
        saving French silk industry beginning
1867   beginning of bicycle manufacture in Paris
1868   Morris and Company design Luncheon (Green)
        Room at the Victoria and Albert Museum
1869   John Wesley Hyatt invents celluloid, early form of
        plastic for film and other products
1869   Suez Canal opened
1870   Franco-Prussian War
c.1870 advertising posters in Paris
1872   James Whistler's Peacock Room
1873   World's Fair in Vienna

1876–1900

1876   Philadelphia Centennial Exhibition
1877   Queen Victoria proclaimed Empress of India
1878   World's Fair in Paris
1879   Louis Comfort Tiffany founds company for
        interior decoration
1881   Sears catalog debuts
1882–1886
        developments in printing technology: linotype,
        monotype, half-tone screen for printing
        photographs
1888   George Eastman perfects Kodak Box Camera
1888   mass production of aluminum
        World's Fair in Paris 1889 (debut of Eiffel Tower)
        and 1900
1890   first steel-framed buildings (Chicago)
1893   World Columbian Exposition, Chicago
1894–1895
        Lumière Brothers invent motion picture camera
        and cinematography
1895   Samuel Bing opens Maison de l'Art Nouveau
        showrooms in Paris
1895   H. G. Wells's *The Time Machine*
1896   *Die Jugend* and *Simplicissimus* begin publication
        in Munich
1897   first Zionist Congress held in Basel
1897   Tate Gallery donated to British people
1898   Spanish–American War
1900   Gustav Stickley founds Craftsman Workshops
1900   Sigmund Freud's *The Interpretation of Dreams*

Twentieth century
1901–1920

1901   Societé des Artistes Décorateurs established
        in France
1901   Theodore Roosevelt becomes US president
1902   World's Fair in Turin
1903   brothers Orville and Wilbur Wright successfully
        fly airplane
1903   Wiener Werkstätte founded
1904   World's Fair in St. Louis
1905   first neon signs
1905   first regularly operating cinema in USA
        (Pittsburgh)
1906   Upton Sinclair's *The Jungle* (exposing conditions
        in meatpacking plants)
1906   Food and Drug Act reforms US meatpacking
        industry
1907   Deutscher Werkbund founded
1908   Applied Arts exhibition in Munich
1909   Futurist Manifesto published
1909   Ballets Russes opens in Paris
1910   Igor Stravinsky's *The Firebird*
1911   Salon d'Automne, Paris

1912   F. W. Woolworth Store founded
1912   Maison Cubiste
c.1913   Model T Ford production in Highland Park, Michigan, with moving assembly line
1914   Werkbund exhibition in Cologne
         World War I 1914–1918
1915   Christine Frederick's *Principles of Household Management*
1917   *De Stijl* journal begins
1917   revolution in Russia, Czar abdicates, Vladimir Lenin named First Commissar
1919   Bauhaus founded in Weimar, Germany
1919   Constructivism emerges at schools and in exhibitions in Russia
1919   Benito Mussolini founds Fascist Party in Italy
1919–1920
         League of Nations formed with headquarters in Paris (later Geneva)
1920   suffrage for women in USA
1920   prohibition of sale of alcoholic beverages adopted as 18th amendment in USA

1921–1940

1920   Mahatma Gandhi emerges as leader of Indian independence
1921   KDKA radio (Pittsburgh) transmits first radio program
1922   La Mâtrise boutique in Galleries Lafayette Department Store, Paris
1923   Le Corbusier's (Charles Edouard Jeanneret's) *Vers une Architecture*
1923   Milan Triennale at Monza
1925   Paris International Exhibition of Decorative and Industrial Art
         Ku Klux Klan violence peaks in southern USA 1918–1927
         Frankfurt Kitchen 1925–1930
1927   Jan Tschichold's *The New Typography*
1927   Ludwig Mies van der Rohe's Weissenhof Seidlung (apartment complex) in Stuttgart, Germany
1927   General Motors Art & Color Section
1927   Ford introduces Model A
1927   fluorescent lighting developed
1927   *Jazz Singer*, first talking motion picture
1928   first moving electric sign on NY Times Building in New York
1929   Museum of Modern Art (MoMA) founded in New York
1929   Union des Artistes Modernes (UAM), France
1929   World's Fair, Spain
1929   Wall Street Crash, October
         Dr. Mehemed Fehmy Agha art director at American *Vogue* and *Vanity Fair* 1929–1943
1930   *Fortune* magazine launched
1932   molded plywood furniture, e.g. Aalto for Paimio Sanitorium, Finland

1933   Bauhaus closes
1933   SS *Normandie* launched
1933   Hitler elected as Chancellor of Germany, granted dictatorial powers
1933–1934
         Chicago Century of Progress Fair
1934   Machine Art exhibition at MoMA in New York
1935   continuous rolling technology for steel used in automobile manufacturing
         Spanish Civil War 1935–1938
1936   synthetic fabric nylon used for stockings patented by Wallace Carothers (Dupont)
1937   Exposition Internationale des Arts et Techniques dans la Vie Moderne
1937   *Life* magazine launched
1939   New York World of Tomorrow Fair
1940   Battle of Britain

1941–1960

1941   Germany invades USSR
1941   Japan invades Pearl Harbor
1941   USA declares war on Japan, Germany, and Italy
1944   *Seventeen* magazine launched in the USA
1945   USA drops atom bomb at Hiroshima, Japan
1946   "Britain Can Make It" exhibition
1946   Vespa motor scooter for Piaggio
1947   Le Corbusier Unité d'Habitation low-cost housing apartment building, Marseilles,
1947   Indian independence declared
1947   Dior pioneers "New Look" for fashion
         First Levittown in Hempstead, New York 1947–1951
1948   Postwar Milan Triennale exhibitions begin
1948   Gandhi assassinated
1948   Marshall Plan
1949   Mao Tse Tung proclaims People's Republic of China
         Number of television sets in USA rises from 2 million to 41 million 1949–1957
1950   Low-Cost Furniture exhibition at MoMA
1950   Good Design exhibitions at MoMA
1951   Color television introduced in USA
1953   Hochschule für Gestaltung opens in Ulm, Germany
1954   first nuclear power reactor
1955   Disneyland opens in California
1957–1958
         Guggenheim Museum built by Frank Lloyd Wright
1958   Brussels World's Fair
1958   USA establishes National Aeronautics and Space Administration (NASA)
1959   American National Exhibition (featuring kitchen debate) in Moscow
1959   USSR reaches moon with rocket with two monkeys aboard

1961–1980

1960s Popularity of the Beatles and British rock 'n' roll
1961 Reyner Banham's *Architecture and Theory in the First Machine Age*
1961 Jacobs's *Death and Life of American Cities*
1961 Berlin Wall constructed
1962 Pop Art exhibition, Sidney Janis Gallery, New York
1962 audio cassette invented
1963 Betty Friedan's *The Feminine Mystique*
1964 Terence Conran's Habitat store opens in London
1964 graphics for Tokyo Olympic Games by Yoshiro Yamashita
1964 New York World's Fair
1967 Montreal Expo 67 World's Fair
1967 Arab–Israeli 6-day war
1968 Hochschule für Gestaltung at Ulm closed
1968 Superstudio and Archizoom groups founded in Italy
1968 assassination of Martin Luther King, Jr.
1968 student protests and riots in Paris, Italy, and elsewhere in Europe
1969 US manned landing on moon (Apollo 11)
1969 Woodstock Rock Music Festival opens with over 300,000 in attendance
1970 World's Fair in Osaka, Japan
1971 Victor Papanek's *Design for the Real World*
1971 videocassette recorder (VCR) commercially marketed
1971 tabletop microwave ovens
1972 design group Pentagram formed in London
1972 Italy: The New Domestic Landscape exhibition at MoMA
1972 Robert Venturi et al.'s *Learning from Las Vegas*
1973 Cuisinart food processor
1975 death of Spanish dictator Francisco Franco popularity of Japanese cars in USA with launch of Honda Civic and Accord mid 1970s
1979 Ergonommi Group founded in Sweden
1979 cellular phones introduced

1981–2000

1981 Memphis Design Group formed in Milan
1981 Music Television (MTV) debuts
1982 journal *Emigre* begins publication
1983 Design Since 1945 exhibition at Philadelphia Museum of Art
1984 CD ROM invented
1986 Design Now exhibition in Frankfurt, Germany
1986 25,000 AIDS cases reported in USA
1987 Black Monday stock market crash
1989 Design Museum London opens
1989 prototypes for Photoshop software tested by Adobe Systems

1989 World Wide Web Internet Protocol created
1989 Berlin Wall demolished
1991 Rick Poynor's *Typography Now: The Next Wave* (book on computer graphics) collapse of Communist regime in USSR 1985–1991
1993 EU formed
1993 "Don't Ask, Don't Tell" policy adopted by US armed forces with regard to homosexuality among service persons
1997 178 nations agree to Kyoto protocol for climate control against global warming
1998 Michael Graves's Whistling Tea Kettle and other products for Target
1998 Google launched
2000 SmartCar debuts
2000 "Rebirth of Design" featured in *Time*
2000 reality TV shows become popular

Twenty-first century
2001–2010

2001 Human genome sequenced
2001 destruction of World Trade Center in New York
2001 Toyota Prius hybrid car introduced worldwide (in Japan 1997)
2001 Apple iPod introduced, subsequent versions (mutations) introduced 2003–2005, 206 million sold by 2008
2002 Skin, Surface, Substance, and Design exhibition at Cooper-Hewitt Museum
2003 invasion of Iraq by US and coalition armies
2004 social networking website Facebook launched
2005 Safe: Design Takes on Risks exhibition at MoMA
2005 YouTube launched
2005 Guitar Hero video game released
2006–2007 Design Life Now national design triennial at Cooper Hewitt Museum in New York
2007 Amazon's Kindle digital reader debuts
2007 Apple iPhone introduced
2008 Design and the Elastic Mind exhibition at MoMA
2008 China Now exhibition of contemporary Chinese design at Victoria and Albert Museum worldwide credit and economic crisis begins late 2008
2008 China conducts first spacewalk
2008 Hewlett Packard introduces eco-friendly reusable packaging to return used printer cartridges
2008 Barack Obama elected US President
2010 Apple iPad introduced

Suggestions for Further Reading

The following sources provide a starting point for further investigation of many of the topics treated in the 2nd edition of *History of Modern Design*. Students may also browse the full bibliography beginning on page 416, including sections for dictionaries and encyclopedias of design as well as source material anthologies. The Internet also is an increasingly valuable search tool for locating examples of design, particularly via museum websites that often contain photographs and accurate descriptions of holdings and exhibitions. Another resource for information are the art/design/antique sections of newspapers, especially in their weekend or Sunday editions; these often comment upon trends in design, report on current exhibitions and auctions, or present reviews of products, particularly electronic products.

Introduction and Part I: Demand, Supply, and Design (1700–1800)

State-owned manufactures form part of the introduction to John Heskett, *Industrial Design* (1980), and are treated, along with guilds, specialization, and the typology of furniture in the 18th century, in Edward Lucie-Smith, *The Story of Craft: The Craftsman's Role in Society* (1981). The illustrations from Denis Diderot and Jean le Rond d'Alembert, *Encyclopédie* have also been published in facsimile (1978). For furniture in particular, see Alexandre Pradère, *French Furniture Makers: The Art of the Ébéniste from Louis XIV to the Revolution* (1989). On Gobelins tapestries, see Roger-Armand Weigert, *French Tapestry* (1962). The role of the *marchand mercier* is documented in an excellent study by Carolyn Sargentson, *Merchants and Luxury Markets: The Marchands Merciers of 18th-Century Paris* (1996). Entries on individual craft masters, manufactures, and furniture types for all periods, are found in Hugh Honour and John Fleming, *The Penguin Dictionary of Decorative Arts* (rev. edition 1989); for materials and techniques see Lucy Trench, *Materials and Techniques in the Decorative Arts: An Illustrated Dictionary* (2000). On the Sèvres manufactory, see Svend Eriksen and Geoffrey de Bellaigue, *Vincennes and Sèvres 1740–1800* (1987). For revolutionary and post-revolutionary furniture, see Denise Ledoux-Lebard, *Les Ébénistes du XIXe Siecle 1795–1889: leurs oeuvres et leurs marques* (1965).

Although its introduction may be less suitable for undergraduates, Leora Auslander's *Taste and Power: Furnishing Modern France* (1996) is an excellent study of furniture in relation to the competing interests of the monarchy, guilds, and aristocracy. For fashion, see Aileen Ribeiro, *Dress in 18th-Century Europe, 1715–1789* (2002) and Caroline Weber's informative and entertaining *Queen of Fashion: What Marie Antoinette Wore to the Revolution* (2006).

For 18th-century typography, see Meggs and Purvis, *Meggs' History of Graphic Design* (2006). Daniel Berkeley Updike's *Printing Types. Their History, Forms, and Use* (1962, first publ. 1927) still provides useful analyses of printers and typefaces. Students may also consult the facsimile of the *Manuale tipografico del cavaliere Giambattista Bodoni, Parma, Presso la vedova, 1818* (1960). There are several histories of printing that cover 18th-century developments, including Chappell and Bringhurst, Febvre, and others listed in the bibliography.

For England, see Michael Snodin and John Styles's *Design & the Decorative Arts: Britain 1500–1900* (2001), an outstanding accompaniment to the reinstallation of the British galleries in London's Victoria and Albert Museum. The dynamic interplay between production and consumption is the subject of Neil McKendrick, John Brewer, and J. H. Plumb, *The Birth of a Consumer Society: The Commercialization of 18th-Century England* (1985), as well as Ann Bermingham and John Brewer, *The Consumption of Culture 1600–1800: Image, Object, Text* (1995). See also Adrian Forty's case study of Wedgwood in *Objects of Desire: Design and Society Since 1750* (1986).

For Chippendale, see *The Gentlemen and Cabinet-maker's Director* (1966) and Christopher Gilbert, *The Life and Work of Thomas Chippendale* (two vols., 1978). The furniture and interiors of Robert Adam are the subject of Eileen Harris *The Genius of Robert Adam: His Interiors* (2001). For fashion, once again, see Ribeiro (2002).

Part II: Expansion and Taste (1800–1865)

An overview of technological progress, reform, and social change in the early 19th century is found in Paul Johnson, *The Birth of the Modern: World Society 1815–1830* (1991). The World's Fairs material cited below and catalogues of those exhibitions are useful in providing an overview of the explosion of manufacturing in the early 19th century; for England in particular, see Snodin and Styles, cited above.

For the history of printing technology, including lithography, see Michael Twyman in *An Illustrated History of its Development and Uses in England* (1970), while the standard work on the expansion of Victorian typography remains Nicolete Gray, *Nineteenth Century Ornamented Typefaces* (1976, first publ. 1938). For an informative survey of wallpaper design, see Brenda Greysmith, *Wallpaper* (1976). For the United States, see Jeffrey Meikle, *Design in USA* (2005). David Hounshell's *From the American System to Mass Production 1800–1932: the Development of Manufacturing Technology in the United States* (1984) is indispensable for an understanding of the history of manufacturing. Students should also consult Regina Blaszczyk, *Imaging Consumers: Design and Innovation from Wedgwood to Corning* (2000) for design in relation to everyday household items in ceramics and glass for this period.

The career and oeuvre of Augustus Pugin are the subject of *Pugin: a Gothic Passion* (1994). for the Gothic Revival more generally, see Michael J. Lewis, *The Gothic Revival* (2002). Examples of Gothic Revival furniture are also illustrated in Charlotte Gere and Michael Whiteway, *Nineteenth Century Design from Pugin to Mackintosh* (1994) and in Snodin and Styles (2001). Owen Jones's *Grammar of Ornament* (1856) is accessible online as well as in numerous reprints, for instance by Dover (1991), along with Charles Eastlake's *Hints on Household Taste* (1969, first publ. in 1868).

For popular imagery and reform see Patricia Anderson, *The Printed Image and the Transformation of Popular Culture 1790–1860* (1991). I am not aware of a monograph devoted to Sir Henry Cole, but the Great Exhibition of 1851 is the subject of Thomas Richards' *The Commodity Culture of Victorian England: Advertising and Spectacle* (1991) and more recently Jeffrey Auerbach, *The Great Exhibition of 1851* (1999). For the British Schools of Design see Quentin Bell, *The Schools of Design* (1963). The *Crystal Palace Exhibition Illustrated Catalogue* appears as a reprint (1970), and for general background to the world's fairs see Greenhalgh's *Ephemeral Vistas: The Expositions Universelles, Great Exhibitions and World's Fairs, 1851–1939* (1988). Examples of Richard Redgrave's paintings form part of the Sheepshank collection at the Victoria and Albert Museum, and the collection is discussed in an excellent study by Dianne Sachko Macleod, *Art and the Victorian Middle Class: Money and the Making of Cultural Identity* (1996). For Charles Dickens's *Hard Times* as a gauge of public reaction to design reform, see Ernst Gombrich, *Sense of Order: A Study of the Psychology of Decorative Art* (1979). On illustration and book printing see Ruari McLean, *Victorian Book Design* (1963), while once again Twyman (1970), Meggs and Purvis (2006), as well as the more recent surveys of Eskilson (2007) and Drucker and McVarish (2008) treat the development of chromolithography.

The two standard books on Thomas Nast are Morton Keller, *The Art and Politics of Thomas Nast* (1968) and Albert B. Paine, *Thomas Nast, his Period and his Pictures* (1904). For Louis Prang, several examples are illustrated in Peter Marzio, *Chromolithography 1840–1900. The Democratic Art. Pictures for a 19th-Century America* (1979). Popular graphics in the form of trade cards and early posters are also treated in Meggs and Purvis (2006) and in the more recent surveys mentioned above.

Part III: Arts, Crafts, and Machines – Industrialization: Hopes and Fears (1865–1914)

For the Arts and Crafts Movement in England, see Gillian Naylor, *The Arts and Crafts Movement* (1980) and Isabelle Anscombe and Charlotte Gere, *Arts and Crafts in Britain and America* (1978). In addition to monographs on individual designers (Morris, Mackmurdo, Ashbee, and others), there are several recent catalogues, including Wendy Kaplan, *The Arts and Crafts Movement in Europe & America* (2004), ibid., *The Art That is Life: The Arts and Crafts Movement in America, 1875–1920* (1987), Janet Kardon (ed.), *The Ideal Home 1900–1920* (1993) and Linda Parry (ed.), *William Morris* (1996). Gustav Stickley publications, including furniture catalogues compiled from *The Craftsman*, have been reprinted by Dover Publications (for example, Victor M. Linoff, ed., 1991), while Elbert Hubbard's Roycroft community was the subject of Marie Via and Marjorie Searl, *Head, Heart and Hand: Elbert Hubbard and the Roycrofters* (1994). In addition to Tim Hilton's 2-volume biography, *John Ruskin* (1995–2000), there are a few useful paperback anthologies of writings by both Ruskin and Morris, including *William Morris: News from Nowhere and Other Writings* (ed. Clive Wilmer 1993), and *John Ruskin: Selected Writings* (1991).

William Morris's printing venture is the subject of William Peterson, *The Kelmscott Press: A History of William Morris, Typographical Adventure* (1991); for the Private Press movement generally see Colin Franklin, *The Private Presses* (1969), and a number of sensitive essays in Alexander Lawson, *Anatomy of a Typeface* (1990). For printing technology (monotype, linotype, half-tone) see Purvis and Meggs (2006), Twyman (1970), as well as the newer graphic design history surveys listed above.

For Christopher Dresser, see Stuart Durant, *Christopher Dresser* (1993) and Michael Whiteway, *Christopher Dresser: 1834–1904* (2001). Two of Dresser's books have also been reprinted, *Principles of Victorian Decorative Design* (1995) and *Traditional Arts and Crafts of Japan* (1994). For the Aesthetic Movement, see Charlotte Gere and Michael Whiteway, *19th Century Design from Pugin to Mackintosh* (1994) and Charlotte Gere, *The House Beautiful: Oscar Wilde and the Aesthetic Interior* (2000).

Among the most comprehensive sources for the centers of Art Nouveau is *Art Nouveau 1890–1914* (2000, ed. Paul Greenhalgh), based upon the exhibition at the Victoria and Albert Museum in London. It also contains extensive additional bibliography.

For the broad topic of Japanese influence in Western art in the 19th and 20th centuries see Siegfried Wichmann, *Japonisme: Japanese Influence on Western Art since 1858* (1981) as well as Gombrich (1979) and Gere (2000). More recently on this topic in relation to France, see Gabriel Weisberg, *The Origins of l'Art Nouveau: the Bing Empire* (2004).

For Lafarge and Tiffany in the context of the Aesthetic Movement, see Doreen Bolger Burke, *In Pursuit of Beauty:*

Americans and the Aesthetic Movement (1986). The subject of women and craft production in the United States is also treated in Bolger Burke (1986), while the political, economic, and social context for women's domestic roles during the 19th and 20th centuries is the subject of Dolores Hayden, *The Grand Domestic Revolution: A History of Feminist Design for American Homes, Neighborhoods, and Cities* (1981). The broader role of women in the decorative arts and design is the subject of Pat Kirkham (ed.), *Women Designers in the USA, 1900–2000: Diversity and Difference* (2000).

On Charles Frederick Worth, see Edith Saunders, *The Age of Worth: Couturier to the Empress Eugénie* (1955) and Diana de Marly, *Worth: Father of Haute Couture* (1990). Students may also appreciate the plates illustrating luxury fashions in Gary Tinterow and Philip Conisbee (eds.), *Portraits by Ingres. Image of an Epoch* (1999) and Aileen Ribeiro, *Ingres in Fashion: Representations of Dress and Appearance in Ingres's Images of Women* (1999). On the early history of the department store, see Michael Miller, *The Bon Marché: Bourgeois Culture and the Department Store, 1869–1920* (1981).

On the political and social context for Art Nouveau in France, see Debora Silverman, *Art Nouveau in Fin-de-Siècle France: Politics, Psychology, and Style* (1989). On French painters working as muralists and in graphic media see Gloria Groom (ed.), *Beyond the Easel: Decorative Painting by Bonnard, Vuillard, Denis, and Roussel 1890–1930* (2001). Posters are treated in a section ("The Age of Paper") in Greenhalgh (ed.), *Art Nouveau 1890–1914* (2000) and in monographs of individual artists listed in the bibliography.

The career of Charles Rennie Mackintosh is outlined in the context of industrialization and urbanization in Scotland in David Brett, *C. R. Mackintosh: The Poetics of Workmanship* (1992), while his oeuvre is more comprehensively presented in Wendy Kaplan (ed.), *Charles Rennie Mackintosh* (1996). For Austria and the Wiener Werkstätte, see Werner Schweiger, *Wiener Werkstätte, Design in Vienna 1903–1932* (1984).

Henry van de Velde is the subject of a monograph by Klaus-Jurgen Sembach (1989), and the Belgian contribution to late 19th-century design is treated in surveys of Art Nouveau such as Greenhalgh (ed.) (2000) and Fahr-Becker (1997). For Jugendstil in Munich the standard treatment is Kathryn Hiesinger (ed.), *Art Nouveau in Munich: Masters of Jugendstil from the Stadtmuseum, Munich and other Public and Private Collections* (1988) as well as the surveys of Art Nouveau cited above.

Sections on Art Nouveau in Scandinavia and Italy also are contained in the Art Nouveau surveys: Greenhalgh (ed.) (2000), Escritt (2000), and Fahr-Becker (1998). Art Nouveau ceramics in Hungary are the subject of Csenkey and Steinert (eds.), *Hungarian Ceramics from the Zsolnay Manufactory, 1853–2001* (2002), while glass from Eastern Europe in the early 20th century is the focus of *Glass of the Avant-Garde: The Torsten Bröhan Collection from the Museo Nacional de Artes Decorativas* (2001). On Barcelona in this period see William Robinson, et al., *Barcelona and Modernity* (2006).

Frank Lloyd Wright's contributions to design are discussed by Heskett (1980) as well as in Alan Crawford, *C. R. Ashbee: Architect, Designer, and Romantic Socialist* (1985). For illustrations of Wright interiors with furniture, see Thomas A. Heinz, *Frank Lloyd Wright Interiors and Furniture* (1994). Again, Greenhalgh (ed.), *Art Nouveau* (2000) devotes a section to Chicago that includes a wider range of Chicago designers, many well represented in the permanent collection of the Art Institute of Chicago. Mechanized production is treated by Peter Ling in *America and the Automobile: Technology, Reform and Social Change 1893–1923* (1990), David Hounshell (1984), and the first chapter of Terry Smith, *Making the Modern: Industry, Art, and Design in America* (1993). Scientific management has been the subject of several studies, including Robert Kanigel, *One Best Way: Frederick Winslow Taylor and the Enigma of Efficiency* (1997). My first encounter with Taylor was in Spiro Kostof, *America by Design* (1987); Taylor's own *Principles of Scientific Management* (1911) has also been reprinted in numerous editions.

For Germany, a basic source is John Heskett, *German Design 1870–1918* (1986), while the history of the AEG during this period is the subject of Tilmann Buddensieg, *Industriekultur: Peter Behrens and the AEG, 1907–1914* (1984). For the Werkbund see Joan Campbell, *The German Werkbund: The Politics of Reform in the Applied Arts* (1978); Lucius Burckhardt (ed.), *The Werkbund: History and Ideology 1907–1933* (1980, first publ. 1977); and Frederic J. Schwartz, *The Werkbund: Design Theory and Mass Culture before the First World War* (1996).

PART IV: AFTER WORLD WAR I: ART, INDUSTRY, AND UTOPIAS (1918–1944)

Barbara Tuchman, *The Guns of August* (1962) introduces the events precipitating the war and the disparity among ideologies, rhetoric, and the realities of warfare in the new century. More comprehensive is Paul Fussell, *The Great War and Modern Memory* (1975). The reactions of avant-garde artists to World War I are the subject of a chapter ("The Faces of Power") in Robert Hughes, *The Shock of the New* (1982) and a more nuanced study by Kenneth Silver, *Esprit de Corps: the Art of the Parisian Avant-Garde and the First World War, 1914–1925* (1989). Dan Silverman, *Reconstructing Europe After the Great War* (1982), presents an economic view of the aftermath of World War I. On posters from World War I, see Richard Hollis's overview in *Graphic Design: a Concise History* (2001).

On Paris and Art Moderne, see foremost Nancy J. Troy, *Modernism and the Decorative Arts in France: Art Nouveau to Le Corbusier* (1991). An early introduction to Art Moderne (Deco) is Bevis Hillier, *Art Deco of the 20s and 30s* (1968). More recent and comprehensive is Tim Benton, et al., *Art Deco 1910–1939* (2003), based upon the Victoria and Albert Museum exhibition of that year. Entries on individual designers appear in Honour and Fleming, *Penguin Dictionary of the Decorative Arts* (1989) as well as other general works and monographs cited in the bibliography.

On the Ballets Russes see Lynn Garafola, *Diaghilev, Ballets Russes* (1989). For illustrations of costumes and sets see Militsa Pozharskaya and Tatiana Volodina, *The Art of the Ballets Russes: The Russian Seasons in Paris 1908–1929* (1990). Poiret's patronage of modern art and its reception after the outbreak of World War I is explored in Silver (1989). Also on Poiret see Alice Mackrell, *Paul Poiret* (1990) and Nancy J. Troy, *Couture Culture: a Study in Modern Art and Fashion* (2003).

For Le Corbusier, see Troy (1991); the Paris Exposition is the subject of Tag Gronberg, *Designs on Modernity: Exhibiting the City in 1920s Paris* (1998) and is also treated extensively in Benton, et al. (2003). Several examples of modern chairs and other furniture in metal from the 1920s are described and illustrated in Alexander von Vegesack et al. (eds.), *Masterpieces of Furniture from the Vitra Design Museum Collection* (1996). Von Vegesack is also the author of *Jean Prouvé: the Poetics of Technical Objects* (2005).

For 20th-century Modernism, see Christopher Wilk, *Modernism: Designing a New World 1914–1939* (2006), based upon the comprehensive exhibition at the Victoria and Albert Museum. A thought-provoking account of innovation in modern typography in the context of avant-garde visual art, poetry, and semiotics is Joanna Drucker, *The Visible Word: Experimental Typography and Modern Art, 1909–1923* (1994). On Futurism and graphic design, see Alan Bartram, *Futurist Typography and the Liberated Text* (2006) and *DeperoFuturista: Rome-Paris-New York and more* (1999) from the exhibition at the Wolfsonian Museum.

For De Stijl, see Paul Overy, *De Stijl* (1991) as well as Nancy J. Troy, *The De Stijl Environment* (1983), the latter with useful comparisons and variations among the movements of the "first machine age" in Europe. Also on De Stijl see Hans Ludwig Jaffé, *De Stijl 1917–1931: The Dutch Contribution to Modern Art* (1986). On Weissenhof, the standard survey is Richard Pommer and Christian F. Otto, *Weissenhof 1927 and the Modern Movement in Architecture* (1991).

For Constructivism, see Christine Lodder, *Russian Constructivism* (1983). For encyclopedic visual material on this movement as well as several critical essays, see *The Great Utopia. The Russian and Soviet Avant-Garde, 1915–1932* (1992). Constructivism in graphic design in Russia, and related developments in Europe, are also treated in Meggs and Purvis (2006), Hollis, and others.

Frank Whitford's *Bauhaus* (1984) is a good introduction to the school, while Gillian Naylor presents an excellent assessment of its shifting and competing ideologies in *The Bauhaus Reassessed: Sources and Design Theory* (1985). A good source for documents and illustrations is Hans M. Wingler, *The Bauhaus: Weimar, Dessau, Berlin, Chicago* (1969), while the textile workshop is the subject of Sigrid W. Weltge, *Women, Work: Textile Art from the Bauhaus* (1993). Studies of individual students and faculty are cited in the Part IV bibliography.

For German graphic design not directly related to the Bauhaus, see Jeremy Aynsley, *Graphic Design in Germany 1890–1945* (2000). The career and contributions of Jan Tschichold are the subject of a monograph by Ruari McLean (1975), Christopher Burke's *Active Literature: Jan Tschichold and New Typography* (2007), and Tschichold's own *The New Typography: A Handbook for Modern Designers* (1995). The Frankfurt Kitchen is discussed by Heskett (1980), Woodham, *20th Century Design* (1997), and Wilk (2006).

For British design in the interwar period, see James Peto and Donna Loveday (eds.), *Modern Britain 1929–1939* (1999). Typography is treated by Twyman (1970), while Frank Pick is the subject of a chapter in *Forty* (1986) and an article by Nicholas Pevsner, *Studies in Art, Architecture and Design: Victorian and After* (1968). For Scandinavia, see Eileen Beer, *Scandinavian Design* (1971) and David McFadden (ed.), *Scandinavian Modern Design 1880–1980* (1982). The works of several Scandinavian designers are illustrated and discussed by Kathryn Hiesinger and George Marcus in *Landmarks of 20th Century Design: An Illustrated Handbook* (1993). For Alvar Aalto, see Peter Reed, *Alvar Aalto: Between Humanism and Materialism* (1998).

There are several well-illustrated sources for the study of American design in the interwar period, including Alastair Duncan, *American Art Deco* (1986). Craft aspects are treated in Janet Kardon (ed.), *Craft in the Machine Age 1920–1945* (1995), while a combination of craft and industrial design is illustrated in Stewart J. Johnson, *American Modern: 1925–1940 – Design for a New Age* (2000). On Elsie de Wolfe, see Penny Sparke, *Elsie de Wolfe: the Birth of Modern Interior Decoration* (2005). Industrial design is the focus of Jeffrey Meikle's illuminating *20th Century Limited: Industrial Design in America, 1925–1939* (rev. edition 2001, first publ. 1979), with a chapter on the 1939 New York World's Fair. The same author's *Design in the USA* (2005) also gives an excellent account of this material. Monographs on industrial designers such as Henry Dreyfuss and Raymond Loewy are listed in the bibliography, while the careers of several interwar modern graphic designers are the subject of Roger R. Remington and Barbara J. Hodik, *Nine Pioneers in American Graphic Design* (1989). The relationship between fine art and illustration is thoughtfully explored by Michele H. Bogart, *Advertising, Artists, and the Borders of Art* (1995), while advertising is the subject of Roland Marchand, *Advertising the American Dream: Making Way for Modernity 1920–1940* (1985) and Richard Wightman Fox and T. J. Jackson Lears (eds.), *The Culture of Consumption: Critical Essays in American History 1880–1980* (1983). Industrial technology, labor, art, advertising, public relations, and corporate strategies are combined in a study of modernity with a focus on the Ford Corporation by Terry Smith mentioned above (1993). The history of the Herman Miller Corporation is the subject of a monograph by Ralph Caplan (1976), and an introduction and several entries on austerity in design during World War II are provided by Hiesinger and Marcus (1993). On the use of aluminum in design see Sarah Nichols, et al., *Aluminum by Design* (2000), while for the reception of Modernism in the domestic interior in the 1930s see Kristina Wilson, *Livable Modernism: Interior Decorating and*

Design during the Great Depression (2004). On Fiestaware and other developments in the glassware and ceramics industries in the United States see Blaszczyk, *Imagining Consumers* (2000).

Part V: Humanism and Luxury: International Modernism and Mass Culture after World War II (1945–1960)

Many of the products of "good design" appear in Kathryn Hiesinger and George Marcus, *Design Since 1945* (1983). See also by the same authors *Landmarks of 20th Century Design: An Illustrated Handbook* (1993). The topic of "good design" is also presented by Peter Dormer, *Design Since 1945* (1993), and by Martin Eidelberg, *Design 1935–1965: What Modern Was: Selections from the Liliane and David M. Stewart Collection* (1991). There are several company histories and monographs on individual designers, among them Charles and Ray Eames, Henry Dreyfuss, Russel Wright, George Nelson, Cipe Pineles, Herman Miller, Knoll, Philips, and Sony Corporation, all listed in the bibliography.

For graphic design, including scientific illustration in this era, see Remington and Hodik (1989) and more recently Remington's *American Modernism: Graphic Design 1920–1960* (2003). Sections in Meggs and Purvis (2006) and other graphic design surveys also treat this material, as well as Ellen Lupton (1999).

Examples of Scandinavian furniture are amply illustrated in Hiesinger and Marcus (1982 and 1993) and are the subject of Eileen Beer (1971), and McFadden (1980), both cited above, as well as the catalogue of the Alvar Aalto Show at MoMA (Reed, 1998). For Britain, see *Austerity to Affluence: British Art & Design 1945–1962* (1997) and Anne Massey, *Modernism and Mass Culture in Britain 1945–1959* (1995). For Italy a good source is Penny Sparke, *Design in Italy: 1870 to the Present* (1988) as well as entries in Hiesinger and Marcus (1983 and 1993). For Germany see Michael Erloff (ed.), *Designed in Germany Since 1949* (1990). On the design school at Ulm, see the relevant section in Woodham (1997) and Herbert Lindinger, *Ulm Design: the Morality of Objects* (1991, first publ. in German, 1987).

On the International Typographic Style, see Richard Hollis, *Swiss Graphic Design: the Origins and Growth of an International Style 1920–1960* as well as books and manuals by the practitioners themselves, including Armin Hofmann, *Graphic Design Manual: Principles and Practice* (1965), Karl Gerstner, *The New Graphic Art. Le nouvel art graphique* (1959), and Josef Müller-Brockmann, *A History of Visual Communications: From the Dawn of Barter in the Ancient World to the Visualized Conception of Today* (1971). While graphic design comprises only a very small part of the literature on semiotics, students may consult the introduction and conclusion in Joanna Drucker (1994), and two contributions by Ulm graduate Gui Bonsiepe, reprinted in Michael Bierut, Jessica Helfand, et al. (eds.), *Looking Closer 3: Classic Writings on Graphic Design* (1999).

For Buckminster Fuller, see his *Utopia or Oblivion: the Prospects for Humanity* (1969) and for Richard Neutra, see his *Survival Through Design* (1954). For postwar Japan see the catalogue for an exhibition at the Philadelphia Museum of Art by Kathryn Hiesinger and Felice Fischer, *Japanese Design: A Survey Since 1950* (1994).

Design and corporate policy are the subject of Wally Olins, *The Corporate Personality: An Inquiry into the Nature of Corporate Identity* (1978), and John and Avril Blake, *The Practical Idealists: Twenty-five Years of Designing for Industry* (1969). Students may also consult relevant chapters in Dormer (1993) and Woodham (1997) with additional bibliography. Studies of design for individual corporations are cited above. For corporate identity and graphic design, see Meggs and Purvis (2006), as well as Hollis (2001), Eskilson (2007), and Drucker and McVarish (2008).

For the economic context of postwar Modernism, see James Sloan Allen, *The Romance of Commerce and Culture: Capitalism, Modernism, and the Chicago-Aspen Crusade for Cultural Reform* (1983), and the essay by Herbert Gans in Hiesinger and Marcus, *Design Since 1945* (1983). For the political context of Modernism on both sides of the Iron Curtain, see the recent important contribution to the field by David Crowley and Jane Pavitt, *Cold War Modern: Design 1945–1970* (2008), from the Victoria and Albert Museum exhibition of that year, with its own extensive bibliography.

For mass culture in the postwar era, students may enjoy David Halberstam, *The Fifties* (1993), and David Riesman, *The Lonely Crowd: A Study of the Changing American Character* (first publ. 1950), documenting the shift in focus from product to reception in American society. For mass design see Thomas Hine, *Populuxe* (1986) while the critical appreciation of the phenomenon forms the basis for articles by Reyner Banham, collected by Penny Sparke in *Reyner Banham: Design by Choice* (1981). For Banham's reconsideration of and objections to the tenets of "good design" see Banham, *Theory and Design in the First Machine Age* (1960). These are also summarized by Sparke (1986) and analyzed more recently by Nigel Whitely, *Reyner Banham: Historian of the Immediate Future* (2002). Students may find useful a collection of essays edited by C. W. E. Bigsby in *Superculture: American Popular Culture and Europe* (1975), as well as John Docker, *Postmodernism and Popular Culture: A Cultural History* (1994). Also useful is Karel Ann Marling, *As Seen on TV: The Visual Culture of Everyday Life in the 1950s* (1994), which includes a chapter on the "New Look" in fashion and its repercussions in middle-class dress. Invectives against mass culture include Vance Packard, *The Hidden Persuaders* (1957), and are also discussed by Penny Sparke (1986). For the role of aluminum in the postwar era, see again Nichols (2000); for plastic see Stephen Fenichell, *Plastic: the Making of a Synthetic Century* (1997), and Jeffrey Meikle, *American Plastic: a Cultural History* (1995).

For fashion design, students may find useful essays contained in Amy de la Haye and Elizabeth Wilson (eds.), *Defining Dress: Dress as Object, Meaning, and Identity* (1999), and Juliet Ash and Elizabeth Wilson (eds.), *Chic Thrills: A Fashion Reader* (1993). Fashion designers are listed in a number of encyclopedias and surveys, including Richard Martin, *Fashion Encyclopedia: A Survey of Style from 1945 to the Present* (1996). See also Douglas Russell, *Costume, History and Style* (1983). A recent chronological treatment is Aileen Ribeiro, *The Gallery of Fashion* (2000).

Part VI: Progress, Protest, and Pluralism (1960–2010)

Hiesinger and Marcus (1983) remains a reliable source for international modernism in the 1960s and 1970s; see also Dormer (1993) and Hiesinger and Fischer (1994), along with Philippe Garner, *Sixties Design* (1996), and Lesley Jackson, *The Sixties: Decade of Design Revolution* (1998), Caplan (1976), *Knoll Design* (1981), Sparke (1988), Fenichell (1997), Meikle (1995), and Nichols (2000).

For graphic design see relevant chapters in Meggs and Purvis (2006), as well as the newer graphic design surveys and Erlhoff, *Designed in Germany Since 1949* (1990). Individual designers are featured in monographs that present an overview of their activity. These include *Vignelli – Design* (1981), Gertrude Snyder and Alan Peckolik, *Herb Lubalin: Art Director, Graphic Designer and Typographer* (1985), and Milton Glaser, *Milton Glaser – Graphic Design* (1983). Also see Steven Heller and Paul Scher, *Seymour: the Obsessive Images of Seymour Chwast* (2009). Examples of the persistence of craft in this period are found in Hiesinger and Marcus (1983), and in Margot Coatts (ed.), *Pioneers of Modern Craft* (1997).

The literature on ergonomics and anthropometrics is extensive and often specialized, of interest both to historians as well as practitioners. Students can, however, examine the diagrams in Henry Dreyfuss, *The Measure of Man: Human Factors in Design* (rev. edition 1960), as well as in Alexander Kira, *The Bathroom* (1976). Students might also consult essays on the practice of design from a number of different perspectives in Richard Buchanan and Victor Margolin (eds.), *Design: Explorations in Design Studies* (1995). The critical appreciation of design for mass culture is found in Robert Venturi, Denise Scott Brown, and Steven Izenour, *Leaving Las Vegas* (1998, first publ. 1972) and is considered as well in John Docker (1994).

The theme of protest and art is among the topics discussed by Thomas Crow in *The Rise of the Sixties: American and European Art in the Era of Dissent* (1996), while a broad social and political study of the decade is Arthur Marwick, *The Sixties: Cultural Revolution in Britain, France, Italy, and the United States c. 1958–c. 1974* (1998). For oppositional tendencies in Italian design in the 1960s see Sparke (1988) and Emilio Ambasz in *Italy: The New Domestic Landscape: Achievements and Problems of Italian Design* (1972). On this topic see also Andreas Huyssen, *After the Great Divide: Modernism, Mass Culture, Postmodernism* (1985). For graphic design in relation to protest, see relevant pages in Meggs and Purvis (2006), Eskilson (2007), and Drucker and McVarish (2008).

Ralph Nader's efforts on behalf of consumers and against the automobile industry in the 1960s are the subject of Thomas Whiteside, *The Investigation of Ralph Nader: General Motors vs. One Determined Man* (1972). Students may still consult Nader, *Unsafe at any Speed: the Designed-in Dangers of the American Automobile* (1965), while Victor Papanek, *Design for the Real World: Making to Measure* (1972) also remains worthwhile reading. Papanek's views are also the starting point for Nigel Whiteley, *Design for Society* (1993), presenting arguments for socially and environmentally responsible design.

The broad issues of pluralism, late capitalism, and post-industrialism that form the basis for the presentation of Postmodernism in this book are treated in numerous studies in a variety of disciplines that include but are not limited to art and design history. The consumer underpinnings of Postmodern design are characterized clearly by Whitely (1993) as a foil for alternative approaches to design. Consumption is the subject of several books by sociologists, economists, and anthropologists that include Mary Douglas and Baron Isherwood, *The World of Goods: Towards an Anthropology of Consumption* (1996, first publ. 1979) and Daniel Miller, *Material Culture and Mass Consumption* (1987). Since some of these studies take as their starting point a Marxist economic model and make use of its vocabulary, one might note Karl Marx and Frederick Engels, *Capital*, volume I (1996, first publ. 1867) for the meaning of terms like "exchange," "use value," and "commodity fetishism." The wider meanings of consumption in relation to products and especially to advertising, popular entertainment, and fashion also form the basis of studies by French scholars Jean Baudrillard, *The System of Objects* (1996, first publ. 1968) and Roland Barthes, *Mythologies* (1972, first publ. 1957). On post-industrialism see Daniel Bell, *The Coming of Post-Industrial Society: An Adventure in Social Forecasting* (1999, first publ. 1973).

For an introduction to the critique of Postmodernism, see also Fredric Jameson, *Postmodernism, or the Cultural Logic of Late Capitalism* (1991). Postmodern perspectives on design, involving materials technology and including "Soft Design" form the basis of seminal essays in John Thackara (ed.), *Design After Modernism: Beyond the Object* (1988). Several of these issues are also treated in collections of essays edited by Victor Margolin, *Design Discourse: History-Theory-Criticism* (1989), and by the same author in collaboration with Richard Buchanan, *The Idea of Design: A Design Issues Reader* (1995). The expansion of design more generally to the field of information and artificial intelligence is found in Herbert Simon's *Sciences of the Artificial* (first publ. 1969 but available in numerous subsequent editions), and Klaus Krippendorf, *The Semantic Turn* (2006). At a more everyday level as an approach to design focusing upon information and mapping in products and systems, see Donald Norman, *The Design of Everyday Things* (1988), as well as more recent titles by the same author.

Recent materials technology in relation to products is the focus of Ellen Lupton, *Skin: Surface, Substance, and*

Design (2002). For other more product-oriented surveys of Postmodern design, see Barbara Radice, *Memphis: Research, Experiences, Results, Failures and Successes of New Design* (1984), Michael Collins and Andreas Papadakis, *Post-Modern Design* (1989), and Volker Fischer (ed.), *Design Now: Industry or Art?* (1989). A recent glimpse into design in the new millennium, focusing upon furniture and high-tech gadgets, is provided by Charlotte and Peter Fiell, *Designing the 21st century = Design des 21: Jahrhunderts = Le design du 21e siècle* (2001). Entries and brief biographies on contemporary individual designers may also be found in Honour and Fleming (1989), Byars (1994), Julier (1993), and Hiesinger and Marcus (1983 and 1993).

Also important are several recent exhibitions on contemporary design and their catalogues, including Paola Antonelli, *Safe: Design Takes on Risks* (2005), ibid., *Design and the Elastic Mind* (2008), and Ellen Lupton, et al., *Design Life Now* (2006).

On graphic design and the Punk scene, see Mark Sladen and Ariella Yedgar, *Panic Attack: Art in the Punk Years* (2007), as well as John Wozencroft, *The Graphic Language of Neville Brody* (1988). An industrial aesthetic as applied to architecture and furnishings is the subject of Joan Kron and Suzanne Slesin, *Hi-Tech: The Industrial Style and Source Book for the Home* (1978).

For social and environmental responsibility in design see Whiteley (1993), and Jonathan Porritt, *Seeing Green: the Politics of Ecology Explained* (1985). The literature on contemporary graphic design and interactive graphics is expanding rapidly in response to new software as well as industry and educational demand. For graphic design in the computer age, see Rudy VanderLans, et al., *Emigre (The Book): Graphic Design into the Digital Realm* (1993) and Rick Poynor and Edward Booth-Clibborn (eds.), *Typography Now: the Next Wave* (1994, first publ. 1991). Landmarks in the history of the graphic design profession are documented in bullet-point fashion by Steven Heller and Elinor Pettit, *Graphic Design Timeline: A Century of Design Milestones* (2000).

There are several studies of contemporary craftspeople, such as Donald Kuspit, *Chihuly* (1997), of craft in general, such as Peter Dormer (ed.), *The Culture of Craft: Status and Future* (1997), and David Pye, *The Nature of Design* (1964). Glenn Adamson's *Thinking Through Craft* (2007) is a recent and engaging attempt to describe the nature of craft mostly in relation to craft as it has been treated in the literature of art history with a thorough grasp of the historiography of the subject; new examples of contemporary craft are regularly acquired and exhibited by major museums throughout the world. Many titles devoted to individual artists/ artisans tend to be of the coffee table variety, and the best appreciation is still gained by making time to visit fairs and exhibitions, which often provide an opportunity to interact with the artisans themselves.

Select Bibliography

GENERAL

Albus, Volker, Reyer Kraus, and Jonathan M. Woodham, *Icons of Design: the 20th Century*, Munich and New York, Prestel, 2000

Auslander, Leora, *Taste and Power: Furnishing Modern France*, Berkeley and Los Angeles, University of California Press, 1996

Barthes, Roland, *Mythologies*, selected and translated by Annette Lavers, New York, Hill and Wang, 1972 (first publ. 1957)

Baudrillard, Jean, *The System of Objects*, trans. James Benedict, London and New York, Verso, 1996 (first publ. 1968)

Bayley, Stephen, Philippe Garner, and Deyan Sudjic, *Twentieth Century Style & Design*, London, Thames & Hudson, 1986

Blaszczyk, Regina Lee, *Imagining Consumers: Design and Innovation from Wedgwood to Corning*, Johns Hopkins University Press, 2000

Buchanan, Richard, and Victor Margolin, *Design: Explorations in Design Studies*, Chicago, University of Chicago Press, 1995

Coatts, Margot (ed.), *Pioneers of Modern Craft*, Manchester and New York, Manchester University Press and St. Martin's Press, 1997

Conway, Hazel, *Design History: A Student's Handbook*, London, Allen & Unwin, 1987

Dormer, Peter, *Design Since 1945*, New York and London, Thames & Hudson, 1993

Ibid., *The Meanings of Modern Design: Towards the Twenty-first Century*, London, Thames & Hudson, 1990

Douglas, Mary, and Baron Isherwood, *The World of Goods: Towards an Anthropology of Consumption*, rev. edition, New York, Routledge, 1996 (first publ. 1979)

Fenichell, Stephen, *Plastic: the Making of a Synthetic Century*, New York, HarperBusiness, 1997

Fiell, Charlotte and Peter, *Design of the 20th Century*, Cologne, Taschen, 2000

Forty, Adrian, *Objects of Desire: Design and Society Since 1750*, London, Thames & Hudson, 1986

Ibid., *Words and Buildings: A Vocabulary of Modern Architecture*, London, Thames & Hudson, 2000

Geijer, Agnes, *A History of Textile Art*, London, Sotheby Parke Bernet, 1979

Giedion, S., *Mechanization Takes Command: A Contribution to Anonymous History*, New York, Oxford University Press, 1948

Gombrich, E. H., *The Sense of Order: A Study of the Psychology of Decorative Art*, The Wrightsman Lectures, Ithaca, Cornell Press, 1979

Greenhalgh, Paul, *Ephemeral Vistas: The Expositions Universelles, Great Exhibitions and World's Fairs, 1851–1939*, Manchester University Press, 1988

Greysmith, Brenda, *Wallpaper*, New York, Macmillan, 1976

Heskett, John, *Industrial Design*, New York and Toronto, Oxford University Press, 1980

Ibid., *Toothpicks and Logos: Design in Everyday Life*, Oxford University Press, 2002

Hiesinger, Kathryn B., and Felice Fischer, *Japanese Design: A Survey Since 1950*, Philadelphia Museum of Art, 1994

Hounshell, David A., *From the American System to Mass Production 1800–1932: the Development of Manufacturing Technology in the United States*, Baltimore, Johns Hopkins University Press, 1984

Hughes, Robert, *The Shock of the New*, New York, Alfred A. Knopf, 1982

Kirkham, Pat, (ed.), *Women Designers in the USA 1900–2000: Diversity and Difference*, New Haven, Yale University Press, 2000

Lucie-Smith, Edward, *Furniture: A Concise History*, New York, Oxford University Press, 1979

Marx, Karl, and Frederick Engels, *Capital*, volume I, in *Collected Works*, volume 35, New York, International Publishers, 1996 (first publ. in German, 1867)

(McFadden, David Revere, general ed.), *Scandinavian Modern Design 1880–1980*, New York, Harry N. Abrams, 1982

McKellar, Susie, and Penny Sparke (eds.), *Interior Design and Identity*, Manchester University Press, 2004

Meikle, Jeffrey L., *American Plastic: a Cultural History*, New Brunswick, NJ, Rutgers University Press, 1995

Ibid., *Design in the USA*, Oxford, Oxford University Press, 2005

Nichols, Sarah, et al., *Aluminum by Design*, Pittsburgh, Carnegie Museum of Art, 2000

Pevsner, Nikolaus, *Pioneers of Modern Design*, Harmondsworth, Penguin, 1960

Pye, David, *The Nature of Design*, London, Studio Vista, 1964 (also New York, Reinhold, 1964)

Snodin, Michael, and John Styles (eds.), *Design & the Decorative Arts: Britain 1500–1900*, London, V&A Publications, 2001

Sparke, Penny, *Design in Italy: 1870 to the Present*, New York, Abbeville Press, 1988

Ibid., *An Introduction to Design and Culture in the Twentieth Century*, New York, Harper and Row (Icon Editions), 1986 (paperback)

Von Vegesack, Alexander, Peter Dunes, and Mathias Schwartz-Clauss (eds.), *100 Masterpieces of Furniture from the Vitra Design Museum Collection*, Weil am Rhein, Vitra Design Museum, 1996

Walker, John A., *Design History and the History of Modern Design*, London, Pluto Press, 1989

Woodham, Jonathan M., *Twentieth Century Design*, Oxford and New York, Oxford University Press, 1997

GRAPHIC DESIGN

Armstrong, Helen (ed.), *Graphic Design Theory: Readings from the Field*, Princeton, Princeton Architectural Press, 2009

Aynsley, Jeremy, *Graphic Design in Germany 1890–1945*, Berkeley and Los Angeles, University of California Press, 2000

Bartram, Alan, *Five Hundred Years of Book Design*, New Haven, Conn.: Yale University Press, 2001

Bierut, Michael, et al. (eds.), *Looking Closer: Classic Writings on Graphic Design*, New York, Allworth Press, 1994

Ibid., *Looking Closer 2: Classic Writings on Graphic Design*, New York, Allworth Press, 1997

Ibid., *Looking Closer 3: Classic Writings on Graphic Design*, New York, Allworth Press, 1999

Ibid., *Looking Closer 4: Classic Writings on Graphic Design*, New York, Allworth Press, 2002

Ibid., *Looking Closer 5: Classic Writings on Graphic Design*, New York, Allworth Press, 2007

Chappell, Warren, and Robert Bringhurst, *A Short History of the Printed Word*, 2nd edition, revised and updated, Point Roberts, Washington, 1999 (first publ. 1970)

Drucker, Johanna, and Emily McVarish, *Graphic Design History: A Critical Guide*, Upper Saddle, NJ, Prentice-Hall, 2008

Elam, Kimberly, *Expressive Typography: The Word as Image*, New York, Van Nostrand Reinhold, 1990

Eskilson, Steven, *Graphic Design: A New History*, New Haven, CT, Yale University Press, 2007

Febvre, Lucien, and Henri-Jean Martin, *The Coming of the Book: The Impact of Printing 1450–1800*, trans. David Gerard, London, Verso, 1976 (first publ. 1958)

Heller, Steven, *Merz to Emigre and Beyond: Avant-garde Magazine Design of the Twentieth Ventury*, New York and London, Phaidon, 2003

Heller, Steven, and Georgette Ballance (eds.), *Graphic Design History*, New York, Allworth Press, 2001

Heller, Steven, and Philip B. Meggs, (eds.), *Texts on Type: Critical Writings on Typography*, New York, Allworth Press, 2001

Heller, Steven, and Elinor Pettit, *Graphic Design Timeline: A Century of Design Milestones*, New York, Allworth Press, 2000

Hollis, Richard, *Graphic Design: A Concise History*, London and New York, Thames & Hudson, 2001

Jubert, Roxane, and Serge Lemoine, *Typography and Graphic Design: From Antiquity to the Present*, Paris, Flammarion, 2006

Lawson, Alexander, *Anatomy of A Typeface*, Boston, David R. Godine, 1990

Lupton, Ellen, *Design Writing Research: Writing on Graphic Design*, London and New York, Phaidon, 1999

Meggs, Phillip, and Alston Purvis, *Meggs' History of Graphic Design*, 4th edition, Hoboken, Wiley, 2006

Müller-Brockmann, Josef, *A History of Visual Communications: From the Dawn of Barter in the Ancient World to the Visualized Conception of Today*, Switzerland, Arthur Niggli, Ltd., 1971

Remington, R. Roger, and Barbara J.Hodik, *Nine Pioneers in American Graphic Design*, Cambridge, MA, MIT Press, 1989

Swanson, Gunnar (ed.) *Graphic Design & Reading: Explorations of an Uneasy Relationship*, New York: Allworth Press, 2000

Twyman, Michael, *Printing 1770–1970: An Illustrated History of its Development and Uses in England*, London, Eyre & Spottiswoode, 1970

FASHION DESIGN

Baumgarten, Linda, *What Clothes Reveal*, Yale University Press, 2002

Breward, Chris, and Caroline Evans (eds.), *Fashion and Modernity*, Berg, 2005

Davenport, Millia, *The Book of Costume*, vols. II and III, U.S.A., Crown Publishers, 1948

de la Haye, Amy, and Elizabeth Wilson (eds.), *Defining Dress: Dress as Object, Meaning and Identity*, New York, Manchester University Press, 1999

English, Bonnie E., *A Cultural History of Fashion in the Twentieth Century: From the Catwalk to the Sidewalk*, New York and Oxford, Berg, 2007

Martin, Richard (ed.), *The St. James Fashion Encyclopedia: A Survey of Style from 1945 to the Present*, Detroit, Visible Ink Press, 1996

Russell, Douglas, *Costume History and Style*, Englewood Cliffs, Prentice-Hall, 1983

PRIMARY SOURCE ANTHOLOGIES AND HISTORIOGRAPHY READERS

Benton, T., Benton, C. (eds.), *Architecture and Design: 1890–1939, An International Anthology of Original Articles*, New York, Watson-Guptill, 1975

Doordan, Dennis (ed.), *Design History: an anthology*, Cambridge, MA, MIT Press, 1995

Frank, Isabelle (ed.), *The theory of decorative art: an anthology of European and American writings 1750–1940*, New Haven and London, Yale University Press, 2000

Gorman, Carma R. (ed.), *The Industrial Design Reader*, New York, Allworth Press, 2003

Greenhalgh, Paul (ed.), *Quotations and Sources on Design and the Decorative Arts*, Manchester and New York, Manchester University Press, 1993

Highmore, Ben, *The Design Culture Reader*, London, Routledge, 2008

Lees-Maffei, Grace, and Rebecca Houze, *Design History Reader*, London and New York, Berg, 2010

Margolin, Victor, and Richard Buchanan (eds.), *The Idea of Design: A Design Issues Reader*, Cambridge, MA, and London, MIT Press, 1995

Margolin, Victor (ed.), *Design Discourse: History-Theory-Criticism*, Chicago University Press, 1989

DICTIONARIES AND REFERENCE

Byars, Mel, *The Design Encylopaedia: The Museum of Modern Art*, London, Laurence King Publishing, 2004

Campbell, Gordon, *The Grove Encyclopedia of Decorative Arts*, 2 vols., Oxford, Oxford University Press, 2006

Fleming, John, and Hugh Honour, *The Penguin Dictionary of Decorative Arts*, London, Viking, new edition, 1989

Hiesinger, Kathryn B., and George H. Marcus, *Landmarks of Twentieth Century Design: An Illustrated Handbook*, New York, Abbeville Press, 1993

Jervis, Simon, *The Facts on File Dictionary of Design and Designers*, New York, Facts on File, 1984 (also publ. by Penguin Books, Harmondsworth, 1984)

Julier, Guy, *The Encyclopedia of Twentieth-Century Design and Designers*, New York, Thames & Hudson, 1993

Ibid., *The Thames & Hudson Dictionary of Design since 1900*, London and New York, Thames & Hudson, 2004

McCracken, Penny, *Women Artists and Designers since 1800: An Annotated Bibliography*, 2 vols., New York, G. K. Hall & Company, 1998

Trench, Lucy (ed.), *Materials and Techniques in the Decorative Arts: An Illustrated Dictionary*, Chicago, University of Chicago Press, 2000

Webb, Pauline and Mark Suggitt, *Gadgets and Necessities: an Encyclopedia of Household Innovations*, Santa Barbara, CA, ABC-CLIO, 2000

Woodham, Jonathan, *A Dictionary of Modern Design*, Oxford University Press, 2004

PART I

Bermingham, Ann, and John Brewer, *The Consumption of Culture 1600–1800: Image, Object, Text*, London and New York, Routledge, 1995

Bodoni, Giambattista, *Manuale Tipografico del Cavaliere Giambattista Bodoni, Parma, Presso la Vedova, 1818*, London, Holland Press, 1960

Braudel, Fernand, *Civilization and Capitalism 15th–18th centuries*, 3 vols., trans. Sîan Reynolds, New York, Harper & Row, 1979

Brewer, John, and Roy Porter, *Consumption and the World of Goods*, London and New York, Routledge, 1993

Chippendale, Thomas, *The Gentlemen and Cabinet-maker's Director*, New York, Dover, 1966 (first publ. 1754)

Crow, Thomas E., *Painters and Public Life in Eighteenth-Century Paris*, New Haven and London, Yale University Press, 1985

Darnton, Robert, *The Business of Enlightenment: A Publishing History of the Encyclopédie 1775–1800*, Cambridge, MA, and London, The Belknap Press of Harvard University, 1979

Diderot Encyclopedia: the Complete Illustrations 1762–1777, 5 vols., New York, Harry N. Abrams, 1978

Dolan, Brian, *Josiah Wedgwood: Entrepreneur to the Enlightenment*, HarperCollins, 2004

Eriksen, Svend, and Geoffrey de Bellaigue, *Sèvres Porcelain: Vincennes and Sèvres 1740–1800*, London and Boston, Faber and Faber, 1987

Gilbert, Christopher, *The Life and Work of Thomas Chippendale*, 2 vols., London, Studio Vista, 1978

Harris, Eileen, *The Genius of Robert Adam: his Interiors*, New Haven, Yale University Press, 2001

Holland, Vyvyan, *Hand-Colored Fashion Plates 1770–1899*, London, Batsford, 1955

Honour, Hugh, *Chinoiserie: The Vision of Cathay*, New York, E. P. Dutton, 1962

Lucie-Smith, Edward, *The Story of Craft: The Craftsman's Role in Society*, New York, Phaidon, 1981

McKendrick, Neil, John Brewer, and J. H. Plumb, *The Birth of a Consumer Society: The Commercialization of Eighteenth-Century England*, Bloomington, Indiana University Press, 1985

Pradère, Alexandre, *French Furniture Makers: The Art of the Ébéniste from Louis XIV to the Revolution*, trans. Perran Wood, Malibu, CA, The J. Paul Getty Museum, 1989

Reddy, William M., *The Rise of Market Culture: the Textile Trade and French Society, 1750–1900*, Cambridge, Cambridge University Press, 1984

Ribeiro, Aileen, *Dress in Eighteenth-Century Europe, 1715–1789*, New Haven, Yale University Press, 2002 (first publ. 1984)

Sargentson, Carolyn, *Merchants and Luxury Markets: The Marchands Merciers of Eighteenth-Century Paris*, London, Victoria and Albert Museum in assoc. with the J. Paul Getty Museum, 1996

Thornton, Peter, *Baroque and Rococo Silks*, New York, Taplinger, 1965

Updike, Daniel Berkeley, *Printing Types: Their History, Forms, and Use*, Cambridge, MA, Harvard University Press, 1962, 2 vols. (first publ. 1922)

Watson, F. J. B., *The Wrightsman Collection*, 3 vols. (vol. I, Furniture), New York, The Metropolitan Museum of Art, 1966

Weber, Caroline, *Queen of Fashion: What Marie Antoinette Wore to the Revolution*, New York, Henry Holt & Co., 2006

Weigert, Roger-Armand, *French Tapestry*, trans. Donald and Monique King, London, Faber and Faber, 1962

PART II

Anderson, Patricia, *The Printed Image and the Transformation of Popular Culture 1790–1860*, Oxford, Clarendon Press, 1991

Atterbury, Paul, and Clive Wainwright (eds.), *Pugin: A Gothic Passion*, New Haven, Yale University Press, 1994

Auerbach, Jeffrey, *The Great Exhibition of 1851*, New Haven, Yale University Press, 1999

Bell, Quentin, *The Schools of Design*, London, Routledge and Kegan Paul, 1963

The Crystal Palace Exhibition Illustrated Catalogue, London 1851: an unabridged republication of the Art-journal special issue, New York, Dover Publications, 1970

Eastlake, Charles L., *Hints on Household Taste. The Classic Handbook of Victorian Interior Decoration*, New York, Dover, 1969 (first publ. 1868)

Gray, Nicolete, *Nineteenth Century Ornamented Typefaces*, Berkeley and Los Angeles, University of California Press, 1976 (first publ. 1938)

Hope, Thomas, *Household Furniture and Interior Decoration*, New York, Dover Books, 1971 (first publ. 1807)

Jackson, Peter, *George Scharf's London: Sketches and Watercolours of a Changing City, 1820–1850*, London, John Murray, 1987

Johnson, Paul, *The Birth of the Modern: World Society 1815–1830*, New York, HarperCollins, 1991

Jones, Owen, *The Grammar of Ornament*, New York, Dover Publications, 1991 (first publ. 1856)

Keller, Morton, *The Art and Politics of Thomas Nast*, New York, Oxford University Press, 1968

Ledoux-Lebard, Denise, *Les Ébénistes du XIXe Siecle 1795–1889: Leurs oeuvres et leurs marques*, Paris, Les editions de L'Amateur, nd (first publ. 1965)

Lewis, Michael J., *The Gothic Revival*, New York, Thames & Hudson, 2002

McLean, Ruari, *Victorian Book Design and Colour Printing*, New York, Oxford University Press, 1963

Morley, John, *Regency Design, 1790–1840: Gardens, Buildings, Interiors, Furniture*, New York, Harry N. Abrams, 1993

Nouvel-Kammerer, Odile, *Symbols of Power: Napoleon and the Art of the Empire Style, 1800–1815*, New York, Abrams, 2007

Ottomeyer, Hans (ed.), *Biedermeier: The Invention of Simplicity*, Milwaukee, WI., Milwaukee Art Museum, and Ostfildern, Germany, Hatie Cantz, 2006

Paine, Albert Bigelow, *Thomas Nast, his Period and his Pictures*, New York and London, Macmillan, 1904

Richards, Thomas, *The Commodity Culture of Victorian England: Advertising and Spectacle 1851–1914*, Stanford, Stanford University Press, 1990

The Second Empire: Art in France under Napoleon III, Detroit, Wayne State University Press, 1978

Twyman, Michael, *Lithography 1800–1850: The Techniques of Drawing on Stone in England and France and their Application in Works of Topography*, London, Oxford University Press, 1970

Part III

Anscombe, Isabelle, and Charlotte Gere, *Arts and Crafts in Britain and America*, NY, Rizzoli, 1978

Artistic Houses: Interior Views of a number of the Most Beautiful and Celebrated Homes in the United States, New York, Benjamin Blom, Inc., 1971 (reprint), first publ. 1883

Arwas, Victor, Jana Brabcova-Orlikova, and Anna Dvorak, *Alphonse Mucha: The Spirit of Art Nouveau*, Virginia, Art Services International, 1998

Backmeyer, Sylvia, and Theresa Gronberg (eds.), *W. R. Lethaby, 1857–1931: Architecture, Design and Education*, London, Lund Humphries, 1984

Beecher, Catherine, and Harriet Beecher Stowe, *The American Women's Home: or, Principles of Domestic Science; being a guide to the formation and maintenance of economical, healthful, beautiful, and Christian homes*, New York, Arno Press, 1971 (first publ. 1869)

Bolger Burke, Doreen, et al., *In Pursuit of Beauty: Americans and the Aesthetic Movement*, New York, Rizzoli, 1986

Brett, David, *C. R. Mackintosh: The Poetics of Workmanship*, Cambridge, Harvard, 1992

Broido, Lucy, *The Posters of Jules Cheret: 46 full-color plates and an illustrated catalogue raisonné*, New York, Dover Publications, 1980

Buddensieg, Tilmann, et al., *Industriekultur: Peter Behrens and the AEG, 1907–1914*, trans. Iain Boyd Whyte, Cambridge, MIT Press, 1984 (first publ. 1979)

Burckhardt, Lucius (ed.), *The Werkbund: History and Ideology 1907–1933*, trans. Pearl Sanders, Woodbury NY, Barrons, 1980 (first publ. 1977)

Campbell, Joan, *The German Werkbund: The Politics of Reform in the Applied Arts*, Princeton, Princeton University Press, 1978

Carron, Christian, *Grand Rapids Furniture: The Story of America's Furniture City*, The Public Museum of Grand Rapids, Grand Rapids, MI, 1998

Cave, Roderick, *The Private Press*, 2nd ed., New York and London, R. R. Bowker Co., 1983

Clark, Kenneth (ed.), *John Ruskin: Selected Writings*, London, Penguin Books, 1991 (first publ. 1964)

Cooper, Jeremy, *Victorian and Edwardian Furniture and Interiors*, London, 1987

Crawford, Alan, *C .R. Ashbee: Architect, Designer, and Romantic Socialist*, New Haven and London, 1985

Csenkey, Éva, and Ágota Steinert (eds.), *Hungarian Ceramics from the Zsolnay Manufactory 1853–2001*, New Haven, Yale University Press, 2002

Cumming, Elizabeth, and Wendy Kaplan, *The Arts and Crafts Movement*, London, Thames & Hudson, 1991

Cunningham, Patricia A., *Reforming Women's Fashion, 1850–1920: Politics, Health, and Art*, Kent State University Press, 2003

de Marly, Diana, *Worth: Father of haute couture*, New York, Holmes & Meier, 1990

Dresser, Christopher, *Principles of Victorian Decorative Design, with 184 illustrations*, New York, Dover Publications, 1995

Ibid., *Traditional Arts and Crafts of Japan*, New York, Dover, 1994 (first publ. 1882 under the title *Japan: Its Architecture, Art and Art Manufactures*)

Duncan, Alastair, *Art Nouveau*, New York, Thames & Hudson, 1994

Durant, Stuart, *Christopher Dresser*, London, Academy Editions, 1993

Engen, Rodney K., *Kate Greenaway*, New York, Harmony Books, 1976

Ibid., *Randolph Caldecott: Lord of the Nursery*, London, Oresko Books, 1976

Escritt, Stephen, *Art Nouveau*, London, Phaidon, 2000

Fahr-Becker, Gabriele, *Art Nouveau*, Cologne, Konemann, 1997

Fiell, Charlotte and Peter (eds.), *1900–1910 Decorative Art: a Sourcebook*, Cologne, Taschen, 2000

Franklin, Colin, *The Private Presses*, London, Studio Vista, 1969

Freeman, Dr. Larry, *Louis Prang: Color Lithographer. Giant of a Man*, Watkins Glen, New York, Century House Inc., 1971

Frelinghausen, Alice Coonley, *Louis Comfort Tiffany and Laurelton Hall: an Artist's Country Estate*, New York, The Metropolitan Museum of Art, New Haven, Yale University Press, 2006

Gere, Charlotte, *The House Beautiful: Oscar Wilde and the Aesthetic Interior*, London, Lund Humphries in association with the Geffrye Museum, London, 2000

Gere, Charlotte, and Michael Whiteway, *Nineteenth Century Design from Pugin to Mackintosh*, New York, Harry N. Abrams, 1994 (first publ. in Britain 1993)

Green, Nancy E., *Byrdcliffe: An American Arts and Crafts Colony*, Ithaca, NY, Cornell University Press, 2004

Greenhalgh, Paul (ed.), *Art Nouveau 1890–1914*, New York, Harry N. Abrams, 2000

Groom, Gloria, *Beyond the Easel: Decorative Painting by Bonnard, Vuillard, Denis, and Roussel 1890–1930*, New Haven and London, Yale University Press, 2001

Halén, Widar, *Christopher Dresser*, Oxford, Phaidon, 1990

Hayden, Dolores, *The Grand Domestic Revolution: A History of Feminist Design for American Homes, Neighborhoods, and Cities*, Cambridge, MA, and London, MIT Press, 1981

Heinz, Thomas A., *Frank Lloyd Wright Interiors and Furniture*, London, Academy Editions, 1994

Heskett, John, *German Design 1870–1918*, New York, Taplinger, 1986

Hiesinger, Kathryn Bloom (ed.), *Art Nouveau in Munich: Masters of Jugendstil from the Stadtmuseum, Munich and other Public and Private Collections*, Philadelphia Museum of Art in association with Prestel Verlag, 1988

Hilton, Tim, *John Ruskin*, 2 vols., New Haven, Yale University Press, 1995–2000

Howe, Katherine S., et al. (eds.), *Herter Brothers: Furniture and Interiors for a Gilded Age*, New York, Harry N. Abrams, 1994

Kanigel, Robert, *One Best Way: Frederick Winslow Taylor and the Enigma of Efficiency*, New York, Viking Press, 1997

Kaplan, Wendy (ed.), *Charles Rennie Mackintosh*, New York, Abbeville Press, 1996

Ibid., *The Art That is Life: The Arts and Crafts Movement in America, 1875–1920*, Boston, Little, Brown, 1987

Ibid., *The Arts and Crafts Movement in Europe & America: Design for the Modern World*, New Haven, Yale University Press and the Los Angeles County Museum of Art, 2004

Kardon, Janet (ed.), *The Ideal Home 1900–1920*, New York, Harry N. Abrams and the American Craft Museum, 1993

Kostof, Spiro, *America by Design*, Oxford and New York, Oxford University Press, 1987

Macleod, Dianne Sachko, *Art and the Victorian Middle Class: Money and the Making of Cultural Identity*, Cambridge, Cambridge University Press, 1996

Marzio, Peter, *Chromolithography 1840–1900. The Democratic Art. Pictures for a 19th-Century America*, Boston, David R. Godine, 1979

Miller, Michael B., *The Bon Marche: Bourgeois Culture and the Department Store, 1869–1920*, Princeton, Princeton University Press, 1981

Muthesius, Hermann, *Das englische Haus*, 3 vols. (Berlin, 1904), trans. J. Seligman, London, 1979

Naylor, Gillian, *The Arts and Crafts Movement*, Cambridge, MIT Press, 1980 (first publ. 1971)

Ohmann, Richard, *Selling Culture: Magazines, Markets, and Class at the Turn of the Century*, New York, Verso, 1996

Parry, Linda (ed.), *William Morris*, New York, Harry N. Abrams, 1996

Peck, Amelia, *Candace Wheeler: the Art and Enterprise of American Design 1875–1900*, New Haven, Yale University Press, 2001

Peterson, Wm. S., *The Kelmscott Press: A History of William Morris's Typographical Adventure*, Berkeley, University of California Press, 1991

Pevsner, Nikolaus, *Studies in Art, Architecture and Design: Victorian and After*, Princeton, University Press, 1968

Pitz, Henry C., *Howard Pyle: Writer, Illustrator, Founder of the Brandywine School*, New York, Clarkson N. Potter, 1975

Reed, Cleota, *Henry Chapman Mercer and the Moravian Pottery and Tile Works*, Philadelphia, University of Pennsylvania Press, 1996

Robinson, William H., Jordi Falgás, and Carmen Bellen Lord, *Barcelona and Modernity: Picasso, Gaudí, Miró, Dalí*, Cleveland, Museum of Art and New Haven, Yale University Press, 2006

Saunders, Edith, *The Age of Worth: Couturier to the Empress Eugénie*, Bloomington, Indiana University Press, 1955

Schwartz, Frederic J., *The Werkbund: Design Theory and Mass Culture before the First World War*, New Haven and London, Yale University Press, 1996

Schweiger, Werner, *Wiener Werkstätte, Design in Vienna 1903–1932*, New York, Abbeville Press, 1984

Sembach, Klaus-Jurgen, *Henry van de Velde*, trans. Michael Robinson, New York, Rizzoli, 1989

Silverman, Debora L., *Art Nouveau in Fin-de-Siecle France: Politics Psychology, and Style*, Berkeley, Los Angeles, and London, University of California Press, 1989

Soros, Susan Weber (ed.), *E. W. Godwin. Aesthetic Movement Architect and Designer*, New Haven and London, Yale University Press and the Bard Graduate Center for Studies in the Decorative Arts, 1999

Stickley, Gustav, *The 1912 and 1915 Gustav Stickley Furniture Catalogs*, New York, Dover Publications, 1991

Via, Marie, and Marjorie Searl (eds.), *Head, Heart and Hand: Elbert Hubbard and the Roycrofters*, Rochester, University of Rochester Press, 1994

Weisberg, Gabriel, and Elizabeth K. Menon, *Art Nouveau: A Research Guide for Design Reform in France, Belgium, England, and the United States*, New York and London, Garland Publishing, 1998

Weisberg, Gabriel P., Edwin Becker, and Évelne Posséme, *The origins of l'art nouveau: the Bing empire*, Amsterdam, Van Gogh Museum, Paris, Musée des arts décoratifs, Antwerp, Mercatorfonds, 2004

Weiss, Peg, *Adelaide Alsop Robineau: Glory in Porcelain*, Syracuse, Syracuse University Press, 1981

Whiteway, Michael, *Christopher Dresser: 1834–1904*, Milan, Skira, 2001

Whiteway, Michael (ed.), *Christopher Dresser: A Design Revolution*, V&A Publications in association with Cooper-Hewitt National Design Museum, Smithsonian Institution, 2004

Whitford, Frank, *Klimt*, London, Thames & Hudson, 1999

Williams, R. H., *Dream Worlds: Mass Consumption in Late Nineteenth Century France*, Berkeley, 1982

Wilmer, Clive, (ed.), *William Morris: News from Nowhere and Other Writings*, London, Penguin Books, 1993

Part IV

Aav, Marianne and Nina Stritzler-Levine, (eds.), *Finnish modern design: Utopian Ideals. Everyday realities, 1930–1997*, New Haven, Yale University Press, 1998

Armi, C. Edson, *The Art of American Car Design. The Profession and Personalities*, The Pennsylvania State University Press, University Park, 1988

Arwas, Victor, *Art Deco*, New York, Abradale Press, 2000

Banham, Reyner, *Theory and Design in the First Machine Age*, Cambridge, MIT Press, 2nd ed., 1960

Baroni, Daniele, *The furniture of Gerrit Thomas Rietveld*, New York, Barron's, 1978

Bartram, Alan, *Futurist Typography and the Liberated Text*. New Haven: Yale University Press, 2006

Benton, Tim, Charlotte Benton, and Ghislaine Wood (eds.), *Art Deco 1910–1939*, London, Victoria and Albert Museum, 2003

Blake, Peter, *Le Corbusier: Architecture and Form*, Baltimore, Penguin, 1964

Blaser, W., *Mies van der Rohe, Furniture and Interiors*, Woodbury, NY, Barron's, 1982

Bogart, Michele H., *Advertising, Artists, and the Borders of Art*, Chicago and London, University of Chicago Press, 1995

Bröhan, Torsten (eds.), *Glass of the Avant-Garde: The Torsten Brohan Collection from the Museo Nacional de Artes Decorativas, Madrid*, Munich, London, and New York, Prestel Verlag, 2001

Bruckner, D. J. R., *Frederic Goudy*, New York, Harry N. Abrams, 1990

Burke, Christopher, *Active Literature: Jan Tschichold and New Typography*, London, Hyphen Books, 2007

Cohen, Arthur A., *Herbert Bayer: The Complete Work*, Cambridge and London, MIT Press, 1984

Ibid., *Sonia Delaunay*, New York, Harry N. Abrams, 1975 (reprinted 1988)

Compton, Susan, *Russian Avant-Garde Book 1917–34*, Cambridge, MA, MIT Press, 1993 (first publ. 1992)

De Fusco, Renato, *Le Corbusier, Designer: Furniture, 1929*, Woodbury, NY, Barron's, 1977

DeperoFuturista: Rome-Paris-New York 1915–1932 and more, Milan, Skira, 1999

Drucker, Joanna, *The Visible Word: Experimental Typography and Modern Art, 1909–1923*, Chicago and London, University of Chicago Press, 1994

Duncan, Alastair, *Art Deco Furniture: the French Designers*, New York, Thames & Hudson, 1992

Duncan, Alastair, *American Art Deco*, New York, Harry N. Abrams, 1986

Ibid., *Art Deco*, New York and London, Thames & Hudson, 1988

Ibid., *The Encyclopedia of Art Deco*, New York, Knickerbocker Press, 1998

El Lissitzky 1890–1941: Architect, Painter, Photographer, Typographer, Eindhoven, Municipal Van Abbemuseum, 1990

Ericsson, Anne-Marie, et al., *The Brilliance of Swedish Glass, 1918–1939: an Alliance of Art and Industry*, New Haven, Yale University Press, 1996

Fiell, Charlotte and Peter (eds.), *20s Decorative Art: a Sourcebook*, Cologne, Taschen, 2000

Ibid., *30s and 40s Decorative Art: a Sourcebook*, Cologne, Taschen, 2000

Fox, Richard Wightman, and T. J. Jackson Lears (eds.), *The Culture of Consumption: Critical Essays in American History 1880–1980*, New York, Pantheon Books, 1983

Franciscono, Marcel, *Walter Gropius and the Creation of the Bauhaus: the Ideals and Artistic Theories of its Founding Years*, Urbana, University of Illinois Press, 1971

Garafola, Lynn, *Diaghilev's Ballets Russes*, New York and Oxford, Oxford University Press, 1989

Garner, Philippe, *Eileen Gray: Design and Architecture 1878–1976*, Köln, Benedikt Tashcen Verlag, 1993

The Great Utopia: The Russian and Soviet Avant-Garde, 1915–1932, New York, The Guggenheim Museum, 1992

Gronberg, Tag, *Designs on Modernity: Exhibiting the City in 1920s Paris*, Manchester and New York, University of Manchester Press, 1998

Hillier, Bevis, *Art Deco of the 20s and 30s*, London, Studio Vista, 1968

Hitchcock, Henry-Russell, and Philip Johnson, *The International Style*, New York/London, W. W. Norton, 1966 (first publ. 1932)

Holtzman, Harry, and Martin S. James (eds. and trans.), *The New Art – the New Life: the Collected Writings of Piet Mondrian*, Boston, G. K. Hall & Company, 1986

Jaffé, Hans Ludwig C., *De Stijl 1917–1931: The Dutch Contribution to Modern Art*, Cambridge, Belknap Press and Harvard University Press, 1986 (first publ. 1956)

Johnson, J. Stewart, *American Modern 1925–1940 – Design for a New Age*, Harry N. Abrams, 2000

Kahn-Magomedov, Selim O., *Rodchenko: the Complete Work*, Cambridge, MA, MIT Press, 1987 (first publ. 1986, Idea Books Edizioni)

Kardon, Janet (ed.), *Craft in the Machine Age 1920–1945*, New York, Harry N. Abrams and the American Craft Museum, 1995

Kaufmann, Edgar Jr., *Prize Designs for Modern Furniture from the International Competition for Low-cost Furniture Design*, New York, Museum of Modern Art, 1950

Kirke, Betty, *Madeleine Vionnet*, San Francisco, Chronicle Books, 1998

Koda, Harold, and Andrew Bolton, *Poiret*, New York, The Metropolitan Museum of Art, and New Haven, Yale University Press, 2007

Le Corbusier, *Towards a New Architecture*, London, Architectural Press, 1974 (first publ. 1923)

Les Années UAM, 1929–1958 (exh. cat.), Paris, Musée des Arts Décoratifs, 1988

Ling, Peter, *America and the Automobile: Technology, Reform and Social Change 1893–1923*, Manchester, Manchester University Press, 1990

Lodder, Christina, *Russian Constructivism*, London and New Haven, Yale University Press, 1983

Loewy, Raymond, *Never Leave Well Enough Alone*, New York, Simon & Schuster, 1951

Mackrell, Alice, *Paul Poiret*, New York, Holmes & Meier, 1990

Marchand, Roland, *Advertising the American Dream: Making Way for Modernity 1920–1940*, Berkeley, University of California Press, 1985

Marcilhac, Felix, *Dunand*, New York, Harry N. Abrams, 1991

McLean, Ruari, *Jan Tschichold: Typographer*, Boston, David R. Godine, 1975

Meikle, Jeffrey L., *Twentieth Century Limited: Industrial Design in America, 1925–1939*, Philadelphia, Temple University Press, 1979 (revised 2001)

Mouron, Henri, *A. M. Cassandre*, trans. Michael Taylor, New York, Rizzoli, 1985

Naylor, Gillian, *The Bauhaus Reassessed: Sources and Design Theory*, New York, E. P. Dutton, 1985

Noyes, Eliot F., *Organic Design in Home Furnishings*, New York, The Museum of Modern Art, 1969 (reprint edition), first publ. 1940

Overy, Paul, *De Stijl*, London, Thames & Hudson, 1991

Ozenfant, Amedee, and C-E. Jeanneret, "Le Purisme" (trans.), in Herbert, Robert L. (ed.) *Modern Artists on Art: Ten Unabridged Essays*, Englewood Cliffs, NJ, Prentice Hall, 1964, pp. 58–73

Peto, James, and Donna Loveday (eds.), *Modern Britain 1929–1939*, London, Design Museum, 1999

Poggi, Christine, *In Defiance of Painting: Cubism, Futurism, and the Invention of Collage*, New Haven, Yale University Press, 1992

Ibid., *Inventing Futurism: the Art and Politics of Artificial Optimism*, Princeton, Princeton University Press, 2009

Pommer, Richard, and Christian F. Otto, *Weissenhof 1927 and the Modern Movement in Architecture*, Chicago and London, University of Chicago Press, 1991

Porter, Glenn, *Raymond Loewy: Designs for a Consumer Culture*, Wilmington, DE, Hagley Museum and Library, 2002

Pozharskaya, Militsa, and Tatiana Volodina, *The Art of the Ballets Russes: The Russian Seasons in Paris 1908–1929*, New York, Abbeville Press, 1990

Silver, Kenneth, *Esprit de Corps: the Art of the Parisian Avant-garde and the First World War, 1914–1925*, Princeton, Princeton University Press, 1989

Silverman, Dan, *Reconstructing Europe After the Great War*, Cambridge, MA,, Harvard University Press, 1982

Smith, Terry, *Making the Modern: Industry, Art, and Design in America*, Chicago and London, University of Chicago Press, 1993

Sparke, Penny, *Elsie de Wolfe: the Birth of Modern Interior Decoration*, New York, Acanthus Press, 2005

Spencer, Herbert, *Pioneers of Modern Typography*, New York, Hastings House, 1970 (first publ. 1969)

Stritzler-Levine, Nina (ed.), *Josef Frank, Architect and Designer: An Alternative Vision of the Modern Home*, New Haven and London, Yale University Press, 1996

Troy, Nancy J., *Couture Culture: a Study in Modern Art and Fashion*, Cambridge, MA, MIT Press, 2003

Ibid., *Modernism and the Decorative Arts in France: Art Nouveau to Le Corbusier*, New Haven and London, Yale, 1991

Ibid., *The De Stijl Environment*, Cambridge, MA, MIT Press, 1983

Tschichold, Jan, *The New Typography: A Handbook for Modern Designers*, trans. Ruari McLean, Berkeley and Los Angeles, University of California Press, 1995

Von Vegesack, Alexander, *Jean Prouvé: the Poetics of Technical Objects*, Weil am Rhein, Vitra Design Museum, 2005

Weltge, Sigrid Wortmann, *Women's Work: Textile Art from the Bauhaus*, San Francisco, Chronicle Books, 1993, also publ. by Thames & Hudson, 1993

Whitford, Frank, *Bauhaus*, London, Thames & Hudson, 1984

Wilk, Christopher, *Marcel Breuer, Furniture and Interiors*, New York, The Metropolitan Museum of Art, 1981

Wilk, Christopher (ed.), *Modernism: Designing a New World 1914–1939*, London, Victoria and Albert Museum, and New York, Harry N. Abrams, 2006

Wilson, Kristina, *Livable Modernism: Interior Decorating and Design during the Great Depression*, New Haven, Yale University Press, 2004

Wingler, Hans M., *The Bauhaus: Weimar, Dessau, Berlin, Chicago*, trans. Wolfgang Jabs and Basil Gilbert, Cambridge, MA, MIT Press, 1969

PART V

Abercrombie, Stanley, *George Nelson: The Design of Modern Design*, Cambridge and London, MIT Press, 1995

Adamson, Glenn (ed.), *Industrial Strength Design: How Brook Stevens Shaped Your World*, Cambridge, MA, MIT Press, 2003

Albrecht, Donald, et al., *Russel Wright: Creating American Lifestyle*, New York, Harry N. Abrams (in conjunction with the Cooper-Hewitt National Design Museum), 2001

Allen, James Sloan, *The Romance of Commerce and Culture: Capitalism, Modernism, and the Chicago-Aspen Crusade for Cultural Reform*, Chicago and London, University of Chicago Press, 1983

Austerity to Affluence: British Art & Design 1945–1962, London, Merrell Holberton, 1997

Bayley, Stephen, *Sony: An Exhibition in the boilerhouse at the Victoria & Albert Museum*, London, 1982 (The Conran Foundation)

Ibid., *Harley Earl*, London, Trefoil, 1990 (Design Heroes, Series Editor: Martin Pawley)

Beer, Eileene Harrison, *Scandinavian Design: Objects of a Lifestyle*, New York, Farrar, Straus and Giroux, 1975

Bigsby, C. W. E. (ed.), *Superculture: American Popular Culture and Europe*, Bowling Green, Bowling Green University Popular Press, 1975

Blake, John and Avril, *The Practical Idealists: Twenty-five Years of Designing for Industry*, London, Lund Humphries, 1969

Bonsiepe, Gui, and Silvia Fernandez (eds.), *Historia del Diseno en America Latina y el Caribe. Industrialización y comunicación visual para la autonomía*, São Paulo, Editora Blucher, 2008

Brino, Giovanni, *Carlo Mollino. Architecture as Autobiography: Architecture, Furniture, Interior Design 1928–1973*, New York, Rizzoli, 1987

Caplan, Ralph, *The Design of Herman Miller*, New York, Whitney Library of Design, 1976

Coqueval, Guy, and Giampiero Bosoni (eds.), *Il Modo Italiano: Italian Design and Avant-garde in the Twentieth Century*, Milan, Skira, 2008

Crowley, David, and Jane Pavitt (eds.), *Cold War Modern: Design 1945–1970*, London, V&A Publishing, 2008

Dreyfuss, Henry, *The Measure of Man: Human Factors in Design*, revised and expanded 2nd edition, New York, Whitney Library of Design, 1960

Eidelberg, Martin (ed.), *Design 1935–1965: What Modern Was: Selections from the Liliane and David M. Stewart Collection*, New York, Harry N. Abrams, 1991

Erlhoff, Michael (ed.), *Designed in Germany Since 1949*, Munich, Prestel-Verlag, 1990

Fiell, Charlotte and Peter (eds.), *50s Decorative Art: a Sourcebook*, Cologne, Taschen, 2000

Finch, Christopher, *Highways to Heaven*, New York, HarperCollins, 1992

Fleck, Glen (ed.), *A Computer Perspective: by the office of Charles and Ray Eames*, Cambridge, MA, Harvard University Press, 1973

Flinchum, Russell, *Henry Dreyfuss, Industrial Designer: the Man in the Brown Suit*, New York, Cooper-Hewitt National Design Museum and Rizzoli, 1997

Fuller, R. B., *Utopia or Oblivion: the Prospects for Humanity*, New York, Overlook Press, 1969

Gans, Herbert, *The Levittowners: Ways of Life and Politics in a New Suburban Community*, New York, Pantheon Books, 1967

George Nakashima and the Modernist Movement, Steven Beyer, curator, Doylestown, PA, James A. Michener Museum, 2001

Gerstner, Karl, *Die neue Graphic. The new graphic art: Le nouvel art graphique*, Switzerland, Arthur Niggli Ltd., 1959

Greenberg, Clement, *Art and Culture: Critical Essays*, Boston, Beacon Press, 1961

Guilbaut, Serge, *How New York Stole the Idea of Modern Art: Abstract Expressionism, Freedom, and the Cold War*, trans. Arthur Goldhammer, Chicago, University of Chicago Press, 1983

Halberstam, David, *The Fifties*, New York, Villard Books, 1993

Heskett, John, *Philips; A Study of the Corporate Management of Design*, London, Trefoil Publications, 1989

Hiesinger, Kathryn B., and George H. Marcus (eds.), *Design Since 1945*, Philadelphia, Philadelphia Museum of Art, 1983

Hine, Thomas, *Populuxe*, New York, Knopf, 1986

Hofmann, Armin, *Graphic Design Manual: Principles and Practice*, New York, Reinhold, 1965

Hollis, Richard, *Swiss Graphic Design: the Origins and Growth of an International Style 1920–1965*, New Haven, Yale University Press, 2006

Jackson, Kenneth T., *Crabgrass Frontier. The Suburbanization of the United States*, New York and Oxford, Oxford University Press, 1985

Jackson, Lesley, *The New Look – Design of the Fifties*, New York, Thames & Hudson, 1991

Ibid., *Robin and Lucienne Day: Pioneers of Modern Design*, New York, Princeton Architectural Press, 2001

Jacobs, Jane, *The Death and Life of Great American Cities*, New York, Random House, 1961

Kira, Alexander, *The Bathroom*, rev. edition, New York, Viking Press, 1976 (first publ. 1966)

Kircherer, Sibylle, *Olivetti: a Study of the Corporate Management of Design*, New York, Rizzoli, 1990

Kirkham, Pat, *Charles and Ray Eames: Designers of the Twentieth Century*, Cambridge, MA, MIT Press, 1995

Lapidus, Morris, *Too Much is Never Enough*, New York, Rizzoli, 1996

Larson, Jack Lenor, *Jack Lenor Larson: A Weaver's Memoir*, New York, Harry N. Abrams, 1998

Lindinger, Herbert (ed.), *Ulm Design: the Morality of Objects*, trans. David Britt, Cambridge, MA, MIT Press, 1991

Lonberg-Holm, K., and Ladislav Sutnar, *Catalog Design Progress*, New York, Sweet's Catalog Service (Division of F. W. Dodge Corporation), 1950

Maldonado, Tomás, *Design, Nature, and Revolution: Toward a Critical Ecology*, trans. Mario Domandi, New York, Evanston, San Francisco, and London, Harper and Row, 1972 (first publ. 1970)

Marcus, George H., *Design in the Fifties: When Everyone Went Modern*, New York, Prestel, 1998

Marling, Karal Ann, *As Seen on TV: The Visual Culture of Everyday Life in the 1950s*, Cambridge, MA, Harvard University Press, 1994

Massey, Anne, *Modernism and Mass Culture in Britain 1945–1959*, Manchester and New York, Manchester University Press, 1995

Melson, Holland R. (ed.), *The Collected Writings of Alvin Lustig*, New York, Thistle Press, 1958

Mumford, Lewis, *The City in History: Its Origins, Its Transformations, and Its Prospects*, San Diego, New York and London, Harcourt Brace Jovanovich, 1961

Nelson, George, and Henry Wright, *Tomorrow's House: A Complete House for the Home-Builder*, New York, Simon & Schuster, 1946

Neutra, Richard, *Survival Through Design*, New York, Oxford, 1954

Olins, Wally, *The Corporate Personality: An Inquiry into the Nature of Corporate Identity*, New York, Mayflower Books, 1978

Packard, V., *The Hidden Persuaders*, Harmondsworth, Penguin, 1960, or New York, David McKay, 1957

Rand, Paul, *Thoughts on Design*, New York, Reinhold, 1970 (first publ. 1947)

Remington, R. Roger, *American Modernism: Graphic Design 1920–1960*, London, Laurence King Publishing, 2003

Reed, Peter, *Alvar Aalto: Between Humanism and Materialism*, New York, The Museum of Modern Art, 1998

Riesman, David, with Nathan Glazer and Reuel Denney, *The Lonely Crowd: A Study of the Changing American Character*, New Haven and London, Yale University Press, 2001 (first publ. 1950)

Rouland, Steven and Linda, *Knoll Furniture 1938–1960*, Atglen, PA, Schiffer Publishing, 1999

Scotford, Martha, *Cipe Pineles: A Life of Design*, New York, W. W. Norton & Company, 1999

Sparke, Penny (ed.), *Reyner Banham: Design by Choice*, London, Academy Editions, 1981

Sutnar, Ladislav, *Package Design: The Force of Visual Selling*, New York, Arts Inc., 1953

Tufte, Edward, *The Visual Display of Quantitative Information*, Cheshire, CT, Graphics Press, 1983

Wichmann, Hans (ed.), *Armin Hofmann: His Work, Quest and Philosophy*, trans. D. Q. Stephenson, Basel and Boston, Birkhäuser Verlag, 1989

Wolfe, Tom, *The Kandy-Colored Tangerine Flake Streamline Baby*, New York, Bantam Books, 1999 (publ. earlier by Farrar, Strauss, & Giroux, 1965)

Part VI

Adamson, Glenn, *Thinking Through Craft*, Oxford and New York, Berg, 2007

Ambasz, Emilio, *Italy: The New Domestic Landscape: Achievements and Problems of Italian Design*, New York, The Museum of Modern Art, New York, in collaboration with Centro Di, Florence, 1972

Antonelli, Paola (ed.), *Design and the Elastic Mind*, New York, The Museum of Modern Art, and London, Thames & Hudson, 2008

Antonelli, Paola, et al., *Safe: Design Takes On Risk*, New York, The Museum of Modern Art, 2005

Ash, Juliet, and Elizabeth Wilson (eds.), *Chic Thrills: A Fashion Reader*, Berkeley and Los Angeles, University of California Press, 1993

Bell, Daniel, *The Coming of Post-Industrial Society: An Adventure in Social Forecasting*, New York, Basic Books, 1999 (first publ. 1973)

Blackwell, Lewis, *The End of Print: the Grafik Design of David Carson*, London, Laurence King, 2000

Bloemink, Barbara J., and Joseph Cunningham, *Design =Art: Functional Objects from Donald Judd to Rachel Whiteread*, London and New York, Merrell, 2004.

Bloemink, Barbara, Brooke Hodge, Ellen Lupton, and Matilda McQuaid, *Design Life Now: National Design Triennial 2006*, New York, Cooper-Hewitt, National Design Museum, 2006

Brown, David E., *Inventing Modern America: From the Microwave to the Mouse*, Cambridge, MA, MIT Press, 2002

Brownlee, David, David G. DeLong, and Kathryn B. Hiesinger, *Out of the Ordinary. Robert Venturi, Denise Scott Brown and Associates. Architecture, Urbanism, Design*, Philadelphia, Philadelphia Museum of Art, 2001

Chwast, Seymour, *The Push Pin Graphic: a Quarter century of Innovative Design and Illustration*, San Francisco, Chronicle Books, 2004

Collins, Michael, and Andreas Papadakis, *Post-Modern Design*, New York, Rizzoli, 1989

Crow, Thomas, "Modernism and Mass Culture in the Visual Arts," H. D. Buchloh, Serge Guilbaut, and David Solkin (eds.), *Modernism and Modernity: the Vancouver conference papers*, Halifax, N. S., The Press of the Nova Scotia College of Art and Design, 1983, pp. 215–264

Ibid., *The Rise of the Sixties: American and European Art in the Era of Dissent*, New York, Harry N. Abrams, 1996

Csikszentmihalyi, Mihaly, and Eugene Rochberg-Halton, *The Meaning of Things: Domestic Symbols and the Self*, Cambridge, Cambridge University Press, 1981

De la Haye, Amy, and Elizabeth Wilson (eds.), *Defining Dress: Dress as Object, Meaning, and Identity*, Manchester, Manchester University Press, 1999

Docker, John, *Postmodernism and Popular Culture: A Cultural History*, Cambridge, Cambridge University Press, 1994

Ewen, Stuart, *All Consuming Images: the Politics of Style in Contemporary Culture*, New York, Basic Books, 1988

Fiell, Charlotte and Peter (eds.), *Designing the 21st century = Design des 21: Jahrhunderts = Le design du 21e siècle*, Cologne, Taschen, 2001

Ibid., *60s Decorative Art: a Sourcebook*, Cologne, Taschen, 2000

Ibid., *70s Decorative Art: a Sourcebook*, Cologne, Taschen, 2000

Fischer, Volker (ed.), *Design Now: Industry or Art?*, Munich, Prestel Verlag, 1989

Foster, Hal, *Design and Crime (And Other Diatribes)*, New York, NY, Verso, 2002

Garner, Philippe, *Sixties Design*, Cologne, Taschen, 1996

Glaser, Milton, *Milton Glaser – Graphic Design*, Woodstock, NY, Overlook Press, 1973

Greiman, April, *Hybrid Imagery: The Fusion of Technology and Graphic Design*, New York, Watson Guptill, 1990

Harper, Laurel, *Radical Graphics Radicals*, San Francisco, Chronicle Books, 1999

Harvey, David, *The Condition of Postmodernity; An Enquiry into the Origins of Cultural Change*, Cambridge, Blackwell, 1989

Heller, Steven, and Paula Scher, *Seymour: the Obsessive Images of Seymour Chwast*, San Francisco, Chronicle Books, 2009

Hughes, Robert, *Culture of Complaint: The Fraying of America*, Oxford, Oxford University Press, 1993

Huyssen, Andreas, *After the Great Divide: Modernism, Mass Culture, Postmodernism*, Bloomington, 1985

Jackson, Lesley, *The Sixties: Decade of Design Revolution*, London, Phaidon, 1998

Jameson, Frederic, *Postmodernism, or the Cultural Logic of Late Capitalism*, Durham, NC, Duke University Press, 1991

Jones, Richard A. L., *Soft Machines: Nanotechnology and Life*, Oxford and New York, Oxford University Press, 2004

Julier, Guy, *The Culture of Design*, London, Sage Publications, 2000

Krippendorf, Klaus, *The Semantic Turn: A New Foundation for Design*, Boca Raton, Florida, Taylor & Francis, 2006

Kron, Joan, and Suzanne Slesin, *Hi-Tech: The Industrial Style and Source Book for the Home*, New York, Clarkson N. Potter, 1978

Kuspit, Donald B., *Chihuly*, New York, Harry N. Abrams, 1997

Labaco, Ronald T., *Ettore Sottsass: Architect and Designer*, with contributions by Dennis Doordan, et al., London and New York, Merrell Publishers in association with Los Angeles County Museum of Art, 2006

Lupton, Ellen, *Skin: Surface, Substance, and Design*, New York, Princeton Architectural Press, 2002

Marwick, Arthur, *The Sixties: Cultural Revolution in Britain, France, Italy, and the United States c. 1958–c. 1974*, Oxford and New York, Oxford University Press, 1998

Miller, Daniel, *Material Culture and Mass Consumption*, Oxford, Blackwell, 1987

Nader, Ralph, *Unsafe at any Speed: the Designed-in Dangers of the American Automobile*, New York, Grossman, 1965

Norman, Donald, *The Design of Everyday Things*, New York, Basic Books, 1988

Papanek, Victor, *Design for the Real World: Making to Measure*, London, Thames & Hudson, 1972

Polhemus, Ted, *Streetstyle: from Sidewalk to Catwalk*, London, Thames & Hudson, 1994

Porritt, Jonathon, *Seeing Green: the Politics of Ecology Explained*, Oxford and New York, B. Blackwell, 1985

Poyner, Rick, *No More Rules: Graphic Design and Postmodernism*, Laurence King Publishing, 2003

Poynor, Rick, and Edward Booth-Clibborn (eds.), *Typography Now: the Next Wave*, London, Internos Books, 1991

Radice, Dorothy, *Memphis: Research, Experiences, Results, Failures and Successes of New Design*, New York, Rizzoli, 1984

Sladen, Mark, and Ariella Yedgar (eds.), *Panic Attack: Art in the Punk Years*, London and New York, Merrell, 2007

Snyder, Gertrude, and Alan Peckolik, *Herb Lubalin: Art Director, Graphic Designer and Typographer*, New York, American Showcase, Inc., 1985

Thackara, John (ed.), *Design After Modernism: Beyond the Object*, New York, Thames & Hudson, 1988

VanderLans, Rudy, Zuzana Licko, with Mary E. Gray, *Émigré (The Book): Graphic Design into the Digital Realm*, New York, Van Nostrand Reinhold, 1993

Venturi, Robert, Denise Scott Brown, and Steven Izenour, *Learning from Las Vegas*, Cambridge, MA and London, MIT Press, rev. edition 1998 (first publ. 1972)

Venturi, Robert, *Complexity and Contradiction in Architecture*, New York, The Museum of Modern Art, 1977 (first publ. 1966)

Von Vegesack, Alexander, and Mathias Remmele, (eds.), *Vernor Panton: the Collected Works*, Weil am Rhein, Vitra Design Museum, 2000

Whitely, Nigel, *Design for Society*, London, Reaktion Books, 1993

Whiteside, Thomas, *The Investigation of Ralph Nader: General Motors vs. One Determined Man*, New York, Arbor House, 1972

Wozencroft, Jon, *The Graphic Language of Neville Brody*, New York, Rizzoli, 1988

Picture Credits

8.24 A. E. Gallatin Collection. Photo: Graydon Wood, 1992/© ADAGP, Paris and DACS, London 2010
8.25 © Tate, London 2002
8.27 © ADAGP, Paris and DACS, London 2010
8.28 Special Collections, Davidow Archives, Box A5
8.30 © FLC/ADAGP, Paris and DACS, London 2010
8.31, 8.32, 8.34, Vitra Design Museum
8.33 Vitra Design Museum/© ADAGP, Paris and DACS, London 2010

9.1 Private Collection/© DACS 2010
9.2, 9.3 Private Collection/© DACS 2010
9.4, 9.16, 9.17 © DACS 2010
9.5 Courtesy of the University of Iowa
9.6, 9.8, 9.11 Frank den Oudsten Associates
9.7 Gemeentemuseum den Haag
9.9 Frank den Oudsten Associates/© DACS 2010
9.12 © DACS 2010
9.13 Historical Museum, Vienna
9.14 Tate Modern/Andrew Dunkley and Marcus Leith
9.16 Merrill C. Berman Collection. Photo by Jim Frank/© DACS 2010
9.17 David King Collection, London
9.18, 9.24 David King Collection, London/DACS 2010
9.19 TopFoto/The Granger Collection/© ARS, New York and DACS, London 2010
9.21 Private Collection/© Rodchenko and Stepanova Archive, DACS 2010
9.22 David King Collection/© Rodchenko and Stepanova Archive, DACS 2010
9.23 Novosti (London)/© ARS, New York and DACS, London 2010
9.21 Private Collection/© DACS 2010
9.25 Private Collection
9.26 © VG Bild-Kunst, Bonn
9.27 Staatliche Bildstelle, Berlin
9.28, 9.34 Bauhaus-Archiv, Berlin
9.29, 9.45 © DACS 2010
9.30 © VG Bild-Kunst, Bonn/Hattula Moholy-Nagy © DACS 2010
9.31 Image © The Art Institute of Chicago/© DACS 2010
9.32 The Cynthia Hazen Polsky Fund, 1989. Photo: Mark Darley © 1989 The Metropolitan Museum of Art
9.33 Purchase, Theodore R. Gamble Jr. Gift, in honor of his mother Mrs. Theodore Robert Gamble. Photo: © 1981 The Metropolitan Museum of Art/© DACS 2010
9.41, 9.42 Private Collection
9.43 © DACS 2010
9.44 © The Heartfield Community of Heirs/VG Bild-Kunst, Bonn and DACS, London 2010
9.50, 9.57, 9.58 London Transport Museum
9.54 Courtesy and © Penguin Books
9.56 © Peter Kent, London
9.59 Orrefors Glass Museum/© DACS 2010
9.63 © Ole Woldbye

10.2 Gift of William E. Levis, 1936.36
10.5 Photo: © The Metropolitan Museum of Art
10.6 The John Axelrod Collection, 2008.1416. Photograph © 2010 Museum of Fine Arts, Boston
10.8 John C. Waddell Collection, Promised Gift of John C. Waddell to The Metropolitan Museum of Art. Photo: © 2000 The Metropolitan Museum of Art
10.10 Purchased with funds from the Libbey Endowment, Gift of Edward Drummond Libbey, 1993.60
10.11 Gift of Kenn Darity and Ed Murchison (1995.51.1-3)
10.13 N. Wright/National Motor Museum
10.14 Vogue © Condé Nast Publications Inc.
10.15, 10.16, 10.26, 10.31 Private Collection
10.18 Hulton Getty
10.20 Gift of David A. Hanks, 1986. Photo: © 2000 The Metropolitan Museum of Art
10.22 Photo: Author
10.23 John C. Waddell Collection, Gift of John C. Waddell to The Metropolitan Museum of Art 2002. Photo: © 2000 The Metropolitan Museum of Art
10.24 AKG London

10.27 Photo: © The Museum of Modern Art, New York
10.30 John C. Waddell Collection, Promised Gift of John C. Waddell to The Metropolitan Museum of Art. Photo: © 2000 The Metropolitan Museum of Art
10.32 Photo: Courtesy of Daimler/Chrysler Corporation Archives
10.33 Courtesy Volkswagen Archives
10.34 Photo: Courtesy Airstream Inc.
10.35 Collection of John C. Waddell. Photo: © 2000 The Metropolitan Museum of Art
10.40 Harriet Russell Stanley Fund, 1953.21. Photo: Arthur Evans/© T. H. Benton and R. P. Benton Testamentary Trusts/VAGA, New York/DACS, London 2010
10.41 Edward Steichen/Vanity Fair © Condé Nast Publications Inc.
10.42 Vanity Fair © Condé Nast Publications Inc.
10.43 John C. Waddell Collection, Promised Gift of John C. Waddell to The Metropolitan Museum of Art. Photo: © 2000 The Metropolitan Museum of Art/© DACS, London VAGA, New York 2010
10.44 Courtesy Eames Office
10.45 Liliane and David M. Stewart Collection, gift of the American Friends of Canada through the generosity of Geoffrey N. Bradfield
10.46 Hulton Getty
10.47 Decorative Arts Purchase Fund, 1998.4
10.48 Second Century Acquisition Fund, 2000.9.1.1-2
10.49 Scala, Florence
10.50 Courtesy and © Paul Rand Archives

11.1 Gift of Tupperware Home Parties, 1982. Photo: Will Brown
11.2 Gift of Howard Miller Clock Company. Photo: Will Brown, 1983
11.6 Purchased with funds contributed by Mr. and Mrs. Adolph G. Rosengarten in memory of Calvin S. Hathaway
11.7, 11.16, 11.43 Private Collection
11.8 Photo: Josh Raizman
11.9 Courtesy Herman Miller
11.10, 11.27 Ezra Stoller © Esto
11.12 Courtesy Walter Dorwin Teague Associates
11.13 Courtesy Walker Art Center, Minneapolis
11.16 Courtesy and © Paul Rand Archives
11.18 Courtesy New Directions Publishing Corp.
11.20 Courtesy Esquire Magazine, New York
11.22 © 2010 Richard Avedon Foundation
11.23, 11.24 Rochester Institute of Technology
11.28 © Ole Woldbye
11.30 Liliane and David M. Stewart Collection, by exchange
11.31 Designor Oy, Arabia, Finland
11.32, 11.33 Courtesy Louis Poulsen Lighting
11.34 Courtesy Saab Automobile AB, Sweden
11.35 Design Council Slide Library, Manchester Metropolitan University
11.37, 11.42 Philippe Garner
11.38 Courtesy Warner Archive
11.40 Courtesy Fine Art Society PLC/Target Gallery
11.44 Hulton Getty
11.45 Courtesy Fiat
11.46, 11.47, 11.48, 11.49 Courtesy Associazione Archivio Storico Olivetti
11.50 Courtesy Ponti Archive
11.51 Gift of Atelier International, Ltd. Photo: Graydon Wood, 1990
11.52 Courtesy Arflex International
11.53 Courtesy Flos
11.54 Courtesy Vittorio Bonacina
11.55 National Motor Museum
11.56 © Aoi Huber Kono
11.57, 11.58 Courtesy Braun GmbH
11.59 Courtesy BMW
11.60 Courtesy Bizerba GmbH & Co. KG
11.61 Owner: Die Neue Sammlung-The International Design Museum Munich/Photo: A. Laurenzo, Die Neue Sammlung

11.62, 11.64 © DACS 2010
11.66 © DACS 2010
11.69 Bridgeman Art Library/Galeria Nazionale d'Arte Moderna, Rome/© DACS 2010
11.76 Courtesy Leica
11.78 Gift of Tendo Company Ltd.
11.81 Courtesy Chermayeff & Geismar Inc.
11.87 Courtesy Eames Office

12.3 © Austin J. Brown/Aviationpictures.com
12.4 Courtesy GM Archives
12.6 Gift of the Brooks Stevens Family and the Milwaukee Institute of Art and Design
12.12 Courtesy Givenchy Archives
12.13 © Richard Hamilton 2010. All Rights Reserved, DACS
12.19 Gift of Silver & Stål. Photo: Eric Mitchell, 1982/© DACS 2010

13.1 Courtesy Hille Educational Products Ltd.
13.2, 13.3 Philippe Garner
13.4 Purchased with funds contributed by Mr. and Mrs. John W. Drayton, 1973. Photo: Graydon Wood, 1990
13.5, 13.31 Courtesy Herman Miller
13.6 Digital Image, The Museum of Modern Art, New York/Scala, Firenze
13.7 Courtesy Artifort
13.8 Christie's Images Ltd.
13.9 Courtesy Artemide
13.10, 13.11, 13.12 Courtesy Associazione Archivio Storico Olivetti
13.13, 13.14 Courtesy Sony Corporation
13.15 Solari Udine
13.16 Courtesy Braun GmbH
13.18 Courtesy Ingo Maurer
13.22 Courtesy Lufthansa
13.23 Courtesy National Park Service
13.26 Herb Lubalin Archive, Rochester Institute of Technology
13.27, 13.28 Private Collection
13.29 Courtesy Associazione Archivio Storico Olivetti
13.32 Courtesy Tendo Company Limited
13.35 Courtesy Marimekko Oyj, Helsinki
13.37 Gift of Jack Lenor Larsen, 1984. Photo: Mark Darley © 1989 The Metropolitan Museum of Art
13.38 Gift of Dr. Irwin R. Berman, in memory of his father, Allan Lake Berman, 1979. Photo: Mark Darley © 1989 The Metropolitan Museum of Art
13.39 Getty Images/Hulton Archive/Fotos International
13.40 Courtesy Dale Chihuly Studio

14.4 Courtesy Eames Office
14.6 National Motor Museum
14.7 Hulton Getty
14.8 Photo: Hickey-Robertson, Houston/© The Andy Warhol Foundation for the Visual Arts, Inc./ARS, NY and DACS, London 2010
14.9, 14.17 Philippe Garner
14.10 © Apple Corps Ltd.
14.11 Private Collection/© ADAGP, Paris and DACS, London 2010
14.13 Christie's Images Ltd.
14.14 Gift of the American Contemporary Art Foundation Inc., Leonard A. Lauder, President. Photo: Jerry L. Thompson
14.15 Scala Images/MoMA/© Estate of Tom Wesselmann/DACS, London/VAGA, New York, 2010
14.18 Advertising Archives
14.21 Courtesy Stewart Brand

15.2 Courtesy Memphis S.r.l./Photo: Roberto Gennari
15.3 Courtesy Studio Mendini
15.4 Given by Collab. Photo: Graydon Wood, 2000
15.5 Courtesy Driade
15.6 Christie's Images Ltd.
15.8 Gift of Mr. and Mrs. David N. Pincus, 2000/ © ARS, New York and DACS, London 2010
15.9 Courtesy Jame Reid/© Sex Pistols Residuals 2003

Sources and Credits for Quotations

While every effort has been made to trace the present copyright holders, we apologize
in advance for any unintentional omission or error and will be pleased to insert
the appropriate acknowledgement in any subsequent edition.

Part I
Page 34
Josiah Wedgwood (Papers E25-18167, nd, probably
September 15, 1767), in Robin Reilly, *Josiah Wedgwood
1730–1795*, London, Macmillan, 1992, 42.

Page 37
Jane Austen, *Mansfield Park*, James Kinsley (ed.), Oxford,
University Press, 1998, 384.

Part II
Page 55
Adam Smith, *An Inquiry into the Nature and Causes of the
Wealth of Nations*, Laurence Dickey (ed.), Indianapolis and
Cambridge, Hackett Publishing Company, 1993, 4.

Page 58
Thomas Carlyle, *Past and Present*, Richard B. Attick (ed.),
New York, New York University Press, 1998, 7. Reprinted
with permission of New York University Press.

Page 60
A. Welby Pugin, *The True Principles of Pointed or Christian
Architecture*, reprint of 1st edition (1841), London,
Academy Editions/New York, St. Martin's Press, 1973, 1.

Page 67
Charles Dickens, *Hard Times*, 2nd edition, George Frod
and Sylvère Monod (eds.), New York and London,
W. W. Norton and Company, 1990, 11.

Page 68
Owen Jones, *The Grammar of Ornament*, London, Bernard
Quaritch, 1868, 5 and 6.

Page 70
Charles L. Eastlake, *Hints on Household Taste. The Classic
Handbook of Victorian Interior Decoration*, New York,
Dover, 1969, 114 (first publ. 1868).

Page 77
Fernand Braudel, *Civilization and Capitalism 15th–18th
centuries*, vol. 2: *The Wheels of Commerce*, trans. Sian
Reynolds, New York, Harper & Row, 1979, 482.

Part III
Page 81
John Ruskin, *The Stones of Venice*, vol. II, chapter VI, § 16
(Kenneth Clark (ed.), *John Ruskin: Selected Writings*,
London, Penguin Books, 1991, first publ. 1964, 282–3).

Page 82
John Ruskin, *The Seven Lamps of Architecture*, V, § 24,
(Kenneth Clark (ed.), *John Ruskin: Selected Writings*,
London, Penguin Books, 1991, first publ. 1964, 236).

Page 82
John Ruskin, *The Stones of Venice*, vol. II, chapter VI, § 15,
italics added (Kenneth Clark (ed.), *John Ruskin: Selected
Writings*, London, Penguin Books, 1991, first publ. 1964,
282).

Page 82
John Ruskin, *The Seven Lamps of Architecture*, V, § 24,
(Kenneth Clark (ed.), *John Ruskin: Selected Writings*,
London, Penguin Books, 1991, first publ. 1964,
235–236).

Page 83
William Morris, "The Lesser Arts" ("The Decorative
Arts"), lecture given to the Trades Guild of Learning, 1877,
reprinted in *Hopes and Fears for Art*, London 1882 (Clive
Wilmer (ed.), *William Morris: News from Nowhere and
Other Writings*, London, Penguin Books, 1993, 233–4).

Page 83
William Morris, *The Ideal Book: Essays and Lectures on
the Arts of the Book*, William S. Peterson (ed.), Berkeley,
California, University of California Press, 1982, 1.

Page 84
William Morris, evidence given to the Royal Commission
on Technical Instruction (1882), reprinted in Gillian
Naylor (ed.), *William Morris by himself: Designs and
Writings*, Boston, Little, Brown and Company, 1988,
page 212.

Page 85
William Morris, "How I Became a Socialist," published in
Justice, 16 July 1894 (Clive Wilmer (ed.), *William Morris:
News from Nowhere and Other Writings*, London, Penguin
Books, 1993, 379).

Page 85
William Morris, "The Lesser Arts" ("The Decorative
Arts"), lecture given to the Trades Guild of Learning, 1877,
reprinted in *Hopes and Fears for Art*, London 1882 (Clive
Wilmer (ed.), *William Morris: News from Nowhere and
Other Writings*, London, Penguin Books, 1993, 250).

Page 85
William Morris, "Some Hints on Pattern-Designing",
lecture given at the Workingmen's College, London, 1881,
(Clive Wilmer (ed.), *William Morris: News from Nowhere
and Other Writings*, London, Penguin Books, 1993, 270).

Page 86
William Morris, *News From Nowhere or An Epoch of Rest,
being some chapters from a Utopian Romance*, serialized in
the *Commonweal*, 11 January to 4 October 1890, published
in book form and revised, Boston 1890 and London, 1891
(Clive Wilmer (ed.), *William Morris: News from Nowhere

and Other Writings*, London, Penguin Books, 1993,
122–123).

Page 88
Arthur Mackmurdo, from Gillian Naylor, *The Arts and
Crafts Movement*, Cambridge, MIT Press, 1980 (first publ.
1971), 116.

Page 89
William Lethaby, from Gillian Naylor, *The Arts and Crafts
Movement*, Cambridge, MIT Press, 1980 (first publ. 1971),
181.

Page 89
Charles Ashbee, from Gillian Naylor, *The Arts and Crafts
Movement*, Cambridge, MIT Press, 1980 (first publ. 1971),
167.

Page 100
Frank Lloyd Wright, "The Art and Craft of the Machine,"
1901, in Bruce Brooks Pfeiffer, *Frank Lloyd Wright
Collected Writings*, vol. 1 1894–1930, New York, Rizzoli
in association with the Frank Lloyd Wright Foundation,
1992, 64.

Page 106
Oscar Wilde, "The Critic as Artist," *The Artist as Critic:
Critical Writings of Oscar Wilde*, Richard Ellman (ed.), New
York, Random House, 1968, 398.

Page 106
Christopher Dresser, *Principles of Victorian Decorative
Design, with 184 illustrations*, New York, Dover
Publications, 1995, 17, footnote.

Page 106
Christopher Dresser, *Traditional Arts and Crafts of Japan*,
New York, Dover, 1994, 180 (originally published 1882
under the title *Japan: Its Architecture, Art and Art
Manufactures*).

Page 132
C. R. Mackintosh, Letter, in Werner Schweiger, *Wiener
Werkstätte, Design in Vienna 1903–1932*, New York,
Abbeville Press, 1984, pages 26–27. The letter was
probably addressed to Fritz Waerndorfer, a wealthy
patron of the Wiener Werkstätte, dating to March 17,
1903, and is a German translation from the English,
probably by Waerndorfer for Hoffmann.

Page 140
Kathryn Bloom Hiesinger (ed.), *Art Nouveau in Munich:
Masters of Jugendstil from the Stadtmuseum, Munich and
other Public and Private Collections*, exh. cat. Philadelphia
Museum of Art in association with Prestel Verlag, 1988,
95, from a drawing by Bruno Paul for *Simplicissimus*.

Page 148
Hermann Muthesius, *The English House*, ed. Dennis Sharp, trans. Janet Seligman, London, Crosby, Lockwood, Staples, 1979, 52. Reprinted by Permission of Frances Lincoln Ltd.

Page 151
Robert Kanigel, *The Best Way: Frederick Winslow Taylor and the Enigma of Efficiency*, New York, Viking, 1997, 214.

Part IV
Page 163
Henri Matisse, "Notes of a Painter," in Roger Benjamin, *Matisse's "Notes of a painter": criticism, theory, and context, 1891–1908*, Ann Arbor, MI, UMI Research Press, 1987, 208 (original in French, pp. 741–742, also reproduced in its entirety in Benjamin).

Page 167
René Gimpel, *Diary of an Art Dealer*, trans. John Rosenberg, New York, Farrar, Strauss and Giroux, 1966, 138.

Page 178
Amedee Ozenfant, and C-E Jeanneret, "Le Purisme" (trans.), in Robert L Herbert (ed.), *Modern Artists on Art: Ten Unabridged Essays*, Englewood Cliffs, NJ, Prentice Hall, 1964, 64.

Page 182
Filippo Marinetti, "Futurist Manifesto," 1909, in Umbro Apollonis (ed.), *Futurist Manifestos* (The Documents of 20th Century Art), New York, Viking, 1973, 21–22, or R. W. Flint (ed.), *Let's Murder the Moonshine: Selected Writings F. T. Marinetti*, trans. R. W. Flint and Arthur A. Coppotelli, Los Angeles, Sun & Moon Classics, 1991. Reprinted by Permission of Green Integer Books.

Page 184
From *De Stijl*, vol. 2, no. 1, November 1918, translated in Paul Overy, *De Stijl*, London and New York, Thames & Hudson, 1991, 47.

Page 184
From *De Stijl*, vol. 2, no. 1, November 1918, 102–103, translated in Nancy Troy, *The De Stijl Environment*, Cambridge, MA, MIT Press, 1983, 22.

Page 185
Piet Mondrian, "Neo Plasticism: The General Principle of Plastic Equivalency," published in French by the Galerie de L'Effort Moderne, Paris, 1920, in Harry Holtzman and Martin S. James (eds.), and translators, *The New Art – the New Life: the Collected Writings of Piet Mondrian*, Boston, G. K. Hall & Company, 1986, 139–140. Reproduced by permission. www.cengage.com/permissions.

Page 185
Piet Mondrian, "The New Plastic in Painting," published in De Stijl, 1917, in Harry Holtzman and Martin S. James, eds. and translators *The New Art – the New Life: the Collected Writings of Piet Mondrian*, Boston, G. K. Hall & Company, 1986, 50. Reproduced by permission. www.cengage.com/permissions.

Page 185
Piet Mondrian, "The Realization of Neo-Plasticism in the Distant Future and in Architecture Today," published in De Stijl, 1922, in Harry Holtzman and Martin S. James (eds.), and translators *The New Art – the New Life: the Collected Writings of Piet Mondrian*, Boston, G. K. Hall & Company, 1986, 167. Reproduced by permission. www.cengage.com/permissions.

Page 187
Nancy Troy, *The De Stijl Environment*, Cambridge, MA, MIT Press, 1983, 133.

Page 192
Gillian Naylor, *The Bauhaus reassessed: sources and design theory*, New York, E. P. Dutton, 1985, 97.

Page 197
Manifesto of the Bauhaus, April 1919, Hans Wingler,

Bauhaus, Cambridge and London, MIT Press, 1996, 31. Reprinted by Permission of MIT Press.

Page 198
Paul Klee, in a letter to Alfred Kubin dated May 12, 1919, in O. K. Werckmeister, *The Making of Paul Klee's Career 1914–1920*, Chicago, University of Chicago Press, 1989, 177–178.

Pages 199–200
Gillian Naylor, *The Bauhaus reassessed: sources and design theory*, New York, E. P. Dutton, 1985, 99.

Page 206
Josef Frank, *Josef Frank, Architect and Designer: An Alternative Vision of the Modern Home*, Nina Stritzler-Levine (ed.), New Haven and London, Yale University Press, 1996, 24.

Page 206
Josef Frank, *Josef Frank, Architect and Designer: An Alternative Vision of the Modern Home*, Nina Stritzler-Levine (ed.), New Haven and London, Yale University Press, 1996, 51.

Page 209
Jan Tschichold, *The New Typography: A Handbook for Modern Designers*, trans. Ruari McLean, Berkeley and Los Angeles, University of California Press, 1995, 67; 70.

Page 214
Herbert Spencer, *Pioneers of modern typography*, New York, Hastings House, 1970, 4 (first publ. 1969).

Page 221
Gunnar Asplund, "Rationalism and Man," speech delivered May 1935 at a meeting of the Swedish Arts and Crafts Society, in Stuart Wrede, *The Architecture of Erik Gunnar Asplund*, Cambridge, MA, MIT Press, 1980, 153. (See also Schildt, Göran (ed.), *Sketches*, trans. Stuart Wrede, Cambridge, MA, MIT Press, 1978.)

Page 229
Henry Ford, as told to John Anderson (attorney), 1903, reprinted in Nevins, Allan, with the collaboration of Frank Ernest Hill, *Ford. The Times, the Man, the Company*, vol. 1, New York, Scribners, 1954, 276.

Page 230
Vogue advertisement copy, April, 1923.

Page 248
Roland Marchand, *Advertising the American Dream: Making Way for Modernity 1920–1940*, Berkeley, University of California Press, 1985, 154.

Page 252
Paul Rand, *Paul Rand: A Designer's Art*, New Haven, Yale University Press, 1985, 233.

Part V
Page 268
Paul Rand, *Thoughts on Design*, New York, Van Nostrand Reinhold, 1970 (first publ. 1947), 36

Page 270
Alvin Lustig, in *The Collected Writings of Alvin Lustig*, Holland R. Melson (ed.), New York, Thistle Press, 1958, 73.

Page 271
Cipe Pineles, from a speech given to the AIGA (1958), in Martha Scotford, *Cipe Pineles: A Life of Design*, New York, W. W. Norton & Company, 1999, 66. Reprinted by Permission of Professor Martha Scotford.

Page 274
K. Lonberg-Holm, and Ladislav Sutnar, *Catalog design progress*, New York, Sweet's Catalog Service (Division of F. W. Dodge Corporation), 1950, Introduction (unpaged).

Page 294
Karl Gerstner, *Die neue Graphic. The new graphic art. Le nouvel art graphique*, Switzerland, Arthur Niggli Ltd., 1959, 148.

Page 310
Chuck Berry, *No Particular Place to Go*, released 1964 by Chess Records. Used by permission of Opus19 Music Company, Ventura, California.

Page 314
Bruce Springsteen, Academy Awards Presentation, March 21, 1994, from *Atlanta Journal and Constitution*, March 22, 1994, Section D, 6.

Page 319
Lewis Mumford, *The City in History: Its Origins, its Transformations, and its Prospects*, San Diego, New York and London, Harcourt Brace Jovanovich, 1961 and renewed 1989 by Lewis Mumford, 486. Used with Permission from the Estate of Lewis and Sophie Mumford.

Page 323
Robert Hutchins, in James Sloan Allen, *The Romance of Commerce and Culture. Capitalism, Modernism, and the Chicago-Aspen Crusade for Cultural Reform*, rev. edition, Boulder, CO, University Press of Colorado, 2002. Reprinted by permission of the University Press of Colorado.

Page 324
Vance Packard, *The Hidden Persuaders*, Harmondsworth, Penguin, 1960, or New York, David McKay, 1957, 4–5.

Part VI
Page 354
Ronny and the Daytonas, *GTO*, 1964 (Renewed) Warner-Tamerlane Publishing Corp. and Warner Chappell Music Ltd. All rights reserved. Used by Permission of Alfred Publishing Co. Inc.

Page 356
Ken Garland, "First Things First," published 1964, reprinted in Michael Bierut, Jessica Helfand, Steven Heller, and Rick Poyner (eds.), *Looking Closer 3*, New York, Allworth Press, 1999, 154–155.

Page 359
Emilio Ambasz, *Italy: The New Domestic Landscape. Achievements and Problems of Italian Design*, New York, The Museum of Modern Art, New York, in Collaboration with Centro Di, Florence, 19–20.

Page 364
Victor Papanek, *Design for the Real World: Human Ecology and Social Change*, New York, Random House (Pantheon Books), 1971, xxi.

Page 364
Victor Papanek, *Design for the Real World: Human Ecology and Social Change*, New York, Random House (Pantheon Books), 1971, 51.

Page 376
Neville Brody, in Jon Wozencroft, *The Graphic Language of Neville Brody*, New York, Rizzoli, 1988, 60.

Page 380
Herbert Simon, "The Science of Design: Creating the Artificial," *The Sources of the Artificial*, Cambridge, MA, MIT Press, 1969, 54.

Page 383
Quoted from the "Values" link on the Body Shop website: http://thebodyshop.com (2000) "our future planning will be based upon achieving a balance between the need to limit the environmental impact of our business whilst not compromising our long term commercial viability."

Page 391
Jonathon Porritt, *Seeing Green: the politics of ecology explained*, Oxford (UK) and New York, B. Blackwell, 1985 (c.1984), xiii, and 15.

Pages 402–403
Rudy VanderLans and Zuzana Licko, with Mary E. Gray, *Émigré (The Book): Graphic Design into the Digital Realm*, New York, Van Nostrand Reinhold, 1993, 23.

Index